Participatory Methodologies to Elevate Children's Voice and Agency

A volume in
Research in Global Child Advocacy Series
Ilene R. Berson and Michael J. Berson, *Series Editors*

Participatory Methodologies to Elevate Children's Voice and Agency

edited by

Ilene R. Berson
University of South Florida

Michael J. Berson
University of South Florida

Colette Gray
Stranmillis University College

INFORMATION AGE PUBLISHING, INC.
Charlotte, NC • www.infoagepub.com

Library of Congress Cataloging-in-Publication Data

A CIP record for this book is available from the Library of Congress
http://www.loc.gov

ISBN: 978-1-64113-546-7 (Paperback)
      978-1-64113-547-4 (Hardcover)
      978-1-64113-548-1 (ebook)

Printed in the United States of America

CONTENTS

PART I

CRITICAL PERSPECTIVES ON CHILDREN'S VOICE AND AGENCY: ETHICAL ISSUES AND DILEMMAS

v

PART II

METHODOLOGICAL APPROACHES
TO PARTICIPATORY RESEARCH WITH CHILDREN

PART III

ISSUES OF REPRESENTATION IN THE ANALYSIS
AND INTERPRETATION OF CHILDREN'S PERSPECTIVES

PART IV

CROSS-NATIONAL PERSPECTIVES
ON PARTICIPATORY RESEARCH WITH CHILDREN

PREFACE

This book, the seventh volume in the Research in Global Child Advocacy Series, explores participatory methodologies and tools that involve children in research. Perspectives on the role of children have transitioned from viewing children as objects of research, to children as subjects of research, to acknowledgement of children as competent contributors and agents throughout the inquiry process. Researchers continue to explore approaches that honor the capacity of children, drawing on diverse methodologies to elevate children's voices and actively engage them in the production of knowledge. Nonetheless, despite these developments, questions over the extent to which children can be free of adult filters and influence merits sustained scholarly attention.

The book highlights the diverse perspectives of early childhood researchers from around the world. Each chapter critically examines methodological approaches that elevate the role of children in the research process. Contributions include empirical research that operates from an empowerment paradigm and demonstrates the agenic capacity of children to contribute their perspectives and voices to our understanding of childhood and children's lives. Some chapters also present conceptual pieces that challenge existing theoretical frameworks, critique research paradigms, and analyze dilemmas or tensions related to ethics, policy and power relations in the research process. Despite divergent perspectives and critical discourse, the chapter authors elaborate on their situated decision-making and consider the epistemological and methodological advantages and pitfalls of their approaches to achieve child-centric research objectives while ensuring contextual relevance and cultural appropriateness.

CRITICAL PERSPECTIVES ON CHILDREN'S
VOICE AND AGENCY: ETHICAL ISSUES
AND DILEMMAS OF POWER

Part I includes chapters that explore issues of power and agency when conducting research with children. In *Participatory Research with Children: Critical Reflections*, Tiffany Barnikis, Maggie MacNevin, and Rachel Berman set the tone for the volume by introducing ethical and methodological issues in participatory research with children. They illustrate the need to challenge traditional boundaries in research and engage in ongoing critical reflection to move beyond pre-established conceptualizations of children. Susan Groundwater-Smith and Nicole Mockler also explore impediments and opportunities for engaging children and young people as participatory actors in the conduct of research in their chapter entitled *Student Voice Work as an Educative Practice*. The authors are concerned with the ways researchers may authentically employ student voice as part of school reform. Edith Jolicoeur, Joanne S. Lehrer, Julie Ruel, Johanne April, and Mathieu Point reiterate the importance of finding non-intrusive and anxiety-reducing approaches to help support communication with children. In their chapter *Researching the Perspectives of Children with Additional Support Needs during their Transition to School: Ethical and Methodological Considerations,* the authors encourage researchers to consider children's characteristics and interests when selecting methodological approaches.

Joseph Levitan's *The Role of Reflexivity in Performing Collaborative Student Voice Research* encourages adult researchers to reflexively uncover their personal assumptions about one's role in an educational space, who holds knowledge, what constitutes knowledge, and how power is lived and experienced. In order to foster youth voice and agency, Levitan challenges adults to let go of some forms of power and develop approaches to relating and communicating with students that create authentic and equitable interpersonal dynamics (while still recognizing differences in positionality and experience). *Amplifying Youth Voice Through Public Engaged Research* by Ross VeLure Roholt and Michael Baizerman further extends discussions on illuminating youth voice as part of the research enterprise. The authors embrace creative methods to involve youth in public engaged scholarship, drawing on young people's actionable knowledge to address their everyday lived experiences. Amanda Ajodhia's chapter on *Reflexively Conducting Research with Ethnically Diverse Children with Disabilities* asserts that children with disabilities have a right to express personal views and to have these views be heard, specifically concerning matters impacting their school life. This right extends to collaborating throughout the research process, and Ajodhia encourages researchers to seek approaches in managing impairments to facilitate maximum research participation among children with disabilities.

Each of the chapters in Part I extend the reader's conceptual repertoire surrounding voice, communication, and language in research with strategies to move beyond conventional speech to access children's perspectives.

METHODOLOGICAL APPROACHES TO PARTICIPATORY RESEARCH WITH CHILDREN

Chapters in Part II call for diverse methods that value children's capacity to share their ideas and lived experiences as participants as well as engage children in the design, implementation, analysis, and dissemination of research. Carlo Fabian and Timo Huber's chapter, *Participating in Creating Open Spaces with and for Children: A Kind of Participatory Action Research?*, aims to show that the best outcomes are achieved through direct participation of children in the creation of their lifeworlds. The authors empower and support children through a community-based action research project. Other chapter authors also employ elements of participatory action research while drawing on diverse modalities to acknowledge the children's expertise and agency throughout the research process.

Several chapters explore the use of digital technologies to promote participatory engagement of children. Colette Gray, Jill Dunn, Pamela Moffett, and Denise Mitchell's chapter *Child Mentors, Virtual Tours and Adult Protégées: Young Children's Experiences with Tablet Devices* describes how they integrate child-led virtual tours into their research methodology. Myriam Savage also relies on digital tools as part of her arts-based narrative method she discusses in *Personal Public Service Announcements: Collaborating with Young Women Adopted from Foster Care using Narradrama and an iPad during Arts-Based Narrative Inquiry*. Similarly, Heilyn Camacho's chapter *Lego Serious Play as a Participatory Research Method to Involve Children in Action Research Projects* introduces the methodology of Lego Serious Play to create an interaction space between children and researchers in which children's feelings, actions, and experiences may be stimulated and accessed. In *Medical Play: From Intervention to Participatory Research*, Cara Sisk and Jane Baker also focus on multidimensional research approaches to elevate children's voices in the research process. They describe how researchers may use medical play as a child-centered method to access the various modalities of expression (i.e., verbalizations, visual representations, and play) used by children. By partnering with children with special health care needs and disabilities, researchers gain insight on how to positively impact pediatric health care based on the perspectives of children with limited communication skills. Each of the methodologies highlighted in Part II reframe children as collaborators in the research process rather than merely objects of study.

ISSUES OF REPRESENTATION IN THE ANALYSIS AND INTERPRETATION OF CHILDREN'S PERSPECTIVES

Part III of the text centers on children's expertise throughout the research process. In *Diffractive Lenses Catching Stories – The Meaning of Belonging Through the Voice of Adolescents*, Hanne Vandenbussche, Elisabeth De Schauwer, and Geert Van Hove use film making with adolescents as a materialization of belonging. Just as they critically reflect on their decisions as researchers and how to negotiate the sharing of decision-making power, Harry Shier considers the fundamental questions that underlie research with children and adolescents in his chapter *An Analytical Tool to Help Researchers Develop Partnerships with Children and Adolescents*. Children live within social and physical worlds that can promote or constrain their actions and reactions. As such, it is essential that researchers promote and sustain collaborative research with children – where children's perspectives, experiences, and responses are valued. Rosemary D. Richards reminds us to carefully conceive research methodologies that consider the relationships between theories, data construction processes, and research-based interactions around the phenomenon under study. Her chapter on *Young Children's Photography within Collaborative Research: Implications for Research Relationships* showcases how young children can be competent and confident photographers and narrators and, through their use of digital photography, they can actively generate knowledge and co-construct understandings about their perspectives on the world. In *Removing the Medical Paradigm—Making Children's Voices Visible in the Context of Problematic Eating: Participatory Action Research in a Clinical Setting* Colleen McMillan similarly suggests that creative and multimodal approaches may reveal the lived experiences of children. She warns that researchers must not underestimate the importance of relationship building with children. Authenticity is critical toward establishing trust.

CROSS-NATIONAL PERSPECTIVES ON PARTICIPATORY RESEARCH WITH CHILDREN

Part IV considers cultural norms and diverse methods of participatory research with children across global contexts. Ilene R. Berson, Michael J. Berson, Joyce Esi Bronteng, and Aaron Osafo Acquah's chapter entitled *Hu m'ani so ma me nti na atwe mmienu nam (Blow the Dust from my Eyes): Making the Voices of Ghanaian Kindergarteners Visible through the Use of Video-cued Ethnography in a Study of Citizenship* explores the use of video-stimulated interviews with kindergarteners in Ghana. The multi-modal research methods intentionally created a conversation space in which children and adults came together in dialogue in and about classroom interactions connected with children's role. Michelle Finnerty also highlights the importance of using interactive methods to listen to children in her chapter *Sounds from Within: Exploring the Role of Ethnographic Fieldwork to Elevate Children's Perspectives and Voices in the Study of Children's Musical Cultures in Ireland.* The growing popularity of technology and the user-friendliness of cameras and videos have led to an increase in the use of visual-oriented tools. The value of narrative inquiry as a methodological approach that provides participatory methods of research to elevate children's voices continues as a theme in *Adolescent Voices: Empowering Haitian Immigrant Youth through Privileging Narratives* by Lauren Christian Gibson. Narrative inquiry approaches, where stories of experiences are shared and re-shared around children's genuine interests, not only honor and elevate their views but also enhance their experiences of being listened to and influential within their worlds. Despite the value of these approaches, Myriam Denov, Natasha Blanchet-Cohen, Alusine Bah, Leontine Uwababyeyi, Jean Kagame, and Andie (Saša) Buccitelli remind us of the messiness and difficulties of this work in their chapter *Co-Creating Space for Voice: Reflections on a Participatory Research Process with War-Affected Youth Living in Canada.* Finding ways to engage in culturally sensitive research requires a reflexive approach that is grounded in participatory methods that contest the objectification of children as participants.

Throughout this volume the contributors' shared vision for participatory research with children has led to innovative insights about how our perspectives on children, research, and theory influence our practices as scholars. The authors encourage us to honor the agency and voice of children while also critically reflecting on the tensions in situating children as co-researchers or collaborators. By acknowledging these ethical issues and dilemmas of power, we may disrupt traditional adult-centric enactments and more authentically situate children as agentic and capable collaborators. Ultimately, we hope this volume supports the continued exploration of creative methodologies inclusive of children as participants in the research process.

—Ilene R. Berson
Michael J. Berson

ACKNOWLEDGMENTS

This book would not be possible without the amazing contributions and assistance of others. We express our tremendous appreciation to all of the contributors of the volume who embarked with us on this journey to explore ethical and methodological issues regarding participatory research with children. Each contributor shared their insightful and creative work from around the world and inspired us with their thought-provoking perspectives. We gratefully acknowledge their collaboration and collegiality throughout this endeavor.

The editors would like to extend our gratitude to George F. Johnson, our publisher, for his assistance in developing this book series and promoting learning and research in global child advocacy. We are very appreciative of his vision and assistance in highlighting this important work. We also are thankful for our colleagues and doctoral students who assisted in the editing and revision of the book to ensure that the words and innovative insight of the scholars whose work we have collected can speak with clarity and capture the essence of the topic.

Our children are always close to our hearts and provide us with the richness and depth of understanding through the lived experience of their own growth and development. They inspire and challenge us with their sense of agency and of endless possibilities to explore the expansiveness of the world around them. It is therefore with great warmth, love and joy that we thank Elisa and Marc. Their inquisitive presence constantly engages us in reflecting on our research as we continue our exploration of new horizons.

PART I

CRITICAL PERSPECTIVES ON CHILDREN'S VOICE
AND AGENCY: ETHICAL ISSUES AND DILEMMAS

CHAPTER 1

PARTICIPATORY RESEARCH WITH CHILDREN

Critical Reflections

Tiffany Barnikis, Maggie MacNevin, and Rachel Berman

ABSTRACT

In this chapter, the three authors discuss ethical issues and dilemmas of power connected to experiences of conducting research with children in three qualitative studies. All of the children participating in these research studies were enrolled, or had been enrolled, in a laboratory school childcare setting, and ranged in age from 2½ to 6½ years. Two projects, one building upon the other, explored children's perceptions of their experiences in two different learning environments. Another project sought to explore children's perceptions of "race" and racial identity. The authors reflect upon their experiences with the goal of provoking further thought and discussion on how we might move toward a more equitable and fuller participation for children in research. Uncertainty and new and unanswered questions emerge through the discussions of the various stages of the research process. More specifically, we consider issues of: adult-initiated research, researcher positionality and social location, gatekeepers, consent and assent, and conversation and drawing as data generation methods. Looking toward future research, recommendations based on lessons learned are offered.

Participatory Methodologies to Elevate Children's Voice and Agency, pages 3–23
Copyright © 2019 by Information Age Publishing
All rights of reproduction in any form reserved.

Research with children strives for "an acceptance that children's knowledge of their own worlds is owned by them and that they are the experts in knowing and recording their own worlds" (Burke, 2005, p. 31). This is consistent with a wider tradition in qualitative research that seeks to democratize the research process. As Karnieli-Miller, Strier, and Pessach (2009) explain, "drawing predominantly on constructivist and critical paradigms of understanding, qualitative research fosters a rebalancing of power in the researcher-participant relationship and encourages a focus on marginalized understandings and experiences (O'Conner and O'Neill, 2004)" (p. 280). Researchers who seek to elevate children's voices tend to utilize participatory methods; such methods aim to empower children through active engagement in the research process. Typically, there is an emphasis on *doing* something (e.g., photography, drawing) with the understanding that such active participation produces "better" knowledge than more traditional methods (e.g., interviews, observation).

However, it is worth noting that Gallacher and Gallagher (2008) problematized the claim that participatory methods always democratize the research process, empower young participants and exist in binary opposition to nonparticipatory methods, arguing that the "very notion of 'empowerment' implies that, without aid and encouragement from adult-designed 'participatory methods,' children cannot fully exercise their 'agency' in research encounters" (p. 503). A researcher's conceptualization of power is always embedded within discussions of participatory research with children. For example, perceiving power as a commodity that can be exchanged among individuals perpetuates the notion that by employing particular research methods, the researcher can transfer power in predetermined ways (Gallacher & Gallagher, 2008). In contrast, they note it is important to recognize that the ways in which "research participants can, and do, act places them beyond the control of the researcher and his or her techniques" (p. 503). Our concept of power aligns best with that of Foucault (1981): power is not a fixed object of possession, but rather a process that is reinforced and reconsidered by discourse in interactions. We therefore acknowledge that power imbalances in research can never be eliminated, and that participation is a slippery concept.

In this chapter, we discuss ethical issues and dilemmas of power related to conducting research with children in three qualitative projects. To support this objective, we adhere to advice from a seminal article written by Punch in 2002, where she maintained that when conducting research with children, it is imperative that researchers remain critically reflective during all stages of the research project, not only remaining sure to carefully consider their role and assumptions, but to be mindful of their choice and utilization of particular methods. All stages of these studies were framed within the sociology of childhood, whereby children are viewed as active participants in their lives, and in the world around them (Mason & Danby, 2011; Mayall, 2002; Prout & James, 1997). All three studies were also grounded in a child-rights approach, which draws from the United Nations Convention on the Rights of the Child (1989) and acknowledges children as citizens who possess distinct human rights and should be recognized as active members in society. Articles 12 and 13 of the Convention on the Rights of the Child clearly state that children have the right to be consulted on matters that affect them and further state that children have a right not only to voice their views, but for these opinions to be listened to and to be given due weight. Tiffany's work was also in keeping with ideas from critical theory, while Rachel's and Maggie's research project engaged with ideas from critical race theory (CRT; Delgado, & Stefancic, 2012).

We share our experiences in this chapter with the goal of provoking further thought and discussion about how we might move toward more equitable and fuller participation for children in research. We grapple with uncertainty and emerging issues that need consideration. In keeping with the theme of incorporating individual voices, we have chosen to adopt a narrative style in which each researcher reflects upon their experiences post-project.

THE RESEARCH PROJECTS

Tiffany: In the first two projects, one building upon the other, I explored twelve children's perceptions of their experiences in both a university laboratory school and in their current elementary school setting with the goal of better understanding how children experience two different learning environments and how they compared these experiences, directly and indirectly. During these qualitative studies, children aged 4 to 6 years expressed their thoughts and opinions about learning in the two different educational settings through semi-structured conversations and child-produced drawings. The present discussion focuses on the research process; for more details about the projects, please see Barnikis (2015).

Maggie & Rachel: The third project, entitled *Can we talk about race? Confronting color blindness in early childhood settings* (hereafter, CWTAR), was begun in 2014. The main research question was as follows: "How we can support early childhood educators (ECEs) to foster conversations about race in early childhood settings to best support children's positive identification with race and difference?" Data generation was multipronged and involved document analysis, interviews with early childhood professionals, participant observation in a preschool classroom, and interviews with 21 children aged 2½ to 5 years. The current discussion focuses on the process of conducting research with children; for more details on the project, including findings, please see MacNevin and Berman (2017) and Berman, Daniel, Butler, MacNevin, and Royer (2017). All projects were approved by the university's Research Ethics Board.

PLANNING THE PROJECTS

Adult-Initiated Research

Tiffany: It is critical for researchers to identify their theoretical and conceptual frameworks and social location because "all research emanates from the researcher's implicit or explicit theory of the phenomenon under investigation" (Rocco & Plakhotnik, 2009, p. 121). Through these projects, my goal was to explore children's perceptions of their experiences at school, but it is important to acknowledge that I, an adult, established the research questions, design, and intentions. I also co-constructed the conversations with the children, but still framed, analyzed, and interpreted the data alone. Dockett and Perry (2005a) ask how adult researchers can "faithfully represent children's knowing and understanding" (p. 518). However, most scholars agree that even when children are involved in the generation of data, data analysis, and interpretation often demands "different knowledge than that generally available to children, in order to explicate children's social status and structural positioning" (Mayall, 1994, p. 11). Such discussions, however, are not unique to research with children, but are consistent with social research with adults where researchers analyze and discuss the findings with reference to academic theories, concepts, and knowledge (Punch, 2002). Throughout all stages of these research projects, however, I tried to remain mindful of my position as an adult researcher, and of children's marginalized position in society, to help ensure that the findings and analysis best represented the children's perceptions of their experiences.

Rachel: As a project lead, I submitted a proposal for funding to the Social Sciences and Humanities Research Council of Canada and, once funded, directed the research activities. The CWTAR project was motivated by the lack of voices of children in Canadian research about children and "race." To me, it was important that the researchers collecting data with children had an understanding of the sociology of childhood, and experience working directly with children so as to have a certain comfort level and ease interacting with them, in a way serving as an insider (Berman & MacNevin, 2017; Gregory & Ruby, 2011). Therefore, the three research assistants hired for the project were registered early childhood educators (ECEs) with master's degrees and considerable experience working in the field directly with children. Moreover, one of the three research assistants worked in the university laboratory childcare center where the data were to be collected. The goal was to minimize the social distance between researchers and participants. Data generation would involve interviews with children as they drew and participant observation as children engaged in open-ended play. Before we began, the research team discussed the role researchers would adopt during participant observation: that of "caring participant observer" (Birbeck & Drummond, 2005). This (supposed) insider status was beneficial in some ways, but as discussed below, it also caused some unanticipated issues in the way some of the child participants (and some adults within the setting) engaged in the co-construction of Maggie's identity (Raffety, 2015). The "races" of researchers and children also have effects, which we have discussed elsewhere (Berman & MacNevin, 2017).

Rachel & Maggie. Although there is ample evidence that children are aware of and beginning to attach meaning to concepts of "race" around age three, researchers have found that ECEs tend not to believe "race" or racism is a relevant topic of inquiry for young children (Boutte, Lopez-Robertson, & Powers-Costello 2011; Husband, 2012). Our interviews with adults during the CWTAR study yielded similar findings; adults tended to deny that racial issues ever occurred in this setting, and used particular discursive strategies to diminish or reframe such incidents when they did speak about them (Berman et al., 2017). Thus, although the CWTAR project was initiated without input from children, it was developed with the knowledge that children are seldom given space and opportunities to talk about "race." Coupled with our commitment to children's participation rights, this underscored the importance of listening to children's thoughts and experiences. According to CRT, racism is normalized to such an extent that it is difficult to identify and thus to discuss it; furthermore, young children may pick up on adult cues that mark race and difference as uncomfortable or even taboo topics of discussion (Pahlke, Bigler, & Suizzo, 2012). Previous research has also suggested that among ECEs, the prevailing response to difference is to take a "colorblind" approach, characterized by the beliefs that children are too young to understand racism and that lessons like "we're all the same on the inside" are adequate (Boutte et al., 2011; Vittrup, 2016). Therefore, as researchers in the context of this project we felt a clear responsibility to amplify and share children's voices, while also being aware that there would likely be much that they could not express or were not comfortable saying aloud. Guided by the ethical responsibility to name and expose racial oppression, we also felt it was necessary to interpret and analyze what was said (or not said) by the children using conceptual frameworks that were unknown and inaccessible to them. This choice led to the emergence of some problematic questions: Are we distorting the meanings of the participants' voices? Could/should the children be brought into the analysis (Coad & Evans, 2008). Should they be brought into the telling?

This chapter only features the voices of three adult researchers. These issues are not isolated to research with children as Tiffany has noted previously, and are relevant to most qualitative research. As Karnieli-Miller and
colleagues (2009) explain:

> The right of participants to play a significant role can lead to the denial of
> the researcher's right to intellectual and academic freedom and to an over-
> simplification of the theoretical construct that can potentially emerge for the
> research. In light of these constraints, qualitative research oscillates between
> the desire to offer a less hierarchical and more reciprocal, transparent frame-
> work and the need to respect the theoretical foundations, methodological
> discipline and ethical boundaries of qualitative scholarship. (p. 285)

One stated goal of the project was to contribute to the development of
tools to support educators in having more meaningful discussions about
racism with young children, in turn providing children with needed information and language. In the future, participants in similar projects should
be better equipped to articulate their experiences and understand the researchers' analysis. This will help encourage a more comprehensive model
of participation.

Researchers' Position and Social Location

Tiffany: I had a preexisting relationship with the children participating
in the studies. They knew me as a parent of one of their peers, and as an
ECE employed by the university laboratory school. Throughout both research studies, my pre-established relationship with the children and their
families presented both challenges and advantages. During recruitment,
I did not want my relationship with the children and their families to influence the decision to participate. To help minimize this possibility, the
manager of the university laboratory school was the first person to contact
possible participants, on my behalf, through an introductory email. Furthermore, on the consent form sent to the families, it was explicitly stated
that participation was entirely voluntary. I was aware that my relationship
with the children might influence their decision to participate. Throughout the data generation stage, discussed below, I made it clear that the children's participation in the study was completely voluntary and they could
stop or withdraw from the study at any time.

Maggie: Like Tiffany, I had a preexisting relationship with the children
in the study. My own involvement as a research assistant with the CWTAR
project was both complicated and enriched by the fact that I was concur-
rently employed as an ECE at the university childcare center. My relationships with the children, the parents, and staff predated the launch of the

project, so I was positioned as an "insider." Any input that I brought to the project during its conceptualization and design was intrinsically influenced by my experiences working as an ECE with the children who would become our research participants. In hindsight, I question whether I should have used my insider's knowledge of the children differently; that is, to act as their voice during the research design. I may have missed an opportunity to bring some of the children's own questions or issues to the table, rather than using my position as an insider to suggest ways to get our adult-initiated questions answered more easily.

Tiffany: At times during the generation of data, my relationship with the children created some unanticipated challenges. I sometimes found myself asking the children for information that I already knew, and which they were aware that I knew. For example, when discussing the rules of the classroom, one child said, "Do not play guns, except you know that one already right?" At other times, I asked the children to expand on certain classroom practices or layouts with which I was familiar. My intent was to uncover what aspects of the classroom were of importance to the children; however, in doing so I was asking the children to accept me in a certain role (i.e., researcher) to which they were not accustomed. Was it respectful to my participants to ask them to "pretend" I did not know the answers to the questions I was asking them? In future research, I will try to make this kind of request clearer to the participants through the project description, and through the assent process.

In some ways, my preexisting relationships with the children were quite beneficial during data generation. Many researchers have referred to the importance of building rapport with children prior to generating data (Cameron, 2005; Fleet & Harcourt, 2018; Irwin & Johnson, 2005; Punch, 2002; Stephenson, 2009). I believe my prior relationships with the children increased their comfort level, because we were accustomed to speaking with each other. For example, when I first sat down with one child, she immediately recalled an art activity I had done with her at the university laboratory school and we spent several minutes reflecting on it. This discussion of our previous relationship created a level of comfort from the onset, which I think would have been difficult to achieve if I were a stranger. After I thanked another child for taking the time to speak with me, he turned to me and asked, "Want to play?" further illustrating his comfort with me. Thus, my preexisting relationships with the children allowed for a comfortable rapport during the conversations and aided in establishing a degree of intersubjectivity.

I believe that my experience, when properly acknowledged and attended to, yielded more insight into the research. My background and experiences with the children allowed me to take an emic approach, which considers research from within the system itself (Gardiner & Kosmitzki, 2010), and can therefore provide a greater understanding of the social and cultural context of the setting. This insider approach, although it had its challenges, allowed me to conduct research from within a familiar context.

Maggie. I found that it was not always easy to separate my two roles of researcher and educator. Prior to beginning each interview, I attempted to explain my dual role to the participants as part of the assent process (discussed in more detail shortly). Although I cannot be sure, I sensed that the children did not fully understand the meanings of *research* and *researcher* that were offered. Support for my hunch came later, while engaging in participant observation: Although I explained that I was in the classroom as a researcher and observer, children repeatedly treated me as a teacher (e.g., by asking permission to go the bathroom, or seeking my help in resolving conflicts over materials). During interviews, I expected that the children would be very comfortable with me. To my surprise, this was not always the case. Two of three participants from my own class were markedly uncomfortable during the interviews, exhibiting nonverbal signs of discomfort and speaking very little. Both children were very open, communicative and affectionate with me when I was in my ECE role, so the interview experience changed how we interacted. I was behaving differently than I normally did: asking unusual, out-of-the-blue questions; using a more formal tone of voice; and not singing or being playful. It was also rare for me to be alone with one child during our normal daily routine, so the interview context was very unusual. Although some participants seemed more at ease than others, in all cases I found it more difficult to establish rapport during interviews than I had expected.

I believe these issues connected to role confusion could be improved by increasing the length of engagement in the research environment. Stephenson (2009) described how longer engagement created opportunities to not only build deeper relationships with participants but also to better understand their unique knowledge, perspective, and use of language. If I could have stayed in my researcher role for a longer period of time, the participants may have developed a stronger understanding of the meaning of research (and I would likely have improved my ability to explain it, while also becoming more adept at switching roles).

RECRUITMENT AND PARTICIPATION

Gatekeepers

Tiffany: When conducting research with children, researchers must obtain the cooperation of a variety of different "gatekeepers" (Berman & MacNevin, 2017; Cree, Kay, & Tisdall, 2002). Within the research process, children "may have less power and often don't have the practical ability to simply say 'yes' or 'no' to participation in research, for example, without other people's permission" (Thomas, as cited in Smith & Greene, 2014, p. 212). Parents, educators, and school administrators are a few groups whose cooperation and permission are required prior to that of the child. This raises many ethical considerations, as gatekeepers may permit or forbid access to children based on their personal assessment of the validity, relevance, or appropriateness of the study. Under the guise of protection, some gatekeepers may avoid studies that involve "sensitive" or "contentious" subject matter. With regard to the notion of "children's voices," Ennew (as cited in Smith & Greene, 2014) noted:

> In today's mistaken political and academic context children have "voices," but only adults have opinions. Until it is recognized that children have valid opinions and are not just decorative additions to political life, their human rights will continue to be violated—often by the very people who think they are helping. (p. 81)

Gatekeepers who believe they are doing a service by protecting children from certain "issues" may not only further silence a marginalized group, but may also perpetuate dominant conceptualizations of children as inferior and innocent. Gatekeepers may prohibit children from taking part in data generation that they believe is too challenging for children (i.e., using certain data generation tools such as cameras or audio recorders). This privileges the gatekeepers' preconceived notions of children's competencies above the children's actual competencies. It is, however, important to note that gatekeepers do occupy an important role in protecting participants from unethical or poorly thought-out research. However, many questions remain. Should the highly subjective decision of research "merit" and/or "appropriateness" fall on gatekeepers, and to what extent do the various gatekeepers influence which voices are accessed and promoted and subsequently which are silenced?

Tiffany: In order to gain access to participants, I approached the manager of the university laboratory school and asked her to send an introductory email to the parents of children who had recently transitioned from the laboratory school to the elementary school system. For both studies, I provided the manager with a brief outline of the research objective and asked her to inquire, by email, whether any parents would be interested in participating. As discussed above, this email sent by the manager of the laboratory school helped ensure that my preexisting relationship did not affect the voluntary nature of participation. Families wishing to participate then contacted me directly.

Rachel & Maggie: For the CWTAR project, we chose to be physically present at the childcare site to recruit participants in person. Given that discussing race and racism can be considered a sensitive topic, we thought that parents would be more likely to consent to their children's participation if they had the opportunity to meet some of the researchers and ask questions. In fact, many parents did take the opportunity to ask questions and share their thoughts about the research topic. Perhaps not surprisingly, a few parents did seem to take on a protective role, as Tiffany discussed above, by questioning the relevance or appropriateness of the topic for young children. However, many parents did consent to their children's participation, including some who were initially hesitant.

While Maggie was a familiar figure to all the children and most of the parents at the childcare center, this was the first time the children had seen two of the other research assistants. Recruitment took place on the playground as parents arrived to pick up their children, and several interactions took place among the children and the research assistants. Children who noticed their parent talking with a researcher sometimes approached and asked what was being discussed. Within a participatory framework, this would be considered a good time to introduce the project to the children. However, ethical guidelines required us to obtain written consent from parents before discussing the research with their children; in any case, parents usually took the lead in responding to their children's questions with some version of "I'm talking to Maggie for a minute, we'll be done soon."

Consent and Assent

Tiffany: During the data generation stage of my research projects, the children were provided with a choice to participate by the use of an assent form. Dockett, Einarsdottir, and Perry (2009) stressed the importance of gaining children's assent to participate, even after parental consent has been granted. This assent process provided further confirmation to the voluntary nature of participation in the studies. Although assent is gained at the beginning of the data generation, it is critical that assent is continuously considered throughout the process (Cocks, 2007). Through the assent form, it was made clear that the children had the choice to participate and could choose to stop participating in the research project at any time. Researchers should be aware of clues, visual or verbal, that children may provide to indicate that they no longer wish to participate in the study. I was vigilant to these clues, and asked whether they still wanted to participate throughout our conversations. When applicable, I respected their request to end data generation. This awareness of visual and verbal cues aided in confirming the voluntary nature of participation.

One encounter with a child offered some insights into the assent process. Upon arrival at his house, the child, who I had not seen for about nine months, greeted me at the door with a surprised and confused look on his face, and asked me what I doing there. It became apparent that he was unaware of the research project, suggesting that his parents had agreed to the research and set up the meeting without consulting him. He did agree to speak with me, however, during the conversation it became clear (through verbal and nonverbal cues) that he was not very interested in the project, so my data generation concluded early. This encounter revealed some of my preconceived notions of conducting research with children. Drawing from my own social location, I assumed all families would discuss the research with their children and ask if they would like to participate, before filling out the consent form. This did not appear to be the case with this child. In my future research projects, consent forms will include a request that families discuss the research project with their child, and whether it would be of interest to them to participate.

Maggie: The CWTAR interview process also began with requesting assent. To ensure consistency among all interviewers, this involved reading a script. Although all the children with whom I spoke agreed to be interviewed and indicated verbally that they understood the nature of the project and their participation, numerous indications suggested that they were not attending to and/or not understanding the information I was providing. For example, several interrupted me to ask questions about the drawing materials or the audio recorder. Some were silent but appeared to be fully engrossed in handling the materials, while I saw others paying attention to sights or sounds outside the interview area. It should be noted that we did not collect any audio recordings of conversations about the assent process, because we decided not to begin recording until participants were fully informed and had agreed to be recorded. Thus, my recollections of the assent process are based on reflective notes that I wrote as soon as possible after each interview. In a recent class discussion about research methods where I was a guest speaker, I was lamenting the lack of audio data of the assent conversations to be used for analysis and reflection. A graduate student offered a simple solution that should have been obvious: ask permission to record at the outset. If a child declined to participate after learning more about the research, the recording of the assent conversation could be erased.

As discussed earlier, a longer engagement (Stephenson, 2009) would have allowed the children to develop a deeper understanding of the nature of the research over time. Others have considered the question of how much to tell children about a research project, especially when sensitive issues are involved (e.g., Dockett & Perry, 2010). I am unsure whether our assent script provided too much or too little information, or was not well communicated. This issue will require more consideration, because it is our ethical responsibility to ensure that participants fully understand what they are being asked to take part in, particularly given that this has not always been a priority for those researching with (or on) children.

Rachel: Harcourt (Fleet & Harcourt, 2018), in her discussion of informed consent and inviting children to participate in research, notes that in her experience, children prefer to be informed in small groups, "as they are able to help each other in establishing and negotiating shared meanings" (p. 170). She points out as well that teaching professionals may be particularly skilled at working with groups of children, unlike those adults who may only have experience working with individual children. I am not exactly sure how this approach might have helped with some of the issues Maggie relayed, but it may have been an approach that led to a different kind of participation on the part of the children. Maggie and the two other research assistants certainly had the requisite skills to facilitate such a process. It is worth noting that Harcourt (Fleet & Harcourt, 2018) takes the position, as do others, that children are capable of informed consent and that, therefore, informed consent, not assent, should be sought from children.

REFLECTION ON RESEARCH METHODS

Conversations

Tiffany: To generate data for the research project, I engaged in semi-structured conversations with the children. Prior to data generation, I created a semi-structured conversation guide intended to provide children with broad areas of discussion. Alderson and Morrow (2011) noted that semi-structured interviews allow participants to have more "control and choice in what they say" (p. 37). Participants built on the conversation guide, directing the conversations by discussing points that were of interest to them, and I followed up on the development of these ideas as they emerged. Mayall (2008) referred to engaging children in conversations where "an opening gambit could lead wherever children wished" (p. 112). My guide included probes to help conversations proceed and ensure the comfort of participants.

Spratling, Coke, and Minick (2012) wrote that "establishing a connection with the child during the interview [is] critical to successful research outcomes" (p. 48). I believe, a semi-structured format encourages rapport between child and researcher, as the child can talk freely and guide the direction of the conversation, so the child can "talk about things that are important to them, not just what is important to the researcher" (Spratling et al., 2012, p. 52). I began each conversation by asking the child some introductory questions to help establish a connection and ease anxiety. Cameron (2005) referred to this as a period of "free narrative," which serves a dual role in helping the child become more comfortable with the research process and giving the researcher time to assess the child's communication style and individual needs and concerns.

Drawings

Tiffany: During our conversations, I asked the children to draw a map of their current classrooms as well as to draw their past classrooms. I had not visited the children's current classrooms, so their drawings helped me visualize these spaces as well as serving to highlight areas of the classrooms the children thought to be important, and which they wished to discuss. I asked them to describe what they were drawing as they completed the task. This allowed us to move past the physical representation of their drawings and to explore how they perceived their learning environments. Within this context, the act of drawing became "a constructivist process of thinking in action, rather than developing ability to make visual references to objects in the world" (Cox, 2005, p. 123). In other words, what the children were saying while drawing was as important as what they were drawing, and neither could be analyzed apart from the other. This kind of method aligns well with a constructivist approach and helps ensure that the interpretation of the drawing lies with the child participant and not with the adult researcher (Dockett & Perry, 2005a).

Maggie: In the CWTAR project, we used drawings not as a source of data, but rather as a means to facilitate conversation and make participants feel more comfortable by having a task to focus on (MacNaughton & Davis, 2009). Participants were asked to draw a self-portrait, using a mirror for help if desired, and a picture of a friend. While each child drew, the interviewer asked related questions (e.g., "What color is your skin?" "What color hair does your friend have?" "Is there another color of skin that you would like to have?"). Although the drawings themselves were not used for analysis, interesting data arose as children created the drawings. For example, we discovered that some White children chose a light beige marker to draw their skin, but did not know what to name the color; others identified their skin as "white" and then felt some confusion over the lack of a white marker.

Tiffany: In my research projects, the drawings of classrooms provided me with a sense of the visual layout of the rooms, as well of the furniture and specific materials in the different classrooms. These drawings served as visual tours, where the children were tour guides and showed me what was important to them in each setting, not only the points of interest that I, as a researcher, believed to be important. This process allowed the children to guide the direction of some of the data generation by choosing which aspects of their classrooms they wished to discuss.

Task-based methods such as drawing may help children feel more at ease with the data generation process, but it is critical that researchers remain reflective and do not choose to employ such methods simply because they believe they are more enjoyable for children, but because they can also yield meaningful and useful data (Punch, 2002). I selected drawing, along with conversations, because I wanted to provide children with a familiar activity and an alternative means of communication, as well as ensuring I collected the most relevant data to answer my research questions.

Drawing offers children, who may have challenges expressing themselves verbally, a means of expression. It can help them express their lived experiences as well as "the unrecognized, unacknowledged or 'unsayable' stories that they hold" (Leitch, 2008, p. 37). Punch (2002) stated that drawings, which are fluid and can be changed, allow children the time and control to shape what they wish to express. I found that throughout the drawing process, children revised parts of their drawings. For example, one participant revised an area of his drawing that depicted a table with chairs around it. He took a marker, crossed out a chair, and said, "this chair is deleted actually, I made a mistake." He then went on to further describe the activities that took place at the table.

Researchers should be careful not to assume that drawing is a "simple, 'natural' method to use with children" (Punch, 2002, p. 331). Because this data generation tool depends on children's comfort with drawing, and their actual ability to draw, it is important to acknowledge that not all children wishing to participate in a research study may want to draw. Some children believe they cannot draw, or think that their drawings are "no good" (Einarsdottir, Dockett, & Perry, 2009; Merewether & Fleet, 2014). When I asked one child if he could draw a picture of his current classroom, he replied, "I don't really know how to draw the things." He went on to tell me that instead he would draw the blocks, with which he enjoyed playing. Although he appeared unsure of his capabilities of drawing his classroom, he wanted to draw, and continued to do so throughout the interview. Near the end of our conversation, I asked him, "Do you want to stop now? Or do you want to keep drawing or talking?" and he replied, "Drawing." Einarsdottir et al. (2009) noted that asking children to draw during data generation might make them feel more comfortable, as they do not need to maintain eye contact with the researcher and are engaged in a familiar activity. This appeared to be the case with this child; although he did not draw his past or current classrooms, he appeared to enjoy, and feel comfortable with, drawing while conversing.

Maggie: We had assumed that drawing during the interview process would be an appealing task for the children and make them feel comfortable. This turned out not to be true for all participants. Most were attracted by the new, "good" markers (a rare treat in a busy childcare setting) and the stand-up mirror we brought to the interviews, and many seemed to genuinely enjoy working on their drawings while talking to the interviewer. However, a few seemed anxious about the request to draw. For example, one participant seemed disappointed in his drawing and said in a sad tone of voice, "I can't make a circle." Another hesitated before starting his drawing and asked, "How do you draw my friends?" Although we clearly told the children they did not have to participate, and were vigilant for verbal and nonverbal signs that they did not wish to start or continue the interview, we failed to explicitly provide them with the option to participate without drawing. Offering choices to children regarding *how* they participate respects them as complex individuals; relying on broad assumptions such as "all children like to draw" can create an uncomfortable experience for some participants.

Tiffany: One child did not wish to draw at all during the data generation process. When I asked him if he could draw a picture of his current classroom, he replied, "Or you could visit my class" and went on to state, "I don't really remember what it looks like." Dockett and Perry (2005b) argued that researchers do not have the right to demand information: Some children may wish to remain silent and it is important to respect their choice. This particular child, especially near the end of the conversation, responded to various questions by saying he did not remember. Although this could be interpreted as a lack of memory, when paired with his body language, it appeared to indicate that he did not want to continue with the interview. After engaging with this particular child for a period, his body language and words shifted to indicate that he was no longer interested in participating in the research. I asked him if he would like to stop talking, and he replied, "Yes." I then thanked him for his time and concluded the session.

Maggie: Some participants in the CWTAR project seemed willing, even eager, to draw, and yet chose not to draw what the interviewer requested (i.e., a self-portrait and a picture of a friend). For example, one child responded to each of my requests by asking, several times, if he could draw various animals. Another child did not ask but simply informed me that he was going to draw a superhero. Another drew a series of concentric circles. These actions can be interpreted in a few ways. Dockett and Perry (2010) noted that children may use actions like this to exercise some control over their level of participation. Perhaps the children felt compelled in some way to participate in the study and chose to draw something other than requested as an act of resistance. It is also possible that their actions reflected an inadequate knowledge of the purpose of the research because we failed to clearly explain it at the outset. The request to draw oneself and one's friend should have been easily understood by all participants, so perhaps their resistance was intended to signal that they did not see any real point in drawing what was asked. During interviews I was sometimes frustrated by what I characterized as "nonparticipation." My preoccupation with the desire to get "good" data may have caused me to miss opportunities to fully hear what participants were saying (verbally and nonverbally), and to engage and respond.

FINAL THOUGHTS

This chapter has focused on the importance of thoughtful research design, and presented some examples of when our research did not proceed as planned. Child participants should be considered social actors in the research process, and therefore the assumption that a child participant will act in a certain manner (i.e., by narrowly defining "participation" and expecting certain methods to elicit predictable behavior and "good data" from children) is unreasonable and unethical, and may be counter to the expressed goals of participatory research. Rather than privileging participatory methods above others, Gallacher and Gallagher (2008) argued instead for a shift in methodological attitude: to one of immaturity and uncertainty in which "Researchers are not simply reporting a world that exists 'out-there,' but are creating and experimenting with an emergent one" (p. 512). In future research, possibilities for elevating children's voices may not be rooted solely in the planning stages, but rather in moments of unpredictability. We are not dismissing the importance of thoughtful research design, but openness to the unexpected—which by its very nature promotes openness to negotiation—may support more reciprocal and equitable research relationships. Encounters between researcher and participant that are guided by past experience, but open to uncertainty, can encourage reimagining and reconsideration.

These possibilities for reconsideration extend past the research relationship, to that of our notions of children themselves. As discussed above, adults are influenced by dominant constructions of children, and often decide which children are exposed to which research. Our research studies illustrate the need to challenge these boundaries and hear children's voices within environments that are often heavily "controlled" (e.g., classrooms) and about topics from which they may be "protected" (e.g., race). It is our hope that this chapter has shed light and broadened conversations on some of the methodological challenges related to participatory research with children. Moving forward, it will be important to engage in continual critical and ethical reflection to move beyond pre-established conceptualizations of children. We need to reconsider children's participation and encourage continual negotiations where children are not *given* voice—rather, where their own voices are elevated throughout the research process.

Questions for Reflection

1. Issues of **power**, present in all research encounters, are heightened when adults do research with children. We question the conventional approach to minimizing social difference that Raffety (2009) describes as one which "inevitably presumes control to be located in the researcher and the research design, and tends to reproduce understandings of difference from the perspective of the researcher rather than the informant or the child" (p. 417). Further, we acknowledge child participants can act in unanticipated ways and engage in acts of resistance, calling into question the assumption that children do not have any power unless adults empower them. *What are some understandings of agency, power, and empowerment, and how may we consider the issues and dilemmas these may present when thinking through conducting research with children?*

2. There is a tension in **adult-initiated research** between the desire to reduce power imbalances by involving participants more fully in all stages of the research process, and the need to employ knowledge and theoretical understanding that may not be available to the participants. *Researchers often interpret and analyze what is said, or not said, by children using conceptual frameworks that are unknown and inaccessible to the children themselves. In doing so, however, are researchers distorting the meanings of the participants' voices? Should child participants be brought into the analysis stage of research projects?*

3. The researcher's **social location** influences all aspects of a research project and should be identified and reflected upon throughout the project. Researchers having "insider status" (i.e., a preexisting relationship with participants) can help create a sense of ease and comfort for children, but it can also, in some cases, lead to children feeling compelled to participate (e.g., if the researcher has a dual role as a teacher or other authority figure). *How else can the researcher's social location either support or restrict children's equitable participation in research?*

4. A variety of **gatekeepers** typically control children's participation in research. They may base their decisions on their beliefs about the appropriateness of the research project, and their conceptualizations of children and their capacities. *How should we balance the need to protect children from unethical research with children's right to have a voice? To what extent do gatekeepers influence which voices are accessed and promoted, and subsequently which are silenced through the research process?*

5. Researchers working with children typically must seek **consent** from parents/guardians and **assent** from the children themselves. Assent should be continuously considered; children may give verbal or nonverbal indications that they would like to stop even after they

have agreed to participate. *How much or little information about the research project should be provided to children? How can it be explained in a way that promotes full understanding, thereby respecting children's participation rights?*

6. When considering which **methods** to employ, it is important to note "perceiving children as competent social actors does not necessarily mean that research should be conducted in the same way as with adults" (Punch, 2002, p. 338). *Are there, or more specifically should there be, "child friendly" research methods? How do conversations regarding research with children change when researchers shift from considering child capability to examining power imbalances innately present in adult-child relationships? What are the possible benefits or dangers associated with labeling certain research methods as 'child-friendly' (or should these methods be labeled as "research friendly")? How may this label further contribute to discussions of children's marginalized position in society?*

Suggestions for Further Reading

Assent and Consent

Graham, A., Powell, M. A., Taylor, N., Anderson, D., & Fitzgerald, R. (2013). *Ethical research involving children*. Florence: UNICEF Office of Research—Innocenti.

Harcourt, D., & Conroy, H. (2011). Informed consent: Process and procedures seeking research partnerships with young children. In D. Harcourt, B. Perry, & T. Waller (Eds.), *Researching young children's perspectives: Debating the ethics and dilemmas of educational research with children* (pp. 38–51). London, England: Routledge.

Mayne, F., Howitt, C., & Rennie, L. J. (2017). Using interactive nonfiction narrative to enhance competence in the informed consent process with 3-year-old children. *Journal of Inclusive Education, 21*(3), 299–315.

Drawing as a Method of Data Generation

Einarsdóttir, J., Dockett, S., & Perry, B. (2009). Making meaning: Children's perspectives expressed through drawings. *Early Child Development and Care, 179*(2), 217–232.

Elden, S. (2012). Inviting the messy: Drawing methods and 'children's voices.' *Childhood, 20*(1), 66–81.

Participatory Research With Children

Groundwater-Smith, S., Dockett, S., & Bottrell, D. (2015). *Participatory research with children and young people*. London, England: SAGE.

Tisdall, E. K. M. (2016). Participation, rights and 'participatory' methods. In

A. Farrell, S. L. Kagan, & E. K. M. Tisdall (Eds.), *The SAGE handbook of early childhood research* (pp. 73–88). London, England: SAGE.

Voice

Gray, C., & Winter, E. (2011). Hearing voices: Participatory research with pre-school children with and without disabilities. *European Early Childhood Education Research Journal, 19*(3), 309–320.

Spyrou, S. (2016). Researching children's silences: Exploring the fullness of voice in childhood research. *Childhood, 23*(1), 7–21.

REFERENCES

Alderson, P., & Morrow, V. (2011). *The ethics of research with children and young people: A practical handbook.* London, England: SAGE.

Barnikis, T. (2015). Children's perceptions of their experiences in early learning environments: An exploration of power and hierarchy. *Global Studies of Childhood, 5*(3), 291–304.

Berman, R., & MacNevin, M. (2017). Adults researching with children. In X. Chen, R. Raby, & P. Albanese (Eds.), *The Sociology of Childhood and Youth Studies in Canada* (pp. 24–46). Toronto, Canada: Canadian Scholars' Press.

Berman, R., Daniel, B.-J., Butler, A., MacNevin, M., & Royer, N. (2017). Nothing, or almost nothing, to report: Early childhood educators and discursive constructions of colorblindness. *International Critical Childhood Policy Studies Journal, 6*(1), 52–65.

Boutte, G. S., Lopez-Robertson, J., & Powers-Costello, E. (2011). Moving beyond colorblindness in early childhood classrooms. *Early Childhood Education Journal, 35*(5), 335–342.

Birbeck, D., & Drummond, M. (2005). Interviewing, and listening to the voices of, very young children on body image and perceptions of self. *Early Childhood Development and Care, 176*(6), 579–596.

Burke, C. (2005). "Play in focus": Children researching their own spaces and places for play. *Children, Youth, and Environments, 15*(1), 27–53.

Cameron, H. (2005). Asking the tough questions: A guide to ethical practices in interviewing young children. *Early Child Development and Care, 175*(6), 597–610.

Coad, J., & Evans, R. (2008). Reflections on practical approaches to involving children and young people in the data analysis process. *Children & Society, 22*(1), 31–52.

Cocks, A. (2007). The ethical maze: Finding an inclusive path towards gaining children's agreement to research participation. *Childhood, 13*(2), 247–266.

Cox, S. (2005). Intention and meaning in young children's drawing. *International Journal of Art & Design Education, 24*(2), 115–125.

Cree, V. E., Kay, H., & Tisdall, K. (2002). Research with children: Sharing the dilemmas. *Child & Family Social Work, 7*(1), 47–56.

Delgado, R., & Stefancic, J. (2012). Introduction. *Critical race theory: An introduction* (2nd ed., pp. 1–14). New York, NY: NYU Press.

Dockett, S., Einarsdottir, J., & Perry, B. (2009). Researching with children: Ethical tensions. *Journal of Early Childhood Research, 7*(3), 283–298.

Dockett, S., & Perry, B. (2005a). Researching with children: Insights from the starting school research project. *Early Child Development and Care, 175*(6), 507–521.

Dockett, S., & Perry, B. (2005b). 'You need to know how to play safe': Children's experiences of
starting school, *Contemporary issues in early childhood, 6*(1), 4–18.

Dockett, S., & Perry, B. (2010). Researching with young children: Seeking assent. *Child Indicators Research, 4*(2), 231–247.

Einarsdottir, J., Dockett, S., & Perry, B. (2009). Making meaning: Children's perspectives expressed through drawings. *Early Child Development and Care, 179*(2), 217–232.

Fleet, A., & Harcourt, D. (2018). (Co)-Researching with children. In M. Fleer & B. van Oers (Eds.), *International Handbook of Early Childhood Education* (pp. 165–201). Dordrecht, Netherlands: Springer.

Foucault, M. (1981). The order of discourse. In R. Young (Ed.), *Untying the text: A post structuralist reader* (pp. 348–378). Boston, MA: Routledge & K. Paul.

Gallacher, L. A., & Gallagher, M. (2008). Methodological immaturity in childhood research? Thinking through 'participatory methods.' *Childhood, 15*(4), 499–516.

Gardiner, H., & Kosmitzki, C. (2010). *Lives across cultures: Cross-cultural human development* (5th ed.). Boston, MA: Allyn & Bacon.

Gregory, E., & Ruby, M. (2011). The 'insider/outsider' dilemma of ethnography: Working with young children and their families in cross-cultural contexts. *Journal of Early Childhood Research, 9*(2), 162–174.

Husband, T., Jr. (2012). "I don't see color": Challenging assumptions about discussing race with young children. *Early Childhood Education Journal, 39*(6), 365–371.

Irwin, L. G., & Johnson, J. (2005). Interviewing young children: Explicating our practices and dilemmas. *Qualitative Health Research, 15*(6), 821–831.

Karnieli-Miller, O., Strier, R., & Pessach, L. (2009). Power relations in qualitative research. *Qualitative Health Research, 19*(2), 279–289.

Leitch, R. (2008). Creatively researching children's narratives through images and drawings. In P. Thomson (Ed.), *Doing visual research with children and young people* (pp. 37–57). New York, NY: Routledge.

MacNaughton, G., & Davis, K. (Eds.). (2009). *"Race" and early childhood education: An international approach to identity, politics, and pedagogy.* New York, NY: Palgrave Macmillan.

MacNevin, M., & Berman, R. (2017). The Black baby doll doesn't fit the disconnect between early childhood diversity policy, early childhood educator practice, and children's play. *Early Child Development and Care, 187*(5–6), 827–839.

Mason, J., & Danby, S. (2011). Children as experts of their lives: Child inclusive research. *Child Indicators Research, 4*, 185–189.

Mayall, B. (1994). Introduction. In B. Mayall (Ed.) *Children's childhoods: Observed and experienced* (pp. 1–12). London, England: Falmer Press.

Mayall, B. (2002). *Towards a sociology for childhood: Thinking from children's lives.* Buckingham, England: Open University Press.

Mayall, B. (2008). Conversations with children: Working with generational issues. In P. Christensen & A. James (Eds.), *Research with children: Perspectives and practices* (2nd ed.; pp. 109–124). New York, NY: Routledge.

Merewether, J., & Fleet, A. (2014). Seeking children's perspectives: A respectful layered research approach. *Early Child Development and Care, 184*(6), 897–914.

Pahlke, E., Bigler, R. S., & Suizzo, M. (2012). Relations between colorblind socialization and children's racial bias: Evidence from European American mothers and their preschool children. *Child Development, 83*(4), 1164–1179.

Prout, A., & James, A. (1997). A new paradigm for the sociology of childhood? Provenance, promise and problems. In A. Prout & A. James (Eds.), *Constructing and reconstructing childhood: Contemporary issues in the sociological study of childhood* (2nd ed.; pp. 7–32). London, England: Falmer Press.

Punch, S. (2002). Research with children. *Childhood, 9*(3), 321–341.

Raffety, E. L. (2015). Minimizing social distance: participatory research with children. *Childhood, 22*(3), 409–422.

Rocco, T., & Plakhotnik, M. (2009). Literature reviews, conceptual frameworks, and theoretical frameworks: Terms, functions, and distinctions. *Human Resource Development Review, 8*(1), 120–130.

Smith, C., & Greene, S. (2014). *Key thinkers in childhood studies.* Bristol, England: Policy Press.

Spratling, R., Coke, S., & Minick, P. (2012). Qualitative data collection with children. *Applied Nursing Research, 25*(1), 47–53.

Stephenson, A. (2009). Horses in the sandpit: Photography, prolonged involvement and 'stepping back' as strategies for listening to children's voices. *Early Child Development and Care, 179*(2), 131–141.

United Nations. (1989). *United Nations Convention on the Rights of the Child.* Geneva, Switzerland: United Nations.

Vittrup, B. (2016). Early childhood teachers' approaches to multicultural education & perceived barriers to disseminating anti-bias messages. *Multicultural Education, 23*(3–4), 37–41.

CHAPTER 2

STUDENT VOICE WORK AS AN EDUCATIVE PRACTICE

Susan Groundwater-Smith and Nicole Mockler

ABSTRACT

This chapter explores the challenges and dilemmas associated with engaging with children and young people as active agents in research in the context of school education, where the purpose is to enlighten and inform schooling as an *educative practice*. It argues that educative practice is that which is strategic and underpinned by transformative research that is inclusive of the consequential stakeholders—the students themselves. Our discussion will address the notion of engaging student voice work as a *practice-changing practice*. Through the development of two case studies of student voice work enacted in different contexts, we use practice theory, specifically the theory of practice architectures to explore how educative practice is formed, reformed and transformed through the engagement of young people as contributors to research—doing research, being in research and themselves relating research to local policy and enactment. As well as contributing to the extant literature regarding participatory methodologies in relation to engaging with children and young people in research, the chapter aims to bring to readers' attention the critical nature of context as understood through the lens of practice architectures with respect to the engagement of student voice.

Participatory Methodologies to Elevate Children's Voice and Agency, pages 25–46
Copyright © 2019 by Information Age Publishing

25

> **Luke:** Master, moving stones around is one thing. This is totally different!
> **Yoda:** [irritated] No! No different! Only different in your mind. You must unlearn what you have learned.
> **Luke:** [focusing, quietly] All right, I'll give it a try.
> **Yoda:** Try not, do or do not, *there is no try.*

Our stance in writing this chapter on the ways in which student voice can and should contribute to educative practice is to keep alive the matter of not only the essential "why" of education—a matter too rarely addressed; but also the "what" and the "how" of education. It is strongly normative and eschews the burgeoning process of consulting young people as pawns, selected to legitimate decisions that have already been made on their behalf (Mockler & Groundwater-Smith, 2015). Participation by children and young people is understood as a contested practice, particularly in the context of school education. For example, Hanson (2016) and Horgan, Forde, Martin and Parkes (2017) suggest that too often the practice is a performative one as illustrated by the use of school organizations, such as Student Representative Councils, whose formation is based upon the selection of students least likely to be disruptive or difficult.

The chapter will discuss the challenges and dilemmas associated with engaging with children and young people as active agents in research in the context of school education where the purpose is to enlighten and inform as an *educative practice.* We will argue that educative practice is that which is strategic and underpinned by transformative research that is inclusive of the consequential stakeholders—the students themselves. Practice, in this case, is understood as that by which we learn and unlearn. The practice of, as Maxine Greene (1977) puts it, "being wide awake."

Our discussion will address the notion of authentic, transformative student voice work as a *practice-changing practice* (Kemmis, 2007). We are concerned here with coming to know "how to go on in practice" (Kemmis et al., 2014, p. 207), understanding those factors which enable and constrain practice on an institutional level such that practices might become sustained and sustainable. Additionally, we are concerned that participation by children and young people in research and inquiry in schools is enacted as a critical democratic practice that provides a firm basis for decisions about, among other things, policy formulation and the provision of resources. Further, that such participation should constitute a capacity building practice employing dialogue and communication (Johnson, 2017). Thus the chapter will explore how educative practice has the possibility to be formed, reformed, and transformed through the engagement of young people as contributors to research—doing research, being in research and themselves relating research to local policy and enactment. Importantly, the chapter will address the knowledge that is developing around the engagement of young people both *about* educational practice and *in* educational practice, by utilizing the framework of practice architectures (Kemmis et al., 2014). Here we will explore the sayings, doings, and relatings enabled and constrained by the cultural-discursive, material-economic, and social-political arrangements of sites of practice in which the emergent traditions associated with the engagement of children and young people might flourish.

To achieve this end two case studies, undertaken by the authors, will be presented: one a year-long study in the middle years of an independent school involving 12 to 13 year old girls. Here, a committee of students made an ongoing contribution to addressing ways of assessing student learning in Years 6 and 7 that encompassed encounters in one specific intersubjective space with its own history and arrangements. The other is a statewide consultation with adolescents, 14 to 17 year olds, undertaken with regard to the impact of a major policy change in the form of a mandatory raising of the school leaving age (Groundwater-Smith & Mockler, 2012, 2015a). The outcome of this study is, even several years later, still uncertain. This leads us into a discussion regarding the ways in which state wide policy formulation may or may not be responsive to the contributions that students may make to educative practice.

While the first of these may be constructed as having more participatory characteristics than the second we shall argue that authentic consultation that goes beyond asking children and young people to complete a superficial student satisfaction questionnaire, for example, may contribute to features of educative practice not hitherto imagined. "Unwelcome truths" (Kemmis, 2006) may be exposed. For example, an Australian historian investigating the teaching and learning of history in secondary schools nationally conducted extensive and penetrating interviews with students across all of the secondary school years (Clark, 2008). She found that, on the whole, students regarded their country's history as something to be endured rather than actively engaged with—in particular the history of its political formation; and that its First Nation people's dispossession was poorly taught and understood; it is a history "that is taught to death, but not in *depth*" (Clark, 2008, p. 67). Such consultation with young people, with the express purpose of bringing to light the unwelcome truths which might then shape responses in policy and practice goes far beyond that envisaged on the bottom "rungs" of various ladders or hierarchies of participation in research by young people (for example, Fielding, 2011; Hart, 1992). Indeed, much depends on the nature of the questions being asked, the form of the interaction and what is at stake.

As well as contributing to the extant literature regarding participatory procedures in relation to engaging with children and young people in research, the chapter will also bring to readers' attention the critical nature of context as understood through the lens of the theory of practice architectures.

SCHOOLING AS EDUCATIVE PRACTICE

As Collingwood (1924) put it:

> Education does not mean stuffing a mind with information; it means helping a mind to create itself, to grow into an active and vigorous contributor to the life of the world. The information given in such a process is meant to be absorbed into the life of the mind itself. (p. 316)

Schools provide a context in which teaching and learning are in a constant state of play, with all of those participating having multiple roles and responsibilities. In his book, *The Beautiful Risk of Education,* Gert Biesta (2007) asks that we "give teaching back to education"(p. 44). He argues that "we should understand the teacher as someone who, in the most general sense, brings something new to the educational situation, something that was not already there" (p. 44). He further argues that, all too often education is constructed as an economic transaction with the learner positioned as consumer and the educator as the provider with education, itself, a commodity (Biesta, 2006).

We would rather see learners as active agents, engaged in dialogue with their teachers, their peers, and their environment. Considering the relationship with teachers, Noddings (2006) asserts that there are widespread misgivings about dialogue in schools. She states: "It is not just talking to each other; dialogue requires listening and a genuine respect for the partner in dialogue, [it] asks for a mutual commitment to inform, learn and make decisions" (p. 80). In this chapter we seek to explore partnerships between teachers and learners that are purposeful and designed to investigate the conditions of teaching and learning practices such that they contribute to ongoing authentic transformation, by working together to create structures and processes that are ever more fair and just. We are mindful of not underestimating the power dimensions associated with such cooperative partnerships, being concerned not to perceive learners as mini clones of their teachers (Ergler, 2017). As Freire (1972) reminds us, education is not a gift to be bestowed, and neither is it an act of knowledge transmission. Rather, education is a continuing process of emerging political and personal consciousness that evolves by acting upon the world dialogically with others in order to transform it. Some might believe that this is a far cry from what young people in schools are capable of, but we assert that given a voice students are well able to articulate the nature and value of their experiences; the why, what, and how of their schooling.

PARTICIPATORY ACTION RESEARCH AND STUDENT VOICE

Much has been written on the nature of student voice in various forms of participatory inquiry (e.g., Alderson, 2012; Fielding, 2004, 2007; Groundwater-Smith, Dockett, & Bottrell, 2015; Kim, 2016; Mockler & Groundwater-Smith, 2015). Valuing young people as those able to contribute to research in schools enables them to come into contact with their teachers and decision makers in ways that may not have been hitherto imagined. As we have asserted, dialogue is central to their participation. Traditionally, dialogue in schools has its limits, positioning students as learners, rather than as speakers. What is required is a change to those fundamental procedures that are mediated by overt and subtle forms of power. Students as authentic responders and active researchers may be seen as a radical interruption to the normal asymmetries inherent in school relations, where adults make the important decisions, and children and young people are the consequential stakeholders. Who will be consulted? How will they be enabled to speak? To what extent will they be fully participative beyond being data sources, acknowledging that this in itself may be a first step. Will they have sufficient agency to inform the consequent decisions arising from any inquiry?

Being inclusive of young people as responders and active researchers finds its rationale in the 1989 United Nations Convention on the Rights of the Child. The convention is comprehensive and entitles children to a broad range of rights, including the right to have their best interests treated as a primary consideration in all actions concerning them, including decisions related to their care and protection (such as their education). In particular, Article 12 states that children have the right to say what they think in all matters affecting them, and to have their views taken seriously (Reynaert, Bouverne-de-Bie, & Vandevelde, 2009). One outcome of the widespread ratification of the Convention that has taken hold globally with few exceptions, is that the perception of autonomy and participation rights for children has become the new norm. It has been widely acknowledged that young people are, in effect, expert witnesses to their experiences of schooling. Even so, perception is one thing, actualization is another. True participation, that is the exercise of authentic agency, must address matters of power.

There can be no denying that power in schools and school systems is increasingly centralized, governed by rules and regulatory frameworks as part of a competitive global scenario over which students (and indeed, teachers) have little control. As Taylor and Robinson (2009) have observed, there is "an uncritical view of the entrenched, hierarchical power relations in schools" (p. 166), with the result that student consultation and research activities are often little more than tokenistic interventions serving established power.

Typically the manifestation of student engagement is embodied through student representative groups that are enabled to run charity events, social occasions, or gatherings such as school assemblies. While in this way they might be enabled to make contributions to discussions regarding such matters as school uniforms and offerings at the school canteen, rarely are they enabled to have an input into the ways in which teaching and learning is conducted. This is resonant with Stoecklin's (2013) concern that

> structured channels of consultation such as youth forums or youth councils only grasp a part of what children and young people are actually able to do, and their filtering effect increases the representational problem linked to the difficulty of reaching a diversity of voices. There are powerful social and economic forces limiting children's voice, and invisible networks perpetuate a culture of non-participation where children and young people feel that decisions are always taken elsewhere and end up frustrated or cynical. (p. 4)

Nonetheless, there are exceptions to these limitations. The State of Victoria in Australia has long established a requirement for student representation on school-governing bodies, a position that gives them both power and legitimacy. Mayes (2016, p. 7) points out six key benefits to student representation on school councils as identified by the students themselves, these being:

- Students have experiential knowledge that other adults may not have.
- Young people and adults learn and connect through dialogue.
- Students have a right to have influence on decisions that affect them.
- Student representation can improve communication between the school council and the broader student body.
- Student representatives benefit individually.
- Students feel heard and valued when changes happen.

There is also a growing acknowledgement that young people in schools are the "consequential stakeholders" (Mockler & Groundwater-Smith, 2012) who bear the brunt of decisions made on their behalf and thus they *should* be participative in making those decisions. However, many of the arguments are of a narrow instrumental kind, seeking to "improve" student learning outcomes within the existing frameworks of practice. As Prout (2003) has recognized, "Listening to children's voices has become so ubiquitous that is has become part of the 'rhetorical orthodoxy'" (p. 11). However, when it comes to wider policy formulation both within and beyond the school little credence is given to the ways in which young people may have a legitimate perspective. We maintain that participatory research with and by young people is effectively, a practice-changing practice which can be understood using the theory of practice architectures.

PRACTICE ARCHITECTURES AND
PRACTICE-CHANGING PRACTICES

Kemmis (2009) argued that authentic action research, aimed at transformation, is in fact a practice-changing practice. He held that action research aims to change practitioners' practices, their understanding of their practices, and the conditions under which their practice is enacted. He wrote:

> Transforming our practices means transforming what we do; transforming our understandings means transforming what we think and say; and transforming the conditions of practice means transforming the ways we relate to others and to things and circumstances around us. (p. 463)

Engaging with student voice work in the context of participatory action research, such as we advocate here, is, accordingly, a practice-changing practice. Elsewhere, we have written of the implications of engaging authentically with student voice in terms of curriculum, pedagogy, and assessment, understood holistically as classroom practice:

> In the context of classroom practice, this might involve an emphasis on student agency in learning, through support of student decision-making in terms of the con-tent, processes and products of learning. Furthermore, it requires teachers to foster authentic dialogue with students regarding their learning experiences and a willing-ness to adapt and tailor learning experiences according to the experience, needs and preferences of students. The notion of privileging student voice in the context of classroom practice raises questions for practitioners regarding supporting students to 'find' and express their voice in relation to their learning, not necessarily a simple task, and also developing strategies for themselves that lead to good listening, an equally complex endeavour. (Mockler, 2014, pp. 154–155)

We understand student voice work, in its best execution to be transformative of both teachers' and students' practice: to herald a different orientation to teaching and learning, a qualitatively different *learning relationship*.

Practice, however, does not occur in a vacuum, and neither is it a simple or unidimensional thing. The theory of practice architectures (Kemmis & Grootenboer, 2008; Kemmis et al., 2014) can provide us with a way of understanding practices, such as the practice of engaging with student voice, in all their complexity. The theory holds that practices are comprised of *sayings, doings* and *relatings*, "bundled together" in the *projects* (or purpose) of practice and the *dispositions* or *habitus* of practitioners. Practices are enabled and constrained (often simultaneously) by their *practice architectures*, the cultural-discursive (e.g., language and ideas), material-economic (e.g., objects, buildings), and social-political (e.g., relationships) arrangements found in or brought to a site of practice. These *practice architectures* are bundled together in characteristic ways in *practice landscapes* and *practice traditions.* Practitioners' characteristic sayings are realized in *semantic space,* in the medium of *language,* their characteristic doings are realized in physical space-time, in the medium of *work* and *activity,* and their characteristic relatings are realized in social space, in the medium of *power* and *solidarity.*[1]

Engaging student voice, then, might be seen as a practice, or set of practices that includes a range of characteristic sayings, doings, and relatings. Furthermore, while for student voice work to be authentic, transformational, and sustained, particular types of practice architectures are required. While the very idea of a "recipe" or checklist for schools and teachers wishing to engage in this kind of work is antithetical to an understanding of practice as highly contextualized and contingent, it is safe to say that this kind of work would be unlikely to flourish in a strongly authoritarian site with its attendant arrangements.

PRACTICE ARCHITECTURES IN ACTION:
AN EXAMINATION OF TWO CASE STUDIES

By way of exploring student voice work using the lens of practice architectures, we present two case studies that, as noted in the introduction, vary greatly in their aims and scope. Following our abbreviated portrayal of these two cases we will use the theory of practice architectures to explore the potential of student voice work to operate as a practice-changing practice.

Young People Investigating (In)Formative Assessment

Soriah College[2] is an independent girls' school catering for young people Kindergarten to Year 12. It was established in the late 1800s and has a long tradition of adhering to liberal Catholic values as expressed in its mission statement:

> Soriah College...educates students to achieve personal excellence, to act with justice and compassion, and to embrace the future with an optimistic global vision.

Years 6 and 7, catering for 12 to 13 year olds, are designated within the school as the "middle years," a phase between primary and senior school. There have been a number of ways in which the middle years of schooling have been characterized but there is agreement that they are a critical point in the cognitive, emotional, and physical development of students, often beset by a misunderstanding of the great variance between individuals and the need to attend to the requisite differentiation. It is a time when basic values and attitudes are forming and for some students, solidifying. It is a time of contradictions; these young people are seen to be reaching out for independence yet seeking for security as they take increasing risks in becoming autonomous (Groundwater-Smith, Mitchell, & Mockler, 2007; Groundwater-Smith & Mockler, 2015b; Pendergast & Bahr, 2010).

The focus of the project was related to the matter of authentic and reflective assessment of learning with high expectations, in particular an exploration of formative assessment in the middle years of schooling at Soriah College, and aimed to address the following two questions:

- How can teachers, through participatory action research collect information that contributes to a better understanding of assessment for learning and assessment in learning?
- How can the processes be sustained by busy teachers and their students so that their joint work becomes increasingly positive and enjoyable?

Following consultation with the school's academic partner (one of the authors of this chapter) it was decided that understanding the nature of (in) formative assessment would be greatly enhanced by engaging students as active participants and researchers in the project.

Consequently, a steering committee composed of twelve students and three teaching staff was formed. The student body was invited to submit expressions of interest for inclusion in the steering committee, with an understanding that they would be sacrificing time to the project from May to December. In sifting through the expressions, staff were enjoined to consider some "outliers," that is students who were known to be nonconformists. Several early meetings with the steering committee and mentor teachers were devoted to participatory research methods outlined in a resource booklet devised specifically for the purpose of informing practitioner research in schools (Groundwater-Smith & Mockler, 2003). The steering committee was not only familiarized with a range of data gathering methods (both qualitative and quantitative) but also the necessary ethical conditions that would be required when they were working with their peers, in particular in relation to matters of informed consent and confidentiality.

An important development was the recasting of the project's key questions to:

- How do I know myself and what contributes to my learning?
- How do I know I am learning?
- How do *you* know I am learning?
- What do we need to do next?

The students perceived that by asking these questions they were broadening the understanding of the nature of assessment that recognized the part played by the students themselves in terms of self-assessment and the development of learning as a joint project.

It is in relation to the first two of these questions that this case study focuses. The steering committee decided to design a full day in which all students in Year 6 and 7 would participate, referred to as "Have Your Say Day." This was no small task, students had carefully examined a number of appropriate methods for collecting data; the challenges associated with analyses and reporting and the logistics of moving a student body through a series of activities. Students progressed through a number of "stations;" see below for a brief summary of each with short observations made by steering committee members:

1. *Myself the Learner.* Students had been asked to consider an animal and its characteristics and the ways in which they could relate to it as a learner. In their analysis the small group saw that the range of responses was significant and that many were related to quietness, efficiency and growth. But they also expressed concern that some young people represented themselves as slow moving and preferring to "work in the shadows."

2. *The Graffiti Wall.* Participants were asked to consider what made learning difficult for them at times and to "scribble" a response "on the wall." This group identified the major issue of distractions, both in terms of noise in open spaces and the multiple uses of technology. They noted concerns about bullying and that technology has consequences, both positive and negative for engagement and learning.

3. *Learning Cartoons.* Students worked in groups to complete a six-frame storyboard that illustrated learning something new. The group selected as key themes the power of watching/observing, practicing, and achieving. They saw the following attributes as important for learning: being courageous, curious, open to risk, self-motivated, and persistent.

4. *The Learning Robot.* Students worked in groups and selected the components of the robot, assembling them in terms of the ways in which it might be able to do tasks that they find difficult. It was noted that responses could be divided into physical capabilities, mental capacities (being fast and staying organized and on task), and social engagement. They distinguished between "what could be done" and "what we are capable of doing."

5. *Posters—Good learning is...* Students observed that much of the time was spent skimming through the magazines in an endeavour

to find topics of interest rather than images of learning. Nonetheless, the steering committee group identified these themes: the power of motivation for success; being able to manage "not always winning" and learning from mistakes; growing, developing, and changing.

6. *The route to learning.* Here students were required to trace the route taken in order to learn something new.

It was noted that although the results were fairly limited the major issue to emerge from this activity was to do with the process—that in constructing a route to learning more time was needed for thinking before committing to paper.

Following several debriefing sessions, steering committee students developed a questionnaire in relation to both the process and outcomes of the day and this was administered online via Survey Monkey. It was clear that the student body from middle years classes, all of whom participated in the survey, found a great deal of value in their engagement on the day, but did not fully realize its purpose. To deal with this the steering committee made a short film, *Small Voices: Big Ideas* that was shown at a school assembly. Steering committee students then turned their attention to ways of further investigating the second key question of the study: *How do I know I am learning?* To this end, immediately after viewing the film, students were invited to respond to a survey developed by the steering committee. A number of extracts from student responses to this survey are provided below. The steering committee complemented their findings from the student survey by conducting a small number of focus group interviews with their peers.

How do I know I am learning?

- When my head feels funny because knowledge is seeping into my head.
- When I want to learn more and when I can go home and tell my parents what I've done and be proud of it.
- When I am productive and when I have been listening to the teacher and it goes into my brain.
- I just know because it gets easier to do.
- When I feel proud of myself when I am not talking.
- If I am intrigued with the lesson and I concentrate and am interested.

What helps you remember what you have learned?

- When I write it down.
- When I use silly strategies such as songs and rhymes.

- Revision helps (but it's not fun) and games help me with it. If it is something that I am interested in I will often remember.
- By doing it over and over again.
- I don't like writing notes because it distracts me from what I'm being taught, but I do like going over it a lot after I have learned it and if it really sticks in my mind.

How do you prove that you have learned something?

- Being able to talk and present on a subject.
- When I can write descriptively about what is asked.
- When I can go back and remember it and I can write it down afterwards.
- If someone asks me what I have learned and I can explain what I'm doing without saying "um."
- When I'm confident and tell someone about the topic, or if I succeed in a test and feel good during class or at home or sport.
- By covering it and then trying to remember it.
- By tests.

When I have learned something, what does it feel like?

- My brain feels funny.
- I feel productive and I have achieved something.
- I have finally done something correctly.
- I feel proud that I have achieved something and learned something that I didn't know before.
- I feel knowledgeable and feel I have concentrated.
- I feel happy and relieved.
- It feels like happiness and freedom.
- Achievement and self-accomplishment.
- I feel happy that now I have understood and then look forward to learning something (more).

The focus group leaders also noted that during the conversations that this group of students much preferred using digital means to handwriting, and that they enjoyed having music in the background when they were concentrating on a task. They liked working independently but also saw merit in working in groups as they had to learn to deal with disagreements.

In the debrief surrounding both the survey and the focus group discussions a number of points were raised, among them the distribution of learning time. Steering committee members reported that students appeared to enjoy the longer blocks of time, but also would like to have longer break periods. Students commented on homework and that teachers did not always appreciate how many different assignments were set. Students indicated that they would like an acknowledgement that provision should be made for the interspersed quiet times between active learning and that greater attention should be paid to student differences. They would also like opportunities to engage in outside learning, making use of the school's extensive grounds, and to have more recognition of student ideas when teachers are planning. Subsequent focus group discussions with middle years' teachers indicated that these recommended arrangements were quite "doable" and school policies could accommodate them.

Returning to the matter of the ways in which teachers know their students are learning, this remains a work in progress. Suffice to say here that the teachers of students in the middle years found the depth of the student inquiry, as demonstrated in a 48-page report, illuminating and informative. An important outcome of the project was seen to be the commitment to change and the contribution that it made to the teachers' own professional learning, which resonates with the work of Bourke & Loveridge (2016).

Giving the last word to a student who wrote in a response to "Have Your Say Day":

> I enjoyed today a lot. I think it really got us thinking about ourselves and how we learn, also what helps us to and also what doesn't help us as learners. I think this has really made us reflect on ourselves and the way we learn.

The sayings, doings, and relatings that comprised the process of engaging in this student voice initiative were complex. On the part of both students and teachers, it required an openness to speaking and hearing the "truths" of student learning in the middle years. In terms of doings, it required a level of joint enterprise, where students were able to shape the inquiry while at the same time being supported as partners by the adult members of the steering committee. In terms of relatings, it required a rebalancing of student–teacher relationships to bring students into more than an advisory or consultative role. The cultural-discursive, material-economic, and social-political arrangements within the school were such that the practices associated with engaging student voice were able to be supported, and this is evident in the valuing and placement of the project, both on an institutional level and a personal level on the part of the teachers involved and in the dedication of time and space within the school year to the project.

Case 2 Impact of the Raising of the School Leaving Age

In New South Wales, Australia's most populous state, compulsory school attendance was set at 15 years of age in 1943. This arrangement remained until 2010 when, by virtue of legislation, all students were required to remain at school until they turned 17 years of age, unless they were engaging in full-time education, training, paid work, or a combination of these activities until they turned 17 years of age (NSW Department of Education and Communities, 2012).[3]

In its community consultation report designed to elicit responses to changing the school leaving age the NSW Department of Education (2008) argued:

> The opportunities for young people with high level qualifications are greater than ever before. Research consistently demonstrates that those who stay longer at school receive higher wages, have less unemployment throughout their lives and are more likely to go on to further study—which is itself increasing in importance in the current job market.

As a consequence the new policy was announced with a law being passed by the New South Wales Parliament in May 2009 to increase the school leaving age from 15 years of age in 2009 to 17 years of age. This law has operated from January 1, 2010.

The claims regarding the benefits to young people with respect to income and career opportunities have not gone uncontested. Dockery's (2005) compelling report seeks to assess the benefits of additional years of schooling for those Australian young people who may not be well suited to further education. He argues that policies around increased retention are based upon the superior outcomes for those completing schooling relative to those who leave early.

> It seems dangerous to paint all young people with the same brush and surely there are some young people who are simply not well suited to the schooling environment, either in terms of their individual preferences or in terms of the benefits that they can expect to gain. (p. 39)

From a policy perspective, he questions

> that there is sufficient empirical evidence to support mandated increases in the level of schooling...Heterogeneity in the returns to schooling exist because individuals are heterogeneous. The objective of policy should be to ensure that there are *alternative pathways and institutional arrangements available to meet the varying needs, abilities and preferences of young people and to make available the information that they require to make informed decisions on what is optimal for them.* (p. 42, emphasis added)

Concerns regarding the impact of changing the school leaving age upon statewide policies and practices were such that two consultants (the authors of this chapter) were appointed to investigate the ways in which students themselves, were responding to the conditions under which they now found themselves, both students who intended to stay on in the senior years of schooling and those who would otherwise have left (for a full report of this study, see Groundwater-Smith & Mockler, 2012, 2015a). The study followed a sequential mixed methods approach (Creswell, 2005) in which there was a qualitative phase (focus group interviews) that was succeeded by a quantitative phase (online survey).

It was determined that students from 12 NSW high schools, one from each of the 10 regions of the state and two from the more populous regions would participate in the focus group discussions and following online survey. In total 236 students (representing 15 to 17 year olds) participated in the conversations. Given that the study sought for the explication of the meanings of the experience of the senior years of secondary schooling, as held by the participants, criterion based selection of sites and participants was warranted—the criteria being social and geographical distribution, ensuring that some, but not all schools, catered for students from challenging socioeconomic backgrounds.

Six hundred thirteen students from the case study schools participated in the online survey, representing a response rate of approximately 20%. The student survey was developed iteratively based on the themes emerging from the focus group discussions, the intention being to "test out" these themes with a broader group of young people. The survey was developed by the project facilitators in consultation with staff from the Student Engagement Bureau of the NSW DEC, and administered by the then Educational Measurement and School Accountability Directorate. The survey remained "open" for 3 weeks, and schools determined the processes by which students engaged with the survey, in some cases merely emailing the link to students for them to complete in their own time while in other cases orchestrating a session in which students could choose to complete their survey. In all cases, students were informed that their participation was optional.

Five key findings emerged that became known as the *New School Leaving Age Student Feedback Study* (Groundwater-Smith & Mockler, 2012), and were deemed worthy of further consideration to the development of appropriate policies and procedures within the NSW Department of Education:

1. *Flexibility and choice.* While for a majority of students the options offered within schools and the structures that support these options are appropriate to their needs, it is clear that for the group of students who find themselves marginalized by the new school leaving age policy, these pathways could be expanded and/or improved. While it is clear that student experience in this area varies from

school to school, this issue emerged as one where schools might be given further support and direction.

2. *Intersection between students' aspirations and teacher expectations:* Some of the emerging evidence in relation to this issue is contradictory, and clearly much depends on the individual experience of students within their school context and the particular teachers with whom they work. Regardless of students' capabilities in terms of achievement, it is important that they are accorded a respect for what is possible, and the data indicate that while this is the case for a large majority of students, for some this lack of respect and regard is highly problematic and painful.

3. *Pedagogy and student engagement:* As a consequence of the overcrowding of the senior curriculum across all Key Learning Areas and the associated high stakes assessment, teachers may find themselves somewhat compromised in terms of the provision of student-centered, differentiated, active learning as encouraged in a range of policies referring to quality teaching. In order for reluctant students to become substantially engaged in their senior studies, it is critical that teachers find ways of conceptualizing and enacting curriculum and pedagogy such that these students see that school *is* for them, drawing on principles of adult learning that many students find to be very compelling in their TAFE (technical and further education) courses.

4. *"Fun:"* It is clear that student expect and want school to be enjoyable, and indeed that a large number of students do, especially in relation to the social dimension of schooling. However, it is not clear what students understand "fun" to be within the context of their classrooms and academic work, and how this concept fits with notions of challenge and academic effort. School clearly needs to be understood as a "whole package," but it is necessary to also appreciate what "fun" might look like in settings other than the social.

5. *Social geography:* Schooling varies in relation to place and space. Small isolated schools have fewer opportunities to fully capitalize on the options available in large urban schools, for example. On the other hand, close relationships between the school and local community develop more readily in remote and rural settings, and this can bring a series of benefits not often seen in urban schools. As yet, schools appear to have not fully taken advantage of their capacity to employ technological solutions to provide greater equity of access through such provisions as provided by digital media.

The report is laced with extracts derived from the encounters with students, many of which are somewhat disturbing in terms of student engagement in learning:

> The teachers did not make them feel welcome, they were not asked in class to answer questions, teachers provided them with few or limited explanations, they experienced verbal put downs in class from teachers, they felt that they were treated with less regard than high-achieving students, teachers had favourites, (and that) less time was spent on students that required assistance. (Groundwater-Smith & Mockler, 2012, pp. 25–26)

In this same report, the suggestions offered by the student interviewees on engaging reluctant students were insightful and informative. They suggested that schools should provide mentors to assist with academic studies, integrate VET courses into school studies, make extracurricular activities available, have active learning in the classroom, and provide further information about the range of careers available (Groundwater-Smith & Mockler, 2012, pp. 19–24).

The main outcome of the study was the republication of a series of case studies of schools that have successfully engaged with their senior students in the senior years. The case studies were collected *prior* to the student feedback study but continue to be offered as examples of "best practice" for the ways in which public secondary schools in New South Wales have demonstrated their capacity to respond to the changes to the school leaving age (NSW Department of Education, 2008). No further publications or policy directions have emerged from the department with relation to the engagement of students in the senior years, although anecdotal evidence suggests that individual schools and school communities have used the input of the students as a starting point for considering their own response. This provides a salient reminder of the difficult relationship between policy and practice as enacted in a large employing authority such as the NSW Department of Education such that local practice is less enabled to be formed, reformed, and transformed in relation to student voice.

The sayings, doings, and relatings that comprised the practice of wide scale and authentic consultation in this student voice initiative were different but no less complex than those involved in Case Study 1. Again, an openness to speaking their truth was required of the students involved, and this in turn required from them a level of trust in the project and in the consultants involved. From the consultants it required creating the right kind of intersubjective space into which students felt emboldened to speak. The sayings and doings were thus very intertwined in this case. In terms of relatings, it required the requisite trust to be built such that, as far as possible, students felt that their voices would be listened to and reported with integrity and honesty. The cultural-discursive, material-economic, and social-political arrangements that enabled the practice of authentically consulting young people on the impacts of a policy decision were, arguably, an artifact of a particular "moment in time," wherein individuals and units within the Department of Education were, for various reasons, willing and able to support such an initiative. A radical restructure which took place shortly after the conclusion of the project caused significant shifts in all three groups of arrangements that meant that this work has not been sustained on a large, systemic scale.

CONCLUSION

Engaging student voice holds the potential to be an educative practice, for schools, teachers and students themselves. While the configuration of practices and practice architectures varies enormously from site to site, there are particular types of sayings, doings, and relatings embedded in student voice work that aim to privilege the voices of children and young people and redress traditional hierarchies in schools that would position adults' voices as more powerful than those of students, as Lundy reminds us "voice is not enough" (2007, p. 927). These in turn rely on cultural-discursive, material-economic, and social-political arrangements within the site to support and sustain the emergence of such practices. While the building of these practice architectures on varying scales within the many and varied "sites" of educational practice is undeniably complex, they begin with a commitment to the educative nature of student voice work on a local level.

Our opening gambit in this chapter was to quote from the interaction between two *Star Wars* principals: Luke and Yoda. Luke believed that he might be better able to undertake a different practice by trying; Yoda enjoined him not to try but to do. We perceive that by engaging children and young people as active agents in educative practice, by "doing" it is conceivable that a transformation can occur. In this sense merely "trying" implies that the commitment is limited, that many with authority in education are not prepared to "unlearn" practices and reset their intentions. Our advice and that which we hear from those consequential stakeholders, the students themselves, is to have the fortitude to change habits and practices to the benefit of all.

Questions for Reflection

1. There would seem to be many impediments to the authentic employment of student voice in school reform—what do you see these to be and how might they be addressed?
2. How useful, for you is the concept of *practice architectures* as a framing device to better understand the ways in which schools can become more deeply involved in participative inquiry with their learners?

Suggestions for Further Reading

Hart, R. (1992). Children's participation: From tokenism to citizen-ship. *Innocenti Essay*. Florence: UNICEF Innocenti Research Centre. *This is critical to an understanding of the impact of the Declaration of the Rights of the Child in giving weight and consideration to the voices of children and young people.*

James, A., Jenks, C., & Prout, A. (1998). *Theorising childhood*. Cambridge, England: Polity Press. *This is a classical reference that has been drawn upon extensively by researchers, and practitioners in the field.*

Percy-Smith, B., & Thomas, N. (Eds.). (2010). *A handbook of children and young people's participation*. London, England: Routledge. *This work contains a range of readings, both in relation to methods and critique.*

Shier, H. (2001). Pathways to participation: Openings, opportunities and ob-ligations. *Children and Society, 15*(2), 107–111. *This reading provides a model for evaluating the extent of participation and builds on wider community consultative practices.*

Tisdall, K., Davis, J., Prout, A., & Hill, M. (2006). *Children and young people and social inclusion: Participation for what?* Bristol, England: Polity Press. *An oft-cited work that draws together theories of childhood and the contexts for participation.*

Wyness, M. (2013). Global standards and deficit childhoods: The contested meanings of children's participation. *Children's Geographies, 11*(3), 340–353.

NOTES

1. This explanation is effectively a "writing out" of the "theory of practice archi-tectures" figure that appears on p. 38 of *Changing Practices, Changing Education* (Kemmis et al., 2014). For a more fulsome explanation of the theory, consult Chapter 2 of the same book.

2. The name has been changed.

3. The NSW Department of Education was known as the NSW Department of Education and Communities until 2015.

REFERENCES

Alderson, P. (2012). Rights-respecting research: A commentary on "The right to be properly researched: Research with children in a messy, real world." *Children's Geographies, 10*, 233–239.

Biesta, G. (2006). *Beyond learning*. Boulder, CO: Paradigm.

Biesta, G. (2007). Why 'what works' won't work: Evidence-based practice and the democratic deficit in educational research. *Educational Theory, 57*(1), 1–22.

Bourke, R., & Loveridge, J. (2016). Beyond the official language of learning: Teachers engaging with student voice research. *Teaching and Teacher Education, 57,* 59–66.

Clark, A. (2008). *History's children: History wars in the classroom.* Sydney, Australia: New South.

Collingwood, R. (1924). *Speculum mentis.* Oxford, England: Clarendon Press.

Creswell, R. (2005). *Educational research: Planning, conducting and evaluating quantitative and qualitative research* (2nd ed.). Upper Saddle River, NJ: Merrill.

Dockery, A. (2005). Assessing the value of additional years of schooling for the non academically inclined. *LSAY Research Reports,* 42. Retreived from https://www.ncver.edu.au/research-and-statistics/publications/all-publications/assessing-the-value-of-additional-years-of-schooling-for-the-non-academically-inclined

Ergler, C. (2017). Beyond passive participation: From re- search on to research by children. In R. Evans, L. Holt, & T. Skelton (Eds.), *Methodological approaches* (pp. 1–19). Singapore: Springer Singapore.

Fielding, M. (2004). 'New wave' student voice and the renewal of civic society. *London Review of Education, 2*(3), 197–217. doi: 10.1080/1474846042000302834

Fielding, M. (2007). Beyond "voice": New roles, relations and contexts in researching with young people. *Discourse: Studies in the Cultural Politics of Education, 28*(3), 301–310.

Fielding, M. (2011). Patterns of partnership: Student voice, intergenerational learning and democratic fellowship. In N. Mockler & J. Sachs (Eds.), *Rethinking educational practice through reflexive inquiry: Essays in honour of susan groundwater-smith* (pp. 61–75). Dordrecht, Netherlands: Springer.

Freire, P. (1972). *Pedagogy of the oppressed.* London, England: Penguin.

Greene, M. (1977). Toward wide-awakeness: An argument for the arts and humanities in education. *Teachers College Record, 79*(1), 119–125.

Groundwater-Smith, S., Dockett, S., & Bottrell, D. (2015). *Participatory research with children and young people.* Los Angeles, CA: SAGE.

Groundwater-Smith, S., Mitchell, J., & Mockler, N. (2007). Learning in the middle years: More than a transition: South Melbourne, Australia: Thomson.

Groundwater-Smith, S., & Mockler, N. (2003). *Learning to listen: Listening to learn.* Sydney, Australia: University of Sydney.

Groundwater-Smith, S., & Mockler, N. (2012). *New school leaving age: Consulting young people. A student feedback project conducted for the NSW department of education and communities.* Sydney, Australia: NSW Department of Education and Communities.

Groundwater-Smith, S., & Mockler, N. (2015a). Why global policies fail disengaged young people at the local level. In H. Proctor, P. Brownlee, & P. Freebody (Eds.), *Controversies in education: Orthodoxy and heresy in policy and practice.* Dordrecht, Netherlands: Springer.

Groundwater-Smith, S., & Mockler, N. (Eds.). (2015b). *Big fish, little fish: Teaching and learning in the middle years.* Melbourne, Australia: Cambridge University Press.

Hanson, K. (2016). Children's participation and agency when they don't 'do the right thing.' *Childhood, 23*(4), 471–475.

Hart, R. (1992). Children's participation: From tokenism to citizenship. *Innocenti Essay*. Florence, Italy: UNICEF Innocenti Research Centre.

Horgan, D., Forde, C., Martin, S., & Parkes, A. (2017). Children's participation: Moving from the performative to the social. *Children's Geographies, 15*(3), 274–288.

Johnson, V. (2017). Moving beyond voice in children and young people's participation. *Action Research, 15*(5), 104–124

Kemmis, S. (2006). Participatory action research and the public sphere. *Educational Action Research, 14*(4), 459–476.

Kemmis, S. (2007). Action research as a practice-changing practice. Retrieved from https://www.researchgate.net/profile/Stephen_Kemmis/publication/233133766_Action_research_as_a_practice-based_practice/links/544da2b60cf24b5d6c42b872.pdf

Kemmis, S. (2009). Action research as a practice-based practice. *Educational Action Research, 17*(3), 463–474.

Kemmis, S., & Grootenboer, P. (2008). Situating praxis in practice: Practice architectures and the cultural, social and material conditions for practice. In S. Kemmis & T. Smith (Eds.), *Enabling praxis: Challenges for education* (pp. 37–62). Rotterdam, Netherlands: Sense.

Kemmis, S., Wilkinson, J., Edwards-Groves, C., Hardy, I., Grootenboer, P., & Bristol, L. (2014). *Changing practices, changing education*. Dordrecht, Netherlands: Springer.

Kim, C. (2016). Why research "by" children? Rethinking the assumptions underlying the facilitation of children as researchers. *Children & Society, 30*, 230–240.

Lundy, L. (2007) Voice is not enough: Conceptualising article 12 of the United Nations convention on the Rights of the Child. *British Educational Research Journal, 33*(6), 927–942.

Mayes, E. (2016). Student representation on schools governance councils. Report prepared for the Victorian Student Representative Council. Retrieved from https://gallery.mailchimp.com/f4c8b5faedc14e0aa5a5fe825/files/VicSRC_Students_and_school_governance_report_131216.compressed.pdf

Mockler, N. (2014). When 'research ethics' become 'everyday ethics': The intersection of inquiry and practice in practitioner research. *Educational Action Research, 22*(2), 146–158.

Mockler, N., & Groundwater-Smith, S. (2012). Weaving the web of professional practice: The coalition of knowledge-building schools. In B. Lingard, P. Thomson, & T. Wrigley (Eds.), *Changing schools: Making a world of difference*. London, England: Routledge.

Mockler, N., & Groundwater-Smith, S. (2015). *Engaging with student voice in research, education and community: Beyond legitimation and guardianship*. Dordrecht, Netherlands: Springer.

Noddings, N. (2006). *Critical lessons: What our schools should teach*. Cambridge, England: Cambridge University Press.

NSW Department of Education. (2008). Consultation report on the new school leaving age (Vol. 2017). Sydney, Australia: NSW DET.

NSW Department of Education and Communities. (2012). *New south wales auditor general's report performance audit: Impact of the raised school leaving age*. Sydney, Australia: NSW DEC.

Pendergast, D., & Bahr, N. (Eds.). (2010). *Teaching middle years: Rethinking curriculum, pedagogy and assessment.* Sydney, Australia: Allen & Unwin.

Prout, A. (2003). Participation, policy and the changing conditions of childhood. In C. Hallett & A. Prout (Eds.), *Hearing the voices of children. Social policy for a new century* (pp. 11–25). London, England: Routledge Falmer.

Reynaert, D., Bouverne-de-Bie, M., & Vandevelde, S. (2009). A review of children's rights literature since the adoption of the united nations convention on the rights of the child. *Childhood, 16*(4), 518–534.

Stoecklin, D. (2013). Theories of action in the field of child participation: In search of explicit frameworks. *Childhood, 20*(4), 443–457.

Taylor, C., & Robinson, C. (2009). Student voice: Theorising power and participation. *Pedagogy, Culture & Society, 17*(2), 161–175.

CHAPTER 3

RESEARCHING THE PERSPECTIVES OF CHILDREN WITH ADDITIONAL SUPPORT NEEDS DURING THEIR TRANSITION TO SCHOOL

Ethical and Methodological Considerations

**Edith Jolicoeur, Joanne S. Lehrer, Julie Ruel,
Johanne April, and Mathieu Point**

ABSTRACT

Research and policy target children with "difficulties" or "special needs" as needing additional support during the transition to school. While we employ a critical perspective with regards to labeling children and normalizing specific childhoods, we question the exclusion of children identified as requiring additional support from research on children's perspectives during the transition from child care to school. This conceptual article explores ethical dilemmas, such as whether informed consent is possible, and reflects

Participatory Methodologies to Elevate Children's Voice and Agency, pages 47–72
Copyright © 2019 by Information Age Publishing
47

on how to carry out empowering research with children who often experience high levels of anxiety when elements of their daily routine are altered. We discuss the need to coordinate multiple participants and institutions in a multi-sectorial context, ensure that soliciting children's perspectives does not increase anxiety related to starting school, and question whether focusing exclusively on children identified as having additional support needs leads to further stigmatization and marginalization. We explore methodological possibilities for listening to young children's voices when those children do not communicate typically, drawing on research with toddlers, children with learning difficulties, and with intellectually "disabled" adults. We conclude with implications for future research, such as the importance of significant and long-lasting relationships between researchers and children, including adults who already play a significant role in children's lives on the research team, and the possibility of involving all children as researchers into their own transition experiences.

TRANSITION AS A TIME OF CHALLENGE AND POSSIBILITY

The transition to school has been conceptualized as setting the tone for children's school experience (Dockett & Perry, 2001; Gray, Prunty, Logan, & Hayes, 2015; Pianta, Cox, Taylor, & Early, 1999) and as a time of "opportunity, expectation, aspiration, and entitlement" (Dockett & Perry, 2015, p. 123). Transition researchers focus on the months or years before and after children enter formal schooling, a period that is often characterized as one of mutual adjustment where children, families, and educational settings adapt to one another in order to build relationships and ensure a positive start to school (Dockett & Perry, 2001, 2015; Gray et al., 2015; Pianta et al., 1999).

In Québec, children generally begin school at the age of 5, when they enter kindergarten. Although kindergarten attendance is not mandatory, the majority of children (97.3%) attend (Ministère de l'Éducation, du Loisir et du Sport [MELS], 2013). During the 2015–2016 school year, 2.7% of the children enrolled in kindergarten were identified as "handicapped" by the Ministry of Education and Higher Education (Ministère de l'Éducation et de l'Enseignement Supérieur [MEES], 2017). These children can attend either "regular" or "specialized" classes. Among kindergarten students, in 2015–2016, 62.6% of those identified as disabled attended the regular class while the others attended specialized classes or other types of class (MEES, 2017).

We employ a critical perspective with regards to labeling children (Dockett, 2014; Petriwyskyj, 2014) normalizing certain childhoods and pathologizing others (Heydon & Iannacci, 2009), and deficit-oriented thinking (Graham & Iannacci, 2013). We instead define children with additional support needs as those presenting atypical developmental patterns who find themselves in situations where the educational setting does not have the resources necessary to adapt to them and meet their needs (Fougeyrollas, Cloutier, Bergeron, Côté, & Saint-Michel, 1998; Riddell & Weedon, 2017). For example, these children may communicate differently, either verbally or nonverbally, have additional needs related to self-help skills and autonomy, or demonstrate particularities in the context of social interactions.

The transition experience depends on a number of factors. Ruel (2011) identified five possible challenges, adapted from Wolery's (1999) work with elementary children identified as having disabilities, that children with additional support needs experience during the transition to school. These include challenges related to the child, challenges related to the family, challenges related to the educational setting, administrative and intersectorial challenges, and finally, challenges related to relationships.

During the transition process, challenges related to the child can be more complex for children identified as having additional support needs (Rosenkoetter, Hains, & Dogaru, 2007). For example, before they begin school, these children may receive services through different organizations and in different locations, such as rehabilitation services (speech therapy, occupational therapy, physical therapy, etc.) and childcare services. Planning a positive transition for these children requires supports and processes to coordinate the participation of multiple professionals in order to maintain intersectorial collaboration during the transition (Rous, Myers, & Stricklin, 2007).

In addition, the transition to school is a stressful period for families, even more so for children identified as having additional support needs, where the type of school program the child will attend may be uncertain (Rosenkoetter et al., 2007). As illustrated in Vignette 3.1, families of children with additional support needs often experience multiple transitions before the child enters school. These additional transitions often continue during the first few years of schooling (and during subsequent transitions), as parents worry about how the new setting will adapt to their child.

VIGNETTE 3.1—MULTIPLE TRANSITIONS

John is the youngest in a family of three children. He was diagnosed with Down Syndrome at birth. His parents had a hard time finding a childcare center. He was cared for by a neighbor briefly until they found a home childcare center to send him to. After a month, the educator explained that John required too much of her attention, and she recommended the parents find alternate arrangements. They enrolled him in a second home childcare center a month later, where he remained until the age of three, although this educator also complained that caring for John had a negative impact on the other children in her group. Finally, when he was 3 years old, his parents were informed that there was a spot for him at the local publicly funded and regulated early childcare center. A few months before he turned 5, his parents discussed his upcoming school entry with his educator. The educator was worried because John was not as autonomous as his peers. His parents formally applied to delay his schooling another year. John was placed in a regular kindergarten class, with a specialized educational technician assigned to the class in order to support the teacher and assist John. At the end of the school year, although John had learned many new skills and abilities, the special education team at the school recommended that John be placed in a special education class at another school. His parents hesitated, they wanted their son to remain in a regular class. The principal suggested that they observe their son in class, and then observe the Grade 1 class at that school and the special education Grade 1 class at the other school. After these observations, the parents decided that the special education class would be the best place for John to continue his education. Within his first 7 years, John experienced six vertical transitions, not to mention the multiple horizontal transitions he experienced while he was at the childcare center: the biweekly visits to specialists at the health and social services clinic, the rehabilitation center, and the community organization, that often took place in the middle of the day.

Administrative and intersectorial challenges include difficulty collaborating amongst institutions offering services to children and families. Children with additional support needs in Québec often receive services from diverse health and social service professionals, complexifying their coordination. Conscious of this challenge, the MEES published a guide to support this first educational transition, in collation with the ministry of family (responsible for childcare services) and the ministry of health and social services (MELS, 2010).

Finally, relationship challenges focus on both relationships between families and professionals as well as relationships amongst professionals who work with the same child(ren). Too often, families feel judges or blamed for their child's difficulties (Deslandes & Bertrand, 2001). Also, the interactions between parents and the adults who care for their children change as children begin school; informal daily verbal communication is replaced by formal, infrequent written communication (Lehrer, Bigras, & Laurin, 2017; Rimm-Kaufman & Pianta, 2005). The focus on deficiencies or dysfunction also contributes to difficult relations between families and schools (Miron & Tochon, 2004).

In addition, Québec's policies single out these children with regards to early childhood education and the transition to school. Article 1 of Québec's Educational Childcare Act specifies that one of the main goals of educational childcare is to ensure equality of opportunity for children with "*special needs* or who live in precarious socio-economic situations" (Gouvernement du Québec, 2006). In 2009, Québec's Minister of Education published a 13-point plan to promote school success. The only point to address the early childhood period proposes to, "prepare children in disadvantaged areas and *children with difficulties* for starting school" (MELS, 2009, p. 12, emphasis added).

This focus on the challenges related to starting school with additional support needs identified in no way detracts from the possibilities, opportunities, and affordances that this transition can offer to all children and families (Dockett & Perry, 2015). As this transition is predictable, it can be planned in advance.

Research on the transition to kindergarten for children with additional support needs often focuses on ensuring continuity between the different environments that the children frequent; preparing the setting to welcome children and families, adapt to the children's needs, and ensure a partnership with parents and other professionals; as well as preparing the children for their transition to the new environment (Ruel, Moreau, & Bourdeau, 2008; Wolery, 1999). Within this context, we assert our commitment to inclusive practice and inclusive research. However, in preparing to carry out research on children's perceptions of their transition experiences, we acknowledge certain methodological challenges, particularly when children are nonverbal (Kelly, 2010). The following sections expose our ongoing reflections regarding ethical and methodological issues that require consideration in order to proceed with this type of project, based on an extensive and multidisciplinary literature review.

RESEARCH ON CHILDREN'S PERSPECTIVES

More and more, children are being viewed as experts on their own lives, and as active participants in research where their point of view is solicited (Baird & Grace, 2017). This emphasis on "giving voice" to children is also seen as important in order for them to become autonomous learners who make decisions, express their ideas and opinions and develop a positive sense of self (Bruce, 2005; Roberts, 2002). Consistent with an image of the strong, competent child (Malaguzzi, 1993), children are seen as members of society and citizens in their own right (Miller, 1997; Uprichard, 2010). We believe that research on children's transition to school should include children' voices (Di Santo & Berman, 2012; Dockett & Perry, 2003; Einarsdottir, Dockett, & Perry, 2009) as well as their collaboration in the research process (Pole, Mizen, & Bolton, 1999; Schäfer & Yarwood, 2008; Yardley, 2011), and that these perspectives should inform political decisions.

Articles 12 and 13 of the United Nations Convention on the Rights of the Child, signed on November 20, 1989, assert that children can express their opinions freely on all matters that affect them, that those opinions should be considered, and that children have the right to seek, receive, and impart information.

More recently, the European Early Childhood Education Research Association published an *Ethical Code for Early Childhood Researchers* (EECERA, 2015). Building on the UN Convention on the Rights of the Child, the EECERA document lists ethical principles for conducting research with young children. The document proposes research practice guidelines, including responsibilities towards participants. In particular, ensuring "meaningful and child-friendly" (p. 6) voluntary and informed consent is discussed. All participants must be provided with truthful and complete information on the content, purpose, and process of the project and must be able to choose not to participate, or to cease participation at any point within an active and ongoing process of obtaining informed consent.

In addition, the EECERA document suggests that researchers "take all necessary steps to reduce the sense of intrusion, pressure or stress" that participation in a research project may entail (EECERA, 2015, p. 7). If the research is taking place during the transition to school, a period that can be a source of stress for all children (Rimm-Kaufman & Pianta, 2000), and often a source of anxiety for children with additional support needs (McIntyre, Eckert, Fiese, DiGennaro Reed, & Wildinger, 2010; Rothe, Urban, & Werning, 2014), this concern is particularly salient.

Despite these concerns, we agree with the EECERA Ethical Code's proposal that the selection of participants should be inclusive and nondiscriminatory, and that no child should be excluded from research seeking to understand their opinions during their transition to school, as long as the children and their parents want them to participate. However, our literature review did not reveal any studies that specifically sought out the point of view of children with additional support during the transition to school. While there are multiple studies about children's perspectives during the transition to school (e.g., Di Santo & Berman, 2012; Dockett & Perry, 2003; Einarsdottir, 2007; Einarsdottir et al., 2009; Niesel & Griebel, 2001), these studies do not specify whether or not children with additional support needs are included.

Given that Québec's policies single out these children (Gouvernement du Québec, 2006; MELS, 2009), as well as the additional challenges they face during the transition, the explicit inclusion of the points of view of children with additional support needs in research on children's transition to school in Québec seems crucial. As these children are often voluntarily excluded from or marginalized within research on children's perspectives (Kelly, 2010), we reaffirm our commitment to an explicitly inclusive approach. The question is not whether or not to include young children with additional support needs in research on their experiences, but how to do so in ethically and methodological rigorous ways. The following sections explore obtaining informed consent, including children as research collaborators, and the advantages and limits of various methods for collecting children's opinions and experiences.

OBTAINING INFORMED CONSENT

Ensuring that children understand that they have the right to decline an invitation to participate, and to stop participating at any time, is of particular concern when children do not speak, have limited social competence, or atypical intellectual development. Skanfors (2009) asserts that respecting children's wishes and integrity is imperative throughout the research project, especially when they are very young or not able to communicate their consent in explicit ways. It also bears reflecting upon whether children are asked only whether or not they wish to participate in the data collection activities, or whether the goals of the project are explained to the children. For example, should children be informed when requesting consent that their words or drawings or photographs will be shared at academic conferences and in publications, and that the goal of the project is that their ideas will change educational practices and policy?

It is important to specify that although the child's ongoing consent is essential, this does not replace parental consent. Although the age of majority in Québec is 18 years, the civil code considers a child capable of providing consent at 14 (Code civil du Québec, 1991). Before this age, a parent or legal guardian must provide consent in order for a child to participate in research. We believe that researchers must require children's consent, regardless of age or the presence of additional support needs, in order to act ethically and respectfully. In most research projects, child consent is only requested after their participation is negotiated with people who held power over them, such as school administrators and parents, which can also pose ethical challenges (Flewitt, 2005; McGettigan & Gray, 2012; Pole et al., 1999). In the following section, collaborative consent between parent and child, adapting the content of the information, and reaffirmed consent with nonverbal children will be presented as possible strategies.

COLLABORATIVE CONSENT

After contacting preschools and parents, Flewitt (2005) met with parents and 3-year-old children together at their homes, explained and jointly negotiated times and duration of meetings, allowed children to explore the video recording equipment that would be used in the research, and emphasized to the children that they could change their mind at any time. She then asked parents to continue discussing the project with the children and to inform the researcher and the staff at the preschool center where the project was taking place of their responses. Within this process, children were able to express their concerns, such as whether participation would interfere with outdoor playtime or their ability to play with their friends.

ADAPTING AND SIMPLIFYING THE CONTENT

Adapting and simplifying the content of consent forms to make it accessible appears to be a common strategy used in research with young children (Baird & Grace, 2017; Skanfors, 2009). The Pavillon du Parc, a readaptation center for people with intellectual disabilities and autism spectrum disorders (ASD), the city of Gatineau, and the research chair on literacy and inclusion of the University of Québec in Outaouais developed a guide (Ruel, Kassi, Moreau, & Mbida-Mballa, 2011) to increase access to information for people with low literacy levels. Vignette 3.2 illustrates a consent form. We recommend the addition of images to make the child version even more accessible.

VIGNETTE 3.2—SIMPLIFIED CONSENT FORM

Excerpt From the Parent Version	**Excerpt From the Child Version**
Participation in the Research Project	
To better understand the transition of children with additional support needs to school, we would like to know your children's opinion. To do this, in an individual meeting lasting approximately 10 minutes, we will ask your child to make two drawings and explain what they mean to him or her.	*The Activity* Make two drawings and explain them.
In order for the child to familiarize him or herself with the person who will attend this meeting, they will take part in the child's daily activities next Monday and Tuesday. At the end of these 2 days, a consent form will be read aloud to the child and the child can write a distinctive mark on the form if they wish to participate.	*How long?* About 10 minutes (as long as recess). *Will it be recorded?* Yes, there will be a video camera.
The drawing and discussion part will take place during a subsequent visit, the day following the 2 days of familiarization. This will take place in the room adjacent to the classroom where the children eat lunch. Before starting the activity, the consent form will be reread to your child.	*Where will it take place?* In the lunchroom. *When?* Tomorrow.
For research purposes, the meeting will be filmed.	*With whom?* Alone with me.

REAFFIRMING CONSENT

Even if consent is obtained at the beginning of the project, consent must be renegotiated with children at each meeting or research period during which data will be collected (Cocks, 2006). The researcher must remain vigilant throughout the project to children's verbal, paraverbal and nonverbal clues. Some authors reread the information form at the beginning of each stage of the project (Baird & Grace, 2017; Gray, 2017; O'Rourke, O'Farrelly, Booth, & Doyle, 2017). Baird and Grace (2017) propose that children sign a special mark that represents their signature, while Wahle, Ponizovsky-Bergelson, Dayan, Erlichman, and Roer-Strier (2017) recorded children giving consent on video. Kelly (2010), in a project with nonverbal children identified as having learning disabilities, used communication cards as part of the interview protocol. Children had access to a "stop" card at all times, and were informed during pre-research familiarization visits that they could hold it up at any time to stop participating. A similar card could also be used so that the child can indicate when he or she would like to take a break.

Remaining vigilant to children's nonverbal cues throughout the research project is suggested by various authors. For example, despite limited language, some children are able to verbalize the word "no" or can indicate their refusal through gesture by shaking their head. When children ignore the researcher, or do not respond, or when the researcher is uncertain as to their intention, this should be interpreted as a desire not to participate in the project (Cocks, 2006; Skanfors, 2009). When this happens, Cocks (2006) suggests that as children are not in a position of power with respect to the adult, it is important to err on the side of caution and leave the space (see Vignette 3.3). Although this may be frustrating when attempting to collect data, from an ethical point of view the child's refusal is positive and demonstrates that the researcher was able to support the child in his or her right to accept or refuse participation.

VIGNETTE 3.3—PHYSICAL INDICATORS OF NON-CONSENT

Amy and Paul's class has been chosen for a research project on children's perspective of the kindergarten classroom environment. This class includes five children with ASD who have severe deficits in verbal and nonverbal social communication. Consent was obtained from the parents of four of these children, but only Amy and Paul initially agreed to participate after the researcher had spent 2 weeks becoming familiar to the children in the classroom.

During the five data collection periods following this period, the two children behave differently. Amy demonstrates signs of anxiety each time as she attempts to pinch the researcher when he approaches her and exhibits more severe echolalia than usual. Paul, on the other hand, has difficulty sitting still during the first three visits, but seems to become more interested in the researcher's image cards as time goes on. These image cards are used to collect the children's point of view.

After reflection and discussion with the class teacher and the special services technician, the researcher determines that Amy is not interested in participating in the research project. However, the adults determine that Paul appears interested in continuing.

Two additional constraints should also be taken into account. First, if the research is taking place at school, extra attention must be paid as school activities are often obligatory for children who may view the researchers as surrogate teachers who would judge their abilities, making it difficult for children to understand that their participation in the research project is truly their choice and potentially introducing a social desirability bias into the data (Pole et al., 1999). Also, children may be influenced by the decisions of their peers. Waller (2006) suggests requesting consent in a group setting and individually with children.

INCLUDING CHILDREN AS RESEARCH PARTNERS AND COLLABORATORS

Beyond simply participating in the data collection process, some researchers advocate for the inclusion of children as research partners or collaborators at all stages of the project from study design to the data analysis and dissemination of results (Kelly, 2010; Pole et al., 1999; Schäfer & Yarwood, 2008; Uprichard, 2010; Yardley, 2011). This increased intensity of participation introduces additional challenges, not only for children identified as having additional support needs.

Transferring these reflections to studies involving younger children, particularly very young children and those with additional support needs, leads to questions about whether or not it is possible and desirable to include children in determining research questions, selecting the methods for sharing their experiences, analyzing the data and disseminating the findings. In addition, if children receive credit as co-investigators and co-authors, they cannot maintain anonymity.

METHODS TO IDENTIFY CHILDREN'S POINTS OF VIEW

This section discusses the advantages and difficulties encountered when researchers enter children's worlds. Then, the use of pictograms, artifacts, and screens to support communication will be explored. Finally, different methods of data collection will be addressed. While each of these methods presents distinct advantages, they also entail challenges related to participant characteristics, which will also be discussed. It is up to researchers, ideally in collaboration with practitioners and parents, to evaluate which of these methods best meet the objectives of their project. This section also includes suggestions drawn from our own research projects. Often these were not directly related to the perspectives of children with additional support needs during the transition to school, but we feel they allow for further illustration and reflection.

Introduction of the Researcher Into the Child's Natural Environment

Entering a childcare center, readaptation center, or school as a researcher involves both advantages and disadvantages. In terms of advantages, when the researcher is on site, he or she can make decisions in real time in order to facilitate data collection. In addition, in a transitional context, a researcher who is present occasionally in multiple contexts can be a familiar reassuring face for children.

However, introducing a new adult, particularly one who will be present only occasionally and temporarily, involves additional concerns. The presence of an unknown person can be a source of additional stress for children who are experiencing anxiety or have difficulty adapting to change. Because of this, if the researcher decides to enter the setting, he or she must reflect upon how to do so in a way that is ethical. In order to gain children's trust, many researchers spend a lot of time building relationships with the children. For example, Baird and Grace (2017), spent 2 days a week during 4 to 6 weeks, establishing relationships with the children by playing with them and spending time with them before beginning their project. The researcher became a familiar face. He also spent time building relationships with the children's parents. Ruel, Moreau, Kassi and Prud'homme (2016), in an action research project with adults with intellectual disabilities, noticed that the more time they spent with the participants, the more the participants felt at ease, and the more fluidly they were able to express themselves.

Building relationships with children takes time. Cocks (2006) explains that he began by sitting near the child, observing the other children and sometimes the one participating in the research project. When he felt like his presence had been accepted by the child, he moved closer and then finally sat next to the child. This gentle approach allowed him to access the point of view of a child who often refused to interact with others.

According to Cocks (2006), there are consequences and implications that come with taking the time to build relationships with children, especially children who do not easily open to others. Losing this relationship could prove difficult or even harmful to the child. When this is likely, Cocks (2006) suggests that the researcher's departure should be planned just as thoroughly as the researcher's entry into the setting.

In order to guide researchers, another source of inspiration are the ethical guidelines of the Critical Indigenous Research Methodology (Hohepa & McIntosh, 2017). These guidelines focus on the following five elements: relationality (establishing relationships based on mutual respect), responsibility (the researcher is responsible to the relationships), respect (participant's universes need to be held in high regard), reciprocity (whatever is received makes its way back to others), and accountability (the researcher is accountable to all involved at all time). We feel that these guidelines are applicable to our context with children.

In order to overcome the disadvantages involved with introducing an external researcher into the child's setting, another option is to have someone already involved in the child's life collect the data. This would involve a collaborative approach to research and a vision of knowledge as co-constructed. Vignette 3.4 illustrates how a project can benefit from not only the perspective of the child, but also that of a parent. As well, in a participatory research context, the perspective of adults already engaged in the child's life can enrich the research design, and in some complex situations, the child's perspective will need to be filtered through those that know him or her best. Eskelä-Haapanen, Lerkkanen, Rasku-Puttonen, and Poikkeus (2016) sought out children's perspectives on starting school through interviews with parents. Similarly, Sheldrick, Neger, Shipman, and Perrin (2012) used *parent proxy reports* where the parents indicated how they thought their child would respond if the child was asked the question. These authors identified a large correlation between the adolescent children's responses and those of their parents, when the parents were asked to respond as they thought their child would. When the parents were asked for their own perception of the situation, the correlations with the adolescent responses were much weaker. However, results from another study (Bray, Noyes, Harris, & Edwards, 2017) showed that, even if a correlation existed between parents' proxy scores and their children's, their responses on a health-related quality of life measure were significantly different. Mobility-impaired children provided higher ratings compared to their parents' proxy answers. These authors suggest not relying on parent proxy reports alone, and finding other ways to engage children directly. Similarly, Hemmingsson, Ólafsdóttir, and Egilson's (2017) systematic review found that parents in their study tended to under evaluate health related assessments when compared to their children. According to these authors, these discrepancies indicate different perspectives, both of which are valuable and should be taken into consideration in research projects.

However, when one or multiple people already present in the setting become responsible for collecting the data, extra time must be accorded to make sure the person understands the research protocol and the objectives of the project. For example, simulations or a pilot study can be carried out, similar to the training of a research assistant.

In sum, deciding who will carry out the data collection should not be arbitrary or based on convenience. If a person external to the setting is chosen, they need to invest the time required to gain the children's trust, and reflect carefully about how they will leave the setting at the end of the project. If, however, someone with a prior relationship with the child collects the data, they should be involved at all stages of the project, and efforts should be made to separate their own points of view with the views collected from the children.

VIGNETTE 3.4—TOWARDS A CO-CONSTRUCTED VISION

As part of her doctoral research project, a researcher asked a child to take pictures that represent play to her, in the child's home and neighborhood. Then, the child was asked to select her favorite photos and explain them. First, the child used the opportunity to engage in one of her favorite activities, art making, by placing her toys in intricate symmetrical designs, toys she never played with otherwise, and photographing them against the carpet in her bedroom. Then, she suggested to the researcher that they go to her favorite park, the one her parents had not taken her to since her younger brother had been born a few months ago. Once at the park, she handed the camera to the researcher and ran off to play on the climbing structure. During the second phase of the project, when the researcher reviewed the photos with the child, their conversation did not allow the researcher a straightforward answer to her research question about the meaning of play to this child. A conversation with the girl's parent may have allowed the researcher to better understand the background context, as the girl's manipulation of the research situation for her own goals of play may have provided more insights than her original methodology. In addition, adapting the research process or spending more time getting to know the child and her family may have provided the researcher with additional, unanticipated data (Merriam, 1988).

Using Pictograms, Artifacts, and Screens to Support Conversations With Children

Most children transitioning to school do not yet read, but are able to understand that written characters represent spoken messages (Ehri, 1998). Cihak (2007) suggests that for children with ASD, pictograms are useful for communicating different information such as requests, turn-taking, and their preferences. In their study on the social participation of adults with intellectual disabilities, Letscher and colleagues (unpublished manuscript) associated themes with pictograms in order for the participants to have a tangible support to allow them to situate themselves within the discussion. In their action research project outlined above, Ruel and colleagues (2016) used a visual support with illustrations in order to encourage participation and elicit reactions and comments from participants.

The use of artifacts, such as toys to manipulate, is another interesting avenue for research with children. For example, Millei and Rautio (2017) describe conversations with children during free playtime in the house center. Similarly, Crump's (2014) study involved offering children craft materials, books to read, toys to play with, and games to play in the children's homes, in an effort to establish an informal situation where the child would feel comfortable engaging in conversation with the researcher. In the context of a study on children's transition to school, a school corner could be set up in order to encourage symbolic play that would elicit children's feelings about starting school while they were in child care. Similarly, a childcare corner, or toys from and photographs of the childcare center could be used to provoke memories and comparisons once the children started school.

Finally, children with ASD seem to be interested in computers and children's films (Althaus, de Sonneville, Minderaa, Hensen, & Til 1996). Others assert that these children are more attentive and perform better when instructions are provided by an electronic character than a human (Moore & Calvert, 2000; Shane et al., 2012). The use of a computer or video seems like an important avenue to consider when attempting to engage children with ASD in research projects.

METHODS OF DATA COLLECTION

This section discusses capturing video, drawings, photography, interviews, artistic creation, and the mosaic approach.

Capturing Video

Filming video sequences is used in research on young children's perspectives to analyze interactions amongst children and between children and educators (Harrison, Sumsion, Bradley, Letsch, & Salamon, 2017), and to prompt interviews with educators and parents about children's daily activities (Fleer, Tonyan, Mantilla, & Rivalland, 2009; Wineberg & Chiquette, 2009). For children who are nonverbal or who have difficulty expressing themselves, video recording allows researchers to capture nonverbal and paraverbal communication (Cohen, Manion, & Morrison, 2000; Harrison et. al., 2017). However, as Harrison and colleagues (2017) mention, analyzing video sequences does not automatically lead to capturing the perspectives of the people filmed. It is often useful to watch the filmed sequences with children in order to capture their point of view. It must also be noted that, while filming hours of video can be enjoyable, analyzing hours of video can be tedious (Walsh, Bakier, Byungho, Chung, & Chung, 2007).

Drawing

Drawing allows young children to express themselves in ways that are often more accessible than through verbal interviews (Einarsdottir et al., 2009). For example, Wahle and colleagues (2017) asked children to draw locations that were inaccessible to photograph. Peccia (2012) and Einarsdottir and colleagues (2009) used drawing to access children's feelings about starting school. These drawing can be completed individually with a researcher or research assistant, or in a small group or whole group setting (Einarsdottir et al., 2009).

The drawings can be analyzed for content, and can also be accompanied by a verbal interview as the child draws. Children can also be asked to explain their drawing once they have completed it (Lehrer & Petrakos, 2011; Wahle et al., 2017; see Vignette 3.5). For children who experience difficulty with verbal language or fine motor skills, an alternative can be to present drawings to the child and ask him or her to choose the ones that correspond to his or her opinion or experience.

VIGNETTE 3.5—USE OF DRAWINGS

Mary is conducting research on children's perspectives of their upcoming transition in a childcare center. She asks the children to draw a picture of something they are excited about when they start school. At another point in time, she asks them to draw something they are worried about when starting school. Rachel has cerebral palsy and struggles with fine motor activities. Instead of excluding Rachel from this part of the research project, Mary and Nancy, the educator, decide to allow Rachel to use a tablet application to electronically create her drawings. All children are audio recorded during the drawing session and as they presents their completed drawings to Mary.

Photography

Photography is another interesting avenue for children less at ease with drawing. Digital cameras, smartphones, and tablets provide instant results and allow children to conserve or discard images at will. Holm (2008) explains that photographs can be used in different ways as part of data collection:

1. Images produced by the children: The researcher invites children to photograph images that capture aspects of their lives (also called Photovoice) and often includes a discussion with children to explain what the photograph means to them (Prosser & Burke, 2008). Dockett, Einarsdottir, and Perry (2017) paired children while they took photos. One child had the camera and the other had a video recorder that allowed them to capture the conversations that accompanied the decision-making about what to photograph. In this way, the researchers were able to collect information about the process of taking photos, the photos themselves, and the children's reactions to the photos.
2. Images produced by the researcher: The researcher uses photography to document events or situations, such as transition practices. This method allows the researcher to capture children's reactions, similar to the process of pedagogical documentation (Buldu, 2010). The photographs can also be manipulated by the children who can use them to create sequences or stories, select or eliminate different images, and express their point of view (Epstein, Stevens, McKeever, & Baruchel, 2006).
3. The use of preexisting photographs: For example, the researcher can provide children with photos of their future school and classroom and record their reactions. They can also show children who have begun school pictures of themselves at the childcare center, in order to provoke memories (Epstein et al., 2006).

Other Creative Approaches

Yardley's (2011) study with older children relied on the children exploring their lives and experiences through the creation of art and performance. The author compares this work to "playspaces" in early childhood settings, "a learning environment designed to allow cognitive, emotional, intellectual, social, relational, and (in the broadest sense) spiritual discovery to take place" (p. 199). The children in Yardley's study created montages of images and texts that they translated into digital forms and then accompanied with live performances. They experimented with different forms of data and creative work, allowing the methodology to emerge from their explorations and to interpret and reinterpret data as they engaged in the process. Simply observing children engaging in dramatic or creative play, or supporting them in a research-creation process revolving around their interests related to the transition to school is an interesting avenue for potential exploration.

Interviews

Interviewing children is often used as a complement to another method or to elicit children's meaning-making. For example, Baird and Grace (2017) used children's drawing and photographs to provoke conversations and focus children's attention on the research subject. These authors recommend interviewing the children multiple times for very short periods (up to 15 minutes, depending on their attention span). In order to encourage children to speak freely, dolls, puppets, cars, or other toys and manipulatives can be made available to the children, either to allow them to create scenarios or to occupy them while the researcher asks questions. Tobin, Hsueh, and Karasawa (2009) suggests presenting a film at the beginning of a group interview that becomes a reference for a conversation. For example, O'Rourke and colleagues (2017) presented children with specific scenarios and then posed questions about the scenarios they had viewed. Finally, in order to encourage children to discuss and share their opinions, Gray (2017) suggests alternating information meetings with structured small group discussions.

Interviews can pose certain challenges for young children who may be intimidated to share their opinion with an adult. Some children are unsure what is expected of them. For example, in small group interview, when children repeat the same answer, we suggest modifying the procedure and conducted individual interviews in order to obtain richer data that seemed like a better reflection of individual children's perspectives. For children who were shy or those that chose not to speak to the researcher, we suggest using a communication application on a tablet to solicit their responses. Wahle and colleagues (2017) add that researchers need to be aware of power dynamics, and that certain actions, like getting down to children's level, or sitting on the floor or at a round table, can make them feel more at ease.

Letscher and colleagues (unpublished manuscript) asked participants to attend interviews accompanied by someone they trust. These people were able to support the participants in sharing their experiences, for example by prompting them such as, "Do you remember what you told me yesterday about that?"; reformulating certain questions to make them easier for the participants to comprehend, or reformulating the participants' answers to allow the researchers to better understand. Ruel and colleagues (2016) used this same procedure. Both of these studies involved adults with intellectual disabilities, but interviewing children with a trusted peer, educator, or family member is a possible option. Similarly, Schäfer and Yarwood (2008) argue that peer-led interviews can lead to more equitable power relations and more of a partnership approach to research with young people. Children can interview each other as part of a collaborative research project.

The Mosaic Approach

The mosaic approach was developed to allow very young children to document their point of view about issues that concern them. The method is flexible, and involves multiple forms of data collection, including photography, mapmaking, guided tours, drawing, and audio or video recording (Clark, 2005; Clark & Moss, 2011). In their study about the daily life of children with and without additional support needs, Gray and Winter (2011) created dyads of children with and without additional support needs. Then, they offered the children a choice of methods to express what they appreciated and what they did not about their childcare setting. For example, the children were offered stickers, artifacts, drawing and painting materials, a disposable camera, and an audio recorder. Even if the authors concluded that children often chose the same materials, they believe that the variety of choice was important to their study (see Vignette 3.6).

**VIGNETTE 3.6—CHANGE AS A RESULT
OF THE MOSAIC APPROACH**

As part of a research project, kindergarten children are asked to identify what they like about their new school and what they would like to change. Provided with red and green sticky tack, the children each identify three things they strongly believe should stay the same (green) and three things they think need to improve or be removed (red). The majority of the children put red sticky tack on the construction area in the classroom. During a whole group discussion (circle time), the children explained that in their childcare center last year there were many different types of blocks and peripheral toys (figurines, cars, etc.). The block center in the kindergarten classroom had only wooden blocks and the children often argue and have to wait their turn to play there. The teacher shared these results with the school principal who agreed to provide a small budget to buy new material.

To conclude this section, we would like to draw attention to Pascal and Bertram's (2009) work over the course of 15 years, during which they carried out different projects experimenting with methods to include young children in research studies. Through the use of photography, filmmaking, bookmaking, collage, guided tours by children, and discussions about concrete events, the authors conclude, "It is clear that supporting and catching children's voices is complex, challenging and multi-layered, involving a profound paradigm shift in the values, actions and thinking of researchers and practitioners" (p. 260).

CONCLUSION

After reviewing the importance of including children with additional support needs in research into children's perspectives during the transition to school, this chapter explored ethical and methodological issues to consider when undertaking such research. We discussed various ways to obtain and reaffirm informed consent throughout the research process, involving children as research partners, considerations and options for researchers entering and leaving a research site, as well as supporting professionals already involved in the children's lives or parents to collect data. We presented examples of various types of data to collect as well as adaptions for children with additional support needs, drawn from research with very young children as well as with adults with additional support needs. We conclude with a commitment to the importance of seeking out children's perspectives, including children with additional support needs in our research projects, and relying on these perspectives to inform policy and practice. We also believe that children should be involved in all phases of a research project, if they so desire. As Uprichard (2010) asserts, there is "no reason not to [...] approach children as competent, knowledgeable informants who can be involved in social research in order to learn more about the world" (p. 9).

Questions for Reflection
1. Why is it important to invest time in getting to know children prior to beginning a project?
2. What considerations and options should you reflect upon when preparing to leave the research setting?
3. If you choose to have someone who is already familiar with the child collect the data, how will you include that person? How will you explore that person's point of view?
4. What materials or artifacts could help encourage children to share their perspectives with you?

Suggestions for Further Reading
Clark, A., & Moss. P. (2011). *Listening to young children: The mosaic approach* (2nd ed.). London: National Children's Bureau.
Dockett, S., Einarsdottir, J., & Perry, B. (2017). Photo elicitation: Reflecting on

multiple sites of meaning. *International Journal of Early Years Education, 3*, 225–240.

Gray, C., & White, E. (2011). Hearing voices: Participatory research with preschool children with and without disabilities. *European Early Childhood Education Research Journal, 19*(3), 309–320.

McIntosh, N. (2000). Guidelines for the ethical conduct of medical research involving children. *Archives of diseases of childhood, 82*, 177–182.

Murray, J. (2017). Welcome in! How the academy can warrant recognition of young children as researchers. *European Early Childhood Education Research Journal, 25*(2), 224–242.

Skanfors, L. (2009). Ethics in child research: Children's agency and researchers' 'ethical radar.' *Childhoods Today, 3*(1), 1–22.

Waller, T. (2006). 'Don't come too close to my octopus tree': Recording and evaluating perspectives on outdoor learning. *Children, Youth and Environments, 16*(2), 75–104.

REFERENCES

Althaus, M., de Sonneville, L. M. J., Minderaa, R. B, Hensen, L. G. N., & Til, R. B. (1996). Information processing and aspects of visual attention in children with the DSM-III-R diagnosis "pervasive developmental disorder not otherwise specified" (PDDNOS). Focused and divided attention. *Child Neuropsychology, 2*(1), 17–29.

Baird, K., & Grace, R. (2017). Do young children perceive change in the daily lives of their families during participation in a therapeutic family support programme? *European Early Childhood Education Research Journal, 25*(2), 258–271.

Bray, N., Noyes, J., Harris, N., & Edwards, R. T. (2017). Measuring the health-related quality of life of children with impaired mobility: Examining correlation and agreement between children and parent proxies. *BMC Research Notes, 10,* 377.

Bruce, T. (2005). *Early childhood education.* London, England: Hodder and Stoughton.

Buldu, M. (2010). Making learning visible in kindergarten classrooms: Pedagogical documentation as a formative assessment technique. *Teaching and Teacher Education, 26*(7), 1439–1449.

Cihak, D. F. (2007). Teaching students with autism to read pictures. *Research in Autism Spectrum Disorders, 1*(4), 318–329.

Clark, A. (2005). Ways of seeing: Using the mosaic approach to listen to young children's perspectives. In A. Clark, A. T. Kjørholt, & P. Moss (Eds.), *Beyond listening: Children's perspectives on early childhood services* (pp. 29–49). Bristol, England: Bristol University.

Clark, A., & Moss, P. (2011). *Listening to young children: The mosaic approach* (2nd ed.). London, England: National Children's Bureau.

Cocks, A. J. (2006). The ethical maze: Finding an inclusive path towards gaining children's agreement to research participation. *Childhood, 13*(2), 247–266.

Code civil du Québec. (1991). Code civil du Québec–CCQ-1991. Québec, Canada: Gouvernement du Québec.

Cohen, L., Manion, L., & Morrison, K. (2000). Research methods in education (5th ed.). London, England: Routledge Falmer.

Crump, A. (2014). "But your face, it looks like you're English": LangCrit and the experiences of Japanese-Canadian children in Montréal (Unpublished doctoral dissertation). McGill University, Montréal, Canada.

Deslandes, R., & Bertrand, R. (2001). L'école et ses liens avec la communauté. *Le Point en administration scolaire, 4*(1), 13–17.

Di Santo, A., & Berman, R. (2012). Beyond the preschool years: Children's perceptions about starting kindergarten. *Children & Society, 26*, 469–479.

Dockett, S. (2014). Transition to school: Normative or relative? In B. Perry, S. Dockett, & A. Petriwyskyj (Eds.), *Transitions to school: International research, policy and practice* (pp. 187–200). New York, NY: Springer.

Dockett, S., Einarsdottir, J., & Perry, B. (2017). Photo elicitation: Reflecting on multiple sites of meaning. *International Journal of Early Years Education, 3*, 225–240.

Dockett, S., & Perry, B. (2001). Starting school: Effective transitions. *Early Childhood Research & Practice, 3*(2). Retrieved from http://ecrp.uiuc.edu/v3n2/dockett.html

Dockett, S., & Perry, B. (2003). Children's views and children's voices in starting school. *Australian Journal of Early Childhood, 28*(1), 12–17.

Dockett, S., & Perry, B. (2015). Transition to school: Times of opportunity, expectation, aspiration and entitlement. In J. M. Iorio & W. Parnell (Eds.), *Rethinking readiness in early childhood education implications for policy and practice* (pp. 123–140). Basingstoke, England: Macmillan.

Ehri, L. C. (1998). Grapheme–phoneme knowledge is essential for learning to read words in English. In J. Metsala & L. Ehri (Eds.), *Word recognition in beginning literacy* (pp. 3–40). Mahwah, NJ: Erlbaum.

Einarsdottir, J. (2007). Research with children: Methodological and ethical challenges. *European Early Childhood Education Research Journal, 15*(2), 197–211.

Einarsdottir, J., Dockett, S., & Perry, B. (2009). Making meaning: Children's perspectives expressed through drawings. *Early Childhood Development and Care, 179*(2), 217–232.

Epstein, I., Stevens, B., McKeever, P., & Baruchel, S. (2006). Photo elicitation interview (PEI): Using photos to elicit children's perspectives. *International Journal of Qualitative Methods, 5*(3), 1–11.

European Early Childhood Education Research Association. (2015). *EECERA Ethical Code for Early Childhood Researchers*. Retrieved from https://www.eecera.org/about/ethical-code/

Eskelä-Haapanen, S., Lerkkanen, M.-K., Rasku-Puttonen, H., & Poikkeus, A.-M. (2016). Children's beliefs concerning school transition. *Early Childhood Development and Care, 187*(9), 1446–1459.

Fleer, M., Tonyan, H. A., Mantilla, A.-C., & Rivalland, C. M. P. (2009). Play and learning in Australia. In I. Pramling-Samuelsson & M. Fleer (Eds.), *Play and learning in early childhood settings* (pp. 51–80). New York, NY: Springer.

Flewitt, R. (2005). Conducting research with young children: Some ethical considerations. *Early Childhood Development and Care, 6*(175), 553–565.

Fougeyrollas, P., Cloutier, R., Bergeron, H., Côté, J., & Saint-Michel, G. (1998). *Processus de Production du Handicap, Classification québécoise* [Processes of production of handicap, Quebec classification]. Québec, Canada: Réseau International sur le Processus de Production du Handicap.

Gouvernement du Québec. (2006). *Loi sur les services de garde éducatifs à l'enfance* [Educational Childcare Centre]. Québec, Canada: Author.

Graham, B., & Iannacci, L. (2013). Reconceptualizing "special education" curriculum in a bachelor of education program: Teacher candidate discourses and teacher educator practices. *Canadian Journal of Disability Studies, 2*(2), 10–34. Retrieved from http://cjds.uwaterloo.ca/index.php/cjds/article/view/79/129

Gray, C. (2017). Crossing cultural barriers: Children's views on the recuperative holiday experience. *European Early Childhood Education Research Journal, 25*(2), 321–339.

Gray, C., Prunty, A., Logan, A., & Hayes, G. (2015). *Managing early years' inclusive transition practices.* Report funded by the Standing Conference on Teacher Education, North and South (SCoTENs). Retrieved from https://www.researchgate.net/publication/283487023_Managing_Early_Years_Inclusive_Transitions_to_School

Gray, C., & Winter, E. (2011). Hearing voices: Participatory research with preschool children with and without disabilities. *European Early Childhood Education Research Journal, 19*(3). 309–320.

Harrison, L. J., Sumsion, J., Bradley, B., Letsch, K., & Salamon, A. (2017). Flourishing on the margins: A study of babies and belonging in an Australian aboriginal community childcare centre. *European Early Childhood Education Research Journal, 25*(2), 180–205.

Hemmingsson, H., Ólafsdóttir, L. B., & Egilson, S. T. (2017). Agreements and disagreements between children and their parents in health-related assessments. *Disability and rehabilitation, 39*(11), 1059–1072.

Heydon, R. M., & Iannacci, L. (2009). *Early childhood curricula and the de- pathologizing of childhood.* Toronto, Canada: University of Toronto Press.

Hohepa, M., & McIntosh, L. (2017). Transition to School for Indigenous Children. In N. Ballam, B. Perry, & A. Garpelin (Eds.), *Pedagogies of educational transitions: European and Antipodean research.* Dordrecht, Netherlands: Springer.

Holm, G. (2008). Visual research methods: Where are we and where are we going? In S. N. Hesse-Biber & P. Leavy (Eds.), *Handbook of emergent methods* (pp. 325–341). New York, NY: Guilford Press.

Kelly, B. (2010). Methodological issues for qualitative research with learning disabled children. *International Journal of Social Research Methodology, 10*(1), 21–35.

Lehrer, J., Bigras, N., & Laurin, I. (2017). Relations entre la famille et des intervenants lors de la transition d'un centre de la petite enfance vers la maternelle: une étude de cas Québécoise [Relationships between families and professionals during the transition from a childcare centre to kindergarten: a case study from Quebec]. In S. Rayna & P. Garnier (Eds.), *Transitions dans la petite enfance: Recherche en Europe et au Québec* [Transitions in early childhood: research in Europe and Quebec] (pp. 121–145). Brussels, Belgium: Peter Lang.

Lehrer, J., & Petrakos, H. (2011). Parent and child perceptions of grade one children's out-of-school play. *Exceptionality Education International, 21*(3), 74–92. Retrieved from http://ir.lib.uwo.ca/eei/vol21/iss2/8/

Letscher, S., Jolicoeur, E., Beaupré, P., Milot, É., Point, M., & Julien-Gauthier, F. (Unpublished manuscript). *Barriers and facilitators related to social participation and inclusion of people with intellectual disabilities.*

Malaguzzi, L. (1993). For an education based on relationships. *Young Children, 49*(1), 9–12.

McGettigan, I. L., & Gray, C. (2012). Perspectives on school readiness in rural Ireland: The experiences of parents and children. *International Journal of Early Years Education, 20*(1), 15–29.

McIntyre, L. L., Eckert, T. L., Fiese, B. H., DiGennaro Reed, F. D., & Wildinger, L. K. (2010). Family concerns surrounding kindergarten transition: A comparison of students in special and general education. *Early Childhood Education Journal, 38*, 259–263.

Merriam, S. (1988). *Case study in education: A qualitative approach.* San Francisco, CA: Jossc-Bass.

Millei, Z., & Rautio, P. (2017). "Overspills" of research with children: An argument for slow research. *Children's Geographies, 15*(4), 466–477.

Miller, J. (1997). *Never too young.* London, England: National Early Years Network.

Ministère de l'Éducation, du Loisir et du Sport. (2007). *L'organisation de services éducatifs aux élèves à risque et aux élèves handicapés ou en difficulté d'adaptation ou d'apprentissage* [The organization of educational services for students who are at-risk, handicapped, or have adaptation or learning difficulties]. Québec, Canada: Gouvernement du Québec.

Ministère de l'Éducation, du Loisir et du Sport. (2009). *L'école j'y tiens! Tous ensemble pour la réussite scolaire* [I care about school! All together for student success]. Québec, Canada: Gouvernement du Québec.

Ministère de l'Éducation, du Loisir et du Sport. (2010). *Document d'appui à la réflexion, Rencontre sur l'intégration des élèves handicapés ou en difficulté* [Reflection document, Meeting regarding the integration of students with disabilities or in difficulty]. Québec, Canada: Gouvernement du Québec.

Ministère de l'Éducation, du Loisir et du Sport. (2013). *Indicateurs de l'éducation, 2012* [Educational indicators, 2012]. Québec, Canada: Gouvernement du Québec.

Ministère de l'Éducation et de l'Enseignement supérieur. (2017). *TSE, DGSEG, DIS, Portail informationnel, Système Charlemagne, données au 2017-01-26* [TSE, DGSES, DIS Information portal, Charlemagne system, data retrieved 26-01-2014]. Québec, Canada: Gouvernement du Québec.

Miron, J.-M., & Tochon, F. (2004). La difficile reconnaissance de "l'expertise parentale" [The difficult recognition of "parental expertise"]. *Recherche et Formation, 47*(1), 55–68. Retrieved from http://www.persee.fr/doc/refor_0988 -1824_2004_num_47_1_1927

Moore, M., & Calvert, S. (2000). Brief report: Vocabulary acquisition for children with autism: Teacher or computer instruction. *Journal of Autism and Developmental Disorders, 30*(4), 359–362.

Niesel, R., & Griebel, W. (2001, August–September). *Transition to schoolchild: What children tell about school and what they teach us.* Paper presented at the 11th

European Early Childhood Education Research Association Conference, Alkmaar, Netherlands. Retrieved from http://extranet.edfac.unimelb.edu.au/LED/tec/pdf/ griebelniesel4.pdf

O'Rourke, C., O'Farrelly, C., Booth, A., & Doyle, O. (2017). "Little bit afraid 'til I found how it was": Children's subjective early school experiences in a disadvantaged community in Ireland. *European Early Childhood Education Research Journal, 25*(2), 206–223.

Pascal, C., & Bertram, T. (2009). Listening to young citizens: The struggle to make real difference participatory paradigm in research with young children. *European Early Childhood Education Research Journal, 17*(2), 249–262.

Peccia, S. (2012). *Children's perspectives of Kindergarten and Grade One: An analysis of narratives and drawings* (Unpublished master's thesis). Concordia University, Montréal, Canada.

Petriwyskyj, A. (2014). Critical theory and inclusive transitions to school. In B. Perry, S. Dockett, & A. Petriwyskyj (Eds.), *Transitions to school: International research, policy and practice* (pp. 201–218). Dordrecht, Netherlands: Springer.

Pianta, R. C., Cox, M. J., Taylor, L., & Early, D. (1999). Kindergarten teachers' practices related to transition into schools: Results of a national survey. *Elementary School Journal, 100,* 71–86.

Pole, C., Mizen, P., & Bolton, A. (1999). Realising children's agency in research: Partners and participants? *International Journal of Social Research Methodology, 2,* 39–54.

Prosser, J., & Burke, C. (2008). Image-based educational research: Childlike perspectives. In J. G. Knowles & A. L. Cole (Eds.), *Handbook of the arts in qualitative research: Perspectives, methodologies, examples, and issues* (pp. 407–419). Thousand Oaks, CA: SAGE.

Riddell, S., & Weedon, E. (2017). Social justice and provision for children with additional support needs in Scotland. *Education, Citizenship, and Social Justice, 12*(1), 36–48.

Rimm-Kaufman, S., & Pianta, R. C. (2000). An ecological perspective on the transition to kindergarten: A theoretical framework to guide empirical research. *Journal of Applied Developmental Psychology, 21*(5), 491–511.

Rimm-Kaufman, S. E., & Pianta, R. C. (2005). Family-school communication in preschool and kindergarten in the context of a relationship-enhancing intervention. *Early Education and Development, 16*(3), 287–316.

Roberts, R. (2002). *Self-esteem and early learning.* London, England: Paul Chapman Educational.

Rosenkoetter, S. E., Hains, A. H., & Dogaru, C. (2007). Successful transitions for young children with disabilities and their families: Roles of school social workers. *Children & Schools, 29*(1), 25–34.

Rothe, A., Urban, M., & Werning, R. (2014). Inclusive transition processes—Considering socio-economically disadvantaged parents' views and actions for their child's successful school start. *Early Years: An International Research Journal, 34*(4), 364–376.

Rous, B., Myers, C. T., & Stricklin, S. B. (2007). Strategies for supporting transitions of young children with special needs and their families. *Journal of Early Intervention, 30*(1), 1–18.

Ruel, J. (2011). *Travail en réseau, savoirs en partage et processus en jeu en contexte d'innovation: Une transition planifiée vers le préscolaire d'enfants ayant des besoins particuliers* [Networking, sharing knowledge and processes at stake in contexts of innovation: A planned transition to preschool for children with special needs] (Doctoral dissertation). Gatineau, Canada: Université du Québec en Outaouais. Retrieved from http://www.archipel.uqam.ca/4192/1/D2192.pdf

Ruel, J., Kassi, B., Moreau, A. C., & Mbida-Mballa, S. L. (2011). *Guide de rédaction pour une information accessible. Critères de lisibilité, d'intelligibilité et de langage simplifié pour soutenir la rédaction de documents destinés aux personnes ayant des compétences réduites en littératie* [Writing guide for accessible information. Criteria of readability, intelligibility, and simplified language to support drafting documents for people with limited literacy competencies]. Gatineau, Canada: Pavillon du Parc. Retrieved from http://w3.uqo.ca/litteratie/documents/guide2011_000.pdf

Ruel, J., Moreau, A. C., & Bourdeau, L. (2008). Démarche de transition planifiée et continuité éducative [Planned transition and educational continuity process]. *Revue francophone de la déficience intellectuelle, 19*, 41–48.

Ruel, J., Moreau, A. C., Kassi, B., & Prud'homme, M. (2016). Éléments clés, enjeux et retombées d'une démarche de rédaction inclusive réalisée avec des adultes ayant de très faibles compétences en littératie [Key elements, issues, and benefits of an inclusive writing approach with adults who have very low literacy competencies]. *Language and Literacy, 18*(3), 113–131.

Schäfer, N., & Yarwood, R. (2008). Involving young people as researchers: Uncovering multiple power relations among youths. *Children's Geographies, 6*(2), 121–135.

Shane, H. C., Laubscher, E. H., Schlosser, R. W., Flynn, S., Sorce, J. F., & Abramson, J. (2012). Applying technology to visually support language and communication in individuals with autism spectrum disorders. *Journal of Autism and Developmental Disorders, 42*(6), 1228–1235.

Sheldrick, R. C., Neger, E. N., Shipman, D., & Perrin, E. C. (2012). Quality of life of adolescents with autism spectrum disorders: Concordance among adolescents' self-reports, parents' reports, and parents' proxy reports. *Quality of Life Research, 21*, 53–37.

Skanfors, L. (2009). Ethics in child research: Children's agency and researchers' 'ethical radar.' *Childhoods Today, 3*(1), 1–22.

Tobin, J., Hsueh, Y., & Karasawa, M. (2009). *Preschool in three cultures revisited.* Chicago, IL: University of Chicago Press.

United Nations. (1989). *Convention on the rights of the child.* New York, NY: Author. Retrieved from http://www.unicef.org/crc/crc

Uprichard, E. (2010). Questioning research with children: Discrepancy between theory and practice? *Children & Society, 24*, 3–13.

Wahle, N., Ponizovsky-Bergelson, Y., Dayan, Y., Erlichman, O., & Roer-Strier, D. (2017). On the margins of racism, immigration and war: Perspectives on risk and protection of young children of Ethiopian origin in Israel. *European Early Childhood Education Research Journal. 25*(2), 305–320.

Waller, T. (2006). 'Don't come too close to my octopus tree': Recording and evaluating perspectives on outdoor learning. *Children, Youth, and Environments, 16*(2), 75–104.

Walsh, D. J., Bakir, N., Byungho, L., Chung, Y. H., & Chung, K. (2007). Using digital video in field-based research with children: A primer. In J. Amos Hatch (Ed.), *Early Childhood Qualitative Research* (pp. 43–62). New York, NY: Routledge.

Wineberg, L., & Chiquette, L. (2009). Play and learning in Wisconsin. In I. Pramling-Samuelsson & M. Fleer (Eds.), *Play and Learning in Early Childhood Settings* (pp. 155–171). Netherlands: Springer.

Wolery, M. (1999). Children with disabilities in early elementary school. In R. C. Pianta & M. J. Cox (Eds.), *The transition to kindergarten* (pp. 217–251). Baltimore, MA: Brookes.

Yardley, A. C. (2011). Children as experts in their own lives: Reflections on the principles of creative collaboration. *Child Indicators Research, 4*(2), 191–204.

CHAPTER 4

THE ROLE OF REFLEXIVITY IN PERFORMING COLLABORATIVE STUDENT VOICE RESEARCH

Joseph Levitan

ABSTRACT

This chapter discusses the how of collaborative student voice research methods, specifically focusing on the role of reflexivity for developing equitable, positive, and productive relational dynamics with students. I utilize phenomenological methods to reflect upon a research project undertaken with Quechua (Indigenous) young women students to create a culturally grounded education program. As there are well-documented issues with suppression of youth and nondominant groups' voice and agency, this chapter offers approaches to facilitate more engagement and voice with youth. I argue that to create an equitable space for collaborative research that elevates students' voices and agency the fundamental framework of student–teacher relational and power dynamics must shift. It is the responsibility of adults to construct an equitable learning and research space, which requires significant reflexivity, an understanding of multiple perspectives, and understanding research-

Participatory Methodologies to Elevate Children's Voice and Agency, pages 73–92
Copyright © 2019 by Information Age Publishing
73

er/teacher positionality. Reframing the educational space to create more distributed power dynamics, and framing adults' roles as thoughtful colleagues, provides opportunities for youth-adult research groups to more genuinely investigate their inquiry topic. In this chapter I discuss how to undertake reflexive learning in order to shift power-dynamics between youth and adults to foster more productive engagement with students and support students' in claiming their voices and agency.

When performing participatory, collaborative research with youth, issues of power and positionality between youth and adults are inevitable in the process (Delpit, 2006; 2012; Levinson, 2011). Adults—teachers, administrators, researchers, and so on—claim most of the power within educational spaces (even if adolescents often contest adults' power). However, engaging in collaborative work means that the power dynamics must shift to become more equitable so that students can increase their voice and agency. To accomplish this shift, adults need to become deeply aware of their positionality and relational dynamics—the ways in which they frame their approach to communicating with students. This self-reflective or reflexive work can open space and encourage students to claim and develop their voices and agency.

However, the "how" of collaboration, or achieving a positive shift in relational dynamics, is a challenging and under-researched aspect of collaborative research and teaching (Lassiter, 2008). Adjusting one's framework, or the subtle ways in which adults construct spaces and relationships, requires a high degree of self-awareness, and a skillful balancing of structure, freedom, and responsibility. This chapter examines the inner workings of learning the how of collaborative research through a reflexive case study. I examine learning moments during a collaborative youth research project to contribute to scholarship on equitable and productive relational dynamics with students as an essential aspect of inquiry. The research project focused on the learning aspirations of students from Indigenous communities in the Peruvian Andes to create culturally grounded learning opportunities. The case, and the various positions of the different individuals working on this project, offers a contribution to understanding reflexivity in action.

BACKGROUND AND CHAPTER STRUCTURE

In 2014 and 2015 I undertook a collaborative research project with young women who are the first in their families to enroll in secondary school (Levitan, 2018). In this chapter I write about one way to engage in reflection and interpretation when working with students in a collaborative research process to foster their voices and agency. I discuss the process of framing collaborative work, as well as discussing tensions and power issues within the process.

The collaborative research project was undertaken to develop a culturally grounded, identity responsive curricula. The research also served to elevate the students' voice and agency within their own education. The 14 young women co-investigators are secondary school students ranging in age between 14 and 17 years old, and are bilingual Quechua and Spanish speakers from rural Indigenous communities.

As an adult from a different cultural background than the students, there are issues of epistemology, positionality, and power at play. I interrogate my epistemology, power, and positionality to discuss the reflexive and relational aspect of developing a collaborative project with students. As a contribution to collaborative and student voice research methods literature (Mitra, 2007; 2009), I argue that reflexivity is an essential aspect of collaborative student voice research, as it allows the researcher/practitioner to uncover the ways they frame their relational dynamics with students and reframe those dynamics towards collaboration, which in turn allows students to more readily claim their voices and agency. Reflexivity also allows the adult researcher to cultivate more thoughtful listening, which helps foster more voice and engagement from the student co-investigators. As this process is still somewhat mysterious, this chapter serves as one example for consideration. It also puts forth an argument that reflexivity includes an understanding and appreciation of multiplicity, which may be better facilitated through reflection upon experience from multiple theoretical frameworks (Levitan, 2018).

The chapter is organized as a phenomenological case study (Van Manen, 1990). In what follows, each step of the collaborative project is discussed through brief descriptions of events and practices, and then reflexively analyzed. First, I outline the context of the research project and briefly share some of the theoretical and methodological foundations for the study. I then discuss the reflexive examination of the research process. Finally, I offer suggestions about self-reflection in collaborative student voice research for those who wish to undertake this type of research work.

CONTEXT AND PARTICIPANTS

The research took place in a small town in the Peruvian Andes at an educational nonprofit with a social justice mission. The town sits about 10,000 feet above sea level, nestled in a fertile mountain valley. This town serves as the main hub for approximately 50 Quechua communities that reside up the mountain paths. These communities can be as far as 8 hours away on foot. The primary occupation of most residents in the town and surrounding area is agriculture.

As recently as 1993, the town did not have electricity (and about half of the surrounding Quechua communities still do not have electricity at the time of this writing). However, in the town, an influx of tourism—due to the town's location along the way to Machu Picchu—has created economic and development opportunities. Tourist dollars have allowed for infrastructure development, such as electricity, Internet, and paved roads, but the influx of money and tourism has also created tensions within and between various groups in the community, and produced a complex cultural and social space within the region.

For example, some community members worry that the influence of "Western" ideas is eroding Quechua culture and community structure. The erosion of a Quechua way of life is seen as negative from most groups. However, those who are becoming relatively wealthy from tourism embrace Western ideology, in the sense of Western business practices. At the same time, there is a significant and growing awareness within these communities that women have been historically marginalized (Sumida Huaman, 2013) and the configuration of male dominated decision-making has denied access to certain forms of power to women, such as governing roles. Yet, feminist ideas from the West have provided opportunities for women to claim some more power and agency (Holmes & Crossley, 2004). Yet, it is often the men who are gaining wealth and embracing neoliberal, Western, economic opportunity who also wish to deny women power, claiming traditional values. This context provides evidence for the complex nature of "development" in a globalized age (Adelman, 2006; Sumida Huaman, 2013).

In addition to these complexities, the individual and social consensus about the state of Quechua communities and the social fabric of the town is constantly shifting. This means that simple interpretations about "good" and "bad" social and individual realities are unhelpful for guiding thinking about education policy. In other words, the constant interaction with international visitors in the region has had mixed influences on the town's way of life based on the accounts of the members of the town.

This is the context within which the educational nonprofit was created. The mission of the nonprofit is to (a) ensure that girl students from rural Quechua communities are able to go to secondary school and become leaders in their communities, and (b) ensure that students' Quechua identities are valued and that students have a space to cultivate and celebrate their identities (Levitan, Carr-Chellman, & Carr-Chellman, 2017).[1]

Girls in rural Quechua communities are often unable to access secondary school because the only secondary schools are 2 to 8 hours away from their homes. Each rural community does have a one or two room primary school, however, and girls are encouraged to attend primary school. This was not always the case. As recently as a generation ago, girls were actively discouraged to go to school (see Levitan, 2015). Once girls reach secondary school age, however, the ability to attend school becomes more difficult.

Because girls are seen as essential help to the household, there is an opportunity cost if adolescents are gone for most of the day at school (Ames & Rojas, 2010; Lewis & Lockheed, 2007; Stromquist, 2001). In primary school, the school day is usually only about four hours and young children leave school in the middle of the day to go check on their herds of goats, cows, and sheep. This practice cannot be done in secondary school, as it is a longer school day, and secondary schools are far from the home. Furthermore, going to secondary school requires buying a uniform (all public schools have uniforms), paying school fees, and purchasing school supplies, which often cost too much for rural Quechua families to afford (Ilahi, 2001; UNESCO, 2012).

In addition, it is not feasible for students to commute at least 2 hours each way everyday, so if students want to go to secondary school they need to find a family in the town who is willing to exchange work for room and board. However, this option is more dangerous for girls than boys, as girls can become targets of aggression, sexual abuse, and/or exploitation by men and women. Therefore, poverty and safety issues often prohibit girls from rural Indigenous communities from attending secondary school (Levitan, 2015).

To respond to these issues the founders of the educational nonprofit built a dormitory near the secondary school that provides a safe space, supplementary education, nutritious meals, school supplies, and uniforms. Girl students from the rural communities stay at the dormitory during the school week, and then go home over the weekend to stay connected to their community and to help with their family's farms. The dormitory has a Quechua speaking house mother/house director who stays with the students overnight during the week.

As the students begin secondary school mostly speaking Quechua, and with less academic (but many more practical) skills than their town-dwelling counterparts, the project brings in professional and volunteer tutors to help with academics, language, and to help facilitate students' abilities to claim their voices and agency. My contribution to this project is in the educational policy and administrative aspects of the work we do with the community.

Participants

Based on the above considerations, it is safe to say that the students come from one of the more historically marginalized and oppressed positions in the current sociopolitical climate of a globalizing world. The students with whom I work have been placed in lesser positions of power as girls from rural Quechua communities. Although each of the students is unique, they share similar experiences due to their shared positions within society, they share similar backgrounds.

The students (and their families) decided to make a significant sacrifice in going to school. Adolescents are highly productive farmers, herders, and cooks, as well as craftspeople, so as mentioned above, the families are losing key individuals in their work force (not to mention emotional and familial supports) in order to try to provide their children with better opportunities. As the mother of one of the students told me:

> I stay here alone with the cows and the fields so that all of my daughters can go to school and have a better life. My husband works [as a cook on the Inca Trail] every week and is away so that he can make enough money [to pay for his eldest daughter's college]. We both sacrifice everything for our children to go to school and make good happy lives. (Levitan, 2015, p. 66)

This sacrifice is not lost on the students, and they are aware that there are significant expectations for them to achieve their goals (and the goals their parents have for them).

As I have worked with the community for 8 years at the time of writing this chapter, I have come to understand the importance of the web of relationships and mutual expectations within Quechua extended communities, which plays a major role in parents' aspirations for their children. The concept of *ayni*, which is a Quechua word that can be roughly translated as reciprocity (although it carries much deeper meaning), plays a significant role in how parents' frame and understand their expectations of their children. Once an individual becomes part of the community, and children are born into the community, there are a number of important relationships that carry mutual obligations in order to ensure that all members, and the community as a whole, are afforded the material, social, emotional, and spiritual support necessary to live, grow, and thrive—the deeper meaning of *ayni*, at least as the author has come to understand it.

Researcher Positionality

In contrast to the students' backgrounds, I come from one of the more privileged and empowered positions in the current sociopolitical climate, as I am a formally educated man with a PhD who is a citizen of the United States. Although I have mixed ethnicities and am Jewish, I am viewed as a "White" man, but I am not "really" White in the sociopolitical context where I was raised. This requires navigating how to express my identities, which has lead to difficulty and even overt bigotry against me.

My experiences have caused me to feel, as well as think about, the need for social justice from multiple perspectives—defined by the individuals who feel and experience oppressive structures. I see my well-being as deeply connected with others' well-being. So, I strive to work with individuals and groups who have been denied choice, mobility, power, and agency to help facilitate their self-determination. As I have the privileges of choice, mobility, and power, which are denied to many others (such as the students and their parents) who have different social positions, I feel a sense of responsibility to facilitate justice through education.

At the time of this research project I was working as the director of education for the nonprofit because I was asked to serve in this role by a friend. So, I held a position of significant power in the context of the collaborative research project and the students' education.

I express these details and analysis here because my positionality informs the interpretive framework I take. In addition, in the current social and academic climate, who one "is"—one's background, education, experiences— is as important as what one says when it comes to issues of social justice and discussion about privilege, power, and agency. These reflections inform the approach, and my understandings of positionality, which will be important for the analysis below.

Intersubjective Context

In the context of this research, there seems to be a wide gulf between the students and the researcher/educator in terms of cultural background, historical levels of agency and power, and epistemology, which have important implications for how members of the research group (students and adults) understand each other. This also affects how each person understands the context and content of the research. Both the students and I speak Spanish, but we also both speak another language in our home communities, Quechua and English, respectively.

So, how can a man from a very different background constructively work with Indigenous young women to facilitate developing their voices and agency? How might this person do so without falling into the traps that historical precedents of colonizing students' thinking or silencing their voices, have shown to be the legacy of Westerners (Adelman, 2006; Mansfield, 2014; Said, 1979; Spivak, 1988; Sumida Huaman 2013; Sylvester, 1999)? These questions are significant and important for collaborative work with people from different backgrounds in many contexts. The spirit of the question—"How can someone from a position of power work productively with individuals from positions of less power to help them claim their voices and agency?"—can be asked in many contexts where teachers and students work together. Misunderstandings and mistakes often happen when assumptions diverge and relational dynamics are not trusting and open. So, although the analysis that follows focuses on a specific case, there is considerable applicability and transferability (Lincoln & Guba, 1990) to other contexts in terms of the process of reflection in order to reframe dynamics. What follows will critically reflect on a process that addresses the questions and the ways forward in response to them.

FRAMEWORK

This chapter contains two main arguments. First, researchers, teachers, and leaders (all of whom are labeled adults in this chapter) benefit from reflexively and iteratively interpreting students' voices from multiple theoretical perspectives as part of their research method process (Levitan, 2018). Second, an essential part of the research process is for the adult researcher to learn how to uncover their implicit, assumed frameworks, and reframe or position themselves as thoughtful and knowledgeable colleagues and co-learners to develop positive relational dynamics with students. These two activities allow the adult researcher to accomplish two things: (a) productively interpret the meanings underlying the students' words in order to create an iterative process of meaning-making with them, and (b) make the collaborative research process truly collaborative while still acknowledging the differences of experience between participants. This requires a shift from understanding experience and knowledge in the common hierarchy of "knowledgeable" teacher and "novice" student into understanding that all collaborators have knowledges, though each person has different knowledges, with different expertise and levels of depth.

The first argument, that utilizing multiple theoretical perspectives to iteratively interpret students' ideas, might seem counterintuitive for common methods in research design (Merriam, 2014). However, in working collaboratively with youth, the complex and emerging nature of the students' ideas and voices—ideas that are in development and voices that are finding themselves—means that the adult researcher is engaging in a delicate process of critical thinking with the students. From this process students will be able to uncover their own insights and gain new understandings of their ideas. When approached thoughtfully, the adult researcher is in a good position to help facilitate this process as a sounding board for understanding and refining the implications of the students' ideas. This process requires both structure and flexibility from the adult researcher. A fully free-flowing or emergent process of developing a theory is likely to be too fluid, but a single theoretical orientation will likely limit and co-opt the many ideas discussed within a given group of students. Comparative, theoretical reflection is an important (and under researched) aspect of deep listening to understand the intentions and the motivations behind others' words (Levitan, 2018).

RESEARCH DESIGN

The design of this research used two complementary methods and approaches, collaborative ethnography (Lassiter, 2008) and student voice methods (Mitra, 2007; 2009). I then undertook phenomenological reflection to write the case study of this reflective process (Van Manen, 1990).

Collaborative ethnography, as a method, is about building action-oriented coalitions *with* participants to identify issues and questions for investigation. This entails developing community grounded avenues for uncovering or addressing those issues or questions, and then for analyzing the findings for thoughtful action forward within the community, or presenting findings and solutions to a wider audience (Lassiter, 2008). Collaborative ethnography is related to action-research methodologies (Levitan, Carr-Chellman, & Carr-Chellman, 2017), but is focused specifically on working with certain communities to address issues of voice, power, and agency, as well as issues of social justice. The collaborative ethnography process was the method I utilized when engaging with the students in developing the research project for building their education programming—simultaneously working with students so that they may productively utilize their voice and agency to steer their learning process, as well as to develop their self-efficacy as agents in their lives and their communities' lives.

Phenomenological research serves as the basis for reflections about working as a co-researcher and facilitator. Phenomenology examines the subtly and connections between pre-reflective experience and the process of interpretation to make meaning out of that experience in order to provide more understanding, and qualitatively improved action in the future (Van Manen, 1990). I pull from this methodology because analysis utilizing this framework has allowed me to find, through 8 years of experience working with youth in schools in the United States and Peru, why some teachers are able to generate productive educational relationships with students, and others (who have the same or similar philosophies about social justice or education) may not be as successful. This methodology has also helped me to grow as a teacher and facilitate student's growth for greater opportunities for self-actualization and accomplishment. Finally, phenomenology offers a method for understanding the processes and orientations to discover: (a) what social justice looks like and feels like for the community of students I am working with; and (b) how to facilitate achieving social justice with them. Therefore, phenomenology is the methodology I use to reflect upon and generate meaning from the experiences within the collaborative educational project that I discuss below.

RESEARCH PROCESS

This section outlines the steps of the collaborative student voice research project. As will be discussed below, much of the work to increase students' voices and agency occurred as framing and "background work" where students were offered a space to bring their own creative ideas, and/or analytical issues to community-wide discussion, which spurred more in-depth investigation. The research project then sprung from this background work, and was accomplished in five steps.

Step 1: Creating a Space

For this participatory research project the research team (students and adults) worked together to better understand each person's values and aspirations, as well as the values and aspirations of the students' parents, in order to design more responsive curricula for the nonprofit. The collaborative student voice project began because the students came up with a topic for exploration during a weekly student-run seminar.

In order to create a space where students can generate their own ideas, we created an hour-long discussion circle. Each week, one of the students or one of the teachers would bring a subject to discuss, or would share an issue that they wanted support to figure out. The adults were an equal part of the seminar format, so each student, and each of the teachers had a turn to bring in a topic.

Placing students and adults on equal footing, taking turns, and sharing opinions worked better for us than maintaining a separation between the students and adults, which would have entailed a student-run discussion circle only. Creating an open space of discussion is a useful approach for cultivating students' voices, and although it takes some time for the students to get used to the freedom and responsibility of running a discussion, it can become a way for students to feel empowered to speak up about issues important to them.

Creating a space for students to bring and develop their voices is the foundation for generating a relational dynamic where students feel that they can bring their voices and develop them with adults and work alongside adults, in contrast to opposing, or avoiding adults. Much of the work of a facilitating adult is to facilitate a space where adults are present and able to collaborate, without overpowering students' voices and opinions. Although it takes a significant amount of time, the shift in relational dynamics is crucial for quality collaborative research, as well as productive dynamics in the classroom.

Step 2: Identifying an Issue

The collaborative student voice research project was initiated during one of the seminars. One of the students began discussing aspirations. The discussion began with students talking about the jobs they wanted, and then turned into a nuanced conversation about the details and implications of their aspirations and how their education would help them achieve their goals. In order to understand the implications of their goals, one of the teachers asked the students about what their parents were hoping for them. The students did not really know the details about what their parents wanted from them, and so began the collaborative research project.

The students were also not particularly clear about the details of their own aspirations, so we decided to explore them in more depth as part of the research project, as the adults also wanted to know how adjust the educational initiatives and programming to better help students achieve their, and their communities', goals to make more responsive educational decisions. The students and the adults were also interested in the parents' aspirations for their children. As parents sacrifice a lot to send their children to school, it was a salient question.

Step 3: Generating a Method and Collecting Data

In the third step, we started to develop a method to better understand the students' aspirations as well as to find out what the parents wanted for the students. As an adult researcher I facilitated some of the methodological decisions. We decided to create an interview protocol to be used with the parents, and as a reflection tool for the students, as framing questions is an essential part of finding answers (Levitan, 2016). To do this, the adult researchers created some sample questions for the students to see as an example, and then the students developed their own questions (see Levitan, 2018). During this process the students also answered the questions and discussed the answers amongst themselves as part of the reflective focus group exercise. This discussion was revealing about certain assumptions students had concerning their futures, as well as exposing certain areas where the students could learn more—for example, what work is entailed when working as a "professional."

The adults had (naively) assumed that the students knew what went into the work of a lawyer, doctor, or teacher. We learned that this was not the case, and that their schooling had not discussed with them the different kinds of work that professionals did, or what a professional was, even though all of the students said that they wanted to be a professional (see Levitan, 2018).

To interview the parents, the adults visited the students' homes during the weekend. As the students went home each weekend, a team of two adult researchers—a woman volunteer teacher and I—would go with the students and visit with their family. Students regularly invite the teachers and volunteers to visit their homes, so it was also a social event. The adults audio recorded the interviews, which lasted between 30 and 70 minutes. Then, adults transcribed the interviews, focusing on main points to discuss with the students.

Step 4: Generating findings and Interpreting Data

Once we interviewed each of the students' parents, the volunteer teacher and I transcribed relevant sections of the interviews (skipping small talk) and then analyzed the transcripts for relevant themes. Because we learned that the students did not really know what a professional was or what went into being a professional, even though the students were keen on becoming professionals, we decided to explore what the parents wanted their children to become as a means of exploring their aspirations and the ways in which the school might be able to facilitate learning that the community wanted.

Based on the information we gathered, the students and adults then met another time to reflect as a group. The adult researchers synthesized the parents' responses to create three example profiles of positive women role models: a farmer, a store clerk, and a lawyer. These themes came from the parent interviews about the kinds of lives that the parents wanted for their children. This allowed the students to more quickly analyze the most salient themes from hours of interviews and pages of transcripts.

After reading each of the profiles, the students responded that there was only one professional, and that was the lawyer. Since the students all said they wanted to be professionals in the first focus group, the assumption from the educators was that the students did not value their traditions and their heritage as farmers. The focus on professionalism, and the way in which I first interpreted the students' responses might have lead me to start to build ideas with the students that were geared towards a certain paradigm, such as development and entrée into a neoliberal, globalized society. However, upon self-reflection I realized that the students could mean many different things, which is also what we uncovered in our third focus group to go over the data.

Step 5: Bringing New Knowledge Into Practice

From the findings, it seemed that we were left with data that needed to be interpreted extensively in order to put new knowledge into action. This step required me to think about the interpretations I made and then think about how to reflect those interpretations back to the students, as a way of continuing the iterative process in educational program development. This meant presenting ideas and plans to the students as part of their supplementary education.

For more information about the findings and the ways in which it was interpreted, see Levitan (2018). This chapter is about how positionality, relational dynamics with the students, and assumptions influenced the process of this research, rather than the results of the investigation and how those results influenced the education of the students.

REFLECTIONS, TRANSFORMATIONS, AND UNCOVERING ASSUMPTIONS

During this process, my own assumptions about what a good education looked like were uncovered. These assumptions were postcolonial (Rankin, 2010; Said 1979; Spivak, 1988), critical (Apple, 1995; Freire, 2000), indigenist (Sumida Huaman, 2013; Wilson, 2001), feminist (Doucet and Mauthner, 2006; hooks, 2000), and progressive (Dewey, 2007), as well as a rejection of common development and capitalist ideas (e.g., Becker, 2008), although I live a life imbedded in the context of those last ideas.

In addition, the students and I learned more about each other and about issues of education within Indigenous communities. For example, I came from a strength-based and empowerment paradigm about Indigenous knowledge, but the students and the parents seemed to buy in more to the idea of professionalism, which can be superficially interpreted as Western. Professionalism means wearing a suit and earning a fixed salary to the students, which was perhaps overtly and covertly self-deprecating about their own community way of life (Levitan, 2018).

Within this context I began to ask a number of questions that regularly informed my continuous struggle for balancing the power dynamics between the students and adults. I struggle with each of these questions on a regular basis, as they underlie the issues and tensions inherent in listening to students (including in less complex cultural circumstances), understanding positionality, and working towards just community and collaborative decision-making. I find that questions like those below are important to return to regularly as an adult working with students from marginalized communities.

1. First, is it reasonable or valuable to think that I "know better" about the context of Quechua students' economic, ethnic, and gendered oppression (because I studied it [e.g., Apple, 1995; Delpit, 2012; Adelman, 2006]—though I did not live it)?

2. Are my postcolonial, feminist, and critical orientations correct, just, and/or qualitatively "better" than what the students and parents are saying about what they want (i.e., professionalism)?

3. Have the students and parents bought into the systems that are inherently oppressing them, a phenomenon predicted by Paulo Freire (2000)?

The most important insight as a result of addressing the questions asked above, was that, when the relational dynamics of the students and myself were at a productively balanced point, my concerns with questions 1, 2, and 3 were no longer as relevant as I had previously thought. Once the relational dynamics were more equitable, the assumption underlying those questions (that I had most of the power) was proven baseless. During this exercise, I did not have as much power, so my ideas and opinions became ideas and opinions, instead of decisions.

One difficult aspect of this process for me was learning to be happy with having others take on leadership roles. I was happy about students and parents taking on leadership roles, though it can be challenging to "let go" of decision-making privileges. The process of opening opportunities for students and parents to have decision-making power turned out to be better for the students, and this helped the research project be meaningful.

I also had some feelings of discomfort when I realized that I could not, necessarily, "take back" power, which showed that the power dynamics had really become much more distributed. Of course, because of my positionality, I still retained a high degree of power, but the power I could enact was different, and relied more upon my ability to reason along with, and offer ideas to the students, instead of directing or dictating.

Once I addressed the above questions, I found that there were still deeper questions about relational aspects of my thinking about developing education with students, and questioning my positionality as a White man coming from a critical perspective working with Indigenous students:

4. What is my responsibility as an "elder" who cares about the students' and communities' well-being and success to educate the students about the possibilities and pitfalls of a professional life and the risks to identity, well-being, and what it means to live a good life? In other words, how much should I hold on to my own ideas, instead of listening and prioritizing ideas from the students?

5. How much do I *experientially* know, as compared to having historical and third-hand knowledge? In what ways should I rely upon the historical knowledge, and how much should hold back because of my experiential ignorance?

Questions 4 and 5 are based on a deeper assumption about my responsibility to develop the educational opportunities for the students, instead of seeing decision-making as a process in which consultation with the students and parents allows for developing culturally grounded ways to engage in education. This meant that a process-oriented approach, which relied upon mutual trust, seriousness of purpose, iterative interpretation, and the thoughtful sharing of ideas was the most important area for me to focus on as the facilitator of this form of collaborative leadership in educational decision-making. This is in contrast to normal practices of "stakeholder voice," that does not develop relationships to get at assumptions and deeper levels of meaning (Denzin, 1997). Working on building trusting relational dynamics also allowed me to freely express my ideas, as an elder, without unilaterally seeing those ideas as correct for the students. This lead to a final question that focused more on process and relational dynamics, reframing the above questions into a way forward that seemed more appropriate to context, practice, and social justice.

6. Is there a way to create a process in which my positionality does not impress, oppress, or unduly steer students away from their, and their parents, own desires and aspirations, while also allowing me to share experiences, knowledges, and ideas?

To address Question 6 I began to interrogate my own relational dynamics and skills as a facilitator and listener, skills I have spent time developing but that I could always improve. As a first step, I thought about how to frame my responses to students so that they would feel free to be able to question my ideas and reasoning, or at least feel empowered to compare it to their own and offer different perspectives. For example, I would express an idea as one of a number of options, or talk about the strengths and weaknesses of the idea when presenting it, to model to students that they can and should think about the strengths and weaknesses of my and their ideas as well.

Refining listening and question-framing skills allowed me to open a space for students to develop their voices and agency. I have found that when students begin to see that adults in power are willing to listen to them, make changes based on their suggestions, learn with them, as well as share their own knowledge and experience, then students recognize their own power and their own agency in the "adult world." In turn, the students report that they start seeing other adults, not as indomitable creators of rules (rules to be subverted occasionally), but instead as partners in discussion and exchange. When the students are thoughtful and considerate, then they know they will be listened to and respected. This is an aspect of the difficult and somewhat mysterious background work of framing relational dynamics with students.

This background work also helps develop a strong community-reasoning environment. As a teacher and educational leader, I have found that both the teachers and the students are at times short sighted, and when there is a strong, respectful, and equitable relational dynamic, all member of the community are able to be brought to attention when they are not coming from a thoughtful place. At the same time, all participants are also capable of sharing ideas from a place of reflective experience and wisdom, and when there is a strong relational dynamic, sharing thoughtful considerations seem to happen more often.[2]

Developing a relational dynamic in which community is built around a task of co-learning and improving the individual and collective lives of the students and teachers takes practice, and is one of mutual learning for the adults and students. In framing the somewhat idealized relational dynamics with the students in this chapter, I do not suppose that the teacher should not influence the students or that they should try to be as noninterventionist as possible. Instead, this work requires significant reflection for constructing the right framework for working with students, and the ability to bring in one's own deeply held beliefs to a conversation in a way that does not dominate, but instead offers ideas and questions for pondering. This means being able to separate one's thinking from personal beliefs to think about community-directed goals and principles. This is not easy internal work, but it is worthwhile. Students see the example and fully engage because they see that the teacher is being transparent and sincere.

For example, during step one of the research project I became concerned by the ways in which students' belittled the life of a farmer (see Levitan, 2018). My assumptions about farming were one of respect and admiration for the hard work that goes into farming. However, I had not been a farmer, so I was not able to understand the toils of the life of a farmer. I did not experientially understand why the students thought it was boring. This was a learning moment in which I learned to uncover my assumptions about farming. I framed farming as a noble profession, even though the students did not think that farming was a profession. Instead of chastising them for the way they thought of farming (for the truth was that they knew better than me what went into farming), I asked questions and expressed my opinions about farming as one who learns with them, offering my reasons. This allowed me to reframe the relational dynamic. I was in danger of taking the role of one who "knows best" from a domineering perspective. Instead, I shared my understandings and values, with the transparent and respectful goal of influencing the students to not be so harsh on their families' livelihood.

Striking the right balance of experience and knowledge, as well as acknowledging lack of knowledge, is a difficult aspect of framing a relational dynamic. Most of what I describe above are fairly simple practices that most teachers and researchers engage in to build rapport. However, the details and the tensions that often arise when working on building learning relationships are challenging, and require more research. One of the dangers of doing community research is not framing one's own power and positionality in a way that allows for being truthful, fully one's self as a researcher and/or teacher, while also providing a space for others to do the same.

CONCLUSION

In adolescence most students are often already attempting to find their voices and claim their agency. Adults can become facilitators and interpreters rather than instructors to help them achieve this fundamental goal of entering broad social engagement. However, facilitation requires significant reflective skills from the teacher/researcher in order to develop awareness about the possible implications of the students' ideas. It is also necessary to help generate equitable power dynamics through productive relational dynamics. Yet, the process of this reflection is still somewhat of a mystery in collaborative research methods (Lassiter, 2008).

What I have presented here are reflections and processes inherent in working to create a space where students are able to cultivate their voices and claim their agency. Although this case centered on a specific context, I have found through my work in multiple cultural contexts that the processes inherent in this kind of practice do transfer to others. Although the content of the interactions may look different in other contexts, issues of voice, power, framing and creating a space are inherent in most collaborative work. If the teacher thinks critically and reflectively and takes into consideration the personalities and positionalities of the students, through listening, they are on the road to developing communities to help develop students' voices and agency.

This chapter was meant to offer some insights into the processes, promises, and stumbling blocks (as well as some of the affective and personal challenges) in working to create a collaborative process in which adults' voices were not overly dominant, but instead members of a collaborative community. For adults with other positionalities, their practices will likely be different, but similar issues of managing a space and framing relational dynamics will arise. My hope is that this chapter offers some insights into how to navigate the subtle work of framing collaborative practices.

Questions for Reflection

1. This chapter presented a number of questions as a part of a process-oriented approach to collaborative student voice research. What other questions might you utilize to deepen your reflective process?
2. In what ways does your background and positionality influence your relationships with your students, in your context? How might you utilize an understanding of your background to reframe your relational dynamics?
3. What information from this case study might help inform your collaborative work to raise students' voices and agency? What information do you think is problematic or superfluous?

Suggestions for Further Reading

Kane, R. G., & Chimwayange, C. (2014). Teacher action research and student voice: Making sense of learning in secondary school. *Action Research, 12*(1), 52–77.

Lassiter, L. E. (2008). Moving past public anthropology and doing collaborative research. *Napa Bulletin, 29*(1), 70–86.

Mitra, D. L. (2014). *Student voice in school reform: Building youth-adult partnerships that strengthen schools and empower youth.* Albany: State University of New York Press.

Rankin, K. N. (2010). Reflexivity and post-colonial critique: Toward an ethics of accountability in planning praxis. *Planning Theory, 9*(3), 181–199.

NOTES

1. The nonprofit was first started because one of the founders' goddaughters, who is from a rural Quechua community about two hours from the town, wanted to go to school but could not because of safety and distance issues. She told her godfather that she really wanted to go to school, so he asked three of his friends and colleagues (including the author) to help with founding an educational nonprofit (for more information, see Levitan, 2015).
2. I want to note that this claim does not mean that feelings do not get hurt sometimes, or that students do not have teenager angst, or that there are not moments of misunderstandings. The point is only that these issues and feelings are addressed and resolved in a productive way, instead of being ignored or improperly addressed, which can lead to deeper conflicts.

REFERENCES

Adelman, J. (2006). Unfinished states: Historical perspectives on the Andes. In P. Drake & E. Hershberg (Eds.), *State and society in conflict: Comparative perspectives on Andean crises* (pp. 41–73). Pittsburg, PA: University of Pittsburg Press.

Ames, P., & Rojas, V. (2010). *Change and opportunity: The transition from primary to secondary school in rural and urban Peru.* Retrieved from http://r4d.dfid.gov .uk/PDF/Outputs/YoungLives/WP63-ames-peru.pdf

Apple, M. W. (1995). *Education and power* (2nd ed.). New York, NY: Routledge.

Becker, G. (2008). "Human capital." In *The concise encyclopedia of economics.* Library of Economics and Liberty. Retrieved from http://www.econlib.org/library/ Enc/HumanCapital.html

Delpit, L. (2006). *Other people's children: Cultural conflict in the classroom.* New York, NY: The New Press.

Delpit, L. (2012). *"Multiplication is for White people": Raising expectations for other people's children.* New York, NY: The New Press.

Denzin, N. K. (1997). *Interpretive ethnography.* Thousand Oaks, CA: SAGE.

Dewey, J. (2007). *Experience and education.* New York, NY: Simon and Schuster.

Doucet, A., & Mauthner, N. (2006). Feminist methodologies and epistemology. *Handbook of 21st Century Sociology.* Thousand Oaks, CA: SAGE.

Freire, P. (2000). *Pedagogy of the oppressed.* New York, NY: Continuum.

Holmes, K., & Crossley, M. (2004). Whose knowledge, whose values? The contribution of local knowledge to education policy processes: A case study of research development initiatives in the small state of Saint Lucia. *Compare: A Journal of Comparative and International Education, 34*(2), 197–214.

hooks, b. (2000). *Feminist theory: From margin to center.* Cambridge, MA: South End Press.

Ilahi, N. (2001). *Children's work and schooling: Does gender matter? Evidence from the Peru LSMS panel data.* Retrieved from http://www.wds.worldbank.org/external/ default/WDSContentServer/WDSP/IB/2002/01/18/000094946_ 02010904 095880/additional/122522322_20041117161051.pdf

Lassiter, L. E. (2008). Moving past public anthropology and doing collaborative research. *Napa Bulletin, 29*(1), 70–86.

Levinson, B. A. (2011). *Beyond critique: Exploring critical social theories and education.* Boulder, CO: Paradigm.

Levitan, J. (2015). More than access: Overcoming barriers to girls' education in the Peruvian Andes. In S. L. Stacki & S. Baily (Eds.), *Educating adolescent girls around the globe: Challenges and implications* (pp. 58–73). New York, NY: Routledge.

Levitan, J. (2016). The difference between educational equality, equity and social justice . . . and why it matters. *American Journal of Education Forum.* Retrieved from http://www.ajeforum.com/the-difference-between-educational-equality -equity-and-justice-and-why-it-matters-by-joseph-levitan/

Levitan, J. (2018). The danger of a single theory: Understanding students' voices and social justice in the Peruvian Andes. *Teachers College Record, 120*(2), 1–36.

Levitan, J., Carr-Chellman, D., & Carr-Chellman, A. (2017). Accidental ethnography: A method for practitioner-based education research. *Action Research.* Retrieved from https://doi.org/10.1177/1476750317709078

Lewis, M. A., & Lockheed, M. E. (2007). Getting all girls into school. *Finance and Development, 44*(2), 17.

Lincoln, Y. S., & Guba, E. G. (1990). Judging the quality of case study reports. *International Journal of Qualitative Studies in Education, 3*(1), 53–59.

Mansfield, K. C. (2014). How listening to student voices informs and strengthens social justice research and practice. *Educational Administration Quarterly, 50*(3), 392–430.

Merriam, S. B. (2014). *Qualitative research: A guide to design and implementation.* Hoboken, NJ: Wiley.

Mitra, D. (2007). Student voice in school reform: From listening to leadership. In D. Thiessen & A. Cook-Sather (Eds.), *International handbook of student experience in elementary and secondary school* (pp. 727–744). Dordrecht, Netherlands: Springer.

Mitra, D. (2009). Student voice and student roles in education policy reform. In D. Plank, G. Sykes, & B. Schneider (Eds.), *AERA handbook on education policy research.* London, England: Routledge.

Rankin, K. N. (2010). Reflexivity and post-colonial critique: Toward an ethics of accountability in planning praxis. *Planning Theory, 9*(3), 181–199.

Said, E. (1979). *Orientalism.* New York, NY: Vintage.

Spivak, G. C. (1988). Can the subaltern speak? In R. C. Morris (Ed.), *Can the subaltern speak? Reflections on the history of an idea* (pp. 21–78). New York, NY: Columbia University Press.

Stromquist, N. P. (2001). What poverty does to girls' education: The intersection of class, gender and policy in Latin America. *Compare, 31*(1), 39–56.

Sumida Huaman, E. A. (2013). Conversations on Indigenous education, progress, and social justice in Peru [Conversaciones sobre Educación Indígena, Progreso, y Justicia Social en el Perú]. *International Journal of Multicultural Education, 15*(3), 10–25.

Sylvester, C. (1999). Development studies and postcolonial studies: Disparate tales of the "Third World." *Third World Quarterly, 20*(4), 703–721.

UNESCO. (2012). *World atlas of gender equality of education.* Paris, France: Author.

Van Manen, M. (1990). *Researching lived experience: Human science for an action sensitive predagogy.* Albany: State University of New York Press.

Wilson, S. (2001). What is an indigenous research methodology? *Canadian Journal of Native Education, 25*(2), 175–179.

CHAPTER 5

AMPLIFYING YOUTH VOICE THROUGH PUBLIC ENGAGED RESEARCH

Ross VeLure Roholt and Michael Baizerman

In this chapter, we share the practice of involving young people in public engaged research as a strategy to elevate young people's voice and agency. We came to understand the value and power of involving young people in public engaged research while studying youth civic engagement. Twenty years ago, a growing concern about young people's involvement in formal politics (voting) and their perceived apathy (Bennett, 2000) led to the creation of a wide variety of youth civic engagement initiatives (Gibson, 2001). At that time, scholars, practitioners, and political representatives advocated immediate action believing that if nothing were done, our democracy's future would be in jeopardy.

Many of the proposed solutions involved young people learning about their community and local political issues and working to address one or more of these: to take action. Our research focused then on three different youth civic engagement initiatives that advocated for meaningful youth public participation as a way to support young people's civic engagement

Participatory Methodologies to Elevate Children's Voice and Agency, pages 93–115
Copyright © 2019 by Information Age Publishing
93

then and in their future (VeLure Roholt, 2004). This research was used to define philosophies and practices to support youth civic engagement (VeLure Roholt, Hildreth, & Baizerman, 2009). Eventually, we brought all of this together to describe a form of practice—civic youth work: a collaborative practice inviting young people to name, investigate, and take action on public issues that they care about (VeLure Roholt & Baizerman, 2013). Over time, we have adapted civic youth work to frame young people's involvement in public engaged research, challenging both the perceived technical skill requirements of research and the age-graded definitions of "normal" young people and what they were able to do.

Scholarship on youth participation has challenged many of the taken for granted understandings of young people as inarticulate, incompetent, and apathetic (Lund, 2008). The scholarship also illuminates the influence of traditional attitudes and cultural values (Lund, 2008), as well as institutional structures and environments in shaping context for youth participation (Lieten, 2008). This discussion has generated a nuanced understanding of youth participation with two important conclusions for this chapter. First, scholars from around the globe now advocate for a change in the way we understand and define young people, and second, "there is no such thing as a free-floating agent" (Lieten, 2008, p. xv). It is now common to define young people as competent and as having something to contribute to their communities, and their participation is always context-bound; embedded within their everyday lives, or phenomenologically speaking, the world(s) they live in. Our experience teaches us that involving young people in public engaged research requires less effort to build their capacity to do high quality research (they learn quickly) and more attention to the social and cultural factors that continue to reinforce the idea that they should not be involved; that they are not researchers.

Research typically requires advanced education, extensive apprenticeship experience doing research with scholars, and understanding of complicated technologies and methodologies, all of which work to exclude young people as possible contributors and researchers (Appadurai, 2008). Therefore, participating in social research remains an atypical and non-normal activity for many young people depending on the community they live in, even though abundant case studies have shown their ability to do this work (Cammarota & Fine, 2008). Appadurai (2008) argues, young people have a right to do research that allows them to speak back to, in part to challenge, the negative narratives told by adults (and youth) about them. Crafting with young people a viable and trustworthy study simultaneously challenges public images and social discourses of (young) age, creating new narratives of what it means to be (and to do) self as a child/ youth, and by extension, an adult—and finally as a citizen in our democracy.

We define public engaged research as public work: "A sustained effort by a diverse mix of people that generates lasting civic goods, material or culture" (Boyte, 2008, p. 12). As such public engaged research fits with youth civic engagement and with civic youth work. Much like working with young people in other civic engagement efforts, involving young people in public engaged research has broken new ground in our understanding of social issues and problems (e.g., Tuck, 2008). In this chapter, we provide two case studies of public engaged research with young people, one in a university setting and the other in a community setting. Both cases illustrate how involving young people in public engaged research open spaces for young people to share their ideas, master knowledge and skill, and take informed action in ways thought unusual, if not unlikely, even impossible because of their age and developmental stage (Cammarota & Fine, 2008; Checkoway & Richards-Schuster, 2003; VeLure Roholt & Baizerman, 2013). Through a duoethnographic research approach (Norris, Sawyer, & Lund, 2012), we explore how youth involvement in public engaged research can create an "in-between" space where young people can learn, practice, expand, master, and celebrate new understandings of research, of themselves, and of their own and others worlds. By doing so, public engaged research enhances their voice and agency.

YOUTH INVOLVEMENT IN RESEARCH: CHALLENGING AGE-NORMS

Involving young people in research challenges the "powerful social and cultural tendencies to keep them in their place" (Lloyd-Smith & Tarr, 2000, p. 62). The invitation and opportunity to participate in a research projects are often interpreted as a surprise by young people we have worked with and unusual by adults they know. A challenge to any invitation and involvement in research are age-graded social expectations (Lansdown, 2010). Childhood and youthhood refer both to people of certain ages and describes specific social and cultural roles and institutions, with associated discourses, that teach us who they are and what they can (should) do (James, 1993; Lesko, 2001; Nybell, Shook, & Finn, 2009). We have known for a long time that: "age offers a handy framework for representing social and cultural expectations for individual experiences and roles" (Chudacoff, 1989, p. 184). If age is done as prescribed by a particular context, in a particular historical moment, age as a sociopolitical, socioeconomic, and sociocultural category is kept powerful (Lesko, 2001). All of this works to "simultaneously sustain, reproduce, and render legitimate the institutional arrangements that are based on" age as a category of defining people (West & Zimmerman, 1987).

Age is continually produced and reproduced through actions and activities that come to be seen as age appropriate.

When young people are first invited to be researchers, we have found that even though they easily learn and take on the role of researcher, they often resist naming themselves as researchers. They initially tell us that being researchers sounds boring, and it is simply not something people of certain ages (similar in age to them) do, around here, now. Involving young people in research challenges age-graded social roles that they and others in this context have and enact. "Youth researchers" challenge the definition of normal youth and therefore are seen as different. Involving young people authentically in research work requires more than technique or a set of activities. Rather it requires creating a critical space that invites their voice and agency (Kane, 2000). This is what our case studies will describe.

YOUNG PEOPLE, RESEARCH, VOICE AND AGENCY

Stories of young people involved in and completing meaningful and high impact empirical social research can easily be found. Two sources for this practice are critical education (Friere, 1997) and participatory action research (McIntyre, 2008). These two philosophies and practices challenge the dominant understandings of young people in both education and research. Critical education advocates for teaching and learning as praxis, and describes everyone as a teacher and everyone as a student (Friere, 1997). Participatory action research (PAR) draws from critical education, and "emphasizes the political aspects of knowledge production" and a collaborative approach to doing research (Reason, 1994, p. 47). Critical education has been used to support young people as teachers and leaders, while PAR posed important questions challenging the epistemological and ontological understandings of knowledge and truth (Caraballo, Lozenski, Lyiscott, & Morrell, 2017). Together these scholarly traditions envision the research process as a partnership between those formally trained as researchers working alongside those who are typically seen as research objects. In contrast, this methodology advocates for a collaborative process of youth and adults as researchers as the preferred means to crafting deeper understanding of the research subject and discovering new knowledge about it. The theory and philosophy of critical education provides a discourse and an imagery to support (young) people's involvement in alternative and creative learning opportunities, including research. As a method, PAR provides a road map for their involvement and has been used to successfully support young people as researchers (Cammarota & Fine, 2008).

Grounded in these two philosophies, several texts and accounts of youth PAR can be found and used to guide research practice with young people (Cammarota & Fine, 2008; Morrell, 2004; Schultz, 2008). Scholars who want to involve young people in research now have ample evidence of the substantive value for young people and their surrounding communities, and for building knowledge and taking action on issues and problems (Caraballo et al., 2017). It is a strategy that supports both youth voice and agency. It also is a strategy for developing traditional and unique social scientific knowledge precisely because of youth voice and agency.

The idea that research practice should support voice and agency are also found in the philosophy and theory of public engaged scholarship (PES). As a substantive practice, public engaged scholarship emphasizes collaboration between scholars and community members (Barker, 2004), recognizing the value in "leveraging their different perspectives and competencies to coproduce knowledge about a complex problem or phenomenon that exists under conditions of uncertainty found in the world" (Van de ven & Johnson, 2006, p. 803). It too is a form of participatory inquiry (Reason, 1994) one which emphasizes the added value of diverse stakeholders working together to design, implement, and use findings from research to make a difference in everyday life. As a methodology, PES includes and understands the benefits of diverse experiences and positionality (scholars, community members, you, old, male, female, etc.) joined within a research project. These diverse teams provide new perspectives and when commited to a participatory process create questions that matter to communities, practitioners, scholars and to young people. Here too is found youth voice and agency.

YOUTH VOICE AND AGENCY

As a research methodology, PES can focus on young people—inviting and amplifying their voice and agency. There are two conceptual underpinnings to PES with young people: Youth voice is polyvocal, and youth agency is relational. When we talk about youth voice, it is important to remember that we do not equate this concept with one set of ideas, one voice, or one perspective (Roberts, 2000). Meacham (2004) helps to explain this idea with four metaphors to describe youth voice: essentialist, organismic, mechanical, and contextualist. Together, these begin to capture the multiple possibilities of youth voice; we add a fifth metaphor adapted from the scholarship of Weis and Fine (2005; see Table 5.1).

Youth voice refers to more than young people expressing their opinions. As the metaphors invite, voice includes processes of self-awareness; becoming comfortable talking to others in small groups and publically; collaborating and working with others to not only say what you have experienced but also to join in setting agendas and courses of actions; and finally, to develop ways of negotiating and resisting normal representations of self, others, and

TABLE 5.1 The Many Metaphors of Youth Voice

Metaphor	To have a voice means:	Skills required
Essentialist	To be aware of one's experiences and feelings and to discover the attributes and qualities that represent who one is.	Self-reflection and self-understanding
Organismic	To be able to participate in conversation, exchange thoughts and feelings with others.	Conversation
Machine	To speak one's thoughts and be able to communicate so that others can understand.	Public speaking
Contextualist	To co-operate with others in setting an agenda for action.	Collaboration
Negotiating (Weis & Fine, 2005)	To negotiate with/against "normalized representations" of age, class, gender, orientation, ethnicity, geography, along with the other multitude of identity shaping social scripts, and talk, as well as listen to these.	Critique

young people in general. Youth voice refers to a set of knowledge, skills, and practices that support young people developing social networks with others who care about similar issues and to use these networks to refine and revise their opinions into informed ideas that they together can act towards. These metaphors suggest how to weave together the idea of voice with its corresponding skills. While these skills are not prerequisites for authentic involvement, young people can come as skillful (and many do) or develop these through their involvement in a public engaged research process: The process is pedagogical.

Scholarship on youth voice has demonstrated that this rich portraiture of youth voice does not always receive support in practice. Indeed, youth voice in practice is often defined simply as young people having their say. Under this definition, we know that the impact of youth voice on programmatic, community, or policy change has not been powerful. There are few instances where young people's work, including presenting their opinions, has brought about substantial change in programs, communities, or policies (Barry-Smith & Thomas, 2010). Indeed, seldom are the stories and experiences of youth taken up, addressed, and responded to in substantive ways. There is applause, but little else. It is clear that giving them a platform to express their ideas does little in the longer term to support their voice or change their everyday lived experiences (Barry-Smith & Thomas, 2010) or those of others. Friere (1997) warned against creating spaces where people talk and discuss ideas and opinions without taking action on their ideas or further developing and refining their insights into actionable knowledge. He called this activity "verbalism" (p. 87). Instead, he advocated for praxis, joining discussion to action in a process that promoted both individual and group learning and social change.

The value of praxis is now well understood as a way to support young people's voice and agency (Ginwright & Cammarota, 2002).

Public engaged scholarship respond to these critiques in several ways: by expanding the definition of voice to include both the contextualist and negotiation metaphors. When embedded in practice, these metaphors challenge voice as only "having one's say" and provide an action scaffold for small groups to transform their ideas and opinions into informed action. In public engaged research, voice and agency are not separate concepts; they are intertwined. Such that developing one's voice also sharpens one's ability to take action on meaningful issues. This way of understanding voice resists verbalism (Friere, 1997), as it is found in many youth programs and initiatives. It also recognizes agency as relational, collective, and communal, rather than as a trait or characteristic of individuals.

Agency is typically defined as an individual attribute (Coffey & Farrugia, 2014). We agree more with Edwards (2005) and Kennelly's (2011) definition of agency as relational. Relational agency directs attention to the interactive and collaborative development of agency. Agency emerges "between" individuals, not within an individual. In this frame, agency refers to both the capacity to work with others, noticing and naming individual's talents and contributions (resources), and the bringing together of these to respond to issues the group cares about and wants to and may decide to do something about collectively (Edwards, 2005). This definition highlights that the essence of agency is interactive; it is this which is found within public engaged research groups and their projects, and the form of agency we found in studying youth civic engagement groups (VeLure Roholt, Hildreth, & Baizerman, 2009). Working together, young people alone and also with adults completed many public engaged research projects and took action based on what they learned. Those who accept this idea and want to try it quickly realize this work comes with significant challenges and obstacles. The following two case studies illustrate these processes, the challenges, and issues that emerge when involving young people in public engaged research, with focus on the place of youth voice and relational agency in public engaged research.

METHODOLOGY

The case studies that follow were informed by a duoethnography methodology, with its emphasis on storytelling (Norris et al., 2012). The two authors (Ross and Mike) have worked together for several years; each come to the work with widely different backgrounds and experiences. One author is a senior researcher and youth studies scholar with a wide and deep experience of working with young people over the last 50 years. The other author has worked extensively with young people for the last twenty years, both in the United States and for extended period in Northern Ireland and Japan. Since 2008, both have worked to involve young people in the research process more intentionally. Dr. Baizerman developed and teaches an undergraduate research course in Youth Studies that works each semester with several community partners to develop research questions that matters to both the partners and the students. Over 15 weeks, teams complete a research study that provides data based, empirically derived responses to the selected questions. This has been done for ten years, with over 80 studies completed in this single course. Dr. VeLure Roholt has worked with young people in the community to complete several research and evaluation studies. These are often commissioned by large youth service agencies or smaller youth programs. In these studies, young people also negotiate with the community partner over the research questions and research design, and then present what they have learned to the partner at the end of the process. These differing experiences, one emerging from a university and the other from a community context, comprise the data for the duo-ethnography presented in this chapter.

This chapter is built upon the stories each have shared with the other about the process of working with young people to design and complete public engaged research studies and their own lived experience working with young people and community partners to complete these field studies. Both have talked about these experiences with each other over several years, drafting and rewriting their experiences of working with young people on public engaged research studies. The two stories presented in this chapter, written here as case studies, were crafted over several years and are the product of multiple in-person conversations along with review of each others initial drafts. Through a process of dialogue, debate, and revision, the final stories emerged and are presented next. These have also informed their work in civic youth work (VeLure Roholt & Baizerman, 2013) and in youth civic engagement (VeLure Roholt, Hildreth, & Baizerman, 2009).

YOUTH INVOLVEMENT IN PUBLIC ENGAGED SCHOLARSHIP: TWO CASE STUDIES

Each of the two case studies is described as a series of steps or stages. This facilitates understanding of the overall process but is also misleading. Inviting, supporting, and facilitating youth involvement in public engaged scholarship is not in actual everyday practice a step-by-step process. Rather, it requires the ability to improvise and remain open to being led by, rather than leading, the co-researchers. It is a relational process which emphasizes co-creative and

TABLE 5.2 Comparing Research Process		
Traditional	**Case Study 1: Youth Work in Research**	**Case Study 2: Youth Participatory Research**
Identify the problem or question	Problem-finding	Inviting co-researchers
Review the literature	Reframing concerns as research questions	Constructing questions
Research design	Designing the study	Doing good research
Data collection	Interviewing, visiting, talking with, conversation	Starting small
Data analysis and interpretation	Revise and pre-test	Making sense of what we heard, saw, and read
Reporting	Data collection and report writing	Taking our stand
Presenting	Presentation to class and relevant community agency/group	Sharing our research story

participatory practices. To use another metaphor, this form of practice is like jazz. Improvisation, creativity, and collaboration are key attributes.

Each case study has a philosophical home. The first associates doing research as doing youth work. Here, emphasis is on how being a skillful youth worker requires one to be like a researcher—asking questions, talking to (interviewing) young people, listening for themes, and taking action on what one learns, both in the moment and over time. The second case study is grounded in the scholarship, theory, and philosophy of youth engagement and youth participation. Here emphasis is on how the research process supports young people's personal, cognitive, and social development while also supporting community, neighborhood, and democratic development. Table 5.2 summarizes the case studies stages of research and compares these to each other and to the more traditional understanding of research process.

CASE STUDY 1: YOUTH WORK IS RESEARCH

Undergraduate students in the capstone research course are given a choice of whether to have a formal research course (class meeting twice a week for 15 weeks) or to do a practical, meaningful, and useful study on an issue of interest to them and also to the state or local community—its people, groups, organizations, public and nonprofit youth serving agencies. Of course, they have always chosen to work on a "practical study." I will tell what we do, how we do it, and our reasons for doing as we do—our pedagogic, political, and social justice rationales and goals.

Step 1: Problem Finding

Students in the research course want to work in youth services, typically with teens at the hands-on level. They want to do direct youth work in contrast to indirect youth work, which includes policy, planning, administration, management, supervision, or college or university teaching. My invitation to "do something which matters to you," something "real" and consequential in and for the world, fits well with their vocational calling to serve, help, care, and "bring change." Given that this is usually their last university semester, students easily and quickly choose a research project over a course lecture. They typically ask for examples of past student studies, which I provide. I then ask them to tell me some youth issues they care about, whether from their lives (family, friends, school, etc.), their youth studies community internship, or other university courses, the news, their part-time jobs, and the like. These are written on a whiteboard, and after an hour into the second class session, there is a list of about ten topics. Typical issues include: teen pregnancy; adolescent suicide; gay, lesbian, bi-sexual, transgender, queer issues (such as homelessness); young women's issues and concerns, homeless teens; chemical dependency; youth worker burnout; and police presence in schools. Less often are topics such as Habitat for Humanity's youth focus, the utilization of a research report on homeless youth by community youth agencies, Hmong (Laos) spirituality as a healing practice and its place in pediatric hospital care for Hmong children and adolescents, existential "burnout" of youth workers, and Hmong on Hmong bullying. I end this class period by asking them to think about these topics and others "on which they may want to make a difference" for young people.

In week two, both class sessions are used to return to their list of possible research topics. At this time, I suggest projects which could be done in partnership with local public or not-for-profit, and which could contribute to social justice for young people, which I describe as more inviting and inclusive library or recreation services, better and safer public transportation, better training and supervision of youth workers, and the like. The class finishes with more talk, more ideas, and a beginning clustering of students by topic.

Step 2: Reframing Concerns as Research Questions

While these discussions and negotiations are going on, I "teach" by reframing their issues, concerns, topics as research questions, suggesting that practical studies begin with a question and some forms of the interrogatory work better to focus and complete a study; for example, "what" questions work better and are easier to work with than "why" questions. I casually mention that youth work is research-like because it is about learning from and about youth as experts in and of their lived realities, in their everyday lives, and I suggest that if they learn how to do a practical study, in contrast to an academic or scientific study, this will be a useful skill in 14–20 weeks, when they begin their hoped for full-time employment as a youth worker.

I also review with them the course syllabus and my reasoning for each assignment, emphasizing how the conceptual vocabulary will be important "on the job" and why I ask them to link each term to their research project and also to youth work practice.

Step 3: Designing the Study

In the third week of the course, the two class sessions are used to form work groups, to begin to frame a "big research question," and two or more mid-level, derivative research questions; and also, some simple "practical" questions they want to ask research subjects. This work continues into Week 4. By then, article abstracts related to their research project have been submitted, read, commented on, and returned. Following my guidance, they are thinking about "how to answer their research questions" by asking, looking, and other practical ways of learning what they want to know. Help, consultation, and technical assistance is provided by me or class group leaders; undergraduate and graduate students; former doctoral students; community youth workers; and classmates who know an issue, a neighborhood, a youth population (Hmong gangs, Karen teens), or a youth agency. The work groups typically spread across several campus buildings for one-to-two class periods "to work," along with a consultant. They work at getting a good, important, meaningful, and practical research question and figuring out how to answer it: Research!

At this time in the class they are also asked to imagine that they have completed the study. Then I ask them a question: "So what? Why might this matter to the world?" They are invited to remember that their study has "to matter" to young people. This is my way to keep present the moral, the political, and the vocational.

Step 4: Interviewing, Visiting, Talking With, Conversation

Every student group wants to get information or collect empirical data in the field (from youth in the community). The instructor, along with the team of consultants, lead them in an hour-long role play which shows them the differences between and among interviewing, visiting with, talking with, and conversations. Emphasis in the role play is on power relations between question asker and answerer—and always cultural context—a major ethical concern in research, one easily taught through these role plays. Students come to understand the need to present their study transparently and to provide assurances and guarantees that the data will remain safe and confidential; that if the interviewee agrees to participate, they won't be harmed. We talk about the university's research ethics guidelines. And students develop, practice, and test a *spiel*, an introduction to themselves and to their study. Especially important, they practice taking notes of interviews and observations. They always conclude that two students are more effective than one when the task is to write down interviews and observations, and sometimes three are even better, although at times intrusive and intimidating depending on who is being interviewed. This is an opening to discuss the use of an interview and observation guide, and also how to best lay out a page in the guide and to think about how this can be used later in the data analysis—making sense of what data they collected. All of this is done in concrete and often literal tasks which serve to make research real for them. To them real means concrete and specific–a guide for interviewing, a chart for data analysis.

Step 5: Pretest

In another week or two, they go to the field for a pretest. Most have no private transportation and thus we help them organize and at times even provide transportation to the field. We are available during their field testing and just after to debrief them about their lived-experience; about the youth talks/interviews and observations they just conducted; about what they learned about self, project, and research; and about the often, conflicting role orientations of (a) researcher (of a certain type) and (b) youth worker (of a certain type). Typical is their comment on how hard it was not "to help" the youth with whom they were talking.

Step 6: Revisions and a Smaller Pretest

Their classmates who grew up in worlds in or about which they are doing their study (geographic, ethnic/racial, agency-based) become expert advisors to them on what it is like to grow up in neighborhoods like these and in similar (if not the same) contexts. This creates a cacophony of expert opinion among faculty, consultants, interviewees, and native and local classmates: Who "gets it" best? Whose advice to follow? A practical, real research issue which is also a youth work focus and question. What is expertise? What are the politics of knowing/ knowledge? All along small research groups meet in the classroom or wherever, on campus or off. The faculty member is always in that classroom, 30 class sessions each semester. Students drop-in (or not). They are learning when and how to ask for consultation/ technical assistance; skills they will need as youth workers in a community agency. They are learning to negotiate with power (faculty) and community groups and agencies.

Step 7: Data Collection and Report Writing

Students self-regulate, with consultations, on better ways to collect, store, and analyze "the information" (data). They are guided toward how to analyze "the information." And for our purposes here, how to write a report, one for a busy executive: short, clean, precise, with emphasis on what was learned and what and how this learning can be used to "change the world" for the better. I suggest a report outline which they could use. Some groups do, some don't. These reports are not stylistically "academic." They work in youth agencies: What would the manager want to read about the place, about how teens see it, about staff? Practical, short, *Reader's Digest* prose. And in a risky request from me, suggestions, recommendations, and thoughts about action.

Step 8: Presentation

Students are encouraged to choose an editor from their group to give a single narrative voice to the report, which is typically written by several group members. They are asked to consider a cover with graphics designed by a classmate volunteer. I pay for copying and low-cost binding. Every student group presents their report to our faculty and their guests over a 2–3 hour class session. Each study includes recommendations for action, and often students volunteer to assist the community agency in implementing the recommendations.

This first case study documents how university coursework can teach students about public engaged research opportunity, and how it provided the experience of completing a real, practical, no-cost study, and possibly consequential for a real community agency on a real issue and on their real concerns. Students come to appreciate that the academic studies they read and dissect at university are sanitized, and don't display the many bumps and detours in doing a real study in the real world. This has implications for their intent in going to graduate school, for taking on research when employed as a youth worker, and also, for how "research" is understood and taught to university students. This course is required, and students have some obligation to complete the study: They are being graded! The second case study documents how community young people have been successfully involved in public engaged research.

CASE STUDY 2: YOUTH PARTICIPATORY RESEARCH

Youth engagement and youth participation theory and philosophy provides a useful frame for involving young people in public engaged research. This is especially true for groups of young people who continue to be actively marginalized and silenced in their communities. Involving young people in public engaged research invites them to publicly talk about their own personal experiences. This typically led the group to common experiences. It is at such moments when it becomes clear how their personal concerns touch public issues and problems. In silence, our issues are personal; when talked about and shared, common themes are heard in the stories, and the public issue embedded in our personal experience can be clarified and illuminated as both personal and social/public reality. This process is of course simple, straightforward, and well documented in community organizing, youth organizing, and youth participation (Ginwright, Cammarota, & Noguera, 2005; Watts, Williams, & Jagers, 2003). Involving young people in public engaged research provides one pathway to move beyond simply listening to, even truly hearing young people's stories, and towards guiding them to confront how the personal and public touch. This frame invites them to work at "making a difference" on an issue or concern that matter to them.

Much has been written on youth participatory (action) research (Cammarota & Fine, 2008). Here I want to describe what we have done to involve young people in pubic engaged scholarship, so that their concerns are not simply listened to but also acted upon—by them or others. As in the earlier case study, here we also talk about what we do, how we do it, and our purposes for doing it that way.

Step 1: Inviting Co-Researchers

The research method literature glosses over a critical beginning phase of all research: What does the researcher care about? Youth participants first describe research as a technical process, and research questions and studies as designed from an objective and technical perspective. We often ignore that research responds to issues and ideas researchers and others care about, have a vested interested in learning more about, and are compelled to engage. This set of questions and issues come prior to developing a research question or reviewing the literature. Starting a research project with young people begins by inviting them to be co-researchers. This is done by asking: What do you care about? How do you want to make a difference in the world?

These questions address two initial aims: (a) The questions invite young people into a beginning research role, and (b) the discussion that follows also works to "build a group" that can work together on a research project. Focus at this time is on connecting what they care about to what others in the group care about and then to connect this to public issues. This step can be facilitated when the group is formed around a topic, for example, when young people are recruited to join a group that is focused on a particular issue, such as educational achievement, violence in the neighborhood, or even expanding art or other opportunities for young people in the community. Once concerns and issues have been clarified and discussed, and connection between their personal concerns and larger public issues made, the group begins constructing research questions.

Step 2: Constructing Questions

Questions drive research. They also create several types of spaces: reflective, creative, and critical. Good questions invite collaboration and co-creation. In a public engaged research project, focus is on how to co-construct research questions with young people and community members. Using individual's experiences, either in the group or from invited guests, has been used successfully to craft questions that matter to both the young people involved and to others in their neighborhood and community. Good public engaged research questions invoke action. When the group has constructed a question they care about, they become energized and want to figure out the answer or at least learn how others think it can or should be answered. This is a good time to both act and also reflect on how to proceed on how to do good research.

Step 3: Doing Good Research

Involving young people in research discloses that research textbooks emphasize the technical—designing rigorous studies and using appropriate methods. We "almost" forget about the ethical. In doing collaborative research projects with young people, ethics tends to emerge within ongoing conversations. So to the moral and political: What matter to you? What matters to the community? How do these compare and contrast? Clearly, ethics informs every stage and decision in research from constructing question to sharing the final research story. Focusing early on how ethics provides advice and guidance supports young people in doing good research. This can often start by asking them to gather advice on the group's research question from people whose advice they trust.

We encourage the participants to seek input from others they know and trust to see if the question they are asking makes sense, is important, and should be asked. They are encouraged to find advisors, whether these are peers, friends, parents, aunts, uncles, or neighbors. They bring what they learn back to the group, where each group member talks about what they did, what it was like, what they learned, and then the group talks over what together they have figured out about the question they asked and possible ways to learn how they might go about figuring out how to answer the increasingly clarified question.

It is important that young people are supported to both "do something" and also to talk about what they did, what it was like, and what they learned. All of this can easily be connected to research ethics and how to go about doing a good study. Most often we find that they are curious about how to gather data, but also keenly aware of what it might be like to be asked to answer certain questions. They often have experience as participants in research, and now that they are on the other side, they are more cautious about what they are doing and how.

They are also not "expert" in research and therefore are more hesitant about what they should do and how, having been told there are correct and wrong ways of doing everything in a research study. For example, the group might ask: Can I interview a friend? Here, concerns about confidentiality emerge, as well as about trust. Researchers much learn to balance both so that all are protected and feel safe. Talking about these issues openly provides insightful learning about how to invite more honest and truthful answers to the research and interview questions.

Continuing discussions about everyday research ethics invites the research group to reflect on, consider, and create plans for seeking out research participants; what interview or survey questions can (should) be asked; how to inform participants about the study; and invite them to participate. Embedded in these discussions are the ethic committee concerns about sample procedures, consent process, data security, confidentiality, consent process, data security, and risk. Again, questions often provide excellent doors into research ethics.

Step 4: Starting Small

When the group has a clear understanding of the research question and the actual questions they want to ask, and the research plan has been thoughtfully considered and advice invited, now is the time to rehearse. Depending on the confidence and capacity of group members, this step can be relatively short or take several meetings to complete (and may need to be revisited at a later time). In this step, focus is on how their questions and process can be "field tested."

At this time, the group takes what they have talked about and developed and now puts it into action. Emphasis is again on finding "safe" advisors or community participants that will support group members practicing, interviewing, or completing a survey, as well as, who will provide feedback on the questions and the practice interviews. Every completed field test is talked about in the group. The step accomplishes two objectives. First, the instruments that they have developed get redesigned, changed, and hopefully improved. Second, they become better at using whatever instrument the group developed and also in explaining to others the purpose of their research project. They develop an expertise around this project and the research process they have co-created.

Step 5: Expanding With Partners

Now that group member are comfortable with the idea and practice of collecting data, with explaining the study to others and they have learned how to take notes to bring back for the group to discuss, the study can be fully implemented. A rule we enforce is that no data collection is done by a single individual; it is always done with a partner and when appropriate, in a triad (two group members and one youth worker). Here too are group discussions around two primary concerns: How can we get information that helps us understand our question, and how can we do this in a way that ensures that co-researchers are safe (and that what we learn is useful)?

Step 6: Making Sense of What We Heard, Saw, and Read

While group members continue going into the field, bringing back information, the next step begins: making sense of what they heard, saw, or read. For example, working with a group after school on a youth-led evaluation of arts youth programming, each time group members collected and brought information, it was discussed in the large group. To keep the research plan in mind, meetings began with a check-in, a review of the research plan, and tasks that people were working on. During discussions, group members talk about who was in the field over the last couple of days and who has information to share. If group members have information, then the pair or team of young people present to the larger group.

Initially, the basic structure for analyzing data is presented while the group is field-testing its data instruments, in Step 4 and 5 listed above. The group is asked: So what should we do with what we learn in the field? After discussion, the groups often agree to a three-question guide to data analysis.

1. What is going on?
2. How do we make sense of it?
3. What are the consequences (for whom, now, maybe later)?

These questions provide a structure for the group to get involved with the data collected, and to begin to discuss the meaning of this information group.

The first question opens the conversation by focusing on describing the data collected, in as neutral language as possible, so that the rest of the group can get a clear understanding of what the pair or team saw, heard, or read. When the group begins to interpret the information as good or bad, the facilitator would ask: How come? What makes this description good or bad? These questions push the group to build a rationale for their interpretation: Good data analysis!

As the project continues, new data is first discussed (read) alone and then compared with the information already collected and discussed by the group. This allows for initial interpretations to be challenged in a low-risk way for the group members. Erroneous interpretations may be first challenged by other information. If more and more information emerges that challenges the initial interpretation, the group recognizes that the initial interpretation has to be revised.

Data gathering and analysis usually stops when one of two things occur: (a) Information saturation occurs, more information is not inviting more understanding but just confirming what has been learned; or (b) there is no more time for data gathering and analysis because the study needs to be completed and presented. Many times, studies end because the group has a deadline. Not when the study is done.

Step 7: Taking Our Stand

As the group prepares to share what it learned, more questions emerge: What are you (the group) confident in saying? What evidence do you have to support what you want to say? What stand do you want to take? Here the data analysis moves into data synthesis. Emphasis is on study transparency and the reporting of what has been learned, what can be conclude, and what can be recommended. Discussions often focus on who they are presenting to, and what evidence might they consider to be strong. We make clear that often having good data doesn't necessarily mean that it will have an impact or support the changes in the world they want to bring about. How the data are presented, and to whom, matters. To do this, the group first needs to be clear where it will put its feet: What conclusions do they have most confidence in?

Step 8: Sharing Our Research Story

To make a difference, the research story must be shared with specific audiences, and how what has been learned can be used by the group and others. In academic research, what is learned is most often shared through a publication. While important, young people often want more impact than publication as a diffusion of ideas; they want action based on their study and emergent ideas. Young people often decide to present and tell what they learned in different and creative ways. For example, some groups have created a short skit that they publicly perform and then discuss. Others have created videos or other visual representations. The focus here is to communicate the research story to those who the group believes needs to/should hear it, and to those who can do something about the issues they learned about. They often pick several mediums and media to do this. These choices also show voice and agency.

AMPLIFYING YOUTH VOICE AND AGENCY
THROUGH PUBLIC ENGAGED RESEARCH

Several lessons emerge from the two case studies on involving young people in public engaged research. The case studies illustrate methods for moving beyond sharing opinions to informed action, thereby addressing a major critique of youth voice efforts (Percy-Smith & Thomas, 2010). While young people are often consulted, rarely do their opinions prompt action or change. These case studies suggest how one might move beyond simply giving opinions and ground participation in the everyday lives of young people (Percy-Smith & Thomas, 2010). Through creating strong research teams, gathering credible evidence, and partnering with community members, young people learned how to find and use information to spark action and promote community awareness on issues that matter to them; the beginning process of changing these issues.

In the process, the case studies illustrated how youth involvement in public engaged scholarship supports multiple metaphors of youth voice, as described by Meacham (2004). The process begins with young people reflecting on their own experiences and understanding how these can inform and shape high quality research (essentialist metaphor). Throughout the process, participants have multiple opportunities to begin sharing their ideas with a small group, building their skills in conversation and collaboration, with ongoing feedback (organismic and machine metaphors). As projects progress, young people work with others in several communities to gather data, thereby practicing collaboration and public speaking (contextualist metaphor). Finally, through analyzing data together young people develop skills in critique and in making reasoned arguments based on their information they have gathered. Their final stance moves beyond personal opinion and towards informed ideas and intelligent actions, by both individual and the group (machine and negotiating metaphors). Young people develop ways to communicate research findings and offer to others what they know and care and learned about from their research.

The two, public engaged scholarship case studies created spaces for the imaginary. Involving young people in public engaged research challenges dominant understandings of child and young person, thereby creating spaces for young people to imagine new ways of being, doing (living), and understanding themselves. Here are new age-roles and new possible identities: researcher, community leader, informed citizen; all of these invite them to be who they are and to expand who they image themselves to be. As described in these two case studies, public engaged scholarship is a strategy, an opportunity, that invites self-identity work and creates real world opportunities and social roles for young people. When invited and supported, young people rarely fail as researchers, in our experience and in the literature (Cammarota & Fine, 2008; Tuck, 2008).

A public engaged scholarship process emphasizes thinking about and thinking through how the group can act on what it learned and what actions might work best depending on the community, particular audience, or partners: experiential learning. As a pedagogy, public engaged scholarship invites participants to learn about voice and agency. To learn how they can create actionable knowledge to shape their everyday lives and make a difference on issues that matter to them.

Finally, the case studies illuminate once again that public expectations and even common daily practices are not good predictors of what young people want to do or are capable of doing. Indeed, young people "are used to enquiring, scrutinizing, accepting unexpected results, revising their ideas, and assuming that their knowledge is incomplete and provisional" (Alderson, 2000, p. 245). This is their everyday lived experience of going to school, being a student, holding a job, playing sports. And it can be directed at being and doing citizen, researcher, citizen-researcher.

Why do we not expect young people to play a substantial role in research studies? Or to design and do research on issues and questions that matter to them and to others in their lives? We have seen their enormous interest and passion when they have the opportunity and coaching available to design and complete public engaged research studies (VeLure Roholt, Hildreth, & Baizerman, 2009). It is some of us—usually adults—who are keeping them from learning and contributing as committed citizen scholars and researchers.

Questions for Reflection

1. What opportunities invite young people into roles of researcher and community change agent?
2. How does their involvement in public engaged scholarship support youth voice and build skills for collective action on public issues and common concerns?
3. How does youth involvement in public engaged scholarship raise young people's awareness of their own experiences and feelings, build cooperative communities, and allow young people to create narratives that challenge negative images and stories of young people and what they should do?
4. What resources must be available for youth involvement in pubic engaged scholarship to start, sustain, and flourish?
5. What promising practices can be drawn upon to support youth involvement in public engaged scholarship?

Suggestions for Further Reading

Fine, M. (2018). *Research in contentious times: Widening the methodological imagination.* New York, NY: Teachers College Press.

Ginwright, S., Noguera, P., & Cammarota, J. (Eds.). (2006). *Beyond resistance! Youth activism and community change: New democratic possibilities for practice and policy for America's youth.* New York, NY: Routledge.

Reason, P., & Bradbury, H. (2008). *The SAGE handbook of action research: Participative inquiry and practice* (2nd ed.). London, England: SAGE.

Tuck, E., & Wayne Yang, K. (2013). *Youth resistance research and theories of change.* New York, NY: Routledge.

Velure Roholt, R., & Baizerman, M. (2013). *Civic youth work: A primer.* New York, NY: Peter Lang.

REFERENCES

Alderson, P. (2000). Children as researchers: The effects of participation rights on research methodology. In P. Christensen & A. James (Eds.), *Research with children: Perspectives and practices* (pp. 241–257). London, England: Falmer Press.

Appadurai, A. (2008). The right to research. *Globalisation, Societies and Education, 4*(2), 167–177.

Barker, D. (2004). The scholarship of engagement: A taxonomy of five emerging practices. *Journal of Higher Education Outreach and Engagement, 9*(2), 123–137.

Barry-Smith, P., & Thomas, N. (Eds.) (2010). *A handbook of children and young people's participation: Perspectives from theory and practice*. New York, NY: Routledge.

Bennett, S. (2000). Political apathy and avoidance of news media among generation X and Y: America's continuing problem. In S. Mann & J. Patrick (Eds.), *Education for civic engagement in democracy: Service learning and other promising practices* (pp. 9–28). Bloomington, IN: ERIC Clearinghouse for Social Studies/Social Science Education.

Boyte, H. (2008). Against the current: Developing the civic agency of students. *Change, 40*(3), 8–15.

Cammarota, J., & Fine, M. (2008). *Revolutionizing education: Youth participatory action research in motion*. New York, NY: Routledge.

Caraballo, L., Lozenski, B., Lyiscott, J., & Morrell, E. (2017). YPAR and critical epistemologies: Rethinking education research. *Review of Research in Education, 41*(1), 311–336.

Chudacoff, H. (1989). *How old are you? Age consciousness in American culture*. Princeton, NJ: Princeton University Press.

Coffey, J., & Farrugia, D. (2014). Unpacking the black box: The problem of agency in the sociology of youth. *Journal of Youth Studies, 17*(4), 461–474.

Edwards, A. (2005). Relational agency: Learning to be a resourceful practitioner. *International Journal of Educational Research, 43*(3), 168–182.

Finn, J. (2009). Making trouble: Representations of social work, youth, and pathology. In L. Nybell, J. Shook, & J. Finn (Eds.), *Childhood, youth, and social work in transformation: Implications for policy and practice* (pp. 37–66). New York, NY: Columbia University Press.

Freire, P. (1997). *Pedagogy of the oppressed*. New York, NY: Continuum.

Gibson, C. (2001). *From inspiration to participation: A review of perspectives on youth civic engagement*. Berkeley, CA: The Grantmaker Forum on Community and National Service.

Ginwright, S., & Cammarota, J. (2002). New terrain in youth development: The promise of a social justice approach. *Social Justice, 29*(4), 82–95.

Ginwright, S., Cammarota, J., & Noguera, P. (2005). Youth, social justice, and communities: Towards a theory of urban youth policy. *Social Justice, 32*(3), 24–40.

James, A. (1993). *Childhood identities: Self and social relationships in the experience of the child*. Edinburgh, England: Edinburgh University Press.

Kane, C. (2000). Development of participatory techniques. In P. Christensen & A. James (Eds.), *Research with children: Perspectives and practices* (pp. 136–159). London, England: Falmer Press.

Kennelly, J. (2011). *Citizen youth: Culture, activism, and agency in a neoliberal era*. New York, NY: Palgrave Macmillan.

Lansdown, G. (2010). The realisation of children's participatory rights. In B. Percy-Smith & N. Thomas (Eds.). *A handbook of children and young people's participation: Perspectives from theory and practice* (pp. 11–23). New York, NY: Routledge.

Lesko, N. (2001). *Act your age! A cultural construction of adolescence*. New York, NY: Routledge Falmer.

Lieten, G. K. (2008). *Children, structure, and agency: Realities across the developing world*. New York, NY: Routledge.

Lloyd-Smith, M., & Tarr, J. (2000). Researching children's perspectives: A sociological dimension. In A. Lewis & G. Lindsay (Eds.), *Researching children's perspectives* (pp. 59–70). Buckingham, England: Open University Press.

Lund, R. (2008). At the interface of development studies and child research: Rethinking the participating child. In S. Aitkin, R. Lund, & A. T. Kjorholt (Eds.), *Global childhoods: Globalization, development and young people* (pp. 131–148). New York, NY: Routledge.

McIntyre, A. (2008). *Participation action research.* Los Angeles, CA: SAGE.

Meacham, J. (2004). Action, voice, and identity in children's lives. In P. Pufall & R. Unsworth (Eds.), *Rethinking childhood* (pp. 69–84). New Brunswick, NJ: Rutledge University Press.

Morrell, E. (2004). *Becoming critical researchers: Literacy and empowerment for urban youth.* New York, NY: Peter Lang.

Norris, J., Sawyer, R., & Lund, D. (Eds.). (2012). *Duoethnography: Dialogical methods for social, health, and educational research.* Walnut Creek, CA: Left Coast Press.

Nybell, L., Shook, J., & Finn, J. (2009). Introduction and conceptual framework. In L. Nybell, J. Shook, & J. Finn (Eds.), *Childhood, youth, and social work in transformation: Implications for policy and practice* (pp. 1–33). New York, NY: Columbia University Press.

Reason, P. (1994). Human inquiry as discipline and practice. In P. Reason (Ed.), *Participation in human inquiry: Research with people* (pp. 40–56). Thousand Oaks, CA: SAGE.

Roberts, H. (2000). Listening to children: And hearing them. In P. Christensen & A. James (Eds.), *Research with children: Perspectives and practices* (pp. 225–240). London, England: Falmer Press.

Schultz, B. (2008). *Spectacular things happen along the way: Lessons from an urban classroom.* New York, NY: Teachers College Press.

Tuck, E. (2009). Suspending damage: A letter to communities. *Harvard Educational Review, 79*(3), 409–427.

Van de Ven, A. H., & Johnson, P. E. (2006). Knowledge for theory and practice. *Academy of Management Review, 31*, 802–821.

VeLure Roholt, R. (2004). *Contesting youthhood, crafting democratic citizens: Young people doing the work of democracy.* University of Minnesota, Minneapolis, MN.

VeLure Roholt, R., & Baizerman, M. (2013). *Civic youth work: A primer.* New York, NY: Peter Lang.

VeLure Roholt, R., Hildreth, R. W., & Baizerman, M. (2009). *Becoming citizens: Deepening the craft of youth civic engagement.* New York, NY: Routledge.

Watts, R., Williams, N., & Jagers, R. (2003). Sociopolitical development. *American Journal of Community Psychology, 31*(1/2), 185–194.

Weis, L., & Fine, M. (Eds.) (2005). *Beyond silenced voices: Class, race, and gender in United States schools.* Albany: State University of New York.

West, C., & Zimmerman, D. (1987). Doing gender. *Gender & Society, 1*(2), 125–151.

CHAPTER 6

REFLEXIVELY CONDUCTING RESEARCH WITH ETHNICALLY DIVERSE CHILDREN WITH DISABILITIES[1]

Amanda Ajodhia

ABSTRACT

This reflexive chapter explores the process of engaging ethnically diverse children with disabilities within participatory and narrative research concerning their school life via a multi-method qualitative approach. It contemplates the use of participatory research methods, involving children with disabilities as co-researchers, establishing relaxed research environments, and maintaining qualitative rigor while supporting children's voices and agency. This chapter addresses possibilities of qualitative research to access and amplify voices and differing social experiences of children with disabilities, whilst underscoring their capacity and right to contribute to research regarding their lives. The author advocates re-envisioning ways to conduct ethical research with children with disabilities.

Participatory Methodologies to Elevate Children's Voice and Agency, pages 117–150
117

The United Nations *Convention on the Rights of Persons With Disabilities* (2006) is a human rights treaty promoting and protecting equitable rights, freedoms, and respect of those with disabilities. The convention aims to ensure those with disabilities have opportunities to engage, enjoy, and live to their fullest potential, with societal rights and freedoms respected as any other person. This includes a right to freely share personal understandings and opinions on issues important to their lives. Article 7 of the convention emphasizes "children with disabilities have the right to express their views freely on all matters affecting them...and to be provided with disability and age-appropriate assistance to realize that right" (United Nations, 2006, #3). While children with disabilities (CWD) have a right to express their views, this right neither guarantees they will be asked to share these views (e.g., due perhaps to assumptions regarding the child's communication abilities, or individuals may lack clarity and confidence approaching and engaging the child, etc.) nor does it guarantee they will be heard. In supporting the convention's position toward CWD, I continuously seek ways as a researcher to break down barriers within research processes for involving CWD, providing them opportunities to both speak and be heard on matters affecting their lives. As I invite CWD to engage within the research process, rendering possibilities for them to exercise their right in sharing personal understandings, I also appreciate the importance of establishing ethical safeguards.

The 2013 *International Charter for Ethical Research Involving Children* (ICERIC) is a set of seven commitments addressing researchers' obligations to uphold the rights, dignity, and well-being of all child participants, in all circumstances, while embarking upon ethical quality research (Graham, Powell, Taylor, Anderson, & Fitzgerald, 2013). In doing so the ICERIC highlights the rights of child research participants and specifically draws attention to roles and responsibilities of commissioners and researchers. The charter advocates challenging discriminatory barriers for research participation and providing equitable opportunity for the involvement of all children (Graham et al., 2013). According to the ICERIC it is imperative that researchers engage in steady reflective inquiry and meaning making throughout their work with children. This reflexivity becomes more critical when involving CWD, due to complexities in accessing their voices (Ajodhia-Andrews, 2016). Reflexivity presents space for researchers to contemplate appropriate methods and mediums in accessing the voices of CWD; space to consider and (re)consider techniques better suiting the children involved within the research. Steady reflexivity supports the management of ethical issues that arise when researching with CWD (e.g., ethical precautions, ongoing consent, participant voice and power, member-checking of data, disclosure of the research process, etc.; Ajodhia-Andrews, 2016).

Realizing the diversities within children's lives, including those with disabilities, it is essential to listen to their versions and stories of personal experiences. In doing so, counternarratives transpire narrated by those experiencing societal marginalization, while challenging dominant narratives, discourse, and assumptions about disability (Connors & Stalker, 2007). There is a need to better understand how to create ethical research milieus offering CWD prospects to chronicle and converse about personal experiences and issues as experts of their own lives. Much of the research involving CWD is typically *on rather than with* CWD. Research on CWD pertains to children's deficiencies due to impairment, concentrating on the child's weaknesses and needs, rather than strengths and abilities (Cuskelly, 2005; Gray & Winter, 2011). Furthermore, developmental assessments and standardized measurements are relied upon frequently in research on children, suggesting child development is predictable, linear, and within age appropriate norms (Hogan, 2005); developmental notions of normalcy suggest diversity in development as deficiencies in development (Gabel & Connor, 2008; Grieshaber, 2001; Rauscher & McClintock, 1996; Tisdall, 2012).

To obtain a comprehensive account of disability we must appreciate the interrelationship between impairment, one's response to impairment, and the social environment, recognizing that together these contribute to the advantages and/or disadvantages experienced by CWD (Shakespeare & Watson, 2002; Siebers, 2008). Gaining insight into how the interrelationship between these factors shape different experiences for CWD requires seeking out children's personal understandings. Every CWD uniquely experiences impairment depending on contexts, circumstances, and needs, often resulting in limitations to societal participation within their communities, schools, and so on (Anastasiou & Kauffman, 2013; Barnes, 2012; Connors & Stalker, 2007; Haegele & Hodge, 2016; Oliver, 1990; Watson, 2012), and I argue also research. Although these limitations to fully take part in activities may result from health challenges or lack of technology (Watson, 2012), CWD should have a choice in whether they want to participate regardless of how much or how little their level of participation may be. As Gray and Donnelly (2013) purported, the benefits experienced from self-expression, communication of views, and opportunities to participate in educational research, far exceed any challenges arising with involving children from minority status groups (i.e., disabilities, ethnoculturally diverse backgrounds). In efforts to support accessing and understanding CWD's views, researchers are encouraged to adapt and accommodate where possible to facilitate maximum research participation. Researchers have a responsibility to offer suitable supports for CWD to exercise their right in discussing issues impacting their lives, being involved and heard within the research (United Nations, 2006, Article 7). Recognizing the importance of inviting and valuing young people's voices in educational conversations (Fielding, 2001; Hopkins, 2008; McIntyre, Pedder, & Rudduck, 2005; Messiou, 2006), and in research processes (Johnson, Hart, & Colwell, 2014a), this chapter reflects on my journey of collaborating with a group of CWD in research examining their school life and insights of inclusion.

The following chapter is a personal reflection on how I engaged CWD from ethnoculturally diverse backgrounds within participatory and narrative research concerning their school life and sense of belonging. This chapter explores complicated questions encountered throughout the research process, as I muddled through unchartered territories researching with ethnically diverse young people with disabilities. I also intend to demonstrate possibilities of participatory qualitative research in actively engaging participants as co-researchers.

This inquiry is influenced by my clinical experience as a behavioral therapist for children and youth with developmental disabilities, particularly those with autism spectrum disorder (ASD) and those who communicate through different means (e.g., not always through speech, but through gestures, pictures/visuals, behaviors, etc.). Many of these children were from diverse ethnic and racial backgrounds, practiced various religions, spoke multiple languages, and sometimes lived in lower socioeconomic contexts. These students were often placed in full-time segregated special education classrooms or mainstreamed. Over my many years as a therapist, I never worked with a child receiving inclusive education within an inclusive classroom on a full-time basis. I frequently wondered how these children felt about their schooling experiences, especially those from diverse ethnic backgrounds. I questioned whether these children experienced opportunities to voice personal perspectives, feeling a sense of equitable participation and belonging within their school. A deep interest in further investigating the schooling experiences of CWD, I sought out their personal narratives of diversity and inclusion within a research context. As the research progressed I encountered many questions, dilemmas, and ethical considerations in positioning participants as co-researchers while supporting approaches to accessing and amplifying their voices through the use of agency-driven qualitative methods.

METHODS

This chapter reflects upon the process of conducting a qualitative study exploring the narratives of six Canadian CWD (ages 10–13). The narratives examined their schooling experiences and understandings of differences and school belonging. Gem, Alice, Simon, Mew, Edward, and William (participant pseudonyms) attend a nonprofit center for individuals with disabilities. All participants are from Chinese and/or Vietnamese ethnic heritages, and are bilingual in Mandarin and/or Cantonese and English. Participants' disability diagnosis includes ASD, attention deficit disorder, hyperactivity, global developmental delay, cerebral palsy, and speech and language delays. Some participants have multiple disability diagnoses, however 5 out of the 6 children have an ASD diagnosis. All participants are placed within special education segregated classrooms within mainstream public schools. The five children with an ASD diagnosis also receive partial integration into the general education classroom during the school week. This study was informed and influenced by both participatory and narrative methods.

Participatory Methods

Participatory approaches seek to balance power relations between researcher and participant so that both parties mutually contribute and challenge knowledge in the research process, becoming co-researchers and co-learners (Bergold & Thomas, 2012; Hart, 1992; Williams et al., 2012). Although many scholars define participation differently, the goal of maximizing decision-making opportunities is central. In the context of working with children, Lansdown (2003) noted, "Participation can be defined as children taking part in and influencing processes, decisions, and activities that affect them, in order to achieve greater respect for their rights" (p. 273). Beyond prospects of voicing personal insights, being heard and listened to, children wish for their views to be respectfully discussed, feeling a sense of involvement in decision-making (Williams et al., 2012).

Supporting CWD as co-researchers involves establishing a space of safety, whereby participants freely express experiences and opinions while also maintaining some degree of decision-making (Bergold & Thomas, 2012). For example, to establish a safe research venue, I contemplated details regarding the number of research sessions and its structure, the number of participants' techniques to engage participants through positive behavioral supports, and my personal level of flexibility to adapt and accommodate for participants and the group climate.

Participants engaged in seven *group sessions* of approximately 90 minutes each. Group sessions elicit stories among young people in narrative research, presenting a more natural and relaxed research context when conversing about salient issues in their lives that are rarely discussed, particularly relating to peer culture, health, well-being, and other sensitive topics (Darbyshire, MacDougall, & Schiller, 2005; Eder & Fingerson, 2003; Engel, 2005; Johnson et al., 2014a). Group interviews may empower children to challenge, encourage, and ask questions of each other, serving as researchers among themselves, thus serving to rebalance existing power dynamics between researchers and child participants (Eder & Fingerson, 2003; Hennessy & Heary, 2005; Johnson et al., 2014a). In using a variety of research methods throughout the study, it was helpful to develop a group *session itinerary* and script guiding facilitation of each session. Yet, I maintained flexibility, adapting the schedule and offering regular breaks to accommodate for the group climate, such as lack of time, participant fatigue, and momentary withdrawal of participation. *Positive behavioural supports* can redirect perceived negative behaviors to allow children in successfully engaging in the research, thus assisting in accessing participant voice and views (Ajodhia-Andrews & Berman, 2009). To create a more exciting experience, I developed what I described to participants as the *Magic Bag* (similar to the *Magic Box*—see Ajodhia-Andrews & Berman, 2009) filled with reinforcing items specific to each child. I also considered the *setting and participant sample size.* All sessions occurred in the nonprofit center, as this environment helped to ensure the children felt safe, comfortable, and relaxed (MacNaughton & Smith, 2005). Using a small sample size (i.e., six) allowed for deeper immersion into topics, group cohesiveness, analysis of narratives (Chase, 2005), and enhanced my ability to attend to each child in supporting their maximum participation.

Hart (1992) developed a well-known model conveying the degrees of participation between young people and researchers. Hart's (1992) "Ladder of Participation" consists of eight levels of young people participation in research projects (see Figure 6.1). The lower three steps of the ladder represent no child participation, whereas steps four to eight represent degrees of child participation. Hart's (1992) Ladder is often criticized for implying progression up the ladder is linear and all research with children should be facilitated at the highest step (Tisdall & Liebel, 2008; Williams et al., 2012). Yet, degrees of participation vary, existing in a state of ebb and flow, as participation highly depends on children's context, access, interests, abilities, mood, and so on. I locate my research on the sixth step (i.e., adult initiated, shared decisions with children), because although participants shared views, made decisions, and served as co-researchers, I initiated many aspects of the research (e.g., research purpose and goals, set of research activities, data collection tools, research venue, etc.). Climbing to this level of the participation ladder is not necessarily a problem, as sometimes it is in the best interest of participants to remain on lower levels of the ladder. In the best interest of this group of CWD, I felt it was critical I initiate and direct certain aspects of the study to maximize individual participation and retain a high level of research engagement.

Narrative Methods

Narratives employ stories as a method to explore others' lived experiences and to examine their understandings of these experiences (Patton, 2002; Polkinghorne, 1988). As children make sense of who they are through

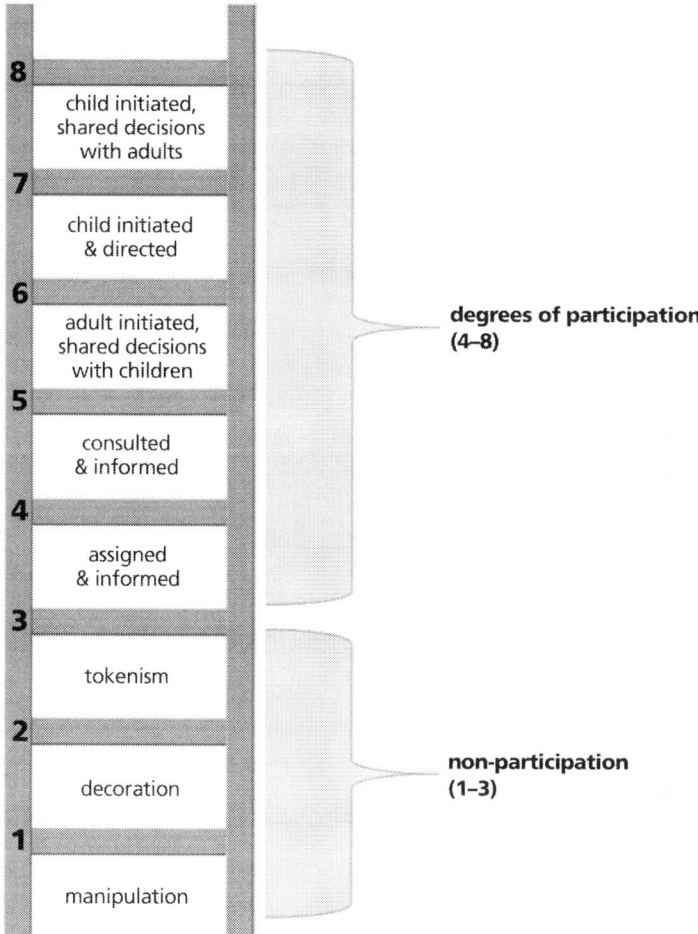

Figure 6.1 Ladder of young people's participation in research (Hart, 1992).

telling and retelling their experiences and stories (Ahn & Filipenko, 2007; Engel, 2005) narrative design works well in accessing children's views, particularly to access silenced schooling experiences of children from minority status groups (He, Chan, & Phillion, 2008; Hendry, 2007).

Participants' narratives were developed orally (dialogue, interviews, story, games), textually (written activities), and visually (drawings, photography). The narrative data was analyzed, establishing patterns and tensions, identifying codes and thematic categories, organizing text, and most critically searching for meaning and making sense of the data (Denzin, 2004; Gray, 2003). To make sense of the children's stories and experiences, I explored their narratives highlighting contexts, characters, key events, and conclusions (Creswell,

2005). Riessman (1993) classified this as "scrutinizing" (p. 57) the data or drafts of texts, for surfacing meaningful patterns, tensions, discourses, and positioning of the narrator as self and with others. Through open coding I segmented the data into categories and subcategories, establishing larger themes related to the purpose of the study (Creswell, 2005).

After coding and searching for emerging themes and patterns, participants and I collaboratively told, retold, wrote, and rewrote their narratives, negotiating which pieces of stories to include, what they thought of surfacing themes and interpretations, where to position texts, and the organization and editing of each narrative (Chase, 2005; Creswell, 2005). Through this dialogue and debate participants and I co-constructed narratives together, whereby I also became part of the conversations, responding to their stories and experiences, thus shaping and restorying their narratives. These narratives become unique to the interaction between myself and participants; if participants shared their stories and understandings with any other person/researcher, the narratives would never be conveyed and told in the same way (Trahar, 2009). This co-construction complicates ownership of the narratives, begging the question of who truly owns the narrative (Trahar, 2009)? I cannot answer this with certainty, as I also surfaced as a storyteller among the children in the telling and retelling, writing and rewriting, and interpreting and organizing of their narratives. However, I sought ways to ensure the children's voices resonated as predominant narrators of their stories, aligning with their beliefs, experiences, and essence of themselves.

ACCESSING VOICES OF CHILDREN WITH DISABILITIES IN RESEARCH

Inclusive research approaches offer CWD the prospect of maximizing participation and engagement within the research process. Participative activities should be appealing, offering a variety of research methods to explore personal experiences of CWD and those from diverse ethnic groups, and these experiences are valued and respected by researchers (Cuskelly, 2005; Gray & Donnelly, 2013; Gray & Winter, 2011; Mishna, Antle, & Regehr, 2004; Williams et al., 2012). Incorporating various creative and engaging methods may complement each other rather than replicate, prevent participant boredom, support triangulation of data, and manage power imbalances between researcher and child (Carrington, Allen, & Osmolowski, 2007; Darbyshire, MacDougall, & Schiller, 2005; Freeman & Mathison, 2009; Moss, Deppeler, Astley, & Pattison, 2007; Punch, 2002). I employed a multi-method data collection approach combining semi-structured interviews with open-ended questions and personal researcher memos, alongside creative mediums to further engage participants in exploring schooling experiences.

Creative Mediums

Utilizing creative approaches when conducting research with CWD may foster a more comprehensive understanding of their experiences, allowing researcher and participants to explore emerging themes from creative mediums to guide discussions. Within the study I included creative mediums, such as artistic writing activities, drawings, storytelling/story games, and visual narratives through photography; methods which entail "inventive and imaginative processes" (Veale, 2005, p. 254). These particular creative mediums supported the children's differing abilities (e.g., not all of the children communicated with speech), and accessed information that may be difficult to share via interviews (e.g., bullying experiences). Mediums involving writing, images (i.e., drawings, photographs), and imaginative stories present CWD with other engaging ways to contribute to research and communicate understandings; ways in which traditional approaches may not offer. These mediums encouraged CWD to create personal forms of their expression and communication, demonstrating that they are well-informed individuals capable of contributing knowledge about their lives and sociocultural contexts. Through these mediums participants explored preselected topics related to school belonging, learning, and diversity.

Artistic writing activities can often effectively provide accounts of children's experiences through writing. Participants engaged in journal writing, brainstorm bubble mapping, and a "Thoughts About Me" booklet. Within each activity, I requested that participants reflect and record their feelings, experiences, ideas, and stories (see Figure 6.2).

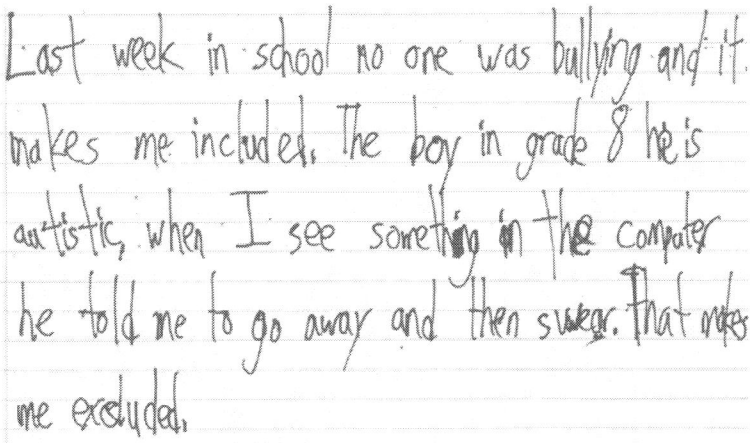

Figure 6.2 Simon's journal writing about personal bullying victimization and exclusion at school.

Figure 6.3 Edward's response in his "Thoughts about Me" booklet, indicating his efforts at school.

To further examine participants' personal insights they completed a booklet I developed entitled "Thoughts About Me" The booklet served as a tool to learn more about participants' schooling experiences, and to re-inforce ideas discussed throughout the interviews (see Figure 6.3). As some of the children preferred not to write I offered choices of typing responses on the computer or scribing (i.e., participants dictated responses aloud and I wrote them down), to support participation in the writing activities.

Through writing activities, the children expressed thoughts and experiences regarding issues that they may not necessarily feel comfortable discussing (e.g., skin color, disability, etc.). It also presents young people with time in the research process to reflect on topics, forming their own opinions and ideas, and extending beyond the researcher's understanding of the topic (Noble-Carr, 2006); thus, balancing the time pressures of providing rushed responses that some young people may experience during interviews. Freewriting may also support accurate recall of personal events, compared to asking children to remember and verbally retell particular details of experiences (Noble-Carr, 2006). However, this medium can be quite time intensive depending on the children's literacy and fine motor abilities.

Drawings can be powerful visual representations of children's understanding of their worlds, serving as a form of communication (Veale, 2005). However, as Veale (2005) noted, for drawings to serve as research data verbal interpretations conveying meanings should accompany the drawings. Asking children to explain their drawings and reasons behind images in the drawings also prevents adult/researcher interpretations of the data (Punch, 2002), as well as enhances the quality and richness of the data, presenting insights which may not have been accessed from only drawings or discussions (Noble-Carr, 2006). As such, participants shared and discussed their drawings in the group (see Figures 6.4 and 6.5).

Drawings more easily convey emotional connections of experiences that may be difficult to express through verbal and/or textual speech (Derry,

School sometimes makes me feel embarrassed and of course, scared. I often feel scared because people keep looking at me...I don't know why.

Figure 6.4 Mew's drawing with accompanying verbal interpretation regarding his feelings about school.

This is me at school when I play UNO. I feel happy

Figure 6.5 Alice's drawing with accompanying verbal interpretation regarding her favorite activity to participate in when at school.

2005). Mew and Alice's drawing and explanation of their schooling experiences clearly convey certain emotions (i.e., scared, embarrassed, happy). Similar to writing activities, drawings are an effective medium in accessing children's voices, because it allows them time to reflect and imagine about topics and how they wish to portray their understandings of these topics, with flexibility to remove or add elements to their drawings (Noble-Carr, 2006; Punch, 2002); this strengthens participants' agency in the data generation process as part of the data collection phase of the research. Yet, drawings may not be an engaging research technique for all young people, particularly older children (Punch, 2002), and thus researchers should consider the children's abilities and interests in artistic drawing.

Storygames provided greater insights into the children's understanding of inclusive education and difference. Storygames entailed each child add one line to an open ended story until it reaches a natural conclusion (Veale, 2005). This method presented participants with opportunities to develop a shared understanding of their respective views to produce an organized and interconnected story (see Figure 6.6).

Imaginative story games may inspire discussion, kindle memories of the children's experiences, and is especially useful when broaching sensitive issues (Noble-Carr, 2006). As such, using fictional characters and pretend scenarios in considering vulnerable topics may present a sense of security for young people, as they remove themselves from personal experiences to invent a story about an issue relatable to their lives. Within story games the children contemplated issues of difference and school inclusion from a make-believe perspective, sharing their own understandings veiled through imaginative stories. Story games may serve as a safe gateway for some children to open up to discussing sensitive issues pertaining to their lives.

Photography complemented participants' responses with the other methods and provided a unique way for the children to express themselves. Using photography and combining it with children's description of their photos presents

---

There once was a girl who was teased and made fun of all the time at school.
She got bullied all the time.
They make fun of her and they say "Your name is stupid."
She always trips all the time and they call her names, like "clumsy."
She cried.
It was cruel.
They called her stupid and all she wanted to do was play UNO with her friends.
She was in the special class.
She was scared and she felt like going home.
She wanted to go home, because she was teased.
The next day, she did not come to school.
Instead she came here, to our centre!
She felt lucky, because she got to come to our centre and she didn't have to go back to school.
She's happy when she's here at the centre.
She feels safe here, safer than her school, away from the people, the classmates, the bully people.
No one bullies her at the centre.
She felt happy.

Figure 6.6 A story told by participants during Storygames about a girl with disabilities being teased at school.

understandings regarding abstract topics, especially if children are uncomfortable discussing these issues through writing or dialogue (Moss, Deppeler, Astley, & Pattison, 2007), or if there is difficulty depicting certain images/actions through drawing (Punch, 2002). Participants used digital photography to preserve and visibly highlight experiences within their narratives. Subsequently, to give life and voice to their images the children created a narrative of their photos, offering meanings that may "…inform a conscious reflection on previously taken-for-granted assumptions" (Carrington et al., 2007, p. 9). I presented participants with digital cameras to capture images representing their schooling experiences. I developed a "Photo Camera Reminders" sheet to guide participants during the photo taking process, and I presented them with an example of my own photo narration. I printed all digital photos and returned them to participants. Working in pairs, participants reviewed images and discussed its significance (see Figures 6.7 and 6.8).

Using photography and combining it with the children's description of their photos, presented their voices, meanings, and insights regarding differences, learning, and inclusion. The children used photography to visibly capture images important in their lives and lived experiences within narratives.

MULTI-METHOD APPROACH

Through a multi-method approach I obtained a more thorough understanding of participants' experiences, triangulating their reports from interviews with their creative activities. Some participants responded more easily to sharing experiences through multiple creative methods, revealing rich data that may be unlikely to access through a single method (i.e., interviews). For example, some of the children more readily wrote rather than

I am graduating this year. Graduating makes me feel involved and like I belong at school. I am going to high school next year! This is my graduation book with pictures!

Figure 6.7   During photo narrations, Gem highlighted that graduating from school provides her with a sense of inclusion.

Sometimes we eat at this restaurant. It means "Tasty House." That's "Tasty House" in Chinese [referring to the restaurant sign]. The name of the restaurant. This is soup that I buy at the restaurant. I don't eat this at school. I don't want to bring this soup to school.

Figure 6.8 During photo narrations, William described his enjoyment of cultural foods, which he reserves for distinct spaces encompassing home and family life, not school.

discussed their experiences. In maintaining an inclusive approach within the research I found it necessary to adapt and tailor research methods better suiting participants' strengths, interests, and preferences (Ajodhia-Andrews & Berman, 2009; Freeman & Mathison, 2009; McDonald, Kidney, & Patka, 2013). This entailed ongoing modification to certain aspects of the research session to foster maximum participation of all children. For instance, I introduced more visual supports (e.g., brainstorm mapping on large boards, large print type outs of all interview questions), modified my delivery and tone of speech (e.g., slow, melodic, short phrasing), offered choices of computer use and scribing, and utilized the Picture Exchange Communication System (PECS) for Gem who has cerebral palsy with significant speech and language delays (see Figure 6.9).

Something that makes me feel included at school is the computer.

Figure 6.9 Through the use of PECS, Gem explained that computers provide her with a sense of inclusion.

As participants moved through these creative mediums they raised sensitive issues that they or others in the group have been dealing with (e.g., difficulty with friendships and bullying [see Figures 6.2, 6.4, 6.6], negotiating appropriate spaces for expressing cultural identity [see Figure 6.8]). Although perhaps eliciting unpleasant memories, these discussions opened doors to further explore taboo and stigmatizing issues related to culture, disability, inclusion/exclusion, and school life in a supportive environment with a group of similar peers. In addition to broaching difficult issues, the children highlighted pleasant experiences through these approaches (e.g.,inclusive experiences at school [see Figures 6.5, 6.6, 6.9], sense of safety and belonging at the nonprofit center [see Figure 6.6]). Such creative mediums presented opportunities for this group of children to inform repertoires of diversity and raise awareness regarding issues impacting their lives.

CHILDREN WITH DISABILITIES AS CO-RESEARCHERS

Consent Process

Considering that children's agency is often passive within the research process, even more so among CWD, I mindfully structured the study to include participants as active co-researchers. I did so by first offering participants decision-making opportunities to engage in the research through verbal and written child assent. I directly asked the children whether they would like to participate in the research. In doing so, I am not suggesting the children knew exactly the meaning of research or consent. However, asking a child to participate in research, as is common practice among adult research participants, demonstrates mutual respect between researcher and child, and I advocate it is part of ethical research involving children. Additionally, in requesting young people for their permission to actively engage in research more likely obtains a sample of children who independently desire with invested interest to be involved. Participants also completed a child assent form. The form addresses the agreement between researcher and child, conveys the child's interest to participate in the study, respects the child's sense of control in the research process, and demonstrates recognition for the rights of the child (Hill, 2005). Requesting for children's assent imparts a sense of empowerment (Mishna et al., 2004), valuing their competency and choice making abilities, thus signifying ownership throughout the research process.

Collaborative Narrative Construction

Moreover, we collaboratively constructed their individual narratives. Participants negotiated which experiences and stories to include, their impressions of surfacing themes/interpretations, and the organization and editing of each narrative (Chase, 2005; Creswell, 2005). Ensuring the analysis and interpretation of narratives were representative of participants' perspectives, I continuously conferred with the children during group sessions, confirming accurate or intended responses. There is the possibility that responses might differ within individual versus group sessions. Yet, as participants had built a rapport with each other and proceeded throughout the entire research within a group session format, I thought it was best to maintain this established and consistent routine to support the children's level of comfort. Maintaining routines (e.g., consistent group session research format) was useful in this research, as it supported engagement of participants with ASD; for young people with ASD routines provide a sense of stability and security, as disruptions to regular schedules or expected practice can often cause distress. Eder and Fingerson (2003) argued that group settings also help reduce to some degree researcher (mis)interpretations and elicits more accurate participant responses; such settings allow children to develop their own "talk" separate from the researcher, and they are often requested to defend these responses among peers in the group. I re-presented (3 times) to participants drafts of their narratives, reassuring appropriate portrayal of their stories as they desired. This particular chapter was not shared with the children for feedback. I shared the data and all drafts of narratives from the original study with them to allow for their decision making regarding narrative interpretation and analysis. Participants were aware from the consent process that I would be presenting their data to others in the form of writing and presentations. However, as previously mentioned, I did not position the children as co-researchers participating at the highest degree of participation (i.e., Hart's [1992] Ladder of Participation, 8th rung), and thus I chose to initiate different scholarly outputs of the research without collaborating with the children. Nevertheless, this does not discount the children's voices as narrators at the center of each narrative (Chase, 2005), participating to a certain degree as co-researchers.

Participants' original interview texts sometimes required rewording or restructuring to support readability of their narratives. All participants maintained some form of communication, language, and comprehension challenges. On occasion, they employed incomplete sentences, incorrect grammar structure, or ambiguously articulated terms and/or phrases. Additionally, participants sometimes provided brief and/or "yes/no" responses requiring ample probing. In such cases, I revised participants' verbatim responses (e.g., editing sentence structure, adding punctuation, pronouns, etc.) to fortify reader comprehension and strengthen participants' personal meanings, ensuring narratives flowed as complete and understandable stories grounded in their experiences. In amending the children's responses, power dynamics shift toward me as the researcher, reflecting perhaps that my voice possesses more power within a research context than my young participants. Although, I think this is always the case in research, whether working with child participants or adult participants; even after member checking and collaborating with participants, the researcher has the ultimate decision-making power to shape the research and disseminate the data in various scholarly forms as they deem suitable. My participants did not have a say in how I shared and presented their narratives to the world, and this may leave them more vulnerable and powerless in the research process. In attempts to restore some of the power imbalance among participants in this particular study, I ensured the children reviewed their narratives after I reworded their verbatim responses. They were offered opportunities to revise or edit my changes, supporting intended meanings and interpretations of their final narratives. To illustrate my amendments of original texts, I present one example for each participant in Table 6.1.

Research Kits

To also support the children's involvement in the research, I provided them with research kits that included personal journals, drawings, photo camera, pencil case, and so on. I developed the kits for participants to further establish a sense of research authority and agency. I hoped the kits incited feelings of belonging and control in the research project. As sessions progressed, participants requested for their kits, decorated and personalized their kits (e.g., stickers, drawings, artwork, etc.), cared for its items, and regularly reviewed their work within the kits, all demonstrating a sense of pride.

QUALITATIVE RIGOR, AGENCY, AND VOICE

Amidst tensions between navigating the realities of carrying out participatory research with a group of CWD and debating strategies to maximize their participation in narrative research emerged issues of agency and voice. Agency and voice are likely shaped by socially constructed circumstances. These circumstances serve to either limit or liberate agency and voice among CWD. For instance, institutional structures of schooling often promote segregated rather than inclusive learning for CWD and structures of medicine promote fixing impairments, both sanctioning normalizing discourses and attitudinal barriers in relation to notions of CWD; thus, influencing a child's sense of agency and voice (Ajodhia-Andrews, 2016; Holt, Lea, & Bowlby, 2012; Rosenbaum & Gorter, 2011). Socially constructed limitations among CWD in research include for example, positioning the child as incapable due to impairment, thus limiting and often excluding

TABLE 6.1a			
Participants:	**Gem**	**Alice**	**Simon**
Context:	Gem and I discussed what makes her feel included at school.	Alice and I discussed understandings of difference and being different.	Simon and I discussed exclusion
Original Interview Text:	**Amanda:** So Gem, what are you going to make in here that makes you feel included? **Gem:** I included in school... I feel school... bus [shows her drawing of school]. **Amanda:** Can you show me what you do at school that makes you feel included [referring to her PECs book]? **Gem:** [Selected Computer PEC]. **Amanda:** Oh, OK. Computer. **Gem:** In School. **Amanda:** In school. It makes you feel included? **Gem:** Yes. **Amanda:** What else? Anything that makes you feel included at school? **Gem:** [Shows the birthday cake PEC]. When have birthday. **Amanda:** Oh, when you celebrate your birthday? **Gem:** Me.	**Amanda:** So, tell me what is different? **Alice:** Good. **Amanda:** So different is good. So, Alice said being different is good. What else? **Alice:** Nice. **Amanda:** Different is nice... What else, Alice? Different is...? **Alice:** Friends. **Amanda:** Oh, different is your friends. Wonderful. Friends are different. **Alice:** Different is good. **Amanda:** Yes. **Alice:** Different is nice. **Amanda:** Yes, different is nice. Being different is...? **Alice:** School. **Amanda:** School... Different is? **Alice:** Spanish. **Amanda:** That means languages. Good job. **Alice:** Yes.	**Simon:** If someone was bullying me, that makes me feel excluded. **Amanda:** Yes. Did that happen to you before? **Simon:** That's... that's... bullying happened to me before and it makes me feel excluded. **Amanda:** Oh, what happened when you were bullied? What did they do? [No response]. Can you remember? **Simon:** I can't remember what it was... **Amanda:** I remember last time [previous session] you said somebody swore at you. **Simon:** Oh, yes. That was the autistic kid. That was grade 8. He swear at me when I go to that boy to see something. He was on the computer. He said "go away" and he sweared. **Amanda:** Oh, he was on the computer and he was in grade 8. **Simon:** Yes. **Amanda:** And he swore at you and said to "go away." And that made you feel...? **Simon:** Excluded.

(continued)

TABLE 6.1a (continued)

Participants:	Gem	Alice	Simon
Narrative Text	This is my school. I am included in school. I feel included in school. I feel included in school, especially on the school bus. Something that makes me feel included at school are the computers. I also feel included at school when my class celebrates my birthday.	I think being different in school is good. I think being different is nice. I see differences at school, like different languages, such as Spanish... Different is my friends.	Amanda: Excluded. And what did you do? Did you go away? Simon: I go away. I ignored it. Amanda: Was he in your special class? Simon: Yes. Bullying makes me feel excluded. Bullying has happened to me before and it makes me feel excluded... There was an autistic kid. He is in Grade 8. He is in the special needs class. He swears at me. I go to that boy to see something, because he was on the computer. He said "Go away" and he swore at me. That made me feel excluded. I went away and I ignored it.

TABLE 6.1b

Participants:	Mew	Edward	William
Context:	Mew shared his understandings of disability during a brainstorming session.	During photo narrations Edward described a photo he took representing exclusion.	During photo narrations William described a photo of his teddy bear, inclusion, and exclusion.
Original Interview Text:	Amanda: What do you think about people that have diabilities? Mew: They're poor. Amanda: Poor, OK. Mew: They're not rich. They have little.	Edward: I think this is exclusion. Amanda: What is it? Edward: When I take a picture of that building. Amanda: Mhm.	Amanda: Do you remember excluded [from previous session]? Makes you feel what, good or bad? William: Bad. Amanda: Bad. So does your teddy bear

(continued)

TABLE 6.1b (continued)

Participants:	Mew	Edward	William
	They don't have money... It's sad when you don't have money... They lost their friends or their life, or their house, or food. **Amanda:** Wow. So you think that people who have autism will lose their friends? Has that happened to you? Have you lost any friends? **Mew:** Maybe if they don't know what you say. **Amanda:** They don't understand. **Mew:** Or, they don't understand another language. **Amanda:** Yeah, understand what you say. **Mew:** Some people doesn't speak the same language as us... Maybe they are inside they are good, but inside their hear is good, but outside they are bad. **Amanda:** Why are they bad outside? Outside in the world? **Mew:** Because they cannot control themselves. **Amanda:** Oh, OK. Outside they are bad because they can not control themselves... like their behaviors? **Mew:** Yeah. Oh, or maybe they take drugs.	**Edward:** And then my mom told me to take a picture because that's where the people goes. **Amanda:** Who people? **Edward:** Other people. **Amanda:** Yeah and why is it exclusion? **Edward:** Because it's almost getting old. **Amanda:** OK. So how does it tell me if people feel left out like they don't belong? **Edward:** They don't belong there, that's why it's an old place. **Amanda:** Uhuh, but people do live there. Are they rich people or poor people or average people? **Edward:** Average people. **Amanda:** OK. **Edward:** Sometimes the apartment got broken wall papers. **Amanda:** Right. Would you want to live there? **Edward:** No. It's too old right now.	make you feel excluded or included? **William:** Included. **Amanda:** Included, OK. Do you wish that the teddy bear was at school? **William:** Uh, nope. **Amanda:** Why? **William:** Not included in school. **Amanda:** What makes you feel excluded, which makes you feel bad? **William:** I can bring this [points to photo of teddy bear]. **Amanda:** To school? **William:** No. **Amanda:** OK. Listen. What makes you feel excluded from school> **William:** This [points to photo of teddy bear]. **Amanda:** Oh, I thought it made you feel included. **William:** This, will bring it. **Amanda:** Yes, but what makes you feel bad? **William:** Bring this. **Amanda:** Bring the teddy bear? **William:** No, people will laugh. **Amanda:** They will laugh at you. **William:** They will laugh at people if you bring a toy.

(continued)

TABLE 6.1b (continued)			
Participants:	Mew	Edward	William
Narrative Text:	I think that people with disabilities are poor and not rich. They have little or no money, and it's sad if they don't have money. I also think maybe on the inside people with disabilities are good . . . inside their heart is good, but outside they are bad. They are bad outside, because they can not control themselves. People with disabilities may lose their life, their house, and food! They may have to take drugs to control their behavior . . . If you have autism you can lose friends if other people don't know what you say . . . if they don't understand you . . . like a different language, and some people don't speak the same language as us.	This building reminds me of exclusion. It's a building where people live. The building where people live. The building is getting old . . . it's an old place. People don't belong there. People that live there are not poor or rich, they are average. Sometimes the apartment has broken wallpaper. I wouldn't want to live there. It's too old right now.	Even though she [teddy bear] makes me feel happy and included, I don't want to bring her to school . . . this will make me excluded and feeling bad. Bear will not make me feel included at school. I will be excluded, because people will laugh at me. The kids laugh at people if you bring a toy. Bear looks like a baby toy. **Amanda:** Oh, why would they laugh at you? **William:** Cause it looks like a baby toy. **Amanda:** Oh, so that would make you feel excluded. **William:** Yes.

them from research rather than presenting adaptations and accommodations to support and access the child's voice (e.g., CWD may be excluded from research because of behavioral difficulties or verbal communication difficulties, etc.; Ajodhia-Andrews & Berman, 2009).

Accessing Voice

In efforts to foster participants' agency through sharing personal views and carrying out degrees of decision making, I retained a distinction between *giving* voice and *accessing* voice; voice is not something given, as we all possess a voice. Yet, although researchers may not give voice we are positioned to modulate how loud and clear these voices ring throughout the research. For instance, depending on the context of a study, level of researcher reflexivity, and consciousness of participant voice, researchers may either amplify or turn down the sound of voices. Employing participatory research methods via creative mediums demonstrated participants' varying stories and supported accessing their unique ways of voicing these stories. Co-construction of the narratives also served to amplify voice and articulate their messages, hopefully allowing them to be heard.

Yet, even with co-constructing of the narratives my voice as the researcher may always hold more power. The researcher filters the data/narratives based on personal context (sociocultural, historical, and political) and experiences, often reflective of the researcher (Creswell, 2007), and s/he has the final say in research dissemination. This is the case with all research participants, whether adult or child or those with or without disabilities. In the end, however, readers must assess the research approach and design, considering how I endeavored to cultivate a safe and empowering research environment involving young people with disabilities, supporting their maximum participation as co-researchers while ensuring narrative presence.

Agency and Power

Voice is connected to agency and power as it implies a sense of presence, particularly narrative presence. Participants' voices as narrators connected with me, the researcher as their audience, and I attempted to access, amplify, and hear their voices; thus, the children maintained a strong sense of narrative presence within the study. I do not use the term presence to simply suggest physical presence in research, as children may physically participate and speak to a researcher and never get heard. The narrative presence of ethnically diverse CWD in research, specifically participatory research, whereby these children contribute to research agendas, processes, and decisions is critical to exploring schooling experiences of marginalized young people (Watson, 2012; Williams et al., 2012).

Researcher reflexivity also fosters participants' agency and voice. I reflected after each session via researcher memo notes capturing details and overall feelings/impressions, and asking questions of myself, participants, and the research process. Reflecting on research methods, I questioned if a particular medium was unsuccessful in accessing participants' voices, and if so, what actions might I take to revise the approach, better inciting the children's stories? What techniques worked well, fully engaging participants' voices, and why? Thus, reflexivity supported my sense of flexibility. This flexibility served as a constant check-in to examine whether I as the researcher did my best to uphold child participants' agency throughout the process while also presenting opportunity for maximum participation (Ajodhia-Andrews, 2016). I contemplated whether I did my best to present children's narratives in ways that they desired while also respecting their agency as co-researchers. Phelan and Kinsella (2013) noted researcher reflexivity supports not only rigor in qualitative research, but also ethical research practices. Through steady reflexivity, I attempted to manage ethical issues of assent, voice, and power, representation of participants within the data, and disclosure of truthfulness.

DISCUSSION AND CONCLUSION

Conducting research with children raises many dilemmas and ethical uncertainties. Such quandaries escalate when researching with CWD, due to complexities of accessing voice and sensitivities surrounding topics. Shifting away from deficit-based positioning of CWD in research, this chapter contemplates ways of maximizing CWD' research participation to support accessing and hearing voice while presenting them decision and choice making opportunities strengthening the researcher-participant partnership.

Researchers are urged to seek ways of emancipating voices of CWD in research projects (Watson, 2012). Participatory methods, particularly through the use of creative mediums, effectively accesses and includes voices of CWD. In their review of research projects involving children and youth with disabilities, Loveridge and Meyer (2010) reported on various projects that successfully used creative mediums to elicit views from CWD. For instance, they described ethnographic creative methods employing arts and crafts, talking mat methods with storyboards and cameras and visual data gathering methods employing picture boards and cameras (Loveridge & Meyer, 2010). These methods present alternative communication/linguistic systems for CWD. Aligning with my study, it was clear these mediums offered participants different options for communication and expression. Through such qualitative creative mediums, participants poignantly shared understandings and experiences of school life relating to inclusion and diversity.

Multiple methods also presented participants with a variety of communicative platforms, with traditional methods combined with creative ones. This supports a suitable balance for preventing boredom and heavy reliance on one research method, while also offering a range of communicative avenues for CWD to choose how they wish to voice their understandings. Multiple qualitative approaches may complement each other, rather than replicate, allowing participants to share different stories and experiences each time they engage in an activity (Darbyshire et al., 2005; Noble-Carr, 2006; Punch, 2002). For example, some research demonstrated employing visual methods combined with interviews and narratives worked well as forms of communication for young immigrant children (Keat, Strickland, & Marinak, 2009) and CWD (Carrington et al., 2007) as they shared personal lived experiences in efforts to foster inclusive schooling. Employing images (e.g., drawing and photos) combined with narratives appropriately suited my participants' interests and abilities, transpiring rich insights. The use of multiple methods is evident in international studies involving research with marginalized young people as they examine issues impacting their lives. For example, West (2014) employed various methods (e.g., games, drawings, mapping, walks, etc.) to understand the challenges of water supply from the perspectives of Tibetan children living in remote villages. In Nepal, Johnson, Hill, and Sapko (2014b) explored through a range of creative and performative mediums (e.g., songs, dance, drawings, mobility maps, etc.), household gender roles and societies. In Scotland, Connors and Stalker (2007) engaged young CWD in research through a variety of methods, including interviews, spider diagrams, picture cards, and word games. In my particular study the number of differing mediums employed with CWD supported their differing forms of communication. It also assisted in acquiring deep and profound understandings of their experiences of inclusion, learning, and diversity. Some of their stories would never have emerged without the combination of the multiple methods.

Safe research milieus, an essential component of participatory research, allow young people to openly and freely share experiences in a trusted environment. I considered ways of building a rapport-filled and trusting research environment for participants to comfortably share personal schooling experiences. Involving children within research entails researchers prioritize creating a safe and enjoyable space for young people to express themselves (Johnson et al., 2014a; MacNaughton & Smith, 2005). For instance, various studies highlight the use of incorporating many research sessions when engaging young people in research (e.g., Connors & Stalker, 2007; Larkins, 2014; O'Kane & Panicker, 2014), as well as the benefits of group sessions (Darbyshire et al., 2005; Eder & Fingerson, 2003;

Einarsdóttir, 2007; Johnson et al., 2014a). Positive behavioral supports may also aid in providing a relaxed venue, functioning to re-engage children in the research process. For example, in describing a study regarding young children's understanding of well-being and ill-being in Peru, Crivello and Arangoitia (2014) reported the use of scheduled playtime with participants throughout activities to re-energize participants. This playtime operated as a positive behavioral support to re-engage the children. Alike my experience, other researchers found value in using an itinerary to guide research work with children, while being aware of the delicate balance between scheduling and maintaining flexibility to provide a supportive research environment (Freeman & Mathison, 2009). All of these collectively impact young people's maximum participation, as well as their ease and comfort in safely participating in the research.

Part of involving children in participatory research includes examining ways to support their voice and maximum participation as co-researchers. One essential means of doing so is providing children with decision making throughout the research process. Receiving young people's consent and assent to engage in research is not only ethical but also empowering, particularly among those with disabilities who experience limited opportunity to be taken seriously within research processes (Connor & Stalker, 2007; Wickenden, 2011). It also acknowledges their capacity to assess the research information for themselves as decision makers (Noble-Carr, 2006). Seeking children's consent and understanding for why they are participating in research and what it may entail affirms the rights of the child, and as such researchers should implement a process for informed consent when engaging in research with children (Johnson et al., 2014a).

Collaborative narrative construction was another important element for establishing the children's agency and voice as co-researchers, and is imperative to narrative research (Chase, 2005; Creswell, 2005). This assisted with ensuring narrative interpretations and the presentation of their stories and images within personal narratives were as participants' wished. Including participants in the process of validating findings and interpretations is a significant factor in engaging young people in research (Johnson et al., 2014a). In my particular study, narrative co-construction provided participants with some ownership over the data, and also accounted for vulnerability of my researcher voice and any assumptions I may have made with interpreting the narratives (Chase, 2005). Qualitative research is not "value-free" (Denzin, 2004, p. 449), but rather an interactive process as both researchers and participants are positioned in diverse contexts, which shape perspectives and interpretations (Denzin & Lincoln, 2005). A prevalent debate in qualitative research with young people concerns researcher interpretation during data transcribing and analysis. In efforts to deal with this conundrum, I clearly state upfront that it was necessary to revise and in a sense "tidy up" the data to support readers' understandings of participants' perspectives. I also concede bringing my own interpretations to the children's schooling experiences and views related to diversity and inclusion. I sought approaches of fostering children's ownership in the research. I offered participants liberty to review and amend personal narratives on multiple occasions and presented various forms of data collection to access and amplify voice; thus providing many opportunities for research participation and personal analysis.

In keeping with participatory research values and approaches I confronted challenges in how to respectfully encourage participant ability and agency. This chapter describes the strategies I employed to foster agency among participants as co-researchers, "giving [the children] as much control over the content and process of the research as practically possible" (Noble-Carr, 2006, p. 12). Strategies included the use of multiple research methods, creative mediums, obtaining participants' informed consent, co-construction of narratives, providing research kits, and maintaining researcher reflexivity. Through these approaches I strove to accurately portray participants' experiences and stories as they intended, exemplifying their meanings and interpretations. Yet, determining what constitutes children's agency is not always straightforward. Children's level of agency in research are sporadically explained throughout the literature, often failing to describe agency, differing levels of agency, and what agency looks like in particular contexts with diverse young people (Prout, 2011; Tisdall & Punch, 2012). In sharing how CWD agencies were enacted in this research, I hope to problematize and convey the complexities involved in taking a concept such as agency from theory-to-practice (Tisdall & Punch, 2012).

The purpose of this chapter is to advance discussion and debate regarding research with CWD based on my reflections of the study I carried out. The qualitative methods and participatory approaches employed to serve as examples guiding researchers in their journey of researching with CWD. Or, at least perhaps serves as a catalyst for thinking about topics raised throughout the chapter as they conduct research with children from traditionally marginalized groups. Despite international recognition and the benefits of participatory child research there are debates regarding children's competency and authenticity, particularly among CWD (Gray & Winter, 2011). This chapter demonstrates that children's competency is not less than those of adult participants or children without disabilities, and employing multi-method techniques may viably access views and voices of CWD. This study highlights the use of creative mediums to rebalance power relations within the research process, as they present forms of inventive communicative possibilities for CWD to express understandings and experiences.

Far too often the rights of CWD in research are dismissed and their voices disregarded due to social exclusions, negative constructions of disability, institutional gatekeepers, and complications of time and accommodations (Ajodhia-Andrews, 2016; Connors & Stalker, 2007; Wickenden, 2011). Yet, perhaps this dismissal results from complexities surrounding disability and childhood issues, methods, approaches, ideologies, and analyses that may limit researchers in participatory work with CWD (Loveridge & Meyer, 2010; Watson, 2012). Considering the multifaceted and messy nature of research within childhood disability, embracing new research approaches may be essential to examining the life of CWD. Watson (2012) suggested these new methods position CWD as active contributors to research agendas in which they comfortably describe personal experiences of disability while also demonstrating intersections of differences (e.g., ethnicity, disability, gender, etc.) highlighting the heterogeneous nature of their social experiences. Through participatory and narrative methods, this chapter addresses possibilities of qualitative research to access and amplify voices and differing social experiences of CWD, while underscoring their capacity and right to contribute to research regarding their lives. It is hoped through these reflections researchers continue (re)imagining and (re)defining ethically, empowering, and socially just ways in conducting research with CWD.

Limitations and Future Research

Many limitations of this study surfaced due to time constraints:

1. This study may have benefited from including one-on-one sessions between myself and participants. This one-on-one time would have allowed for individual interviews to compliment group interviews, and also to review final drafts of the narratives individually with each participant. The children may have provided different responses during these one-on-one sessions, thus allowing for more robust triangulation of the data and perhaps greater depth of information obtained.
2. The sense of safety and trust within the research environment would have been strengthened if I built a rapport and developed a relationship with the children prior to the beginning of the research process (e.g., 1–2 sessions engaging with the children during their program time at the center).
3. Last, participants were not observed in their school environment. Including an observation period may present more insights into the children's schooling experiences, support triangulation of the data, and assist in the interpretation of their narratives. With more time built into the research process these three limitations may be addressed in future research.

Considering the complex nature of facilitating research with young people with disabilities, investigators may continue exploring the researcher's role in deliberating over ethical matters of fostering voice and agency when involving CWD. This may include how to engage young people with disabilities as co-researchers ensuring they are respected and protected throughout the process, while also being attuned to necessary adaptations and accommodations suiting the children's differing abilities in accessing and amplifying their voices. In reflection, for example, I recommend researchers involve children in the scheduling of research activities, as it may further develop their sense of agency as co-researchers. This limitation relates to my itinerary and guide used throughout the study, as it was not created with the children.

Generalizability was not a goal or consideration for this research, and therefore is not a limitation. Each participants' narrative is uniquely their own story representative of personal views, thoughts, contexts, and lived experiences. My primary interest focused upon participants' stories, how they told them, and their understandings of them. This research was about their lives, school world, and personal human experiences as ethnically diverse CWD—I sought ways in which to gain entry, access their voices, listen, and share their stories.

Questions for Reflection

1. How may your research incorporate participatory and inclusive methods to access and amplify diversity among children's voices?
2. What are some biases, assumptions, values, and beliefs influencing your research process with CWD?
3. In what ways can you support agency and voice among CWD while ensuring rigorous research standards?

Suggestions for Further Reading

Ajodhia, A. (2017). Arts/image-based creative co-research with disabled children: Practical dilemmas of the research process. In M. Emme & A. Kirova (Eds.), *Good question! Creative research collaborations with kids* (pp. 92–120). Victoria, BC: The Canadian Society for Education through Art.

Dalli, C., & Te One, S. (2012). Involving children in educational research: Researcher reflections on challenges. *International Journal of Early Years Education, 20*(3), 224–233.

Fleet, A., & Harcourt, D. (2018). (Co)Researching with children. In M. Fleer & B. van Oers (Eds.), *International handbook of early childhood education* (pp. 165–202). Dordrecht, Netherlands: Springer.

Lambert, V., & Glacken, M. (2011). Engaging with children in research:

Theoretical and practical implications of negotiating informed consent/ assent. *Nursing Ethics, 18*(6), 781–801.

Skanfors, L. (2009). Ethics in child research: Children's agency and research-ers' "ethical radar." *Childhoods Today, 3*(1), 1–22.

ACKNOWLEDGMENT

I thank the center's director and program instructor, as well as participants' families for warmly embracing the research. Also, many thanks to Dr. Diane Gérin-Lajoie for her counsel. With sincere appreciation I thank all the children who participated in this study, serving as brilliant co-researchers. This research project received support through an Ontario Graduate Scholarship and the Social Sciences and Humanities Research Council of Canada (Doctoral Fellowship).

NOTE

1. Sections of this chapter were previously published in *The Qualitative Report* (2016) and are re-published here with authorization from the journal.

REFERENCES

Ahn, J., & Filipenko, M. (2007). Narrative, imaginary play, art, and self: Intersecting worlds. *Early Childhood Education Journal, 34*(4), 279–289.

Ajodhia-Andrews, A. (2016). *Voices and visions from ethnoculturally diverse young people with disabilities.* Rotterdam, Netherlands: Sense.

Ajodhia-Andrews, A., & Berman, R. (2009). Exploring school life from the lens of a child who does not use speech to communicate. *Qualitative Inquiry, 15*(5), 931–951.

Anastasiou, D., & Kauffman, J. (2013). The social model of disability: Dichotomy between impairment and disability. *Journal of Medicine and Philosophy, 38*(4), 441–459.

Barnes, C. (2012). Understanding the social model of disability: Past, present and future. In N. Watson, A. Roulstone, & C. Thomas (Eds.), *The Routledge handbook of disability studies* (pp. 12–29). London, England: Routledge.

Bergold, J., & Thomas, S. (2012). Participatory research methods: A methodological approach in motion. *Forum: Qualitative Social Research, 13*(1), 1–23.

Carrington, S., Allen, K., & Osmolowski, D. (2007). Visual narrative: A technique to enhance secondary students' contribution to the development of inclusive, socially just school environments. Lessons from a box of crayons. *Journal of Research in Special Educational Needs, 7*(1), 8–15.

Chase, S. E. (2005). Narrative inquiry: Multiple lenses, approaches, voices. In N. K. Denzin & Y. S. Lincoln (Eds.), *The SAGE handbook of qualitative research* (3rd ed., pp. 651–679). Thousand Oaks, CA: SAGE.

Connors, C., & Stalker, K. (2007). Children's experiences of disability: Pointers to a social model of childhood disability. *Disability & Society, 22*(1), 19–33.

Creswell, J. W. (2005). *Educational research. Planning, conducting and evaluating quantitative and qualitative research.* Upper Saddle River, NJ: Pearson Merrill Prentice Hall.

Creswell, J. W. (2007). *Qualitative inquiry and research design: Choosing among five approaches* (2nd ed.). Thousand Oaks, CA: SAGE.

Crivello, G., & Arangoitia, V. R. (2014). Exploring children's understandings of well-being and ill-being in young lives, Peru. In V. Johnson, R. Hart, & J. Colwell (Eds.), *Steps to engaging young children in research: The guide* (Vol. 1, pp. 75–81). Retrieved from http://www.bernardvanleer.org/files/Steps-to-Engaging-Young-Children-in-Researchvol-1.pdf

Cuskelly, M. (2005). Ethical inclusion of children with disabilities in research. In A. Farrell (Ed.), *Ethical research with children* (pp. 97–111). New York, NY: Open University Press.

Darbyshire, P., MacDougall, C., & Schiller, W. (2005). Multiple methods in qualitative research with children: More insight or just more? *Qualitative Research, 5*(4), 417–436.

Denzin, N. K. (2004). The art and politics of interpretation. In S. Nagy Hesse-Biber & P. Leavy (Eds.), *Approaches to qualitative research: A reader on theory and practice* (pp. 447–472). New York, NY: Oxford University Press.

Denzin, N. K., & Lincoln, Y. (2005). Introduction: The discipline and practice of qualitative research. In N. K. Denzin & Y. Lincoln (Eds.), *Handbook of qualitative research* (3rd ed., pp. 1–32). Thousand Oaks, CA: SAGE.

Derry, C. (2005). Drawings as a research tool for self-study: An embodied method of exploring memories of childhood bullying. In C. Mitchell, K. O'Reilly-Scanlon, & S. Weber (Eds.), *Just who do we think we are? Methodologies for self-study in education* (pp. 34–46). London, England: Routledge.

Eder, D., & Fingerson, L. (2003). Interviewing children and adolescents. In J. A. Holstein & J. F. Gubrium (Eds.), *Inside interviewing: New lenses, new concerns* (pp. 33–53). Thousand Oaks, CA: SAGE.

Einarsdóttir, J. (2007). Research with children: Methodological and ethical challenges. *European Early Childhood Education Research, 15*(2), 197–211.

Engel, S. (2005). Narrative analysis of children's experience. In S. Green & D. Hogan (Eds.), *Researching children's experience: Approaches and methods* (pp. 199–216). London, England: SAGE.

Fielding, M. (2001). Students as radical agents of change. *Journal of Educational Change, 2,* 123–141.

Freeman, M., & Mathison, S. (2009). *Researching children's experiences.* New York, NY: The Guilford Press.

Gabel, S. L., & Connor, D. J. (2008). Theorizing disability: Implications and applications for social justice in education. In W. Ayres, T. Quinn, & D. Stovall

(Eds.), *The handbook for social justice in education* (pp. 377–399). New York, NY: Routledge.

Graham, A., Powell, M., Taylor, N., Anderson, D., & Fitzgerald, R. (2013). *Ethical research involving children.* Florence, SC: UNICEF Office of Research—Innocenti.

Gray, A. (2003). *Research practice for cultural studies.* Thousand Oaks, CA: SAGE.

Gray, C., & Donnelly, J. (2013). Unheard voices: The views of traveller and non-traveller mothers and children with ASD. *International Journal of Early Years Education, 4*(21), 268–285.

Gray, C., & Winter, E. (2011). Hearing voices: Participatory research with preschool children with and without disabilities. *European Early Childhood Education Research Journal, 19*(3), 309–320.

Grieshaber, C. (2001). Equity issues in research design. In G. MacNaughton, S. A. Rolfe, & I. Siraj-Blatchford (Eds.), *Doing early childhood research: International perspectives on theory and practice* (pp. 136–146). Philadelphia, PA: Open University Press.

Hart, R. A. (1992). *Children's participation. From tokenism to citizenship.* Florence, SC: UNICEF International Child Development Centre.

He, M. F., Chan, E., & Phillion, J. (2008). Language, culture, identity, and power: Immigrant students' experience of schooling. In T. Huber-Warring (Ed.), *Growing a soul for social change: Building the knowledge base for social justice* (pp. 119–144). Charlotte, NC: Information Age.

Hendry, P. M. (2007). The future of narrative. *Qualitative Inquiry, 13*(4), 487–498.

Hennessy, E., & Heary, C. (2005). Exploring children's views through focus groups. In S. Green & D. Hogan (Eds.), *Researching children's experience: Approaches and methods* (pp. 236–252). London, England: SAGE.

Haegele, J., & Hodge, S. (2016). Disability discourse: Overview and critiques of the medical and social models. *Quest, 68*(2), 193–206.

Hill, M. (2005). Ethical considerations in researching children's experiences. In S. Green & D. Hogan (Eds.), *Researching children's experience: Approaches and methods* (pp. 61–86). London, England: SAGE.

Hogan, D. (2005). Researching the child in developmental psychology. In S. Green & D. Hogan (Eds.), *Researching children's experience: Approaches and methods* (pp. 22–41). London, England: SAGE.

Holt, L., Lea, J., & Bowlby, S. (2012). Special units for young people on the autistic spectrum in mainstream schools: Sites of normalisation, abnormalisation, inclusion, and exclusion. *Environment and Planning A, 44,* 2191–2206.

Hopkins, E. A. (2008). Classroom conditions to secure enjoyment and achievement: The pupils' voice. Listening to the voice of every child matters. *Education 3–13, 36*(4), 393–401.

Johnson, V., Hart, R., & Colwell, J. (2014a). *Steps to engaging young children in research. Volume 1: The guide.* Retrieved from http://www.bernardvanleer.org/files/Steps-to-Engaging-Young-Children-in-Research-vol-1.pdf

Johnson, V., Hill, J., & Sapko, P. (2014b). Listening to smaller voices in Nepal. In V. Johnson, R. Hart, & J. Colwell (Eds.), *Steps to engaging young children in research. Volume 1: The guide* (pp. 82–84). Retrieved from http://www.bernardvanleer.org/files/Steps-to-Engaging-Young-Children-in-Research-vol-1.pdf

Keat, J. B., Strickland, M. J., & Marinak, B. A. (2009). Child voice: How immigrant children enlightened their teachers with a camera. *Early Childhood Education Journal, 37*(1), 13–21.

Lansdown, G. (2003). The participation of children. In H. Montgomery, R. Burr, & M. Woodhead (Eds.), *Changing childhoods: Local and global* (pp. 273–282). Milton Keynes, England: Open University Press.

Larkins, C. (2014). Children's citizenship and Europe: Learning from the perspectives of marginalised children. In V. Johnson, R. Hart, & J. Colwell (Eds.), *Steps to engaging young children in research. Volume 1: The guide* (pp. 110–114). Retrieved from https://bernardvanleer.org/app/uploads/2016/04/Steps-for -Engaging-Young-Children-in-Research-Volume-1-The-Guide0b91.pdf

Loveridge, J., & Meyer, L. H. (2010). Children and young people with disabilities. In J. Loveridge (Ed.), *Involving children and young people in research in educational settings* (pp. 137–162). Wellington, New Zealand: Ministry of Education New Zealand.

MacNaughton, G., & Smith, K. (2005). Transforming research ethics: The choices and challenges of researching with children. In A. Farrell (Ed.), *Ethical research with children* (pp. 112–123). New York, NY: Open University Press.

McDonald, K. E., Kidney, C. A., & Patka, M. (2013). You need to let your voice be heard: Research participants' views on research. *Journal of Intellectual Disability Research, 57*, 216–225.

McIntyre, D., Pedder, D., & Rudduck, J. (2005). Pupil voice: Comfortable and uncomfortable learnings for teachers. *Research Papers in Education, 20*(2), 149–168.

Messiou, K. (2006). Conversations with children: Making sense of marginalization in primary school settings. *European Journal of Special Needs Education, 21*(1), 39–54.

Mishna, F., Antle, B. J., & Regehr, C. (2004). Tapping the perspectives of children: Emerging ethical issues in qualitative research. *Qualitative Social Work, 3*(4), 449–468.

Moss, J., Deppeler, J., Astley, L., & Pattison, K. (2007). Student researchers in the middle: Using visual images to make sense of inclusive education. *Journal of Research in Special Educational Needs, 7*(1), 46–54.

Noble-Carr, D. (2006). *Engaging children in research on sensitive issues.* Dickson, Australia: Institute of Child Protection Studies.

Oliver, M. (1990, July). *The individual and social models of disability.* Paper presented at the Joint Workshop of the Living Options Group and the Research Unit of the Royal College of Physicians on People with Established Locomotor Disabilities in Hospitals. Retrieved from https://disability-studies.leeds.ac.uk/ wp-content/uploads/sites/40/library/Oliver-in-soc-dis.pdf

O'Kane, C., & Panicker, R. (2014). Exploring street and working children's views and experiences of their rights: India. In V. Johnson, R. Hart, & J. Colwell (Eds.), *Steps to engaging young children in research. Volume 1: The guide* (pp. 105–109). Retrieved from https://bernardvanleer.org/app/uploads/2016/04/ Steps-for-Engaging-Young-Children-in-Research-Volume-1-The-Guide0b91 .pdf

Patton, M. Q. (2002). *Qualitative research & evaluation methods* (3rd ed.). Thousand Oaks, CA: SAGE.

Phelan, S. K., & Kinsella, E. A. (2013). Picture this… Safety, dignity, and voice–Ethical research with children: Practical considerations for the reflexive researcher. *Qualitative Inquiry, 19*(2), 81–90.

Polkinghorne, D. E. (1988). *Narrative knowing and human sciences.* New York, NY: State University of New York Press.

Prout, A. (2011). Taking a step away from modernity: Reconsidering the new sociology of childhood. *Global Studies of Childhood, 1*(1), 4–14.

Punch, S. (2002). Research with children: The same or different from research with adults? *Childhood, 9*(3), 321–341.

Rauscher, L., & McClintock, J. (1996). Ableism curriculum design. In M. Adams, L. A. Bell, & P. Griffen (Eds.), *Teaching for diversity and social justice* (pp. 198–231). New York, NY: Routledge.

Riessman, C. K. (1993). *Narrative analysis.* Newbury Park, CA: SAGE.

Rosenbaum, P., & Gorter, J. W. (2011). The "F-words" in childhood disability: I swear this is how we should think! *Child: Care, Health, and Development, 38*(4), 457–463.

Shakespeare, T., & Watson, N. (2002). The social model of disability: An outdated ideology? *Research in Social Science and Disability, 2,* 9–28.

Siebers, T. (2008). *Disability theory.* Ann Arbor, MI: University of Michigan Press.

Tisdall, K. (2012). The challenge and challenging of childhood studies? Learning from disability studies and research with disabled children. *Children & Society, 26*(3), 181–191.

Tisdall, E., & Liebel, M. (2008, June). *Theorising children's participation in "collective" decision making.* Paper for the European Science Foundation Seminar "Children's participation in decision-making: Exploring theory, policy, and practice across Europe," Berlin.

Tisdall, K., & Punch, S. (2012). Not so "new"? Looking critically at childhood studies. *Children's Geographies, 10*(3), 249–264.

Trahar, S. (2009). Beyond the story itself: Narrative inquiry and autoethnography in intercultural research in higher education. *Forum: Qualitative Social Research, 10*(1). Retrieved from http://www.qualitative-research.net/index.php/fqs/article/view/1218/2653

United Nations. (2006). *Convention on the rights of persons with disabilities.* Retrieved from https://www.un.org/development/desa/disabilities/convention-on-the-rights-of-persons-with-disabilities.html

Veale, A. (2005). Creative methodologies in participatory research with children. In S. Green & D. Hogan (Eds.), *Researching children's experience: Approaches and methods* (pp. 253–272). London, England: SAGE.

Watson, N. (2012). Theorising the lives of disabled children: How can disability theory help? *Children & Society, 26,* 192–202.

West, A. (2014). Children and water supply in Tibet: China. In V. Johnson, R. Hart, & J. Colwell (Eds.), *Steps to engaging young children in research. Volume 1: The guide* (pp. 101–105). Retrieved from https://bernardvanleer.org/app/uploads/2016/04/Steps-for-Engaging-Young-Children-in-Research-Volume-1-The-Guide0b91.pdf

Wickenden, M. (2011). "Talk to me as a teenager": Experiences of friendship for disabled teenagers who have little or no speech. *Childhoods Today, 5*(1), 1–35.

Williams, V., James, N., Barclay, M., Stalker, K., Watson, N., & Hudson, K. (2012). *The conversations project. A report to the steering group of the national review of services for disabled children and young people.* Edinburgh, Scotland: The Scottish Government.

PART II

METHODOLOGICAL APPROACHES
TO PARTICIPATORY RESEARCH WITH CHILDREN

CHAPTER 7

PARTICIPATING IN CREATING OPEN SPACES WITH AND FOR CHILDREN

A Kind of Participatory Action Research?

Carlo Fabian and Timo Huber

ACTION, RESEARCH AND PARTICIPATION: FUNDAMENTALS AND DEFINITIONS

More than 20 years ago P. Alderson "claimed, that the view of children and young people had been generally overlooked in research studies" (Alderson, 1995, p. 40, cf. Aldridge, 2016, p. 31). In order to include the general population, and specifically children, in participatory action research, it is necessary to clarify the following points: (a) What is action research? What is participatory research?; (b) Which fundamental concepts are central to conducting participatory action research with children?; (c) What are the foundations of this kind of research approach?; and (d) What ethical aspects need to be considered? In the following, these points will be addressed in a short overview.

Participatory Methodologies to Elevate Children's Voice and Agency, pages 153–179

What Is Action Research? What Is Participatory Research?

Participatory research is grounded philosophically and ethically on the intention to do research *with* people, not *on* people. Participatory research needs to reconcile questions of rigor and professionalism with the idea of sharing power and competencies with research participants. This is the tension between research and application. Fundamentally, one can ask whether social science research (increasingly) has an obligation to address people's real lifeworlds and to render its products and insights closer to these lifeworlds and, probably, more useful to them. In order for this to work, it is central for researchers to acknowledge people as experts of their lifeworlds and fully integrate them into the research process (Reason & Bradbury, 2008c).

Participatory research is not so much a methodology, but rather a research strategy, or perhaps a research paradigm. Participatory research is a matter of decisions regarding the collaboration between research and application, when it is possible and in what form. A key questions concerns decision-making powers: Do researchers or practitioners decide on the approach, or is it both together on an equal footing?

According to Reason and Bradbury (2008b) there are a number of origins and variants on this research strategy: "Action research is a family of practices of living inquiry that aims, in a great variety of ways, to link practice and ideas in the service of human flourishing" (p. 1). However, it's

Figure 7.1   Relationship between participation, action and research (cf. Hughes, 2008, p. 385).

worth mentioning Lewin here as the founder of this research approach. Lewin's starting point was the conviction that theory and practice are closely related, and he aimed at conducting actual experiments with *naturally occurring social groups* (Lewin, 1951). It is difficult to draw a clear line between *action research* and *participatory research*. Additionally, there is *participatory action research* (McDonald, 2012, p. 40; Reason & Bradbury, 2008a, p. 696f). Hughes (2008, p. 385) provides a useful typology for this chapter.

In this chapter we maintain that participatory action research (PAR) "is an umbrella term covering a variety of participatory approaches to action-oriented research" (Kindon, Pain, & Kesby, 2010, p. 1). As will be explained below, QuAKTIV includes all three elements, that is *participation, action,* and *research*. It doesn't make much sense to try to separate them out, as all three work together, complement each other and should be considered as a whole.

Because of this, we use the concept *participatory action research* (Swantz, 2008, p. 31f). According to Reason and Bradbury, "Action research is part of revisioning our worldview, a paradigm shift, changing what we take as knowledge" (cf. Reason & Bradbury, 2008a, p. 698; see also Kindon et al., 2010, p. 14). In this chapter we discuss the fundamental concepts and key elements, as well as ethical aspects, of PAR. On this basis we present the program QuAKTIV and finally analyze it against the backdrop of PAR and the action research paradigm.

FUNDAMENTAL CONCEPTS OF PARTICIPATORY ACTION RESEARCH WITH CHILDREN

Before considering the foundations, processes, and methods of action research, it is important to clarify the fundamental concepts. In order to participate, formulate a concern, or put forward an opinion on equal terms, a person requires certain competencies. These can be fairly general, such as communication competence, rhetorical competence, bravery, perseverance, and so on. In the context of PAR the following deserve a special mention: *participation, empowerment, emancipation,* and *autonomy*. These will be explained briefly here, and discussed and elaborated later in the chapter.

Participation and Emancipation

Participation in the context of urban development, as it is understood and implemented within QuAKTIV, aims at fostering participation in the development process of a quarter or a specific open space. In this process, those in a position of power (local authorities or local administration, schools, etc.)

enable and organize participation. It is thus embedded in and connected to democratic society. Emancipation involves a step-by-step, procedural, and experimental approach, because emancipation aims to increase the participants' self-determination, autonomy, and recognition, and can be considered an open-ended process of learning and liberation, on an individual and collective level (Oehler, Drilling, Käser, & Thomas, 2017). It always involves liberation from power relations on the one hand, and self-liberation on the other.

Empowerment and Autonomy

An empowerment approach means abandoning paternalistic practice and replacing it with a focus on individual care provision, support, and education, with new strategies specific to target groups, aiming at lifeworld activation and mobilization. Empowerment denotes measures, strategies and concepts that increase autonomy and self-determination in the lives of individuals or communities, that enable them to autonomously champion their interests and independently shape their own environment. Participatory projects also give rise to critical and ethical questions (Salge, Glackin, & Polani, 2014). A central question is *who* should be empowered. Empowerment requires engagement with the needs, concerns, and circumstances of disadvantaged, weaker, or vulnerable people (Fabian, Drilling, Niermann, & Schnur, 2017). But who exactly is considered to be disadvantaged, weak, and vulnerable is determined through the normative gazes of professionals. However, this normative gaze "from above" contradicts the empowerment approach, in which the people affected should be the driving force for change (Salge et al., 2014).

In summary, participatory processes can have emancipatory impacts. Participatory processes have a great potential to strengthen individuals—including children—and even communities and groups in learning and development processes. Participation and emancipation have a number of overlaps and commonalities, but they differ in their starting points, in the difference between *empowerment by others* and *self-empowerment*. But often empowerment by others is a precondition for self-empowerment. Both approaches can thus be considered complementary.

What Are the Foundations of Participatory Action Research?

There are various guidelines and checklists that put forward the foundations and principles of PAR. These won't be detailed here, instead we will rely on a simple system that provides an appropriate foundation for reflection, in order to measure and discuss the quality of processes in PAR, and more specifically in QuAKTIV.[1] The basic principles for participatory research are presented here, following Selenger. He describes seven components to the PAR process (as cited in MacDonald, 2012, p. 39):

1. The problem "originates in the community itself and is defined, analyzed, and solved by the community."
2. "The ultimate goal of PAR research is the radical transformation of social reality and improvement in the lives of the individuals involved; thus, community members are the primary beneficiaries of the research."
3. "PAR involves the full and active participation of the community at all levels of the entire research process."
4. "PAR encompasses a range of powerless groups of individuals: the exploited, the poor, the oppressed, and the marginalized."
5. PAR has the "ability to create a greater awareness in individuals' own resources that can mobilize them for self-reliant development."
6. "PAR is more than a scientific method, in that community participation in the research process facilitates a more accurate and authentic analysis of social reality."
7. "PAR allows the researcher to be a committed participant, facilitator, and learner in the research process, which fosters militancy, rather than detachment."

The description of these seven components shows that expectations are high when it comes to PAR. The practicalities will be discussed using the example of QuAKTIV.

WHAT ETHICAL ASPECTS NEED TO BE CONSIDERED?

This section will sketch some specific ethical aspects that should be considered in relation to PAR projects. Ethical aspects are generally important in the context of research, but also more specifically as soon as work is carried out for or with people. Ethics does not prescribe what or how something is to be done, instead it helps us establish principles and rules, and determine which actions are right and which wrong (Manzo & Brightbill, 2010, p. 31). Manzo and Brightball state: "Participation will not, in and of itself, make research 'ethical'; the approach can be deployed to support a researcher's pre-existing agenda, or to further the interests of a particular group" (p. 39).

In addition to existing ethical principles in research, that is "respect for the person," "beneficence," and "justice" (Manzo & Brightbill, 2010, p. 34), Manzo and Brightbill (2010, p. 37f) put forward the following points:

- *Representation*: Everybody's knowledge and concerns matter and are important.
- *Accountability:* to an ethical review board.
- *Social responsiveness*: Researchers must listen and respond to participants' concerns and include their perspectives in the process.
- *Agency*: PAR inspired approaches promote ethical principles by following them in their execution and demanding them from all participants.
- *Reflexivity*: Ethical aspects are important beyond the planning stage, and should be continuously reflected upon.

QuAKTIV was not presented as a PAR project from the very beginning. However, as previously mentioned, QuAKTIV implemented lots of different elements and aspects of PAR. Because of this, it is important to discuss the ethical aspects of this program.

The Participatory Action and Research Program Quaktiv

"QuAKTIV" is shorthand for enhancing activities in the neighborhood (www.quaktiv.ch). Children participated in different project phases, like *analysis of the situation plan, design, and concept* or *realization*. The starting point for the program was an acknowledgement of the lack of communal planning and implementation in previous programs for children and youth, as well as in aspects of the design of place and natural spaces. The University of Applied Sciences and Arts Northwestern Switzerland FHNW, School of Social Work carried out QuAKTIV in collaboration with three pilot communities, as well as various experts in the canton of Aargau (Switzerland) between 2013 and 2016.

The aim was to develop and evaluate adequate processes, methods, and structures in the community, and with the community, in order to gain insights and develop methods that can be made available to a wider public. In the three locations various different methods were tested, dynamic processes realized, supporting structures installed and experiences gained. The participatory processes in QuAKTIV included several methods and can be subsumed as PAR, even though the project was not declared as such from the beginning. The insights acquired were discussed with all stakeholders (children, adults, experts) and the children were part of the decision-making process. Research and practice came very close and certainly profited from one another.

Participation and Participating Children in Quaktiv

The best outcomes are achieved when children participate directly in the design of their lifeworlds, which were areas of open space in the program QuAKTIV. Participation does not mean that adults keep children informed and ask for their ideas, rather it takes place when children help shape and are involved in the decision-making process. Ideally they will even take on some of the responsibility (for example caring for the open space). Within the program QuAKTIV, the working basis for the participatory processes was a project cycle with five working phases, as shown in Figure 7.2.

Throughout all phases, there was a different distribution of the number of participating children (see Table 7.1). Pilot Project 1 and 2 took place in a school context. Pilot Project 3 was about an open space in a neighborhood

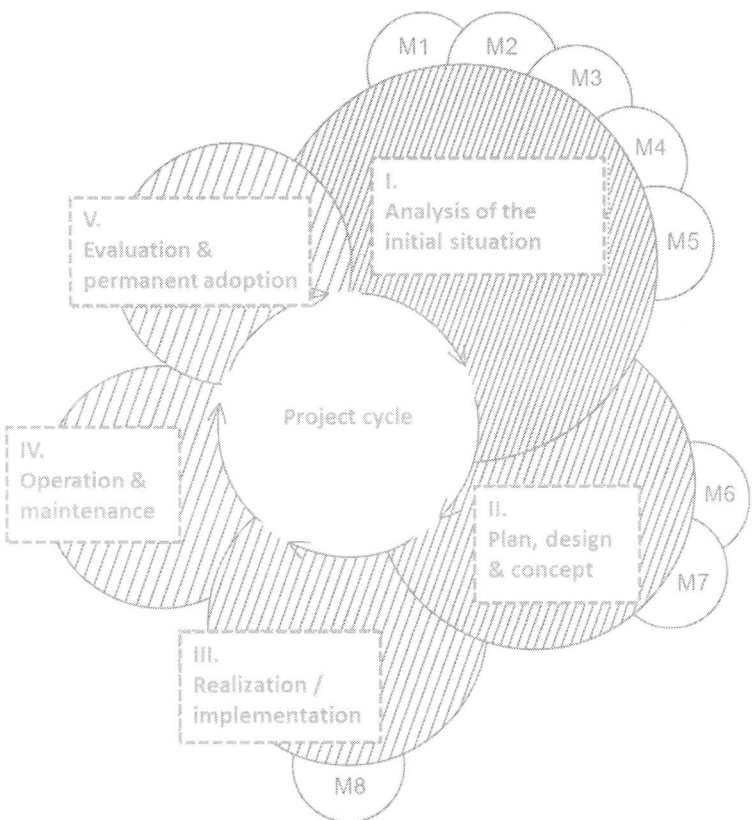

Figure 7.2 Project cycle and working phases (Fabian, Huber, Käser, & Schmid, 2016, p. 19).

TABLE 7.1 Participating Children in QuAKTIV Pilot Projects' Different Working Phrases			
Participating children	Phase I	Phase II	Phase III
Pilot project 1			
Age 4–9	16f / 17m	10f / 8m	15
Age 9–12	24f / 31m	9f / 9m	25
Pilot project 2			
Age 4–6	14f / 17m		
Age 6–9	12f / 8m	11f / 9m	
Age 9–12	24f / 22m	17f / 14m	15
Pilot project 3			
Age 6–8	8f / 5m		
Age 12–13	8f / 9m		

with many children and a lack of play options for the specific age group. The distribution of age and gender was balanced. Several selection procedures were used. In Phase I in Pilot Projects 1 and 2 all children from the school concerned were part of the participation process. In Pilot Project 3, the teachers chose to participate with the respective class. In Phase II and III in Pilot Project 1, the children could show their interest and it was decided by lottery. Pilot Project 2 allowed all interested children to attend across all classes. The children of Pilot Project 3 were not able to participate any further because the project had to be aborted due to lack of funding. For Phases IV and V, it is not possible to provide further information because these phases are outside the QuAKTIV project period.

Particularly during the first three phases, the children's participation played an especially important role, and was decisive for the success of the project, to reap the health benefits and positive factors relating to democracy. The basis for this participation was a four-level model (see Figure 7.3). This model encompasses a theoretical concept, social values, and a concrete working method all at the same time. Within this model, *information* constitutes the first step. It is the basis for all participation processes, but it is usually only a precursor to participation. Real participation begins with active *contribution and collaboration*, when the affected parties become participants, join the discussions, and can co-develop and co-create during idea generation, the planning and the shaping phase. The following step is for participants *to take part in decisions* concerning concrete designs and realization. Finally, under certain circumstances children can be included to take *co-responsibility* for some of the outcomes. The QuAKTIV program sought to foster participation that included all of the above steps, including information and co-design, as well as decision-making. The participatory processes

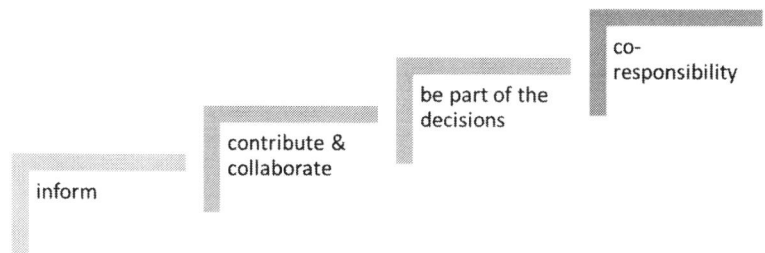

Figure 7.3   Participation steps in QuAKTIV (Fabian et al., 2016, p. 16).

brought about a variety of effects. By contributing and collaborating, the children experienced firsthand that their rights are taken seriously and that they have opportunities to shape their local community.

Through being involved in relevant design and decision-making processes, the children developed competences such as debating, developing their own opinions, and advocating or abandoning their position to reach a compromise as part of a group. Children could also take on different roles and experiment with them. Children emerge as creative individuals and negotiation partners, who can provide important feedback during discussions and negotiations. At the same time, encounters between children, young people, and grown-ups are facilitated, bridging class, gender, age, and cultural differences. In this way children experience that they can take responsibility for their current and future environment, in an age appropriate way.

Participation Methods Used in QuAKTIV

Depending on the working phase, particular methods were used in QuAKTIV. A common theme in all methods is that children share and negotiate their observations, perceptions, recollections, and assessments amongst themselves and, whenever possible, with the experts. The *QuAKTIV-Team* was always actively involved. Part of the team's work was to incorporate a *feedback element* between experts and the children, to ensure that children had really understood the plans and decisions formulated by the experts, and to check if any changes or further developments were necessary. In the following we describe the main methods used (Fabian, Huber, Käser, & Schmid, 2016, S. 38f). The descriptors M1 to M8 correspond with the respective links to the work phases in the project cycle (see Figure 7.2).[2]

The methods M1 to M5 in Phase I "analysis of the initial situation" have the same overarching aim, which is to define, situate, and describe the crucial open spaces in the quarter and community. In communication and exchange with the children concerning their impressions, perspectives, and experiences of the open spaces, we aimed to understand their relevance and meaning. In the *Pin Method* (M1) children are presented with a large map in which they mark the open spaces in their quarter or community (for example informal meeting points or recreational spaces) with a pin and name a specific quality (such as "friendly," "dangerous," etc.). Children sketch what they consider to be the most important places and open spaces with the help of *Subjective Maps* (M2), and then explain and present them in more detail. During the *Walk-through* (M3) children move freely through their quarter or community and comment on the open spaces, their function, and meaning. The outcomes are written down and photographed. In *Auto-Photography* (M4) children choose open spaces (e.g., meeting points, open spaces in nature for retreat and relaxation) and take photographs of them. This creates a collection of impressions, which are then discussed. *Exploration and Assessment* (M5) means that children encounter and assess specifically the open space that is going to be redesigned.

In Phase II, "plan, design, and concept," the children visit the open space as part of the method *Planning-Drawing Workshop* (M6). They then take their ideas and proposals about the redesign process and work it into a drawing. The method *Model Construction* (M7) involves the children building models of the open space, including their ideas for the new design, using handicrafts and natural materials. The models and ideas are then discussed and evaluated and can also be discussed with the planning experts.

The method *Participatory Building Days* (M8) is part of Phase III, "realization and implementation." Here children join in with the building work to transform the open space, for example helping with landscaping, the artistic arrangement of a specific zone or working with plants. It is important that this work involve mostly natural materials, such as sand, stone, and earth.

Organization and Cooperation in the Program and Pilot Projects

It is worth clarifying the program structure of QuAKTIV in order to show which people and institutions were involved. QuAKTIV was organized as a program and included three pilot projects (project level). The project level consisted of the overall management team with responsibility for (a) the implementation of the pilot projects, (b) bringing together the insights gained, (c) experience exchange between the participating communities, (d) communication with external agencies and participants (a workshop took place with planning and design experts, who were not involved in QuAKTIV), and (e) the organization of a final conference with a number of participants from different professional contexts. This responsibility fell to the QuAKTIV team from the University of Applied Sciences and Arts Northwestern Switzerland (FHNW). On a strategic level the team was accompanied by a steering group, made up of representatives from the canton of Aargau.

On the project level in the *pilot communities*, the aim was to implement the project on a local level. The communities led on the local projects and formed a local working group. The community also ensured the collaboration of relevant experts and local departments, employed experts like landscape architects, gardeners, and people to oversee the participation process, and were responsible for diverse aspects of the natural design and open spaces. The communities took part in the knowledge exchange workshops and the final conference, consented to disseminating the experience gained from the pilot project and confirmed their interest in sustainable engagement with the theme within the community. They also needed to ensure that there was plenty of time to enable the participatory process, agreeing to the timetable proposed on the program level.

The main responsibility of the *QuAKTIV team* consisted in the participatory work with the children, as well as ensuring that exchange occurred between the children and other stakeholders. Furthermore, the team conducted a number of evaluations concerning the methods and processes (Schmid, 2015a, 2015b; Schmid, Käser, Huber, & Fabian, 2015) and wrote reports (Huber, Fabian, Käser, & Schmid, 2015a, 2015b). There was also one external evaluation that investigated the participatory procedures and democratic aspects of the project (Widmer & Stutz, 2016).

To sum up, there was intense cooperation and significant exchange between the QuAKTIV leadership, stakeholders in the community and canton, and children. The work processes have enabled and supported the overlapping and complementary areas of action, research, and participation in multiple ways.

Conclusion of the Structures, Processes, and Methods

Based on the experience gained in the QuAKTIV program, the following conditions and foundations need to be in place so that participatory methods with a focus on children can be successfully implemented.

- The responsible parties in the community share the position that children *must* be included in the development projects that concern them. This commitment confirms and emphasizes their belief that decisions that are to be made *for* children can only be made *with* children.
- Children are given a *fair opportunity* to adequately participate during *all the phases* of the project.

- Those responsible see and accept children as *experts in their lifeworlds*.
- Children *help define* which places and open spaces in their environment are considered, inspected, visualized, and discussed.
- Children assess the open spaces, considering various qualities such as presence, attractiveness, opportunities for exchange and for retreat, sport, relaxation, and adventure, but also unease, fear, barriers to access, and so on.
- The children develop their ideas and wishes regarding how these open spaces could be designed according to their needs. They provide ideas on what *activities* they would like to carry out there, what *functions* the spaces should fulfill, what *elements* they would like to include and what materials and plants they prefer.
- The children's discussions, comments, assessments, wishes, and ideas are noted in the form of a report, photos, video, or models. The children thus receive a *documented voice*.
- *Experts* are brought in from the areas of planning and construction, such as landscape architecture, planning, gardening, and so on. This also includes representatives from local administration and government. Thus exchange takes place between *partners*; that is, between *children* and the *adult experts*.
- Other *adults*, such as parents, people working in children and youth services, or educational personnel from schools and kindergartens are included. They work alongside everybody else (e.g., participatory building site) or support the processes and work stages (e.g., model building)

RESULTS AND FINDINGS

In the following section we will present the results and findings from the program QuAKTIV. This is based mainly on the research project itself, evaluation, and further reflection.

Participation and Democracy

The project QuAKTIV has prompted the question: To what extent can children's participation in the development of open spaces contribute to the development or preservation of democracy at a community level? This question is relevant to this contribution because, in our view, the promotion and support of participation for "weaker" or "vulnerable" groups, in this case children, is central to PAR. The more these criteria are fulfilled, the stronger the participative element in a PAR project will be. At the same time ethical aspects will be better addressed. This question has been addressed in the external evaluation mentioned earlier (Widmer & Stutz, 2016). The dimensions that are central to the question of relevance to democracy are (Widmer & Stutz, 2010, p. 20):

- *Inclusion:* reaching the target group and facilitating participation with the chosen methods.
- *Justice:* with regards to the behavior towards participants and non-participants.
- *Quality of the participation:* reaching qualitatively high-value participation processes, in other words deep, continuous participation with a fair, balanced, and unbiased procedure.
- *Transparency:* information for participants and nonparticipants.
- *Socialization:* influence on the behavior and attitudes towards participation among those involved.
- *Embeddedness:* inclusion of the new forms of participation in the existing democratic processes.

When considering PAR it is the first four dimensions that are most relevant, and these will be explored in more detail. The program-specific analysis from Widmer and Stutz (2016, p. 10) shows that the potential for a democratic contribution from participation processes with a group without the right to vote varies (which affects young people specifically), and is dependent on the framework conditions in the community (different structures, values, and traditions). In the following we describe how QuAKTIV implemented the previously described dimensions of democracy (Fabian et al., 2016; Schmid et al., 2015; Widmer & Stutz, 2016).

In order to ensure *inclusion* and thus participation, QuAKTIV chose and implemented age-appropriate and low-threshold methods (cf. above). Creative and activating elements were built into the methodology, such as nonverbal negotiation and exchanges, in order to ensure the inclusion of younger children or those children with speech or articulation difficulties. For this to work it was decisive to use experienced and trained staff to plan and carry out the methods. The staff were familiar with the methods and were experienced with regards to interacting with children and young people, allowing real participation to emerge.

QuAKTIV aimed to ensure that children of all age groups were represented and that a gender balance was achieved within the participation processes. In order to achieve this *justice,* the children were all included during 1 week of the project and then, for example, on another occasion, selected by chance on a quota basis (with the selection criteria being age and gender). According to Widmer and Stutz (2016), it was possible to ensure *justice* within QuAKTIV through good representation, despite not all people in the target groups participating.

QuAKTIV made constant communication and exchange of interim results and decisions to the group of participating children a priority. Processes without prejudging the outcome were continually favored, although always keeping within the constraints imposed by the time and budget available (a new swimming pool was not, for example, considered doable). Following Widmer and Stutz (2016) we achieved *high quality and deep participation*. The fact that the same children were part of the long process also increased the participation quality.

Following Widmer and Stutz (2016) a good level of *transparency* was achieved in most cases. The children were given information about QuAKTIV at various points. The aims and objectives of QuAKTIV were explained in a way that the children understood and the role of those present was clarified. Both the potential of the project and the limitations due to the available budget was made clear. This was done to avoid the creation of false expectations (p. 10).

The results of the evaluation (Widmer & Stutz, 2016) on the dimension *socialization* shows that the participation process had a positive effect on all parties. It was a good experience for the children to be asked for their opinion, and they did not take it for granted. The workshops in which feedback was given about the development of the project led to discussions, which were also experienced positively by the children. They felt that they were taken seriously and valued. Other people involved in the process, such as planning experts and decision-makers took something away from the process, including new insights. Most of the children would take part again in a similar participation process, which suggests at least a short term positive socialization effect (Widmer & Stutz, 2016, p. 11). The children involved in the location with a project that had to be cancelled had a less positive experience.

Participation and Emancipation

The foundation for emancipation is the ability to think rationally and recognize one's own interests. Children need practice to learn to think rationally and to recognize their own interests. In order to get this practice, they are dependent on a social environment that communicates to them that they can, and should, have their own opinions. As the experience in QuAKTIV shows, it is crucial that preconditions (structures and processes) are built or kept that support and enable this process, at home, at school, and in the community. Children can build on this to reflect on their lifeworlds and put forward an idea. The different experiences in the pilot projects from QuAKTIV have shown how important it is for children to have the time and space to interact with their own lifeworlds and the relevant open space to be able to analyze, judge, and formulate ideas for a new design or transformation.

To create this space and time for them, it is necessary to break down the process into small parts, provide feedback sessions, and add more in-depth processes where necessary. It is also key to designing the processes in a way that means children have the best possible opportunity to take part, so that fairness is ensured. These processes and experiences support children on their path to independence, self-efficacy, and finally maturity.

In this context, it is important to consider the level of the individual children who benefit from the opportunity to analyze their lifeworld and their own individual learning process. The kind of political education that comes with participation in a project such as QuAKTIV supports children in their ability to formulate their own projects in the future. In this sense, participative projects aimed at developing open spaces can be seen to lay the foundations for future emancipative projects. Participation is thus a step towards emancipation, as was seen in at least one of the three QuAKTIV projects, in which young people went to their community with wishes after the formal project had finished. Thus, the learning process transforms what is initially a more top-down process (participation in QuAKTIV) into a bottom-up approach.

The meaning of the paired terms *participation and empowerment* is in many ways similar to the paired terms *participation and emancipation*. The move from participation to emancipation is in fact empowerment. Both emancipation and participation are contingent on a certain openness in the process, which is to some extent a gamble that allows experimentation and a willingness to relinquish power. Participatory processes at the level of *contribution and collaboration* lead to experiences and learning processes which give the participants the potential to join other projects at a higher participation level, and thus prepare them to take emancipative action.

The Health Benefits of Participation

The Participatory Process as a Space of Experience

Participation does not only foster democracy and shared outcomes (in the case of QuAKTIV the design and identification of the open space), but also has an *effect on those taking part*. The design process influences, amongst other things, the health prospects and health resources of those participating (Vis, Strandbu, Holtan, & Thomas, 2011, see also Hartung, 2012). In the case of participating children, their experience is manifold: to be heard and taken seriously as a resident with both an opinion and a voice, integration in the community, social contact and exchange with other people and other generations, to experience empathy from grown-ups and other children. If this experience is felt as positive, children's health resources may be strengthened. These resources are to be seen as factors that safeguard or strengthen resilience, that can be fostered and are empirically measurable (Bengel, Meinders-Lücking, & Rottmann, 2009). These factors will be outlined in the following paragraphs.

Empowerment and Autonomy

The concepts of empowerment and autonomy were introduced earlier in the chapter. It should be emphasized again, that the empowerment approach means that researchers and practitioners attempt to depart from paternalistic practices of traditional social work focused on individual care, support and education. Instead such practices attempt to encourage autonomous action and mobilization among the target beneficiaries. The term empowerment describes measures, strategies, or concepts that increase the autonomy and self-determination of individuals or communities, allow them to champion their interests and independently shape their environment (Salge et al., 2014). Here, autonomy is always in a state of tension with decisions taken elsewhere, and also with other individuals or a community. An opportunity for individuals to resolve this tension for themselves promotes health. In participatory projects such as QuAKTIV, children can experience and witness how their concerns and ideas are taken up by the public authorities and planners, and are integrated into the final design. Children experience that they really can build and mold the world around them through a process of exchange, and also negotiation. Through this realization they obtain power and their autonomy is strengthened. It is thus a matter of reconciling the tension between *autonomy* and *community* and experiencing it as malleable.

Self-Efficacy

The concept of perceived self-efficacy is important in the area of health and is well validated. Perceived self-efficacy is defined as the subjective certainty that new or difficult situations or conditions can be overcome based on one's own competences (Schwarzer & Warner, 2013). Such practices go beyond the routine and demand effort and perseverance. The concept differentiates between the perception of the consequence (conviction that the conduct will lead to success) and the perception of competence (expectation about one's self, about one's own ability to carry out the action; Bandura, 1997). There is a strong relationship between perceived self-efficacy and health or healthy behavior (Schwarzer, 2008; Schwarzer & Warner, 2013). Fostering self-efficacy is an important intervention, especially in the context of prevention projects and projects that promote health (e.g., in the area of substance abuse, violence, civil courage). Self-efficacy shows a clear preventative effect in these contexts. The most effective way to strengthen perceived self-efficacy is through *firsthand experience* and observing *behavioral models* (Schwarzer & Warner, 2013, p. 146). Participatory projects such as QuAKTIV provide many such experiences.

Attribution and Locus of Control

A central component of perceived self-efficacy is the idea that, as an individual, one can influence events and conducts—or that one cannot. This locus of control is subdivided into an *internal* and an *external locus of control*. We speak of an internal locus of control when somebody is convinced that the outcome of a particular action is due to their contribution. In contrast, in the case of external locus of control, external circumstances are seen as the cause of the outcome. People with a stronger internal locus of control are often healthier and have a better sense of well-being (Schwarzer & Warner, 2013). When participatory processes in projects like QuAKTIV give children the experience of influencing (controlling) part of their lifeworld and contributing to decisions and solutions, then their internal locus of control is strengthened, along with its method of attribution.

Sense of Coherence

In his model of salutogenesis, A. Antonovsky (1979) places center stage the question of what keeps a person healthy. The concept of the *sense of coherence* emerged in this context and has three components: *Comprehensibility* is an individual's expectation that everyday stimuli, situations, and experiences are orderly and predictable, and that they can be understood as consistent and structured. This allows a consistent picture of the world to be built. *Manageability* describes the expectation that difficult situations or challenges can be solved and overcome. The individual's resources and competences are important here, but also the belief that other people will help master the difficulties. Finally, *meaningfulness* describes the expectation that life is meaningful. The feeling of purpose motivates individuals to face the challenges and manage. A person's sense of coherence correlates with their health. A strong sense of coherence means that a person can react flexibly in the face of challenges and stress, and that they can effectively activate required resources. The decisive influences on the development of the sense of coherence are participation and decision-making processes, such as those that occur within QuAKTIV (Sagy & Antonovsky, 2000).

REFLECTION ON AND DISCUSSION OF QUAKTIV

In this section, QuAKTIV will be discussed in relation to the principles of PAR and to the ethical aspects, leading to some final insights and discussion points.

QuAKTIV and the PAR-Principles

The PAR principles based on the work of Selenger (as cited in MacDonald, 2012, p. 39) will be used for the reflection of QuAKTIV.

Defining the Starting Position as Close to the Lifeworld of the Community Members

The problem "originates in the community itself and is defined, analyzed, and solved by the community" (Selenger, as cited in MacDonald, 2012, p. 39). Depending on the definition and interpretation of *community*, this point is at least partly fulfilled by QuAKTIV. If community is defined not only as the main target group of the program (children in the case of QuAKTIV), but instead includes the wider circle of stakeholders (including residents, administration, and local government departments), it can be argued that the problem originates in the community. Following on from this, experts from the administration and wider practice on the level of the canton (Aargau) have, based on their experience, formulated the aim to address place-making projects with more participatory, ecological, and pedagogical aims for children in a *shared* and *integrated* approach. To achieve this aim, the university was asked to support the canton. The development of the program, including the questions asked and the approach used, was developed in close cooperation with the representatives of the community. However, the children were *not* included in this initial phase. The children were included early on and comprehensively in the framework of the three local projects, and were able to shape the project from the "analysis of the initial situation" phase. But the decision whether or not to pursue QuAK-TIV was made by adults and the administration.

In hindsight, the question arises about to what extent this first principle of PAR can be fulfilled in projects with children. As was discussed earlier, in order for people to become active themselves and to be able to formulate and express concerns, they first need to hold certain competences and have undergone emancipatory processes. These are processes that are more likely to work in the domain of older children and young adults. In this respect the principle may be considered as fulfilled on the level of the children being the target group of the research: In the local projects they were involved early on. In addition, it may be assumed that the participatory processes of QuAKTIV supported the development of a more emancipatory outlook and initiative and thus contributed to the fulfillment of the PAR principle.

Transformation of Society

"The ultimate goal of PAR research is the radical transformation of social reality and improvement in the lives of the individuals involved; thus, community members are the primary beneficiaries of the research" (Selenger, as cited in MacDonald, 2012, p. 39). Radical transformation of social reality is a visionary goal, an indeed a hardly realistic goal for a single, limited project. However, once this goal is transferred to the lifeworlds of the community, with particular emphasis placed on children, QuAKTIV can be seen to make an important contribution to transformation in the social reality in this context. Beyond the realization of new free and play spaces with all their advantages (play, movement, social contacts, etc.), which are all important elements of a transformed social reality, it became evident in the project that the *participatory processes* aiming at the autonomous design of lifeworlds have great potential to empower and support children. Furthermore, QuAKTIV has (in locally specific ways) contributed to the enhancement of participation specific principles, values, and cultures.

If we want to work together to (co-)shape lifeworlds in a responsible way, and through this work transform them, there are certain prerequisites that need to be in place, including empowered and emancipated individuals, participation that also includes weaker members of the community and an understanding of democracy. This is the case even when only small steps are taken, with radical transformation remaining a larger endeavor.

Full and Comprehensive Participation

"PAR involves the full and active participation of the community at all levels of the entire research process" (Selenger, as cited in MacDonald, 2012, p. 39). As was made clear while discussing the other principles, children as the main beneficiaries of the project were closely and intensely involved in the local projects. However, during the preparation and organization work-phases of the program and projects the involvement from the communities was limited to key adult stakeholders.

It is important to carefully consider and negotiate who the community is and which members can and must be present at particular points in time, not only when reflecting back using the PAR principles, but more importantly during the planning and realization of PAR projects. This means that in some cases it will not make sense for particular groups to be involved in certain phases, as in our case, where the children weren't involved from the very beginning. However, this question cannot be answered in any final sense based on principles alone, but needs to be addressed in a situated manner. As powerful adults, we are responsible for including children and allowing them to participate as extensively as possible. This is a challenge as well as an ethical question.

Focusing on Weaker Members of Society

"PAR encompasses a range of powerless groups of individuals: the exploited, the poor, the oppressed, and the marginalized" (Selenger, as cited in MacDonald, 2012, p. 39). Generally speaking, children are among the weakest members of society. Children have rights (see the UN Convention on the Rights of the Child), however, these come into effect in very different ways. In the QuAKTIV projects children were intensively included using new and alternative forms of participation, also alongside key members of their community. The prerequisites for this were the previously discussed points regarding power sharing in questions of design and decision-making.

As mentioned earlier, processes like QuAKTIV, which are broadly supported, methodologically sound, and lasting, may contribute to the strengthening of children. PAR projects like QuAKTIV work beyond their direct impact on the beneficiaries by supporting and developing structures, values, and attitudes (like the importance of democracy and participation). Presumably such impacts can be achieved best when not only considered theoretically, but in a combination of participation–action–research, as exemplified in QuAKTIV.

The Development of Individual Resources and Competencies

PAR has the "ability to create a greater awareness in individuals' own resources that can mobilize them for self-reliant development" (Selenger, as cited in MacDonald, 2012, p. 39). This point was put into practice very successfully in QuAKTIV. As was explained above, specifically children were strengthened through involvement in the participatory processes in QuAKTIV, but also the adults involved and some of the structures, such as the community administration. The development of self-reliance mentioned in the principles is to be understood in the contexts of autonomy, empowerment, and especially emancipation, as discussed previously.

QuAKTIV, as an example of a PAR project, shows that our own resources can be fostered, and that this can be done consciously. The decision to foster resources has positive consequences (e.g., health benefits).

A Realistic Analysis of Social Reality

"PAR is more than a scientific method, in that community participation in the research process facilitates a more accurate and authentic analysis of social reality" (Selenger, as cited in MacDonald, 2012, p. 39). Based on the evaluation and project reports of QuAKTIV, as well as the methods of participation and the construction and organization of the program and its local projects, it can be argued that this research project was conducted in a comprehensive and integrative way, in particular with regards to the realization of open spaces. Not all members of the community were involved (for example, adults without children or older people were not asked to participate). However, the main beneficiaries, children, as well as the other key stakeholders were intensively

In our view, the diversity of participatory methods used within QuAKTIV as well as the commitment to repeatedly feedback intermediate results to all participants, including a process of reflection, led to an authentic analysis of social reality.

Researching on an Equal Footing With Participants

"PAR allows the researcher to be a committed participant, facilitator, and learner in the research process, which fosters militancy, rather than detachment" (Selenger, as cited in MacDonald, 2012, p. 39). We believe that QuAKTIV fulfilled this principle very successfully. As department of social work and part of a university of applied sciences, we are always striving to work close to practice and application, working for and with beneficiaries, with respect and aiming at mutual utility. To enable such work, we always aim to also learn in our projects and to make results available broadly (in publications, presentations, and teaching). We learnt a number of key things in QuAKTIV, including: cooperation with administration, key stakeholders, and children; communication on all levels; implementation of adequate means of participation; design of organizational processes. To work respectfully with children, partners, and other key stakeholders requires the ability to meet them as equals. To work with children on an equal footing is particularly challenging, and this is evidenced purely physically: Adults tower above children. It is important to constantly reflect on dominance and power, to choose methods and communicate adequately, and to permanently reflect and adjust accordingly.

In order to be able to work with all participants in the community on an equal footing (specifically children), become their supporters and learn in the process, it is necessary to clarify values and attitudes in advance. It is only possible to do justice to this principle by recognizing that children are experts in their lifeworlds and showing a willingness to share power and the decision-making process.

QuAKTIV and Ethical Aspects

The ethical aspects introduced earlier in the chapter will be summarized and discussed here in relation to QuAKTIV. The results relating to democratic research are particularly relevant. Although ethical aspects were not as such explicitly addressed in QuAKTIV, they emerged as part of the processes and attitudes, especially as part of decision-making questions, such as: What do we want to do? Which methods should we apply? How do we make sure that all children take part, including disadvantaged children? How do we make sure that the children's wishes and ideas are taken into account? How do we deal with the fact that a power gap exists between children and adults, and yet we want to work on an equal footing? and so on. These questions occupied us on a daily basis.

Looking back at QuAKTIV we believe that key PAR principles like *respect for the person, beneficence,* and *justice* were fundamentally fulfilled, because children as main beneficiaries as well as a wider community (adults, and key stakeholders) participated intensely in the processes, were *often involved in joint decision-making* and *repeatedly reflected* on the processes. By and large, the children profited greatly (attractive, child-friendly, and natural open spaces were created, individuals were strengthened), and the same was true for the community (adults) also (development of attitudes, understanding of the value through participation). QuAKTIV's processes and basic assumptions (everyone is an expert in their lifeworld, also children, and has the right to contribute their insights and desires) contributed to the fulfillment of the principles *representation, social responsiveness,* and *reflectivity.*

QuAKTIV did not have to be examined by an ethical review board at any point (*accountability*). However, ethical concerns were debated and reflected on during all phases with the steering group and internally in the team, thus working towards this principle in a different way. As a stakeholder the steering group lacked neutrality, however it did provide space for reflection. Despite this, ethical aspects were more unconsciously part of the project and the decisions made. In this way QuAKTIV probably contributed to the principle of *agency.* We cannot estimate how large this contribution was.

Is this all sufficient? Upon reflection, we believe that QuAKTIV would have benefitted from a more conscious and explicit consideration of ethics as part of the PAR process. We never clarified how decisions had to be done exactly, who had to be involved, who was allowed to be involved, how to deal with dissent, and what to do when no decision could be reached, etc. It would have been beneficial to have followed more systematic procedures and explicitly ethically guided processes, potentially leading to more (and better) outcomes and impacts.

Insights on the Research Methodology

Projects for and with children present a particular challenge. Children are not adults. It is thus not enough simply to ask them questions or involve them. Children think differently, perceive differently, have different needs, communicate differently, and so on. Precisely because of this it is not only an exciting opportunity, but also a duty, to promote and allow children to participate by putting in place the appropriate attitudes and adequate methods and processes. This is especially the case with regards to questions that affect children's lives, such as the design and transformation of their lifeworld. For this to occur, there are certain preconditions with regards to competences, structures and attitudes, that will either already be in place or can be developed. PAR can be an appropriate measure to achieve this. The central basic concepts and preconditions in PAR are, in our opinion, the previously described points of autonomy, empowerment, and emancipation. In addition to these, the basic principles of PAR and the ethical aspects need to be considered, integrated, and continually reflected upon.

If the requirement for PAR projects is that they *completely* and comprehensively fulfill the previously described PAR principles, then implementation may become difficult, as was shown using the example of the QuAKTIV program. If, however, it is viable to fulfill *as broad a range* of these principles *as possible* and to aim at these principles, then PAR is the appropriate approach. The key question, specifically in work with children, seems to be whether it is more useful to wait until the community and children become active themselves, in order to follow the PAR principle that the concern "originates in the community itself and is defined, analyzed, and solved by the community"; or whether it is more useful to intervene from the outside, from the world of adults and administration, in order to initiate projects that resemble PAR in the attempt to strengthen children and the community.

We strongly believe that the latter option is the better one. The decisive factor is that the prerequisites we mentioned earlier, namely reflections on power and decision competencies, are in place. On balance, projects such as QuAKTIV are a good opportunity to elevate children's voice and agency. Even if aspects of the program could have gone better and further, children gained a voice and the communities were supported in taking a step towards recognizing and integrating this voice.

Questions for Reflection
1. What image of children do you have? What are children like? What can, may, and must they do? What can, may, and must they not do?
2. What are the advantages for children if they are involved in projects that are relevant for them? What are possible obstacles or traps? What are your concerns?
3. Does it make sense to also initiate and support such processes "top down," or should these issues always arise "bottom up," that is from the community?
4. Under what conditions would you commit yourself with conviction to PAR projects with children? Which conditions would have to be fulfilled in order that you would actively participate?
5. Related to your field of action and its contexts:
   a. To what extent do you consider alternative, new forms of democratic participation as an opportunity? Which ones? What are their limits?
   b. How can an attitude be established that regards children as experts in their life worlds?
   c. How can the "powerful people " from politics and administration be supported and enabled to cooperate with children and share power for some decisions?

6. What are other useful and practicable ways to support children and make their living environments child-friendly?

Suggestions for Further Reading

Aldridge, J. (2016). *Participatory research. Working with vulnerable groups in research and practice.* Bristol, England: Policy Press.

Manzo, L. C., & Brightbill, N. (2010). Toward a participatory ethics. In S. Kindon, R. Pain, & M. Kesby (Eds.), *Participatory action research approaches and methods: Connecting people, participation and place* (pp. 33–40). London, England: Routledge.

Reason, P., & Bradbury, H. (Eds.). (2008c). *Action research. Participative inquiry and practice* (2nd ed.). Los Angeles, CA: SAGE.

Stoecker, R. (2003). Are academics irrelevant? Approaches and roles for scholars in community based participatory research. In M. Minkler & N. Wallerstein (Eds.), *Community-based participatory research for health* (pp. 98–112). San Francisco, CA: Jossey-Bass.

Swantz, M. L. (2008). Participatory action research as practice. In P. Reason & H. Bradbury (Eds.), Action research. Participative inquiry and practice (2nd ed., pp. 31–48). Los Angeles, CA: SAGE.

NOTES

1. For further information on the foundations of PAR, see Bergold & Thomas, 2012; Cook (n.d.); Kindon et al., 2010, p. 14; 2012; McTaggart, 1989.
2. The documentation providing practical help for the project includes a description of the methods in German. They are also illustrated, so that they can be understood without words (-> www.quaktiv.ch).

REFERENCES

Alderson, P. (1995). *Listening to children: Children, ethics and social research.* London, England: Barnardo's.

Aldridge, J. (2016). *Participatory research. Working with vulnerable groups in research and practice.* Bristol, England: Policy Press.

Antonovsky, A. (1979). *Health, stress and coping.* San Francisco, CA: Jossey-Bass.

Bandura, A. (1997). Self-efficacy: Toward a unifying theory of behavioral change. *Psychological Review, 84*(2), 191–245.

Bengel, J., Meinders-Lücking, F., & Rottmann, N. (2009). *Schutzfaktoren bei Kindern und Jugendlichen. Stand der Forschung zu psychosozialen Schutzfaktoren für Gesundheit* [Protective factors for children and adolescents. State of research on psychosocial protective factors for health]. (Vol. 35). Köln, Germany: Bundeszentrale für gesundheitliche Aufklärung.

Bergold, J., & Thomas, S. (2012). Participatory research methods: A methodological approach in motion. *Forum: Qualitative Social Research, 13*(1). Retrieved from https://search.proquest.com/docview/1012106019?accountid=14745

Cook, T. (n.d.). *Ensuring quality: Indicative characteristics of participatory (health) research.* Retrieved from http://www.icphr.org/uploads/2/0/3/9/20399575/qualtiy_criteria_for_participatory_health_research_-_cook_-_version_15_08_21__1_.pdf

Fabian, C., Drilling, M., Niermann, O., & Schnur, O. (2017). Quartier und Gesundheit–Klärungen eines scheinbar selbstverständlichen Zusammenhangs [Neighbourhood and health—Clarifications of a seemingly self-evident context]. In C. Fabian, M. Drilling, N. Olivier, & O. Schnur (Eds.), *Quartier und Gesundheit. Impulse zu einem Querschnittsthema in Wissenschaft, Politik und Praxis* [Neighbourhood and health. Impulses for a transversal topic in science, politics and practice] (pp. 9–37). Wiesbaden, Germany: VS Verlag Fachmedien.

Fabian, C., Huber, T., Käser, N., & Schmid, M. (2016). *Naturnahe Freiräume für Kinder und mit Kindern planen und gestalten. Grundlagen, Vorgehensweise und Methoden. Praxishilfe.* [Plan and design nature-oriented open spaces for children and with children. Basics, procedures and methods. A guideline]. Basel, Switzerland: FHNW.

Hartung, S. (2012). Partizipation-wichtig für die individuelle Gesundheit? Auf der Suche nach Erklärungsmodellen. [Participation—important for individual health? In search of explanatory models]. In R. Rosenbrock & S. Hartung (Eds.), *Partizipation und Gesundheit. Handbuch* [Participation and health. Handbook] (pp. 57–78). Bern, Switzerland: Hans Huber.

Huber, T., Fabian, C., Käser, N., & Schmid, M. (2015a). *Naturnahe, kinder- und jugendgerechte Quartier- und Siedlungsentwicklung im Kanton Aargau. Projektbericht Birmenstorf* [Nature-oriented, child- and youth-friendly neighbourhood and settlement development in the canton of Aargau. Project report Birmenstorf]. Basel, Switzerland: FHNW-HSA.

Huber, T., Fabian, C., Käser, N., & Schmid, M. (2015b). *Naturnahe, kinder- und jugendgerechte Quartier- und Siedlungsentwicklung im Kanton Aargau. Projektbericht Herznach* [Nature-oriented, child- and youth-friendly neighbourhood and settlement development in the canton of Aargau. Project report Herznach]. Basel, Switzerland: FHNW-HSA.

Hughes, I. (2008). Action research in healthcare. In P. Reason & H. Bradbury (Eds.), *Action research. Participative inquiry and practice* (2nd ed., pp. 381–393). Los Angeles, CA: SAGE.

Kindon, S., Pain, R., & Kesby, M. (2010). Introduction—Connecting people, participation and place. In S. Kindon, R. Pain, & M. Kesby (Eds.), *Participatory action research approaches and methods—Connecting people, participation and place* (pp. 1–5). London, England: Routledge.

Lewin, K. (1951). Field theory in social science: Selected theoretical paper (D. Cartwright, Ed.). New York, NY: Harper & Row.

MacDonald, C. (2012). Understanding participatory action research: A qualitative research methodology option. *Canadian Journal of Action Research, 13*(2), 34–50.

Manzo, L. C., & Brightbill, N. (2010). Toward a participatory ethics. In S. Kindon, R. Pain, & M. Kesby (Eds.), *Participatory action research approaches and methods: Connecting people, participation and place* (pp. 33–40). London, England: Routledge.

McTaggart, R. (1989). 16 tenets of participatory action research. Retrieved from http://www.caledonia.org.uk/par.htm

Oehler, P., Drilling, M., Käser, N., & Thomas, N. (2017). Soziale Arbeit und Stadtentwicklung—Emanzipation als neue Leitperspektive? [Social work and urban development—Emancipation as a new guiding perspective?]. In P. Oehler, N. Käser, M. Drilling, J. Guhl, & N. Thomas (Eds.), *Emanzipation, Soziale Arbeit und Stadtentwicklung. Eine programmatische und methodische Herausforderung* [Emancipation, social work and urban development. A programmatic and methodological challenge] (pp. 11–32). Opladen, Germany: Budrich UniPress.

Reason, P., & Bradbury, H. (2008a). Concluding reflections: Whither action research. In P. Reason & H. Bradbury (Eds.), *Action research. Participative inquiry and practice* (2nd ed., pp. 695–707). Los Angeles, CA: SAGE.

Reason, P., & Bradbury, H. (2008b). Introduction. In P. Reason & H. Bradbury (Eds.), *Action research. Participative inquiry and practice* (2nd ed., pp. 1–10). Los Angeles, CA: SAGE.

Reason, P., & Bradbury, H. (Eds.). (2008c). *Action research. Participative inquiry and practice* (2nd ed.). Los Angeles, CA: SAGE.

Sagy, S., & Antonovsky, H. (2000). The development of the sense of coherence: A retrospective study of early life experiences in the family. *International Journal of Aging and Human Development, 51*(2), 155–166.

Salge, C., Glackin, C., & Polani, D. (2014). Empowerment—An introduction. In M. Prokopenko (Ed.), *Guided self-organization: Inception. Emergence, complexity and computation* (Vol. 9; pp. 67–114). Berlin, Germany: Springer.

Schmid, M. (2015a). *Ergebnisse Abschlussevaluation Birmenstorf* [Results final evaluation Birmenstorf]. Basel, Switzerland: FHNW-HSA.

Schmid, M. (2015b). *Ergebnisse Abschlussevaluation Herznach* [Results final evaluation Herznach]. Basel, Switzerland: FHNW-HSA.

Schmid, M., Käser, N., Huber, T., & Fabian, C. (2015). *Naturnahe, kinder- und jugendgerechte Quartier- und Siedlungsentwicklung im Kanton Aargau. Bericht Zwischenevaluation in Birmenstorf und Herznach* [Nature-oriented, child- and youth-friendly neighbourhood and settlement development in the canton of Aargau. Interim evaluation report in Birmenstorf and Herznach]. Basel, Switzerland: FHNW-HSA.

Schwarzer, R. (2008). Modeling health behavior change: How to predict and modify the adoption and maintenance of health behaviors. *Applied psychology, 57*(1), 1–29.

Schwarzer, R., & Warner, L. M. (2013). Perceived self-efficacy and its relationship to resilience. In S. Prince-Embury & D. H. Saklofske (Eds.), *Resilience in children, adolescents, and adults* (pp. 139–150). New York, NY: Springer.

Selenger, D. (1997). *Participatory action research and social change.* New York, NY: Cornell University.

Swantz, M. L. (2008). Participatory action research as practice. In P. Reason & H. Bradbury (Eds.), *Action research. Participative inquiry and practice* (2nd ed., pp. 31–48). Los Angeles, CA: SAGE.

Vis, S. A., Strandbu, A., Holtan, A., & Thomas, N. (2011). Participation and health—A research review of child participation in planning and decision-making. *Child and Family Social Work, 16,* 325–335.

Widmer, T., & Stutz, M. (2016). *Evaluation des Demokratiebeitrags von QuAKTIV. Schlussbericht zur externen Evaluation des Demokratiebeitrags neuer Partizipationsformen in drei Pilotprojekten des Programms "QuAKTIV—Naturnahe, kinder- und jugendgerechte Quartier- und Siedlungs-entwicklung im Kanton Aargau"* [Evaluation of the democratic contribution of QuAKTIV. Final report on the external evaluation of the democratic contribution of new forms of participation in three pilot projects of the programme "QuAKTIV—Nature-oriented, child and youth-friendly neighbourhood and settlement development in the canton of Aargau"]. (Vol. 16). Zürich, Switzerland: Universität Zürich.

CHAPTER 8

CHILD MENTORS, VIRTUAL TOURS, AND ADULT PROTÉGÉES

Young Children's Experiences With Tablet Devices

Colette Gray, Jill Dunn, Pamela Moffett, and Denise Mitchell

ABSTRACT

This chapter reports findings from a multi-method, multi-stage research project designed to shed light on children's familiarity and experiences with digital technology; specifically tablet devices. Nested within the participatory right-based approach and informed by the sociocultural conceptualizations of learning (Vygotsky, 1978), whereby mental processes are viewed as social in origin and mediated through interaction using symbolic representations, such as language and cultural artifacts that have evolved over time, we employed a range of participatory methods to engage young children in the research process. Our new approach, termed a *virtual tour*, acknowledges children's expertise and positions the child as a digital mentor to an adult protégée. Findings from the research are discussed using exemplars from child-led virtual tours.

Participatory Methodologies to Elevate Children's Voice and Agency, pages 181–201

While traditional child-friendly research methods yield important information, they are inherently flawed. Consequently most researchers draw on a range of methods to ensure the rigour, veracity, and integrity of their findings. In our investigation (see Gray, Dunn, Moffett, & Mitchell, 2017) we employed a number of traditional approaches, including classroom observations, focus groups with children, teacher interviews, and parental surveys to determine young children's experience of, access to, and familiarity with digital technology. Despite offering a wealth of data, we sought to delve deeper by actively involving the child in the research process. Having trawled the research literature and been frustrated with current approaches, we developed a method to capture and acknowledge the child's expertise and competence with digital technology by positioning them in the role of digital mentor to an adult protégée. We termed this new approach a *virtual tour*. It is this addition to the toolbox of early years enquiry that informs the current chapter.

To set the study in context, we begin with a brief overview of the burgeoning literature on the role of digital technology in children's lives before considering the need to extend the toolbox of research methods employed by participatory researchers who strive to give prominence to the child's voice.

DIGITAL NATIVES

From birth to adulthood, children in the Western world are immersed in a social and cultural world of technological innovation (Chaudron, 2015; Plowman, Stephen, & McPake, 2010). By the time they start school as many as 70% have gained the skills, knowledge, confidence, and lexicon necessary to engage with a wide range of multi-modal digital tools including laptop computers, smartphones, and tablet devices (Arnott, 2017; Gray et al., 2017). Terms such as swiping, drag and drop, apps, tapping, and cropping are commonly used and understood by young children, many with otherwise limited vocabulary. Such is their proficiency with digital technology that Prensky (2001) concluded it is an innate skill. Without a genetic marker there is of course no evidence to support claims regarding innate technological abilities. Since the field of enquiry is relatively new, Wolfe and Flewitt (2010) point out that further research is warranted to determine how early learning experiences are influenced by technology.

The prominence of digital technology in young children's lives is without dispute. According to a survey by CHILDWISE (2015) as many as 73% of under-fives are estimated to have access to a tablet device or a computer and 1 in 3 preschoolers (35%) use a parent's mobile phone, half of them twice a week or more. Whereas younger children aged between 2–4 tend to play with educational apps, older children aged between 5–7 prefer popular games such as Angry Birds, Club Penguin, and Moshi Monsters or games associated with popular films (Marsh, 2010; 2011). Likewise, an Ofcom report (2017) provided evidence that as many as 21% of 3 to 4 year olds own their own tablet with 83% of children aged between 12 and 15 owning a smartphone. YouTube use appears to increase with age from 37% amongst 3–4 year olds to 87% amongst 12–15 year olds. There are variations in the type of information downloaded by younger children who showed a preference for nursery rhymes, children's films, and cartoons as compared to older children who download games and adult films.

To test understanding and self-confidence with a range of digital technologies amongst 800 children and 2000 adults, Ofcom devised a test that culminated in a digital quotient; akin to an intelligence quotient. The scores achieved by 6 year olds were equivalent to those obtained by 45 year old adults, with 14–15 year olds outperforming all other age groups. This led some researchers to label today's generation of children "Digital Natives," "High Tech Tots," "Millennials," "Nexters," "Generation Y," and "Generation Why" (Berson & Berson, 2010; Prensky, 2001; Zevenbergen, 2007). Labeling tends, however, to denote a homogeneous group and in this instance assumes that all children have the same access to, familiarity with, and expertise in the use of digital technology. Ignoring within and between group differences, these claims have no empirical basis (Buckingham, 2007). While many children appear proficient in the use of technology, others remain dependent on adult support to navigate and access a range of digital devices (Chaudron, 2015; Karagiannidou, 2017). Given the cost of digital devices and toys, many children may have no or limited access to technology at home.

TABLET DEVICES: DIVERGENCE AND CONVERGENCE

The popularity of tablet devices is attributed by researchers to the malleability and portability of touch screen technology which enables children as young as 12–18 months to open, navigate and use touch game and drawing apps (Arnott, 2017; Chaudron, 2015; Merchant, 2009; Ofcom, 2017). Mapping the interactions of infants aged 6 months to 1 year with tablet devices, O'Connor (2017) found that 6 month olds were more attracted by the sounds and images of touchscreens and interacted with them interacted with them more often than with books. By 1 year, they could open an app by touching it and swipe through photos stored on the device. Further support for the notion that children immersed in a technological world develop skills unknown to previous generations comes from a range of studies. Levy (2009), for example, observed children aged 3–5 making sense of digital texts and using them with independence before starting school.

Developing the discourse, in a study of iPad use amongst children aged between 4 and 5, Flewitt, Messer, and Kucirkova (2015) found that children communicated more effectively, collaborated more with their peers, and displayed higher levels of independence, concentration and motivation when using digital devices as opposed to traditional pen and paper approaches to teaching and learning.

Another body of evidence suggests that digital technology has a negative impact on the developing brain (e.g., Ferranti, 2016; Kardaras, 2016). By way of example, it is claimed that exposure to digital technology can diminish important aptitudes such as empathy and concentration and undermine a school's ability to settle pupils (Luckin, 2018). Concern with the impact technology may exert on neural development has led a number of international government agencies (England [Public Health England, 2013]; Canada [Lipnowski & LeBlanc 2012]) to advise parents that children from birth to 2 years of age should have zero or minimal screen time. A caveat, however, is proffered by Choudhury and McKinney (2013) who question the evidence base used to support negative impact theories, describing it as thin and ambiguous. Support for this latter contention comes from a large scale UK study that explored the impact of a variety of digital devices on children's mental health and well-being. The authors (Przybylski & Weinstein, 2017) found that time spent using digital technology has a negligible impact on children's mental well-being. In contrast to negative impact theories, Przybylski and Weinstein report a significant correlation between poor mental well-being and zero exposure to digital technology, whereas moderate use had a small but positive effect on children's mental well-being. Moreover, they argue, opponents ignore the well-documented advantages that digital technology has on the developing brain, such as improvements in multitasking, decision-making, and problem solving. Evidence also suggests that babies aged between 6 and 18 months learn faster from interactive apps with sound and moving pictures than from books (Bedford, Saez de Urabain, Cheung, Karmiloff-Smith, & Smith, 2016). Equally it has the potential to improve a young child's fine motor skills, hand/eye coordination, and visual attention.

Tensions also surround the role of digital technology in children's creative play and in their early years education. Employing highly emotive terms, Palmer (2007) asserts that technology pollutes childhood rendering it "toxic." Concern has also been voiced by Levin and Rosenquest (2001) who believe that electronic devices threaten children's ability to engage in imaginative play. This notion is countered by Kjällander and Moinian (2014, p. 29) and Fleer (2014), amongst others, who note that digital technology can lead to new forms of play with a "positive influence on the content of more traditional forms of play." Similarly evidence suggests that the interaction between the virtual and physical world offers children new opportunities to develop complex imaginative play episodes (Marsh, 2010). Marsh cautions researchers and early years advocates against dismissing the role of the virtual world in children's play. To gain insight into how the virtual world impacts play, she argues, children should be positioned as co-constructors of meaning in the research process. In essence digital and non-digital play should be examined from the child's rather than the adult's perspective.

DIGITAL TECHNOLOGY IN THE EARLY YEARS CLASSROOM

The digital/non-digital binary continues to exert influence on the role of technology in the early years classroom fuelled by two firmly entrenched beliefs. The first premised on the notion that iPads will revolutionize education and provide a panacea to underachievement. According to Kucirkova (2014) proponents of this position have "a tendency to perceive technology, including iPads, as a quick fix solution for outstanding educational problems, without giving due consideration to the idiosyncrasies of individual educational contexts" (p. 1). The adoption of technology by schools has also been described as a hot trend used by schools to attract higher pupil numbers (Clarke & Abbott, 2016; Clark & Luckin, 2013).

The second theory positions traditional classroom resources in opposition to technology rather than on a continuum that offers blended multimodal learning opportunities. Opponents of digital technology believe it undermines rather than enhances classroom teaching and learning (Kay, Benzimra, & Li, 2017). Support for this proposition is typically drawn from a report by the Organisation for Economic Co-operation and Development (OECD, 2015) that noted no appreciable improvement in student achievement in reading, mathematics, or science in countries that have invested heavily in information and communication technologies for education. This large scale report is based on findings that required pupils to respond to test questions using a computer keyboard and mouse. Consequently, they cannot be generalized to touch screen modalities. Worthy of note, however, both hypotheses situate the child as a passive recipient in the learning process rather than as an active participant who exerts their influence on the learning process.

In contrast, another body of research suggests that children are engaged deeply and creatively in story-making apps and shows how tablets can empower children to form new identities as good spellers and good readers (Flewitt et al., 2015). It is also argued that children are more actively engaged, appear more enthused, motivated, and stay on task for longer periods when completing a group task using a tablet then when completing similar tasks independently on work sheets (Fekonja-Peklaj & Marjanovič-Umek, 2015; Gray et al., 2017). Gray et al. (2017) observed children between the ages of 4 and 6 years old working collaboratively to complete tasks by offering problem solving solutions and then calling the teacher to admire their completed efforts on iPad. The same excitement and level and depth of conversation were not apparent when the work was completed individually using pen and paper.

INNOVATIONS IN RESEARCH METHODS: EXTENDING THE TOOLBOX OF ENQUIRY

The veritable explosion of digital technology onto a consumer hungry market was preceded by a new methodological paradigm. Termed the participatory rights-based approach advocated by the United Nations Convention on the Rights of the Child, it challenges researchers to find effective methods to elicit the voice of the child (see Gray & MacBlain, 2015 for a full review). This position was not without challenge. On the one hand, Christensen and James (2000) point out that child-friendly research methods are redundant in research that respects their competence. On the other, researchers who perceive children as competent but as having different abilities to adults have developed a broad spectrum of research tools that afford them a pivotal role in the research process.

Irrespective of their perspective, the vast majority of researchers have drawn on a range of traditional methods of enquiry to address the key aims of their study, many of which are argued to be flawed and position the child as a passive rather active participant with rights. Although this argument is well rehearsed, worthy of mention is the inevitable power differential that typically favors adults in research situations and may inhibit a child's response in question and answer situations. Whilst a number of strategies can be employed to bridge the physical and psychological divide between the adult and child (Gray & Winter, 2011), age differences are a power dynamic that may doubly disadvantage a child. There is also an assumption that young children understand the researcher's questions, have the ability to articulate their response and the confidence to engage in conversation with a stranger (Einarsdóttir, 2007; Clark, McQuail, & Moss, 2003; Punch, 2002). In a number of studies these assumptions are flawed.

Clark (2007) offers a salutary lesson when she reports how her carefully scripted questions about the outdoor provision available to nursery school children aged between 3 and 4 evoked unexpected answers. Asked "if you wish to be by yourself in nursery school where would you go?" children variously replied:

Chrissie: At my Mum's house
Helen: In the playdough
Julie: I'd go back home

Jules: Outside place
Nicholas: I go with my Mum and Dad. I was sitting over there when I saw you
Sally: To the book corner (Shhh)
John: Right here (book corner) (p. 18)

In interview sessions, young children have also claimed to dislike activities that they were later observed enjoying (Einarsdóttir, 2007). It was, however, the adult observer's interpretation that the child was enjoying the activities when they might merely have demonstrated compliance or enjoyed engaging with their peer rather than the activity.

In light of previous research shortcomings, in an evaluation of a multiagency network of services Clark and Moss (2001) developed the Mosaic approach to offer a multi-method, participatory, reflexive, and adaptable approach to listening to children. More recently, Clark (2011) took listening to children to a new level within the Mosaic approach, recognizing that children can use multimodal instruments she included mapmaking, walking tours, photography, and art as a means of capturing their authentic voice and views. Utilizing a similar approach, Chaudron (2015) had a child or child with their parent escort a researcher around their house pointing out their favorite devices and activities. The children aged between 0–8 in seven countries also demonstrated their favorite apps, drew pictures of their favorite digital device (typically a smartphone or a tablet), and were interviewed in a follow-up 1 hour session about their digital preferences. Acknowledging that the interviews were overlong, Chaudron notes that due to problems with participant recruitment the majority of children were from middle class homes with the research conducted within the child's home. No mention was made of the power differential between the child and adult, nor was there an acknowledgment that the presence or absence of a parent might impact the dynamics of the situation.

METHODS

To further extend the toolbox of enquiry we utilized a range of methods with the emphasis placed on developing a child-friendly engagement task that would actively involve the child in the research process. In acknowledgment of the children's expertise and competence with digital technology, they were positioned in the role of mentor to an adult novice protégée. Working individually and in pairs with a researcher, the children led us on a virtual tour of a tablet device. Demonstrating considerable proficiency as they navigated the tablet, they described the apps they most preferred, their experience with mobile technology at home and how tablet devices were used in the classroom. They also shared their thoughts on work presented across modalities and the difficulties they experience. The selected method reflects our commitment to the sociocultural approach that embraces the notion that children's learning is defined by interpersonal, institutional, and sociopolitical circumstances (Vygotsky, 1978).

THE PRESENT STUDY

From more than 100 applicants five primary schools from areas of multiple in the Greater Belfast area (Northern Ireland) participated in this study. The project was funded by the Belfast Regeneration Office under the auspices of the Education Authority. The program focused specifically on the impact of iPad devices on young children's educational experience. After preliminary teacher training, the devices were introduced into Year 1 (4.2–5.10) and Year 2 (5.2–6.10) classrooms with the aim of using technology to engage, enthuse, and motivate young learners. Tablet devices were rolled out into Year 3 (6.2–7.10) classes in each of the participating schools. The study involved principals, teachers, parents, and children. Here we focus on the virtual tour which actively engaged young children in the research process.

Ethical permission was sought from the University Research Ethics Committee, the Education Authority (NI), the participating school principals, teachers, parents, and children at each stage of the research process. The investigation is fully compliant with the European Early Childhood Education Research Association's Ethical Code for Childhood Researchers (Bertram, Formosinho, Gray, Pascal, & Whalley, 2015, p. 3). It was considered essential before involving the children to ensure that they were fully conversant with their right to withdraw at any stage from the research process. In the event, all of the children were keen to be involved and would have stayed on task for much longer than necessary. To protect each child's anonymity, pseudonyms are used throughout.

In each of the five participating schools, four children (2 boys and 2 girls: total = 20) were selected from each Year 1 and 2 class by their class teacher on the grounds that they were of differing educational ability levels and showed an interest in digital devices. Working individually and in pairs children led a researcher on a virtual tour of a tablet device. As they navigated the device, the children (aged between 4.6 and 5.10, in years and months respectively) demonstrated educational apps used to support mathematics and literacy development, explained the differing levels of the apps, their favorite and least favorite app and discussed their experience with varying levels of authority about their experience with digital devices. Each session lasted approximately 15–20 minutes, was recorded, transcribed and analyzed thematically by the research team.

CASE STUDIES

Case Study 1 demonstrates how a child can find greater success with the trial and error approach embedded in a number of numeracy apps that offer increasing/decreasing levels of difficulty than with pen and paper worksheets. Aaron (5.11 years and months) is in the bottom reading and maths set in his Year 2 class. While he understands he is not good at maths and gets the answers wrong on his worksheets, he believes he has a greater chance of success when he completes work on the tablet. Aaron has a slight speech delay and initially points at the screen using mono-symbolic speech. When he realises that he has greater expertise than the researcher his language becomes more fluent and expansive.

Case Study 1: Snakes and Ladders

> **R:** "Hi Aaron, I don't know about iPads but I've been asked to find out. Would you please help me by switching it on and showing me where the apps are? Is that the right word apps?"
> *Aaron starts the iPad, swipes the screen and points to the apps.*
> **A:** "That's an app."
> **R:** "Really, that little thing there?"
> **A:** "Yes b . . . b . . . but . . . its . . . [he points again] . . . bigger inside, it's very big inside. See [taps on the app] . . . its . . . its . . . bigger."
> **R:** "You made that look easy, can I try?"
> *The researcher fails to open the app and Aaron laughs and taps it.*
> **A:** "Tap it see [he opens and points again]."
> *Aaron laughs as the researcher tries again and after several attempts opens the app.*
> **R:** "Well now what do you do with it?"
> **A:** "See you pick a . . . level . . . you play the levels."
> **R:** "What's a level? Can you show me how to play this app Maths 3–5, is it any good? Do you use it in class or at home?"
> **A:** ". . . *mumbles* . . . ok, see you swipe and it opens . . . then . . . p . . . p . . . pick a level. See 1st level is easy stuff, bigger levels do harder stuff. I don't have a tablet at home. I borrow my brother's but he uses it a lot for games all the time."
> **R:** "You did that really well, finding and opening the app. I bet you're really good at your school work."
> **A:** "No, I'm . . . b . . . b . . . bottom set . . . 'cause I'm not . . . g . . . g . . . good at sums and reading. I'm good at my work but I d . . . d . . . do better sums on the tablet."

R: "You find it easier on the tablet than when you have to write the answers down?"

A: "It's easier [on the tablet] 'cause it gives you more chances. When you get it wrong a noise says 'uh uh' and 'try again.' When it's right balloons come up and you pop them . . . worksheets is harder. You get it wrong [sum] and scribble it out and try again and scribble it out and then the teacher gives it a big X and says it's all messy."

R: "Do you rub out the wrong answer?"

A: "No, you're not allowed to rub out and then it gets all messy and it looks stupid."

R: "You have more chances on the tablet to get it right then when you write. Is that why you prefer the tablet?"

A: "Yes I get some right on the tablet so it's better, I don't get sums right on the worksheets. You can go down a level [using the app on the tablet] if it's too hard or up a level if it's too easy and then you get some right. I don't like the worksheets."

R: "Which app do you like best?"

Aaron points to Puppet Pals.

R: "Puppet Pals, is that your favorite? Why do you like it?"

A: "b . . . b . . . because it's my favorite one."

R: "It plays music; does it do that all the time?"

A: Aaron laughs and says "Yeah. Look I can change the color of the background. There are lots of colors, you pick a color and it changes the background." Aaron shows the researcher how to do it. "See it's easy; you can d . . . d . . . do the colors if you want to."

R: "I see you are walking along the street. I suppose you could make up a story."

A: "Yeah, I'm going to the shop to b . . . b . . . buy sweets. Then I'm going to eat all the sweeties. Lollipops, I'll b . . . b . . . buy lots of lollipops. There's another App with a shop with lots of sweeties and you can put them in the b . . . b . . . basket." He opens the App and points to the sweets.

R: "Goodness that an awful lot of sweets. It sounds like a good story but do you have to type it?"

A: "No see you can talk into the computer and then you can hear it again." Aaron records his story and plays it for the researcher.

R: "That's a great story, I think you're very clever, well done and you've taught me a lot about how to use the iPad and the apps and levels. Do you like all the apps or is there one you don't like?"

A: "I d . . . d . . . don't like snakes and ladders because I always lose."

R: "We could play it together; I'm not good at games so you might win."

A: Aaron opens the snakes and ladders app, they play for a few minutes and Aaron wins. He is delighted and laughs and claps his hands shouting "I won, I won."

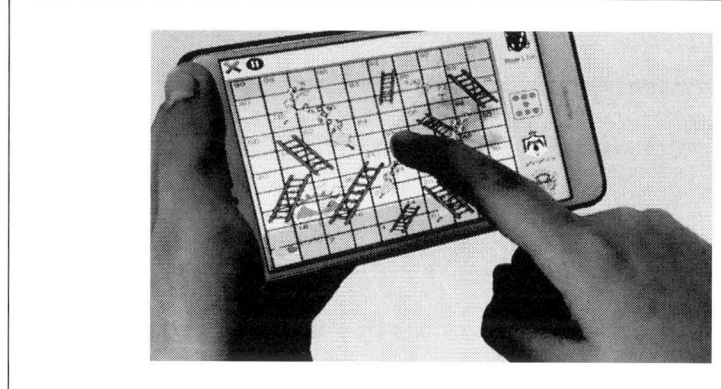

One of the major challenges for teachers, according to Hedegaard (2012), is to gain an insight into the individual needs of children whilst working with the class group and meeting curriculum targets. Although her focus was on engaging children in a range of pedagogical research activities, her suggestion that children be included in discussions concerning their learning is relevant in this instance. Throughout the virtual tour Aaron displayed poor self-regard and low self-efficacy in terms of his written work. Yet as his accomplishments in navigating the tablet were recognized and praised, he became an enthusiastic, patient, and encouraging teacher to his novice protégée. Steeped in technology from an early age, Aaron is a digital native with a sound understanding of the virtual world. Given he lives in an area of endemic social deprivation with the highest level of academic underachievement in Northern Ireland (Perry, 2016), early intervention is essential. Supporting his learning may require a reshaping of his educational experience to position technology as a key modality in his everyday learning. Whilst the factors influencing educational underachievement are complex and multifaceted, schools can operate as a powerful intervening mechanism to reverse established trends as depicted in the schematic illustration included below (Perry, 2016). The challenge for Aaron's class teacher lies in seamlessly integrating technology into the curriculum to encourage active engagement and positive learning experiences across modalities, thus ensuring better educational outcomes.

In Case Study 2, Shannon (a pseudonym) a Year 1 pupil aged 4 years and 8 months demonstrated how her favorite app can be used to plant seedlings in the ground, water them to encourage growth, and once the plant produces fruit, count, pick, and place the tomatoes in the basket presented on screen. The app selected forms part of a series of free online educational resources that the teacher incorporates into her lesson plans and encourages the children to explore and play with during "golden time" (rewarded free play) on a Friday afternoon. Widely-used in primary and early years settings, the golden time strategy is argued to promote good behavior and raise academic standards (Mosley & Sonnet, 2005). Shannon is a confident child with good communication skills. She has limited access to a tablet device at home. She explained, "It's really my mummy's tablet and she doesn't like me using it unless she's there. But if I'm really, really good then I can play with it for 15 minutes." Shannon is excited at the prospect of demonstrating her technical skills.

Case Study 2: Growing Tomatoes

Shannon easily navigates the tablet, locates and opens the app. She explains that this will help show how things grow. Music plays softly in the background as an expanse of earth with bamboo sticks appears on screen with a hand holding a seed. Shannon guides the hand then drops the seeding using a drag and drop approach, the screen hand pats the seed into position. She repeats this process until all the seeds are planted and a watering can appears. Excitedly she describes this part of the process as "magic, it's just magic, wait and see." As she moves the watering can it pours water on top of the seed and green sprouts appear. The more water she aims at the plant the higher and bushier it grows. She continues until all the seeds have sprouted and counts 10 plants. Once all the plants have produced tomatoes a basket appears on screen and she guides the hand to pick each of the tomatoes placing it in the basket whilst counting. Shannon's counting skills are challenged as she concentrates on picking the fruit and explaining what she is doing. Several times she loses the count but concludes that she must have picked 8 tomatoes.

Throughout the activity, Shannon remained focused and enthusiastic. She displayed a strong self-image and considered herself "good" at using tablet devices. To paraphrase Flewitt et al. (2015), children's immersion in digital communication occurs at a critical period in their lives when their emerging identity as competent and effective learners is moulded by the conventions of their social and cultural world.

Shannon explained that the class would use their iPads to take pictures of plants in the school grounds. She commented, "...But that's not until springtime, it's too cold now...and we'll make story books with our pictures in and we can talk the words into our story and Miss XXX [class teacher] says that she'll make our stories into real books to take home." In recognizing the creative potential of digital technology and embedding it into the children's learning experience, Shannon's teacher has developed short and long term goals that meet a large number of targets within the Northern Ireland Foundation Curriculum, including enabling children "to learn in a practical way" (p. 2); developing the fundamental skills of literacy, numeracy and oral communication" (p. 3); bringing the "physical world" (p. 8) into the classroom to extend children's understanding of nature and in relating to the "pupil's immediate and known environment" (p. 2).

Case Study 3 demonstrates children's ability to work collaboratively while involving the novice researcher in the virtual learning experience. It also serves to highlight some of the strategies children use to manipulate technology to their own ends.

Harley and Cody-Lee are in Year 2 of primary school. Aged 5 years and 10 months and 6 years and 2 months respectively, they are best friends. Both are underachieving in maths and literacy and have limited communication skills. Despite being younger, Harley is the more dominant of the two. He takes charge of the tablet and throughout the virtual tour describes the challenges he experiences with written work and how he and Cody-Lee use technology to mask their difficulties.

Case Study 3: Strategic Learning

R: "Is it easy to use an iPad?"

C&H giggle, "It's really easy."

Asked who taught them how to use it, they laugh and say they, "Just knew." Harley opens the device and points out the apps he "hates" including High Frequency Words and Maths apps, describing them as "rubbish" and "really, really hard." Cody-Lee agrees saying "Them sums is hard and the words [high frequency] is hard. We like the games [on the tablet] best." Asked for an example of a high frequency word the boys whisper amongst themselves before correctly identifying "and, the, as." They giggle then ask for Puppet Pal 2 and Cbeebies. Harley clicks on Puppet Pal 2 selects the farm background and tells the researcher that he can put her face into the story. He uses the iPad to take her picture which he circles, crops, and drags onto one of the characters. The boys laugh and talk as they decide on a story to record. Asked if they want to type a title for their story Harley mumbles "...my name." Harvey records a story about the researcher who goes to the farm rides a horse, falls off and lands in poo. The horse runs away and she is "all smelly and stinky." The boys laugh as they both repeat the words "poo, smelly and stinky."

Asked if they could write the story on the tablet rather than record it, Harley says "Yes." He points to a letter writing app and Cody-Lee explains that you have "to use a stylus but... its thick like a crayon... me and Harvey doesn't like writing much." Asked if they prefer to write using the tablet or with a pencil and paper, neither appealed and Harvey replied, "We don't like writing much." In contrast to this finding, other research reports higher levels of motivation, engagement, and better handwriting skills for children using stylus interface technology or pentop technology (Couse & Chen, 2010). It has also been claimed that children are intrinsically motivated to complete computer-related activities and are more focused on tasks presented on screen than on non-computer related tasks (Talley, Lance, & Lee, 1997). Our findings suggest otherwise.

Working in unison, Cody-Lee and Harvey evade writing by using the recording function. Harvey further minimizes his written input into the story by writing his name rather than giving the work a title. The boys have also devised strategies to mask the fact that they are not progressing to the higher maths ability levels expected by their class teacher. Harvey explained, "We're in sets. Me and Cody we just play Levels 1 and 2 then when she [the teacher] comes we pretend we're at 3 and 4 [the boys giggle] and she moves on."

While the relationship between underachievement and social disadvantage is well rehearsed (see for example Perry, 2016; Sharples, Slavin, Chambers, & Sharp, 2011), in colluding to avoid failure Harvey and Cody-Lee are establishing a pattern that may prove detrimental in the longer term.

Yet despite their early learning difficulties both boys show considerable expertise in taking pictures using the tablet, and cropping, dragging, and dropping a picture into their story. They understand the record and delete functions and how to manipulate the various app levels. Arguably, Harvey and Cody-Lee are displaying facets of the *possibility thinkers* described by Craft et al. (2012, p. 1), who positions children as capable and potent users of technology who pose "what if" and "as if" questions. In essence, in electing to circumvent the aspects of the apps they find most challenging the boys demonstrate a different toolbox of skills based on their mastery of technology.

DISCUSSION

The development of the virtual tour approach to actively engage children in the research process offered important insights into each child's familiarity, expertise, and use of mobile technology. Individual differences were noted in their proficiency with educational apps and in their ability to transfer their learning across modalities. Given children are products of their social and cultural environment, the role of the teacher is paramount in providing multiple-cross-modality opportunities to hone young children's early learning skills. This poses a challenge to traditional teaching and learning methods and requires an immersion approach that integrates mobile technology across all subject areas rather than positioning it on the periphery of children's learning. It also necessitates a trained and confident teaching workforce keen to embrace technology in all aspects of the learning environment. Whereas Shannon's teacher encouraged children to take pictures inside and outside the classroom, other teachers confined tablets to table top activities. Access to devices was strictly controlled by teachers and in several cases available only on a Friday afternoon during Golden Time which offers a reward for good behavior across the week. In restricting access to technology, it may be argued, that teachers are limiting children's educational experience. As Gray et al. (2017) contend the inclusion of tablet devices in the learning process offers a powerful teaching tool with the capacity to motivate and challenge young children, expand their perception of the world, and enhance their language and thinking. Moreover, the increased use of mobile technology in classrooms would offer a bridge between the child's experience at home and at school.

According to Perry (2016) there is a need for schools in Northern Ireland to operate as buffers between the child's home circumstances, personal characteristics, and subsequent outcome using all the resources available to them (see Figure 8.1). Despite living in areas of social disadvantage and high social deprivation, each of the four children included in our case studies has access to a range of mobile devices at home including games consoles, smartphones and laptops, and to a wide range of games apps including Super Mario, Angry Birds, Batman, Crayola Color Studio, Pokémon, Princess Fairy Tale Maker, and Frozen. The children also talked about downloading Youtube clips and films to watch in bed or in the car. It is unsurprising therefore that they find it easy to navigate a tablet and demonstrate considerable skill in swiping, dragging, dropping, cropping, taking pictures, and making story books.

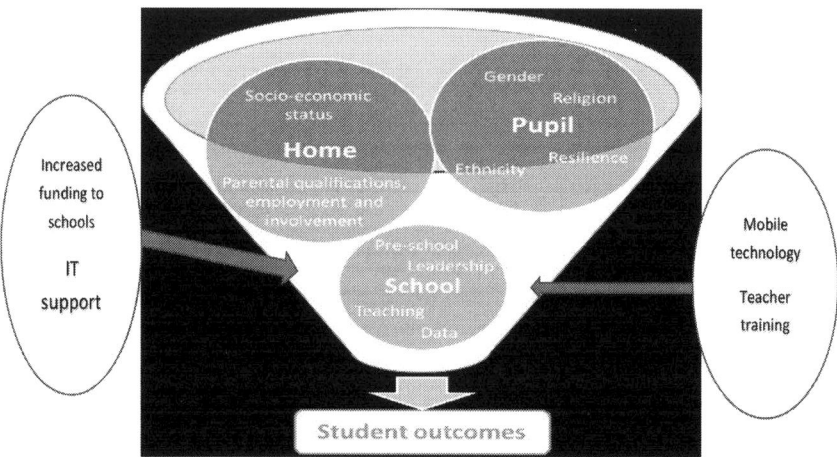

Figure 8.1 Schematic overview: Enabling schools to enable pupils.

In contrast to their proficiency with technology, the boys struggled with worksheets and Aaron, in particular, displayed a sense of low self-esteem and low self-competence. Whereas Harvey and Cody-Lee have devised strategies to mask their underperformance, Aaron described himself as "stupid." In our study, the lack of confidence displayed by boys was particularly evident when they talked about completing work using traditional pen and paper approaches. They understand and can navigate digital technology to their advantage and show confidence, aptitude and self-confidence in their ability to use devices to a level well beyond that of many adults. Given the long tail of underachievement amongst boys in areas of high social deprivation in Northern Ireland (Perry, 2016), it is essential for schools to use enablers to address their attainment including greater flexibility in the delivery of curricular subjects. Moreover, the cost of underachievement to society is high given its impact on a child's self-concept, self-efficacy, and motivation to learn (Retelsdorf, Schwartz & Asbrock, 2015). For example, underperforming boys are at greater risk of anxiety, depression, bullying, and of leaving schools with fewer qualifications than their achieving peers. As Flewitt et al. (2015) note, "digital technologies have a role to play in developing children's identity as effective learners in the classroom, through their potential to offer not only stimulating and varied pathways into literacy but also 'figured worlds' (Holland et al., 1998) that are empowering for young learners in mainstream and special education" (p. 305).

In conclusion, the innovative virtual tour methodology described in this chapter complements and extends existing tools that seek to explore children's experiences of digital technology. The depth of information gleaned using this approach, we argue, would be difficult to equal using any another method. Moreover, this innovation enhances existing methodological approaches and may be used to ensure the rigor of research findings involving children. At this point, the sophistication and evolution of mobile technology continues unabated. It offers an important social and cultural tool that bridges the child's experience at home and school. In harnessing the potential of these devices, teachers can engage children in a more active learning experience that may be tailored to suit their individual needs. Moreover, respecting the rights of the child requires educationalists and educational researchers to investigate how digital artefacts can be immersed throughout the curriculum to offer children a seamless learning experience. Thus empowering children and raising achievement levels.

In the final analysis, from a rights-based, social-constructivist perspective, we argue against the use of terms that label children and suggest they represent a homogeneous group, for example "digital natives." Instead we believe that children have the right to be viewed as individuals with differing levels of expertise, access to and involvement with technology; as demonstrated using the virtual tour approach.

Questions for Reflection

1. Consider the range of technological tools available in your early years setting. How would you use them to (a) promote young children's communication skills?; (b) improve their attention span?; and (c) enhance their motivation for learning?
2. To improve the early years setting, you want to know what children most and least enjoy. What steps would you take to reduce the power differential between adult and child to capture a child's authentic voice?
3. As Harvey and Cody-Lee's teacher, what strategies will you employ to ensure that both boys achieve to the fullest potential?

Suggestions for Further Reading

Arnott, L. (Ed.). (2017). *Digital technologies and learning in the early years.* London, England: SAGE.

Berson, I. R., & Berson. M. J. (Eds.). (2010). *High tech tots: Childhood in a digital world.* Charlotte, NC: Information Age.

Gray, C., Dunn, J., Moffett, P., & Mitchell, D. (2017). *Mobile devices in early learning: Evaluating the use of portable devices to support young children's learning.* Report Commissioned by the Education Authority for Northern Ireland, Belfast, Ireland. Retrieved from http://www.stran.ac.uk/media/media,756133,en.pdf

Luckin, R. (2018). *Enhancing learning and teaching with technology.* London, England: UCL IOE Press.

REFERENCES

Arnott, L. (Ed.). (2017). *Digital technologies and learning in the early years.* London, England: SAGE.

Bedford, R., Saez de Urabain, I. R., Cheung, C. H. H., Karmiloff-Smith, A., & Smith, T. J. (2016). Toddlers' fine motor milestones achievement is associated with early touchscreen scrolling. *Frontiers in Psychology, 7.* Retrieved from https://www.frontiersin.org/articles/10.3389/fpsyg.2016.01108/full?

Berson, I. R., & Berson, M. J. (Eds.). (2010). *High tech tots: Childhood in a digital world.* Charlotte, NC: Information Age.

Bertram, T., Formosinho, J., Gray, C., Pascal, C., & Whalley, M. (2015). *Ethical code for early childhood researchers.* Retrieved from http://www.eecera.org/documents/pdf/organisation/EECERA-Ethical-Code.pdf

Buckingham, D. (2007). *Beyond technology: Children's learning in the age of digital culture.* Cambridge, England: Policy Press.

Chaudron, S. (2015). *Young children (0–8) and digital technology. A qualitative exploratory study across seven countries.* European Commission, Joint Research Centre.

Institute for the Protection and Security of the Citizen. Luxembourg: Publications Office of the European Union.

CHILDWISE. (2015). *The monitor pre-school report 2014: Key behaviour patterns among 0 to 4 Year Olds*. Norwich, England: CHILDWISE.

Choudhury, S., & McKinney, K. A. (2013). Digital media, the developing brain and the interpretive plasticity of neuroplasticity. *Transcultural Psychiatry, 50*(2), 192–2015.

Christensen, P., & James, A. (Eds.). (2000). *Research with children: Perspectives and practices*. London, England: Falmer Press.

Clark, A. (2007). *Early childhood spaces: Involving young children and practitioners in the design process* (Working Paper 45). The Hague, The Netherlands: Bernard van Leer Foundation.

Clark, A. (2011). Multi-modal map-making with young children: Exploring ethnographic and participatory methods. *Qualitative Research, 11*(3), 311–330.

Clark, A., McQuail, S., & Moss, P. (2003). *Exploring the field of listening to and consulting with young children. Exploring the field of listening to and consulting with young children*. Thomas Coram Research Unit. Department for Education and Skills. Research Report RR445. Queen's printer. ISBN 1844780260

Clark, A., & Moss, P. (2001). *Listening to young children*. London, England: National Children's Bureau and Rowntree Foundation.

Clarke, L., & Abbott, L. (2016). Young pupils', their teachers' and classroom assistants' experiences of iPads in a Northern Ireland school: Four and five years old, who would have thought they could do that? *British Journal of Educational Technology, 47*(6), 1051–1064.

Clark, W., & Luckin, R. (2013). *What the research says: iPads in the classroom*. London, England: Institute of Education.

Couse, L. J., & Chen, D. W. (2010). A tablet computer for young children? Exploring its viability for early childhood education. *Journal of Research on Technology in Education, 43*(1), 75–96.

Craft, A., Cremin, T., Burnard, P., Dragovic, T., & Chappell, K. (2012). Possibility thinking: Culminative studies of an evidence-based concept driving creativity? *Education 3-13, 41*(5), 538–556.

Einarsdóttir, J. (2007). Research with children: Methodological and ethical challenges. *European Early Childhood Education Research Journal, 15*(2), 197–211.

Fekonja-Peklaj, U., & Marjanovič-Umek, L. (2015). Positive and negative aspects of the IWB and tablet computers in the first grade of primary school: A multiple-perspective approach. *Early Child Development and Care, 185*(6), 996–1015.

Ferranti, S. (2016). How screen addiction is damaging kids' brains. *VICE*. Retrieved from https://www.vice.com/en_ca/article/5gqb5d/how-screen-addiction-is-ruining-the-brains-of-children

Fleer, M. (2014). *Theorizing play in the early years*. New York, NY: Cambridge University Press.

Flewitt, R., Messer, D., & Kucirkova, N. (2015). New directions for early literacy in a digital age: The iPad. *Journal of Early Childhood Literacy, 15*(3), 289–310.

Gray, C., Dunn, J., Moffett, P., & Mitchell, D. (2017). *Mobile devices in early learning: Evaluating the use of portable devices to support young children's learning*. Report Commissioned by the Education Authority for Northern Ireland, Belfast,

Ireland. Retrieved from http://www.stran.ac.uk/media/media,756133,en.pdf

Gray, C., & MacBlain, S. (2015). *Learning theories in childhood* (2nd ed.). London, England: SAGE.

Gray, C., & Winter, E. (2011). The ethics of participatory research involving young children with special needs. In C. Harcourt, B. Perry, & T. Waller (Eds.), *Researching young children's perspectives* (pp. 26–37). London, England: Routledge.

Hedegaard, M. (2012). Analysing children's learning and development in everyday settings from a cultural-historical wholesome approach. *Mind, Culture, and Activity, 19*(2), 127–138.

Karagiannidou, E. (2017). Children's technology learning journeys. In L. Arnott (Ed.), *Digital technologies and learning in the early years* (pp. 20–31). London, England: SAGE.

Kardaras, N. (2016, August 27). It's 'digital heroin': How screens turn kids into psychotic junkies. *New York Post.* Retrieved from https://nypost.com/2016/08/27/its-digital-heroin-how-screens-turn-kids-into-psychotic-junkies/

Kay, R., Benzimra, D., & Li, J.(2017). Exploring factors that influence technology-based distractions in bring your own device classrooms. *Journal of Educational Computing, 55*(7), 974–995.

Kjällander, S., & Moinian, F. (2014). Digital tablets and applications in preschool—Preschoolers' creative transformation of didactic design. *Designs for Learning, 7*(1), 10–33.

Kucirkova, N. (2014). iPads in early education: Separating assumptions and evidence. *Frontiers in Psychology, 5,* 715.

Levin, D., & Rosenquest, B. (2001). The increasing role of electronic toys in the lives of infants and toddlers: Should we be concerned? *Contemporary Issues in Early Childhood, 2*(2), 242–7.

Levy, R. (2009). 'You have to understand words . . . but not read them': Young children becoming readers in a digital age. *Journal of Research in Reading, 32,* 75–91.

Lipnowski, S., & LeBlanc, C. M. A. (2012). Healthy active living: Physical activity guidelines for children and adolescents. *Paediatric Child Health, 17*(4), 209–10.

Luckin, R. (2018). *Enhancing learning and teaching with technology.* London, England: UCL IOE Press.

Marsh, J. (2010). Young children's play in online virtual worlds. *Journal of Early Childhood Research, 8*(1), 23–39.

Marsh, J. (2011). Young children's literacy practices in a virtual world: Establishing an online interaction order. *Reading Research Quarterly, 46*(2), 101–118.

Merchant, G. (2009). Literacy in virtual worlds. *Journal of Research in Reading, 32*(1), 38–56.

Mosley, J., & Sonnet, H. (2005). *Better behaviour through Golden Time.* London, England: L.D.A.

O'Connor, J. (2017). Under 3s and technology. In L. Arnott (Ed.), *Digital technologies and learning in the early years* (pp. 87–98). London, England: SAGE.

OECD. (2015). *New approach needed to deliver on technology's potential in schools.* Retrieved from http://www.oecd.org/education/new-approach-needed-to-deliver-on-technologys-potential-in-schools.htm

Ofcom. (2017). *Children and parents: Media use and attitudes report.* Retrieved from https://www.ofcom.org.uk/__data/assets/pdf_file/0034/93976/Children-Parents-Media-Use-Attitudes-Report-2016.pdf

Palmer, S. (2007). *Toxic childhood.* London, England: Orion Press.

Perry, C. (2016). *Underachievement: A brief overview.* Research and information briefing note. The Northern Ireland Assembly, Paper 52/16, NIAR 299-16. Retrieved from http://dera.ioc.ac.uk/27348/1/5216.pdf

Plowman, L., Stephen, C., & McPake, J. (2010). *Growing up with technology: Young children learning in a digital world.* London, England: Routledge.

Prensky, M. (2001). Digital natives, digital immigrants. Part 1. *On the Horizon, 9*(5), 1–6.

Przybylski, A., & Weinstein, N. (2017). A large-scale test of the goldilocks hypothesis: Quantifying the relations between digital-screen use and the mental well-being of adolescents. *Psychological Science, 28*(2), 204–215.

Public Health England. (2013). *How healthy behaviour supports children's wellbeing.* London, England: Health & Wellbeing Directorate, Public Health England. Retrieved from https://assets.publishing.service.gov.uk/government/uploads/system/uploads/attachment_data/file/232978/Smart_Restart_280813_web.pdf

Punch, S. (2002). Research with children: The same or different from research with adults? *Childhood, 9*(3), 321–341.

Retelsdorf, J., Schwartz, K., & Asbrock, F. (2015). "Michael can't read!" Teachers' gender stereotypes and boys' reading self-concept. *Journal of Educational Psychology, 107*(1), 186–194.

Sharples, J., Slavin, R., Chambers, B., & Sharp, C. (2011). *Effective classroom strategies for closing the gap in educational achievement for children and young people living in poverty, including white working-class boys.* Centre for Excellence and Outcomes in Children and Young People's Services (C4EO). Retrieved from www.c4eo.org.uk.

Talley, S., Lancy, D., &, Thomas, L. (1997). Children, storybooks and computers. *Reading Horizons, 38.*

Vygotsky L. S. (1978). *Mind in society: The development of higher psychological processes.* Cambridge, MA: Harvard University Press.

Wolfe, S., & Flewitt, R. (2010). New technologies, new multimodal literacy practices and young children's metacognitive development. *Cambridge Journal of Education, 40*(4), 387–399.

Zevenbergen, R. (2007). Digital natives come to preschool: Implications for early childhood practice. *Contemporary Issues in Early Childhood, 8(1),* 19–29.

CHAPTER 9

PERSONAL PUBLIC SERVICE ANNOUNCEMENTS

Collaborating With Young Women Adopted From Foster Care Using Narradrama and an iPad During Arts-Based Narrative Inquiry

Myriam D. Savage

ABSTRACT

This chapter describes an arts-based narrative inquiry in which four young women (ages 16 and 18) who had been adopted from foster care conducted research on matters of self-identity through the use of narradrama and a new drama therapy exercise called the *personal public service announcement*, which is a make-believe PSA created via mask work and a digital design app on an iPad. The chapter examines the psychosocial and developmental challenges of females adopted from foster care, who are seldom represented in adoption research and whose personal stance as youth experiencing adolescent individuation is rarely investigated. Five themes that emerged from this collaborative inquiry, which encourages the exploration of personal stories, are discussed. Additional research may further inform families, social services professionals,

Participatory Methodologies to Elevate Children's Voice and Agency, pages 203–227

educators, and other communities by providing useful data on therapeutic benefits and a method for supporting voices that deserve to be understood.

PROCESSING INEQUITIES IMPOSED ON CHILDREN

My previous job as a drama therapist on a children's inpatient unit (CIP) of a Los Angeles psychiatric hospital introduced me to a predominance of foster care children, ages 5 to 12, who had repeatedly been admitted as patients through Child Welfare Services (CWS). Drama therapy, which is one of the creative arts therapies, is influenced by various schools of thought in psychology, theatre arts, anthropology, and philosophy, among others. Certified drama therapists facilitate groups and work with individuals to enhance psychosocial well-being in clinical, educational, and social justice settings through the intentional use of theatre arts, such as improvisation and role play, and psychology. In my role on the CIP, I became increasingly aware of the psychosocial adjustments these marginalized children were required to make as they experienced, sometimes frequently, the abrupt loss of family, physical home, school, and community.

Given their histories, I wondered about the long-term developmental challenges of a childhood filled with displacement, inconsistencies, interruptions, medication, diagnoses, labels, neglect, abuse, and overall loss, and sought to learn how they would experience the onset of adolescence and individuation. On the unit, I investigated and facilitated ways of supporting their creativity and self-expression in order to alleviate dissociative, disordered, and depressed behaviors by using drama therapy within the time limits of rapid patient turnover in a critical care hospital that relied heavily on psychotropic medications. Eventually, I designed and tested ways to do arts-based narrative research (Clandinin & Connelly, 2000) with marginalized youth who were similar to the patients I had come to know and care about through mutually constructed age-appropriate play (Cabe, 2005; Emerson & Shelton, 2001; Ryan & Nalavany, 2003; Thomson & Hall, 2008; Winnicott, 1971).

THE SOCIALLY SITUATED RESEARCHER: WHY CONDUCT ARTS-BASED NARRATIVE RESEARCH WITH THIS POPULATION?

The literature of foster care and adoption contains little information on child-centered, creatively empowering interventions or research with children. It offers few examples of collaborative methods of generating qualitative data with this special needs population (Ryan & Nalavany, 2003; Smith,

Howard, & Monroe, 2000; Thomson & Hall, 2008), who suffer from behavioral issues that typically stem from the trauma of abusive, neglectful childhoods (Anyon, 2011; Hort, 2000). State and national CWS-funded programs aimed at helping children cope with trauma-filled life narratives, pre- or post-adoption, are largely nonexistent (Anyon, 2011). Feigelman (2005) argues that "adoptees have endured a long history of being demonized and pathologized in the popular and social scientific press" (p. 207). Therefore, more studies with these young people as active research participants and more resources for inquiries that employ specific, child-centered methods in collaboration with children from foster care would not only benefit them, but also inform social service systems and government funding entities regarding best practices to use for these children's well-being.

Narrative inquiry (Clandinin & Connelly, 2000) offers a framework within which I can creatively and authentically collect data *with* young women about their serious issues rather than positioning me in a hierarchical, elevated researcher role, which can impede the relationship's development. For instance, the arts-based narrative approach invites roles of "teller and told" that can be shared (Leitch, 2008, p. 38). This method of inquiry and constructing data offers a natural, albeit novel, fit with the method of drama therapy I use with youth, narradrama (Dunne, 2006; 2009), which is influenced by narrative therapy (White, 1995, 2000). As discussed later in the chapter, narradrama methods aim to re-story problem-saturated self-identifications. Furthermore, collaborative interaction, which is a component of arts-based narrative inquiry and narradrama methods, complements the active role of the "socially situated researcher" (Denzin & Lincoln, 2005, p. 641), which I take on. When doing research with these marginalized young women (referred to here as *participant collaborators*), I consider the following:

> Nothing stands outside representation. Research involves a complex politics of representation. The socially situated researcher creates, through interaction and material practices, those realities and representations that are the subject matter of inquiry. (Denzin & Lincoln, 2005, p. 641)

LOCATING THE SELF IN RESEARCH: ACCOUNTING FOR MY BIASES

My stance as a drama therapist and social science researcher has been personally affected by intergenerational trauma stemming from my French mother's experiences of childhood neglect, abuse, and the inept government childcare system that funneled abandoned youth like her and her four sisters onto farms to be used for child labor during and after World War II in France. Based on my inherited narrative, and previous work in psychiatric units, and because adopted girls' specific challenges are particularly under-represented in the literature, I invited four young women (ages 16 and 18) adopted from Child Welfare Services (CWS) to explore their expertise in self-identity with me by participating in narradrama.

In this chapter, I review the psychosocial concerns of young women adopted from foster care, which must be discerned before embarking on an arts-based narrative project. I also argue for the creative use of digital design applications and narradrama as tools for research with young women adopted from foster care. Lastly, I review this method of inquiry, which I conducted in collaboration with young adopted females by exploring narradrama and a novel digital media application exercise called the personal public service announcement (PPSA). I include aspects of my own personal narrative, which were the result of collaboration and reflection in the course of narrative inquiry.

PSYCHOSOCIAL CHALLENGES FOR ADOLESCENT FEMALES ADOPTED FROM FOSTER CARE

Special Needs Defined

To comprehend the participant collaborator's psychosocial history and the significance of adoption from foster care in the United States, or even the need for appropriate qualitative inquiry specifically devised for this population, it is important to understand the label *special needs*. According to CWS, the categorical term defines youth whose non-White race, ethnicity, older age, sibling group status, sexuality, gender nonconformity, or mental, medical, developmental, or physical disabilities may hinder adoption (Hussey, Falletta, & Eng, 2012). Therefore, the term applies to the majority of youth from foster care.

Approximately 85% of children at any given time who are waiting to be adopted from foster care in the United States are considered to have special needs (Hussey et al., 2012), with 60% to 85% of nearly 500,000 foster youth in the United States meeting the criteria for a psychiatric diagnosis (Grant, 2011). Research has demonstrated that children (age 6 through adolescence) who are categorized as having special needs frequently show "self-defeating, negative behaviors that often do not respond to traditional interventions" (Smith et al., 2000, p. 539). Once adopted, youth from CWS, such as the participants in this research, are disproportionately referred to psychiatric care compared to non-adopted youth outside of social services (Feigelman, 2001; Goldberg & Wolkind, 1992; Sharma, McGue, & Benson, 1998), and their families receive more financial subsidies and clinical, educational, medical, and crisis counseling than other adoptive families (Wind, Brooks, & Barth, 2007).

Relationship to Trauma

The adoption literature reveals that adolescent females, especially those adopted late from foster care, have a propensity for certain psychosocial difficulties that can be evidenced during adolescent individuation. This is typically due to harmful factors that were present before they were removed from their birth families by CWS, or while they were under CWS supervision. In particular, females adopted from foster care experience substantially higher rates of sexual abuse compared to adopted boys or non-adopted girls (Burrow, Tubman, & Finley, 2004; Edmond, Auslander, Elze, & Bowland, 2006; Feigelman 2001; Grotevant et al., 2006; Hussey et al., 2012; Kohler, Grotevant, & McRoy, 2002; Ryan & Nalavany 2003; Smith et al., 2000). According to Hussey et al. (2012), "experiencing sexual abuse may indicate a particularly ubiquitous level of risk for children adopted from the public child welfare system" (p. 278). Post-traumatic stress disorder (PTSD), which may cause physiological changes in the brain and endocrine system, is common in sexually abused foster youth and victims of any type of abuse before age four (Smith et al., 2000). Early childhood abuse, such as the instances identified in this inquiry, may trigger self-blame, a sense of helplessness, and challenging behavior in a person at particular junctures of development. Researchers have correlated these behaviors with repeated and compounded loss and grief experiences—which, if left unresolved and unmourned, can lead to serious psychological and emotional damage (Neil, 2012; Smith et al., 2000).

Specific to adolescent females adopted from foster care, the literature posits that they may be more prone to depression, nonaggressive antisocial behavior (NAASB), PTSD, psychosomatic problems, and intense search ideation for birth parents than adolescent adopted boys (Burrow et al., 2004; Edmond et al., 2006; Feigelman, 2001; Grotevant et al., 2006; Hussey et al., 2012; Kohler et al., 2002; Ryan & Nalavany, 2003; Smith et al., 2000).

DEVELOPMENTAL CONSIDERATIONS IN RESEARCH WITH ADOPTED YOUNG WOMEN

The young women in this study were experiencing mid- and late-adolescent individuation-separation (Erikson, 1968; Winnicott, 1971), which involves the developmentally appropriate, transitional movement toward autonomy. This requires emotional separation from caretakers and personal identity resolution, which is a twofold endeavor for the adopted adolescent, who may become more conscious of childhood trauma while simultaneously identifying and separating from adoptive parents and known or unknown birth parents (Smith et al., 2000). Thus, stages of development that conflate self-identity and adoption awareness in children require substantial relational support. For instance, Van der Kolk (1989) and Cabe (2005) advised against therapies with foster youth that rely solely on cognitive behavioral therapy (CBT) approaches. They argued CBT reinforces the intellectual aspects of brain function but not the midbrain and limbic system, where healing response through active and relational play can be stimulated because emotional and maternal attachment connections to trauma exist there (Cabe, 2005; Van der Kolk, 1989; Winnicott, 1971). Children from foster care who are "stuck with old behaviors" (Cabe, 2005, p. 18) due to PTSD must restore their damaged memory systems through play in order "to learn new behaviors and memories" (Cabe, 2005, p. 18). This also applies to action-based collaborative research that offers therapeutic benefit for adopted populations.

Ryan and Nalavany's (2003) narrative research stresses that "particularly lacking in existing adoption studies is input from the adolescent" (p. 491). Input, an important component of encouraging agency and healthy individuation for this age group, offered adopted participants in their inquiry, the opportunity to disclose their desire for strengthened inner support systems and help in gaining coping skills for ongoing grief and isolation.

INVITING AGENCY THROUGH CREATIVE EXPRESSION AND CONVERSATIONAL INPUT

Notably, an examination of the literature reveals a paucity of studies on adolescent-centered research that could support the adopted adolescent's needs described above. Moreover, few studies have focused on giving voice specifically to adolescent females adopted from foster care (Hussey et al., 2012; Ryan & Nalavany, 2003; Smith et al., 2000; Wind et al., 2007). However, Emerson and Shelton (2001) point to the success of female gender-specific, creative art therapy programs for juvenile offenders who were exposed to domestic abuse and who suffered from PTSD, which is a prevalent condition in girls experiencing long-term institutionalization (Burrow et al., 2004; Cabe, 2005; Edmond et al., 2006; Feigelman 2001; Grotevant et al., 2006; Hussey et al., 2012; Ryan & Nalavany, 2003). In a similar vein, another study (Snow & D'Amico, 2015) of adolescent girls living in a residential group home found that they benefited greatly from art, drama therapy, and public performance, and ascribed this to their "authentic expression,"

(p. 214) of their lived experiences "inside the system" (p. 206) of youth welfare services.

Critical participatory researchers (Huntley & Owens, 2013; Martin,1998 as cited by Reissman & Speedy 2007; Zeller-Berkman, Muñoz-Proto, & Torre, 2016) remain acutely aware of the systems that negatively impact children, as well as the power differentials that can be present in research between adults and youth, and strive to enable the opinions and narratives of their young co-researchers, who are mutually or independently generating data about these systems. Martin addressed the potential of adult input to unfairly bias young participants' data by creating and employing direct scribing (Martin, 1998, as cited by Reissman & Speedy 2007, p. 441), a therapeutic practice method that directly generated data via conversations she had with transition age youth from foster care (TAY), who "felt strongly that child welfare files misrepresented their reality" (Martin, 1998, p. 2, as cited in Reissman & Speedy, 2007). While in conversation with participant collaborators, Martin typed their spoken stories verbatim on a computer screen, then member-checked the text, and eventually published a collection of the narratives that aimed to "amplify muted voices of young people in child protection" (Reissman & Speedy, 2007, pp. 441–442).

Overall, the adoption literature confirms the value of including adolescent perspectives; appropriate discussion of the adoption story by family members, connection to birth mothers, and family acceptance of changing developmental, adoption-related needs were beneficial components of adoptive family counseling. Attention to the inevitable changes in identity development is especially critical for good adoptive parenting, supportive counseling, and for productive research with adopted youth (Bach, 2007; Ryan & Nalavany, 2003; Smith et al., 2000; Von Korff & Grotevant, 2011).

DIGITAL DESIGN APPLICATIONS AS COLLABORATIVE TOOLS IN RESEARCH

Pertinent to this study, which implemented a visual digital animation app on an iPad, Carlton (2014) argues that the relevance of using digital media in creative art therapies and research is that their use reflects current cultural influences and encourages the self-identity of individuals. Also, digital media are typically easily accessed by youth, who may be reticent about self-expression in other forms (Thomson & Hall, 2008). However, Malchiodi (2009) cautions that the use of electronics and apps in creative art therapy could lead to relational client-patient over-distancing due to inadequate tactile stimulation and social interaction, which would be detrimental for children who yearn for connection. Still, Orr (2005) argues that current art therapy trends that use iPads or smartphones can positively facilitate youth because they are accessible to the population. Novy (2003) and Halverson (2010) further maintain that there is a positive correlation between adolescent identity formation and storytelling or personalized narrative construction using digital video; Halverson states, "Identity is concretized through the narratives we tell of our own lives" (p. 2355). In a similar vein, in working with foster care youth to create digitally animated characters and games, Austin (2010) proposes that "adolescents may gain psychological relief because the image [digital character] functions as a container to hold affect" (p. 202). Therefore, Austin and the results of this study support the developmental needs of marginalized youth from foster care by providing therapeutic mirroring and containment via expressive play interventions using digital apps. This also occurs through relationships that use playful action, expressive arts, and symbolic metaphor that may parallel much needed and appropriate mother-child connectivity (Cabe, 2005; Leitch, 2008; Savage, 2016; Thomson & Hall, 2008; Winnicott, 1971).

NARRADRAMA AS AGENTIVE METHOD

The drama therapy method narradrama (Dunne, 2009) is influenced by postmodern, narrative therapy (White, 1995, 2000) approaches that use language as an externalizing tool to negotiate and separate problem-saturated identities from the whole person. Narradrama adds the use of theatre and expressive arts to its method, which allows for more embodied perspectives. Psychodramatic concepts such as *concretization* (Dunne, 2009) invite participants to enact something physically or portray a restraining thought or idea symbolically with expressive arts and body movement, which allow problem or preferred thoughts to become more clearly felt and cognitively understood. Narradrama exercises such as the PPSA help differentiate preferred self-identity from problem(s) through concrete actions.

The eight-step narradrama method used in this inquiry (described below) invites role play, role reversal, and expressive arts in witnessed environments, which supports children's developmental processes and avoids power differentials between facilitator and participant collaborator. For example, when employed in a group home with adolescent females in foster care, narradrama intervention techniques have been shown to successfully aid identity formation and group collaboration (Dunne, 2004). One exercise in particular, which is relevant to this study, is the "self-commercial" (Dunne, 2009, p. 184), which invites a person to role play the part of a unique product being advertised on television, thereby "re-storying any negative self-images and affirming positive ones" (Savage, 2016, p. 198). Exercises such as this may appeal to young, marginalized populations because they are engaging and fun, and offer personal agency.

The PPSA Exercise

A novel therapeutic exercise used in this research, the PPSA, combines the format of a public service announcement (PSA), which usually involves voicing expertise on a socially relevant topic, and Dunne's (2009) afore-mentioned self-commercial, with the added component of a plaster or face paint self-mask. Previous to this study, to explore the potential of using digital media tools in research that focused on self-identity for adopted youth (Savage, 2015), I adapted Dunne's self-commercial exercise (using digital video and computer editing) for a narrative study I conducted with five early adolescent males who were members of an adoption support group. All of the editing and data generated were my responsibility. In contrast, research using the PPSA exercise allows participant collaborators hands-on, facile interaction with art making, role play, editing, and data generation through the use of an iPad and a digital design app that animates their self-masks with their own words (Savage, 2016).

Creating self-masks from plaster or face paint quickly advanced the relational aspect of this inquiry. As part of making the PPSA, the process required trust between the participant collaborator and me, because while applying the materials to the person's face, it was essential that I remain sensitive to her psychological and physical comfort levels (Dunn-Snow & Joy-Smellie, 2000). In previous research and during this study, self-masks offered anonymity and a way to externalize or safely distance internalized negative issues, and thereby avoid re-traumatization while creatively addressing pressing current problems or past trauma (Dunn-Snow & Joy-Smellie, 2000). Landy (1986) argues that masks allow a person to express a new identity that arises from a group, a social role, or conflicting issues or dreams.

By helping these young women create animated, verbal self-masks using an app, I wanted to avoid any triggers that could further marginalize them. Therefore, we followed a safe guideline making certain that "the PPSA is not a platform for pitching, selling or advertising oneself as a valuable, attractive type of product" (Savage, 2016, p. 198), which might further *other* a person into the category of special needs. An objective of this exercise was to offer participant collaborators a safe, fun way to voice their personal narratives about lived experiences that involved adoption and foster care through protected anonymity, collaborative relationship with a facilitator, agency, and the opportunity to be witnessed as they announced their expertise on self-identity via drama therapy.

METHOD

Narrative inquiry is both a product of and a method to study personal stories (Clandinin & Connelly, 2000; Creswell, 2013), and arts-based methods that safely initiate the journey to answer the research question are helpful when collaborating with young people who have trauma-filled pasts or limited access to deeply embedded feelings. This was a natural methodological choice for the study, based on documented uses of narrative inquiry with marginalized youth (Clandinin & Connelly, 2000; Gilligan, Spencer, Weinberg, & Bertsch, 2003; Leitch, 2008; Martin, 1998; Rockquemore & Laszloffy, 2003; Thomson & Hall, 2008). Additionally, the method explores the construction of meaning, permits open interpretations of identity, and celebrates multiple perspectives (de Mello 2007; Moen 2006), all of which complement narradrama approaches. Narrative inquiry and therapy follow the theory that "people, places, and things are becoming rather than being" (Clandinin & Connelly 2000, p. 145), and because adolescents are in ongoing states of developmental transition, this method of inquiry seemed particularly appropriate.

Thus, I followed the three-dimensional inquiry guidelines by listening for layers of time, place, and relationship in narratives (Clandinin & Connelly, 2000), and recorded and deciphered emerging story threads while being in relationship with participants who were engaged in sharing. Through this method, I sought to respond to the following three research questions:

1. How do adopted adolescent females who have special needs, as defined by Child Welfare Services, and who have a history of being in foster care, experience creating the PPSA?
2. How does the experience of creating the PPSA contribute to the self-identity of adopted adolescent females who have special needs, as defined by Child Welfare Services, and who have a history of being in foster care?
3. How does the articulated experience of adopted adolescent females who have special needs, as defined by Child Welfare Services, and who have a history of being in foster care contribute to understanding what this population needs on a more global level for the various fields of expressive therapies and other therapeutic, educational, or social support services?

Participants

I invited four adolescent female participant collaborators (with institutional review board approval), referred by a therapist or from an adoption support service organization sponsored by CWS, to participate. The participant collaborators consisted of one White European American, two African Americans, and one Latina-White European American. Two were 16 and two were 18 years old, and they had been adopted from foster care at ages

12 months, 24 months, 30 months, and at age 15. Each lived in a two-parent home in a suburban setting outside Los Angeles. Of the four participant collaborators, three had been separated from birth siblings, and one did not know her birth history. Two were prescribed psychotropic medications for ADHD. One participant collaborator had been in foster care for several years before being adopted by her biological uncle at age 15. One girl, who believed she had been born to her adoptive family, was unexpectedly informed at age 13 that she had been adopted. Another, who had been placed six times before being adopted at age 2, suffered physical assault by her birth mother, which damaged her pancreas and subsequently led to the onset of diabetes at age 14.

Setting: Time and Place

In the course of six home visits with each participant collaborator, narradrama exercises took place in a private or semi-private family room or kitchen, and mask making occurred in a bathroom or kitchen. Sessions took place during a summer month and culminated with a luncheon and screening of the PPSAs with an invited audience, which included a Q&A session led by participant collaborators for family, friends, and social services staff.

Data-Collection Procedures

I was a participant who observed and collaborated in the field with the young women, and adhered to Creswell's (2013) guide for narrative inquiry, which includes reflexivity and having a small sample. Dunne's (2006) eight steps of narradrama were part of the four data-collection phases, and were elements of the six individual sessions per participant and a final, culminating group celebration.

Phase 1: Narradrama Sessions
These sessions, which consisted of a warm-up, central activity, and closure, were consecutive, occurred two or three times a week, and were 60 to 75 minutes in length. I led each session, while a research assistant, who was a registered drama therapist (RDT), took field notes. Three plaster self-masks and one face painting combined with a paper mask were photographed on an iPad and animated via the digital design app Morfo (Anon, 2013). Each session resulted in a 30 second, digitized, and enacted audio narrative based on the session instruction: "Create a mask and monologue that represent your preferred self-identity—who you are." The following

descriptions list the exercises used and the corresponding step(s) from the eight steps of the narradrama method:

- Session 1: Narradrama exercises on environment and self-identity occurred using fabrics, an empty box, or Matryoshka stack dolls; sample television PSAs and the Morfo computer application (Anon, 2013) on an iPad were introduced; narrative-based questionnaires were administered and discussed. This session used narradrama Step 1: New descriptions of identity and environment.
- Session 2: Self-portrait masks with plaster, decoupage, and paint were applied, created and discussed, making certain of participant comfort levels. This session employed narradrama Steps 3 and 5: possibility extension and personal agency.
- Session 3: A writing exercise, "Story of Myself," was facilitated and discussed. Masks were painted, embellished, and completed. Script writing and improvisation were introduced. The session ended with a discussion. This session made use of narradrama Steps 1, 4, and 5: new descriptions, externalizing choices, and personal agency.
- Session 4: The narradrama restorative hand drawing (hand tracing) exercise was done, in which a positively attributed self-portrait was created and discussed. The mask was worn, explored with physical movement, and photographed via Morfo application. Sample scripts of actual PSAs were practiced. Participants were invited to write or record an autobiographical life story to bring to the next session. This session made use of narradrama Steps 5, 6 and 7: personal agency, alternative story, and re-story.
- Session 5: Their PPSA scripts were completed. Participants rehearsed and recorded their PPSAs via Morfo, ending with a discussion. This session made use of narradrama Steps 1, 2, and 7: new descriptions, externalize the problem, and re-story.
- Session 6: The participant and I viewed the finished PPSA on the iPad. Final interviews were recorded and gift certificates given to the participant. This session made use of narradrama Step 8: ritual and reflection.
- Witnessing session: Participant collaborators invited family members, friends, and social workers to view PPSAs on a large screen in a performance and luncheon venue. A guided discussion of the exercise followed, and viewers completed questionnaires. Certificates of research completion, finished self-masks, and copies of the recorded PPSAs were presented to participant collaborators in gift boxes, along with letters of thanks to participating families. This session made use of narradrama Step 8: ritual and reflection (Savage, 2016).

Phase 2: Interview Method

I used the adapted life story interview (Atkinson, 1998) during the final recorded interview, which invited participant collaborators to disclose their narratives more freely as I guided open-ended conversations based on the collaborative experience of making the PPSA.

Phase 3: Member Checking and Reflective Witnessing

Upon viewing the PPSA, participant collaborators and their families and social workers served as reflective witnesses for triangulation. Member checking of narrative data occurred throughout, which affirmed the participant collaborator's voice and how or what she wanted to express.

Phase 4: Listening Community or Peer Review

A "listening community" (Gilligan et al., 2003) or peer review was consulted on the transcribed texts from the conversations recorded during the six visits, which provided constructive insight and triangulation of resulting thick data.

Analysis and Synthesis

I generated thick description by transcribing the final session's recorded interviews, the semi-structured recorded interviews from other sessions, and the PPSA audio-video data. I included the autobiographical life stories written by participants as part of data. Member checking occurred throughout the transcription phase and afterward when discussing PPSAs and the invited screening, with Q&A responses from the audience. My initial step in data analysis, *portraiture* (Lawrence-Lightfoot & Davis, 1997; see p. 193 for method), allowed me to compose and contextualize scenes from collaborative research experiences and the environment, while providing reader information on participants' personal and social histories as well as my personal predisposition and biases during our meetings. Detailed storied portraits (not included in this chapter), which shaped and defined the data and captured the essence of the young women at the time, prepared me for more analysis of their expressed truths using Gilligan et al.'s (2003) listening guide. Thus, Lawrence-Lightfoot and Davis's (1997) qualitative narrative method of portraiture helped contextualize initial data about participant collaborators.

Post portraiture, I used the listening guide (Gilligan et al., 2003), which entailed doing *I-poems* (explained below) that functioned as succinct units of data (Saldana, 2009) for further, deeper analysis in order to cull themes. The listening guide's sequential "listenings" (Gilligan et al., 2003, p. 159)— a method originally devised for research with adolescent girls—consist of four steps that offer "a way of systematically attending to the many voices embedded in a person's expressed experience" (p. 157).

1. Listening for plot by reading and rereading transcribed text with added insight from peer reviewers (Gilligan et al., 2003, pp. 159–161).
2. Creating I-poems by focusing on the speaker's voice, isolating underlined I pronouns within each passage along with the verb and important words at first, until finally honing a poem-like format via a two-step iteration method resulting in streamlined passages and stanzas that evolve into minimally worded lines (pp. 159–164).
3. Listening for contrapuntal voices by rereading interviews and identifying and sorting out different strands in the stanzas that relate to the research question with color-coded underlining of each "*voice*" (p. 159) until the transcript begins to provide a visual way (pp. 164–165) of showing the relationship of voices on the page and the meaning behind the words for potential counterpoints.
4. Composing an analysis and synthesizing meaning to research questions. This final step requires pulling all the themes together from in vivo portrait accounts (an added component I chose to contribute for thick data) and I-poems, and determining their connection to the research question (p. 168).

Additionally, the PPSA audiovisuals (embedded in this chapter) were analyzed by Bach's (2007) method of constructing visual narrative composites following the three-dimensional inquiry (Clandinin & Connelly, 2000) of observing place, time, and relationship using inward, backward, and forward perspectives. I devised an additional step—a form of imaginal dialogue (McNiff, 2008) and doubling (Moreno, 1985)—in which I dialogued with the audiovisual components of the PPSA data and assessed in-vivo remarks that best contextualized them (included in this chapter accompanying the PPSAs) and epitomized their meaning. I then member-checked my interpretations for further clarity with each participant collaborator.

Issues of Trustworthiness: Validation Strategies

As a guide for generating extensive data that ensures a more collaborative approach with youth, I followed Creswell's (2013) "validation strategies" (p. 250) for narrative inquiry, such as prolonged engagement and persistent observation. I kept a journal and field notes, and triangulated data to avoid and include bias, using various sources for "corroborating evidence'" (Creswell, 2013, p. 251), such as my research assistant's notes and participant interviews, artwork, and questionnaires. Member checking, peer review, and supervision provided researcher reflexivity throughout. I embedded my own narrative in the inquiry in order to check subjectivity, and transparency, credibility, and to create thick description from our mutually constructed narratives to provide context, rigor, and depth.

RESULTS

The intent of this research was to discover how adolescent females who had been adopted from foster care and defined as having special needs experienced narradrama and making the PPSA. The research also asks whether creating the PPSA contributes to identity awareness, and whether it offers information on participants' needs. Five prevalent themes emerged from data analysis of interviews and the PPSAs. Results are presented by describing the themes and subsequent in vivo remarks that emerged from the data.[1]

Themes

Each themed section also includes an example of the first iteration of an I-poem (Gilligan et al., 2003) that I created from transcribed interviews with each participant collaborator in order to better listen to her voice and intent. Finally, the PPSAs (inclusive of my own) follow this section. Each person is referred to by a pseudonym she chose that correlates to the favorite color she used to make the PPSA self-mask. The themes are:

1. Self-expression and creativity.
2. Self-identity, or who I am and how I like to identify myself.
3. Adolescent independence, or how I want to live my life.
4. Self-love, or how I accept myself.
5. Survival that contends with being stuck, or what I do with loss.

Self-Expression and Creativity
Self-expression directly pertained to the initial research question: How do adopted adolescent females who have special needs, as defined by Child Welfare Services, and who have a history of being in foster care, experience creating the PPSA?

Participant collaborators' statements on this theme included the following: "I always wanted to tell my story," "Freedom of expression," "I get to let someone know how I feel," and "It made me not think about some things." Three out of four of the young women stated that they were hesitant about the research process until the second session, which involved plaster or face-paint mask making. Fuchsia's I-poem revealed:

I had to get comfortable and that's what
I did, so
I'm going inside of me—going inside of you with the mask and
then coming out
with words—like kids that are shy to overcome—
kids that are holding things in and can't express to people and
they can express things through the mask
I really, really never told anybody so . . .
I got to let someone know how
I feel.

Self-Identity

The remaining research questions and whether the PPSA contributed to self-identity were connected to the action and discovery of self-expression, which was a conduit to the four other emergent themes revealed in the data. In vivo remarks on self identity include: "I've been struggling with the fact and have asked myself why me?"; "Your family defines who you are"; "I just couldn't feel no way"; and "I just couldn't call a house my home." For example, despite childhood neglect, Purple stated that the PPSA exercise "helps open your eyes" about adoption and who you are. Turquoise's revelation on discovering identity was:

I'm an open book.
I guess it means like everyone just knows who
I am
I don't keep secrets
I guess.
I don't try to do what everyone else does—
I do my own thing.
I guess
I stand out.
I'm different.

Independence

In the midst of processing her friend's untimely death during the research, for instance, one participant collaborator said, "I can talk now and have my own mind." Turquoise remarked, "I'd rather be hated for who I am than to be loved for someone I'm not." She stressed, "I'm strong and independent." Other participant collaborator statements were, "I don't let anybody push me over" and "I'm a big fish in a little pond." Fuchsia's pronouns *I* and *you* interchange in the following I-poem:

I just
I don't let anybody push me over or—like my mom always taught me

you have to be a woman of your word.
You can't just let anybody do
you over and
you just be weak.
You have to be strong about it.
I was adopted.

Self-Love, or How I Accept Myself

The theme of self-love or acceptance was evident with each participant collaborator. Defining herself as a "tomboy," Turquoise remarked that adolescence is about "finding yourself," and admitted, "I'm not perfect, I have flaws." Fuchsia clarified, "I said you have to learn how to love yourself first." For Purple, the feeling of accomplishing tasks was correlated with self-acceptance and identity:

> It was like
> It looks cool
> It's like a little masked
> Me imitating me
> I got the shape of my face—got to steal
> My identity.
> I felt satisfied finishing the mask—finished the
> mask—accomplished—when
> I finish something.

Survival

Remarks about survival and strength coincided: "I'm trying not to trust people," "I was stuck," "I got to keep living my life," "I'm a sailboat that has to sail and never break down and never once fail," "You don't have to be stuck on the foster care stuff," "I've, uhm, been through it," and "It's really important to me—strength." Orange's I-poem expresses how survival corresponds to trust:

> I meet people they have to earn
> My trust.
> I'm trying not to trust people.
> I just—like now
> I'm getting older
> I'm just like, um nah,
> I don't trust you.
> I don't know if it has to do with my birth mom but kinda feels like
> it does.
> I feel like everything is like building up since
> I was little cuz

I kept it in and now
I can like—talk now and have my own mind.

Personal Public Service Announcement Data

Embedded PPSA data are included here with member-checked in vivo statements that epitomize and substantiate the participant collaborator's meaning, which provides more depth in data analysis. URLs are included for PPSA data viewing, inclusive of my own (Green):

- Orange: http://youtu.be/fPs7EF8CfJA
  "I'm starting to. I don't know. That's all I have."
- Turquoise: http://youtu.be/0eL4486qWo8
  "I know some days, it's easier to just give up . . . It's all about finding yourself . . . I meet my own standards."
- Fuchsia: http://youtu.be/MHZ72_3PQeA
  "In school, I ask questions because I want to be sure. I want to know. I want to know what's supposed to be done. Then, I feel for sure."
- Purple: http://youtu.be/y176Eyb0Eok
  "It's all a combination of sibling love, potion, and bunches of fun. I am a sailboat that has to sail and never break down and never once fail."
- Green: https://youtu.be/MWzdyNioj2g
  "I no longer want that role. I define myself."

DISCUSSION

Through this arts-based narrative inquiry, I collaborated with young women to make PPSAs while exploring their sense of identity, particularly during this challenging phase of adolescence. Two central lessons from the study were identified from the five emergent themes pertaining to the research questions. First, narradrama and the PPSA promoted safe, creative self-expression; second, the nontraditional method of doing research *with* participants enabled them to process developmentally appropriate challenges concerning identity in relation to their adoptive histories.

Lessons Learned

Narradrama and the PPSA Promoted Safe, Creative Self-Expression
Participant collaborators were able to design and complete a digitized self-portrait that symbolized and actualized how they wanted to be seen via

the tactile creation of a self-mask and PPSA that afforded self-identification, along with concealment, protection, and even transformation (Dunn-Snow & Joy-Smellie, 2000). For instance, one person stated that the PPSA process allowed her to go "inside" and come out with words, which enabled her to more freely express herself and collaborate. "Externalizing" (Dunne, 2009, p. 184) narradrama tools invited participant collaborators to use art, movement, and creative autobiographical writing and took them outside of themselves in a fun way, evidenced when I applied plaster or face paint during the second session.

Participants Processed Developmental Self-Identification Challenges

Developmental challenges related to adoptive histories and current lived experiences were processed such as childhood abuse, shame, self-acceptance, independence, peer pressure, and personal loss. Therefore, 30-second make-believe PSAs permitted these young women to create roles and speak private thoughts. For instance, individuals reported feeling "different" from school peers and believing that they needed to be "strong," which are common challenges for adopted youth (Cabe, 2005; Edmond et al., 2006; Ryan & Nalavany, 2003). However, by stepping away from the conflict of parents, siblings, school, mourning, and the travails of adolescence during this inquiry, participant collaborators were able to focus on constructing a creative product based entirely on their self-representation. Orange and Turquoise stated the discussion after the invited PPSA screening aided them in processing personal challenges. These processes also offered access to self-preservation via self-identity awareness. For instance, while creating her PPSA and grieving a schoolmate's sudden death, Orange said, "I got to keep living my life."

Limitations of the Study

Narrative inquiry purposely requires a small sample, and therefore generalizability was not feasible; also, constructing representation instead of objectivity was the goal in the re-storying of narratives from transcribed data (Denzin & Lincoln, 2008, p. 7). Furthermore, a qualified research assistant was available to offer additional psychosocial support to youth; however she was not able to attend all 25 meetings, which affected the triangulation of data. Additionally, the participant collaborator, Purple was preparing to attend a state college and chose not to do member-checking or to attend the PPSA screening. Finally, ideally I would have preferred an even more collaborative role in data analysis by the young women who participated.

Implications for Research: Including Young People's Narratives

As discussed by invited family, social services, and the participant collaborators during the invited screening of the completed PPSAs, the use of this exercise may serve as an accessible method of addressing the psychosocial issues of adopted young women by opening up conversations between them and supportive adults (Huntley & Owens, 2013; Von Korff & Grotevant, 2011). This may in turn, enable them to process personal histories and provide them with a sense of security connected to positive identity formation that comes from being unconditionally witnessed by a nurturing parental figure (Leitch, 2008; Thomson, 2008; White, 1995; Winnicott, 1971; Zeller-Berkman et al., 2016). Nurtured witnessing through expressive therapy in research parallels a necessary developmental stage of sharing the potential or transitional space of creativity within a trusting relationship between caretaker and infant (Glaveanu 2011; Leitch, 2008; Winnicott, 1971) and may provide essential therapeutic mirroring by creating opportunities for the adolescent girl who has a history of maternal loss, to be seen and heard in the manner she wants and needs. Further research on creating the PPSA with adopted adolescent girls and other populations will determine its usefulness.

CONCLUSION: REFLECTION

The arts-based narrative method that anchored this inquiry offers a framework of possibility, a way to alleviate adverse and negative effects of childhood maltreatment that informs those who help this population. My mother once asked me to take her to the now-empty farmhouse near Bordeaux, France, where she lived as a ward of the state. There, she shared much of her story about childhood abandonment and abuse, and I listened as she constructed meaning for herself and me. From her story and this inquiry, which offers a method to include young people in research, I learned that the compounding effects of trauma ripen during adolescence and reappear over time (Romeo & McEwen, 2006). An entry in the journal my mother shared with me about her wishes as an adolescent foster child was "that one day, I would be free to do, to say, to express my ideas, my heart—to share with other people, if I could for the rest of my life" (A. Savage, personal communication, December 25, 2012). I believe the desire to freely express oneself is universal, and this inquiry offered me an opportunity for self-discovery and a way to explore the expertise of adopted young women who want to be heard and need to be understood.

Questions for Reflection

1. Barone and Eisner (2012) claim that arts-based inquiry has the ultimate goal of evocation and illumination for its participants, researchers, and audience by bringing us all closer to what can only be represented in creativity—closer to evoking and understanding *feeling* in meaning or data. Considering this, why would you want your research data to be represented in nonquantitative forms such as poems, letters, video diaries, or photo voices? And what does conveying meaning in ways that are not measurable capture in research?
2. What is the connection between technology, expressivity, and research in your opinion? What would be the benefit of applying this triad concept as practice in your own research and with what populations? How would you approach it?
3. "Arts based research is at its deepest level about artistic and aesthetic approaches to raising and addressing social issues" (Barone & Eisner, 2012, p. 57). How is meaningful engagement affected by cultural difference in your research or practice, and how significant to your work are implementing certain materials or even types of questionnaires that consider the personal, cultural, and sociopolitical backgrounds of the children or adults who are your participants and/or collaborators?

Suggestions for Further Reading

Barone, T., & Eisner, E. W. (2012). *Arts based research*. Thousand Oaks, CA: SAGE.

Carlton, N. (2014). Digital culture and art therapy. *Arts in Psychotherapy, 41,* 41–45.

McNiff, S. (2008). Arts-based research. In J. G. Knowles & A. L. Coles (Eds.), *Handbook of the arts in qualitative inquiry* (pp. 29–40). Thousand Oaks, CA: SAGE.

Novy, C. (2003). Drama therapy with pre-adolescents: A narrative perspective. *Arts in Psychotherapy, 30,* 201–207.

Snow, S., & D'Amico, M. (2015). The application of ethnodrama with female adolescents under youth protection within a creative arts therapies context. *Drama Therapy Review, 1*(2), 201–218.

Thomson, P., & Hall, C. (2008). Dialogues with artists: Analyzing children's self-portraits. In P. Thomson (Ed.), *Doing visual research with children and young people* (pp. 147–163). New York, NY: Routledge.

NOTE

1. Examples of narrative data adapted from "Listening to the Voices of Young Women Adopted From Foster Care Through Personal Public Service An-

nouncements" by M. Savage, 2016, *Drama Therapy Review*, 2(2), 203–205. Copyright 2016 by Drama Therapy Review. Adapted with permission.

REFERENCES

Anon. (2013) Morfo Version 2.2.1, i-Pad, i-Phone application. SunSpark Labs. Retrieved from www.morfoapp.com

Anyon, Y. (2011). Reducing racial disparities and disproportionalities in the child welfare system: Policy perspective about how to serve the best interests of African American youth. *Children and Youth Services Review, 33*, 242–253.

Atkinson, R. (1998). *The life story interview.* Thousand Oaks, CA: SAGE.

Austin, B. (2010). Technology, art therapy, and psychodynamic theory: Computer animation with an adolescent in foster care. In C. H. Moon (Ed.), *Materials and media in art therapy: Critical understandings of diverse artistic vocabularies* (pp. 199–213). New York, NY: Routledge.

Bach, H. (2007). Composing a visual narrative inquiry. In J. D. Clandinin (Ed.), *Handbook of narrative inquiry: Mapping a methodology* (pp. 280–307). Thousand Oaks, CA: SAGE.

Burrow, A., Tubman, G., & Finley, G. (2004). Adolescent adjustment in a nationally collected sample: Identifying group differences by adoption status, adoption subtype, developmental stage, and gender. *Journal of Adolescence, 27*, 267–282.

Cabe, N. (2005). Adolescents in foster care: Grounded play therapy. In L. Gallo-Lopez & C. Schaefer (Eds.), *Play therapy with adolescents* (pp. 177–209). Plymouth, England: Jason Aronson.

Carlton, N. (2014). Digital culture and art therapy. *Arts in Psychotherapy, 41*, 41–45.

Clandinin, J. D., & Connelly, M. F. (2000). *Narrative inquiry: Experience and story in qualitative research.* San Francisco, CA: Jossey-Bass.

Creswell, J. W. (2013). *Qualitative inquiry and research design: Choosing among five approaches.* Thousand Oaks, CA: SAGE.

de Mello, D. M. (2007). The language of arts in a narrative inquiry landscape. In D. J. Clandinin (Ed.), *Handbook of narrative inquiry: Mapping a methodology* (pp. 203–223). Thousands Oaks, CA: SAGE.

Denzin, N.K., & Lincoln, Y. S. (2005). Methods of collecting and analyzing empirical materials. In N. K. Denzin & Y. S. Lincoln (Eds.), *The SAGE handbook of qualitative research* (3rd ed., pp. 641–680). Thousand Oaks, CA: SAGE.

Denzin, N. K., & Lincoln, Y. S. (2008). The discipline and practice of qualitative research. In N. K. Denzin & Y. S. Lincoln (Eds.), *Strategies of qualitative inquiry* (pp. 1–8). Thousand Oaks, CA: SAGE.

Dunne, P. (2004). *Exploring narradrama* [Video]. Retrieved from http://www.psychotherapy.net/video/narradrama-pam-dunnewww.psychotherapy.net/video.narradrama-pam-dunne

Dunne, P. (2006). *The narrative therapist and the arts* (2nd ed.). Los Angeles, CA: Possibilities Press.

Dunne, P. (2009). Narradrama: A narrative approach to drama therapy. In D. R. Johnson & R. Emunah (Eds.), *Current approaches in drama therapy* (pp. 172–204). Springfield, IL: Charles C. Thomas.

Dunn-Snow, P., & Joy-Smellie, S. (2000). Teaching art therapy techniques: Mask-making, a case in point. *Art Therapy: Journal of the American Art Therapy Association, 17*(2), 125–131.

Edmond, T., Auslander, W., Elze, D., & Bowland, S. (2006). Effects of child sexual abuse on youth: Signs of resilience in sexually abused adolescent girls in the foster care system. *Journal of Child Sexual Abuse, 15*(1), 1–28.

Emerson, E., & Shelton, D. (2001). Using creative arts to build coping skills to reduce domestic violence in the lives of female juvenile offenders. *Issues in Mental Health Nursing, 22*, 181–195.

Erikson, E. H. (1968). *Identity, youth, and crisis.* New York, NY: Norton.

Feigelman, W. (2001). Comparing adolescents in diverging family structures: Investigating whether adoptees are more prone to problems than their non-adopted peers. *Adoption Quarterly, 5*(2), 5–37.

Feigelman, W. (2005). Are adoptees at increased risk for attempting suicide? *Suicide and Life-Threatening Behavior, 32*, 206–216.

Gilligan, C., Spencer, R., Weinberg, K., & Bertsch, T. (2003). On the listening guide: A voice-centered relational model. In P. M. Camic, J. E. Rhodes, & L. Yardley (Eds.), *Qualitative research in psychology* (pp. 157–172). Washington, DC: American Psychological Association.

Glaveanu, V. P. (2011). How are we creative together? Comparing sociocognitive and sociocultural answers. *Theory and Psychology, 21*(4), 473–492.

Goldberg, D., & Wolkind, S.N. (1992). Patterns of psychiatric disorder in adopted girls: A research note. *Journal Child Psychology Psychiatry, 33*(5), 935–940.

Grant, R. (2011). The mental health needs of children in foster care. *American Academy of Child & Adolescent Psychiatry.* Retrieved from https://www.aacap .org/AACAP/Families_and_Youth/Facts_for_Families/FFF-Guide/Foster-Care -064.aspx

Grotevant, H. D., van Dulman, M. H. M., Dunbar, N., Nelson-Christinedaughter, J., Christensen, M., Fan, X., & Miller, B. C. (2006). Antisocial behavior of adoptees and non-adoptees: Prediction from early history and adolescent relationships. *Journal of Research on Adolescents, 16*, 105–131.

Halverson, E. R. (2010). Film as identity exploration: A multimodal analysis of youth-produced films. *Teachers College Record, 112*(9), 2352–2378.

Hort, K. A. (2000). Is twenty-two months beyond the best interest of the child? AS-FA's guidelines for the termination of parental rights. *Fordham Urban Law Journal, 29*(6). Retrieved from http://ir.lawnet.fordham.edu/ulj/vol28/iss6/6

Huntley, J., & Owens, L. (2013). Collaborative conversations: Adolescent girls' own strategies for managing conflict within their friendship groups. *International Journal of Adolescence and Youth, 18*(4), 236–247.

Hussey, D. L., Falletta, L., & Eng, A. (2012). Risk factors for mental health diagnosis among children adopted from the public child welfare system. *Children and Youth Services Review, 34*(10), 2072–2080.

Kohler, J. K., Grotevant, H. D., & McRoy, R. G. (2002). Adopted adolescents' preoccupation with adoption: The impact on adoptive family relationships. *Journal of Marriage and family, 64*, 93–104.

Landy, R. J. (1986). *Drama therapy concepts and practices.* Springfield, IL: Charles C. Thomas.

Lawrence-Lightfoot, S., & Davis, J.D. (1997). *The art and science of portraiture.* San Francisco, CA: Jossey-Bass.

Leitch, R. (2008). Creatively researching children's narratives through images and drawings. In P. Thomson (Ed.), *Doing visual research with children and young people* (pp. 37–58). New York, NY: Routledge.

Malchiodi, C. (2009). Art therapy meets digital art and social multimedia. *PsychologyToday: The Healing Arts.* Retrieved from http://www.psychologytoday.com/blog/the-healing-arts/200911/art-t

Martin, F. E. (1998). Tales of transition: Self-narrative and direct scribing in exploring care-leaving. *Child and Family Social Work, 3*(1), 1–12.

McNiff, S. (2008). Arts-based research & the spectrum of possibilities. In J. G. Knowles & A. L. Coles (Eds.), *Handbook of the arts in qualitative inquiry* (pp. 1–21). Thousand Oaks, CA: SAGE.

Moen, T. (2006). Reflections on the narrative research approach. *International Journal of Qualitative Methodology, 5*(4), 1–10. Retrieved from https://journals.library.ualberta.ca/ijqm/index.php/IJQM/article/view/4360

Moreno, J. L. (1985). *Psychodrama: First volume.* Ambler, PA: Beacon House.

Morfo. (2013). Version 2.2.1, i-Pad, i-Phone application. *SunSpark Labs.* Retrieved from www.morfoapp.com

Neil, E. (2012). Making sense of adoption: Integration and differentiation from the perspective of adopted children in middle childhood. *Children and Youth Services, 34,* 409–416.

Novy, C. (2003). Drama therapy with pre-adolescents: a narrative perspective. *Arts in Psychotherapy, 30,* 201–207.

Orr, P. (2005). Technology media: An exploration for "inherent qualities." *Arts in Psychotherapy, 32,* 1–11.

Riessman, C. K., & Speedy, J. (2007). Narrative inquiry in the psychotherapy profession: A critical review. In D. J. Clandinin (Ed.), *Handbook of narrative inquiry: Mapping a methodology* (pp. 426–456). Thousand Oaks, CA: SAGE.

Romeo, R. D., & McEwen, B. S. (2006). Stress and the adolescent brain. *Annals of the New York Academy of Science, 1094,* 202–214.

Rockquemore, K. A., & Laszloffy, T. A. (2003). Multiple realities: A relational narrative approach in therapy with Black-White mixed-race clients. *Family Relations, 52*(2), 119–128.

Ryan, S., & Nalavany, B. (2003). Adopted children: Who do they turn to for help and why? *Adoption Quarterly, 7*(2), 29–52.

Saldana, J. (2009). *The coding manual for qualitative researchers.* Thousand Oaks, CA: SAGE.

Savage, M. D. (2015). *Making personal public service announcements with adopted young women from foster care: A narrative inquiry* (Doctoral dissertation). Available from ProQuest Dissertations & Theses. (UMI No. 3706869)

Savage, M. D. (2016). Listening to the voices of young women adopted from foster care through personal public service announcements, *Drama Therapy Review, 2*(2), 195–209.

Sharma, A. R., McGue, M. K., & Benson, P. L. (1998). The psychological adjustment of United States adopted adolescents and their non-adopted siblings. *Child Development, 69*(3), 791–802.

Smith, S. L., Howard, J. A., & Monroe, A. D. (2000). Issues underlying behavior problems in at-risk adopted children. *Children and Youth Services, 22*(7), 539–562.

Snow, S., & D'Amico, M. (2015). The application of ethnodrama with female adolescents under youth protection within a creative arts therapies context. *Drama Therapy Review, 1*(2), 201–218.

Thomson, P., & Hall, C. (2008). Dialogues with artists: Analyzing children's self-portraits. In P. Thomson (Ed.), *Doing visual research with children and young people* (pp. 147–163). New York, NY: Routledge.

Van der Kolk, B. A. (1989). The compulsion to repeat the trauma: Re-enactment, re-victimization, and masochism. In B. James (Ed.), *Handbook for the treatment of attachment-trauma problems in children* (pp. 389–406). New York, NY: Free Press.

Von Korff, L., & Grotevant, H. (2011). Contact in adoption and adoptive identity formation: The mediating role of family conversation. *Journal of Family Psychology, 25*(3), 393–401.

White, M. (1995). *Re authoring lives: Interviews and essays.* Adelaide, Australia: Dulwich Centre Publications. Retrieved from http://www.narrativetherapylibrary.com/free-

White, M. (2000). *Reflections on narrative practice: Essays and interviews.* Adelaide, Australia: Dulwich Centre Publications. Retrieved from http://www.dulwichcentre.com.au/articles-about-narrative-therapy.html

Wind, L. H., Brooks, D., & Barth, R. P. (2007). Influences of risk history and adoption preparation on post-adoption services use in U.S. adoptions. *Family Relations, 56*(4), 378–389.

Winnicott, D. W. (1971). *Playing and reality.* London, England: Routledge.

Zeller-Berkman, S., Muñoz-Proto, C., & Torre, M. E. (2016, October). A youth development approach to evaluation: Critical participatory action research, *Non Profit Quarterly.* Retrieved from http://nonprofitquarterly.org/2016/10/06/youth-development-approach-evaluation-critical-participatory-action-research/

CHAPTER 10

LEGO SERIOUS PLAY AS A PARTICIPATORY RESEARCH METHOD TO INVOLVE CHILDREN IN ACTION RESEARCH PROJECTS

Heilyn Camacho

ABSTRACT

Lego Serious Play (LSP) is a thinking, communication, and problem solving methodology for teams making use of Lego bricks, play theory, metaphorical thinking, imagination, and storytelling as a process to create a shared understanding. The methodology was created for developing business strategies but has subsequently been adapted for use in many different fields, including few cases as a research method. The aim of this chapter is to discuss whether LSP methodology could be used as a method to involve students in participatory research. The chapter analyzes the data from LSP workshops conducted as part of two different action research projects in rural schools in Costa Rica.

Participatory Methodologies to Elevate Children's Voice and Agency, pages 229–249
Copyright © 2019 by Information Age Publishing

Findings from these events suggest that LSP enhances the engagement of students in action research projects by creating a childlike space along with a concrete process that facilitates the construction of knowledge as well as the materialization of students' tacit knowledge, experience, and feelings. Furthermore, LSP makes use of visual representation, imagination, creativity, and two-way communication to embrace the voice of children. This approach allows participants to assume ownership of the process, to construct a joint narrative that includes the perspectives of students with different backgrounds, and to co-construct understanding among students and between students and researchers. Finally, the workshops themselves turned out to be a significant experience for the participants, which is relevant to the learning principle of action research projects.

Recent research on listening and responding to the voice of students and on the involvement of children in the research process has been extensive (Langhout & Thomas, 2010; Leitch & Mitchell, 2007; Rudduck & Flutter, 2004), and it is clear that the growth of this movement has affected educational practice and drawn attention to the need for participatory methods to engage children in research processes (Leitch et al., 2007).

Research methodologies define the values, belief, and assumptions of researchers; they also determine the methods for the collection and analysis of data and construct the relationship between researched and researcher. In a very early stage of my research career, I felt called to use action research because my trajectory as a person and professional has predisposed me to believe that people can improve and grow beyond their original perspectives. Within the action research approach, researchers aim not only to understand and explain the world, but also change the world through collaboration between participants and researchers. My challenge as an action researcher is knowing how to approach people, how to facilitate an environment that engenders honest, mutual learning and promotes change. In the last 2 years, I have worked with low performance high schools in rural areas in Costa Rica; methodological challenges have arisen for me on occasions when I genuinely needed to involve students.

The fundamental principles of action research are participation, democracy, change, and learning (Lewin, 2008). Therefore, the study of social interactions, contextual phenomena and situated behaviors are fundamental for action research, making it indispensable to use multidimensional research methods that allow a deep understanding of individual and group perspectives toward their created social reality, which changes through interactions.

There are many different schools of action research; this chapter falls within Lewin's original approach emphasizing planned changes (Burnes, 2004; Burnes & Cooke, 2013; Lewin, 2008). Lewin argues that for change to take place, the overall situation must be taken into account, as leaving some parts outside of the analysis will misrepresent the overall picture.

Most action research projects directed toward organizational change in schools do not directly involve students as actors carrying ownership within the educational system, who can contribute to the understanding of the overall picture and organizational change. Students are typically seen as beneficiaries rather than participants in these processes. The most frequently involved stakeholders are the principal, teachers, parents, and surrounding community, which is a weakness of the research design. On the other hand, as mentioned by Leitch and Mitchell (2007), giving students the right to speak about educational issues can rise significant challenges regarding the means by which their feelings, thoughts, and experiences are stimulated, accessed, and captured. A central concern for action researchers within the educational field is how the collaborative research process can be driven by the participation of students who will be affected by the organizational changes that are being developed. The chapter discusses the potential of Lego Serious Play (LSP) methodology as a way to involve students in action research projects aiming at transformation in schools.

WHAT IS LEGO SERIOUS PLAY?

LSP is a methodology, mediated by Lego bricks, to foster thinking, communication, and problem solving. In this approach, a shared understanding is sought through the externalization of thoughts represented by Lego construction and the use of metaphors and storytelling to communicate the meaning of these externalized insights.

This methodology was originally created with the goal of facilitating creative strategic thinking in business organizations (Roos, Victor, & Statler, 2004); more recently, this methodology has been applied in many different fields including education (Barton & James, 2017), design of new technologies (Frick, Tardini, & Cantoni, 2014), creative thinking (Gauntlett, 2015), and social research (Hinthorne & Schneider, 2012), to mention a few.

According with Kristiansen and Rasmussen (2014) the methodology is composed of three sets of principles to be used systematically: one concerning group dynamics, one for the use of the Lego bricks, and one set of techniques composed of a core process for LSP and seven application techniques. The group dynamics principles include the following practices: everyone participates all the time, everyone participates in all the phases of the LSP process, the person leading the workshop is a facilitator and not a consultant, trainer, teacher, or instructor, and time is given to reflect and gather thoughts before anyone begins to speak. The principles for the use of Lego bricks are: They are to be used to unlock and construct new knowledge, there is no "right" way to build with the Lego bricks, all participants have the obligation to build and the right to share their stories, builders own their models and their stories, each builder's construction and story must be accepted, and questions and comments must be about the Lego model not about the person.

The core process of LSP is based on four steps: posing questions (the facilitator presents a challenge to the participants), construction (the participants build an answer using Lego bricks; this construction is called a model), sharing (each participant shares the stories and meanings assigned to the models), and reflection (the facilitator encourages participants to reflect on the models, the explanations, and own thought process). The seven application techniques are: (a) building individual models (participants unlock knowledge from their individual perceptions, display that knowledge in a way that everybody can see), (b) building shared models (the individual models merge into a common model to reach a shared understanding of a specific issue), (c) creating a landscape (a team analyses additional variables to create a bigger picture), (d) making connections (participants identify relationships between different elements of the model and build physical links between them), (e) building a system (the team explores and identifies systems and their impact), (f) playing with emergence and decision-makings (scenarios are played out to explore how the system would respond to potential circumstances), and (g) extracting simple guiding principles (these principles come from the previous activities and serve as guidelines to support strategic decision making). It is important to note that those techniques are progressive: To use Application 3, you should have performed 1 and 2. The techniques are chosen depending the complexity of the challenge on hands and are based on the core steps. Workshops using these techniques can last from 2 hours to 2 days (Kristiansen & Rasmussen, 2014).

What is the Theoretical Grounding of LSP?

LSP is built on the interlocking of different theoretical perspectives, combining constructivism, constructionism, play, hand and mind connections, flow theory, imagination, storytelling, and metaphorical thinking. Following a constructivist approach, LSP engages people as theory builders who use their previous experience and knowledge to construct new knowledge or rearrange their existing perceptions (Kristiansen & Rasmussen, 2014). Likewise, LSP follows constructionism in its emphasis on learning by making; creativity, art, and imagination are involved in a process where individuals create tangible objects representing abstract ideas and participants represent their individual perspectives in a unique way (Papert, 1991). The description of what initially inspired Papert's theory of constructionism describes equally well the process taking place in LSP workshops: "It allowed time to think, to dream, to gaze, to get a new idea and try it and drop it or persist, time to talk, to see other people's work and their reaction to yours" (Papert, 1991, p. 4). The Lego bricks are an expressive medium in which to externalize people's knowledge and abstract thoughts. They allow tacit thoughts to be transformed into concrete, tangible representations that could be discussed, negotiated, and shared.

Two concrete theoretical concepts can be used to describe the Lego models: *shared objects of thought* (Kirsh, 2009) and *object-mediated communication* (Roos, 2006). Kirsh's research concerns the relevance of external representations and their influence on processes of sense-making, problem-solving, and understanding (Kirsh, 2009). The externalization of thoughts (through diagrams, drawings, figures, etc.) makes the process of sense-making easier by encoding our projections visually, allowing us to process complex situations more efficiently, while creating forms through which we can share our thoughts with others (Kirsh, 2017). Kirsh argues that once we make our thoughts visible, they can be reliably identified, discussed, reformulated, rearranged, and transformed, and become shared objects of thought. An object of thought occurs whenever a thinker can grasp the referent, but a shared object of thought implies that "different thinkers share mechanisms for agreeing on attributes of the referent" (Kirsh, 2009, p. 1105). Similarly, Roos is investigating how construction can mediate serious and authentic conversations (Roos, 2006). According to his research, objects allow us to know, agree, and cope differently. Object-mediated communication results from conversations and interactions among participants who have made use of various materials (Lego bricks, pencil, clay) to mediate communication. According to Roos and Said (2006) the "possibility of externalizing mental items and sharing them through rich imagery, gives us an overview and facilitates conversations of complex themes" (p. 95); furthermore, the objects enabling this communication become an ensemble of artifacts, rather than a collection of individual objects.

The third key theoretical aspect of LSP is the concept of serious play. Here, I draw on the work of Roos et al. (2004), the creators of LSP methodology, to understand the concept of serious play within LSP. Their research presupposed that changing the mode and medium of the strategy process (including its constraints) would also affect the content generated. Traditionally, in business, strategic processes prioritize cognitive over emotional and social aspects and strategy makers focus primarily on data-driven considerations, leaving aside the social and emotional modes of experience. They identify this way of approaching strategy processes as *work mode*. In their action research project, Roos and colleagues propose to transform the work mode of strategic process into a *serious play mode*. They define this serious play mode as "a mode of activity that draws on the imagination, integrates cognitive, social and emotional dimensions of experience and intentionally brings the emergent benefits of play to bear on organizational challenges" (Roos et al., 2004, p. 563). Furthermore, they understand play as a process that can be encouraged, enabled, and supported but not forced.

This serious play mode is intentionally created in the same way within an LSP workshop. According to Kristiansen and Rasmussen (2014), three aspects must be considered in relation to serious play:

1. The workshop is an intentional gathering to apply the imagination (it requires active participation, not an observer stance). The group is meeting on purpose and with a purpose; they know there is a challenge but do not know the solution, so they work out a solution in a playful way.
2. The activity involves preparing and exploring a solution, but not implementing it. The intention is to unlock tacit knowledge, and arrive at a common understanding, which may lead to the implementation of a more effective solution later on.
3. Finally, there are a set of rules that should be followed, as described in the previous section.

The fourth theoretical aspect is imagination. For Roos (2006), imagination is more than an intellectual exercise; it requires thinking that is accompanied by hands-on activities. He argues that imagination relates to three dimensions: what we do (the behavioral dimension), what we use (the material dimension), and how we think (the conceptual dimension). LSP makes use of imagination in three different ways:

1. Descriptive imagination evokes images that describe a complex and confusing world. This type of imagination is used to rearrange data and information to identify patterns and make sense of what is happening here and now; furthermore, it provides insights for new possibilities and opportunities.
2. Creative imagination aims to find new possibilities by combining, rearranging, and transforming things or concepts; it has the features of visioning, innovation, and creativity.
3. Challenging imagination is equivalent to starting from scratch; this aspect does not work to improve existing practices but to invent new ones (Kristiansen & Rasmussen, 2014).

The last three theoretical building blocks of LSP involve storytelling, metaphors, and flow theory. Through the core process of this methodology, participants are asked a question, construct an answer, and share this answer; through the construction of the sharing processes they make use of metaphors and stories. These two elements help them to make sense of the challenge and to communicate their thoughts. Gibbs (2008) defines a metaphor as a "fundamental scheme by which people conceptualize the world and their own activities" (p. 3). Metaphors are a means to generate new ways to understand things; stories are part of organizational memory and are always under construction (Roos, 2006), furthermore, they help us to "structure how we perceive, how we think, and how we do" (Lakoff & Johnson, 1980, p. 3). In this understanding, the models created in LSP workshops, based on metaphors, provide a medium to tell, exchange, and construct stories.

Finally, to provide the environment to facilitate play, externalization of thoughts, reflection, and so on, LSP makes use of the concept of flow theory, defined as "a subjective state that people report when they are completely involved in something to the point of forgetting time, fatigue, and everything else but the activity itself" (Csikszentmihalyi, Abuhamdesh, & Nakamura, 2014, p. 230). Csikszentmihalyi and colleagues note three aspects in particular that promote the experience of flow: (a) a clear set of goals for the activity, (b) a balance between skills and the challenges, and (c) immediate feedback.

LSP WORKSHOPS IN RURAL SCHOOLS IN COSTA RICA

First, I acknowledge that my data was not initially collected to explore LSP as a method for involving children in research. Furthermore, I did not involve the students fully as researchers: They were not involved in defining the research question, did not collect data, and were not involved in the data analysis. In the evidence presented here, they had the role of key actors that could contribute to an understanding of the school system. Nevertheless, I understand that action research aims to involve all who are affected by a change, so students were involved in the process with the belief that understanding their perspectives and opinions about school issues were relevant to the action research undertaken.

The participation of the students was approached through an LSP workshop (following the description presented in "What is LSP?" above), which aimed to provide a space for students to express themselves concerning the culture of the school and the challenges they faced, as well as the opportunity to share their identities in their own words without the interpretation of their teachers or parents.

The data analyzed in this chapter resulted from two different workshops I led with students in the southern part of Costa Rica, in August 2015 and September 2016. These workshops were part of two different research projects.

These studies took place in rural high schools in a canton called Buenos Aires, one of the less developed cantons of Costa Rica. Both projects dealt with low socioeconomic status schools, where most of the students came from families with very low educational background and incomes. In Costa Rica, high school is a 5-year system finishing at 11th grade; therefore, the participants in the studies were between 13 and 18 years old. To protect the identity of the schools and the students, the schools are identified as School A and School B.

The project in School A aimed to provide the students with an opportunity that would support their self-development and increase their opportunity to overcome their vulnerable situation through education; to achieve this, the school needed to go through a process of transformational change. The aim of the research project in School B was to identify why this school performed so well when they have the same conditions as the other schools in the canton, to determine how other schools could learn from them.

Workshop in School A

In this intervention, the aim was to get to know the student's identity, their motivation to study, the school's constraints, and the type of teaching conditions that they would like to have. The whole workshop took 3 hours and was divided in three parts: telling "who I am" (using LSP), "my life trajectory" (using drawings), and "the school that we would like to have" (using a critique and visioning process). I only used the data from the first part. The LSP technique used in this case was "building individual models and stories;" 17 students represented the five grades at the school.

Workshop in School B

In this intervention, the aim was to get to know the school organizational culture (Schein, 2010) from the student's point of view. I used the "creating landscape" technique, and the workshop lasted less than three hours. Only LSP was used as a method; 15 students participated in the workshop, three from each grade.

Both workshops were partially video-recorded, mainly when students were presenting and explaining their constructions as well as some periods when they were building. The full workshop was not recorded, so that the students would not be made uncomfortable. This chapter is based on the 30 minutes of video from School A and 40 minutes of video from School B, recorded at various times during the workshops.

Potential of LSP as Research Method: Data Presentation

The analysis presented here does not correspond to the aim of the workshops, because this chapter is not about organizational change but rather methodological in emphasis, examining the potential of LSP to involve students in the research process. I went through the videos several times, sometimes scrutinizing a specific scene from the video and at other times watching it as a movie, allowing the data to speak about the key events and products that took place during the workshops. Subsequently, I transcribed the students' descriptions of their models and took notes about the interactions that took place. The following is an extract of the evidence that emerged from the LSP workshops in the two schools.

The workshop in School A started with a bunch of Lego bricks and figures in the center of a big table surrounded by the students (Figure 10.1). Upon entering the room, the students were excited and showed a desire to play with the Lego; the signs of this were somatic as well as verbal, suggesting a certain immersion with their bodies in the workshop space. In School B, the workshop started in a normal classroom setting, where the Lego was presented after a short introduction to the aim of the workshop. The same emotional expressions were identified in School B. This emotional response of participants when Lego is introduced has been discussed by McCusker (2014), who states that the introduction of Lego opens the door to play. This playful environment was maintained throughout the workshops; there were a lot of laughter, smiling, joking, sharing, and generally having a good time, as was highlighted by Lotts (2016) after conducting 20 LSP workshops for librarians. This playful and enjoyable experience is captured very well in the comment of a student when he heard that we needed to hurry up because of an approaching deadline, "do not take away our illusions." This comment and the playful environment in general suggests that the LSP workshop becomes an experience in itself, promoting open discussion and sharing, as pointed out by Barton and James (2017).

In School A, the workshop started right away with the use of LSP; after a short skill-building exercise, the students were asked to construct who they were, and had 7 minutes to build the model. All participants built freely

Figure 10.1   Students immersed in the LSP workshop in School A.

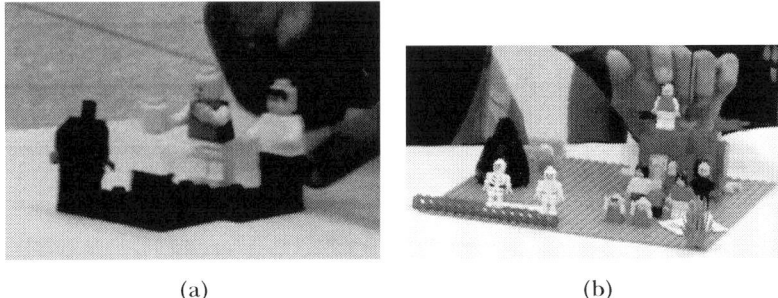

(a)   (b)

Figure 10.2   Student representation.

using bricks of their own choice and were not restricted or pushed in any way about what to emphasize; they were only reminded of the social norms of LSP. The results included very elaborate models and quite simple ones. In total, 11 of the models were judged elaborate and six not elaborate. For example, the creator described Figure 10.2a saying, "This me, my father, my grandmother, and my grandfather." Interpreting Figure 10.2b, the student placed his mother higher than the other members of the family, saying: "This represents my home and she is my mom. This represent a castle. My mom is my princess and the core of my family." He continued to explain the model by pointing out its different elements; when he pointed to the skeletons, he said, "These represent the people that come and leave our life." The constructions to the rear represented his hobbies and his love for various activities, while the black structure symbolized a rocket, representing his dreams to become a professional.

The presentation of the models took very little time, a maximum of 1 minute per participant. Looking through the details emphasized by different participants, emotional, affective, and nonlinguistic dimensions are represented in the models; this has been noted in previous research on LSP (Barton & James, 2017).

Continuing the workshop in school A, students were asked to elaborate on their model, now adding an element that represented "Why are you in this school?" Here students started to reveal more sensitive or personal issues. However, the environment (laughter, smiling, interaction) seemed to soften the impact of those aspects.

Concerning the model shown in Figure 10.3a, the student shared "Well…I have…I have something like a history. Many people think that they cannot do something because they failed the same level many years…I, I have been in all the high schools of Buenos Aires, so this [the object next to the Lego girl] represents the years that I lost. I am there because of that, because I lost many years…but I still can do it."

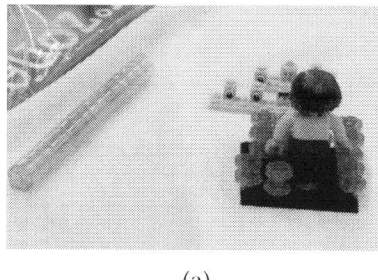
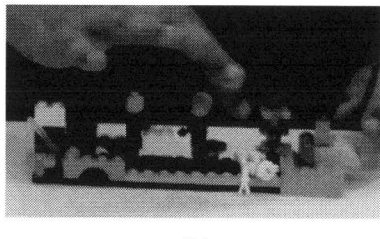

(a)   (b)

Figure 10.3 Student representation.

While the student was visibly nervous telling the story behind the Lego model, the focus on the model seemed to help. Also, she added humor to the story, that shifting attention away from the "sensitive" aspect of the story behind the model. After she shared that aspect, two other participants also mentioned that they had attended several high schools, in their later presentations.

The student presenting Figure 10.3b said "This skeleton also represents what I was [at this point, she raised her hand, made a fist, and gently but firmly hit the table], in the moment that I had no illusions left, where I stayed stuck. I finished school [meaning primary school] and went to work in a house. I had to stay there, and could not get out of that situation. I was like that [she pointed to the skeleton very emphatically]. When I saw the opportunities the high school provided . . . it re-animated me." The model expressed many of the student's feelings about who she was, her current aspirations, and her desire to grow.

In these two examples, it is clear to see that the bricks (the tube constructed in 3a and the skeleton used in 3b) facilitate the externalization of thoughts and allow the physical representation of abstract experiences, their meanings, and the creator's feelings about them (Gauntlett, 2015).

In the workshop at School B, the students were divided into two groups with each group given the task to use Lego to introduce the school to somebody who did not know anything about it. The students were then given 15 minutes to build what they wanted to present; each group would present its model and everyone would be allowed to ask questions. The subsequent task was for all students to build a common model, merging the two group models. Throughout the whole workshop, I asked questions about the school's organizational culture that arose from the students' comments; at times I also introduced topics without them being mentioned by the participants.

Figure 10.4, shows the model constructed by the first group. They used the physical infrastructure of the school to communicate the tacit school environment. For example, one of the key elements of their model

Figure 10.4   The model of the school produced by the first group at School B.

represented the social places where students interact informally, identified as *los pollitos* (the benches), as well as the harmonious environment created by the ornamental plants of the school (in the area circled).

When presenting their model, the group pointed to the classrooms, multisport facilities, the eating room, and toilets and said "pollitos, pollitos, and more pollitos." I asked, "Why are they on benches?"

> **Student 1:** They are having lunch. Also during breaks, many sit on benches to talk, to converse.
>
> **Student 2:** We want to represent the areas that we as students use the most... the plants are very important because they create a calm environment... also, the benches are a very, very important part because they represent students gathering together, they represent a space outside of classrooms where students can work also. They are a place where groups of

students can share knowledge, so they benches here in the high school are very, very, very important.

Student 3: They are social spaces, where all the students gather.

Student 4: All the students share those spaces, sometimes from different grades.

The model included small details that were used to go deeper into what was going on in the school and to identify relationships, roles, and aspects relevant to the students. After the second group had presented and the students started to build their common model, some members of the first group offered an interpretation of one aspect of their model (Figure 10.4) not mentioned in their presentation. The following conversation took place:

Researcher: Who else is part of the high school?

Student 1: The teachers.

Student 2: Here they are, see?

Student 3: He is teaching

Student 4: The teachers also help us work.

[They continued presenting]

Student 5: Here is Mr. John [the principal].

Reseacher: Ahhh, where is Mr. John?

Student 6: Mr. John is one of the key promoters of the green areas so here he is [close to the plants]; also, he shares a lot with the students, with us, so he has two roles [when explaining this, she moved the Lego figure from the bench to the plants and back to the bench].

This dialogue revealed the students' opinion of the principal and his role in the school environment. An interesting aspect was that the principal was not aware of the value the students attributed to the green environment and the benches. He attended the workshop, and told me afterward that it was eye-opening to hear their opinion about the green areas. He simply liked plants and flowers, and started bringing them to decorate the school as if it was his house, without knowing the impact it would have on the students.

The second group also included the benches in their model and their presentation, but addressed additional aspects related to the meaning of being at school. They explained, "Here are the benches where people from different grades sit and share. They are not separated, but can mix and can share things, and have lunch; it is a very important space because it is not only about to study, but also about to enjoy nature, and to work in a group..." Another student added, "As he was saying, [meaning the school] it is not only about studying, but also to have fun, to relax, and a space to get along socially; for example, here in the greenhouse [another space represented in the model] there are also many places to share and hang out...."

It is worth noting how these pollitos become a physical representation of a phenomenon that is not at all physical. What the students are representing is not the bench itself, but the interaction that takes place in that specific physical space, which is so important to them. This is a clear example of how LSP allowed students to communicate what really mattered to them. This physical representation allowed all participants, students as well as researcher, to examine, discuss, and understand that specific aspect and its meaning for the students. This confirms the findings of previous research (Barton & James, 2017; Gauntlett, 2015; Geithner & Menzel, 2016), which has argued that Lego bricks allow participants to externalize and describe abstract concepts more profoundly, in ways that are not possible without object-mediated communications.

As the students at School B moved to construct their common model, I started posing questions about the model and also about things that they had not mentioned up to that point. I repeated the question, "Who else is part of the school?" The students replied, mentioning elements that were present in the models and elements that had not been represented. For example, parents and the school board were not included in the model. Recognizing that those elements were not reflected in the model, the students felt that they needed to add them but also negotiated where they should be represented. In this negotiation, the students discussed aspects of the situation that revealed how they interpreted the involvement of the parents with the school and in their lives. Using Legos, they were able to "add" the parents and "move" them to a place that better represented their connection to the school. In this sense, they were constructing the meaning of the parents' relationship with the school, sharing how they see the parents' role. As they negotiated where to place them and why, they were also negotiating meaning (Barton & James, 2017).

The students continued to finish the construction process for another 10 minutes. When they presented the model I asked some additional questions, first about the model, then for the last 15 minutes, the conversation did not focus on the model. We discussed many different aspects of the students' experience such as school values, future plans, identity development, and many anecdotes voicing aspects that mattered to them individually, but I am not going to detail them.

A general analysis of both workshops reveals four concepts that relate most closely to the process of sense-making and of exploring complex problems, previously identified by Hansen, Mabogunje, and Haase (2009): (a) the bricks as a neutral language—participants can articulate their knowledge succinctly, and different participants can contribute in the common understanding of a problem in a short time; (b) a democratized process, giving participants time to reflect upon issues concretely and the opportunity to explain and interpret their models; (c) shared experience of improvising, where the sense-making process is driven by the tacit knowledge of participants and the ensuing group dynamic; and (d) a shared experience of collective commitment, where members of the team experience strong attachment to their decisions.

DISCUSSION: WHY IS THIS VISUAL, THREE-DIMENSIONAL, CREATIVE METHOD ADVANTAGEOUS TO RESEARCH INVOLVING STUDENTS IN ACTION RESEARCH PROJECTS?

The quick answer to this question is because, as action researchers, we need to provide space for participants to describe their views and their socially constructed realities; sometimes it is quite difficult for a participant, for students in this case, to articulate their meanings using words or text alone. Human beings are complex and multidimensional; to understand our being in a situated context we need methods that can model and capture that complexity.

LSP has great potential to serve as a participatory research method, to involve students in action research projects; I have identified four aspects to be cultivated in this work. First a friendly and safe space must be created, to facilitate interaction and understanding. In this space, power distance should be reduced so that knowledge can be shared on equal terms; it should be a space where students and researchers come together to seek common understanding of their needs, feelings, values, and concerns. Various terms have been used to identify this space; for example, in research with indigenous people, Hall (2014) refers to it as a "third space of understanding," meaning that nonindigenous researchers and indigenous participants should find a way to understand each other and to respect their different ways of knowing, which demands "ongoing negotiated reciprocal relationships" (Hall, 2014, p. 384). Hall argues for a research design that includes methods to promote shared dialogue and mutual understanding.

Within the field of participatory design, researchers refer to a *third space*, which is described as encompassing such methods as workshops, stories, games, drama, and photography, that bridge between two spaces (the world of technology designers and users). In this space, people meet, willing to explore differences and foster understanding, interacting on the basis of knowledge-sharing, exchange of knowledge, and reciprocal learning (Muller & Druin, 2012). Another concept that can be used to explain the space created through LSP is the concept of *Ba* within the process of knowledge creation proposed by Nonaka and Konno (1998). According to these authors, knowledge creation cannot take place without context; it is context-specific in terms of *who* participates and *how* they participate. The *Ba* consists in both the physical space and the mental space, which includes emotion, cognition, and meaning.

A second aspect relates to the externalization of abstract concepts and meanings for deeper, shared understanding. LSP allows the communication of complex thoughts and makes tacit knowledge explicit, which is very relevant to support students expressing themselves in an additional modality, beyond oral or written communication. This strength of LSP has been pointed out by other researchers (Barton & James, 2017; Gauntlett, 2015; Hansen et al., 2009; Montesa-Andres, Garrigós-Simón, & Narangajavana, 2014). In this regard, one could classify LSP as a generative tool that engages people in telling, making, and enacting. Regarding generative tools, Brandt, Binder and Sander (2013, pp. 159–160) state that, "It is a full palette of predominantly visual components that enable participants to explore and express playful landscapes of past, present, and future experiences. These tools can be used to encourage and challenge people to express their tacit and latent needs, aspirations and dreams." In this understanding, LSP becomes a method enabling students to describe and interpret their reality (composed of explicit, tacit, unconscious, and abstract elements) through making things themselves.

The third element relates to the multiple theoretical aspects of LSP, providing the possibility of a multidimensional method. Drawings (Leitch et al., 2007), metaphors (Black-Hawkins & Amrhein, 2014), storytelling, and visual methods (Young & Barrett, 2001) have each demonstrated their capacity to lend voice to the experiences, feelings, dreams, and concerns of children or others who might be silenced or marginalized. All of these methods strongly support engagement and participation, while stimulating reflection and children's ownership of the research process. These aspects are also integrated into LSP methodology, which even strengthens the aspects involving imagination, creation, and collective activity. Furthermore, the theoretical basis of LSP is consistent with social constructivist research, revealing realities as they are constructed socially and making co-constructed understandings visible.

The fourth element concerns the core LSP process and involves the group dynamics governing how to interact and use the Lego bricks; these principles promote democracy and participation while giving voice to all participants. This methodology has at its core a deep respect for the people who have built the model and the meanings that an individual or group has attributed to it. Therefore, this method genuinely fosters the centrality of research participants, enabling them to explore what matters to them rather than relying on the researcher's worldview (Black-Hawkins & Amrhein, 2014; Hall, 2014). Also, the seven LSP application techniques specify how they are to be applied but remain open to an unbounded range of challenges. Therefore, this approach will support the exploration and deepening interpretation at many different levels of complexity and in various fields of study.

These four aspects demonstrate the potential of LSP as an unconventional participatory research method, providing a means for children and youth to express themselves using a rich, visual, imaginative, emotional, and dialogical set of techniques that disclose important insights that a more traditional oral-text oriented research method might not uncover. However, the participation principle is not implied in the method per se, but relies on the values of researchers. As Gauntlett and Holzwarth (2006) have stressed, this kind of creative method recognizes and embraces the creativity and reflexivity of people, which is the most appropriate attitude for researchers. LSP is based on the sincere belief that with appropriate tools, people can thoughtfully communicate their own meanings and understandings. This approach does not emphasize what researchers want to hear or a hypothesis that they want to confirm, but offers the assurance and the question, "I want to understand you; would you tell me? I will honestly listen to you." Without this commitment by researchers, the LSP approach would be useless.

CONCLUSION

I began this chapter by arguing that at the core of participatory methodologies is an unshakable commitment to ensuring that those who will be affected by any changes as a result of the research should play a critical role in the process. Furthermore, action research projects aiming to promote organizational changes in schools should involve students so that they can achieve their goals, but a space should be created to support interaction between students and researchers. After reviewing the evidence, I argue that LSP can enable the participation of students who are affected by research processes and resulting proposals for change. LSP creates a space enabling investigation, understanding, mutual learning, and collective reflection. It provides a process that is driven by social interaction, commitment, and engagement. This method allows the construction of scenarios, objects, and ideas through which students can express themselves, think differently, and contribute to the research process. Furthermore, it is a childlike approach, which is coherent with the values, philosophy, and theory of action research.

Although my research involved students as key actors for understanding the school system, the same method could be used for different levels of participation, from children or young people as informants to their role as researchers. This chapter provides examples of how the LSP could look in practice, discussing the process, related values, and the theoretical underpinnings of LSP along with the kinds of interaction seen with young participants.

Finally, it is important to recognize that LSP presents challenges, as does any other method. The main challenges I have identified relate to the focus of the workshop, the allotted time, and materials. The students become so engaged in the play aspect that facilitators must respond flexibly to ensure that the session does not become just "fun" for participants or degenerate into a building competition. The second challenge is the requirement for a skilled facilitator, to get the full benefit of the LSP methodology. One of the most important facilitation skills is the capacity to ask meaningful and explorative questions. When building models, students add many small meaningful details, which they may skip over when presenting their models; it is the task of the facilitator to discover these by posing questions about the model. Another significant challenge is the amount and richness of data received and determining how to analyze it. According to Gauntlett and Holzwarth (2006), when analyzing the data from this kind of methodology, researchers should not go beyond interpretations expressed by the participants, because doing so would impose their own interpretation on someone else's work. This issue of interpretation has also been discussed in research with children using drawing. The recommendation for both LSP and drawings, is that interpretation should be done in situ, not later. However, this issue would require further discussion if LSP comes to be used for participatory research. Two final aspects concern availability of time and materials. It requires time to design, run, and analyze LSP workshops, as well as access to the actual LSP kits.

Questions for Reflection

1. Think about the last time that you engaged in a conversation where you used materials. How can you relate that experience with the concept of object-mediated communication?
2. How do you understand the concept of serious play and how it differs from just playing? Could you think in an example of each of these types of plays?
3. I argue that children construct meaning and understanding while they build their mind with Legos, to what extent do you agree or disagree with me?
4. What is the impact of cultural differences in using Lego to involve children in research? How will this methodology work in your culture?

Suggestions for Further Reading

Barton, G., & James, A. (2017). Threshold Concepts, LEGO® SERIOUS PLAY® and whole systems thinking: Towards a combined methodology. *Practice and Evidence of Scholarship of Teaching and Learning in Higher Education, 12*(2), 249–271.

Bjørndahl, J., Fusaroli, R., Østergaard, S., & Tylén, K. (2014). Thinking together with material representations: Joint epistemic actions in creative problem solving. *Cognitive Semiotics, 7*(1), 103–123.

Gauntlett, D., & Holzwarth, P. (2006). Creative and visual methods for exploring identities. *Visual Studies, 21*(1), 82–91.

Kristiansen, P., & Rasmussen, R. (2014). *Building a better business using the Lego Serious Play method.* Hoboken, NJ: Wiley.

Roos, J., & Said, R. (2006). Object-mediated communication. In J. Roos (Ed.), *Thinking from within: A Hands-on strategy practice* (pp. 77–96). New York, NY: Palgrave Macmillan.

Roos, J., Victor, B., & Statler, M. (2004). Playing seriously with strategy. *Long Range Planning, 37*, 549–568.

REFERENCES

Barton, G., & James, A. (2017). Threshold Concepts, LEGO® SERIOUS PLAY® and whole systems thinking: Towards a combined methodology. *Practice and Evidence of Scholarship of Teaching and Learning in Higher Education, 12*(2), 249–271.

Black-Hawkins, K., & Amrhein, B. (2014). Valuing student teachers' perspectives: Researching inclusively in inclusive education? *International Journal of Research & Methods in Education, 37*(4), 357–375. https://doi.org/10.1080/174372 7X.2014.886684

Brandt, E., Binder, T., & Sanders, E. (2013). Tools and techniques: ways to engage telling, making and enacting. In J. Simonsen & T. Robertson (Eds.), *Routledge international handbook of participatory design* (pp. 145–181). New York, NY: Routledge.

Burnes, B. (2004). Kurt Lewin and the planned approach to change: A re-appraisal. *Journal of Management Studies, 41*(6), 977–1002. doi:10.1111/j.1467 -6486.2004.00463.x

Burnes, B., & Cooke, B. (2013). Kurt Lewin's field theory: A review and re-evaluation. *International Journal of Management Reviews, 15*(4), 408–425. doi:10.1111/ j.1468-2370.2012.00348.x

Csikszentmihalyi, M., Abuhamdesh, S., & Nakamura, J. (2014). Flow. In M. Csikszntmihalyi (Ed.), *Flow and the foundations of positive psychology* (pp. 227–238). Springer. doi:10.1007/978-94-017-9088-8

Frick, E., Tardini, S., & Cantoni, L. (2014). Lego Serious Play applications to enhance creativity in participatory design. In F. Reisman (Ed.), *Creativity in business—Research papers on knowledge, innovation and enterprise volume II.* KIE Conference Book Series. Retrieved from http://www.kiecon.org/Creativity %20in%20Business%202014.pdf

Gauntlett, D. (2015). Chapter 7: The LEGO System as a tool for thinking, creativity, and changing the world. *Making media studies: The creativity turn in media and communications studies.* New York, NY: Peter Lang.

Gauntlett, D., & Holzwarth, P. (2006). Creative and visual methods for exploring identities. *Visual Studies, 21*(1), 82–91.

Geithner, S., & Menzel, D. (2016). Effectiveness of learning through experience and reflection in a project management simulation. *Simulation & Gaming, 47*(2), 228–256.

Gibbs, R. (2008). Metaphor and thought: The state of the art. In R. Gibbs (Ed.), *The Cambridge handbook of metaphor and thought* (pp. 3–13). Cambridge, England: Cambridge University Press.

Hall, L. (2014). "With" not "about"—Emerging paradigms for research in a cross-cultural space. *International Journal of Research & Methods in Education, 37*(4), 376–389.

Hansen, P. K., Mabogunje, A., & Haase, L. M. (2009). Get a grip on sense-making and exploration dealing with complexity through serious play. In *2009 IEEE International Conference on Industrial Engineering and Engineering Management* (pp. 1593–1597). Retrieved from http://ieeexplore.ieee.org/stamp/stamp.jsp?tp=&arnumber=5373107&isnumber=5372873

Hinthorne, L., & Schneider, K. (2012). Playing with purpose: Using Serious Play to enhance participatory development communication in research. *International Journal of Communication, 6,* 2801–2824.

Kirsh, D. (2009). Interaction, external representations and sense making. In N. Taatgen & H. van Rijn (Eds.), *Proceeding of the 31st Annual Conference of the Cognitive Science Society* (pp. 1003–1008). Austin, TX: Cognitive Science Society.

Kirsh, D. (2017). Thinking with external representations. In S. Cowley & F. Vallée-Tourangeau (Eds.), *Cognition beyond the brain* (pp. 61–84). Cham, Switzerland: Springer.

Kristiansen, P., & Rasmussen, R. (2014). *Building a better business using the Lego Serious Play method.* Hoboken, NJ: Wiley.

Lakoff, G., & Johnson, M. (1980). *Metaphors we live by.* Chicago, IL: University of Chicago Press.

Langhout, R., & Thomas, E. (2010). Imagining participatory action research in collaboration with children: An introduction. *American Journal of Community Psychology, 46*(1–2), 60–66.

Leitch, R., Gardner, J., Mitchell, S., Lundy, L., Odena, O., Galanouli, D., & Clough, P. (2007). Consulting pupils in assessment for learning classrooms: The twists and turns of working with students as co-researchers. *Educational Action Research, 15*(3), 459–478.

Leitch, R., & Mitchell, S. (2007). Caged birds and cloning machines: How student imagery "speaks" to us about cultures of schooling and student participation. *Improving Schools, 10*(1), 53–71.

Lewin, K. (2008). *Resolving social conflicts & field theory in social science.* Washington, DC: American Psychological Association.

Lotts, M. (2016). On the road, playing with Legos®, and learning about the library: The Rutgers University Art Library Lego playing station, part two. *Journal of Library Administration, 56*(5), 499–525.

McCusker, S. (2014). Lego®, seriously: Thinking through building. *International Journal of Knowledge, Innovation and Entrepreneurship, 2*(1), 27–37.

Montesa-Andres, J., Garrigós-Simón, F. J., & Narangajavana. (2014). A proposal for using Lego Serious Play in education. In M. Peris-Ortiz, F. J. Garrigós-Simón, & I. Gil Pechuán (Eds.), *Innovation and teaching technologies: New directions in research, practice and policy* (pp. 99–107). Cham, Switzerland: Springer.

Muller, M., & Druin, A. (2012). Participatory design: The third space in HCI. In J. Jacko (Ed.), *The human–computer interaction handbook* (pp. 1125–1154). Boca Raton, FL: CRC Press.

Nonaka, I., & Konno, N. (1998). The concept of "ba": Building a foundation for knowledge creation. *California Management Review, 40*(3), 40–54.

Papert, S. (1991). Situating constructionism. In S. Papert & I. Harel (Eds.), *Constructionism.* New York, NY: Ablex.

Roos, J. (Ed.). (2006). *Thinking from within: A Hands-on strategy practice.* New York, NY: Palgrave Macmillan.

Roos, J., & Said, R. (2006). Object-mediated communication. In J. Roos (Ed.), *Thinking from within: A Hands-on strategy practice* (pp. 77–96). New York, NY: Palgrave Macmillan.

Roos, J., Victor, B., & Statler, M. (2004). Playing seriously with strategy. *Long Range Planning, 37*, 549–568.

Rudduck, J., & Flutter, J. (2004). *How to improve your school: Giving pupils a voice.* London, England: Continuum Press.

Schein, E. (2010). *Organizational culture and leadership* (4th ed.). San Francisco, CA: Jossey-Bass.

Young, L., & Barrett, H. (2001). Adapting visual methods: Action research with Kampala street children. *Area, 33*(2), 141–152.

CHAPTER 11

MEDICAL PLAY

From Intervention to Participatory Research

Cara Sisk and Jane Baker

ABSTRACT

Working with children as research participants may seem impractical to some, yet children are qualified and capable of reliably sharing their experiences and telling their stories (Spratling, Coke, & Minick, 2012; Vogl, 2015). Child-centered research methods may facilitate and encourage children's participation (Clark, 2011). *Medical play* is one child-centered data collection method that encourages participation and highlights the voices of children with special health care needs. Children's participation in health care research aligns with the patient- and family-centered care philosophies of child life programs. Certified Child Life Specialists provide psychosocial services within pediatric health care settings (Association of Child Life Professionals, 2017; American Academy of Pediatrics, 2014). One tool of the Certified Child Life Specialist is medical play. With medical play, children are encouraged to explore medical items and express their thoughts and feelings regarding their health care experiences (McCue, 1988). Originally created as an intervention tool, medical play is a natural fit for engaging children in participatory research. Using

Participatory Methodologies to Elevate Children's Voice and Agency, pages 251–272
Copyright © 2019 by Information Age Publishing

images and the children's words, this chapter reviews a study that utilized medical play to highlight the perspectives and experiences of children with special health care needs and disabilities (Sisk, 2016). The primary goal of the research was to highlight the voices of children with special health care needs and positively influence pediatric health care practices. Listening to the voices of children via participatory research is necessary for the advancement of pediatric health care.

* * *

Medical play revealed the impacts of Alex's pain and coping experiences. Alex picked up the syringe, pulled out the plunger, and put it back in saying: "Ah, this won't hurt a, but a second, ok? One, that leg on the count of ten. One, this is the kid, 1, 2, 3, 4, 5, 6, 7, 8, 9, 10. Ready? Hang on, hang on, it's ok, it's ok, don't hurt, don't hurt. (He quickly gets the Band-Aid.) And we got it! We got it! We've got to do another one" (Alex, 7 years). Alex provided supportive, coping statements to his doll patient as he administered the shot, despite his own dislike of needle sticks, or as he stated, "get sticked."

—Sisk, 2016, p. 141

Children with special health care needs (CSHCN) are an unlikely population to be identified as research participants, which is evidenced by the lack of research highlighting the perspectives of these children. However, CSHCNs are ideally suited to be research participants. Despite various, multiple challenges that CSHCNs face, they are the ultimate experts on their health care experiences. Researchers and professionals may facilitate partnerships with these children by asking proper questions in therapeutic environments and collecting data with diverse child-centered modalities. The results of such research partnerships are authentic, realistic, reliable, and enlightening.

Informed by Sisk's[1] (2016) research, the aim of this chapter is to describe the population known as children with special health care needs and highlight their abilities to broaden our knowledge of their health care experiences. Partnering in research with children who have special health care needs enhances pediatric health care services and positively impacts the children and their families. Topics examined in this chapter include children's voice in qualitative inquiry, the value of child-centered participatory research, and *medical play* as a research method.

This chapter is relevant to both practitioners and researchers who work with children and families in health care settings. Such professionals are uniquely positioned to listen to and learn from children who have special health care needs. Investing in these research partnerships will assist with fuller understanding of the children's health care experiences. Descriptions of case studies (including photos of the child participants' medical play dolls) provide further insight into their perceptions. Resources for further learning are provided, as well as reflective questions to spark creative inquiry regarding participatory research with children who have special health care needs.

CHILDREN WITH SPECIAL HEALTH CARE NEEDS

Children with special health care needs (CSHCN), a classification of children in American Health and Human Services (Arango et al., 1998), were defined by the Maternal and Child Health Bureau as those who "have or are at increased risk for a chronic, physical, developmental, behavioral, or emotional condition and who also require health and related services of a type or amount beyond that required by children generally" (Arango et al., 1998, p. 138).

The Children with Special Health Care Needs Screener, a 5-question parent survey, developed by Bethell et al. (2002) is used to determine if children qualify as having special health care needs. The Maternal and Child Health Bureau use the screener for the in-depth National Survey of Children with Special Health Care Needs (NS-CSHCN; van Dyck et al., 2002). The 2009 NS-CSHCN survey sample size was 40,242 households with 15.1% of children screening positive for having a special health care need (Child and Adolescent Health Measurement Initiative, 2012).

Bramlett, Read, Bethell, and Blumberg (2009) created these subgroupings of CSHCNs: (a) Rx meds only, (b) elevated services only, (c) Rx meds and elevated services, and (d) functional limitations (p. 154). The functional limitations subgroup exhibited the highest needs and required high level interventions. The more criteria a child met on the screener, the more likely the child was to experience decreased health and increased complexity of needs. Conversely, children that met fewer criteria experienced better health and decreased complexity of needs. For example, children in the taking prescription medications only subgroup had less acuity of needs and better physical health.

Houtrow, Okumura, Hilton, and Rehm (2011) identified CSHCN with disabilities as a unique subgroup of the CSHCN population and identified a gap in the research literature for this subgroup. Children with special health care needs and disabilities are a vulnerable population (Eddy & Engel, 2008) who require many health care services for complex medical needs and present more psychosocial issues than CSHCNs without disabilities (Houtrow et al., 2011).

All participants[2] discussed in this chapter qualified on the CSHCN Screener as having special health care needs, with all qualifying in both service use and functional limitations categories, while all but one qualified in the medication dependency category. Using the World Health

Organization's International Classification of Functioning, Disability, and Health (2001) framework, all participants were also classified as having disabilities. The participants in Sisk's (2016) study were in the unique subgroup of children identified by Houtrow et al. (2011) with a combination of special health care needs and disabilities as well.

THE VOICES OF CHILDREN WITH SPECIAL HEALTH CARE NEEDS

Children with special health care needs have voices that need to be heard. Parents' perceptions of children's health care experiences often differ from the children's perceptions; thus, parent proxy (or a parent's interpretation of a child's health care experience) should not be solely relied upon (Garth & Aroni, 2003; Lindeke, Fulkerson, Chesney, Johnson, & Savik, 2009; Spieth & Harris, 1996). Eiser and Morse (2001) noted parent proxy was more congruent with child self-report when identifying outwardly visible characteristics but not more internal characteristics of health-related quality of life (HRQoL). In other words, parents more accurately described their children's physical states but not their cognitive or emotional states. Therefore, it is vital to hear directly from the children, because parents do not necessarily know what their children are experiencing internally.

Varni, Limbers, and Newman (2009) discovered through factor analysis that parental proxy reporting accounted for 10–25% of the variance in children's self-report related to health-related quality of life (p. 186). This finding reinforces the importance of gaining child self-report to learn internal perceptions. Varni, Limbers, and Newman also found proxy reports from health-care providers for quality of life perceptions differed from those of the children. Children's perceptions of health care experiences are covert or internal, thus they should be accessed with developmentally appropriate interview methods. Cindy Dell Clark (2011) in her book *In a Younger Voice: Doing Child-Centered Qualitative Research* emphasized the importance for children to be original, primary sources for data collection. Gathering health care perceptions directly from children via their voices is the most accurate method for learning children's thoughts and feelings.

Hearing the children's voices was a primary focus of the Sisk (2016) research. This goal dictated that the researcher assess each participant's unique perceptions; therefore, medical play was chosen as one data collection method.[3] Medical play allowed the children's voices to be shared verbally, artistically, and kinesthetically. This combination of expressive modalities strengthened the interpretation of the children's voices regarding their health care experiences.

Accessing the voices of children requires more than just listening to them talk. Developmentally, young children are often cognitively more aware of their perceptions than they can verbalize (Hollan & Skinner, 2009). Stressful, emotionally demanding experiences may decrease a child's ability to share his/her perceptions verbally (Gaynard, Goldberger, Laidley, 1991). Thus, to fully hear a child's voice, nonverbal expressive modalities are useful. A child's voice consists of much more than mere verbalizations; it includes the child's visual representations and play demonstrations (Box 11.1). Medical play, as a data collection method, provides an alternative way for children to share their voices through verbalizations, visual representations, and play.

BOX 11.1   CHILDREN'S VOICE

Children's voices include:
- Verbalizations
- Visual Representations (artistic renderings, gestures, facial expressions)
- Play

CHILD-CENTERED RESEARCH METHODS

A qualitative design is most appropriate for researching human experiences and perceptions. Patton (2002) noted the ability of qualitative data to share people's experiences via their own voices. Qualitative inquiry respects subjectivity, pursues individual truth, and gives power to participants (Grbich, 2013). These characteristics made qualitative inquiry the best design for Sisk's (2016) research involving CSHCN and disabilities. Clark (2011), a child-centered proponent, advocated for qualitative methodologies to discover the meanings children attribute to experiences. In addition, child-centered qualitative methodologies fulfill the researchers' responsibilities to authentically and reflexively partner with child participants. Discovering the children's perceptions of and meanings assigned to their health care experiences necessitated the use of child-centered data collection methods in the Sisk (2016) study.

Qualitative, child-centered data collection methods afforded the child participants autonomy and agency to share their stories. Such methodological decisions were reinforced by Clark (2011) who argued children are equipped to influence their worlds in various settings including hospitals, schools, and churches. As practitioners and researchers, we believe that professionals should listen to the children's voices in many, varied settings to improve the experiences of children with and without special health care needs and disabilities.

Partnering with children requires understanding the many facets of "the 'soufflé' that is child-centered inquiry" (Clark, 2011, p. 14). A child's voice is influenced by complex, individual perspectives, parental influences, and social expectations. Despite this confluence of complexities within the soufflé analogy, Clark argued, "Hearing children's voices can be more than an exotic delicacy but part of standard fare in a menu of important discovery" (p. 14). In other words, hearing children's voices through multiple expressive modalities should be the norm, not the exception. Medical play provided the child participants in Sisk's (2016) research a unique way to demonstrate their perceptions of health care experiences.

Clark (2011) identified health care research using a child-centered paradigm to be accessible and inviting to children. The flexibility of qualitative inquiry allows child-centered research methods to be used optimally. Child-centered methods foster children's voice and agency. The participants discussed in this chapter were offered the opportunity to engage in medical play, a unique child-centered method focused on health care experiences.

PLAY

Play is pivotal for children's optimal development and impacts their balance of cognition and emotion (Piaget & Inhelder, 1969). Piaget noted that play provides children a necessary break from life's realities while imitation fosters assimilation of their realities. Play is a key ingredient for children to cognitively and emotionally process their life events with the ultimate outcome being mastery over their experiences while building resiliency. Play is the ideal intervention tool for children in health care, because it optimizes their holistic development and functioning.

Play has a prime role in the lives of children, which makes it an effective tool for expression. See Box 11.2 for the general characteristics of play. Bolig (1990) explained, "Since the 1940s, nondirective/unstructured play has consistently been cited as a means of preventing anxiety, depression, and diminished mastery and control associated with the experience of being hospitalized as a child" (p. 232). As a familiar activity for children, play facilitates their expression of feelings and offers an emotionally safe place, which fosters children's abilities to cope (Lerwick, 2013). Play is an exceptional tool to facilitate children's self-expression, self-efficacy, and self-confidence regarding health care experiences. According to Landreth (2012), "Play is to the child what verbalization is to the adult" (p. 12).

BOX 11.2 GENERAL CHARACTERISTICS OF PLAY

- Intrinsic motivation
- Process not product
- Symbolic
- No external rules
- Active engagement

Rubin, Fein, & Vandenburg (1983)

MEDICAL PLAY

Medical play, a form of play that incorporates health care themes and utilizes health care equipment, (McCue, 1988), provides children an expressive medium with which to balance their affective and intellectual domains. Similar to play in general, McCue described medical play as a pleasurable experience sustained by the child but revolving around medical subject matter. Medical play differs from psychological preparation (or preparation for medical procedures), which gives the adult more control (Bolig, Yolton, & Nissen, 1991). Medical play exhibits the typical attributes of play but also has unique attributes (Box 11.3).

BOX 11.3 ATTRIBUTES OF MEDICAL PLAY

- Includes "medical themes and/or medical equipment"
- Is "voluntarily maintained by the child"
- Is enjoyable yet can be "intense and aggressive"
- Differs from psychological preparation (preparation for medical procedures is not play due to the adult directedness of psychological preparation)

(McCue, 1988, p. 158)

Medical play is a therapeutic modality that assists children's adaptation to their health care realities while assimilating their individual needs. Medical play sessions are nondirective, in other words the children possess the power to play without adult direction. McCue (1988) categorized medical play into four types: (a) role rehearsal/role reversal play, (b) medical fantasy play, (c) indirect medical play, and (d) medical art (Box 11.4). Role rehearsal/role reversal, the most traditional type of medical play, was demonstrated in the Sisk (2016) study. In the role rehearsal/role reversal medical play type, children take on the powerful roles of health-care providers while caring for doll patients using toy medical kits or actual medical equipment (McCue, 1988, p. 158). A doll patient is typically a body outline doll (Gaynard, Goldberger, and Laidley, 1991), that allows the child to project his/her perceptions onto the pretend patient (Figure 11.1). Gaynard, Goldberger, and Laidley discussed the use of cloth body-outline dolls within the Gaynard et al. (1998) Child Life Research Project. While no experimental data was kept on the body outline dolls, child life specialists noted that the dolls were effective for (a) building rapport with patients, (b) assessing patients' thoughts and emotions, (c) psychological preparation, (d) initiating medical play, (e) detecting misconceptions during medical play, (f) assessing children's understandings during medical play, (g) demonstrating appropriate coping, and (h) comforting the patients (pp. 217–222).

Figure 11.1 Body outline dolls.

BOX 11.4   FOUR CATEGORIES OF MEDICAL PLAY

■ **Role Rehearsal/Role Reversal Medical Play**
  Children take on the roles of health care providers demonstrating
  medical procedures on doll patients.
■ **Medical Fantasy Play**
  Children demonstrate medical play with non-medical items that may
  include toys used in their typical play.
■ **Indirect Medical Play**
  Children are provided experiences to educate and familiarize them
  with health care through non-threatening exploration. For example, a
  medical bingo game or a hospital scavenger hunts.
■ **Medical Art**
  Children engage in art activities with medical themes or use medical
  items in non-medical creative ways.

(McCue, 1988)

Intervention

Medical play originated as an intervention in the child life profession.
Emma Plank (1962), a key figure in child life studies (American Academy
of Pediatrics Committee on Hospital Care and Child Life Council, 2014),
developed six goals for this psychosocial health care profession in her book
Working with Children in Hospitals (p. 73). Plank's pioneering work focused
on children in hospitals, their active involvement in play, their interactions
with peers, and their abilities to cope with health care fears while working
through stressful experiences alongside trained professionals.

Recognition of play as vital for children's development in health care
environments has been further supported by Thompson and Stanford's
(1981) seminal work *Child Life in Hospitals: Theory and Practice*, as well as
The Handbook of Child Life: A Guide for Pediatric Psychosocial Care (Thompson,
2009). These foundational works in child life reinforced Plank's original
tenants that child life programs incorporate play for children in health care
settings. Medical play is now recognized as the hallmark therapeutic intervention for Certified Child Life Specialists.

Research studies have deemed medical play, one form of therapeutic
play, to be evidence-based practice for children with health care needs.
While not specifically medical play, therapeutic play was shown as an effective intervention for hospitalized school-age children's anxiety levels
(Clatworthy, 1981). Comparably, children waiting for outpatient neurology
clinic visits without supervised medical play were more anxious and cried

more than those children who participated in the supervised medical play sessions (Ispa, Barrett, & Kim, 1988). Medical play not only alleviates children's anxiousness, but plays a role in pain management. Children who received needle play (a specific type of role rehearsal/reversal medical play utilizing a needle for injections or intravenous line starts on a blank cloth doll patient) demonstrated less objective pain as indicated by pulse rates measured 5 minutes after the participants' blood work procedures (Young & Fu, 1988). In addition to physical benefits, medical play assists children emotionally. Nondirective medical play helped children with illnesses and their siblings express their feelings (Nabors et al., 2013). Research evidence exists to support medical play as a worthy intervention tool that encourages children to share their thoughts and feelings about health care experiences.

Research Method

There is limited research literature on medical play as a therapeutic intervention and less literature discussing the need for medical play as a data collection tool. Medical play is an inviting, hands-on activity that easily engages children. In her clinical experience as a certified child life specialist, Sisk observed when children were involved in activity (drawing, play, video games), the more likely they were to share verbally. Sisk called this the *busy hands, busy mouth* phenomenon. Rollins (2005) named this the "campfire effect" when talking about research interviews and described it as "the result of an activity or experience that provides a focal point shared by the individuals involved that serves to increase conversation in both quantity and intensity" (p. 213). Rollins explained that just like a campfire focuses people's attention, the physical act of drawing focuses the researcher's and participant's attention so the participant feels safe sharing more than he/she might in typical interviews. Medical play as a data collection method offers a therapeutic, active play mode of expression that encourages children's release of various thoughts, feelings, and perceptions. Medical play is an ideal research method to empower children to share their health care experiences and is a powerful data collection method to gather the children's voices.

As play, medical play provides a nonthreatening experience where participants feel free to interact with medical equipment. It is a safe activity, meaning the children uninhibitedly participate and freely express themselves (Lerwick, 2013). Safe engagement with the medical items through play leads children to demonstrate their understandings of health care experiences. Medical play is a versatile data collection method that offers participants safety, pleasure, and therapeutic expression.

Medical play supplies often consist of blank cloth body-outline dolls, markers, and the medical supplies and tools most commonly seen at pediatrician visits or before surgery (Figure 11.2). Participants in the Sisk (2016) study were introduced to the medical items, their names, and functions. The participants freely acknowledged they knew what the items were prior to play. The nondirective approach to medical play allowed the participants to demonstrate their knowledge of medical items. The researcher's typical prompt to engage the children in medical play was "Here's your patient, do what they need today." Often the children verbally explained what they were doing for their doll patients as they played.

At times, participants would include the researcher as an assistant in the medical play to open medical items or hold the patient still. These were child-directed interactions that are typical in role reversal/role rehearsal medical play (McCue, 1988) and maintained the children's control. Medical

• Gloves	• Tourniquet	• Oral syringe
• Hat	• Otoscope	• Swabs
• Mask	• Medicine cups	• Stethoscope
• Shoe covers	• Coban wrap	• EKG lead stickers
• Emesis basin	• Thermometer	• Band aids
• Blood pressure cuff	• Gauze	• Tongue depressors
• Oxygen mask	• Tape	• Alcohol wipes

Figure 11.2 Medical supplies incorporated into the medical play sessions.

play may be approached differently among children. Some participants immediately engaged with each item as it was introduced, but other children waited to see all the medical equipment before playing.

Medical play is a projective modality that affords participants the opportunity to project their experiences onto the body-outline doll. Medical play allowed the researcher to see the children's nonverbal perceptions as they cared for their doll patients with the medical supplies. Visually observing children's medical play provided an additional "voice" for hearing their health care perceptions. Medical play is a child-centered methodology that should be considered for giving children voice and agency when partnering with them in participatory research.

HEARING THE CHILDREN'S VOICES THROUGH MEDICAL PLAY

The following case study data from Sisk's (2016) research illustrate the use of medical play as a child-centered data collection method.

Alex

Alex, 7 years old, was talkative, full of energy, and loved dinosaurs. He was aware of his chronic kidney condition and the daily medical care required to maintain his health. Alex eagerly participated in medical play. Alex's medical play was a prime example of a child's ability to give "voice" to his cognitive understandings of health care realities, as well as the emotions he simultaneously experienced.

> Alex was comfortable with the glove and blew it up like a balloon. He demonstrated proper usage of the otoscope, thermometer, and oxygen mask. He was so familiar and comfortable with the tongue depressor that he called two of them "bang-bangs" and (bangs them on the table like drumsticks), and his mother said he used to bang them together when he was young. Upon his completion of medical play, he stated: "Now he's all better. Except he needs a smiley face." He provided more patient history saying: "He started sad. Cause, cause um, he got, got, like all boo-booed and stuff by the dinosaurs." (Sisk, 2016, p. 120)

Ben

Ben, 7 years old, was diagnosed with a rare brain stem disorder that required he have a tracheostomy tube. He had an easy-going, reserved personality yet was very interactive and able to "voice" his health care knowledge through medical play.

> Ben, having a history of health care experiences since birth, conveyed much knowledge while demonstrating his control of the medical equipment. His combining of an oxygen mask ("gas mask" as he named it) with an IV procedure was evidence of his understanding that the medication typically administered via the mask would eliminate the doll patient's pain. "Ok, now I wanted to put this on him, but I'm going to do a . . . What's it called? Like, ok, I want to put this on me, cause I'm going to do IV" (Ben, 7 years old). (Sisk, 2016, p. 121)

Instinctively, Ben also played out the medical care plan process known as Assessment, Plan, Intervention, and Evaluation (APIE). He demonstrated the APIE process through medical play, assessing his doll patient's temperature (with a thermometer) and throat (using a tongue depressor and otoscope). He swabbed the doll patient's nose and gave his patient the medical diagnosis of the flu with a rash on the doll's throat. He then took the patient's temperature again and gave medication. Ben, having many health care experiences during his young life, observed and absorbed the APIE process to know the appropriate sequence of events for diagnosing and treating a patient.

"VOICING" DEVELOPMENTAL VARIATIONS IN MEDICAL PLAY

The three female participants provided examples of Piaget's stages of cognitive development (Piaget & Inhelder, 1969) during their medical play sessions.

Dena

Dena was 6 years old and full of life. She exuberantly expressed herself in speech, through visual representations of emotions, and through play. She was diagnosed with a heart defect at birth and an intellectual disability. Dena exhibited behaviors that indicated she was in Piaget's pre-operational stage of cognitive development (Piaget & Inhelder, 1969). She utilized the medical equipment on her own body during medical play instead of on her body outline doll. She put a Band-Aid on her ear (because it was hurting that day) and put the thermometer in her mouth to take her own temperature. Egocentrism (the inability to distinguish between self and others) is a characteristic of the pre-operational stage of cognitive development (Piaget

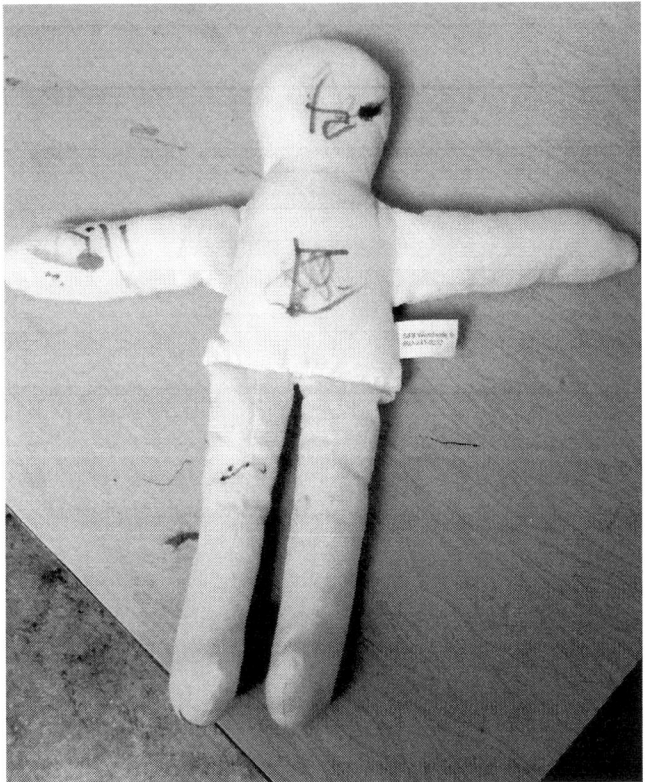

Figure 11.3   Dena's body-outline doll.

& Inhelder, 1969). Dena's use of the medical equipment directly on her own body reflects her egocentric thinking. Perhaps due to her intellectual disability, Dena did not assign any meanings to the markings she made on her body-outline doll. See Figure 11.3 of Dena's body-outline doll.

Fergie

Nine-year-old Fergie exhibited a happy, pleasant personality and enjoyed playing games with her family. She was diagnosed with an unspecified genetic disorder and a developmental disability. She appeared physically petite for her age and her speaking voice was small as well. During medical play, Fergie drew specific body parts on her body outline doll (eyes, hands, mouth, heart, hands, belly button, and knees; Figure 11.4), which was a key indication she was in Piaget's Concrete Operational Stage of Cognitive Development (Piaget & Inhelder, 1969). Initially the mouth she drew was

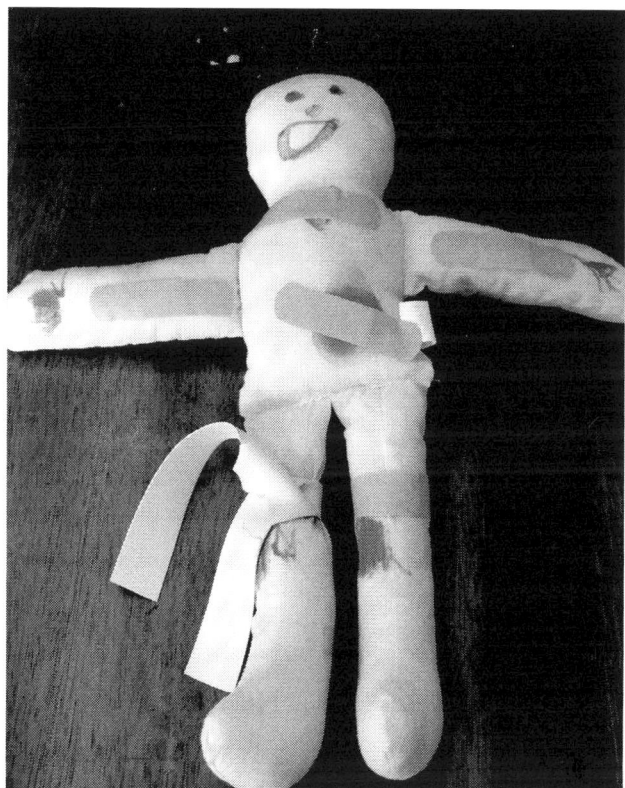

Figure 11.4 Fergie's body-outline doll.

just the bottom lip, but as she engaged in medical play she added a top lip so she could use the tongue depressor with the mouth opened wide. This artistic addition, prompted by her play, reflected that Fergie's thinking was concrete operational in development.

Emily

Emily, the oldest participant at 12 years old, was highly mature for her age, possessing a matter-of-fact personality. She was clearly in Piaget's formal operational stage of cognitive development (Piaget & Inhelder, 1969). Due to her ability to think logically, Emily did not approach medical play in the typical role rehearsal/role reversal style like the cognitively younger participants. McCue's (1988) attributes of medical play (Box 11.3) were evident during Emily's experience, which is why her play is still considered medical play.

Figure 11.5 Emily's body-outline doll.

Emily drew a realistic representation of herself on the body-outline doll. She thoroughly explored and interacted with the medical play supplies while verbally sharing her rich knowledge of previous experiences with each item. Emily discussed two challenging, painful health care experiences during medical play: blood draws and MRIs. While Emily was not engaging in typical role rehearsal/role reversal medical play (due to her cognitive level), the exposure to the medical equipment and the freedom to explore the items provided her a context to discuss her health care experiences.

Emily's formal operational thinking did not prevent her from benefiting from the medical play experience. When Emily completed her medical play session, she commented: "It's a lot more fun than I thought" (Sisk, 2016, p. 115) This statement substantiated the researcher's clinical belief that preteens and adolescents should be encouraged to participate in therapeutic medical play. See Figure 11.5 for Emily's medical play doll.

GENDER DIFFERENCES IN MEDICAL PLAY

Gender differences were notable among the participants in this research. The boys, Alex and Ben (7-year-olds), both assigned imaginative, strong male characters to their body-outline dolls (Figures 11.6 & 11.7). Related to their interests, Alex chose a dinosaur trainer, and Ben chose Superman. Neither boy was opposed to playing with the body outline dolls. The female participants did not assign specific imaginative characters to their body outline dolls, but treated the dolls as patients just as introduced by the researcher.

COMMONALITIES AMONG PARTICIPANTS' MEDICAL PLAY

There were two commonalities within the participants' medical play. First, the roles of doctors and nurses were represented in the youngest four

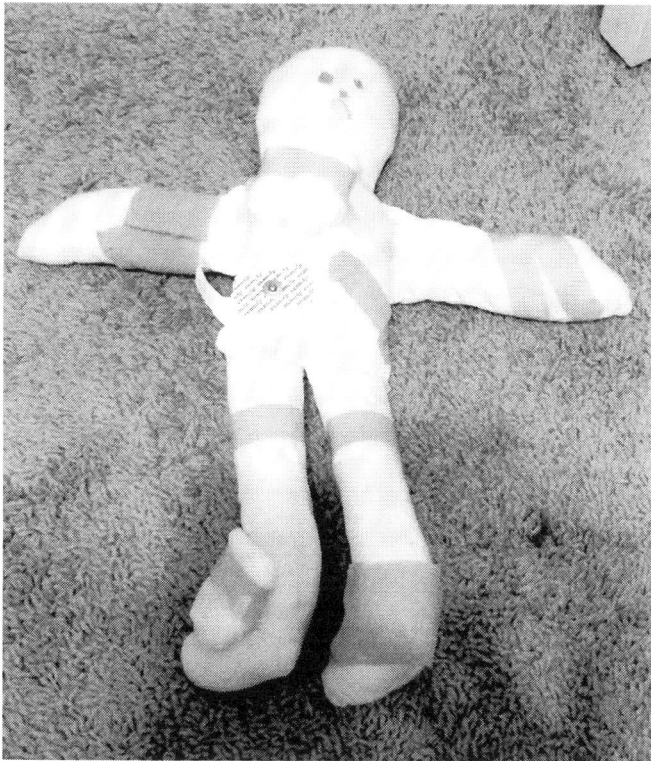

Figure 11.6 Alex's body-outline doll.

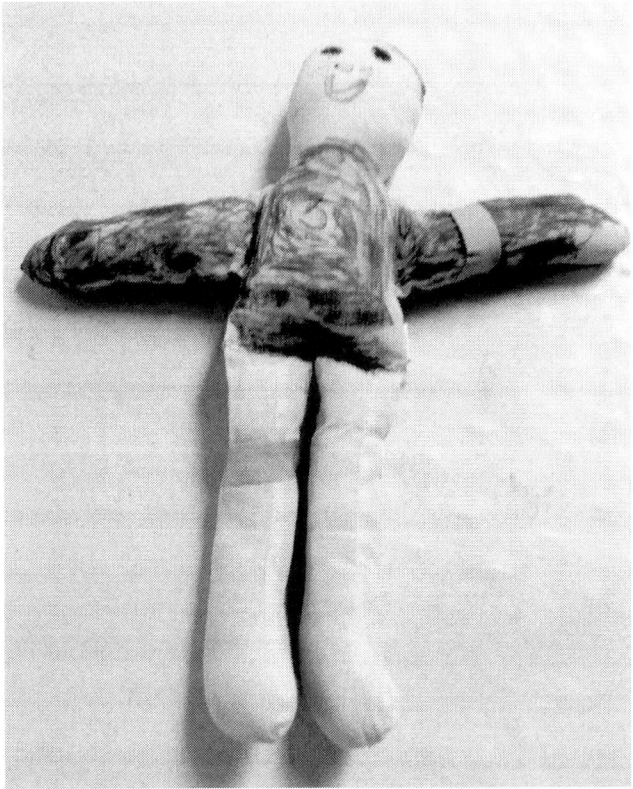

Figure 11.7 Ben's body-outline doll.

participants' medical play sessions. Regardless of their gender, the young participants chose both males and females to take on the doctor roles. Alex (7 years old) initially chose to be a nurse likely due to his mother and stepfather being nurses, but then switched to being a doctor insisting the researcher call him "Dr. Dinosaur Fixer" during the remainder of the medical play session. Dena, the youngest child with the intellectual disability, identified herself as a doctor-nurse combining the two roles. The children's choices of what health care role to assume in role rehearsal/role reversal medical play allowed their voices to be heard and demonstrated their familiarity with professional health care fields. The second commonality, among the younger participants, was the inclusion of medicine during medical play. The children gave their doll patients medications with medicine cups, oral syringes, and pretend needle sticks via injections and IVs (syringes without needles). While Emily (12 years old) did not administer medicine in her play session, she did discuss both doctors and nurses and the medications she received. Children with special health care needs voiced cognizance of their health care providers and the medications they received during medical play. Based on these common themes in participants' medical play, pediatric health care professionals should work to introduce themselves, clarify their titles, and discuss how medications will be administered.

CONCLUSION

Through medical play, the child participants in Sisk's (2016) study demonstrated their familiarity with medical professional roles, medical procedures, and medicine administration. Medical play permitted Sisk to learn more about her child participants' perceptions than if she had relied solely on verbal interviews. Verbal interviews would have produced only surface-level responses, whereas medical play revealed the children's different developmental and gender-related perceptions of their health care experiences. Furthermore, medical play usefully served to reveal Dena's perceptions despite her limited communication and intellectual abilities. The versatility of the medical play data collection method combined with the children's abilities to control the play facilitated the researcher's varied findings across developmental levels and gender.

Children with special health care needs (CSHCN) have stories worth listening to, yet common data collection methods such as parent or professional reports, impersonal surveys, or researcher-directed interviews provide limited access to the children's internal mental states and perceptions. We argue that listening to children's voices should involve more than listening to them talk. We propose an expanded definition of voice to include children's verbalizations, their visual representations (gestures, expressions, artistic drawings), and their play actions. Medical play, previously considered only a therapeutic intervention, offers a child-centered, nonthreatening, developmentally appropriate method for collecting the fuller voices of CSHCNs. Research that values the more comprehensive, more dynamic voices of children has the potential to positively influence practices. Both pediatric health care professionals and researchers can learn from listening to the "voices" of CSHCNs.

Questions for Reflection

1. How do children share their voices verbally, visually, and through play? Consider how the medical play of Alex, Ben, Fergie, and Emily revealed their perceptions and provided voice for their inner states.
2. How might parents' reports of their children's health care experiences mask or misrepresent the voices of children with special health

care needs? How do parents' voices compare to children's voices?
3. How could data collection from medical play add to medical research? How might observations of children's medical play complement other qualitative data collection methods?
4. Are there other therapeutic interventions used with children that would make ideal child-centered research tools?

Suggestions for Further Reading

Bolig, R. (1990). Play in health care settings: A challenge for the 1990s. *Children's Health Care, 19,* 229–233.

Bolig, R., Yolton, K., & Nissen, H. (1991). Medical play and preparation: Questions and issues. *Children's Health Care, 20,* 225–229.

Clark, C. D. (2011). *In a younger voice: Doing child centered qualitative research.* New York, NY: Oxford University Press.

Gaynard, L., Wolfer, J., Goldberger, J., Thompson, R., Redburn, L., & Laidley, L. (1998). *Psychosocial care of children in hospitals: A clinical practice manual from the ACCH child life research project.* Rockville, MD. Child Life Council, Inc.

Houtrow, A., Okumura, M., Hilton, J., & Rehm, R. (2011). Profiling health and health related services for children with special health care needs with and without disabilities. *Academic Pediatrics, 11*(6), 508–516.

McCue, K. (1988). Medical play: An expanded perspective. *Children's Health Care, 16,* 157–161.

Rollins, J. (2005). Tell me about it: Drawing as a communication tool for children with cancer. *Journal of Pediatric Oncology Nursing, 22*(4), 203–221.

Thompson, R. (2009). *The handbook of child life.* Springfield, IL: Charles C. Thomas.

Thompson, R., & Stanford, G. (1981). *Child life in hospitals: Theory and practice.* Springfield, IL: Charles C. Thomas.

NOTES

1. Sisk was the researcher with Baker serving as her dissertation committee chair.
2. Pseudonyms have been used for the participants' names in this chapter.
3. Semi-structured interviews, drawings, and body maps were the other child-centered methods used in Sisk's (2016) research.

REFERENCES

American Academy of Pediatrics Policy Statement Committee on Hospital Care and Child Life Council. (2014). Child life services. *Pediatrics, 133*(5), e1471–e1478.

Arango, P., Fox, H., Lauver, C., McManus, M., McPherson, M., & Newacheck, P. (1998). A new definition of children with special health care needs. *Pediatrics, 102*(1), 137–140.

Association of Child Life Professionals. (2017). *The child life profession: Mission, values, vision.* Retrieved from http://www.childlife.org/child-life-profession/mission-values-vision

Bethell, C., Read, D., Stein, R., Blumberg, S., Wells, N., & Newacheck, P. (2002). Identifying children with special health care needs: Development and evaluation of a short screening instrument. *Ambulatory Pediatrics, 2*(1), 38–48.

Bolig, R. (1990). Play in health care settings: A challenge for the 1990s. *Children's Health Care, 19,* 229–233.

Bolig, R., Yolton, K., & Nissen, H. (1991). Medical play and preparation: Questions and issues. *Children's Health Care, 20,* 225–229.

Bramlett, M., Read, D., Bethell, C., & Blumberg, S. (2009). Differentiating subgroups of children with special health care needs by health status and complexity of health care needs. *Maternal and Child Health Journal, 13,* 151–163.

Child and Adolescent Health Measurement Initiative. (2012). *About the Data Resource Center.* Data Resource Center for Child and Adolescent Health. Retrieved from http://www.childhealthdata.org/about/drc

Clark, C. D. (2011). *In a younger voice: Doing child centered qualitative research.* New York, NY: Oxford University Press.

Clatworthy, S. (1981). Therapeutic play: Effects on hospitalized children. *Children's Health Care, 9*(4), 108–113.

Eddy, L., & Engel, J. (2008). The impact of child disability type on the family. *Rehabilitation Nursing, 33,* 98–103.

Eiser, C., & Morse, R. (2001). Can parents rate their child's health-related quality of life? Results of a systematic review. *Quality of Life Research, 10,* 347–357.

Garth, B., & Aroni, R. (2003). 'I value what you have to say'. Seeing the perspective of children with a disability, not just their parents. *Disability & Society, 18*(5), 561–576.

Gaynard, L., Goldberger, J., & Laidley, L. (1991). The use of stuffed, body-outline dolls with hospitalized children and adolescents. *Children's Health Care, 20*(4), 216–224.

Grbich, C. (2013). Introduction. *Qualitative data analysis: An introduction* (2nd ed.; pp. 3–14). Thousand Oaks, CA: SAGE.

Hollan, W., & Skinner, L. (2009). Assessment and documentation in child life. In R. H. Thompson (Ed.), *The handbook of child life* (pp. 116–135). Springfield, IL: Thomas.

Houtrow, A., Okumura, M., Hilton, J., & Rehm, R. (2011). Profiling health and health related services for children with special health care needs with and without disabilities. *Academic Pediatrics, 11*(6), 508–516.

Ispa, J., Barrett, B., & Kim, Y. (1988). Effects of supervised play in a hospital waiting room. *Children's Health Care, 16*(3), 195–200.

Landreth, G. (2012). *Play Therapy: The Art of the Relationship* (3rd ed.). New York, NY: Routledge.

Lerwick, J. (2013). Psychosocial implications of pediatric surgical hospitalization. *Seminars in Pediatric Surgery, 22,* 129–133.

Lindeke, L., Fulkerson, J., Chesney, M., Johnson, L., & Savik, K. (2009). Children's perceptions of healthcare survey. *Nursing Administration Quarterly, 33*(1), 26–31.

McCue, K. (1988). Medical play: An expanded perspective. *Children's Health Care, 16,* 157–161.

Nabors, L., Bartz, J., Kichler, J., Sievers, R., Elkins, R., & Pangallo, J. (2013). Play as a mechanism of working through medical trauma for children with medical illnesses and their siblings. *Issues in Comprehensive Pediatric Nursing, 36*(3), 212–224.

Patton, M. (2002). Strategic themes in qualitative inquiry. *Qualitative research & evaluation methods* (3rd ed.). (pp. 37–73). Thousand Oaks, CA: SAGE.

Piaget, J., & Inhelder, B. (1969). *The psychology of the child.* New York, NY: Basic Books.

Rollins, J. (2005). Tell me about it: Drawing as a communication tool for children with cancer. *Journal of Pediatric Oncology Nursing, 22*(4), 203–221.

Rubin, K., Fein, G., & Vandenberg, B. (1983). Play. In P. H. Mussen (Ed.), *Handbook of child life psychology: Social development.* New York, NY: Wiley.

Sisk, C. (2016). *Children with special health care needs and disabilities: Perceptions of health care experiences.* (Doctoral dissertation). Retrieved from ProQuest. (Order No. 10242687)

Spratling, R., Coke, S., & Minick, P. (2012). Qualitative data collection with children. *Applied Nursing Research, 25,* 47–53.

Spieth, L., & Harris, C. (1996). Assessment of health-related quality of life in children and adolescents: An integrative review. *Journal of Pediatric Psychology, 21*(2), 175–193.

Thompson, R. (2009). *The handbook of child life.* Springfield, IL: Thomas.

Thompson, R., & Stanford, G. (1981). *Child life in hospitals: Theory and practice.* Springfield, IL: Thomas.

Young, M., & Fu, V. (1988). Influence of play and temperament on the young child's response to pain. *Children's Health Care, 16*(3), 209–215.

van Dyck, P., McPherson, M., Strickland, B., Nesseler, K., Blumberg, S., Cynamon, M., & Newacheck, P. (2002). The national survey of children with special health care needs. *Ambulatory Pediatrics, 2* (1), 29–37.

Varni, J. W., Limbers, C. A., & Newman, D. A. (2009). Using factor analysis to confirm the validity of children's self-reported health-related quality of life across different modes of administration. *Clinical Trials, 6,* 185–195.

Vogl, S. (2015). Children's verbal, interactive, and cognitive skills and implications for interviews. *Quality and Quantity. 49,* 319–338.

World Health Organization. (2001). *International classification of functioning disability and health.* Retrieved from http://www.who.int/classifications/icf/en/

PART III

ISSUES OF REPRESENTATION IN THE ANALYSIS AND
INTERPRETATION OF CHILDREN'S PERSPECTIVES

CHAPTER 12

DIFFRACTIVE LENSES CATCHING STORIES

The Meaning of Belonging Through the Voice of Adolescents

Hanne Vandenbussche, Elisabeth De Schauwer, and Geert Van Hove

ABSTRACT

In this chapter the meaning of belonging is mapped by listening to the voice of adolescents in a secondary school in an urban context in Flanders, Belgium. The first author participated in a class with seven pupils, moving on intersecting axes of ability, ethnicity, socioeconomic status, gender, and so on. Catching the meaning of belonging in the project resulted in filming the multiple voices of the pupils in the class while imagining and practicing their past and future dreams. The stance of the researcher in this exploratory study can be conceptualized as a "bricoleur" or "handywoman" (Lévi-Strauss, 1962/1966; Kincheloe & Berry, 2004; Kincheloe 2005), puzzling the plural and singular voices present and trying to materialize them in a film. Processes of "becoming-in-the-world-with-others" (Shildrick, 2002) from a position in the margin surfaced. For the researcher to see the concept of belonging "at

Participatory Methodologies to Elevate Children's Voice and Agency, pages 275–294
Copyright © 2019 by Information Age Publishing

work," she had to become a part of the complex assemblages arising through the encounters, by listening and following the pupils in their daily actions and environment, connected to people, historicity, places, objects, and so on. A diffractive analysis of the data gave meaning to the complexity and relational character of belonging. The individual voices of the pupils blurred and intra-acted with each other and the relational meshwork they were part of.

CONTEXT

In this chapter, we want to take you on a journey. We attempt an empirical wandering in which we travel along the dreams of seven adolescents attending a secondary school in Ghent, a city in Flanders (Belgium).

Our story begins with a lesson we organized in this class, a sixth-grade vocational training.[1] A class of seven pupils was brought together at school: Rayann, Sam, Sara, Gabrielle, Katarina, Sophie, and Iliana. Their teacher, Emily, joined in. The authors were interested in the meaning of "belonging" according to the pupils. What does this concept mean to them? It became clear that simply asking the question "What does belonging mean to you?" was not helpful for them. They had to make the meaning concrete and lively by showing where it was present in their life stories. The class of seven shared what they consider central in their lives with each other and with the first author. They talked about what they like to do, about who is important in their lives, about what makes their hearts beat faster. They communicated moments they felt excluded and moments they felt included. Sometimes this thinking accompanied strong emotions. Drawing on the portrait they had sketched, they tried to share their stories. After this lesson, their teacher Emily asked them whether they wanted to move on in picturing their future dreams building on what we accomplished there. They needed some time to think; sharing personal things was hard. One of the girls said: "I cannot tell you about some things, it is too close to my heart." However, in the same movement they considered it a fascinating project to finish their secondary school. Their teacher stimulated them and emphasized the great opportunity to work on their own project. Although Emily will be moving behind the scenes a lot in what follows, her part in the creation of these dreams is essential.

We decided together we were going to work with film. Every student of the class got some time to think through the dreams he/she was going to bring in stage. They needed each other to materialize these. The first author used a camera and met the class several times to work on the project to make sure every pupil could visualize their dream. We worked through the scripts when at school, and we walked to the scenes together.

In what follows we will highlight some of their dreams and stories. We will explore three stories in particular: the stories of Gabrielle, Rayann, and

Sam. The other pupils' voices, as well as multiple others, will be interwoven in the stories we will present. We consider "voice" as plural and complex. Voice appears as a "process of couplings and connections of different bodies, places, spaces, times, utterances, and becomings" (Mazzei, 2016, p. 154). Following Mazzei (2016) we do not approach voice as "a" voice that can be linked to an "I" of a humanist subject, but to an unbounded voice.

We aim to conceptualize belonging by listening to the dreams of the pupils and connect this input to some philosophical views and notions, as diffraction (Barad, 2007) and assemblage (Delanda, 2016). The stories will be "cut together apart"[2] (Barad, 2007) to gain insight into the meaning of belonging through the eyes of the storytellers. Before moving on to the stories, we dwell on a framework to read the dreams of the adolescents. The pupils always present their stories through an assemblage that moves and is moved. We will try to map some of these moving assemblages of constellations, of dreams, of voices, of memories, and so on in this book chapter.

ASSEMBLAGES OF INTRA-ACTIONS AND INTRA-ACTING ASSEMBLAGES

In what follows, we will present parts of the stories. We use the concept of *assemblage* as a framework to consider those parts. We regard the concept of assemblage as a moving constellation of intra-acting[3] parts that is taking the perspective of the adolescents into account (Davies, 2014a). Delanda (2016) explains assemblages are constellations where the dangers of "reified generalities" (such as power, resistance, and we would like to add society) can be overcome. We want to use this framework to approach more "precision" and let young pupils living in the margin speak out.

Assemblages are concerned with contingent territories and codes that work through lines of de- and reterritorialization and de- and recoding (Delanda, 2016). These processes are transversing, as such thinking through "assemblage" is helpful to pursue a diffractive reading where ontology and epistemology are not separated from each other.

The work of Gilles Deleuze and Félix Guattari (e.g., Deleuze & Guattari, 1987) helps to give meaning to the concept of assemblage. The term in French is *agencement*. The word in English fails to capture the meaning of the original, where the term refers to the action of matching or fitting together a set of components (*agencer*), as well as to the result of this action: "an ensemble of parts that mesh together well" (Delanda, 2016, p. 1). Deleuze and Guattari use several definitions to give meaning to the concept. One of the definitions catches the meaning we ascribe to it here: "We will call an assemblage every constellation of singularities and traits deducted from the flow—selected, organized, stratified—in such a way as to converge, artificially or naturally. An assemblage is, in this sense, a veritable invention" (Deleuze & Guattari, 1987, p. 406; see also Delanda, 2016, p. 79). We cling writings of Hickey-Moody (2007) and Barad (2007) together to conceive assemblages as always moving multiplicities of connections in a space–time–mattering.

As Wise (2005) notices, assemblage is not a "static term." Assemblage is not a set of predetermined parts that can be put together like a puzzle. Wise (2005) states "there is a sense that an assemblage is a whole of some sort that expresses some identity and claims a territory" (p. 77). The idea of "territory" is crucial. Since it is not considered "any space," these territories have a stake, a claim and they express some specific liaison. An assemblage is characterized by a play of contingency and looking for interconnection. Hickey-Moody (2007) elucidates how an assemblage is a contextual arrangement in which heterogeneous times, spaces, bodies, and modes of operation are connected. Hence, assemblage implies a certain "wholeness" of intra-acting parts, which can be human, nonhuman, material, virtual, imply effects and feelings, time, and so on. This wholeness is characterized by how it starts to exist in interconnection. It is however never a fixed entity, but works as a strong unity opening new possibilities because of the moving composition of the parts. In this way, assemblage is a phenomenon[4] in which meaning is addressed to concepts as belonging because it shows how the concept "works" and "matters" (i.e., literally by giving it material ground and figuratively by gaining insights into what is important to the adolescents speaking here). It has characteristics which open it up and let it grow in multiple directions. On the other hand, it is always coming together and moving apart. Assemblages are entangled in events concentrated in timespaces. Through certain constellations assemblages become organized, but differences in the constellations and the moving character of the assemblage, will also undo this organization and reassemble differently. We consider this phenomenon a fundamental impetus for agency.

DIFFRACTIVELY CUTTING THE STORIES TOGETHER APART

We bring the concepts of bricoleur or handywoman (Lévi-Strauss, 1962/1966; Kincheloe & Berry, 2004; Kincheloe, 2005) and diffraction (Barad, 2007) into play to approach the stories shared by the adolescents. These concepts will be our gazing tools to give significance to "belonging" according to their voice. We will briefly present the meaning of these concepts. After narrating some of the pupils' stories, we will try to put the concepts "at work" in the stories and dreams shared.

Claude Lévi-Strauss developed in his work La pensée sauvage (The savage mind) (1962/1966) the concept of *bricoleur*. In this book, Lévi-Strauss distinguishes two "levels" of scientific knowledge following his anthropological research with several tribes illustrating an extraordinary knowledge of plants and animals living in their environments. Lévi-Strauss argues people from these tribes use empirical observation and imagination as tools to gain knowledge of the world. They make use of all their senses and their intuition in approaching reality. He connects this way of gaining knowledge with a bricoleur. The bricoleur uses materials he finds in his collection to give them a new function and finality. Lévi-Strauss attributes to the bricoleur a perception and a train of thought as "precise." It is a science of the "concrete." The bricoleur works with his/her hands and uses heterogeneous parts collected to get results. Lévi-Strauss contrasts this with a rational representationalist approach still dominating most natural sciences. He states there is a parallel with the "entrepreneur," trying to get power over the world by taking distance and being "objective." Kincheloe and Berry (2004) worked on the theoretical/methodological grounding of the concept.

In this chapter, we try to work as the bricoleur. We will bring some parts together and let the pupils speak by drawing on concepts of Karen Barad and Gilles Deleuze. The bricoleur or handywoman in this case, makes use of a limited number of tools with multiple possibilities to put to work (see e.g., Badley, 2014). We will make a bricolage in connecting it with diffraction and assemblage, as well as parts of film we collected with the class, the multiple and plural voices of the pupils, who so generously shared their feelings, ideas, and stories. We elaborate on constructions and deconstructions of the collected items to bring up the meaning of belonging according to the youths. With the method of bricolage, we do not intend to lift each story out separately and make a collage of them as it were. We hold on to a conception of researching social reality through looking for precision (Bergson, 1946/1997). We intend to find precision by listening closely and by using all our senses to the stories the pupils in this study share (Davies, 2014b).

The position of the researchers as bricoleurs is accompanied by looking with a diffractive lens. We want to interweave diffraction and bricolage in our search to give meaning to belonging.

We borrow the concept of *diffraction* from Karen Barad (2007). She utilizes diffraction as a different conception of *reflection*. It is a concept originating from optical physics that helps to gain insight in phenomena we experience in natural sciences, but also in cultural sciences, social sciences, and so on. The easiest way to envision diffraction is to think about a pond or river where you throw two stones in the water simultaneously. What you perceive are waves overlapping in concentric circles. This is a diffraction pattern. When the waves meet, a higher wave is created. Barad does not only regard diffraction as an optical metaphor, but also as a method and practice that pays attention to material engagement with data and the relations of difference and how they matter (Barad 2007; see also Bozalek & Zembylas, 2016). Barad uses it as a "tool" to highlight the entanglement of material-discursive phenomena in the world. In this chapter, it is helpful to pursue our method of bricolage by looking with a diffractive lens, thus giving meaning to the stories and constant production of difference in mutual entanglement arising in the film scenes.

Diffractively reading implies attentively and carefully reading for differences that "matter" in their fine details (Dolphijn & Van der Tuin, 2012). Diffraction is not just a matter of interference, but of entanglement, an ethico-onto-epistemological matter (Barad, 2007; Van de Putte, De Schauwer, Van Hove & Davies, 2017; De Schauwer, Van de Putte, & Davies, 2018). The several connections present in phenomena all have agential force, human and nonhuman.

The lives we meet show patterns of difference and repetition. The pupils long for belonging by fitting in a suppositious predetermined community. However, during the "performing" and discussing of their dreams they break through these predetermined assumptions by opening other possibilities of living and belonging. Doing a diffractive analysis requires not knowing where you are going in advance, as well as taking the continuous interference of intra-actions seriously (Davies, 2014b). As diffractive researchers, we do not intend to present a representationalist interpretation of what belonging might mean. In the relational onto-epistemological account we draw on, the idea of observing an "entity" from a "distance" and consequently achieving objectivist knowledge about it is problematic. With Davies (2014b) we state:

> The diffractive researcher's task, then, is not to tell of something that exists independent of the research encounter, but to open up an immanent truth—to access that which is becoming true, ontologically *and* epistemologically, in the moment of the research encounter. (p. 3, emphasis in original)

BELONGING THROUGH THE ADOLESCENTS' VOICE

The Story of Gabrielle

Gabrielle connects the meaning of belonging with important people in her life. Her search for her father drove her to Belgium. She has Jamaican roots and misses her country tremendously. She located her father, but life in Flanders with him appeared difficult. She loves her mother, her sister, and brother. She explicitly leaves the father out. In expressing her dreams, she utters a desire to help people. We visualize her dream by going to the center for homeless people in Ghent. The class is eager to know everything about how these people are helped out. "Are small children coming here too?" "How does it work when they have to go to school?"

Also, Gabrielle wants to get married on the beach of Jamaica. The class works together to set the stage for this dream. We will describe the scene of the beach here.

> We go to Blaarmeersen (a local small beach in Ghent), the closest we could get to imagine a Jamaican beach near school. The weather was nice. The sun reflected into the water and enriched the dreamy character of our mission.

> Gabrielle is getting all dressed up, by putting on the wedding dress of her teacher. Sara, another student, helps her to close the buttons of her dress. The other pupils are watching her transforming and stand somewhat lost on the edge of the road. She calls out to them "Come on! I'm not a statue you know!" (laughter of the others).

> She walks to the waterline; her footsteps leaving a trace in the sand. Gabrielle smiles and clearly enjoys this moment. Her eyes twinkle. She has a beautiful red rose in her hair. She holds a bouquet with flowers that they gathered on the road in her hands. Her beautiful dark skin contrasts to the white dress she's wearing. A certain sadness moves over her face: "I came to find my father, but I didn't plan to stay here... (silence)" "I came to Belgium when I was 17. I came here with great expectations about my bond with him. In the end, it does not work out. I don't get along with his new wife. I moved out and live with my aunt now. This I regret, that I came to Belgium for him." Then she starts to talk about her boyfriend, the twinkle is back. She is already engaged and shows the ring on her finger with great pride and a big smile. This dream is going to come true very soon... "He should be respectful. And just stay who he is." She looks up and stares at the water. She plays with her dress. "I also want to have children, three of them. It doesn't matter if they will be boys or girls, or... They are welcome the way they are." She calls out to the others: "Everybody, get behind me and watch out!" The other pupils are looking at her from a distance, but still in close connection to her. She swings the bouquet with flowers over her shoulder [See Figure 12.1]. Sophie catches it with great enthusiasm. She will be next in line! The class is shouting and is very excited.

The story of Gabrielle emphasizes the importance of interrelationships to experience belonging. She expresses a deep need to be connected to and with the people who are important to her. The relationship with her father is confusing. She traveled here from Jamaica to find him, all by herself, to connect with him. The others from the class already told the first author

Figure 12.1 Gabrielle throwing away the bouquet.

it is difficult for her to share this with "strangers." By looking for means to take her voice seriously and opening up the space to make her dreams actual, it felt safe for her to share abundantly.

It was not her intention to stay in Belgium. Still she does. This context and environment offer opportunities for young people to go to school, to find a job, to build out a life on their own, and so on. "It's a better life here." This withholds her to return to Jamaica (at least for now). In everything she does and says, her love for her country is echoed. She performs and plays a part. She is the director, the screenwriter, and the actress. She takes matters in her own hands to connect with her story and to materialize her hopes and dreams. She illustrates how belonging is tied to the sun, the sand, the water, her mother, her house, her brother and sister, and so on. This story is interlaced with the story below.

THE STORY OF RAYANN

Rayann also moved from Jamaica to Belgium. She has been here a bit longer than Gabrielle. For her too, the connection with her father was the reason to come here. This was not a choice, but an obligation. The relationship has been working out, although she is living alone in Ghent at a very young age. She is still in secondary school, but she is determined to work here and earn money to send to her mother in Jamaica. She wants to take care of her family. Rayann dreams about a beautiful house—a place where she can feel free to develop her own skills.

> The class walked together looking for a nice place for Rayann. Sam, Gabrielle, Sara, and Sophie checked an advertisement to buy a house near Ghent. They saw the prices and swallowed. We arrive at a nice neighborhood. Rayann already critically discussed some of the houses she passed by. One of them she adored. She gave suggestions about how she would adapt the color of the house, replace some parts or switch them. We moved on and passed by a house at the Leie (a river). Emily, the teacher, knew the person who lived there and asked if Rayann could buy the house. The man smiled: "This is indeed a nice house. My children love it too... We have the city very near, but on the other hand we have nature, the water, a beautiful view. It's unique in Ghent. It costs a lot of money..." Rayann responded: "Yes... I will have to save a lot." "You can go out and watch the garden." Rayann steps out into the garden. "Oh, this is really nice. It looks like a Jamaican garden. We have chickens too. Some plants over there... Some pineapple growing over here. And then a coconut tree in the middle!" (see Figure 12.2).

She talks about Jamaica. She thinks Belgium can offer her chances to become well-educated and have a diploma. Here she can find a job more easily than at home. It is a way to help out her mother, who doesn't have a lot of money. On the other hand, she criticizes this country: "I will not grow old here. It's crazy

Figure 12.2   Rayann's dream house with "Jamaican" garden.

what you do with older people. When people get old you put them in a rest home where they can do nothing. It is so boring when you get old here. In Jamaica your family takes care of you when you grow old. They don't 'put you away.'"

Rayann was looking for her "American Dream" in Belgium. She already experiences what it means to live alone while still going to school, where she lives her life with the little means she has. She believes in breaking through hegemonic discourses underlying this society and working hard to "gain" more in life. Why would a beautiful garden and a big house located in a rich area in Ghent not be an option for a young Black woman living in straitened circumstances? She realizes what it means to save money. This is what she does to help her mother. It is also this person she names when she's asked who or what is important to her. She struggles with the love for Jamaica and on the other hand the prosperity of the neighborhood she is living in in Belgium. Rayann, but also the others, make difficult choices at a very young age. While materializing her story in a house with a beautiful garden, everything she connects with this materialization is about her longing and belonging of real and virtual places and spaces elsewhere. She reflects in it her striving for another life where she can choose and pick out what she needs to make her life work and be interconnected with those she loves and what she loves, as well as what she urges to be and to become. When trying to connect her image on belonging by visualizing her dream, it becomes clear belonging is about interrelationship, not just with people, but also with nonhuman matters.

The Story of Sam

The third story we want to share is about Sam. Sam wants to run his own pancake house. He has needed extra support during his school career because of learning difficulties. He states to be extremely happy in his class here. He got a second chance to graduate. This opens perspectives for him. He can flourish in an environment where they believe in him and take into account his needs in tempo to exercise some tasks, as well as to understand certain assignments.

> Sam wanted to visualize his dream in a pancake house. He pondered the location. "It would be nice to have it in Bruges. That is a small and romantic city. A little medieval... That should work to attract customers!" The class took the tram to Art House Bavart, an alternative meeting place for artists in the city of Ghent, an ideal location to invent a new pancake house. They dropped in separately. Like a school of fish, they came together again and formed a whole. We were welcomed to come in and prepare the scene. Emily, the school teacher, had baked a lot of pancakes with her other classes to make the dream of Sam

real. He got a white skirt to put on and was requested to start work . . . "No, Sam, not with your hands, you should use a fork and knife." Sam looked scared, as he thought he did something wrong: his back curled up, his shoulders went down and he tried to become invisible. Emily noticed his unease and made a little joke, subsequently telling him he could move on. He smiled and looked a bit shy. He asked the confirmation of Emily as he proceeded: "Is it okay like this?" Then he started to go to the small tables where his classmates were waiting. A little nervous, he asked them what they wanted and went back to prepare their orders. He brought the plates enthusiastically: "A pancake with brown sugar? Here you go!" He enjoyed (t)his moment. After eating their pancakes, he went off to one of the tables where Sara, his best friend, was sitting. He started to chat with her and a trainee (see Figure 12.3). The stress was gone; he was doing a good job. He laughed and was performing his job as a good host wonderfully. He was proud and felt recognized. He talked about his brother who was going to university. "It is very heavy for him. I feel like I must support him. My parents support me, and he supports them . . . Yeah, we all support each other . . . I also dream about getting married and having children, maybe two or one child . . . Not thirteen, that would be too much" (laughter).

Sam adores his family and loves to cook. He would really like to earn his own money and be able to exercise his rights as "a good citizen." In his story the neoliberal citizen who manages to earn good money, who is independent, and knows what hard work is, arises even more explicitly than in the others' dreams. Belonging then is connected to achieving the status of "this good citizen," also echoing his parents' voice. This urge contrasts with his longing for time and chances, even as his needs to function in an environment where warm contacts and understanding set the tone. It seems this desire emerges constantly and is almost a precondition to achieve the dream

Figure 12.3 Sam in "his" pancake house.

of independence and success. He needs to belong in such an entanglement of connections to chase his dream.

DIFFRACTIVE LENSES CATCHING BELONGING

The Meaning of Belonging Produced Through Agential Forces

In the film we made together with the adolescents, a relational ontology is endorsed. The agency the pupils perform is not something they "own," it is a matter of possibilities for reconfiguring entanglements, an enactment. They take response-ability (Barad, 2014) and perform agency in mutual entanglement in how they construct belonging. Agency is about "the power to engage with others in ways that open up the capacity for thought and being" (Davies, 2014b, p. 9). The school these pupils attend, takes their needs to learn by doing and experience seriously. Their teacher, Emily, acted as an important facilitator to help create the liminal spaces[5] to perform their agency. Agency then concerns practice and *doing*, an engagement with mattering.

> Agency itself is a matter of intra-acting, an enactment, not something someone or something has. Agency cannot be designated as an attribute of "subjects" or "objects" (since they do not exist as such). Agency is not an attribute whatsoever. It is "doing" or "being" in its intra-activity. (Barad, 2007, p. 178)

At every moment, particular possibilities exist and these hold a responsibility to intervene in the world's becoming, "to contest and rework what matters and what is excluded from mattering" (Barad, 2007, p. 178). These diffractive thoughts bring forth inventive provocations. They are creative attempts to interpret the world.

Diffractively reading through the stories crisscrossing each other we gain insight into the various entanglements these pupils present/perform. The role of the bricoleur in this part is being attentive to what gets excluded as well as what comes to matter. The diffraction processes deliver the pieces and elements we are matching together to get meaning out of the stories.

We experience Katarina is very bighearted in what "matters" when discussing all she loves: "my family, my boyfriend, my class, I love to act, to perform, to sing, to dance…" This is situated in her local context where she feels belonging. Sophie talks about "Happiness. To have a big house, get married, have two children and earn good money." Gabrielle takes another perspective: "I love my family, my mother, brother, and sister. I want to help people who are poor." What comes to matter is produced by the cutting of the camera, their cutting by expressing their dreams and all the underlying material-discursive discourses constantly (re)shaping dreams (i.e., the independent, autonomous citizen doing a great job in contributing to his/her society economically and socially). Inside these agential intra-actions, belonging gets meaning. In the film, the dreams overlap in lines about work, traveling, and family. In these lines, we recognize a pattern of repetition, and through that repetition, effects of difference arise (Barad, 2007; Deleuze, 1967/1994). Sam comes from a well-off environment; he has learning difficulties which make him dependent on support in the class, a good connection with his speech therapist, "golden teachers" giving him time, his brother and parents, his class, the school, his small village, the train, and so on. Rayann grew up poor. Coming to Belgium, she connected with her father (also bringing her here), with her class, with her small house, Jamaica, the rest home, and so on. For Gabrielle longing for her relatives came up too, as well as feeling at home, Jamaica, the beach, her boyfriend, her class, and so on. They all experience what it means to be surrounded by a complexity of matters and people to get chances and be part of a community.

The adolescents are making claims that are valuable to look at fixed discourses and practices existing in a certain society. Additionally, they illustrate a strong notion about how they see themselves belong in *this* society and how they would intra-act in *this* community to shape their own idea of *their* future, taking into account *their* historicity. They resist and at the same time follow current discourses. Rayann illustrates this when criticizing how she perceives the Belgian way of treating people growing old. In the same movement, Belgium holds chances, freedom, education, which are often missed in the "own," "local" context. In their encounters, they come to matter (Davies et al., 2013).

We recognize this paradoxical attitude in all the pupils' stories. They struggle with abstract ideals closely entwined with a neoliberal focus and meanwhile they resist these ideas almost stubbornly and illustrate how they want to follow their own path.

The dreams the pupils practice and image shift over each other and transform the assemblages arising. Looking through a diffractive lens, both the researchers and the subjects engage in an affirmative way with difference. Belonging then appears as a non-definable ungraspable feeling "at home," constantly changing and moving. Lines of affect and feeling, attach belonging to people significant to them, to places important to them, as well as to chances, and the fundamental freedom to live a life with moveable borders. "Home" is in movement. They connect it with traveling between their "own" country and Belgium, and exploring the world. They associate it with doing something that is important for them (e.g., working in a hospital, helping poor people, working in a rest home). Home is also related to concrete materiality attached to "this home" (e.g., tree, shape, weather). They need the possibility to dream and are aware that all these relations are constantly changing.

This is how we see the diffractive lens operating in and in-between these stories. This makes it clear that we cannot fix belonging; we need to listen to the adolescents' dreams and watch how it works for every one of them, through their overlapping stories in the effects of difference.

(Re)assembling Dreams About Belonging

In each story, assemblages are reassembled several times. However, also between the stories this movement happens constantly.

We see assemblages arise out of the class itself and how the pupils have to connect with each other to make their dreams visible and vivid. Assemblages are transforming in every dream and between the different dreams. They exist of connections with other people, but also with other places and spaces (e.g., Jamaica, Belgium, beach, house), and they relate to other matters as well. We think about the beautiful long white dress of Gabrielle, the symbol of a wedding, which she cannot put on alone. The connection with the sand on the beach, the water, the sun. In Rayann's story we perceive the connection with the garden, where the coconut tree is striking. There was no coconut tree. Her dream is very real in that moment. For Sam the density of the relationship with his parents and brother came up, but Bruges as well, with its tinge of romance, the architecture, the smell of pancakes, the skirt, the class, and so on.

As a researcher, the first author got the permission to follow the moving "class assemblage" as such getting meaning *out of it* and giving meaning *to it*. The class is forming an assemblage of intersectional lines wiring out to different cultures and, among others, countries, abilities, and gender. Some are speaking the local language "Dutch" very well, others intermingle this with their own mother tongue. When we talk about the places the adolescents mention, we do not consider these the bordered countries as we can find them on a map. We do mean the moving territories accompanying an assemblage (Delanda, 2016). Jamaica, Belgium, Bulgaria are reinvented by the youths as they present them in their dreams.

Probyn (2004) sees the constellation of assemblages functioning in a classroom, where an assemblage of bodies meet and are being assembled. This can be hopeful and playful, but it can also create connections of fear and terror. Assemblage according to a Deleuzian reading implies a continuous process of "becoming." Becoming is always "identity-in-motion," an open system of assemblages. It also means undoing categorizations and believing in a fixed, stable identity which can create a feeling of imprisonment. In the stories shared, all is possible, and all is dreamt. We consider the idea of identity as proposed by Bakhtin:

To be, means to be for the other and through him, for oneself. Man has no internal sovereign territory, he is always on the boundary; looking within himself he looks in the eyes of the other or through the eyes of the other. I cannot do without the other; I cannot become myself without the other; I must find myself in the other; finding the other in me in mutual reflection and perception.[6] (Bakhtin, 1984 in Yuval-Davis, 2012, p. 16, emphasis in original)

Identity is not something we can put on as a coat; we inhabit our identities and choices, and they inhabit us (Titchkosky, 2011, p. 112). Probyn (1996) constructs identity as transition, always producing itself through the combined processes of being and becoming, belonging and longing to belong. Rayann is a young black woman who moved to Belgium a couple of years ago. She is no longer the same Rayann as she was when she flew there. She longs for her own country, but also for working in Belgium, as well as to accomplish certain things there. She feels belonging in her class, her school in Ghent, she loves her school teacher, and she has her own small place in Ghent where she lives alone. She is becoming-employee, becoming-caregiver, becoming-Belgian, becoming-woman. What drives her is desire and longing for those close to her and "home." She is assembled manifold with many connections, affects and feelings.[7] When listening to Sam, we hear he longs for independence and especially for making his parents proud. He knew difficulties on the road throughout his school career. In this class assemblage, which is also attached in a bigger school assemblage where the way of following classes is open and respectful, he finds power and energy to express his dream. He feels the safety of sharing his uncertainties, of articulating his feelings of belonging there that make him flourish. His roots are completely different from Gabrielle's, or Rayann's, or those of any other member of the class. The longing to belong and the accompanying pursuit of happiness from a minority position are however very recognizable and opened up by connecting in this film project.

Every one of the adolescents started with the reflection of an "ideal abstract dream." However, through performing it and working together in doing this, they took other lines of flight (Deleuze & Guattari, 1987) where diffraction patterns made these differences matter. The youths proceed on these lines where they pursue chances, possibilities, and potentialities. They are aware they cannot fully escape the organized society as such. They also use the territorialization of this society to walk lines of flight. They bring in narratives from the "margin" and show the potentialities of this position to move to change. Liminal spaces formed the contours in which their imagination got materialized. They open up space-time-matterings through which they show that any human subject is in constant motion, emergent, capable of resistance to categorizations in subordinate categories (e.g., Black, poor, disabled, female). What they do here, matters (De schauwer et al., 2017).

They do not offer a fixed definition of what belonging "means" or "is," instead they show us what it means to them by letting us enter their transforming/transversal contingent and still structured assemblages in all their multiplicity and complexity.

CONCLUSIVE IDEAS

Following our findings and by listening to the voices of the young people sharing their dreams and their memories, their longings and longing to become-in-the-world-with-others (Shildrick, 2002), we see belonging as an "assemblic" concept itself. With the term assemblic we try to catch the double meaning present in the French term *agencement*, in which assemblage is both a process and a constellation. Belonging is a meaning we give to an event, a moment, a dream, a memory when some essential parts for that specific person with their historicity, their multiple connections with other humans and nonhumans make "sense" to uplift a completion of belonging. The pupils often discussed place, although this is not conceived as separate from duration. They connect this idea of place to home. "Home" is not the Jamaican beach. It is all the feelings, affects, connections assembled in a certain historiographical constellation that make "home." Katarina says: "All of my family lives here, my friends live here, I have my hobbies here, I do not feel connected with Slovakia. I speak the language at home, that's it. 'Belgium is my house." Iliana states her dream is "Going 'home', back to Bulgaria where I was cut off from my friends, my school. . . ." The stories reveal patterns of difference and repetition (Deleuze, 1967/1994).

Connecting with these patterns of difference and repetition is necessarily interwoven with society where life histories flood and affect each other as such, making experiences richer and more swollen than when we try to cut them off and draw borders between them. The discourses we see arising— but also contested constantly—are specifically connected with a neoliberal ideal citizen capable of earning good money, living in a nice house and having children who also meet the "ideal standards" (preferably two of them, a boy and a girl). These discourses are included in the assemblages being constituted and being broken down constantly. Discourses, words, meanings, non-corporeal relations are a part of this assemblage (Deleuze & Guattari, 1987). This implies that young people go with the flow of the normate and the normal. In the same stories these discourses are transversed by critical sounds of what this "normal" can be. Is it "normal" that when you grow old you go to a rest home away from your family, and you have little fascinating activities left to do? Is it "normal" that a young Black woman cannot strive for a beautiful house in an expensive neighborhood in a big city? Is it "normal" for a young man having learning difficulties in need of support never to become an independent well-earning self-employed person? They question these discourses by dreaming them differently. They need each other to do this. Every story is manifold and plural-voiced (Mazzei, 2016). They always bring it in an assemblage which in its turn shifts constantly. Next to the class assemblage there are other assemblages emerging in each story, overlapping and doing the diffractive "wavework" in rumpling over each other. Each story is made up of passed memories and future dreams. All of them explicitly emphasize the love for others, their connections with other people, mostly family, but also other places that are part of who they become and are, as well as other matters (e.g., garden, beach, sand, dress).

The cross-cultural assemblages illustrate the richness of the bricolage process. They give ideas about belonging which we see as graspable only in the complexity of "a life" where it unravels the intra-actions present with others and other matters, where past and future get mixed up and blur the idea of the present. The openness of connecting with others and getting chances to make something of your life as any other is for them of the utmost importance. They need the freedom to dream of other places, of home, of their closest family and to do this together. By putting the concepts of assemblage and diffraction at work on their stories we endeavored to create liminal spaces where openings and lines of flight for these young people could be explored (Deleuze & Guattari, 1987). This does not mean they believed all their dreams could come true. It was necessary to truthfully listen to their ideas and voice. They gave significance to what belonging really means by providing it with a ground to put its feet on, although that ground is moving and changing inexhaustibly.

Questions for Reflection

1. Consider your own conception about belonging. What does this concept mean to you? How would you draw the multiple connections between people and matters?
2. How would you put the "methods" of diffraction and bricolage to work in your own research? What new insights would these bring you in your research domain?

Suggestions for Further Reading

Barad, K. (2007). *Meeting the universe halfway. Quantum physics and the entanglement of matter and meaning*. Durham, England: Duke University Press.

Davies, B. (2014). *Listening to children. Being and becoming*. London, England: Routledge.

Delanda, M. (2016). *Assemblage theory (speculative realism)*. Edinburgh, England: Edinburgh University Press.

Kincheloe, J., & Berry, K. (2004). *Rigour and complexity in educational re-search: Conceptualizing the bricolage.* New York, NY: Open University Press.

Yuval-Davis, N. (2012). *The politics of belonging: Intersectional contestations.* Los Angeles, LA: SAGE.

NOTES

1. We begin here, but we are aware we could have started somewhere else, as we always start in the middle of an entangled complexity.
2. Barad uses this idea of cutting-together apart to illustrate that diffraction is about one movement. It troubles the notion of dichotomy in all possible ways (Barad, 2007, 2014). Here we want to give full attention to the complexity and entangled nature of the stories brought in.
3. Barad makes use of the notion intra-action in contrast to the usual 'interaction' which presumes the prior existence of independent entities. This is essential in her onto-epistemological vision (Barad, 2007).
4. Barad calls a "phenomenon" an entanglement of subject and object. This is also how she sees reality. The duality between object and subject is "undone." The apparatus and the observed object entangle and are inseparable (Barad, 2007).
5. We refer to "other places" that imply thresholds to imagine life differently. There is a need to have no restrictions in what is possible to open up the creation of potential newness. The project the pupils engaged in contributed to these possibilities.
6. Bakhtin stays close to an anthropocentric discourse. In this chapter we want to extend this and also see identity in motion through connecting with non-human otherness.
7. This idea of becoming-other is also recognized in the idea of the nomad on which Rosi Braidotti elaborates.

REFERENCES

Badley, G. (2014). Six characters in search of an author: A qualitative comedy in the making. *Qualitative Inquiry, 20*(5), 659–667.

Barad, K. (2007). *Meeting the universe halfway. Quantum physics and the entanglement of matter and meaning.* Durham, England: Duke University Press.

Barad, K. (2014). Diffracting diffraction: Cutting together-apart. *Parallax, 20*(3), 168–187.

Bergson, H. (1997). *The creative mind. An introduction to metaphysics by Henri Bergson.* New York, NY: Carol. (Original work published in 1946)

Bozalek, V., & Zembylas, M. (2016). Diffraction or reflection? Sketching the contours of two methodologies in educational research. *International Journal of Qualitative Studies in Education, 30*(2), 111–127.

Davies, B., De Schauwer, E., Claes, L., De Munck, K., Van De Putte, I., & Verstichele, M. (2013). Recognition and difference: A collective biography. *International Journal of Qualitative Studies in Education, 26*(6), 680–691.

Davies, B. (2014a). Assembling Oscar, assembling South Africa, assembling affects. *Emotion, Space and Society, 13*, 40–45.

Davies, B. (2014b). *Listening to children. Being and becoming.* London, England: Routledge.

Delanda, M. (2016). *Assemblage theory (speculative realism).* Edinburgh, Scotland: Edinburgh University Press.

Deleuze, G. (1994). *Difference and repetition.* New York, NY: Columbia University Press. (Original work published in 1967)

Deleuze, G., & Guattari, F. (1987). *A thousand plateaus: Capitalism and schizophrenia.* London, England: Athlone Press.

De Schauwer, E., Van de Putte, I., Van Goidsenhoven, L., Blockmans, I., Vandecasteele, M., Davies, B. (2017). Animating disability differently: Mobilizing a heterotopian imagination. *Qualitative Inquiry, 23*(4), 276–286.

De Schauwer, E., Van de Putte, I., & Davies, B. (2018). Collective biography: Using memory work to explore the space-in-between normativity and difference/disability. *Qualitative Inquiry, 24*(1), 8–19.

Dolphijn, R., & Van der Tuin, I. (2012). *New materialism: Interviews & cartographies.* Michigan, MI: Open Humanities Press.

Hickey-Moody, A. (2007). Re-imagining intellectual disability: Sensation and the outside of thought. In A. C. Hickey-Moody & P. Malins (Eds.), *Deleuzian encounters: Studies in contemporary social issues.* (pp. 79–98). London, England: Palgrave Macmillan.

Kincheloe, J. L. (2005). On to the next level: Continuing the conceptualization of the bricolage. *Qualitative Inquiry, 11* (3), 323–350.

Kincheloe, J., & Berry, K. (2004). *Rigour and complexity in educational research: Conceptualizing the Bricolage.* New York, NY: Open University Press.

Lévi-Strauss, C. (1966). *La pensée sauvage* [The savage mind]. Paris, France: Librairie Plon. (Original work published in 1962)

Mazzei, L. A. (2016). Voice without a subject. *Cultural Studies Critical Methodologies, 16*(2), 151–161.

Probyn, E. (1996). *Outside belongings.* New York, NY: Routledge.

Probyn, E. (2004). Teaching bodies: Affects in the classroom. *Body & Society, 10*(4), 21–43.

Shildrick, M. (2002). *Embodying the monster. Encounters with the vulnerable self.* London, England: SAGE.

Titchkosky, T. (2011). *The question of access: Disability, space, meaning.* Toronto, Canada: University of Toronto Press.

Van de Putte, I., De Schauwer, E., Van Hove, G., & Davies, B. (2017). Rethinking agency as an assemblage. From change management to collaborative work. *International Journal of Inclusive Education,* 1–17. doi:10.1080/13603116.2017.1412514

Wise, J. M. (2005). Assemblage. In C. J. Stivale (Ed.), *Deleuze: Key concepts* (2nd ed., pp. 77–87). London, England: Routledge.

Yuval-Davis, N. (2012). *The politics of belonging: Intersectional contestations.* Los Angeles, CA: SAGE.

CHAPTER 13

AN ANALYTICAL TOOL TO HELP RESEARCHERS DEVELOP PARTNERSHIPS WITH CHILDREN AND ADOLESCENTS

Harry Shier

ABSTRACT

All researchers whose research involves children and adolescents have decisions to make about how and when to engage with those involved in and/or affected by their research; who to engage with and who to leave out. This chapter offers a tool that researchers can use to help them address these issues in a purposeful and ethical way. The chapter discusses earlier work on child rights-based approaches to research which influenced the approach taken here. However, the main inspiration for the proposal was the author's own research with children working on coffee plantations in Nicaragua; in particular the Transformative Research by Children and Adolescents methodology that was used, and the critical reflection on methodology prompted by this experience. The tool is presented as a matrix which can be used for

Participatory Methodologies to Elevate Children's Voice and Agency, pages 295–315
Copyright © 2019 by Information Age Publishing

planning and designing, as well as evaluating research. It seeks to foster coherent critical thinking around three related dimensions: At what stage in a research process should researchers seek to engage with children and adolescents? What type of engagement is appropriate, particularly in relation to the sharing of decision-making power? And finally who is included in the process and who is excluded? The matrix is used to carry out a reappraisal of a recent research project by the author, showing how this analysis can shed light on a number of issues that might not otherwise be given sufficient attention.

For some academic researchers, children are little more than statistical data, while for others they are actively engaged subjects, advisers or co-researchers (Kellett, 2010a). However, all researchers whose research involves children and adolescents have decisions to make about how and when to engage with those involved in and/or affected by their research; and also, very importantly, who to engage with and who to leave out. These decisions may depend on a range of factors related to the purpose of the research, efficiency, validity, and resources available; but there are also factors that relate to the methodological approach of the researcher and its underpinning paradigm, not to mention the culture and traditions of research establishments. These might include a commitment to (or alternatively a resistance to) community engagement, to the emancipation or empowerment of those involved, and to a children's rights-based approach.

This chapter offers a tool that researchers can use to help them address these issues in a purposeful and ethical way, so that these important decisions are informed and considered. With this aim in mind, the chapter is structured in six sections. Following this introduction, the next section considers the literature on engaging children in research, focusing on two child rights-based approaches to research with children. The third section talks about my own research with children working on coffee plantations in Nicaragua, and in particular the Transformative Research by Children and Adolescents methodology that I used, and the subsequent reflection on this that sparked the development of the tool to be presented here. The fourth section discusses the development and design of the tool, and presents it in its current form. The fifth section discusses how it may be used by researchers, and, by way of a "worked example," uses it to re-evaluate children's engagement in my own research. This is followed by section six which offers a brief conclusion.

THINKING ABOUT HOW ADULTS ENGAGE
WITH CHILDREN IN RESEARCH

There is a large and ever-growing literature on research with children (Black & Busch, 2016; Clark, Flewitt, Hammersley, & Robb, 2014; Ergler,

2015; Kellett, 2010a), in which two basic typologies stand out. Christensen and Prout (2002) identified four ways of seeing children in the research literature: "The child as object, the child as subject and the child as social actor . . . and a nascent approach seeing children as participants and co-researchers" (p. 480). Kellett (2010a) proposes a slightly different fourfold distinction, identifying research *on, about, with,* and *by* children.

Much of the literature focuses on children as the data sources for research by adults, and deals with the nature of adult researchers' interactions with their child subjects (Bolzan & Gale, 2011; McCartan, Schubotz, & Murphy, 2012; Kruger & Mokgatla-Moipolai, 2014; Randall, 2012), and the ethical issues that arise from these interactions (Alderson & Morrow, 1995/2011; Powell, Fitzgerald, Taylor, & Graham, 2012).

Yet there are many other roles that children can take besides being data subjects, and here another important distinction emerges between those roles which locate children as researchers (that is, as the *doers* of research, be it data gathering, analysis, or writing up/reporting), and those that identify them as advisors to adult researchers, but not themselves researchers (Casas, González, Navarro, & Aligué, 2013; Lundy & McEvoy, 2012b; Moore et al., 2016). In the former case, where children do the research themselves, again there is a wide range of possibilities, from small scale school projects with negligible follow-up or impact (Alderson, 2008; Groundwater-Smith, Dockett, & Bottrell, 2015; Spalding, 2011) to larger projects which may have a significant impact (CESESMA, 2012; Save the Children, 2010). In all these cases, questions arise about how child researchers are recruited and selected (Johnson, Hart, & Colwell, 2014); how they give (or withhold) consent at different times (Powell & Smith, 2009); how they are safeguarded (Bradbury-Jones & Taylor, 2015; Graham & Fitzgerald, 2010); how they are guided, facilitated, or manipulated by adults (Johnson et al., 2014; Kim, 2015; Shaw, Brady, & Davey, 2011); how they are rewarded (Bradbury-Jones & Taylor, 2015; Powell et al., 2012); how their findings are disseminated and who gets credit (Robb, 2014); and what, if anything, is done as a consequence of their research, and by whom (Ruxton, 2014; Shier, 2015).

Child Rights-Based Research

The methodological approach that most influenced the proposal being presented here is that of Children's rights-based research. There are two main strands of writing about rights-based approaches to research with children: The right to be properly researched, associated with Judith Ennew and colleagues (Bessell, Beazley, & Waterson, 2017), and the child rights-based approach developed by Lundy and McEvoy. Although these are closely related, because of their distinct origins, conceptual bases and emphases, it is worth considering them separately.

The phrase "the right to be properly researched" appears in Ennew's publications from 2004, but Ennew herself said she started to develop the approach in Jamaica in 1979 (Smith & Greene, 2014, p. 81). Although it thus predates the UN Convention on the Rights of the Child (CRC), Beazley, Bessell, Ennew, and Waterson (2011) mention CRC inspired international advocacy for children's participation rights as one of the factors that influenced its subsequent development, together with the advent of the new sociology of childhood, and a growing interest in children in the field of human geography. However they go on to suggest that these developments alone were insufficient, and that

> the impetus for the development of rights-based research with children was the submission of the first reports to the CRC Committee in 1992, and the Committee's realisation that available data, particularly information that fell outside the conventional health-education-psychology-demography nexus, were insufficient for monitoring the CRC. (Beazley et al., 2011, p. 160)

Thus by 2004 the right to be properly researched was established as both a *vision* for rights-based research with children (Beazley, Bessell, Ennew, & Waterson, 2006), and a step by step how-to-do-it manual (Ennew & Plateau, 2004). By 2009, this had become a boxed set of ten manuals (Ennew et al., 2009).

Proponents of this approach do not claim that the right to be properly researched is itself a legal right (Ennew & Plateau, 2004), but use this expression as a convenient shorthand to describe how "a nuanced interpretation of four key articles of the UNCRC" (Bessell et al., 2017, p. 211) can be used to guide researchers as to how children must be treated, as set out by Ennew and Plateau in Table 13.1.

The approach to research with children that is inferred from the combination of these articles is described as having five key characteristics:

1. It is respectful of children as partners in research (i.e., their participation must be meaningful on their own terms, not imposed by adults).
2. It is ethical, and does not exploit children.
3. It is scientifically valid, using methods that are systematic and can be replicated.
4. It involves robust analysis, both descriptive and statistical.
5. It prioritises local knowledge and expertise. (Beazley et al., 2011, p. 161)

In a sustained critique of this approach, Alderson (2012) raises a number of objections to Beazley and colleagues' insistence that rights-based research

TABLE 13.1 The Right to be Properly Researched	
CRC Article	**What it means for research**
Article 3.3 "States Parties shall ensure that the institutions, services and facilities responsible for the care or protection of children shall conform with the standards established by competent authorities, particularly in the areas of safety, health, the numbers and suitability of their staff, as well as competent supervision."	Research must conform to the highest possible scientific standards. Researchers must be carefully recruited and supervised.
Article 12.1 "States Parties shall assure to the child who is capable of forming his or her own views the right to express those views freely in all matters affecting the child, the views of the child being given due weight in accordance with the age and maturity of the child."	Children's perspectives and opinions must be integral to research.
Article 13.1 "The child shall have the right to freedom of expression; this right shall include freedom to seek, receive and impart information and ideas of all kinds, regardless of frontiers, either orally, in writing or in print, in the form of art, or through any other media of the child's choice."	Methods need to be found, and used, to help children to express their perspectives and opinions freely in research.
Article 36 protects children against "all . . . forms of exploitation prejudicial to any aspects of the child's welfare."	Children must not be harmed or exploited through taking part in research.

Source: Ennew and Plateau, 2004, p. 29.

with children must be participatory in nature, mentioning unresolved issues such as: Who gets the opportunity to participate? How are they paid or rewarded? If everything is reduced to children's level, what happens to theoretical, statistical or systematic-synthetic analysis? And finally, "If anyone can do research with similar competence, what is the point of studying for years to become a postdoctoral researcher?" (p. 237). These are very much the kind of issues that the tool presented here will help researchers to address.

A key feature of the right to be properly researched approach, stressed in all the publications mentioned, is its insistence that all "proper" research with children involves the rigorous application of scientific methods, including replicability. However, researchers from ethnographic, narrative, indigenous, and reflexive traditions may question whether this must always be the case.

The second important strand of thinking about rights-based research with children is that developed by Lundy and McEvoy. Whilst it acknowledges Ennew's work, this draws its conceptual framing in large part from the way human rights-based approaches have coalesced in the field of international development; specifically the three core principles found in the Statement of Common Understanding agreed by the main UN agencies in 2003:

1. All programmes of development co-operation should further the realisation of human rights.
2. Human rights standards must guide all development cooperation and programming.
3. Development cooperation should contribute to the development of the capacities of duty-bearers to meet their obligations and/or of rights-holders to claim their rights. (United Nations, 2003, p. 1)

Lundy and McEvoy reformulate these principles as a new proposal for a children's rights-based approach to research based on the Convention on the Rights of the Child, restating the principles as follows:

> The research aims should be informed by the CRC standards, the research process should comply with the CRC standards; and the research outcomes should build the capacity of children, as rights-holders, to claim their rights, and build the capacity of duty-bearers to fulfil their obligations. Cutting across all of this is a requirement to ensure that the process furthers the realisation of children's rights. (Lundy & McEvoy, 2012a, p. 79)

Using examples from previous field studies, they go on to show how these principles might take effect across the three main phases of the research process: framing, conducting, and disseminating research (Lundy & McEvoy, 2012a, pp. 79–90). The main implications of this analysis are summarized in Table 13.2.

A distinctive feature of this approach is the way every piece of research is supported by at least one Children's Research Advisory Group (CRAG). Children who become members of CRAGs are considered to have an advisory role, and as such are expressly excluded from the category of research subjects. That is, CRAG members may advise adult researchers on formulation of research questions, appropriateness of methods, design of data-gathering instruments, analysis and interpretation of findings, or design of dissemination materials and methods; but do not provide data for the research. This allows children to be engaged in every stage of the research, as appropriate to the circumstances, and with a considerable amount of flexibility. Time-consuming and complex work such as data-gathering and statistical analysis can be left to appropriately qualified adult researchers, but children know that the advice they give on these matters will be taken on board. Also, if the circumstances are appropriate, CRAG members can go on to engage with duty bearers in advocacy activities relating to the research, but are not required to do so, and other methods may be proposed for influencing duty bearers (Lundy & McEvoy, 2012a, pp. 81–86). In critiquing Ennew's approach, Alderson asked In her critique of Ennew's approach referred to above, Alderson asked, if anyone can do research, what is the point of studying to become a professional researcher?

TABLE 13.2 Summary of Lundy and McEvoy's proposal for a Children's Rights-Based Approach to Research

Elements constituting a children's rights based approach	Stages of the research process		
	Framing	Conducting	Disseminating
Overall/cross-cutting requirement: Research furthers the realization of children's rights.	Children's participation in the research design is CRC-compliant.	Researchers' engagement with children is guided by CRC standards.	Children contribute to research outputs, and are informed about how these will be disseminated.
Aims: Research aims are informed by CRC standards.	Research aims to further the realisation of CRC children's rights standards.		
Process: Research process complies with CRC standards.	Research questions are framed with CRC standards and associated jurisprudence (though research questions are often set by funders, there may be opportunities for "translating non-rights-based research questions into rights-based questions").	The conduct of the research respects the rights of the children involved; Research methods are of high quality and appropriate to address the issues investigated; Children are engaged meaningfully in choices about methods and how these are employed.	Ideally children are involved in dissemination of findings, and engaged in influencing duty-bearers (but this is not considered a necessary component).
Outcomes: (a) Research outcomes build the capacity of children to claim their rights.	An objective of the research is to inform children involved about their CRC rights. Children are meaningfully engaged in development of research questions and instruments used, e.g., working with Children's Research Advisory groups, (CRAGs), and building their capacity in relation to the substantive topic of the research as well as the methods involved.	Deliberate steps are taken to ensure that children have opportunities to form and express their views freely across all stages of the research, including the significance or meaning attributed to findings; Children are made aware of who has responsibility for acting on the research findings.	Children are engaged in shaping the dissemination outputs. Deliberate and conscious effort to engage with children in meaningful ways (directly or indirectly) to influence state actors whose policy and practices impact on their lives.
(b) Research outcomes build the capacity of duty-bearers to fulfil their obligations.	An objective of the research is to inform duty-bearers about their obligations.	Where possible, opportunities are harnessed to engage with duty-bearers during the conduct of the research.	Outputs are presented to duty-bearers in ways that build their capacity to fulfil their obligations to children.

Source: Derived from Lundy & McEvoy, 2012a.

Another distinctive aspect of Lundy and McEvoy's approach is their emphasis on building capacity in participating children, particularly those who are members of CRAGs. This emphasis is based on interpretation of three key CRC rights in combination: Article 12 provides the right to form and express opinions which must be given due weight by decision-makers; Articles 13 and 17 provide the right to receive information; and Article 5 permits responsible adults to provide "appropriate direction and guidance" to children on matters relating to the exercise of their rights (Lundy & McEvoy, 2012b). It is, in fact, questionable whether Article 5 applies in the case of researchers carrying out research with children, as the text of the article restricts it to parents, guardians and "other persons legally responsible for the child." However, the underlying principles remain relevant, and so it is proposed that an adult-guided capacity-building process can help children express opinions that are not just "formed" but also "informed," and so enhances their contribution to research.

The central role of capacity-building with children in Lundy and McEvoy's approach does, however, raise an issue about the risk of adult manipulation of children's views. Information-giving is never politically or ethically neutral, and in the case of adult researchers collaborating with child research advisers, there is also a significant power differential (Groundwater-Smith et al., 2015), so it is inevitable that the capacity-builder, whether described as "assisting" children (Lundy & McEvoy, 2012b), or "facilitating" them (Larkins et al., 2015), influences the kinds of (in)formed views that children are assisted towards. Some may approach this in a self-aware, reflexive way, seeking to recognize their own biases, and modifying the way information is selected, presented and discussed to try and counteract these. Others may not be so aware, and influence children's opinion-forming in certain directions without meaning to. Yet others may have beliefs about what kinds of opinions children *should* form about an issue, and seek to assist children to these views, either honestly (e.g., by confessing a religious or political position) or by less honest manipulation (Hart, 1997, pp. 40–42). If the building of children's capacity by adult researchers is to be a central part of rights-based research, further guidance is needed on how to recognize, make explicit and minimize the extent to which adults, knowingly or unknowingly, lead children towards the kinds of views that they, the adults, approve of, instead of uncovering those that children themselves are drawn to.

An important difference between Ennew and colleagues' and Lundy and McEvoy's approaches to child rights-based research is their different orientations. Ennew and colleagues' approach has been packaged and marketed to those doing research in a wide range of institutional settings, including NGOs and community groups, with particular reference to the global South (Ennew et al., 2009). Lundy and McEvoy, on the other hand, are concerned with defining a child rights-based approach that can also inform the kind of research done in universities.

MY RESEARCH IN NICARAGUA

The tool that will be described in the next section developed out of my doctoral research on children's perceptions of human rights in school, which was carried out with children working on coffee plantations in Nicaragua in 2013, informed by the literature discussed in the previous section. This chapter is not concerned with the substantive findings of the research (for which see Shier, 2016), but rather with the methods; and specifically with the outcome of my critical reflection on the experience. The research project will be described briefly here to provide a backdrop for the methodological reflections that follow.

The research project arose out of the recognition that, for the many thousands of children in poor countries who drop out of school and so lose out on the life chances that education might offer them, the notion of a "right to education" has little meaning. Though poverty and child labor were recognized as important factors, lack of respect for human rights in education was seen as a contributing factor for many children. The research was therefore designed to explore how children and adolescents in Nicaragua's coffee sector perceived their human rights in school, in order to provide insights that would contribute to the development of effective human rights-based approaches to schooling, particularly in poor countries where the right to go to school must itself be claimed and defended.

To come as close as possible to understanding how children themselves perceive their rights in school and the issues that concern them, the adult researcher worked in partnership with a team of child researchers in Nicaragua. Using a distinctive methodology known as Transformative Research by Children and Adolescents (CESESMA, 2012; Shier, 2015), a team of 17 young researchers was formed, aged 9–16, and these were facilitated in developing and carrying out a research project using qualitative interviews to address the above issues, while I gathered background information from parents, teachers, and other adult informants. With the young researchers' approval, I subjected their original data to a more thorough thematic analysis, which was compared with their own analysis.

Four main themes emerged as important findings:

1. Developing positive human relations is fundamental for a rights-respecting school, with relations among students (e.g., reducing bullying) seen as every bit as important as student-teacher relations.

2. Students saw some forms of behavior management as rights violations, for example depriving them of playtime as punishment.
3. Lack of attention to the complex relationship(s) between rights and responsibilities had led to confusion and misunderstandings (echoing similar findings in the UK and elsewhere).
4. The child's right to be heard was not an important issue for the children in this research, which raises questions for adult researchers interested in this topic (Shier, 2016).

On completing their research, the young researchers collaborated on a number of significant dissemination activities, specifically: presenting their findings directly to the combined Latin American regional leadership of Save the Children; publishing their report under their own names in a leading Latin American Children's Rights Journal (Niñas y Niños Investigadores, 2014); and participation in an international seminar on children's participation organized as part of the St. Olaf's Festival in Trondheim, Norway (details in Shier, 2016, pp. 111–113). The question of what further outcomes may have come from the process is considered further in the "Discussion" section below.

THE DEVELOPMENT AND DESIGN OF THE MATRIX

The need to justify the use of an unorthodox methodological approach gave rise to deep reflection on the methodological aspects of the research, and in particular on the wide range of possible relationships that may be established between child and adult researchers, and how to develop productive and ethical partnerships between the two. A starting point for this reflection was to recognize that there is no symmetry between adult and child participants in decision-making about research projects. As a rule, adult researchers decide when and how to engage with child participants, and with whom to engage. But how much conscious reflection or evaluation goes into the making of these decisions? A default position of "children are not involved at this stage" may be taken for granted without being given much serious thought.

The model, then, is built on an important normative assumption; namely, that the quality of research is improved if decisions about who is to be involved and how they are to be involved are carefully thought through and justified, rather than taken for granted.

The decisions in question, on engaging children in research processes, involve three distinct dimensions:

1. *When* should children get involved with a research project (i.e., at what stage in the overall process)?
2. *How* should they be involved (i.e., what should be their role or the nature of their engagement with the adult researcher[s])?
3. *Who* should be involved (and, equally significantly, who will be excluded or left out, and how is this justified)?

Though these can be asked as three separate questions, they cannot be answered this way; rather there must be critical reflection leading to an integrated response that deals with all three.

In developing an analytical tool to help guide this reflection, my approach was first to visualize and unpack the "when" and "how" dimensions. Considering first the "when" dimension; every piece of research involves a number of steps or phases. There are many ways to label these, but the following is a simple generic framework derived from Kumar (1999/2014) that works well for the present purpose: (a) deciding on the research question, (b) designing the research and choosing methods, (c) preparing research instruments, (d) identifying and recruiting participants, (e) collecting data, (f) analyzing the data and drawing conclusions, (g) producing a report, (h) dissemination of the report and its findings, (i) advocacy and mobilization to achieve policy impact.[1] It is perfectly possible for children and adolescents to be engaged at any of these moments, or indeed at each and every one of them.

The second dimension, where we consider *how* to involve children, seems more complicated. The wide range of different ways in which children can engage with research was mentioned above, neatly summarized by Kellett's (2010a) conception of research *on, about, with,* and *by* children. Along this dimension, the key variable is the amount of control or decision-making power that children have in relation to adult researchers, and the literature on child participation offers a plethora of models for analyzing different levels or types of participation; some of the best-known being Hart's (1992) ladder of children's participation and Shier's (2001) pathways to participation. Karsten (2012, regularly updated), offers probably the most comprehensive compilation of all the different models available.

However, for our present purposes, clarity and simplicity are key, so the model used here is that of Lansdown (2011), which conveniently reduces the myriad forms of children's participation to three essential "levels of engagement" which are:

1. *Consultation:* When adults ask children for their views, and children are not involved beyond this (so child-to-child or peer consultation falls into one of the other categories).

2. *Collaboration:* When adults and children work together, sharing roles and responsibilities in planning and carrying out an activity.
3. *Pro-activism:* Activities initiated, organized, or run by children and young people themselves (adults may still provide support, though not always necessary).[2]

To these it is necessary to add a fourth level—that of exclusion or "non-involvement."

One of the advantages of Lansdown's model is that it is simple enough to use in discussions with children themselves about how they might wish to engage with a research project.

The idea of assembling these two dimensions as a matrix to produce a tool for researchers was inspired by a similar matrix in Save the Children's Toolkit for Monitoring and Evaluating Children's Participation (Lansdown & O'Kane, 2014). The new matrix was created by using the same column headings (Lansdown's three levels plus the level of non-involvement), while for the vertical axis, replacing the five phases of the development project cycle in the original with the nine stages of the research process listed above.

The issue of *who* is to be involved at each stage (and by inference, who is to be excluded from involvement) was described above as a third dimension, and ideally should be envisaged that way to complete the model. However, in order to design a tool that can be represented on a two-dimensional page, it is easier to show it as an additional vertical column on the right of the matrix. The result is shown in Table 13.3.

Although the final column offers a simple "Who?" question in each box, it is important to stress that each simple "who" represents a series of more complex questions that need to be asked and answered. Depending on whether the matrix is being used to help plan a research project or to evaluate a process, the questions can be rephrased in past, present, or future tense as appropriate:

- Which children, or what kinds of children, got the chance to participate?
- How were they chosen? What were the criteria for inclusion and exclusion? If there was differential treatment, was it relevant and ethically justified? (If not, it was by definition discrimination, and therefore a rights violation.)
- What efforts, if any, were made to identify those children, or groups of children, who might have wanted to participate but faced obstacles to putting themselves forward, who might have needed additional support to play a full and equal role in the process, or who never heard about the project because the information didn't reach them?

TABLE 13.3 Matrix for Analysing Children's Engagement in Research Processes

Phases of the research process ↓	← Dimension of decision-making power or control →				Who is involved and who is excluded?
	Children are not involved	Children are consulted	Children collaborate with adult researchers	Children direct and decide for themselves →	
Deciding on the research question		Children asked about problems that concern them.	Children and adults jointly define research question.	Children choose their own research question.	Who has a say in the research question?
Designing the research and choosing methods		Children consulted on what research methodology to use.	Children and adults deliberate and jointly decide on the methodology to use.	Children decide what methodology they want to use.	Who is invited to get involved in the research design?
Preparing research instruments		Children consulted on (and perhaps test) research instruments before use.	Children and adults work together on design of research instruments.	Children create their own research instruments.	Who gets to work on the research instruments?
Identifying and recruiting participants		Children asked to advise on recruiting participants.	Children and adults jointly identify and recruit participants.	Children identify and recruit research participants.	Who has a say in choosing participants?
Collecting data		Research involves adults interviewing children or surveying their opinions.	Children and adults collaborate on data-gathering activity.	Children organise and carry out data collection activities.	Who gets involved in data collection?
Analysing the data and drawing conclusions		Adults show preliminary findings to children and ask for feedback.	Children and adults work together to analyse data and determine conclusions.	Children analyse data and draw their own conclusions.	Who has a say in what the conclusions are?
Producing a report		Adults consult children on aspects of the final report.	Children and adults work together to produce a report.	Children produce their own report in their own words.	Who gets credit for the report?
Dissemination of the report and its findings		Adults consult children on how to disseminate findings.	Children and adults collaborate on dissemination and awareness-raising activities.	Children undertake activities to disseminate their findings.	Who is actively involved in dissemination?
Advocacy and mobilization to achieve policy impact		Adults consult children about possible advocacy actions.	Children and adults work together on plans for advocacy and mobilisation.	Children develop and implement an action plan for advocacy and mobilisation.	Who is active in follow-up campaigning and advocacy?

DISCUSSION

Essentially all models are wrong, but some are useful.
—Box, 1979, p. 201

This matrix is being offered as a practical tool to help researchers think through important issues in planning, designing, or evaluating research. It is not presented as a model intended to represent reality. For example, Lansdown's three levels of participation may be considered an oversimplification of the complexities encountered in practice, amply discussed in the participation literature, where, as mentioned above, here are many more complex models available. In particular the model as it stands does not interrogate the role of the seemingly invisible, or at least well-hidden, adult supporter/facilitator in the fifth column. Nevertheless, for practical purposes, and particularly for those concerned to involve children directly in their deliberations, this simplified scheme has proved effective.[3] Similarly, not all research projects run through a neatly ordered series of stages as implied here. Some kinds of research, action research for example, have a different internal logic and series of steps. However, the matrix sets out a framework that can easily be adapted to a wide range of different situations.

It would also be a mistake to see the matrix as a set of norms or targets to strive for. Specifically, it would be unfortunate if users got the impression that more pro-active participation is always better. As McCarry (2012) concludes, researchers should be open to questioning "models of participation which assume that the greater the level of involvement the more inclusive and empowering it is for young people, and the stronger research is as a result" (p. 68) and, as a result, should strive to be flexible and accommodating. The matrix is designed to encourage, rather than restrict, this flexibility, by helping researchers decide for themselves what is the most appropriate way to engage with children and adolescents at each stage in a research process. It is possible that at some stages involving children in a limited way, or not at all, is the best way to go. However, using the matrix means that such nonengagement will be the result of a thought through and justified decision, rather than a mere oversight.

Though an individual researcher could work through the matrix themselves, identifying the most appropriate way to engage with children at each stage and asking the relevant "who" questions, it is better seen as an exercise for research teams to work on together or, better still, as an activity to be worked through by researchers with groups of child and/or adolescent advisers.

To give the matrix a practical text, I used it to analyze my own doctoral research project. Drawing on my own intimate knowledge of the process, I determined which cell of the matrix was closest to what had actually happened at each stage. I then marked these on a copy of the matrix and joined the dots. The result is shown in Figure 13.1.

Phases of the research process →	← Dimension of decision-making power or control →				Who is involved and who is excluded?
	Children are not involved	Children are consulted	Children collaborate with adult researchers	Children direct and decide for themselves	
Deciding on the research question		Children asked about problems that concern them.	Children and adults jointly define research question.	Children choose their own research question.	Who has a say in the research question?
Designing the research and choosing methods		Children consulted on what research methodology to use.	Children and adults deliberate and jointly decide on the methodology to use.	Children decide what methodology they want to use.	Who is invited to get involved in the research design?
Preparing research instruments		Children consulted on (and perhaps test) research instruments before use.	Children and adults work together on design of research instruments.	Children create their own research instruments.	Who gets to work on the research instruments?
Identifying and recruiting participants		Children asked to advise on recruiting participants.	Children and adults jointly identify and recruit participants.	Children identify and recruit research participants.	Who has a say in choosing participants?
Collecting data		Research involves adults interviewing children or surveying their opinions.	Children and adults collaborate on data-gathering activity.	Children organise and carry out data collection activities.	Who gets involved in data collection?
Analysing the data and drawing conclusions		Adults show preliminary findings to children and ask for feedback.	Children and adults work together to analyse data and determine conclusions.	Children analyse data and draw their own conclusions.	Who has a say in what the conclusions are?
Producing a report		Adults consult children on aspects of the final report.	Children and adults work together to produce a report.	Children produce their own report.	Who gets credit for the report?
Dissemination of the report and its findings		Adults consult children on how to disseminate findings.	Children and adults collaborate on dissemination and awareness-raising activities.	Children undertake activities to disseminate their findings.	Who is actively involved in dissemination?
Advocacy and mobilization to achieve policy impact		Adults consult children about possible advocacy actions.	Children and adults work together on plans for advocacy and mobilisation.	Children develop and implement an action plan for advocacy and mobilisation.	Who is active in follow-up campaigning and advocacy?

Figure 13.1 The matrix used to give a visual representation of children and adolescents' involvement with the author's doctoral research project in Nicaragua in 2013.

Some issues are immediately apparent: Though the children and adolescents had an impressive level of control in the central stages of the project, it is clear that they had no say at all in deciding what was to be researched, as this had been decided in a foreign country long before they had the chance to get involved.

But should child researchers always choose their own research topics? It seems a good idea, but the issue is complicated and nuanced. A first point to note is that adult researchers do not always get to choose their own research topics, as research agendas are largely set by research funders, and research projects developed accordingly. Should child researchers have a more privileged position, or might it be beneficial for them sometimes to work within this larger reality?

Another factor to consider is the potential research impact. Where research has been commissioned and paid for, this means that someone is interested in hearing the results, so an audience can be guaranteed for the presentation of the findings, thus increasing its likely influence (Lundy, 2007). Conversely, if research is motivated by child researchers' own concerns, it may be harder to get the message across to those who can make a difference. However, in the latter situation, the young researchers may have a stronger sense of ownership and greater motivation to engage with those in power, either face-to-face or indirectly through the media (see for instance the work by Manasa Patil on getting around as the child of a wheelchair user described by Kellett [2010b, p. 201], and my own work with the Young Researchers of Yúcul on alcohol and violence [Shier, 2015, p. 212]).

The figure above supports this hypothesis: Though the young researchers did collaborate on a number of significant dissemination activities as mentioned earlier, they had no significant involvement in advocacy or mobilization for change. Was this because, since they had no say in deciding on the research topic, they felt that getting something done about it was not their concern? (But there is another plausible explanation here: that it was the adults, not the children, who lost interest in the project at this point.)

If the analysis also includes the right-hand "Who" column, it will tell us that the only children who had the chance to participate through various stages of the project were the team of 17 young researchers. Only at the data collection stage were other children involved, as the young researchers interviewed 150 of their classmates to learn about their perceptions of rights in school.

The need to select a small number of participants from a larger target group must raise ethical questions about how one can identify and dismantle the barriers that privilege some children and adolescents and discriminate against others in terms of who gets involved. For example, I was fully aware that there were a number of disabled children living in the catchment area of my doctoral study, but none of them joined my team of young researchers. So I must ask myself: Did they have the same opportunity as everyone else to come forward and get involved in the project? They may not have wanted to, but the crucial question is: Did they have an equal chance to opt in or opt out? For example: Did we identify those children, or groups of children, who might have wanted to join the team but faced obstacles to putting themselves forward? And those who might have needed additional support to play a full and equal role in the team once selected? And what about those who would have loved to participate but never heard about the project because no one made the effort to reach them? In this particular project, with the benefit of hindsight, I don't think we got it right; but, learning through critical reflection, these are now questions to be asked at the start of every future research process.

CONCLUSION

The above is one researcher's reflection, stimulated by applying the matrix tool to one specific research project. It is worth repeating here that this tool cannot tell you the correct way to engage with children and adolescents in your research. What it may be able to do, though, is stimulate critical reflection, either individually or, better, collectively, that will guide you in the direction of wise and ethical decisions.

The reflection inspired by applying the matrix tool to my own research has helped me identify some further questions that we, as researchers, can ask ourselves when planning, designing, or evaluating research that involves children and adolescents, and these are presented in "Questions for Reflection" below. Although the questions mainly deal with methodological considerations, underlying these are more fundamental questions about the very nature of our research; its goals and purposes, whose interests it is designed to serve and who benefits. And behind these are questions asking us to reflect on ourselves and our own interests and attitudes as researchers: our willingness to take risks—or contrariwise, our preference for playing safe. And finally, when it comes to innovation in research, are we up for a challenge?

Questions for Reflection

1. Are our research goals limited to the creation of knowledge, or are we also concerned with impact for social change and/or empowerment of the children and adolescents involved?
2. Where do our research questions come from, and who is involved in defining them?
3. Have we thought about engaging with children throughout our research process, or is it more convenient just to bring them in at a certain stage?

4. Have we considered forming a children's advisory group or reference group for our current research project?
5. If we were to increase the level of engagement of children and adolescents in our research process, what would be the methodological and resource implications? What would be the challenges for us as adult researchers? What would be the risks, if any (and are we under pressure to play safe?), and what would be the potential benefits?

Suggestions for Further Reading

CESESMA. (2012). *Learn to Live without Violence: Transformative research by children and young people*. (H. Shier, Ed.). Preston, England: University of Central Lancashire and CESESMA. Retrieved from http://www.harryshier .net/docs/CESESMA-Learn_to_live_without_violence.pdf

Invernizzi, A., Liebel, M., Milne, B., & Budde, R. (2017). *'Children Out of Place' and Human Rights: In Memory of Judith Ennew*. Dordrecht, The Netherlands: Springer.

Kellett, M. (2010). *Rethinking Children and Research: Attitudes in contemporary society*. London, England: Continuum.

Lansdown, G., & O'Kane, C. (2014). *A Toolkit for Monitoring and Evaluating Children's Participation*. London, England: Save the Children.

Lundy, L., & McEvoy, L. (2012). Childhood, the United Nations Convention on the Rights of the Child and research: What constitutes a "rights-based" approach? In M. Freeman (Ed.), *Law and Childhood* (pp. 75–93). Oxford, England: Oxford University Press.

Shier, H. (2015). Children as researchers in Nicaragua: Children's consultancy to transformative research. *Global Studies of Childhood*, 5(2), 206–219.

NOTES

1. Some researchers may say that this final advocacy phase is beyond their remit, and that is their choice. However, for me it has always been a crucial part of the research process.
2. Lansdown originally labelled this third level "Child-led," but I consider this label problematic, and prefer "Pro-activism" which is the nearest equivalent in English to the Latin American concept of *"protagonismo infantil."*
3. I worked on the international piloting of the Save the Children Toolkit (2011–2013), where the original matrix that inspired this one, and its simplified conceptual scheme, were assessed and validated in practice.

REFERENCES

Alderson, P. (2008). Children as researchers. In P. Christensen & A. James (Eds.), *Research with Children: Perspectives and practices, second edition* (pp. 276–290). Abingdon, England: Routledge.

Alderson, P. (2012). Rights-respecting research: A commentary on "The right to be properly researched: Research with children in a messy, real world." *Children's Geographies, 10*(2), 233–239.

Alderson, P., & Morrow, V. (2011). *The ethics of research with children and young people: A practical handbook.* London, England: SAGE. (Original work published in 1995)

Beazley, H., Bessell, S., Ennew, J., & Waterson, R. (2006). *What children say: Results of comparative research on the physical and emotional punishment of children in South-East Asia and the Pacific, 2005.* Bangkok, Thailand: Save the Children.

Beazley, H., Bessell, S., Ennew, J., & Waterson, R. (2011). How are the human rights of children related to research methodology? In A. Invernizzi & J. Williams (Eds.), *The human rights of children: From visions to implementation* (pp. 159–178). Farnham, England: Ashgate.

Bessell, S., Beazley, H., & Waterson, R. (2017). The methodology and ethics of rights-based research with children. In A. Invernizzi, M. Liebel, B. Milne, & R. Budde (Eds.), *'Children out of place' and human rights* (pp. 211–231). Dordrecht, Netherlands: Springer.

Black, A. L., & Busch, G. (2016). Understanding and influencing research with children. In B. Harreveld, M. Danaher, C. Lawson, B. A. Knight, & G. Busch (Eds.), *Constructing methodology for qualitative research* (pp. 219–235). London, England: Palgrave Macmillan.

Bolzan, N., & Gale, F. (2011). Expect the unexpected. *Child Indicators Research, 4*(2), 269–281.

Box, G. E. P. (1979). Robustness in the strategy of scientific model building. In R. L. Launer & G. N. Wilkinson (Eds.), *Robustness in statistics* (pp. 201–223). Waltham, MA: Academic Press.

Bradbury-Jones, C., & Taylor, J. (2015). Engaging with children as co-researchers: Challenges, counter-challenges and solutions. *International Journal of Social Research Methodology, 18*(2), 161–173.

Casas, F., González, M., Navarro, D., & Aligué, M. (2013). Children as advisers of their researchers: Assuming a different status for children. *Child Indicators Research, 6*(2), 193–212.

CESESMA. (2012). *Learn to live without violence: Transformative research by children and young people.* (H. Shier, Ed.). Preston, England: University of Central Lancashire and CESESMA. Retrieved from http://www.harryshier.net/docs/CESESMA-Learn_to_live_without_violence.pdf

Christensen, P., & Prout, A. (2002). Working with ethical symmetry in social research with children. *Childhood, 9*(4), 477–497.

Clark, A., Flewitt, R., Hammersley, M., & Robb, M. (2014). *Understanding research with children and young people.* London, England: SAGE.

Ennew, J., Abebe, T., Bangyai, R., Karapituck, P., Kjørholt, A. T., & Noonsup, T. (2009). *The right to be properly researched: How to do rights-based, scientific research with children.* Bangkok, Thailand: Black on White Publications, Knowing Children.

Ennew, J., & Plateau, D. P. (2004). *How to research the physical and emotional punishment of children*. Bangkok, Thailand: Save the Children.

Ergler, C. (2015). Beyond passive participation: From research on to research by children. In R. Evans & L. Holt (Eds.), *Methodological approaches: Geographies of children and young people* (pp. 97–115). Singapore: Springer.

Graham, A., & Fitzgerald, R. (2010). Children's participation in research: Some possibilities and constraints in the current Australian research environment. *Journal of Sociology, 46*(2), 133–147.

Groundwater-Smith, S. Dockett, S., & Bottrell, D. (2015). *Participatory research with children and young people*. London, England: SAGE.

Hart, R. A. (1992). *Children's participation: From tokenism to citizenship*. Florence, Italy: UNICEF Innocenti Research Centre.

Hart, R. A. (1997). *Children's participation: The theory and practice of involving young citizens in community development and environmental care*. Abingdon, England: Earthscan.

Johnson, V., Hart, R., & Colwell, J. (2014). *Steps to engaging young children in research*. Brighton, England: University of Brighton Education Research Centre.

Karsten, A. (2012). *Participation models: Citizens, youth, online* (2nd ed.). Berlin, Germany: Retrieved from www.nonformality.org

Kellett, M. (2010a). *Rethinking children and research: Attitudes in contemporary society*. London, England: Continuum.

Kellett, M. (2010b). Small shoes, big steps! Empowering children as active researchers. *American Journal of Community Psychology, 46*(1), 195–203.

Kim, C.-Y. (2015). Why research 'by' children? Rethinking the assumptions underlying the facilitation of children as researchers. *Children & Society, 30*(3), 230–240.

Kruger, M., & Mokgatla-Moipolai, B. (2014). Children as research subjects. In M. Kruger, P. Ndebele, & L. Horn (Eds.), *Research ethics in Africa* (pp. 91–98). Stellenbosch, South Africa: Sun Press.

Kumar, R. (2014). *Research methodology: A step-by-step guide for beginners*. London, England: SAGE. (Original work published in 1999)

Lansdown, G. (2011). *Every child's right to be heard*. London, England: Save the Children.

Lansdown, G., & O'Kane, C. (2014). *A toolkit for monitoring and evaluating children's participation*. London, England: Save the Children.

Larkins, C., Thomas, N., Carter, B., Farrelly, N., Judd, D., & Lloyd, J. (2015). Support for children's protagonism: Methodological moves towards critical children's rights research framed from below. *International Journal of Children's Rights, 23*(2), 332–364.

Lundy, L. (2007). "Voice" is not enough: Conceptualising Article 12 of the United Nations Convention on the Rights of the Child. *British Educational Research Journal, 33*(6), 927–942.

Lundy, L., & McEvoy, L. (2012a). Childhood, the United Nations Convention on the Rights of the Child and research: What constitutes a "rights-based" approach? In M. Freeman (Ed.), *Law and Childhood* (pp. 75–93). Oxford, England: Oxford University Press.

Lundy, L., & McEvoy, L. (2012b). Children's rights and research processes: Assisting children to (in)formed views. *Childhood, 19*(1), 129–144.

McCarry, M. (2012). Who benefits? A critical reflection of children and young people's participation in sensitive research. *International Journal of Social Research Methodology,* 15(1), 55–68.

McCartan, C., Schubotz, D., & Murphy, J. (2012). The self-conscious researcher: Post-modern perspectives of participatory research with young people. *Forum Qualitative Sozialforschung/Forum: Qualitative Social Research, 13*(1), Article 9.

Moore, T., Noble-Carr, D., & McArthur, M. (2016). Changing things for the better: The use of children and young people's reference groups in social research. *International Journal of Social Research Methodology, 19*(2), 241–256.

Niñas y Niños Investigadores. (2014). Aprendiendo de niñas, niños y adolescentes investigadoras/es: Hacia una nueva pedagogía de derechos y deberes [Learning from child researchers: Towards a new pedagogy of rights and responsibilities]. *Rayuela, Mexico, 10,* 131–142.

Powell, M. A., & Smith, A. B. (2009). Children's participation rights in research. *Childhood, 16*(1), 124–142.

Powell, M. A., Fitzgerald, R. M., Taylor, N., & Graham, A. (2012). *International literature review: Ethical issues in undertaking research with children and young people.* Lismore, New South Wales: Southern Cross University Centre for Children and Young People.

Randall, D. (2012). Revisiting Mandell's "least adult" role and engaging with children's voices in research. *Nurse Researcher, 19*(3), 39–43.

Robb, M. (2014). Disseminating research: Shaping the conversation. In A. Clark, R. Flewitt, M. Hammersley, & M. Robb (Eds.), *Understanding research with children and young people* (pp. 237–249). London, England: SAGE.

Ruxton, S. (2014). Achieving policy impact: Researching children's issues at EU level. In A. Clark, R. Flewitt, M. Hammersley, & M. Robb (Eds.), *Understanding research with children and young people* (pp. 250–268). London, England: SAGE.

Save the Children. (2010). *Child carers: Child-led research with children who are carers.* Pretoria, South Africa: Save the Children.

Shaw, C., Brady, L.-M., & Davey, C. (2011). *Guidelines for research with children and young people.* London, England: National Children's Bureau.

Shier, H. (2001). Pathways to participation: Openings, opportunities and obligations. *Children & Society, 15*(2), 107–117.

Shier, H. (2015). Children as researchers in Nicaragua: Children's consultancy to transformative research. *Global Studies of Childhood, 5*(2), 206–219.

Shier, H. (2016). *Children's rights in school: The perception of children in Nicaragua.* Belfast, Ireland: Queen's University Belfast.

Smith, C., & Greene, S. (2014). *Key thinkers in childhood studies.* Bristol, England: Policy Press.

Spalding, V. (2011). *We are researchers: Child-led research, children's voice and educational value* (Research paper). Guildford, England: Centre for Education Research and Policy.

United Nations. (2003). *Statement of common understanding on a human rights-based approach to development co-operation.* New York, NY: United Nations.

CHAPTER 14

YOUNG CHILDREN'S PHOTOGRAPHY WITHIN COLLABORATIVE RESEARCH

Implications for Research Relationships

Rosemary D. Richards

ABSTRACT

When young children have cameras, they can visually record aspects of their experiences and generate new understandings and narratives about their lives, opinions, and perspectives. When their visual and verbal narratives are central to the co-construction of research understandings, through sensitive and supportive interactions with researchers, children competently contribute throughout the inquiry process. Establishing and sustaining participatory research with young children requires careful and conscious interweaving of theoretical frameworks, research paradigms, research methods, and ethical practices. The discussions in this chapter examine these features and consider how these supported participatory research with four young Australian children, aged 4 to 6 years old, when they used digital photography and personal narratives to expand and communicate about their art experiences (Richards, 2012). Elsewhere, focus has been given to how these young

Participatory Methodologies to Elevate Children's Voice and Agency, pages 317–339
Copyright © 2019 by Information Age Publishing
All rights of reproduction in any form reserved.

visual ethnographers were co-researchers as "their cameras afforded a site for art-making and promoted dialogue on interpersonal and intrapersonal planes" (Richards, 2009b, p. 1). This chapter expands on the ways that positive research relationships with these young children was at the heart of this participatory research. The principles that guided research interactions are examined, alongside some of tensions that arose when researching with children who had digital cameras.

RESEARCHING WITH CHILDREN

Responding to disquiets around teachers' roles when interacting with young children engaged in art activities, my initial research focused on children's drawing self-efficacy in relation to the messages they gave and received (Richards, 2009a). This research, which involved 136 children (aged 4 to 9 years) in one New Zealand early childhood center and one school, employed mixed methods in the form of verbal questionnaires with Likert scale, semi-structured interviews and observations. While this research illuminated links between messages exchanged and drawing self-efficacy levels (Richards, 2005, 2009a), little was understood about individual children's art experiences over time and in various contexts, or how transitions between home, early childhood, and school settings influenced their art experiences. Recognizing this gap in understanding, I subsequently undertook longitudinal research in Australia with four children during their last term at preschool and first terms at school. Understanding the nature of these children's art experience, as they transitioned in time and experience between home, early childhood, and school contexts was central to this research. Employing sound theoretical frameworks, ethical research practices, and participatory methodologies that showcased children's voices and images was vital in accessing children's perspectives.

Qualitative and Co-Constructivist Research Paradigms

Functioning within an empowerment paradigm, which values the agentic capacity of children to contribute to their worlds, the research required carefully conceived research methodologies that considered the relationship between theories, data construction processes, and research-based interactions around the phenomena under study. I believe, as others do, that younger children's views and opinions should be taken seriously and their involvement in research should be carefully considered and done well (Darbyshire, Schiller, & MacDougall, 2005).

As with any area of research interest there are multiple realities constructed by those who experience a phenomenon (Ellis, 2006), and the children's voices and photographic images were of central importance as I discerned the significance of what they said in relation to the research focus of understanding the nature of their art experiences. I held that each child-participant actively co-constructed his or her understanding of art experiences within cultural and social environments. Such co-constructions were not merely private affairs; instead children learnt and developed through interactions with people and objects (Vygotsky, 1978, 1986) and they constructed their understandings about their lives within their social and cultural worlds that were rich with defined and evolving histories. How spaces and resources are structured, for example in homes and schools, reflect issues of power and control (Goouch, 2010) and impact on how children make sense of experiences and exercise agency. Thus, working reflexivity within qualitative and co-constructive research paradigms required me to think about theoretical standpoints, how data and themes were generated, how investigations were undertaken, and how children's views were valued and foregrounded within various authentic contexts.

Theoretical Framework: Art as Experience (Dewey)

Dewey's (1934) philosophies on art as experience framed my understandings of children's experiences. In brief, Dewey pointed out that while we often have incomplete experiences, "under conditions of resistance and conflict, aspects and elements of the self and the world that are implicated in this interaction qualify experience with emotions and ideas so that conscious intent emerges" and we have *an* experience (p. 36) with "a single *quality* that pervades the entire experience" (p. 38, emphasis in original). Such experiences have pattern and structure as they involved conscious intent of doing (action) and undergoing (perception). In art experiences the artistic and aesthetic are unified as the active outgoing energies of doing and making are integral to ingoing energies of perception, appreciation, and enjoyment.

Art exists beyond museums and galleries as it exists in the realm of human experience in ways that can be thought of as aesthetic modes of experience (Dewey, 1934/2005), and from this perspective I maintain that children create art. Connecting art with experience highlighted the importance of children sharing their art experiences in ways that illuminated the connections between their artmaking actions, their artworks and their perceptions, thoughts and feelings. The question remained—how does one access young children's opinions and perspectives? After exploring several research methodologies, I became convinced that two research approaches in concert facilitated participatory research with young children. In particular, narrative inquiry (Clandinin, 2007; Clandinin & Connelly, 2000;

Connelly & Clandinin, 2006) made sense of children's stories of experiences and visual ethnography (Pink, 2013) provided viable and visual ways to engage *with* children through their photography.

Young Children Voices and Narrative Inquiry

Narrative accounts of experiences and stories as research have provided a wealth of insights into lived experiences, such as that of Goouch (2010) who worked with early years teachers. At the time of my research I was especially interested in Clandinin and Connelly's (2000, p. 24) notion that individuals lived "storied lives on storied landscapes" as I recognized that as researchers and child-participants interact they co-construct understandings through sharing and re-sharing narratives of experience. Field texts, derived from participants' stories, field notes, observations, photographs, drawings, and other sources, generate research texts in relation to the research questions. When engaging in narrative-based research, Dewey's (1938) notion of significant experiences having situation, continuity, and interactions are considered, as research texts are shared and re-shared and interpretations consider where researchers "and their participants are placed at any particular moment—temporally, spatially, and in terms of the personal and the social" (Clandinin & Connelly, 2000, p. 95). As such, when inquiring narratively with children the researcher is positioned as part of their experiences, rather than one looking from afar. The relationships are such that the children's narratives of experience drive research directions and findings unfold as each child in authentic context is of central importance rather the grand narratives or universal case. Through such processes, knowledge is created rather than extracted (Clark & Moss, 2017) and, as they engage in expressive forms such as sharing stories of experience, children's knowledge counts as important.

Inquiring narratively with young children relies on their ability to voice their experiences and on the researcher's ability to engage in their stories. As an educator, artist, and researcher I felt equipped to meet some of these challenges. However, considering the children's ages (4 to 6 years) and the focus on their art experiences, I anticipated several issues if limiting data generation to verbal interactions and my observations. Firstly, in order to make sense of young children's stories, a researcher reflected upon their own experience of experience (Clandinin & Connelly, 2000) and on dominant theories that informed their understandings. While many of the traditional lenses of inquiry have reinterpreted young children's art experiences through adult perspectives or filtered them through curriculum and political discourse (Richards, 2007a), it was important to make sense of *children's* perspectives on art experience. Secondly, art experiences are understood in ways other than just verbal thought, and even for adults, verbal descriptions of art experiences can be difficult to express. Therefore, expecting young children to describe their art experience through verbal narratives limited how and what they communicated. My interest in arts-based approaches and my capacity to be involved in longitudinal research made visual ethnography, based around children's photography, an attractive research approach. The use of visual media through which to study and share narratives of experiences is a growing field of narrative scholarship (Kim, 2016) and combining narratives and images has been successfully employed in multi-method mosaic approach research with children (Clark & Moss, 2017; Stephenson, 2009).

Young Children, Photography, and Visual Ethnography

In general, ethnographers have extensive contact with participants in authentic contexts and such approaches are valuable in investigating children's experiences, in representing their perspectives and in teasing out the "temporal underpinnings of different presentations of childhood" (James & Prout, 2015, p. 203). Photography can inform ethnographic research and ethnographic approaches can promote the production and interpretation of visual images (Pink, 2013) as photographs are a means of recording data and a medium through which new knowledge and critiques are shaped. As Kind (2013) points out, cameras offer special possibilities and playful ways of seeing and communicating. In order to facilitate young children's competent use of cameras within research processes it is useful to examine and critique how cameras have been used with and by children and the extent to which such provisions lead to empowering children and showcasing their voices, images, and perspectives.

REVIEW OF CHILDREN'S USE OF CAMERAS IN RESEARCH

Research participants can create narratives with and around photographs and Pink (2013) points out that researchers should be interested in both the content of the photograph and how these images are used by the research-participants to make meaning and represent ideas, identities, and emotions. Advances in visual technologies have unlocked new ways of conveying meaning in the construction of ethnographic descriptions, including research with children. For example, when researching with 2- to 4-year-old New Zealand children, Stephenson (2009) noted that the children's photographs provided an effective way for them to share their experiences of the early childhood curriculum. She noted that a researcher's prolonged and sustained involvement in the data-generation period, and a willingness to step back from the research agenda to be open to the less overt messages, aided in developing a deeper understanding of children's perspectives.

An awareness of the strengths and pitfalls of research involving children and visual methods can be achieved by examining research projects in which cameras have been used with and by children in classrooms (e.g., Brooks, 2017; Cook & Hess, 2007; Griebling, 2009; Jorgenson & Sullivan, 2009; Loizou, 2011; Northcote, 2011; Whiting, 2015), early childhood settings (Blagojevic & Thomes, 2008; Einarsdottir, 2005, 2007; Hawkes, 2014; Kelly et al., 2013; Kind, 2013; Kriegler, 2010; Lind, 2005; Quinn & Manning, 2013; Smith, Duncan, & Marshall, 2005; Stephenson, 2009; Terreni, 2010), homes (Jorgenson & Sullivan, 2009; Loizou, 2011), and art galleries (Cook & Hess, 2007; Fasoli, 2003). Children's photographs have helped build better understandings of how they experienced curriculum areas (MacDonald, 2012; Moreland & Cowie, 2005; Northcote, 2011), perceived peers' learning successes (Mykkänen, Määttä, & Järvelä, 2016), and starting school (Dockett & Perry, 2003; Kirova & Emme, 2006). Their photographs and narratives have illuminated aspects of children's everyday and working lives (Brown, Lysaght, & Westbrook, 2007; Mizen, 2005), urban mobility (Kullman, 2012), and perceptions of their physical and social positioning (Orellana, 1999). Photographs with and by children and young persons have been powerful when investigating experiences of homelessness (Joanou, 2009, 2017), chronic ill health (Clark, 1999), of the HIV and AIDS pandemic (Yang, 2015), and being a young carer (Aldridge, 2012; Aldridge & Sharpe, 2007). In preparation for my research, and as I continue to make meanings around the children's visual and verbal narratives, I considered how such studies provided insights into how visual ethnographic methodologies promoted young children's active participation throughout the research processes, while also providing valuable insights into the complex worlds of children.

Harper (2002) believes that images evoke deeper levels of consciousness than do words alone. Thus, in conversations based around children's photographs the children are the experts and, in making sense of their narratives, researchers engage in "everyday listening" (Clark, 2005) as they listen, interpret, and co-construct meanings based on children's knowledge and perspectives. Researcher-participant conversations around photographs also create bridges between their different experiences and understandings and allow participants to be the authors of their own histories and narratives (Joanou, 2009, 2017; Pink, 2013). For example, in Chicago-based ethnographic research, 36 chronically ill children and their families were provided with single-use cameras, and the printed photographs auto drove the interview process from the informants' points of views (Clark, 1999). Through photography, children acted as research collaborators and the researcher was "given privileged access to the child's world, as the child frames it" (Clark, 2010, p. 165).

My interest in art experiences lead me to look at research in this field. When seven children, aged 4 and 5 years, visited an Australian art gallery, digital photographs were taken. Through analysis of these photographs, children's actions were linked to their communities of practice and how they experienced artifacts as mediated entities (Fasoli, 2003). Despite building these understandings, using photographs taken by adults potentially limited insights into children's perspectives on these issues. In other research, children have been the photographers. For example, Cook and Hess (2007) described three research project: In an England-based project, three primary and four secondary students created a book of photographs of their special school; a second study gathered the views and opinions of five young children on aspects of their lives in a reception class, and a third study involved 12 Danish preschool children who visited art museums. In each project the children had disposable cameras, and it was recognized that adults needed to "relinquish some of their predetermined research agenda and methods" (p. 31). Cook and Hess believed that the children's discussions about their photographs provided greater insights into children's feelings than traditional interview processes would have revealed. The research projects ranged from a single art museum visit to seven full-day sessions with children. These studies demonstrated children's ability to take and respond to photographs, but in critiquing these projects I noted that the children were limited by the number and scope of the photographs taken and were not able to view or edit photographs prior to printing.

Orellana's (1999) 3-year ethnographic research into children's views of their social worlds brought together children's comments with their photographs; in this case of the spaces in which they lived. At times, when children took photographs at home and/or school, they had disposable cameras or borrowed Orellana's 35-millimeter film camera. The children's photographs reportedly brought new perspectives to what seemed familiar and "the freedom that kids had to take pictures of their 'choice' was delimited by the degree of spatial autonomy they had at the time they had the camera" (p. 77). Children's social relationships and their culturally constructed photographic traditions also influenced how, when, and why they used the camera and a few children "seemed to feel they had to 'sneak' shots of adults" (p. 80). In reading this research it occurred to me that the young photographers were aware of the rights of other to refuse to be photographed and the control adults usually had over children's actions. All these aspects needed careful consideration as I embarked on my research with children. Also, at the time of Orellana's research, digital cameras may not have been in common use.

In Iceland, Einarsdottir (2005, 2007) investigated 4- to 6-year-old children's perspectives on playschool (prior-to-school setting). In addition to other research methods the children were provided with cameras. One group of 22 children showed the researcher around their playschool as they took between eight and 20 digital photographs of what they thought were important features. A second group of 12 children, who had disposable cameras for a longer period, took photographs of their choice. This group was unsupervised and some children lost interest, others took their photographs quickly while others systematically planned and took photographs. Compared to the supervised children, this group took more photographs in private places and in a more playful manner with many children regarding the camera as a novel plaything (Einarsdottir, 2007). Both groups talked about their photographs and Einarsdottir noted, as others such as Moreland and Cowie (2005) have, that without a child's comments, photographs alone could have been misinterpreted. Furthermore, combining visual and verbal language was "particularly beneficial when working with young children or children with poor written or verbal language skills" (Einarsdottir, 2007, p. 203). Thus, in participatory research, in which children's voices and perspectives are valued, the connection between children's photographs and their comments must be central to generation and interpretation of research narratives.

Sharing verbal understandings can be especially problematic for those children whose racial, linguistic, or ethnic backgrounds differ from the mainstream in their communities, and visual methods provide important links between researchers and participants. Kirova and Emme's (2006) research, which involved six immigrant children taking digital photographs, generated understandings about children's experiences of starting school in Canada. This research embodied aspects of narrative inquiry as the young students retold their experiences and then photographed re-enactments of these. These photographs were "manipulated and arranged in a narrative format" (Kirova & Emme, 2006, p. 4) with some written text to create a fotonovela. Bach (2007), also found value in visual narrative inquiry where participants and researchers constructed meanings about experiences through visual and narrative forms, including through photographs they took and that were taken of them.

In reviewing this body of research, the conditions that promoted or constrained children's agency as active co-researchers were noted. It was clear that providing children with the means to produce photographs and associated narratives enhanced the research experience for researchers and participants. The ways cameras might be used by children were less clear. In many of the reviewed studies, children independently used disposable cameras or, under supervision they used digital cameras. The studies documented the strengths and limitations of using photography, but the time-based connections or disconnection between the child-photographers taking photographs and their viewing of those images, was relatively unexplored. While disposable cameras are relatively inexpensive, such devices do limit the number of photographs taken and, as the children do not see their photographs until they are in the hands of the adult researcher, there is limited capacity to view, edit, or reframe photographs.

Einarsdottir's (2005, 2007) studies provided some useful comparisons between single-use and digital cameras, although the children's photographic experiences varied greatly in terms of the social connections children made during and following their photography sessions. Interactions between children and accompanying adults both constrained (they took fewer photographs) and supported (they remained motivated) one group, while another without adult company was equally inhibited (some lost interest) and liberated (they took a great variety of photographs). Despite these ambiguities, I saw potential in using digital camera in ways that supported and promoted children's independent photography while also developing child–researcher collaborations. As digital cameras allow children to control the production and editing of images, actions, and perceptions are linked, which is a feature of satisfying aesthetic experiences (Dewey, 1934/2005). Kullman's (2012) observation that "seeing the immediate results of filming and photography made the children more aware of their camera work" and encouraged them to "explore various styles of picture-making" (p. 11) adds further support for children's innovative use of digital visual technologies.

Also, central to maintaining children's interest and agency was the relationship that they had with other people in various contexts. While I could not governor the actions and reactions of families and teachers towards a child-as-photographer, I could develop and model supportive and agentic research relationships with each child and their communities. Before discussing the nature of such relationships, the research processes and children's use of cameras within the research is outlined.

FIELDWORK: CHILDREN'S USE OF CAMERAS AND RESEARCH VISITS

Following ethical approval that met university and Australian state requirements, 40 children and their families from one Australian preschool were invited to participate. Information sheets indicated that children would engage in everyday art activities in their homes, early childhood and school settings and that each child would be given a digital camera with which to take photographs of his/her art experiences. Families were informed that participating children would discuss their photographs during the researcher's regular home-based visits; that child-led discussions would be digitally recorded and reflected upon; and that each child's perspectives were of primary importance. Participants and their families had access to ongoing verbal and written summaries and to the completed thesis. At any time, participants could refuse to respond, withdraw consent, exit the study, and ask questions. Based on expressions of interest, home visits were undertaken, which provided further opportunity for the researcher to interact with each child and his/her family, for each party to gauge their genuine interest in being involved, and an opportunity to pose and respond to questions and comments. Factoring each child's and family's inclination to be involved, gender balance, geographical location, and school principals' willingness to participate in the future, two girls and two boys were invited to participate.

Lilly, Sophie, Jackson, and Lee (pseudonyms) were aged between 4 years 11 months, and 5 years and 4 months at the start of the research. They lived in a small Australian city and each had one or two siblings (21–29-month age gap) and two-parent families—three Caucasian families and one Chinese. Throughout the study, each child's consent to participate was treated as an ongoing and dynamic process and children could opt out of engaging with the researcher or research focus at any point in the study. As has been noted, "The more that participants can engage and identify with the topic, the more interest and motivation is generated" (González & Moll, 2002, p. 627) and all children remained enthusiastic throughout the research and were supported by their families and teachers.

Providing Children With Digital Cameras

During the initial home-based visit, each child participant was given a digital camera, hand lanyard, personalized camera bag, rechargeable batteries, and 1GB memory card. Regarding each child as a competent problem solver and learner he/she was introduced to the basic camera functions and encouraged to independently take photographs. Developing shared and negotiated understandings of research intentions and relationships was important, so I did not instruct the children to take specific photos, but instead had several conversations with them about the nature of the project. I discussed how I was very interested in their art experiences and how their photographs and comments helped me to understand children's art experiences better. All four children readily mastered photographic techniques and like Luttrell (2010), I did not encourage the children to take particular kinds of images, but instead honored whatever meanings children gave to their photographs. I listened with genuine interest to their stories of experiences, based around their photographs, and carefully and systematically recorded their visual and verbal narratives.

Over a 10-month period, in their homes, early childhood center and schools, the children photographed their art experiences and talked about their photographs during regular fortnightly home-based visits. Each child expected to see me at their home, school, or preschool at least once a week and my reliability and predictability (in action and demeanor) was important, so children felt safe and valued. The children keenly anticipated the home-based visits and the presence of a siblings and parent appeared to support rather than limit their focus and agency.

From the onset, the children were competent photographers, computer operators, orators, decision-makers, and organizers. During home visits, once the camera card was inserted into a laptop computer, each child managed a slide show and commented on his/her photographs. Occasional prompts helped to clarify artistic motivations, social circumstances surrounding artmaking, and emotional responses. In the main however, each child decided the pace, direction, and topics of conversation and no parent or family member censored or limited the children's discussions or the photographs that they shared. During these visits, recharged batteries and new memory cards were provided and photographs were saved to files and discussions were digitally recorded.

Research collaborations resulted in more than 5,000 photographs and over 30 hours of research conversations. Photography and children's narratives are not an easy data set to organize or navigate as they become complex, vast, and sometimes ambiguous. When dealing with such data the researcher must be open to ambiguity as the children's stories of experiences expand, and what may have seen apparent as an emerging theme is later discarded as new insights and experiences are shared, that leads in new directions. Remaining open to these possibilities is important so the child-participant is not steered towards expressing preconceived notions based on adults' views.

Establishing and maintaining positive research relationships that were agentic for young children was not just a matter of good luck—instead supporting collaborative relationships with the child-participants and their communities was reflectively practiced throughout the research. From the inception of the research careful thought was given to developing and maintaining positive research relationships with the young participants. Building on my previous approaches for building "trusting relationship with children that was perhaps unique from the usual adult roles" (Richards, 2009a, p. 46) I again found useful the notions of the researcher's role as context (Graue & Walsh, 1998), alongside Clandinin and Connelly's (2000) ideas about working narratively at the boundaries of research.

PRINCIPLES THAT GUIDED RESEARCH INTERACTIONS WITH YOUNG RESEARCH PARTICIPANTS

Boundaries can exist between narrative inquiry approaches and reductionistic and formalistic approaches, where all experience is seen in terms of playing out the "hegemonies of politics, culture, gender, and framework" (Clandinin & Connelly, 2000, p. 40) and narrative inquirers need to be conscious of the tensions that may exist when working at these boundaries. Furthermore, Graue and Walsh (1998) suggested that the "act of research is conceived as nested contexts, including the researcher's perspectives on research, theory, and, in this case, children; the role negotiated with/by the participants; and the relationships that ensue over time" (p. 73). Together, these ideas formed the principles that guided my research interactions with young research participants. Specifically, I considered the following:

- How and in what ways did my perspectives on children, research, and theory impact on research processes?
- How and in what ways were my roles with children and other research participants negotiated and dynamic?
- How and in what ways did relationships develop and change over time and experience?
- When working at the boundaries of personal and research site beliefs, histories, and ethics, what tensions arose?

In relation to my research the first three consideration are discussed and, in each case, some of the actual tensions that arose are described.

Perspectives on Children, Research, and Theory

How a researcher regards children's and families' roles within the research processes influences how participants experience the research processes and how relationships develop. Just as indigenous communities should experience benefits "substantially within the foreseeable future" (Ball, 2005, p. 86), I believed that parents should expect their children to benefit from being in the research project. Therefore, prior to participant selection I considered how each child benefited from research experiences and interactions. Principally, I held that children benefited from interacting with a caring adult who was genuinely interested in their perspectives and whose focused attention facilitated and acknowledged their opinions, feelings, experiences, and sense of well-being. My experiences in art, art education and photography, coupled with children's capacity to communicate through words, actions, and photographs could enrich children's experiences of art and thus contribute towards positive art self-efficacy (Richards, 2009a). I held that while research should contribute to expanding knowledge in various domains, this was second to ensuring that the actual research processes were of social, emotional, and cognitive benefit to the child-participants, their families and teachers, and to the researcher if these benefits could not be sustained then the time spend interacting within the research project was of questionable value.

If one holds that children capably and competently contribute to their own and others' lives, then children are capable co-researchers (Alderson, 2000; Jones, 2004; Morrow, 2005) who influence how our research relationships develop. Specifically, through visual ethnography (Pink, 2013) and narrative inquiry (Clandinin & Connelly, 2000), coupled with home-based research meetings, the children exercised some control over research processes as their photographs and comments generated data and informed my research directions and analysis. The research findings were crafted around each child's visual and verbal narratives and written as case studies (Richards, 2012).

While I held that young children are competent contributors who can make informed decisions about their actions and reactions, including photography, tensions arose when others did not share such perspectives. For example, in response to an article about research methods (Richards, 2007b), an anonymous reviewer suggested that young children were unable to competently use digital cameras, and during participation selection processes, some children were excluded because there intended schools prohibited children's camera use at school. In identifying and addressing tensions around child-generated photography a policy on digital photography for research purposes was developed, in consultation with the early childhood center director, and approved by the board of managers. This negotiated approach encouraged respectful interactions within the educational settings and supported the children's use of cameras. This camera policy was subsequently modified and included in the Australian state education research approval process (SERAP) application as a guide for children's use of cameras in school settings.

At an intersection of attitudes about children, research, and theory are ethical approval processes, which are designed to safeguard participants, ensure worthwhile research and meet stakeholders' needs. Approval to research in state schools involved government departments and policies. At the time I submitted a SERAP application, approval processes focused on long-term benefits for students when they left school (MCEETYA, 2000). While these theoretical frameworks, which placed the importance of childhood in relation to children's futures (James & Prout, 2015), risked overshadowing the benefits of art-based research with young children and the importance of interpersonal relationships in research with children, it was important to address these aspects during ethical approval processes.

Role Negotiation With and by Child Participants

As the children interacted with me and their cameras I was mindful of how our roles, manner, and interactions were partly dependent on social and physical contexts. Within the research three key contexts influenced our interactions—children's homes, preschool, and schools. At home the children experienced the most autonomy and this was especially evident with Lee, a bilingual Chinese-Australian boy who was animated and gregarious at home, a place in which he enthusiastically drew, took photographs, and talked about his art and photographs. However, at preschool he was quiet, serious, and largely solitary and his sense of belonging, or lack of it, was sometimes explored through his home-based drawing stories (Richards, 2017). Later, at school, he was industrious, introverted, and reluctant to verbally contribute in group situations. As Lee's manner in these contexts varied I needed to be sensitive to these changing roles, take my cue from him, and modify my behavior accordingly. It was important that the children could count on my adaptability (to situations based on their cues) and dependability (always positive, approachable, and focused on their narratives).

The nature of physical interactions with the children also changed over time and place. For instance, in homes adult–child interactions were often more physical and demonstrative than those in educational settings, the children related differently to me in each situation. For example, at his home, Jackson organized games for us to play while at preschool or school he acknowledged my presence but did not seek my company. Over time, I also found that physicality tended to increase in terms of playful behavior, hugs, and physical proximity. For these reasons, it was important to always have at least one parent present as this not only encouraged the children to feel comfortable with me, but allowed me to check that the parents were comfortable with the interactions between their child and me.

Once again, I encountered tensions when working at the boundaries in that the way the children and I interacted at home, was not the same as our school or preschool interactions. The school environment was especially different to home or preschool as I endeavored to create minimum disruption, while also helping the teachers. One school was concerned that my focused attention on the research participant/s could cause equity issues and the principal stated, "No child should feel more important than any other." To involve the children in the change of my role at school, I talked with them prior to visits, and again after the school visits. The children had experienced being schoolchildren and were supportive of my need to act like a school-adult. As I was an experienced teacher, the classroom teachers often asked me to work with groups or help individuals. In many ways, because I continued to regularly visit the research participants in their homes and our relationships continued to evolve, I felt the children were both my supporters and co-conspirators as we enacted these new roles.

Thus, far from being established entities, our ways of being for the children and I were negotiated between the various people in the research community and in relation to the place in which such interactions took place. The children and I supported each other in enacting roles that were appropriate in each context, without violating the overall integrity of our interpersonal and research relationships.

The ways in which children used their cameras varied across the three contexts of home, early childhood and school settings. At home the children were more likely to take photographs of completed artworks, artworks in progress, and their art activities. At preschool, while the four children took some photographs or prompted others to take photos of them, they were more likely to photograph their paintings and so on when they were at home. My regular visits to the center, and the photographs I took, added to the discussions we had at home. The teachers were also committed to the research project and at times encouraged the children to take photographs or told me about the children's art experiences. The children usually took their cameras to school but they seldom took photographs during class time. Again, my visits contributed towards coherent visual and verbal narratives of their experiences. As the research progressed, I realized that the children had a variety of art related experiences throughout the school day (and not just at scheduled art time) so it was decided that I would be at each school for 3 to 4 consecutive full days. This helped provide context around the children's narratives and artworks and my photographs contributed a focus to some of our discussions. Thus, there was continual role negotiation with and by child participants, myself, their families, and teachers that helped to support the children's communication around their art experiences and the generation of photographs.

Relationships Develop and Change

Relationships with children and families evolved over time. In the beginning, I talked with the parents about the importance of allowing their child to take the lead in the discussions. While the parents' participation in the home-based discussion was not generally verbal, they eagerly looked on as their child showed and discussed his or her photographs. Their presence supported their child, and often a parent communicated with me through facial expressions that prompted me to ask their child to elaborate, or helped me to link together episodes. These types of interactions demonstrated that not only was I building theories about the children's art experience, but so too were the parents and children.

In society in general, child–adult interactions tend to reflect power imbalances. However, researching with children across a variety of contexts that included the children's own homes, helped to address this. In preschool and school contexts, children become accustomed to a variety of adults visiting and interacting with them. However, these same people did not usually visit their homes with the express purpose of interacting with them. As Virginia Morrow (2005) noted in her research, "children are always in a structural relationship to the adults around them: as a child of their families, as somebody's son or daughter, or a 'school' child" (p. 160). Therefore, home visits allowed for unique adult-child relationships and how these relationships developed depended on each child, situation, and time. I was conscious of generating a negotiated role—by acting like neither a childlike friend nor an authoritarian adult. I achieved this in part by focusing my attention on each child, always greeting them first, engaging in his or her banter and humor, and physically engaging in play when invited. All parents were supportive of these relationships and in many ways, the home environment was a safe space for the children to "share their ideas without challenge or critique" (MacNaughton & Smith, 2005, p. 115). In each family parents reported deeper understandings about their child's thoughts and ideas, and they marveled at their child's expanding abilities to articulate complex thoughts and experiences.

Trustworthiness is essential, and I made it clear to the children and their parents that I would not say anything *about* the children that I did not also discuss *with* them. Likewise, I reiterated to all participants and teachers that I would only hold conversations about the children that I could then freely share with them and their parents. I believed that the overt nature of such conversations added to the integrity of the research relationships and strengthened the trust between all research participants.

Over time, our relationships developed in subtle yet dynamic ways. As the research progressed the children became more agentic in driving the direction and nature of my visits, and we developed routines and rituals that allowed the research process to flow. I became most aware of the change in relationships, and potential tensions, when on two occasions parents, who were not usually present at home-based research discussions, were surprised by their child's response to me. One parent asked his son to "stop mucking around"—yet playing hide and seek when I arrived had developed as a fun start to our session. Another parent commented on her daughter's distractibility during my visit but, apart from supporting each child to act in any way he/she felt fit, I had come to realize that these distractions nearly always related to her developing narratives about her art experiences as she often created additional drawings and descriptions.

My active involvement in the children's classroom communities allowed for some continuity between home and preschool research processes. However, once at school, the research participants appeared to assimilate ways of being a schoolchild that influenced the choices they made. For example, while the children all eagerly used the cameras at preschool and home, they were reluctant to use it independently at school unless specifically encouraged to—perhaps appraising that adults made the decisions at school. Therefore, tensions at the boundaries of dominant beliefs or behaviors, and research beliefs and behaviors were also an issue for the children as co-researchers.

Just as starting the research project was problematic, so too was exiting the community formed around the research activities. More than 10 months had elapsed between first home visits and final school visits. While some home visits continued, I prepared the children for the change of routine. I explained that I would write up their stories and discuss these with them, but I would no longer visit them at school, and my visits to their homes would become less frequent. The children appeared to understand this transition as they talked about me going back to my other home in New Zealand. Thus, as the parents and I supported the children in taking the lead in aspects of the research process, unique relationships developed. The children not only displayed the ability to develop fluid relationships, but they showed an understanding of how our relationship changed and developed over time and experience.

CONCLUDING COMMENTS

Positive research relationships are at the heart of participatory research with young children. While cameras provide both a means for making sense of experiences, and a medium through which new meanings can be co-constructed, if trusting relationships are not established and maintained between each child-participant and adult researcher, then children's perspectives may be overshadowed by adults' interests and research agendas.

Developing positive and dynamic research relationships with children that promotes and supports children's active involvement as co-researchers is not a haphazard affair. Instead, the researcher and research team must critically reflect on the ways in which their views, beliefs and practices may impact on children within research. In particular, consideration could be given to how perspectives on children, research, and theory influence research processes; how children's and adults' co-researcher roles are negotiated and dynamic; and how research relationships between participants develop and change over time, context and experience. In addition, viewing and supporting children as powerful storytellers, photographer and change-makers can lead to tensions at the boundary of such beliefs and those dominant in society. Being aware of these tensions can help the researcher to navigate these paths and support children when they too experience such tensions.

Participatory research with young children with cameras and digital technologies provides many opportunities, challenges, and complexities. In my experience, it can be positive, powerful and satisfying for co-researchers—the young and not-so-young!

Questions for Reflection

1. When providing children with cameras, to what extent are they in control of photographic processes? What is the time lap between their photographic actions and their viewing and discussing? How might this impact on the sense made of the photograph and children's potential to control the construction and editing of images and narratives?
2. Interactions with children: How can the research focus be explained and meanings co-constructed with children in ways that they understand and that does not limit their scope for sharing their perspectives?
3. How and in what ways could your perspectives on children, research and theory impact on research processes? What perspectives might child-participants have of you and how might this impact on their interactions with you?
4. How and in what ways could your roles with children and other research participants be negotiated and dynamic? What practices and habits will you develop when interacting with children that will promote safe, supportive and collaborative research interactions?
5. How and in what ways can you allow for relationships to develop and change over time and experience?
6. When working at the boundaries of personal and research site beliefs, histories and ethics, what tensions can you anticipate and how might you respond to these?
7. As visual and verbal data are generated how will you store and arrange this so it remains open for ongoing analysis and fluid interpretations? How can you ensure that children's 'big ideas' or larger interests are acknowledged? How can you share this on-going analysis with children that allows for their responses and re-interpretations?

Suggestions for Further Reading

Aldridge, J. (2012). The participation of vulnerable children in photographic research. *Visual Studies, 27*(1), 48–58.

Clark, A., & Moss, P. (2017). *Listening to young children: The mosiac approach* (3rd ed.). London, England: Kingsley.

Dwyer, R., Davis, I., & Emerald, E. (2016). *Narrative research in practice: Stories from the field*. Singapore: Springer.
Graue, M. E., & Walsh, D. J. (1998). *Studying children in context: Theories, methods, and ethics*. Thousand Oaks, CA: SAGE.
Kim, J.-H. (2016). *Understanding narrative inquiry: The crafting and analysis of stories of research*. Thousand Oaks, CA: SAGE.
Pink, S. (2013). *Doing visual ethnography* (3rd ed.). London, England: SAGE.

REFERENCES

Alderson, P. (2000). Children as researchers: The effects of participation rights on research methodology. In A. Lewis & G. Lindsay (Eds.), *Researching children's perspectives*. Philadelphia, PA: Open University Press.

Aldridge, J. (2012). The participation of vulnerable children in photographic research. *Visual Studies, 27*(1), 48–58. doi: 10.1080/1472586X.2012.642957

Aldridge, J., & Sharpe, D. (2007). *Pictures of young caring*. Loughborough, England: Young Carers Research Group, Loughborough University.

Bach, H. (2007). Composing a visual narrative. In D. J. Clandinin (Ed.), *Handbook of narrative inquiry: Mapping a methodology*. Thousand Oaks, CA: SAGE.

Ball, J. (2005). Restorative research partnerships in Indigenous communities. In A. Farrell (Ed.), *Ethical research with children* (pp. 81–97). Maidenhead, England: Open University Press.

Blagojevic, B., & Thomes, K. (2008). Young photographers. *Young Children, 63*(5), 66–72.

Brooks, M. L. (2017). Drawing to learn. In M. Narey (Ed.), *Multimodal perspectives of language, literacy, and learning in early childhood: The creative and critical "art" of making meaning* (pp. 25–44). Cham, Switzerland: Springer.

Brown, I., Lysaght, P., & Westbrook, R. (2007). Analysing image and text: Voices of children. *Australian Art Education, 30*(2), 40–56.

Clandinin, D. J. (Ed.). (2007). *Handbook of narrative inquiry: Mapping a methodology*. Thousand Oaks, CA: SAGE.

Clandinin, D. J., & Connelly, F. M. (2000). *Narrative Inquiry: Experience and story in qualitative research*. San Francisco, CA: Jossey-Bass.

Clark, A. (2005). Listening to and involving young children: A review of research and practice. *Early Child Development and Care, 175*(6), 489–505.

Clark, A., & Moss, P. (2017). *Listening to young children: The mosiac approach* (3rd ed.). London, England: Kingsley.

Clark, C. D. (1999). The autodriven interview: A photographic viewfinder into children's experience. *Visual Sociology, 14*, 39–50.

Clark, C. D. (2010). *In a younger voice: Doing child-centered qualitative research*. New York, NY: Oxford University Press.

Connelly, F. M., & Clandinin, D. J. (2006). Narrative inquiry. In J. Green, G. Camilli, & P. Elmore (Eds.), *Handbook of complementary methods in education research* (pp. 477–487). Mahwah, NJ: Erlbaum.

Cook, T., & Hess, E. (2007). What the camera sees and from whose perspective: Fun methodologies for engaging children in enlightening adults. *Childhood, 14*(1), 29–45.

Darbyshire, P., Schiller, W., & MacDougall, C. (2005). Extending new paradigm childhood research: Meeting the challenges of including younger children. *Early Child Development and Care, 175*(6), 467–472.

Dewey, J. (1934). *Art as experience.* New York, NY: Penguin Group.

Dewey, J. (1934/2005). *Art as experience.* New York, NY: Penguin Group.

Dewey, J. (1938). *Experience and education.* New York, NY: Collier Books.

Dockett, S., & Perry, B. (2003). Children's views and children's voices in starting school. *Australian Journal of Early Childhood, 28*(1), 12–17.

Einarsdottir, J. (2005). Playschool in pictures: Children's photographs as a research method. *Early Child Development and Care, 175*(6), 523–541.

Einarsdottir, J. (2007). Research with children: Methodological and ethical challenges. *European Early Childhood Education Research Journal, 15*(2), 197–211.

Ellis, J. (2006). Researching children's experience hermeneutically and holistically. *The Alberta Journal of Educational Research, 52*(3), 111–126.

Fasoli, L. (2003). Reading photographs of young children: Looking at practices. *Contemporary Issues in Early Childhood, 4*(1), 32–47.

González, N., & Moll, L. C. (2002). Cruzando el Puente: Building bridges to funds of knowledge. *Educational Policy, 16*(4), 623–641.

Goouch, K. (2010). *Towards excellence in early years education: Exploring narratives of experience* (1st ed.). Abingdon, England: Routledge.

Graue, M. E., & Walsh, D. J. (1998). *Studying children in context: Theories, methods, and ethics.* Thousand Oaks, CA: SAGE.

Griebling, S. J. U. (2009). *Designs for making a tree: An ethnographic study of young children's work in the visual arts* (Doctoral dissertation). University of Cincinnati, Cincinnati, OH.

Harper, D. (2002). Talking about pictures: A case for photo elicitation. *Visual Studies, 17*(1), 13–26.

Hawkes, K. (2014). *Where have all the children gone? Experiences of children, parents and teachers in a changing early childhood education service* (Master's thesis). The University of Waikato. Retrieved from http://researchcommons.waikato.ac.nz/bitstream/handle/10289/9291/thesis.pdf?sequence=3&isAllowed=y

James, A., & Prout, A. (2015). Re-presenting childhood: Time and transition in the study of childhood. In A. James & A. Prout (Eds.), *Constructing and reconstructing childhood: Contemporary issues in the sociological study of childhood* (Classic ed., pp. 202–219). New York, NY: Routledge.

Joanou, J. P. (2009). The bad and the ugly: Ethical concerns in participatory photographic methods with children living and working on the streets of Lima, Peru. *Visual Studies, 24*(3), 214–223.

Joanou, J. P. (2017). Visualising the invisible: Children on the streets of Lima, Peru, realise the self through photographs. *Visual Studies, 32*(2), 133–147.

Jones, A. (2004). Involving children and young people as researchers. In S. Fraser, V. Lewis, S. Ding, M. Kellett, & C. Robinson (Eds.), *Doing research with children and young people* (pp. 113–144). London, England: SAGE.

Jorgenson, J., & Sullivan, T. (2009). Accessing children's perspectives through participatory photo interviews. *Forum: Qualitative Social Research, 11*(1), Art. 8. http://dx.doi.org/10.17169/fqs-11.1.447

Kelly, J., White, J., Dekker, M., Donald, J., Hart, K., McKay, F., . . . Wright, G. (2013). *The Ngahere Project: Teaching and learning possibilities in nature settings.* Hamilton, New Zealand: Wilf Malcolm Institute of Educational Research.

Kim, J.-H. (2016). *Understanding narrative inquiry: The crafting and analysis of stories of research.* Thousand Oaks, CA: SAGE.

Kind, S. (2013). Lively entanglements: The doings, movements and enactments of photography. *Global Studies of Childhood, 3*(4), 427–441.

Kirova, A., & Emme, M. (2006). Using photography as a means of phenomenological seeing: "Doing phenomenology" with immigrant children. *The Indo-Pacific Journal of Phenomenology, 6*(2). Retrieved from http://www.ipjp.org/index.php?option=com_jdownloads&Itemid=25&task=finish&cid=54&catid=15&m=0

Kriegler, L.-A. (2010). Photography: An expressive language for learning. *Australian Art Education, 33*(2), 26–44.

Kullman, K. (2012). Experiments with moving children and digital cameras. *Children's Geographies, 10*(1), 1–16.

Lind, U. (2005). Identity and power, "meaning," gender and age: Children's creative work as a signifying practice. *Contemporary Issues in Early Childhood, 6*(3), 256–268.

Loizou, E. (2011). Disposable cameras, humour and children's abilities. *Contemporary Issues in Early Childhood, 12*(2), 148–162.

Luttrell, W. (2010). "A camera is a big responsibility": A lens for analysing children's visual voices. *Visual Studies, 25*(3), 224–237.

MacDonald, A. (2012). Young children's photographs of measurement in the home. *Early Years, 32*(1), 71–85.

MacNaughton, G., & Smith, K. (2005). Transforming research ethics: The choices and challenges of researching with children. In A. Farrell (Ed.), *Ethical research with children* (pp. 112–123). Maidenhead, England: Open University Press.

MCEETYA. (2000). *National report on schooling in Australia* (ISSN 1036-0972). Melbourne, Australia: Curriculum Corporation. Retrieved from http://www.educationcouncil.edu.au/site/DefaultSite/filesystem/documents/Reports%20and%20publications/Archive%20Publications/National%20Report/ANR%202000.pdf

Mizen, P. (2005). A little 'light work'? Children's images of their labour. *Visual Studies, 20*(2), 124–139.

Moreland, J., & Cowie, B. (2005). Exploring the methods of auto-photography and photo-interviews: Children taking pictures of science and technology. *Waikato Journal of Education, 11,* 73–87.

Morrow, V. (2005). Ethical issues in collaborative research with children. In A. Farrell (Ed.), *Ethical research with children* (pp. 150–165). Maidenhead, England: Open University Press.

Mykkänen, A., Määttä, E., & Järvelä, S. (2016). 'What makes her succeed?' Children's interpretations of their peers' successes in learning situations. *International Journal of Early Years Education, 24*(1), 97–112.

Northcote, M. (2011). Teaching with technology: Step back and hand over the cameras! Using digital cameras to facilitate mathematics learning with young children in K–2 classrooms. *Australian Primary Mathematics Classroom, 16*(3), 29–32.

Orellana, M. F. (1999). Space and place in an urban landscape: Learning from children's views of their social worlds. *Visual Sociology, 14*, 73–89.

Pink, S. (2013). *Doing visual ethnography* (3rd ed.). London, England: SAGE.

Quinn, S. M. F., & Manning, J. P. (2013). Recognising the ethical implications of the use of photography in early childhood educational setting. *Contemporary Issues in Early Childhood, 14*(3), 270–278.

Richards, R. D. (2005). Critically re-examining young children's art experiences. *Early Education, 37*, 15–21.

Richards, R. D. (2007a). Outdated relics on hallowed ground: Unearthing attitudes and beliefs about young children's art. *Australian Journal of Early Childhood, 32*(4), 22–30.

Richards, R. D. (2007b). Self-portraits of young children as art-makers. *Proceedings of the Inaugural Postgraduate Research Conference–Bridging the Gap between Ideas and Doing Research (2006)*, 338–348.

Richards, R. D. (2009a). *Jake just does scribbles but I do pictures: Drawing self-efficacy and the messages four- to nine-year-old children give and receive about their drawing.* Koln, Germany: Lambert Academic.

Richards, R. D. (2009b). Young visual ethnographers: Children's use of digital photography to record, share and extend their art experiences. *International Art in Early Childhood Research Journal, 1*(1), 1–13. Retrieved from http://www .artinearlychildhood.org/artec/images/article/ARTEC_2009_Research_ Journal_1_Article_3.pdf

Richards, R. D. (2012). *Young children's art experiences: A visual ethnographic study with four children in their homes, early childhood centre and schools* (Doctoral dissertation). University of New England, Armidale, NSW. Retrieved from http:// e-publications.une.edu.au/1959.11/11398

Richards, R. D. (2017). Young children's use of drawings and storytelling to mediate complex worlds of cultural and linguistic diversity. In M. Narey (Ed.), *Multimodal perspectives of language, literacy, and learning in early childhood: The creative and critical "art" of making meaning* (pp. 127–148). Cham, Switzerland: Springer.

Smith, A., Duncan, J., & Marshall, K. (2005). Children's perspectives on their learning: Exploring methods. *Early Child Development and Care, 176*(6), 473–487.

Stephenson, A. (2009). Horses in the sandpit: Photography, prolonged involvement and "stepping back" as strategies for listening to children's voices. *Early Child Development and Care, 179*(2), 131–141.

Terreni, L. (2010). Art and ICT: Considering new possibilities for visual art education in early childhood settings. *Australian Art Education, 33*(2), 74–86.

Vygotsky, L. S. (1978). Mind in society: The development of higher psychological processes. In M. Cole, V. John-Steiner, S. Scribner, & E. Souberman (Eds.),

Mind in society: The development of higher psychological processes (pp. 19–120). Cambridge, MA: Harvard University Press.

Vygotsky, L. S. (1986). *Thought and language* (A. Kozulin, Trans.). Cambridge, MA: The MIT Press.

Whiting, L. S. (2015). Reflecting on the use of photo elicitation with children. *Nurse Researcher, 22*(3), 13–17.

Yang, K.-H. (2015). Voice, authenticity and ethical challenges: The participatory dissemination of youth-generated visual data over social media. *Visual Studies, 30*(3), 309–318.

CHAPTER 15

REMOVING THE MEDICAL PARADIGM—MAKING CHILDREN'S VOICES VISIBLE IN THE CONTEXT OF PROBLEMATIC EATING

Participatory Action Research in a Clinical Setting

Colleen McMillan

ABSTRACT

Disordered eating among children and preadolescents is increasing with serious outcomes including death. Currently the third leading mortality among this age group methods of assessment have historically been situated within the medical paradigm characterized by closed opened questions focusing on pathology. Practitioner positions of power silence the voice of the child, and the situation is complicated by screening questions that rest upon the surface of superficiality. Deeper childhood experiences marked by disconnection,

Participatory Methodologies to Elevate Children's Voice and Agency, pages 341–365
Copyright © 2019 by Information Age Publishing
341

abandonment, worries related to growing up, and bullying around "fatness" become masked behind such questions. This chapter is informed by a clinical practice that values participatory action research (PAR) resulting in a study that actively involved 16 girls between the ages of 9 to 11 with the goal of collaboratively creating an assessment template that honored their experiential knowledge. Understanding the spoken word may have previously been harsh in the lives of the girls, methods that supported connection and belonging were used to elicit internal voices dismissed by authority figures, and to establish the critical component of trust. As such, artwork, dance, and games were combined as avenues to create a collective sense of community supporting vulnerable voices to speak to their experiences that manifested negatively through food. By validating these deeper meanings the girls began to feel empowered as knowledge holders and understand the concept of agency. The success of their efforts resulted in two significant outcomes; the development of a feminist informed template of questions for family physicians to use and the hosting of a knowledge dissemination event designed for significant others in their lives to see and hear, through artwork and stories, the hidden contributing factors at play that were missed by traditional medical screening.

Disordered eating among children and preadolescents is increasing with serious outcomes including death. Incidence of restrictive eating disorders in children aged 5 to 12 is twice the incident rate of type II diabetes in all children up to the age of 18 years (NEDIC, 2017). Currently the third leading mortality among this age group, methods of assessment have historically been situated within the medical paradigm characterized by closed opened questions focusing on pathology. Practitioner positions of power silence the voice of the child, and the situation is further complicated by screening questions that rest upon the surface of superficiality. Current screening tools, such as the Eating Attitudes Test 26 (EAT) or SCOFF (which is an acronym for an eating disorders screening tool), collect scant information as to the contributing reasons food becomes problematic; as a result lived experiences become embedded and are at risk to being lost. Narratives focused on feeling disconnected, abandoned, worried about growing up, or being bullied around "fatness" are masked behind clinical questions.

This chapter is informed by a clinical/research methodology that is participatory in nature and celebrates the intuitive and lived knowledge of children and young adolescents channelled through avenues of creativity. Theoretically informed by relational cultural theory developed by Jean Baker Miller (1976) the chapter initially challenges traditional developmental theories that posit psychological separation and individuation is a critical benchmark for healthy development (Mahler, Pine, & Bergman, 1975; Winnicot, 1965). Instead, by using foundational work by Chodorow (1974), Miller (1976), and Gillian (1982) who argue girls develop their sense of self in the context of relationships and desire connection and mutually responsive relationships, I will show how reaching preadolescence marks a transitional intersection where these values are challenged. The collision of these seemingly opposed concepts (connection/interdependency and separation/individuation) positions young girls in what Pipher (1994) calls the paradox of adolescence. Maine (2001) frames this time as one of "relentless pressure" where the preadolescent girl responds by losing contact with her own feelings leading to a "dangerous deficit of self awareness and self-efficacy that can lead to eating disorders" (p. 1302). Friedman (1997) likens this juncture to that of learning a new language as girls attempt to fit into a male dominated culture that values independence over interdependence and self-sufficiency over connectedness.

I practice on the premise the manifesting of voice through the body is an attempt to resolve this constructed dilemma, in that the body communicates these unspoken stories of connection (Brown Brown & Augusta-Scott, 2007; Orbach, 1986; White & Epston, 1990). Referred to as hurting stories, Treasure (2007) posits that symptoms of restriction reflect earlier experiences of relational trauma. My experience has been that such stories become categorized and sanitized by being forced into a plethora of traditional modalities including cookie cutter assessment questionnaires. Steiner-Adair (1986, p. 110) calls children and adolescents "truth tellers" and suggests that they are literally dying to tell a story of an impoverished culture that does not "nourish itself by valuing interrelationships" (p. 110). Traditional methodologies often filter these messy stories (White, 2001) so that what often is from the professional is clinical talk focused on pathology and individual deficit.

Methods aimed to collect these stories through standardized questionnaires and semi- structured interviews focus on issues of calories and food, eliciting responses that do not move beyond the narrow parameters of symptomatology (Tozzi, Sullivan, Fear, McKenzie, & Bulik, 2003). As a result, stories rest at the level of symptoms rather than seek underlying reasons that may support such behavior or make them more understandable. Girls are therefore left no choice by these clinical/research methods other than to "tell their story with their bodies" (Steiner-Adair, 1986, p. 110). Likewise, Oliver (1999) says that in order to understand the "interior layers" of such stories, one must look below surface knowledge and "listen to these voices as they speak from the heart" (p. 221).

Whether it is research or clinical methodologies, I believe current methods that focus on symptoms are flawed in terms of how such stories are collected and understood. Data collection methods individualize stories into fragments that cannot be holistically understood or appreciated when separated from the overall social/cultural/political context. In comparison, methodologies that collect stories holistically, embrace creative energy synonymous with youth and celebrate emerging voices are rich. Approaches that seek to hear voices in a communal way reach deeper into the complexities that challenge youth, experiences holding contradictions that boxes on a questionnaire cannot support. As such, I advocate for a methodology that collects the voices of youth with eating disorders in a communal way valuing connectedness, collectiveness, and mutuality contrasting to traditional approaches that emphasize autonomy and individuality.

CURRENT METHODOLOGICAL APPROACHES

Best practice protocols, also referred to as evidence based, solicit problem saturated dialogue based on questions contained in assessment tools such as the EAT 26 and SCOFF (See Table 15.1). Screening questions are concentrated on eating patterns, and the young patient is asked individualistic questions suggesting the fault or problem is intrapersonal without considering the influence of distal factors. Language is reductionist and inaccessible to a child or early adolescent.

TABLE 15.1 Specific Screening Questions to Identify the Child, Adolescent, or Young Adult With an Eating Disorder
What is the least you ever weighed in the past year? How tall were you then? When was that?
What do you think you ought to weigh?
Exercise: how much, how often, level of intensity? How stressed are you if you miss a workout?
Current dietary practices: ask for specifics—amounts, food groups, fluids, restrictions?
24-hour diet history? • Calorie counting, fat gram counting? Taboo foods (foods you avoid)? • Any binge eating? Frequency, amount, triggers? • Purging history? • Use of diuretics, laxatives, diet pills, ipecac? Ask about elimination pattern, constipation, diarrhea. • Any vomiting? Frequency, how long after meals?
Any previous therapy? What kind and how long? What was and was not helpful?
Family history: obesity, eating disorders, depression, other mental illness, substance abuse by parents or other family members?
Menstrual history: age at menarche? Regularity of cycles? Last menstrual period?
Use of cigarettes, drugs, alcohol? Sexual history? History of physical or sexual abuse?
Review of symptoms: • Dizziness, syncope, weakness, fatigue? • Pallor, easy bruising or bleeding? • Cold intolerance? • Hair loss, lanugo, dry skin? • Vomiting, diarrhea, constipation? • Fullness, bloating, abdominal pain, epigastric burning? • Muscle cramps, joint paints, palpitations, chest pain? • Menstrual irregularities? • Symptoms of hyperthyroidism, diabetes, malignancy, infection, inflammatory bowel disease?

Source: American Academy of Pediatrics (2003)

A further example of questions that divorce the familial, cultural, and social contexts from a more holistic understanding of the young person's experience with food and eating is the SCOFF (Morgan, Reid, & Lacey, 2000). Administration of the questionnaire is described in the following way, "each patient completes a series of five yes-or-no questions that screen for eating disorders, with the typical patient taking just a few minutes to answer them" (Dooley-Hash, Lipson, Walton, & Cunningham, 2013, p. 309). The five survey questions are noted in Table 15.2.

Such questions are problematic for several reasons. First, experiential or lived knowledge is channelled into categorical boxes that remove any possibility of agency, the child, or young person. Physiologically focused questions on body functioning removes wider contexts of family dynamics, peer relationships, school environments, or media influences. The body does not live in isolation, yet such questions suggest that it does. Posing questions that reduce the lived experience to a number on the scale or a BMI rank reinforces the passivity of the young person's ability to voice their narrative. The binary nature of the questions leaves no space for description or explanation; for example, a child who lives in poverty is *naturally* preoccupied with food and eating and experiences fear and worry.

Secondly, such questionnaires assume a level of health literacy, suggesting expertism, or agnotologistic privilege on the part of the practitioner, further distancing the young client from understanding their own experiences because of language. For example, in the EAT 26 Questionnaire many of the 26 questions contain the tone of shame and/or suggest a certain expectation as illustrated in Question 15 that ask the child if they "take *longer than* others to eat my meals." The structure of the question infers that there is a "right" amount of time to consume food. It also opens up the question of who represents the other. Similarly, Question 21 asks "I give *too much* time and thought to food" suggests that there is a correct time, and anything outside of this ambiguous marker represents failure. Time is a developmental concept to children and preadolescents making such questions and those like them not just irrelevant but harmful (Michel, Harb, & Hidalgo, 2012).

TABLE 15.2   SCOFF Questionnaire for Eating Disorders

- Do you ever make yourself throw up (or use laxatives, water pills, or exercise) because you feel uncomfortably full?
- Do you worry you have lost control over how much you eat?
- Have you recently lost or gained more than 10 to 15 pounds in a 3-month period?
- Do you believe yourself to be too fat when others say you are too thin?
- Do thoughts and fears about food and weight dominate your life?

Lastly, such questions ignore the larger contextual world children and young people live in. While the positivist paradigm has persisted to be the tried and true one in which to practice, the current emphasis of how social determinants inform living now suggests a positivist worldview is obsolete and incongruent to how we understand health. Evidence of this shift is reflected by the curriculum offered by some U.S. and Canadian medical schools who teach medical residents how the intersectionality of culture, societal, political, and economic impact the health of individuals (Klein et al., 2011; O'Brien et al., 2014). Aside from the problematic nature of the questions asked of children and young teens, an equally discerning issue positioned within current methodologies concerns the concept of trust. Clinical descriptors of children and adolescents with eating disorders found in the literature terms such as "notoriously difficult and deceitful" (Kaplan, 2002, p. 238) "abnormal, weak, manipulative and inadequate" (Fleming & Szmukler, 1992, p. 436-443) and "vain and responsible for their illness" (Crisafulli, Von Holle & Bulik, 2008, p. 76). Pejorative attitudes towards eating disorders have been identified among primary care physicians, obstetricians and gynaecologists, hospital doctors, and the general public (Album & Westin, 2008; Currin, Waller, & Schmidt, 2009; Fleming & Szmukler, 1992; Hay, de Angelis, Millar, & Mond, 2005: Morgan, 1999). Despite being helping professionals, negative attitudes and stigma were also exhibited by some therapists who work with this vulnerable population presenting a barrier to establishing therapeutic alliance (Walker & Lloyd, 2011). Deeply embedded stigma can result in clinical practices that threaten to undermine therapeutic engagement, such as approaching the young patient with suspicion during assessment. For example, practice guidelines published by the American Academy of Pediatrics advise "physicians to weigh children in a hospital gown because objects may be hidden in clothing to falsely elevate weight" (American Academy of Pediatrics, 2003, p. 204). Clinical approaches mirror research methodologies. A similarly distressing outcome was found in a study conducted by Dignon, Bearsmore, Spain, and Kuan (2006) that used what was labeled as "stimulus" questions to "help stimulate the patient into considering the reasons for *her disorder*" (p. 955, emphasis in original). It was noted by the authors the "patients were honest" in disclosing legitimate responses. This example and the earlier one regarding surveillance beneath hospital gowns construct an assumption that children and youth who experience eating disorders are not to be trusted.

Problem saturated questions framed by language that does not transfer over to a child's lived experience with food, combined with professional stigma toward the diagnosis, manifests in methodologies that are more harmful than helpful. Such approaches keep children and adolescents as clinical objects of surveillance and miss rich opportunities to engage this group as active and willing collaborators in speaking their narratives of experience around food and eating.

SHIFTING TO PARTICIPATORY ACTION METHODS

Abandoning what is currently referred to as evidence-based practices to address eating disorders among children and young adolescents will undoubtedly provoke questions among some readers. Yet, literature is abundant that such practices do not work and in fact, may even cause harm (Walker & Lloyd, 2011). The most recent statistics available reported a 119% increase in hospitalizations between 1999 and 2006 for children under the age of 12 years (Zhao & Encinosa, 2009). Such startling statistics beg for different methodologies to be pursued as preferred responses in working with children and youth who exhibit problematic relationships with food. Lastly, traditional methodologies individualize cultural and societal narratives that are imprinted upon young bodies that have yet to form a strong sense of self and voice. Without a larger communal text to support the emerging voice, individual stories that are shared can feel tentative and fragile.

Several epistemological shifts are needed toward a framework that elevates the voice of children and preadolescents and promote a feeling of agency, a necessary bridge to regain mastery over their lives. This next section will describe four shifts and how the intersectionality of each piece culminates in a methodology that values connection, collaboration, mutuality, and creativity.

Interactive Interviewing or Communal Storytelling

Interactive interviewing is also referred to as *shared interviewing* and *storytelling* (Frank, 2000). Interactive interviewing is described by Ellis, Kiesinfger, and Tillmann-Healy (1997) as a collaborative process where remnants of stories are dislodged from individual experiences, often buried under shame and judgement, to be shared and made sense of in a group setting. The interviewer, in my case the clinician/researcher, is an active contributor to the emerging discussion using selective self disclosure to facilitate discussion as well as contribute to the "intersubjective process to provide a contextual basis for a deeper level of understanding and interpretation" (p. 122). The goal of interactive interviewing is to foster a culture of equality and safety in order to reach an intimate understanding of a sensitive topic such as an eating disorder. Story telling is also a venue for children and young people to develop self-confidence (Short, 2011) and when done collectively, plants the possibility of greater agency toward social action. This approach to interviewing is considered a feminist response to the traditional method of interviewing, and calls for clinician researchers to "acknowledge their personal, political and professional interests" (Ellis & Berger, 2003, p. 158). A defining feature of the interactive interview is the dismissal of the emotional separation characteristic of the traditional interview in favor of developing an active relationship occurring in a context "permeated by issues of power, emotionality and interpersonal process" (Holstein & Gubrium, 1995, p. 159). The hierarchical position that the traditional interview supports restricts researcher participation preventing a reciprocal dialogue and instead supports a static question and answer format (Hertz, 1995).

By shifting to a more reciprocal conversation, as opposed to the traditional extraction of answers, goes far toward fostering the building of trust. Without trust there is no entry to the inner world of the young person's lived habitus. Permission to enter the most secret, and often shameful world because how significant others perceive the disorder, requires an "equal, confidential, and open interaction, and co-operation" (Kyronlampi-Kylmanen & Maatta, 2011, p. 87). The process of storytelling becomes a platform for assembling trust due to the back and forth nature of listening and responding. This culture of acceptance opens the door for deeper and previously hidden meanings to emerge. Feeling accepted as "truth tellers" children and adolescents begin to develop a critical perspective of how their behaviors with food are positioned within different contexts of their young lives. Collective storytelling removes the assumption that individual behaviors are anything but isolated, but instead lie as jigsaw pieces fitting together into overarching social and cultural narratives about being female in a thin obsessed world.

Understanding the Rhythm and Currency of Speech

Children and young adolescents have a unique and specific pattern of speech which is incongruent to traditional interviewing styles found in assessment guides. While this communication pattern is part of storytelling, this aspect is felt to be important enough to discuss on its own merit. The nature of dialogue with children and adolescents tends to be multidirectional and is characterized by what Ambrose and Yairi (1999) refer to as "disfluences." These interruptions of speech are specific to the stage of development of early adolescence and include part or single syllable repetition, injection, abandoned utterances, and "prolongations, blocks and broken words" (Andrade & Martin-Reis, 2007, p. 172). In other words, the speech of older children and young adolescents has its own special rhythm that can be lost in more "adult forms" of interviewing. The binary construction of questions of either "yes" or "no," as seen in Table 15.1 and 15.2, ignore the presence of disfluences and as such, fail to understand and accommodate this dialogical pattern. Conversation is reduced to severed pieces of stories without a framework to support, much less appreciate. In comparison, open-ended questions facilitated by a conversational style of speaking allows for the inclusion of such disfluences. When space is given by the interviewer it infers to the young person what they say is important and their elongated responses will not be prematurely truncated. Related to understanding the rhythm of dialogue is another concept of what I label as *thought currency*. Working with youth over several decades as a therapist has given me the opportunity of witnessing how their thoughts can extend over time and change depending upon contexts. Making alternative space for these emerging fragments is not always possible in real time, and so the provision of another medium they are comfortable with is critical. The use of a blog is such an avenue. Smith (2000) writes that students see the web as a "playful place" that reflects a cultural norm around digital literary for the current generation. Creating a password protected blog actively encourages youth to spontaneously post in a safe space when a thought or comment appears in a written form that is free of being corrected or judged.

Physical Literacy as Communication

The body as a cultural artifact reflecting the social norm of dieting begins by the age of 5 (Hayes & Tantleff-Dunn, 2010). A study by the same authors found that nearly a third of children age 5 to 6 choose an ideal body size that is thinner than their current perceived size. By age 7 one in four children have engaged in some form of food restriction (Klein & Shiffman, 2005). Girls also become much more sedentary by the age of 10 with activity levels dropping by as much as 83% as they reach the stage of adolescence (Wolf et al., 1993; Kimm et al., 2002).

Messages that glorify the thin body are multiple and increasing beyond the mainstream domains of television, music videos movies, and magazines. Social networks sites including Facebook can instigate anxieties around body image when posted pictures are "not liked" or pictures deemed unattractive are shared among sites (Tiggermann & Slater, 2013). Adolescent girls who are Facebook users have been shown to be at greater risk to internalize a drive for thinness and engage in body surveillance than those non Facebook users (Tiggemann & Slater, 2013).

Female girls and teens translate these messages into how they train their bodies not to use more space as a way to appear smaller (McMillan, 2010). As girls age they become acutely aware of the norms constructed around femininity that emphasize smallness in both size and movement (McMillan, 2010). Earlier physical play that celebrated gross motor movements is traded for pastimes that are spatially contained; ensuring body movements are kept to a minimum such as playing with dolls.

Challenging the norm that girls are content to be passive observers (Ridgers, 2009), methods that open up space for girls to celebrate their bodies through movement offers another avenue for the expression of voice. Creating opportunities for safe and creative movement supports a message of female strength and empowerment without the cumbersomeness of words.

Speaking Through Different Mediums

Prior to developing verbal skills children are visual learners who understand the world through pictures. Imagery connects to the earliest ways of knowing and reacting to the external world, therefore "it is not foreign to the experience of learning" and a normal part of development" (Riley, 2001, p. 54). Adolescents are attracted to making symbols and graphic depictions, and this is increasingly more evident with the popularity of social media and emoticons. As a group, adolescents are more attracted to using art as language than to verbal questioning (p. 54) but when combined with open conversational interviewing this medium draws upon all capacities to make meaning of a phenomenon. It also comes as a pleasant surprise because children and youth are socialized to speak rather than to creatively express their feelings.

While acknowledging that art therapy is a specialized clinical modality requiring training, the use of art as a medium is encouraged as a form of data collection within a constructivist context. Code (1991) refers to this as different forms of knowledge retrieval, meaning artwork using mediums such as clay, paint, crayon, or markers can be used to capture internal messages that have yet to take shape. These images represent metonymic spaces, defined by Olausson and Bondas (2009) as the "unsayable" or emotions that are socially labeled as being "unfeminine" such as anger and competitiveness (Levens, 1995). She argues that such feelings over time can be "split off from parts of the self" and become inaccessible to words alone (Levens, 1995, p. 30). Making available avenues to recover these marginalized feelings and transfer to pictorial representations can be an empowering process. Using metaphoric meanings emerging from artwork as a springboard for communal discussion lessens the feeling of being the only one to experience an issue, hence decreasing isolation and aloneness.

Lastly, artwork also externalizes what may feel like an issue, such as a problematic relationship with food, so the young person can begin to distinguish their own autonomy from that of an identified diagnosis. In this way, the artificial boundary between therapy and research disappears, and the mutual outcome of supporting agency and voice among female children and youth becomes synonymous.

In summary, staying within a positivist or medical paradigm characterized by static, predetermined questionnaire boxes to understand the lived experiences and meanings associated with eating disorders by female children and youth reproduces the marginalization of agency and voice among this already vulnerable population. Shifting to a non-hierarchical paradigm that seeks to empower youth encourages internal knowledge to emerge and take shape, and in the process allows young individuals to become active stakeholders in their recovery.

CASE STUDY—PUTTING METHODOLOGY INTO ACTION

Putting new methods into action can trigger some feelings of uncertainty and anxiety on the part of the clinician/researcher especially when working with a vulnerable group such as children and youth experiencing health issues. As with any new endeavor, one should be guided by the highest of ethical standards and professional prudence being mindful of the safe welfare of their participants. This section will describe different contextual factors where the proposed methodology was put into action, including setting, recruitment, and outcomes.

The setting chosen to implement the new methodology was a physician run, community based primary family medicine clinic with a patient case load of approximately 25,000 individuals in Ontario, Canada. The high incidence of older children and young adolescents presenting with problematic relationships with food ranging from disordered eating to eating disorders was identified by the physicians as a critical issue which was further complicated by the lack of treatment facilities in the geographical area. After receiving university ethics clearance, the clinic agreed to allow me as a practicing clinician/researcher to implement the described methodology within their practice. Physicians also agreed that at no time would any traditional screening for eating disorders be done to participants while in the study to respect the methodological shift described earlier. To remain congruent to the belief that female children and adolescents know themselves best (Brown & Augusta-Scott, 2007; Kearny-Cook & Isaacs, 2004) self-referral was invited through recruitment posters in addition to those referred by a physician.

Once a group of older children and young adolescents was recruited and parental consent was obtained, I described the proposed methodology making note of the differences compared to the traditional individual and one session interviewing style they were accustomed to with their physician. A total of 16 girls volunteered for the study with ages ranging between 9 and 14 years. Diversity of ethnic background included British, Italian, South Asian, Aboriginal, Chinese, and German. Due to the developmental differences within such a wide range of age, I divided the group into those aged 9 to 11 and 12 to 14. As it happened, there was an equal number of girls in each group. The described collective and prolonged process initially came as a surprise to the girls who volunteered for the study. Each girl was asked to commit to a time frame of 4 months. As a group we decided to meet at the clinic on a Saturday as to avoid disrupting school to discuss concepts associated with food and eating. The two groups followed the same format of communal storytelling followed by artwork and bodywork activities. The decision was given to each group as to what snacks they preferred over the 3 hour meeting. Parents or caregivers dropped off and picked up their child at the clinic and were not part of the process. To make explicit for the reader how the methodology was implemented, a description of each of the five tents identified in the preceding section will now be explained. Pseudonyms have been used for reasons of confidentiality.

Interactive Interviewing or Communal Storytelling

Transparency framed the group process from the very beginning with girls sharing the reason of why they were either physician or self-referred as inclusion criteria. Each group discussion started with a circle of checking in followed by me suggesting a concept for discussion. For example, one of the concepts discussed was that of "growing up." The girls took turns talking about their lived experiences, private thoughts, and perplexing questions with the discussion evolving into a co-authored, communal narrative. Self reflexivity by me was critical and constant. I had been clinically trained within a positivistic paradigm that valued linear interviewing styles and positions of authority, and so my patience for the very fluid, multi-directional discussions was regularly tested. However, remaining committed to process and trusting in the embedded knowledge of my young participants unequivocally rewarded me after each meeting. I was amazed at how natural the methodology was for the girls demonstrated in the following example. At one of the meetings I suggested we consider talking about their experiences of growing up. What surfaced was a deep, rich, and poignant story that reached into the recesses of why girls may choose to starve themselves, one that a questionnaire would have been woefully inadequate.

The concept of "growing up" was unpacked by the younger girls as having a myriad of meanings associated with independence. A developmental milestone celebrated within Western culture, this group of girls expressed feeling differently. They described feelings of anxiety and reluctance. For example, Clara associated independence with the experience of loneliness, as in "it means that you like to work alone (10 second pause) and to be by yourself." Likewise, Zoe added, "Um, like ... you don't have anyone to help you like when you were young." The element of time was tacked onto the evolving storyline by Emily who said, "When you get a little bit older your parents stop helping you with stuff (5 *second pause*), because you are getting too old to help." After further discussion the concept of independence extended to that of decision making, described by Angela as "just because you hit puberty doesn't mean (*pause*), you know, you know how to make decisions, and all that complicated stuff." Having the space to follow up on this question led to a different kind of discussion on meanings associated with the term *complicated stuff*. Deconstructing this term verbally and through artwork it revealed artifacts related to physical development; the awareness of body odor, negotiating menstruation, and the appearance of underarm hair. Such deeper meanings would be stunted by a questionnaire.

The subject of decision making then detoured into the topic of boys, specifically how boys are treated differently. Angela elaborated upon the differences in this way, "(*long silence*) People expect girls to be more serious, and not have fun like boys do. And, like . . . that's just not fair. Because if we do fool around, they say, they say . . . like . . . we are being foolish." Waiting until no more disclosures were shared also meant waiting for the silence to be broken by one of the girls rather than by me.

It is unlikely these "truths" about growing up and the expressed reluctance to embrace the concept of independence would have surfaced by a questionnaire with a choice of a "yes" or "no" option. The binary notation on eating disorder questionnaires would not have been given credence a feeling expressed by Lauren who poignantly summed up the discussion with the statement: "When I turned 10 I was really, like, um, sad . . . because I know I'd never be a single digit in my life again, and (*4 second pause*), when I turn 13 I going to be really sadder because, then, I'm never going to be a kid ever again . . ."

Understanding the Rhythm and Currency of Speech

The advantage of spending extended time with the girls over 4 months created a degree of relational intimacy allowing me to observe and be mindful of their individual speech patterns or what Ambrose and Yairi (1999) referred to as "disfluences." It was not uncommon for the ebb and flow of speaking to be filled with extended pauses (defined as longer than 5 seconds) and for responses to be circular, eventually returning to the point of initial departure. The following examples make visible the meandering and frequent breaks of thought that occurred during a discussion with the older group of girls regarding independence and the meanings associated with the concept:

> If people are busy or something (*pause*) and, like, (*pause*) I get lonely (*pause*) . . . there was this one time that I asked my mom to help me (*pause*) I can't remember what she was doing (*pause*) was she driving my brother to soccer? (*pause*) What was I saying? (*pause with the girls laughing*) Oh yea! Now I remember (*pause*) then I have to learn how to be independent, I guess that's the way now. (Tiffany)

> Well, you can't always expect to be happy (*pause*) you know...when you do
> things on your own, like (*6 second pause*) never mind...ok, it's just that when
> you want your mom or dad to do something with you it doesn't always hap-
> pen...like when you were little. (Sarah)

The unspoken message of sadness beneath this text allowed me to open up
a space to talk about what some of the girls expressed feeling when parents
expect them to take on new responsibilities as a result of growing older.

Physical Literacy as Communication

As girls mature they begin to absorb the cultural message that smallness
is the preferred body norm defining femininity. This smallness assumes
multiple forms; reduced physical space, verbal space, and spatial presence.
By doing so, researchers and clinicians sever off a valuable avenue of exploration of deeper meanings beneath phenomena. Thinking of voice as
belonging to the *body* expands the paradigm of how to listen to the narratives of young participants. Giving children a concept and allowing them to
translate the concept into movement unleashes a physical creativity that di-
minishes when growing up as often such movement is termed as immature.

Different concepts related to eating disorders including dieting, connection, and independence, among others, were given to the two groups of girls,
and they were asked to create body movements or a game that reflected their
feelings toward the concept. Using the term "dieting" as an example, I described the activity with the question: "If your body could talk, how would
it express the feeling of dieting?" The outcome was powerful. After a short
discussion the older girls formed a circle and began to play dodgeball—taking turns shouting a name and then quickly but forcibly throwing the ball
toward the player. Each girl had to be constantly on alert not knowing when
their name was to be shouted. As an observer there was a paradoxical mixture
combining randomness and strategy. At the end of the game we sat down as
a group to process the thinking and rationale behind this choice of game.

The explanation provided by the girls spoke to the inseparable relationship between the mind and the body, not unlike metaphorically standing at
the cusp of being diagnosed with an eating disorder. They spoke to being
on constant surveillance of being targeted for what Amy stated as "not being the right weight." They agreed that being hit by the ball represented
"people who tell you that you are too fat," but as Jackie said, "never knowing who those people were" so a high degree of vigilance is necessary at
all times. Jessica added that "you need to throw the ball hard," and when
asked why, she replied, "Because that's what, um...it feels like (*pause*)
when someone like your friend or mom says you are fat."

This physical game the girls created spoke to deeper issues including those of body surveillance, rejection by significant others because of weight, and negotiating feelings of ambiguity and fear around what is the "right" weight. Limiting data collection to only verbal methods would have restricted the capacity to reach these deeper embedded meanings within the lived body, reflecting the disingenuity associated to traditional methods of data collection.

Speaking Through Different Mediums

Incorporating artwork through different mediums acknowledges that the voice of children and youth is fluid and multiple, recognizing what Code (1991) refers to as different forms of knowledge specific to girls. As such, a variety of different artwork mediums were available to the girls at each meeting. After talking about a concept related to food and eating, they were asked to draw or sculpt the concept based upon their lived experience. The use of cameras was also used as an art medium to capture meanings of a concept between meetings. Using the concept of dieting as an example, and for purposes of consistency for the reader, the girls externalized the term dieting using paint and clay to share deeper meanings not previously shared verbally. The tension separating hunger and the inability to eat was captured in a oil painting by Clara (Figure 15.1) who described her painting this way:

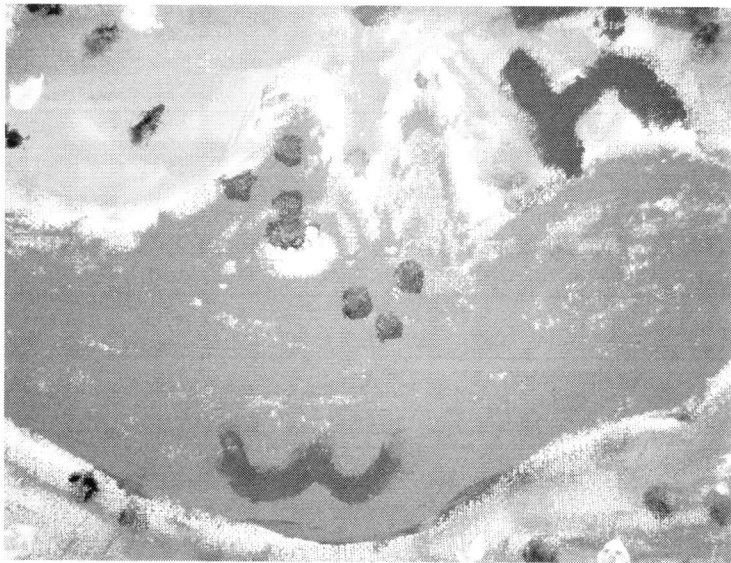

Figure 15.1   What my stomach says about dieting—10 year old Clara

Sometimes I feel there is a war going on in my stomach, my stomach is the red blob with a smile thinking about food, but then, I've got a thing near the top of the picture that looks like a boot, stamping out the hungry feeling (*4 second pause*) like it's a voice saying "stop eating stupid!"

What dieting felt like for 9-year-old Zoe was captured by this photo of a wire mesh cage with rats inside (Figure 15.2). When asked to describe her photo she said, "I feel caged, like, I am trapped like a rat. Rats have to eat leftovers and are always hungry."

Yet another visual depiction of dieting was captured in clay by 12-year-old Jessica who molded two opposing artifacts; a single carrot opposite to a hamburger and French fries (Figure 15.3). Jessica described her reason for creating the clay objects this way: "On one plate is what I eat…like one carrot. One the other plate is really what I want to eat…but I can't because it's bad."

Creating different mediums for youth to channel spoken and unspoken messages into different forms of communicating achieves a number of

Figure 15.2 What dieting feels like to me–9 year old Zoe.

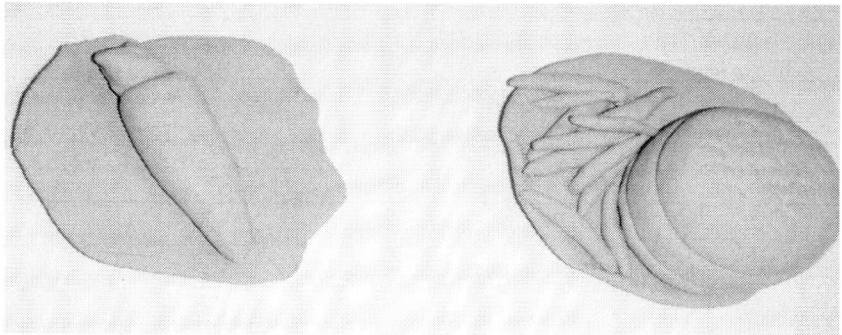

Figure 15.3   Dieting means not eating what I really want—12 year old Jessica

critical methodological outcomes; the capturing of multiple dimensions of a concept, a participatory and non-hierarchal form of research, and equally important, privileging knowledge embodied by children and youth with lived experience of a phenomena such as eating disorders.

FROM PARTICIPATORY ACTION METHODS
TO SOCIAL ACTION

The described participatory action method involving children and youth yielded in-depth and rich outcomes toward understanding a sensitive topic such as eating disorders. Intersecting the various approaches created momentum within the group while supporting data triangulation. However, one of the most powerful outcomes was that of supporting children and youth to feel empowered by the knowledge they held.

At the end of the 4 month data collection process the girls expressed a desire to extend their involvement to that of social action. As young patients within a general practice clinic, they lamented not being heard by health care providers, or as Zoe said, "They just want me to, you know, give answers that fit into boxes." While participatory action models have been used with children in the areas of education (Peña, 2017), child labor (Hastadewi, 2009), health promotion (Suleiman, Soleimanpour, & London, 2006), drug and tobacco use (Berg, Coman, & Schensul, 2009), and community change (Wilson et al., 2007), this study is the first one to use this methodology for eating disorders and for a younger population. Also, the majority of studies using nontraditional approaches, such as a participatory action involving youth, stops short at the action stage for a variety of reasons: resistance from existing dominant institutions who hold the power (Ross, 2011; Suleiman et al., 2006); wavering time and energy due to school and other extracurricular activities by the participants (Bostock & Freeman, 2003; Powers & Tiffany, 2006); questions of validity and rigor (Le Rous, 2016); and increasing transparency regarding personal issues (Ford, Rasmus, & Allen, 2012). None of the noted barriers materialized within this study, and for this reason, I felt responsible to support the momentum of the young participants to the action stage. Being in this position also provided a space for me to use my position of power to advocate within a medical institution reaching those stakeholders (physicians, executive director) that the girls did not have access to.

Intentional discussion with the girls resulted in a decision to move into a social action phase for the predominant reason of informing significant others, mainly parents and physicians, so that "they can really understand what, um, we live with and how hard it is. No one has ever asked me these questions before. So, yea . . . it's important" (Tiffany). The term *social action* was introduced and broken down into language that was accessible for the girls to ensure that they were fully aware of the goals and responsibilities that accompany this phase. Exploring several definitions of participatory action the girls eventually decided upon one offered by Jason, Keys, Suarez-Balcazar, Taylor, and Davis (2003) described as a method focusing on non-expert voices and power, and interested in facilitating social action to solve problems. The girls felt it important to create a template of questions that reflected their lived experience with an eating disorder, rather than the traditional screening questionnaires, previously used on them. They also felt it critical to make explicit the distal factors that inform problematic eating relationships rather than focus on individual deficits and pathology. The idea of an open house was generated by the girls as an opportunistic venue to solicit interest from physicians, nurses, social workers, parents, school teachers, and friends. A weekend date was selected and print invitations were sent out. Making the shift from a participatory research phase to an action phase meant giving the girls control over what they felt others needed to know about living with an eating disorder not captured by traditional interviewing and collection methods. Cornwall and Jewkes (1995) point out that visual methods tend to be popular because they allow individuals to express their perspective in their own language. Visual methods also enable youth to choose particular symbols that represent their lives and share them with others in an easy and accessible manner (Wang, Burris, & Ping 1996). The girls decided to showcase all of their drawings, paintings, photographs, and clay sculptures at the open house accompanied by a cluster of words that spoke to the concepts embedded in their artwork creating a powerful and rich collage for the adult viewer. Despite the sheer enormity of the number of artifacts, I respected their decision for the following reason. To ask the girls to reduce the number of artifacts for display would

Figure 15.4   Why everything needs to be included – it's all connected – 11 year old Emily.

reenact the positivist approach framing their previous experience with traditional reductionist methods. One of the girls captured the rationale beautifully in a painting of connecting circles and squares (Figure 15.4). Emily explained, "It like all comes together—you can't just take away one idea from the others, because, like, everything is connected to something else to make it a whole." The simplicity of Emily's words succinctly captures the meaning of intersectionality of concepts contributing to problematic relationships with food.

Multiple outcomes occurred as a result of the open house: intrapersonal, interpersonal, and structural. These two groups of girls gained self-confidence in their abilities to cause positive change guided by their lived knowledge with parents and family witnessing the deeper meanings associated with their child's diagnosis. Secondly, physicians at the clinic agreed to use alternative questions and avenues when assessing youth for eating disorders. How this case study differs from other participatory methods resulting in wider community intervention in youth issues (Gosin, Dustman, Drapeau, & Harthun, 2003) is that this study was intentionally positioned within a diabolical epistemological paradigm, that of a medical clinic guided by the *DSM* 5. The response by the physicians to adopt the assessment template by this group of girls speaks to the receptiveness of this group of professionals, but equally to the power of the truth based upon lived experience.

CLINICIAN/RESEARCHER REFLEXIVITY

The decision to use a participatory methodology with children and youth comes with great responsibility and a need for constant reflectivity. Working with a vulnerable group I needed to be mindfulness of the principle of beneficence guiding all activities including that of the social action phase. As noted by Ross (2011) because social action challenges existing power structures, it can pose unintentional harm to young participants. Not knowing what the physicians' response might be to the girls suggesting an alternative assessment template for eating disorders at the clinic posed a significant relational risk between themselves and their primary health provider. In addition, the girls' decision to transition from a previously invisible and embedded knowledge to a very visible and public display of lived experience urged me to reflect upon their developmental stage of decision making in regard to risk. Had the outcome been a negative or judgemental one from significant others and authoritative figures, I would be responsible for not fully exploring this consequence and as a result contributed to the consequence of harm.

CONCLUSION

The richness in working with children toward new methodologies that elevate and celebrate voice and agency is not limited by their developmental abilities but rather the lack of creativity by the clinician/researcher. Combined with the reluctance to share power with young children and youth, many practitioners continue to use traditional methodologies that are ineffective and relationally harmful when addressing eating disorders and disordered eating. The juxtaposition of methodological approaches understood by children compared to those favored by professionals speaks to how little we know, or are prepared to change our way of doing. Adding to this inefficiency is the reluctance of researchers and health care providers to mix epistemological practice paradigms, further reducing solutions to complex issues.

This chapter attempts to intentionally move away from traditional methodologies when working with children and youth by abandoning standardized, individualized practices in favor of those that are collaborative and participatory, seeking to reach and support lived experiences as a form of knowledge. The decision to adopt such practices requires the clinician/researcher to relinquish a position of power; assuming a position of "not knowing" by trusting the process of knowledge retrieval as crafted by young participants. If one is able to do so, the results are transformative. The example described in this chapter highlighted the potential offered by participatory methods actively involving youth toward changing how eating disorders are understood by family physicians, refocusing the lens from a reductionist and individual issue to one that speaks to the complexities of growing up in a culture reifying thinness.

Negating the belief that children are only literal thinkers, this chapter also encourages the reader to provide young clients the opportunity to operationalize concepts through a variety of diverse mediums; collaborative storytelling, movement, art and photography. In doing so, these become gifts in which to engage the young person to describe their experience of a diagnosis that ravages growing bodies. Offering a methodology that makes accessible untraditional ways to gain entry into the lived experience of the disorder celebrates both voice and agency of young children and youth. In this way the methodology *becomes* the therapy, supporting the beginnings of a newly found confidence needed to collectively challenge Western norms of independence, maturity and the quest for body conformity.

Questions for Reflection

1. Reflect upon how your childhood experience was acknowledged by adults.
2. What are the internal barriers that may present as challenges when using a participatory method with children?
3. What do you see as risk or ethical dilemmas with this method?
4. What are your thoughts as to whether participatory approaches can be therapeutic? If you think they can be, why do you think they are not used more often?

Suggestions for Further Reading

Beazley, H., Bessell, S., Ennew, J., & Waterson, R. (2009). The right to be properly researched: Research with children in a messy, real world. *Children's Geographies, 7*(4), 365–378.

Bostock, J., & Freeman, J. (2003). 'No limits': Doing participatory action research with young people in Northumberland. *Journal of Community & Applied Social Psychology, 13*(6), 464–474.

Proctor, R., & Schiebinger, L. (Eds.). (2008). *Agnotology: The making and unmaking of ignorance.* Stanford, CA: Stanford University Press.

REFERENCES

Album, D., & Westin, S. (2008). Do diseases have a prestige hierarchy? A survey among physicians and medical students. *Social Science & Medicine, 66*, 182–188.

Ambrose, N., & Yairi, E. (1999). Normative disfluency data for early childhood stuttering. *Journal of Speech Language and Hearing Research, 42*(4), 895–909.

American Academy of Pediatrics. (2003). Identifying and treating eating disorders. Committee on Adolescence. *Pediatrics, 11*(1) 204–211.

Andrade, C., & Martins-Reis, V. (2007). Fluency variation in adolescents. *Clinical Linguistics & Phonetics, 21*(10), 771–782.

Berg, M., Coman, E., & Schensul, J. (2009). Youth action research for prevention: A multilevel intervention designed to increase efficacy and empowerment among urban youth. *American Journal of Community Psychology, 43*(3), 345–359.

Bostock, J., & Freeman, J. (2003). 'No limits': Doing participatory action research with young people in Northumberland. *Journal of Community & Applied Social Psychology, 13*(6), 464–474.

Brown, C., & Augusta-Scott, T. (2007). *Narrative therapy: Making meaning, making lives.* London, England: SAGE.

Chodorow, N. (1974). *Family structure and feminine personality: The reproduction of mothering.* Boston, MA: Brandeis University Press.

Code, L. (1991). *What can she know? Feminist theory and the construction of knowledge.* Ithaca, NY: Cornell University Press.

Cornwall, A., & Jewkes, R. (1995). What is participatory research? *Social Science & Medicine, 41*(12), 1667–1676.

Crisafulli, M. A., Von Holle, A., & Bulik, C. (2008). Attitudes towards anorexia nervosa: the impact of framing on blame and stigma. *International Journal of Eating Disorders, 41*(4), 333–339.

Currin, L., Waller, G., & Schmidt, U. (2009). Primary care physicians' knowledge of and attitudes toward the eating disorders: Do they affect clinical actions? *International Journal of Eating Disorders, 42,* 453–458.

Dooley-Hash, S., Lipson, S., & Cunningham, R. (2013). Increased emergency department use by adolescents and young adults with eating disorders. *International Journal of Eating Disorders, 46*(2), 308–315.

Ellis, C., & Berger, L. (2003). Their story, my story, our story. In J. F. Gubrium & J. A. Holstein (Eds.), *Postmodern interviewing* (pp. 157–187). London, England: SAGE.

Ellis, C., Kiesinger, C. E., & Tillmann-Healy, L. M. (1997). Interactive interviewing: Talking about emotional experience. In R. Hertz (Ed.), *Reflexivity and voice* (pp. 119–150). Thousand Oaks, CA: SAGE.

Fleming, J., & Szmukler, G. (1992). Attitudes of medical professionals towards patients with eating disorders. *The Australian and New Zealand Journal of Psychiatry, 26,* 436–443.

Ford, T., Rasmus, S., & Allen, J. (2012). Being useful: Achieving indigenous youth involvement in a community-based participatory research project in Alaska. *International Journal of Circumpolar Health, 71,* 1–7.

Frank, A. (2000). The standpoint of storyteller. *Qualitative Health Research, 10*(30), 354–365.

Friedman, S. (1997). Decoding the language of fat. In C. Brown & K. Jasper (Eds.), *Consuming passions: Feminist approaches to weight preoccupation and eating disorders* (p. 291). Toronto, Canada: Second Story Press.

Gilligan, C. (1982). *In a different voice: Psychological theory and women's development.* Cambridge, MA: Harvard University Press.

Gosin, M., Dustman, P., Drapeau, A., & Harthun, M. (2003). Participatory action research: Creating an effective prevention curriculum for adolescents in the Southwestern US. *Health Education Research, 18*(3), 363–379.

Hastadewi, Y. (2009) Participatory action research with children: Notes from the field. *Children's Geographies, 7*(4), 481–482.

Hay, P., de Angelis, C., Millar, H., & Mond, J. M. (2005). Bulimia nervosa mental health literacy of general practitioners. *Primary Care and Community Psychiatry, 10*, 103–108.

Hayes, S., & Tantleff-Dunn, S. (2010). Am I too fat to be a princess? Examining the effects of popular children's media on young girls' body image. *The British Journal of Developmental Psychology, 28*(Pt 2), 413–426.

Hertz, R. (1995). Separate but simultaneous interviewing of husbands and wives: Making sense of their stories. *Qualitative Inquiry, 1*, 429–451.

Holstein, J. A., & Gubrium, J. F. (1995). *The active interview.* Thousand Oaks, CA: SAGE.

Jason, L., Keys, C., Suarez-Balcazar, Y., Taylor, R., & Davis, M. (2003). *Participatory community research: Theories and methods in action.* Washington, DC: American Psychological Association.

Kaplan, A. (2002). Psychological treatments for anorexia nervosa: A review of published studies and promising new directions. *The Canadian Journal of Psychiatry, 47*(3), 235–242.

Kearney-Cook, A., & Isaacs, F. (2004). *Change your mind, change your body.* New York, NY: Simon & Schuster.

Kimm, S., Glynn, N., Kriska, A., Barton, B., Kronsberg, S., Daniels, S., & Liu, K., (2002). Decline in physical activity in Black girls and White girls during adolescence. *The New England Journal of Medicine, 347*(10), 709–715.

Klein, M., Kahn, R., Baker, R., Fink, E., Parrish, D., & White, D. (2011). Training in social determinants of health in primary care: Does it change resident behaviour? *Academic Pediatrics, 11*(5), 387–393.

Klein, H., & Shiffman, K. S. (2005). Thin is "in" and stout is "out": What animated cartoons tell viewers about body weight. *Eating and Weight Disorders, 10*(2), 107–116.

Kyronlampi-Kylmanen, T., & Maatta, K. (2011). Using children as research subjects: How to interview a child aged 5 to 7 years. *Educational Research and Reviews, 6*(1), 87–93.

Le Rous, C. (2016). Exploring rigor in autoethnographic research. *International Journal of Social Research Methodology, 20*(2), 195–207.

Levens, M. (1995). *Eating disorders and magical control of the body.* London, England: Routledge.

Mahler, M., Pine, F., & Bergman, A. (1975). *The psychological birth of the human infant.* New York, NY: Basic Books.

Maine, M. (2001). Altering women's relationship with food: A relational, developmental approach. *Psychology in Practice, 57*(11), 1301–1310.

McMillan, C. (2010). *What the body stories of girls tell us about autonomy and connection during adolescence.* (Doctoral dissertation, Wilfrid Laurier University, Kitchener, Canada). Retrieved from https://scholars.wlu.ca/etd/1088

Michel, F., Harb, F., & Hidalgo, M. (2012). The concept of time in the perception of children and adolescents. *Trends in Psychiatry and Psychotherapy, 34*(1), 38–41.

Miller, J. (1976). *Toward a new psychology of women.* Boston, MA: Beacon Press.

Morgan, J. (1999). Eating disorders and gynecology: Knowledge and attitudes among clinicians. *Acta Obstetrica et Gynecologica Scandinavica, 78,* 233–239.

Morgan, J. F., Reid, F., & Lacey, J. H. (2000). The SCOFF questionnaire: A new screening tool for eating disorders. *Western Journal of Medicine, 172*(3), 164–165.

Olausson, S., & Bondas, T. (2009). Photography as a data collection method in intensive care. *International Journal of Qualitative Methods, 8*(4), 20.

Oliver, K. L. (1999). Adolescent girl's body-narratives: Learning to desire and create a "fashionable" image. *Teachers College Record, 101*(2), 220–246.

Orbach, S. (1986). *Hunger strike: The anorectic's struggle as a metaphor for our age.* London, England: Faber and Faber.

Peña, M, (2017). Participatory action research with children in education: The learning process as political praxis. *SAGE Research Methods Cases, Part 2.* doi:10.4135/9781473972841

Pipher, M. (1994). *Revisiting Ophelia: Saving the selves of adolescent girls.* New York, NY: Ballantine Books.

Powers, J. L., & Tiffany, J. S. (2006). Engaging youth in participatory research and evaluation. *Journal of Public Health Management and Practice, 12,* 79–87.

Ridgers, N. (2009). Relationships between maturity status, physical activity, and physical self perceptions. *Journal of Sports Sciences, 28*(1), 1–9.

Riley S. (2001). Art therapy with adolescents. *The Western Journal of Medicine, 175*(1), 54–57.

Ross, L. (2011). Sustaining youth participation in a long-term tobacco control initiative: Consideration of a social justice perspective. *Youth & Society, 43*(2), 681–704.

Short, K. (2011). Inquiry as a way of life. *Language Arts, 89*(2), 125–135.

Smith, C. (2000). Nobody, which means anybody: Audience on the World Wide Web. In S. Gruber (Ed.), *Weaving a virtual web: Practical approaches to new information technologies* (pp. 239–249). Urbana, IL: NCTE.

Steiner-Adair, C. (1986). The body politic: Normal female adolescent development and the development of eating disorders. *Journal of the America Academy of Child and Adolescent Psychiatry, 37,* 352–359.

Suleiman, A., Soleimanpour, S., & London, J. (2006). Youth action for health through youth led research. *Journal of Community Practice, 14*(1–2), 125–145.

Tiggerman, M., & Slater, A. (2013). NetGirls: The internet, Facebook and body image concern in adolescent girls. *International Journal of Eating Disorders, 46*(6), 630–633.

Tozzi, F., Sullivan, P., Fear, J., McKenzie, J., & Bulik, C. (2003). Causes and recovery in anorexia nervosa: The patient's perspective. *International Journal of Eating Disorders, 33*(2), 143–154.

Treasure, J. (2007). The trauma of self starvation: Eating disorders and body image. In M. Nasser, K. Baistow & J. Treasure (Eds.), *The female body in mind* (pp. 57–71). London, England: Routledge Press.

Walker, S., & Lloyd, C. (2011). Barriers and attitudes health professionals working in eating disorders experience. *International Journal of Therapy and Rehabilitation, 18*(7), 383–391.

Wang, C., Burris, M., & Ping, X. (1996). Chinese village women as visual anthropologists: A participatory approach to reaching policymakers. *Social Science & Medicine, 42*(10), 1391–1400.

White, M. (2001). Narrative practice and the unpacking of identity conclusions. *Gecko: A Journal of Deconstruction and Narrative Ideas in Therapeutic Practice, 1,* 28–55.

White, M., & Epston, D. (1990). *Narrative means to therapeutic ends.* New York, NY: W.W. Norton.

Wilson, N., Dasho, S., Martin, A., Wallerstein, N., Wang, C., & Minkler, M. (2007). Engaging young adolescents in social action through photovoice: The youth empowerment strategies (YES!) project. *The Journal of Early Adolescence, 27*(2), 241–261.

Winnicott, D. W. (1965). *The maturation process and the facilitating environment.* New York, NY: International Universities Press.

Wolf, A., Gortmaker, S., Cheung, L., Gary, H., Herzog, D., & Colditz, G. (1993). Activity, inactivity, and obesity: Racial, ethnic, and age differences among schoolgirls. *American Journal of Public Health, 83,* 1625–1627.

Zhao, M., & Encinosa, W. (2009). *Hospitalizations for eating disorders from 1999 to 2006. Statistical Brief #70.* Healthcare Cost and Utilization Project (HCUP). Washington, DC. Retrieved from https://www.hcup-us.ahrq.gov/reports/statbriefs/sb70.jsp

PART IV

CROSS-NATIONAL PERSPECTIVES
ON PARTICIPATORY RESEARCH WITH CHILDREN

CHAPTER 16

HU M'ANI SO MA ME NTI NA ATWE MMIENU NAM (BLOW THE DUST FROM MY EYES)

Making the Voices of Ghanaian Kindergarteners Visible Through the Use of Video-Cued Ethnography in a Study of Citizenship

Ilene R. Berson, Michael J. Berson, Joyce Esi Bronteng, and Aaron Osafo-Acquah

ABSTRACT

In this study video-cued ethnography fostered a culturally responsive approach and contested social injustices in the research enterprise that typically marginalize the voices of children. Video-cued interviews with dyads of Ghanaian kindergarteners created a conversation space in which children came together in dialogue with a familiar peer. Rich data emerged not only from children's verbal reflections but also their physical actions, exhibited through simultaneous reenactment of the observed events depicted in the video.

Participatory Methodologies to Elevate Children's Voice and Agency, pages 369–382
Copyright © 2019 by Information Age Publishing

369

Ghana is a sovereign multinational state and a unitary presidential constitutional democracy. It is located along the Gulf of Guinea and the Atlantic Ocean, in the subregion of West Africa. The country is comprised of eight ethnic groups, including Akan, Mole-Dagbon, Ewe, Ga-Dangbe, Gurma, Guan, Grusi, and Mande-Busanga. The Ghanaian culture is built upon the belief of one nation, one people, with a common destiny, so even with the numerous traditions of the various ethnic groups, they are bound by common values, beliefs, and norms. For example, the proverbial Ghanaian hospitality is exhibited and experienced throughout the country.

Historically, early childhood education (ECE) in Ghana has been rooted in colonialism. It began as part of the missions from abroad that were established to convert the population to Christianity (Morrison, 2000). Since Ghana gained independence from colonial rule in 1957, the new republic has remained committed to educating young citizens. Being the first country in sub-Saharan Africa to become independent and propelled by the ideologies of self-determination and a new national identity, Ghana pursued a rapid expansion of primary education under the Universal Primary Education program, which started in 1952 (Kuyini, 2013; Wilson, 1999). In 1965, the Ministry of Education established the nursery and kindergarten unit to develop preschools. Yet, "the financial strain of supporting cost-free basic education and tertiary education (university, teacher training, and professional) left the government with limited resources to focus on education before the age of 6" (Morrison, 2000, p. 216). Despite this, a grassroots movement in the 1990s propelled preschool expansion by setting up childcare centers across the nation and seeking funds from a variety of nongovernment organizations. The universal primary education program was later enhanced into the Free Compulsory Universal Basic Education (FCUBE) in 1987, and in 2010, free compulsory basic education expanded to include access to kindergarten at age 5 (Republic of Ghana Ministry of Women and Children's Affairs, n.d.; UNESCO International Bureau of Education, 2006). Before then informal systems of education had been the principal way by which Ghanaian communities prepared their members for citizenship.

Despite a commitment to early learning, Ghanaians struggle with how to best educate their citizen apprentices. Educators in schools across Ghana face a challenge as they prepare "citizens who can consider problems in a global context" yet "develop Ghanaian solutions" to those problems (Wilson, 1999, pp. 94–95). This duality of citizenship represents the tension between Western values focused on citizens as contributors to economic development and non-Western understandings of citizens as a collective community with a shared identity that cares for one another and upholds traditional cultural values (Oduro, 2009; Pence & Shafer, 2006; Twum-Danso, 2009b). In Ghana, preparation of the young as citizens is clearly now on the agenda both from the point of view of those wishing to promote national development, as well as those who seek to reduce the social exclusion of young people facing poverty (Arnot, Casely-Hayford, Wainaina, Chege, & Dovie, 2009).

This research is part of a larger comparative multi-case study of civic education in kindergarten classrooms serving low-income students in the United States and Ghana. The African experience has typically been told through the lens of colonial perspectives, denigrating traditional beliefs and practices as primitive. As a result, contributions from the Global South continue to be marginalized in Western academic curricula. This comparative research has facilitated scholarly discourse between research sites and opened "a window to a society, revealing particular histories and cultural values" as well as broadened the researchers' conceptual lenses as they analyze similar issues or topics in different national contexts (Hahn, 2006; 2010). The Ghanaian kindergarteners' video-stimulated interviews are the focus of this chapter. Our goal was to develop a systemic understanding of the challenges and opportunities in Ghana for young children's civic roles and engagement.

CONCEPTUAL FRAMEWORK

Rogoff's sociocultural theory (2003) provides a relevant lens from which to understand ECE as a reflection of the cultures and societies of which it is a part. According to Rogoff, different sociocultural groups have unique beliefs and values that are expressed and reflected differently in their educational systems. Rogoff (1990) used the term apprenticeship to describe individuals' involvement with others in culturally organized activity, which has as part of its purpose the development of mature participation in the activity by the less experienced people.

USING VIDEO-CUED ETHNOGRAPHY TO MAKE CHILDREN'S VOICES VISIBLE

Video data collection is not a new research approach (Morgan, 2007; Robson, 2011; Tobin, Hsueh, & Karasawa, 2009). Video-cued ethnography (VCE) in early childhood contexts has an established history as a methodology that engages children, teachers, and researchers (Tobin et al., 2009) in exploring the "pedagogical complexity of classrooms" (Cutter-Mackenzie, Edwards, & Quinton, 2015, p. 343) while empowering young children as participants (Barratt-Hacking, Cutter-Mackenzie, & Barratt, 2012).

Nonetheless, the "insiders' view" captured through participants' interrogation of video data often privileged the perspectives of the adults not the children who studied in the preschools. More recently, teacher education researchers have explored innovative methods in researching children's perspectives. In particular, video-based methodologies are progressively being utilized for this purpose. The "child-framed" methodological movement (Barratt-Hacking et al., 2012) emphasizes the idea that children are active participants in their communities and as such have the right to contribute their thoughts to research in which they might be involved.

Researchers have used video-cued interviews as a method to address asymmetric power relations inherent in exchanges between children and adults (Christensen, 2004; Rogoff, 2003) and create conditions that privilege children's "interpretations about the motives, goals, and values" (Fleer, 2008, p. 113) of the young participants who are the main actors of interest (Dockett, Einarsdóttir, & Perry, 2011; Einarsdóttir, 2007). Fleer (2008), however, cautions that video-based research methodologies are not necessarily the easy option as it is not a matter of the researcher simply pointing the video camera to capture the children's experience. Taking a video camera into an early childhood setting raises a host of questions centering around issues associated with the ethics of visual data collection, approaches to analyzing data, and the way in which the video works to shape researcher and participant behavior in the educational context.

In order to capture diverse representations of empowering civic engagement in young learners, our research study included a triangulation of data collection procedures involving various information sources, such as document analysis of children's literature and classroom materials, observation of kindergarten classrooms, and interviews of school stakeholders (faculty, caregivers, and children). Our research team videotaped a day in each participating kindergarten class. The video recordings focused on whole group activities as well as small group learning centers during which researchers often moved around the room, documenting exchanges among children and program staff. The visual data became a living archive of the interactions that happened in that space.

We subsequently showed brief, edited versions of this footage to selected kindergarten children. VCE drew upon young children's competencies for participation in research, providing unique modalities for children to communicate and exercise their own agency. The video, which served both as a source of data as well as a cue for discussion, slowed down the act of looking at classroom practices to deeply explore young children's perspectives while simultaneously valuing and validating their views.

BLOW THE DUST FROM MY EYES:
VALUING GHANAIAN KNOWLEDGE

Giving child participants a voice in research in Ghana is at its "teething" stage, even though children have been conceived as active participants in the traditional communities (Boakye-Boaten, 2010; Pence & Marfo, 2008). Twum-Danso (2009a, p. 430) asserts that the Ghanaian values of "respect, reciprocity and responsibility play a crucial role" in how families and communities mediate expectations for children's interactions with adults. Beginning at age 5, Ghanaian children are characterized as having sense to assume responsibility to "not only work for the cohesion of the family, but also to respect parents and elders at all times and to assist them in case of need" (Twum-Danso, 2009a, p. 420). Given this cross-cultural diversity, Rogoff (2003, pp. 3–4) has argued that the context of children's lives "can be understood only in light of the cultural practices and circumstances of their communities."

In order to reflect culturally relevant understanding of citizenship and promote active engagement of young children in the research, video-cued and multivocal methodology gave voice to participants in each community and engaged them in analyzing the institutions of which they are a part. As an international research team of Ghanaian and U.S. scholars, our discussions revealed particular values about belonging, identity, ownership, and choice that frame perspectives on citizenship (Kankam, 2016). These methodological dilemmas of interpretation across cultural chasms elevated indigenous conceptual schemes and helped our team contest normative meanings of "good students," "good work," and the role of children as apprentice citizens (Rogoff, 2003).

To ensure inclusivity of community contexts, we collaborated on a research design that privileged particular histories and cultural values (Hahn, 2010) in Ghana while also critically challenging the binary distinctions between indigenous and Western forms of knowledge. The approach was best reflected in the Ghanaian proverb: *Hu m'ani so ma me nti na atwe mmienu nam* (Blow the dust from my eyes). This had a multiplicity of meanings for how we conducted ourselves as a research team and how we designed our methodology. Ghanaian belief systems have their roots in a culture based on reciprocity and redistribution of knowledge and resources.

This idea of collaboration rather than competition runs through a number of wise sayings in Twi, an Akan language widely spoken among the people of Ghana, including a large percentage of the Ghanaian population who are not Akans. Collaboration is deeply ingrained in the Ghanaian culture, creating a strong disincentive for independence and isolation.

The research team members were driven by a shared epistemological stance that privileged local knowledge and children's perspectives.

Therefore, we aligned the methodology with Ghanaian approaches to civic learning and action that prepared children to contribute to strengthening the community. Children were expected to assume authentic roles and responsibilities to ensure the health, safety, and vitality of the classroom and school community (i.e., cleaning the school, checking on the water supply, etc.; Kankam 2016). These roles reflected societal challenges essential for protection, food production, and mastery of the environment.

Similarly, the research design promoted children's active participation, which aligned with the Ghanaian ethnotheory that children are responsible, aware, motivated, and engaged individuals (Nsamenang, 2008; Pence & Nsamenang, 2008). The visual-cued process elevated the children as active collaborators rather than passive objects of study (Christensen, 2004; Stanczak, 2004). This methodology deconstructed positioning of researchers and participants and allowed for divergent interpretations of the data as the children assumed roles as active social agents.

CONSTRUCTING CONVERSATIONS AND KNOWLEDGE THROUGH VCE

The use of video-based technologies in our research project was informed by the development of a methodology that placed the data analysis in the hands of the children and therefore allowed them a degree of power in the process. Prosser (2007) argues that visual methods are particularly useful for facilitating authentic user involvement: "Emancipatory and participatory research such as photo voice and photo elicitation can gather valuable input from teachers, pupils and others who actually inhabit the built environment" (p. 16). In our study, promoting "children as researchers" diminished the impact of researcher subjectivity and enhanced reflexivity.

The methodology was designed to allow the children to be active participants. The multimodal research methods intentionally created a conversation space in which children and adults came together in dialogue in and about classroom interactions connected with children's roles as apprentice citizens. Use of the video mediated reliance on literacy skills and confidence, which could be expected to vary quite widely across the participants. Prosser and Burke (2008) argue that "words are the domain of adult researchers and therefore can be disempowering to the young. Images, on the other hand, are central to children's culture from a very early age and are therefore empowering" (p. 407). In our research study video clips assisted in the facilitation of conversations with the children, thus enabling them to remain engaged in the reconstruction of knowledge (Einarsdóttir, 2007; Prosser & Burke, 2008). Conversation starters included: "Tell me, what do you think about...?"; "How do you feel when...?"; "What do you like about...?"; "What makes you think that?"; and "What makes you feel that way?" Scaffolding children to express their ideas as fully as possible was emphasized, thereby balancing children's agency with their dependency. Strategies for clarifying, extending, reformulating, and prompting children to elaborate upon their ideas, were all explored, in the context of continuing to check for shared understanding as the conversations unfolded.

The rationale for using the VCE was to assist us, as an international research team guided by contextual ethics (Ebrahim, 2010; Rogoff, 2003), to promote active involvement of our young participants in our quest to examine young learners' civic roles in the kindergarten classrooms in Ghana.

Although focus groups are typically an integral part of the methodological canon for VCE and draw on the group dynamics to reveal participants' perspectives about events in which they were involved, some researchers have concluded that focus groups may be problematic for children under the age of 6 since the young participants may have more limited social or language skills to effectively engage in the group (Heary & Hennessy, 2002). The research team believed that the young Ghanaian children may not be forthcoming in a group but would open up in the intimacy of a one-on-one interview context and more freely share their voices. Moreover, due to limited resources on-site, a single laptop had to be brought to the Ghanaian school setting for the participants to view the clips. No projection devices were available, and they could not be supported by the school infrastructure where electricity was not available in the classrooms. Since the viewing of the video was already a novel experience for the children, individual interviews seemed to be the most ideal approach to facilitate viewing.

The children involved in this research were between 5 to 6 years old and were selected in consultation with classroom teachers before the visits. The purposeful sample involved children identified by the teacher as socially and verbally confident. Nonetheless, when the first kindergartener entered the room to participate in the video-cued interview, the implied power and authority of the adult researcher muted the child's voice. After a series of failed attempts to elicit the child participant into a more engaged response, the session was halted.

The research team reflected on how the children's Ghanaian identity had important implications for the researcher–child relationship. In Ghana children are simultaneously cherished and expected to demonstrate reverence for their rightful place among adults (Boakye-Boaten, 2010; Kankam, 2016; Twum-Danso, 2009a). Much of Ghanaian children's learning in the early years is factored into peer group activities, more so than through adults' interactions (Nsamenang, 2008). Ghanaian ethnotheory views socialization as a generative process by which children's learning occurs in collaboration with peers through their active participation in their cultural communities (Nsamenang, 2008; Rogoff, 2003).

We revised our methodology to use peer-partners (where the interviewee was paired with his or her friend) as a technique to access the voices of the Ghanaian children while still allowing the participants to easily view the video clips on the laptops. The children's familiarity with each other boosted the confidence of those who needed it, and their interaction in the dyad enhanced the data-gathering process, allowing the researcher to clearly track what the children focused on when the video was played back. After a successful pilot of the revised process, we implemented team video-cued interviews throughout the remainder of our research, involving pairs of kindergarteners, a researcher, and videographer.

Co-construction of child discourse pinpointed the experiences that children found most compelling and were evidenced not only in their articulation of concerns and issues but also their physical actions, exhibited through simultaneous reenactment of the observed events depicted in the video. The comments that the children made to each other were often more revealing and as interesting as the responses they offered to the adult-generated questions. Their shared experiences and perceptions cultivated a strong and unique relationship that underscored the importance of multivocality and collaboration in the research process.

Peer interaction seemed to provoke a feeling of empathetic understanding between the children. While the video-cued methods provided both a means for making sense of experiences and a medium through which new meanings could be revealed, the children's pre-established relationships promoted trust that overcame the predisposition of the children to respond to the researchers with a "right answer," thereby enhancing the quality of the conversation. The peer dyads helped ensure that the children's perspectives were not overshadowed by adults' interest and research agendas. A relaxed and comfortable rapport developed between the peers as they naturally engaged in discussion. As the children watched the video together, there were visible signs of mutual enjoyment of the experience, such as laughter, conversation, close physical contact, smiling, singing, and reenactment of activities observed on the video. The inclusion of a playful attitude seemed to facilitate the acquisition of rich data.

As can be seen in Extract 1, the original kindergartener (Yaw) reengaged in a dynamic way when joined by a peer (Francis) in the video-cued interview.

Extract 1
[Video plays]

> **Yaw:** [Stands and joins the class in the video in singing the Ghanaian National Anthem] God bless our homeland Ghana...
>
> **Francis:** [giggles as Yaw stands, and she points to Yaw in the video.] Look you didn't obey Madame.

> **Yaw:** I am obeying now. [Yaw continues to sing along with the video.]
>
> **Interviewer:** What do the words mean?
>
> **Yaw:** I don't know.
>
> **Francis:** Madame says they are the national anthem.
>
> **Interviewer:** Why do you sing that song?
>
> **Francis:** Yaw doesn't sing. He is in trouble with Madame. Yaw, if you respect Madame you will go to Heaven. If you do not respect you will go to Hell.
>
> **Yaw:** No, I am listening. Watch me do my stretching! [follows teacher's voice on the video for stretching.]
> Francis and Yaw laugh.

The video offered a compelling catalyst for discussion in order to gain the perspectives of the children in the kindergarten, rather than serve as a stimulus for recall. In Extract 2, the dyad of children engage in a conversation about what they learned after watching the teacher in the video read the story of Midas to the class.

Extract 2

> **Interviewer:** What did you learn from the video about a good citizen?
>
> **Francis:** A good person doesn't steal. A bad person steals from his mother.
>
> **Yaw:** It is bad to steal from Madame. Stealing is a sin. My mother says that it is bad to beg for money.
>
> **Francis:** We are good if we sweep the class and clean the board.
>
> **Yaw:** Yesterday Madame caned me when I did not sweep the room.
>
> **Francis:** You made a mess and Madame told you to sweep.
>
> **Yaw:** Aunty found out and told me next time to obey. Today Madame told us to cover our mouth with handkerchiefs when coughing and wash our hand when we visit the toilet or else we will infect other people with diseases. I did those things.
>
> **Francis:** [giggles] You didn't wash your hands.
>
> **Yaw:** [laughing] I meant to.

It was clear peers had a far greater knowledge of the classroom context in comparison with the adults who were present. The video elicited children's interpretation of particular events, and their multimodal responses reflected their expressions of meaning.

CONCLUSION

In a democratic society, central tenets of citizenship often are conceptualized as having a voice and influencing change. Such engagement, however, has typically negated young children's perspectives. While some question young children's capacity for such engagement, and others may doubt the age appropriateness of such action, there are still others who question adults' right to search for children's points of view. It has been further noted that perceived benefits of engaging with children's voices are usually defined by adults and not children. This research explored a methodological approach that valued and validated Ghanaian children's insights and recognized child-specific competencies for participation.

Building conceptions of democratic citizenship is paramount in the Ghanaian context because it is an important foundation in the national narrative (Levstik & Groth, 2005). Such ideals help children to honor multiple identities, and search for unifying elements that might be carried into the present and future. In this research, the methodology aligned with Ghanaian approaches to civic learning and action that were embodied in authentic roles and responsibilities that students assumed to ensure the health, safety, and vitality of the classroom and school community (i.e., cleaning the school, checking on the water supply, etc.). These roles reflected societal challenges that needed to be addressed. Similarly, the research design promoted children's participation through hands-on processes, such as being responsible, aware, motivated, and engaged (Pence & Nsamenang, 2008). The visual elicitation process elevated the children as active collaborators rather than passive objects of study (Stanczak, 2004). This methodology deconstructed positioning of researchers and participant and allowed for divergent interpretations of the data as the children assumed roles as active social agents.

Thus, the adult researchers became facilitators and co-interpreters who used the video to create a space where students might cultivate their voices and claim their agency. However, facilitation required significant reflective skills from the researchers in order to develop awareness about the possible implications of the children's ideas, and to help generate equitable power dynamics through productive relational dynamics. As a result the children initiated and encouraged a depth of dialogue with each other that may never have been possible without the peer dyad. Ultimately the video-cued methods provided important links between researchers and participants and shifted the research from surveillance of children to an ethnographic approach based on relationships to deepen our understanding of children's educational experiences across diverse Ghanaian communities.

Our findings moved beyond stereotypes of Ghanaian education to reveal the diversity of communities. Children are simultaneously cherished and expected to demonstrate reverence for their rightful place among adults. Traditions are interwoven with contemporary realities. Our research contested common depictions of African schools as deprived settings. Routinely global media have perpetuated a discourse of pessimism and a childhood in Ghana defined by existential challenges; however, we discovered opportunities exemplified in the educational experiences that celebrate and provide civic outlets for children's fortitude, resilience, creativity, and sense of agency.

This project applied strategies for using technologically situated visual research tools to mediate barriers to young children's authentic participation and engage them in co-constructing data-generated themes. However, future research is needed that continues to explore the ethical and methodological dilemmas in researching children's perspectives with video-based methodologies. Topics include consent, power inequities in the researcher/participant relationship, confidentiality and protection, data interpretation and analysis, and use of ICT in countries throughout the Majority World.

ACKNOWLEDGMENTS

We would like to acknowledge the Spencer Foundation New Civics Grant for their support of this research. We also greatly appreciate our colleagues, Drs. Kafui Felicia Etsey, Alex Kwao, Awo Abena Amoa Sarpong, and Kankam Boadu at the University of Cape Coast, Ghana, for their collaboration on the data collection for this research study.

Questions for Reflection
1. How do you conceptualize citizenship, and what evidence of enacted citizenship is practiced in classrooms?
2. What is video-cued elicitation, and how does this methodology facilitate active engagement of young children in research?
3. How does children's participation in the video elicitation assist researchers in situating their analysis in the social and cultural context of the region?
4. In collaborative, cross-national research what strategies must be considered to contest social injustices in the research enterprise?

Suggestions for Further Reading
Civic Agency
Adair, J. K., Phillips, L., Ritchie, J., & Sachdeva, S. (2017). Civic action and play: Examples from Maori, Aboriginal Australian and Latino communities. Early Child Development and Care, 187(5–6), 798–811.

Payne, K. A. (2015). Who can fix this? The concept of "audience" and first grad-
ers' civic agency. Social Studies and the Young Learner, 27(4), 19–22.

Brown, C. P., Englehardt, J., Barry, D. P., & Ku, D. H. (2018). Questioning
democratic notions of governance: A case study examining how a kindergarten teacher and her students give voice to and enact a neoliberal
framing of schooling. Contemporary Issues in Early Childhood, 1–17.

Global Perspectives

Britto, P., Engle, P., & Super, C. (Eds.). (2013). Handbook of early childhood
development research and its impact on global policy. New York, NY:
Oxford University Press.

Twum-Danso, A. (2011). Searching for a middle ground in children's rights in
Ghana. Journal of Human Rights, 10(3), 376–392.

Twum-Danso, A. (2013). Children's perceptions of physical punishment in
Ghana and the implications for children's rights. Childhood, 20(4),
472–486.

Twum-Danso, A., & Ame, R. K. (2012). Childhoods at the intersection of the
local and the global. Houndmills, England: Palgrave Macmillan.

Video-Elicitation

Cutter-Mackenzie, A., Edwards, S., & Quinton, H. W. (2015). Child-framed
video research methodologies: Issues, possibilities and challenges for
researching with children. Children's Geographies, 13(3), 343–356.

Lewis, H. (2017). Supporting the development of young children's metacog-
nition through the use of video-stimulated reflective dialogue. Early
Child Development and Care, 1–17.

Lynch, H., & Stanley, M. (2018). Beyond words: Using qualitative video
methods for researching occupation with young children. OTJR:
Occupation, Participation and Health, 38(1), 56–66.

Theobald, M. (2012). Video-stimulated accounts: Young children account-
ing for international matters in front of peer. Journal of Early Childhood
Research, 10(1), 32–50.

REFERENCES

Arnot, M., Casely-Hayford, L., Wainaina, P. K., Chege, F., & Dovie, D. A. (2009). Youth
citizenship, national unity and poverty alleviation: East and West African approaches to the education of a new generation (Working paper). Cambridge, England:
RECOUP. Retrieved from https://www.ssoar.info/ssoar/handle/document/
6878?locale-attribute=en

Barratt-Hacking, E., Cutter-Mackenzie, A. N., & Barratt, R. (2012). Children as active researchers: The potential of environmental education research involving

children. In R. B. Stevenson, M. Brody, J. Dillion, & A. E. J. Wals (Eds.), *International Handbook of Research on Environmental Education* (pp. 438–458). New York, NY: Routledge.

Boakye-Boaten, A. (2010). Changes in the concept of childhood: Implications on children in Ghana. *Journal of International Social Research, 3*(10), 104–115.

Christensen, H. P. (2004). Children's participation in ethnographic research: Issues of power and representation. *Children & Society, 18*(2), 165–176.

Cutter-Mackenzie, A., Edwards, S., & Quinton, H. W. (2015). Child-framed video research methodologies: Issues, possibilities and challenges for researching with children. *Children's Geographies, 13*(3), 343–356.

Dockett, S., Einarsdóttir, J., & Perry, B. (2011). Balancing methodologies and methods in researching with young children. In D. Harcourt, B. Perry, & T. Waller (Eds.), *Researching Young Children's Perspectives* (pp. 68–81). New York, NY: Routledge.

Ebrahim, H. B. (2010). Situated ethics: Possibilities for young children as research participants in the South African context. *Early Child Development and Care, 180*(3), 289–298.

Einarsdóttir, J. (2007). Research with children: Methodological and ethical challenges. *European Early Childhood Education Research Journal, 15*(2), 197–211.

Fleer, M. (2008). Using digital video observations and computer technologies in a cultural-historical approach. In M. Hedegaard & M. Fleer (Eds.), *Studying Children: A Cultural-Historical Approach* (pp. 104–117). Maidenhead, England: McGraw Hill, Open University Press.

Hahn, C. L. (2006). Comparative and international social studies research. In K. Barton (Ed.), *Research methods in social studies education* (pp. 139–157). Greenwich, CT: Information Age.

Hahn, C. L. (2010). Comparative civic education research: What we know and what we need to know. *Citizenship Teaching and Learning, 6*(1), 5–23.

Heary, C. M., & Hennessy, E. (2002). The use of focus group interviews in pediatric health care research. *Journal of Pediatric Psychology, 27*(1), 47–57.

Kankam, B. (2016). Citizenship education in Ghana: A traditional and modern perspective in development. *International Journal of Information Research and Review, 3*(4), 2102–2108.

Kuyini, A. B. (2013). Ghana's education reform 2007: A realistic proposition or a crisis of vision? *International Review of Education, 59*(2), 157–176.

Levstik, L., & Groth, J. (2005). Ruled by our own people: Ghanaian adolescents' conceptions of citizenship. *The Teachers College Record, 107*(4), 563–586.

Morgan, A. (2007). Using video-stimulated recall to understand young children's perceptions of learning in classroom settings. *European Early Childhood Education Research Journal, 15*(2), 213–226.

Morrison, J. W. (2000). Under colonialism to democratization: Early childhood development in Ghana. *International Journal of Early Childhood, 32*(2), 24–31.

Nsamenang, A. B. (2008). (Mis)Understanding ECD in Africa: The force of local and global motives. In M. Garcia, A. Pence, & J. L. Evans (Eds.), *Africa's future, Africa's challenge: Early childhood care and development in Sun-Saharan Africa* (pp. 135–150). Washington, DC: World Bank.

Oduro, F. (2009). The quest for inclusion and citizenship in Ghana: Challenges and prospects. *Citizenship Studies, 13*(6), 621–639

Pence, A. R., & Marfo, K. (2008). Early childhood development in Africa: Interrogating constraints of prevailing knowledge bases. *International Journal of Psychology, 43*(2), 78–87.

Pence, A. R., & Nsamenang, B. (2008). *A case for early childhood development in Sub-Saharan Africa.* (Working papers in early childhood development, No. 51). The Hague, Netherlands: Bernard van Leer Foundation.

Pence, A., & Shafer, J. (2006). Indigenous knowledge and early childhood development in Africa: The early childhood development virtual university. *Journal for Education in International Development, 2*(3). Retrieved from http://www.web.uvic.ca/~eyrd/pubs/P7_Schaffer_Pence_IK_FINAL_2006.pdf

Prosser, J. (2007). Visual methods and the visual culture of schools. *Visual Studies, 22*(1), 13–30.

Prosser, J., & Burke, C. (2008). Image-based research: Childlike perspectives. In J. G. Knowles & A. L. Cole (Eds.), *Handbook of the arts in qualitative research: Perspectives, methodologies, examples, and issues* (pp. 407–419). London, England: SAGE.

Republic of Ghana Ministry of Women and Children's Affairs (n.d.). *Early childhood care and development policy.* Retrieved from http://planipolis.iiep.unesco.org/sites/planipolis/files/ressources/ghanaeccdp.pdf

Robson, S. (2011). Producing and using video data in the early years: Ethical questions and practical consequences in research with young children. *Children & Society, 25*(3), 179–189.

Rogoff, B. (1990). *Apprenticeship in thinking: Cognitive development in social context.* Oxford, England: Oxford University Press.

Rogoff, B. (2003). *The cultural nature of human development.* New York, NY: Oxford University Press.

Stanczak, G. C. (2004). Introduction: Visual representation. *American Behavioral Scientist, 47*(12), 1471–1476.

Tobin, J., Hsueh, Y., & Karasawa, M. (2009). *Preschool in three cultures revisited: China, Japan, and the United States.* Chicago, IL: University of Chicago Press.

Twum-Danso, A. (2009a). Reciprocity, respect and responsibility: The 3Rs underlying parent-child relationships in Ghana and the implications for children's rights. *International Journal of Children's Rights, 17,* 415–432.

Twum-Danso, A. (2009b). The construction of childhood and the socialization of children: The implications for the implementation of Article 12 of the Convention on the Rights of the Child in Ghana. In B. Percy-Smith & N. Thomas (Eds.), *A handbook of children and young people's participation* (pp. 133–140). London, England: Routledge.

UNESCO International Bureau of Education. (2006). *Ghana: Early childhood care and education programmes.* Retrieved from http://unesdoc.unesco.org/images/0014/001471/147192e.pdf

Wilson, A. (1999). A global perspective and Ghanaian social studies teachers. *Mate Masie, 1,* 94–95.

CHAPTER 17

SOUNDS FROM WITHIN

Exploring the Role of Ethnographic Fieldwork to Elevate Children's Perspectives and Voices in the Study of Children's Musical Cultures in Ireland

Michelle Finnerty

ABSTRACT

This chapter reports on the use of ethnographic fieldwork as a method of carrying out research with children in middle childhood. This chapter explores several themes and concepts that emerge when carrying out observations and group interviews with children. Original findings on the use of these methods are drawn from an ethnographic study of the musical cultures of children which includes sets of observations and group interviews in three primary school settings and three after-school settings in the south of Ireland. The approach adopted is informed by research that considers children as active research participants and employs ethnographic fieldwork methods and a mutimethod approach to carrying out research with children. This chapter proposes to examine approaches to listening to children and ethical issues of informed consent and informed assent. It documents the interactive methods that were used in the study of children's musical cultures and highlights how

Participatory Methodologies to Elevate Children's Voice and Agency, pages 383–403
Copyright © 2019 by Information Age Publishing
383

these methods facilitated children to engage meaningfully in the research process with due consideration of their role within the study.

In this chapter, I discuss the methodological approach used as part of a research study exploring children's perspectives on their musical worlds in Ireland. I begin with an outline of how research with children has evolved in the last decade, focusing on how children have become more centrally involved in research studies. I discuss two frameworks developed to increase children's active engagement in the research process: First, I outline Hart's ladder of participation (1992), a reference tool used for planning children's participation levels in research studies. Next I discuss the mosaic approach (Clark & Moss, 2001) which is a multimethod approach to carrying out research with children that focuses on a diverse range of methods of carrying out research with children. I discuss the role of ethnographic fieldwork and consider its value to elevate children's voices in research studies. I discuss how ethnographic fieldwork, including sets of observations and semi-structured group interviews with children, were used as part of a research study exploring children's perceptions on their musical worlds in Ireland. I consider the ethical issues that emerged in the planning of research studies with children, and I outline the safeguards that were put in place to overcome these issues. I also discuss the approach used in the analysis of the data and the methods that were used to create the ethnographic narrative.

RESEARCH WITH CHILDREN: HISTORICAL AND CONTEMPORARY DEVELOPMENTS

Up until recently, the direct participation of children in research studies across many disciplines has been limited. The marginalization of children and their views from research studies is often considered to be connected to how children were viewed in society at large. Holloway writes about the historical role of children in sociological research, stating that "children tended to be seen as human becomings rather than human beings, who through the process of socialisation were to be shaped into fully human adult beings" (Holloway et al., 2005, p. 4).

Hogan (2005) suggests that even when research studies have taken place with children, they often have not sought to understand children's "subjective experiences and their worlds" (p. 22). The focus has remained on the views of adults rather than capturing "children's own perspectives on their behaviour, on their feelings, and on their evaluation of the kinds of services they receive" (p. 22). Similarly, Kellett and Ding (2004) emphasize how the focus in research studies has been "on children" and not "with children."

The growing concern for children's rights internationally has influenced the awareness of including their voices in research studies. Since the 1990s children have become more central to many research studies and viewed as "active researchers" or "participants" rather than "objects" of research (Christensen & James, 2017; Greig, Taylor, & MacKay, 2013; Kellett, 2005b, 2010). Emphasizing the importance of children in the research process, Kellett (2005a) states that "children are party to the subculture of childhood which gives them a unique 'insider' perspective that is critical to our understanding of children's worlds" (p. 1). Further research studies highlight the role of children as active participants and advocate for children to be involved as "co-researchers" and provide opportunities for children to be "reflexive" throughout the process (Christensen & James, 2017; Murray, 2016).

FRAMEWORKS FOR ENGAGING CHILDREN IN THE RESEARCH PROCESS

Ethnographic Fieldwork

Ethnographic fieldwork is a central component of ethnomusicological study. Ethnography has been variously defined as: "the study of people in naturally occurring settings" (Brewer, 2000, p. 6); "the study of groups and people as they go about their everyday lives" (Emerson, Fretz, & Shaw, 2011, p. 1); "the observation and description of culture" (Barz & Cooley, 2008, p. 4); and as the "observation of people in situ" (Myers, 1992, p. 23). The term *participant observation* is often used to characterize ethnographic fieldwork. Participant observation is a research process whereby a researcher aims to gain a close and intimate familiarity with individuals or groups of people within a particular setting, through an intensive involvement with people in their environment.

A qualitative approach was adopted for this study as an understanding of the musical cultures of children is not quantifiable in numbers. Denzin and Lincoln define qualitative research as, "multi-method in focus, involving an interpretative, naturalistic approach to its subject matter" (2008, p. 3). They refer to qualitative researchers as people who "study things in their natural settings, attempting to make sense of, or interpret, phenomena in terms of meanings people bring to them" (2008, p. 3). Similarly, Layder (1993) states, "The status of the distinction is ambiguous, because it is almost simultaneously regarded by some writers as a fundamental contrast and by others as no longer useful or even simply as 'false'" (p. 110).

In relation to the use of qualitative methods while researching children's views, Hogan (2005) outlines that it is "an approach designed by openness and inclusiveness, it aims to capture children's lived experiences of the word and the meanings they attach to those experiences from their own perspectives. It allows them to describe those experiences without the level of restraint that is often used in quantitative approaches" (p. 2).

Hogan's study reveals the positive effects on how children behave during the research process. Prout and James (1997) report that ethnography is a particular useful methodology for the study of childhood and that the approach "enables children to have a direct voice and active participation in the production of data."

Hart's Ladder of Participation and the Mosaic Approach

Hart's ladder of participation (1992) and the mosaic approach (Clark & Moss, 2001) are two methodological approaches that focus on increasing awareness of children's active participation in research studies. Hart's ladder of participation (1992) is a reference tool divided into seven stages outlining various participant levels that children can engage in during a research study (see Figure 17.1). Through the development of this approach, Hart advocates for increased levels of participation of children in research studies. The reference tool outlines the levels ranging from nonparticipant (levels/rung 1, 2, 3) to full participation (levels/rung 7, 8). At full participation, adults and children share decisions that affect their lives.

Hart (1992) defines participation as a "process of sharing decisions which affect one's life and the life of the community in which one lives" (p. 5) and he emphasizes the link to a democratic society and how participation is the "fundamental right of citizenship" (Hart, 1992, p. 5). The ladder of participation is created to "serve as a beginning typology for thinking about children's participation in projects" (Hart, 1992, p. 9). Hart explains

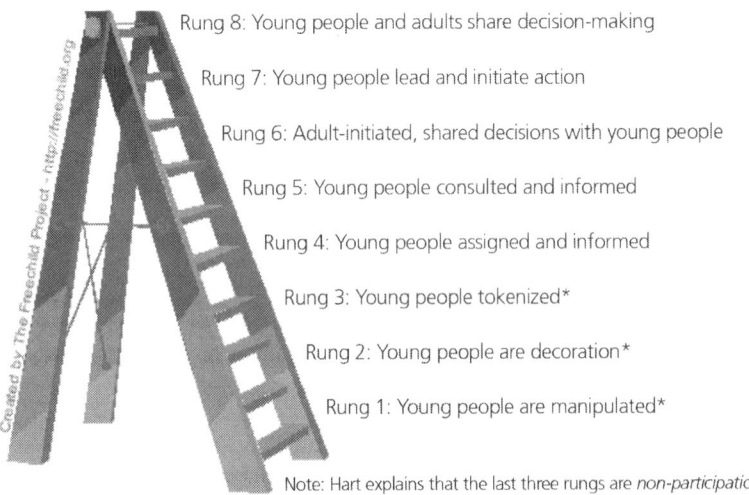

Rung 8: Young people and adults share decision-making

Rung 7: Young people lead and initiate action

Rung 6: Adult-initiated, shared decisions with young people

Rung 5: Young people consulted and informed

Rung 4: Young people assigned and informed

Rung 3: Young people tokenized*

Rung 2: Young people are decoration*

Rung 1: Young people are manipulated*

Note: Hart explains that the last three rungs are *non-participation*

Figure 17.1 Roger Hart's (1992) Ladder of Young People's Participation.

that the first three levels, manipulation, decoration, and tokenism are models of nonparticipation of children. Manipulation is where children are not consulted in any capacity regarding their views and or if they are consulted, they are not given any feedback on the relevance of their ideas. Decoration is where children are included in events but have no knowledge of what it is related to. One example is of children performing in an important event but they are unaware of the meaning of their participation. Tokenism is described by Hart as a process where children are "apparently given a voice" (Hart, 1992, p. 9) but have no opportunity to convey their own opinions on it. Hart refers to the fourth rung of the ladder of participation as "assigned but informed." In this type of project, children "understand the intentions of the project . . . they know who made the decisions concerning their involvement and why . . . and they have a meaningful role" (Hart, 1992, p. 11). The fifth state of the ladder is entitled "consulted and informed," and this is similar to Stage 4 as the projects are run by adults but children's views are treated seriously. The sixth rung, "adult initiated, shared decisions with children," is referred to by Hart as "true participation." Even though these projects are initiated by adults, children are involved in the decision making process. Rung 7, "child-initiated and directed" is a process were children are facilitated to initiate and direct their own research projects with the support of adults. The final stage, Rung 8, "child initiated, shared decisions with adults," refers to projects that are initiated by children but where they collaborate with adults to make informed shared decisions on matters that affect their lives. Hart notes that projects that represent the highest rung of the ladder of participation are rare.

Hart's ladder of participation is an important reference tool that aims to encourage researchers to consider the levels of participation of children in research studies. Since its development, it has been widely used in a range of disciplines that aim to involve children in their research studies; however, it has also received negative criticism for its "over simple linear approach to the concept of participation" (Kellett, 2005a, p. 7). In the context of exploring children's perspectives in the musical cultures of children in Ireland, Hart's ladder emphasizes the importance of considering how children were included in the research process. It also brings to focus some of the limitations that emerge when aiming to involve children as active participants. Similar to the definition of Rung 5, this study was initiated by me, an adult researcher, and the engagement of children's views is informed and highly valued. Later in this chapter, I discuss the ways in which children were encouraged to participate in this research study. I also consider ways in which further studies of children's musical cultures could be developed considering higher levels of participation.

The Mosaic Approach

The mosaic approach is a multi-method framework developed for listening to young children's perspectives on their daily lives. In 1999, the integrated approach was initially devised for working with under 5-year-olds. In recent years, the method has been adapted for use with older children. The mosaic approach aims to involve children in the research process and is considered as "a way of listening while acknowledging children and adults as co-constructors of meaning" (Clark & Moss, 2005, p. 1). The approach combines traditional methods of observing children with participatory methods of interviewing children, including visual and verbal techniques during the interview process. Writing about the concept of the mosaic itself, Clark and Moss (2005) reveal that

> a mosaic is an image made up of many small pieces, which need to be brought together in order to make sense of the whole. The Mosaic approach gives young children the opportunity to demonstrate their perspectives in a variety of ways, calling on their "hundred languages." (p. 1)

The method recognizes the different "voices" or "languages" of children and emphasizes how children are experts in their own lives. A variety of techniques are explored to enable young children to communicate their ideas and feelings to adults in symbolic ways.[1] These techniques are used as a "springboard" for talking, listening, and reflecting with children.

The mosaic framework for listening is outlined in Figure 17.2. Within this framework, a two-stage approach to gathering data is outlined in Figure 17.3. Clark and Moss (2005) argue for the importance of understanding listening as a process which is not confined to the spoken word. They suggest that the "voice of a child" could indicate the transmission of ideas

Multi-method:	recognizes the different languages or voices of children
Participatory:	treats children as experts and agents in their own lives
Reflexive:	includes children, practitioners and parents in reflecting on meanings and addresses the question of interpretation
Adaptable:	can be applied to a variety of early childhood institutions
Focused on children's lived experiences:	looking at lives rather than knowledge gained or care received
Embedded into practice:	a framework for listening, which has the potential to be both used as an evaluative tool and to become embedded into early years practice

Figure 17.2 The Mosaic Framework for Listening—Clark and Moss (2001, 2005).

Stage One:	Children and adults gather documentation and practitioners and parents reflect on what they think life is like for the child(ren)
Stage Two:	Piecing together information for dialogue, reflection and interpretation and practitioners and parents listen to the child(ren's) own perspectives

Figure 17.3   The Mosaic Research Approach—Clark and Moss (2001, 2005).

not only through words. They argue for the importance of listening to children and the need for this to be a "process that is open to the many creative ways young children use to express their views and experiences" (Clark & Moss, 2005, p. 5). Although the value of talking to children is not ignored, the approach suggests other valuable symbolic ways of enabling young children to communicate. Clark and Moss (2005) advocate for a participatory approach to listening that is mindful of children's views and of their silences. They suggest that "it is not only a question of seeing the world from children's perspectives but of acknowledging their rights to express their point of view or to remain silent" (p. 7).

In the next section of this chapter, I discuss the methodological approach used to elevate children's voices in the study of their musical cultures in Ireland. I highlight how the study aims to explore the musical cultures of children by embracing multi-methods of research with children and by focusing on increasing their participation levels and raising their voices using a multi-method approach to data collection.

CASE STUDY: EXPLORING CHILDREN'S VIEWS AND PERSPECTIVES IN THEIR MUSICAL CULTURES

Methods of participant and nonparticipant observations and semi-structured group interviews were used for the research study. The approach is informed by my own acquaintance with the cultures of Irish primary classrooms and after-school clubs and also international studies of children's musical cultures. Observations within the school environment took place in various spaces, including the classroom, playground, supervised excursions within the school day, music workshops, and activities organized and facilitated by visiting music teachers to the school. At all times, a teacher or supervising adult was present in the room. I observed children as they engaged in musical activities in both in-school and out-of-school settings. I also observed children during sports activities, lunchtimes, and free play time in the playground. During my observations, I carried a notepad and pen. I also had a camera and an audio recorder with me. I gathered data from the various sets of observations, using written fieldnotes, written reflections, audio, and video recordings. Throughout my observations, I recorded and collected the various sounds that formed part of the musical soundscape of the children. The fieldnotes were often short words or diagrams that I quickly jotted down to remind me of the physical space and layout of some of the musical activities. These complemented the audio and video recordings that were also gathered and they enhanced the writing up of the observations. Throughout my observations, I often wrote down some questions for further discussion or consideration. These were particularity useful as I began to analyze my observations and consider relevant themes that were emerging. Reflections of my observations were for the most part recorded immediately after the observation or later that day as I had finished my visit to the schools and to the after-school clubs. The use of the recording device provided me with valuable data and an opportunity to reflect on the information gathered. Similar to the approaches outlined by Rice (2017) and Krüger (2008), the collection of data using this variety of techniques were valuable in writing up the ethnography.

This research study involves children as research participants, and as a result, ethical approval was required before commencing. The ethical process required me to focus specifically on the fieldwork plan and the methodological approach. The following section discusses the plan in detail. It outlines the safeguards that were put into place to ensure the safety of all research participants. It also discusses the child-friendly methods of acquiring informed assent and the multi-method approaches to interviewing children that were used.

Six primary schools in Cork city and county were contacted requesting permission to host the research project. Responses were received from all the schools of which three were selected, based on access and their willingness to facilitate the research during the time-periods required. The schools chosen were representative of some of the different categories of primary schools that exist in Ireland.

School A is a single-sex girls school, located in the south of Cork city. It is a designated Delivering Equality of Opportunity in Schools school (DEIS).[2] School B is a coeducational school with the curriculum taught through the medium of the Irish language. It is located in a southern suburb of Cork city. School C is a coeducational school, located in the western suburbs five miles from Cork city. All schools are run by the local Catholic patronage, in association with the board of management.[3] Fieldwork also took place in three after-school settings. The after-school clubs were chosen as they were located close to the areas in which the schools were located. After-school Club A is a community-based voluntary music club, located to the south of Cork city. It is also located in the same community as School A. After-school Club B is a branch of the national CCÉ organization, and classes take place in the school building of school B. After-school Club C takes place in the School C building and is organized by primary school teachers from the school.

Children from ages 6–12 were selected as the main focus of this research study for a number of reasons. Recent research on children and spontaneous music making has focused on children in early years of childhood (ages 0–6 years). There is an absence of research with children in the middle childhood age-group in the national and international context. As interviews were one of the primary methods of data collection, it was felt that children ages 6 and upwards would be able to participate in the type of questioning and activity based interviews I had hoped to use.

Fieldwork for this study took place in two phases. The first phase of study was spent observing musical activities in Primary School A and Primary School B. The second phase focused on return visits to Schools A and B. Further sets of observations took place at these locations along with activity-based semi-structured group interviews. Sets of observations and interviews in School C, After-School A and After-School B also took place during phase two. After initial correspondence with the principal teachers from the schools, meetings were arranged to discuss further details of the research project. The initial meetings with the teachers focused on discussing the aims and objectives of the study and ethical issues, such as parental consent and supervision of the research activities.

Information packs, outlining details of the research, were disseminated to parents of the children. The packs contained documents requesting permission for parents to consent for their children to participate.[4] Information packs were also distributed to principal teachers, assistant teachers, music leaders, and after-school club leaders, requesting their permission to become involved in the research study. An ethics statement was included in the packs alongside child-friendly information leaflets that were created specifically for the research study.

The child-friendly brochure included in the information pack was created in collaboration with an illustrator. The objective was to convey the aims and objectives of the research study with the use of child-friendly images and appropriate language. Two versions of the brochure were created. The first one was designed for children ages 6–8 years and was specifically for parents to read with their children. The second version was aimed at children ages 9–12 years and was designed considering the reading level of children in that age group (see Figure 17.4 for sample of information flyer). Irish language versions of the brochures were also created and distributed with the English language brochures in School B and After-School Club A.

In addition to the distribution of the information packs, information sessions were also carried out in classrooms to further explain elements of the research study. During these sessions, child-friendly illustrations were used by the researcher to discuss the research study with the children. The

What do I do now?

When you have read this leaflet you can decide with your parents if you want to talk to me about music.

If you want to take part, ask your parents to sign the consent form and bring it back to your teacher at school.

Thank you for taking part in this project.

Where can I find out more information?

Phone:
Michelle Finnerty: 086 3142906

Email:
m.finnerty@ucc.ie

Post:
School of Music & Theatre
University College Cork
Cork

Figure 17.4 Children and Music in Ireland information flyer.

(continued)

Hello there!

My name is Michelle Finnerty and I am a student at the School of Music, University College Cork.

I am writing to see if you would like to help me in a project on Children and Music in Ireland.

This leaflet will tell you all about the project.

When you have read this you and your parents can decide if you would like to take part.

So what is the project about?

It is an exciting project to find out about the music children sing, play, and listen to in Ireland today.

I will be spending time with you in your classroom and your school learning about the things you do.

Other students and your teacher will always be there with me too.

Why is the project important?

This project is important because it will help adults to understand what music children are interested in.

It will also be important for people who make decisions about providing music for children in Ireland.

What happens if I take part?

Taking part is easy and will not take too much time.

I will talk to you and the students in your class about the project and why it is important.

I will ask your teacher some questions about music in your school.

I will then talk to you and the students in your class about music in your school.

I will ask you questions like, do you like music?, why do you like music?, and what types of music do you like to sing or listen to?

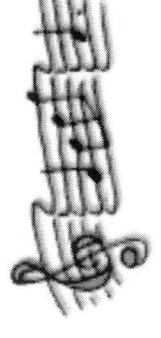

Figure 17.4 (cont.) Children and Music in Ireland information flyer.

information sessions were an important way for children to learn more about the research, to discuss ideas of what a research study is, and to consider their role as research participants. It also served as time for children to get to know the researcher. A poster was displayed in each classroom where children were participating in the study. The poster summarized the research study and provided children with ongoing access to the project details after the session. For any children that might have been absent on the day of the information session, the poster provided them an opportunity to learn about the research project (see Figure 17.5 for poster sample). Student consent forms were also circulated to children in advance of carrying out the interviews. These forms were read to students by the researcher before the interviews, and children could indicate if they did not wish to participate. All children reported they were happy and willing to participate in the interviews.

In the context of this study, the mosaic framework informed elements of my approach to fieldwork. I was mindful of creating multiple ways for children to express themselves and share their ideas on their musical lives. I interviewed children in a variety of different contexts. In some cases, children enjoyed sharing their thoughts while a rehearsal was taking place in the background, or during their free play in the school yard, or during a group activity in the school hall. Others were much more comfortable discussing

Figure 17.5 Children and Music in Ireland classroom poster.

their views in a quieter setting. I explored different methods of data collection, including the traditional methods of observations and interviews with the use of other participatory tools, such as drawings, tours, and images.

The multi-method mosaic framework facilitates what Clark refers to as a "pedagogy of listening" emerging from Reggio Emilia practice.[5] The three strands of listening outlined by Rinaldi (2005) as internal listening, multiple listening, and visible listening informed my fieldwork approach. Clark and Moss' (2005) description of internal listening as a "reflective process for children to consider meaning, make discoveries and new connections and express understandings" (p. 17) informed my decision to use open ended questions in interviews to allow children to respond and express their views and to leave the space for children to consider and reflect on their views during the process. Using open ended question where there are no "wrong" answers facilities children to "explore without the fear that they have to second-guess the intended response…and to support internal listening as a 'creative process' where there is freedom to express a new idea for the first time or in a new way" (Clark & Moss, 2005, p. 17). Multiple listening is a process where "practitioners, groups of children and individual children listen to each other and to themselves" (Clark & Moss, 2005, p. 19). It focuses on a "web of interactions" where space is given for the sharing and discussion of ideas (Clark & Moss, 2005, p. 19). In the context of this study, a multiple listening space was created in some of the larger focus group interviews with children. Visible listening is a process of "documentation…which allows listening to take place at multiple levels and with a range of individuals and groups" (Clark & Moss, 2005, p. 23). Visible listening encourages the sharing of experiences and promotes the sharing and discussion of research experiences with others.

A further methodological challenge is outlined by Holmes (1998) who outlines the limitations of the role of the adult as "outsider" to the children's culture and suggests that the field researcher must attempt to experience the children's way of engaging with the world. She states:

> Adult fieldworkers are never fully accepted into children's cultures because they can never relinquish their adult status. Rather, the fieldworker becomes the learner and the children become the teachers in the fieldworkers' attempt to experience the children's ways of knowing about the world. (p. 19)

In my fieldwork, I was conscious that I might be considered an expert in music, and I was particularly mindful of this when I introduced myself to the research participants and explained my background and role. This was particularly useful in my conversations with the music teachers and facilitators as it was important that they understood my role in terms of research and not as an evaluation of their teaching or pedagogical approach. Barker and Smith (2010) argue that defining the relationship between researcher and participants as "adult as powerful" is "oversimplistic," suggesting that children are a lot more knowledgeable of their own environments that the adult researcher is and could be regarded as a "novice" to the environment.

LISTENING TO CHILDREN: INTERVIEWS

Semi-structured group interviews took place with children, teachers and music facilitators. All of the interviews were audio recorded and were transcribed afterwards verbatim. Pseudonymous were allocated to all respondents to allow anonymity. Interviews were carried out in over fifteen different locations in various in-school and out-of-school contexts. Eighty-one children were interviewed in a variety of small group and larger focus group interviews. Fifty-three were girls and twenty-eight were boys. Informal conversations and interviews were carried out with 10 principals, principal teachers, music teachers, and after-school club leaders. A total corpus of 69,704 words were collected from the children's interviews and 15,205 words were collected from adult interviews. Interviews with children were facilitated by the researcher in collaboration with the classroom teachers or music facilitators. During the interviews with the children, I aimed to facilitate flows in conversations with the children as they engaged in activities. This allowed for a more informal group conversation which was considered to be more appropriate for the children. The activities created an interactive and comfortable environment for the children which in turn allowed them to share their thoughts and views during the conversations. After my initial observations and discussions with children regarding the ways in which they experience music, my aim was to explore the various contexts that they indicated as relevant to their musical experience. Some larger focus group interviews, provided the opportunity for children to listen to each other's thoughts on their musical lives and to comment and share their own ideas. I had originally thought that this process might generate similar ideas and that children might be influenced about what their peers had said. For the most part, this did not appear to be the case. Children were interested in sharing the common experiences that they shared with their peers and were extremely keen to talk about those parts of their musical worlds that were different.

Interviews with adults all took place in a one-to-one capacity and varied from informal spontaneous conversations to semi-structured interviews. In comparison to interviewing children, these interviews were more conversation based and required less prompts. Adults seemed to appreciate the more formal structure and respond to my questions directly. All adult respondents were more than willing to share their ideas with me, however, at times, I felt they were keen to explore some of the ideas that they thought children might think about in relation to music. In all cases, it was important to spend some time talking about the research project aims and objectives and about the desire to facilitate children to share their views on their musical lives.

A multi-method approach was used in the interviews with the research participants. This allowed children to share details of their musical worlds combining the "verbal" and "visual" (Clark and Moss, 2005). Worksheets and drawings were used to allow children to respond to questions using visual tools. A list of sample questions was used as a guide for the interviews. The questions were adapted from a research study of the musical culture of children that took place in a U.S. context (Campbell, 1998, 2010; Campbell & Wiggins, 2013). Campbell's ethnographic narrative highlights that her conversations with children reveal much about themselves and their musical lives. The "initial details" questions provide an opportunity to gauge personal characteristics of the children. Similar to Campbell, they enhanced the writing up of the conversations later as they helped remind me of certain characterizes of the children and the conversations I had with them.

The questions which are listed in Figure 17.6 were used as prompts in the interviews with children. They provided children the opportunity to express their thoughts and ideas on their musical interests. The order of questions varied according to the "flow of the conversation" (Campbell, 1998, p. 230). I also abandoned certain questions where children's "streams of consciousness" led me elsewhere (p. 9).

Interviews were carried out in various locations that were considered most appropriate in each school and after-school setting. Locations included classrooms, school halls, school library, art room, resource room, and playgrounds. It is widely acknowledged that the context in which interviews are carried out have a significant impact on children's ability to participate, engage and respond in an interview setting. Writing about this, Clark and Moss (2005) discusses how young children respond in a more positive way to interviewing if the interview takes place in a familiar environment with a trusted adult. He also stresses the importance of "maintaining rapport" and how "monitoring the child's comfort is an ongoing process" (p. 20).

All interviews were carried out in small group contexts as they were considered to be less overwhelming for the children than one-to-one interviews. In most cases, the teachers choose the groups of children to be interviewed together. In some cases, children decided themselves and as a result, there were some obvious instances where there were close friendships in the groups. This often impacted the conversations I had with children— friends often started to reveal aspects of their musical activities that they engaged in together at their homes. The free-flowing nature of the conversations facilitated children to talk spontaneously about different aspects

Introduction

My name is Michelle. I want to know more about what music you listen to, the music you like and the types of music you do. I play music all the time. I love listening to it, in the car, when I make my dinner and when I am going to bed. Today I want to ask you some questions and do some activities.

Initial Details—The Child and Setting

Name of Child (real for records only)
Pseudonym (assigned by me)
Interview Setting
Teacher
Others in the interview

General Questions

❖ Do you like music?
❖ What do you like about it?
❖ What kind of music do you do?
❖ Do you have a favorite sound?
❖ Do you play a musical instrument? Which one(s)?
❖ How did you learn to play the instrument?
❖ Do you friends or family play musical instruments?

Listening to Music

(Home, school, After-school, Bedroom, Kitchen, Living Room, school Yard, Playground, concerts, car).

❖ Do you listen to music? Where and when?
❖ What kinds of music od you listen to?
❖ Where do you hear music when you get up during the day?
❖ Do you sing when you're at home?
❖ Do you parents sing?
❖ What kinds of songs do they sing /music do they listen to?
❖ Do you ever make up songs?
❖ Do you ever make up tunes?
❖ Do you dance/ do you like to dance to music?
❖ What kind of music do you like to dance to?
❖ Do you like fast/slow music? Loud/soft music?
❖ Do any of your books or toys make music?

Singing

❖ Do you like to sing?
❖ What types of songs do you like to sing?
❖ How did you learn them?
❖ Do you sing songs in school?
❖ Do you have a favorite song? Can you sing some of it for me?

Where you sing or play music

❖ Do you sing or play music in school?
❖ Do you sing or play music outside of school?
❖ Do you sing or play music with your friends?
❖ When you grow up what would you like to be?
❖ Do you sing or play music with your family?
❖ Is there anything about music that you don't like?
❖ You do music at x and y - what kind of music do you like the most?
❖ Is there any music you'd like to do more of in school or at home?
❖ Live music?
Tell me more about that?
What do you mean by that?

Figure 17.6 Music and Children in Ireland—Interview outline.

of their musical lives. There were many instances where the conversations flowed into different areas and some instances of where I was unsure of the exact conversation details. There were other occasions where children spoke about a song or musical artist or computer application that I was not familiar with. In those cases, I invited them to explain more about the unknown references to songs or artists.

Barker and Smith (2010) suggest that the relationships between the researcher and research participants are not fixed and that our identities as researchers are constructed in relation to the research participants (Barker & Smith, 2010). Writing about this, Holmes (1998, p. 19) refers to the importance of adopting the "friend role," where the fieldworker exerts no authority over children and that the key ingredients to achieve this are "expressing positive feelings and a desire to be with the children, the failure to deliver discipline, and treating the children with respect." In the context of this study, the time spent visiting and observing children as they engaged in musical activities provided multiple opportunities for the researcher to develop a strong relationship with children in advance of detailed conversations with them as part of the study. During my conversations, I sat with children in diverse locations. Sometimes we sat at tables, on their chairs, on the floor or close to a school fence outside.

At the end of the interviews with children, I thanked the children for participating and explained that I was now going to listen again to the recordings and start to write about their collective ideas of the role of music in their lives. In the case of adults that participated in the research, I thanked them for participating and assured them of anonymity. I outlined that I was going to write up a thesis, and if they were interested that I would forward them sections of the work including their quotations before submission of a final draft. This process gave the adult participants the opportunity to withdraw or alter any ideas or quotations that had been gathered throughout the interview process. It also gave them the opportunity to submit any additional comments or thoughts that had come to mind after the interview process. One interviewee decided to forward me additional comments via email.

REVIEWING CHILDREN'S PERSPECTIVES: DATA ANALYSIS

The process of analyzing data for this study is informed by approaches to data analysis of ethnographic material and to the creation of ethnographic texts, as outlined by Richards (2005), Crang and Cook (2007), and Maykut and Morehouse (1994). Similarly, literature that focuses on the areas of ethnography (Emerson et al.; 2011; Krüger, 2008) and narrative enquiry (Clandinin & Connelly, 2000) informs the creation of the ethnographic narrative. The transcriptions of the sets of observations and the interviews with children took place after the fieldwork phase was completed. The transcription of any supplementary interviews with adults such as teachers, music coordinators, or visiting music specialists also took place at this time. The transcripts combined with fieldnotes and reflections were used in the analysis of the data. Drawings and images collected during the interviews were also included in the analysis.

Once all of the transcriptions were read and reviewed individually, a system of coding of data began. Keywords and ideas were circled in each interview transcript and inputted into an Excel file. Approximately 120 keywords were created during this method. Writing about this process, Krüger (2008) states that "the coding of data begins at a basic level so as to identify 'meaning units' in the data" (p. 111). She emphasizes how complex this process is and how there often is lack of transparency in how this emerges in ethnographic data analysis. The keywords were reviewed and grouped into the provisional themes and strands. Themes emerged in various ways but most particularly from repeated keywords that were linked or connected. Once the themes were identified, files were created and themed sections of interviews were inserted into the relevant files. In instances where some passages of material linked to more than one theme, the material was colored coded and inserted into two or more themed files. Following Krüger (2008), Richards (2005), Crang and Cook (2007), and Emerson et al. (2011), I analyzed the themes and sub-themes that emerged from the interview and observation data. They are combined into three areas which were further explored in fieldwork analysis.

SUMMARY OF CHAPTER

This chapter explored how children's views have become central in research studies across a wide range of disciplines. It discussed frameworks of participation in research studies and methodological approaches to carrying our research studies that elevate children's voices. Ethical considerations are central to carrying out research with children. Working ethically is vital and parameters exist to how research is carried out with children. This chapter discussed in detail how I carried out the research with due consideration of ethics and how this was negotiated at every stage of the research process. This chapter also provided insight into the approach used in the data analysis and interviews and how this data was used to create the ethnographic narrative that shared children's perspectives and views on their musical worlds. It highlights the importance of using interactive methods to listen to children and the value of ethnographic fieldwork as a methodological approach that provides participatory methods of research to elevate children's voices.

Questions for Reflection

1. Consider how ethnographic fieldwork methods could be incorporated within your own area of research.
2. How can the concept of listening be integrated into research studies that explore children's views and perspectives?
3. How can methods of participant observation provide researchers with opportunities to understand different aspects of children's lives?

Suggestions for Further Reading

Theme: Children as Active Researchers

Greig, A., Taylor, J., & MacKay, T. (2013). *Doing research with children: A practical guide* (3rd ed.). London, England: SAGE.

Kellett, M. (2010). Small shoes, big steps! Empowering children as active researchers. *American Journal of Community Psychology, 46*(1–2), 195–203.

Christensen, P., & James, A. (Eds.). (2017). *Research with children: Perspectives and practices* (3rd ed.). New York, NY: Routledge.

Theme: Ethnographic methods in Ethnomusicological research with children

Barz, G., & Cooley, T. J. (Eds.). (2008). *Shadows in the field: new perspectives for fieldwork in ethnomusicology,* (2nd ed.). Oxford, England: Oxford University Press.

Campbell, P. S. (2010). *Songs in their heads,* (2nd ed.). New York, NY: Oxford University Press.

Campbell, P. S., & Wiggins, T. (Eds.). (2013). *The Oxford handbook of children's musical cultures.* New York, NY: Oxford University Press.

NOTES

1. Techniques include the use of visual and written materials, drawings, child-generated photographs, observations and verbal communication with children, child conferencing (interviews with children), map making, and children led tours of settings.
2. The DEIS programme is run by the Department of Education and Skills and represents a range of national programmes that aim to address educational inclusion throughout the public school system in Ireland. For more information see www.citizensinformation.ie (Accessed November, 2013).
3. In 2012, statistics released by the DES on the profile of schools in Ireland reveals that over 97% of primary schools in Ireland are run by the Catholic Church in association with the board of management and the DES. Alongside

the categories such as single-sex, co-educational, English language medium, and Irish medium language schools, there exists other socio-economic differentiations such as DEIS schools and rural schools and urban schools.

4. Overall, parental consent for their children to become research participants was quite high with over 96% positive response rate from the forms distributed.

5. Reggio Emelia is an educational approach to pre-school education developed in Italy in the 1990s.

REFERENCES

Barker, J., & Smith, F. (2010). Power, positionality and practicality: Carrying out fieldwork with children. *Ethics, Place & Environment, 4*(2), 142–147.

Barz, G., & Cooley, T. J. (Eds.). (2008). *Shadows in the field: New perspectives for fieldwork in ethnomusicology,* (2nd ed.). Oxford, England: Oxford University Press.

Brewer, J. (2000). *Ethnography—Understanding social research.* England: Open University Press.

Campbell, P. S. (1998). *Songs in their heads.* New York, NY: Oxford University Press.

Campbell, P. S. (2010). *Songs in their heads* (2nd ed.). New York, NY: Oxford University Press.

Campbell, P. S., & Wiggins, T. (Eds.). (2013). *The Oxford handbook of children's musical cultures.* New York, NY: Oxford University Press.

Christensen, P., & James, A. (Eds.). (2017). *Research with children: Perspectives and practices,* (3rd ed.). New York, NY: Routledge.

Clandinin, J. D., & Connelly, M. F. (2000). *Narrative inquiry: Experience and story in qualitative research.* San Francisco, CA: Jossey-Bass.

Clark, A., & Moss, P. (2001). *Listening to young children—The mosaic approach* (2nd ed.). London, England: National Children's Bureau.

Clark, A., & Moss, P. (2005). *Spaces to play: More listening to young children using the mosaic approach.* London, England: National Children's Bureau.

Crang, M., & Cook, I. (2007). *Doing ethnographies.* London, England: SAGE.

Denzin N. K., & Lincoln, Y. S. (Eds.). (2008). *Strategies of qualitative inquiry.* Thousand Oaks, CA: SAGE.

Emerson, R. M., Fretz, R. I., & Shaw, L. L. (2011). *Writing ethnographic fieldnotes* (2nd ed.). Chicago, IL: The University of Chicago Press.

Greig, A., Taylor, J., & MacKay, T. (2013). *Doing research with children: A practical guide* (3rd ed.). London, England: SAGE.

Hart, R. (1992). *Children's participation: The theory and practice of involving young citizens in community development and environmental care for UNICEF in 1997.* London, England: EarthScan.

Holloway, S. L., & Valentine, G (2005). *Children's geographies: Playing, living, learning.* London, England: Routledge.

Holmes, R. (1998). *Fieldwork with Children.* London, England: SAGE.

Hogan, D. (2005). Researching the children in developmental psychology. In S. Green & D. Hogan (Eds.), *Researching children's experiences, approaches and methods.* London, England: SAGE.

Kellett, M. (2002, September). *Empowering able 10-year-olds as active researchers.* Paper presented at Annual Conference of the British Educational Research Association, Herriot Watt University, Edinburgh.

Kellett, M. (2003, September). *Enhancing pupils' learning skills through their engagement with research process.* Paper presented at Research in Practice Conference, Westminster Institute of Education, Oxford.

Kellett, M. (2004). Developing critical thinking skills in 10–12 year-olds through their active engagement in research. *Teaching Thinking Skills, 14,* 32–40.

Kellett, M. (2005a). *Developing children as researchers.* London, England: Chapman.

Kellett, M. (2005b). *Children as active researchers: A new research paradigm for the 21st century?* Swindon, England: ESRC.

Kellett, M. (2010). Small shoes, big steps! Empowering children as active researchers. *American Journal of Community Psychology, 46*(1–2), 195–203.

Kellett, M., & Ding, S. (2004). Middle childhood. In S. Fraser, V. Lewis, S. Ding, M. Kellett, & C. Robinson (Eds.), *Doing research with children and young people.* London, England: SAGE.

Krüger, S. (2008). *Ethnography in the performing arts: A student guide.* Liverpool, England: JMU/Palatine.

Layder, D., (1993). *New strategies in social research.* Cambridge, England: Polity Press.

Maykut, P., & Morehouse, R. (1994). *Beginning qualitative research: A philosophic and practical guide.* London, England: Routledge.

Murray, J. (2016). Young children are researchers: Children aged four to eight years engage in important research behaviour when they base decisions on evidence. *European Early Childhood Education Research Journal, 24*(5), 705–720.

Myers, H. (1992). *Ethnomusicology: An introduction.* New York, NY: MacMillan.

Prout, A., & James, A. (1997). *Constructing and reconstructing childhood: Contemporary issues in the sociological study of childhood.* London, England: Falmer Press.

Richards, L. (2005). *Handling qualitative data: A practical guide.* London, England: SAGE.

Rice, T. (2017). *Modelling ethnomusicology.* New York, NY: Oxford University Press.

Rinaldi, C. (2005). Documentation and assessment: What is the relationship? In A. Clark, A. Kjørholt, & P. Moss (Eds.), *Beyond listening: Children's perspectives on early childhood services* (pp. 17–28). Bristol, England: Policy Press.

CHAPTER 18

ADOLESCENT VOICES

Empowering Haitian Immigrant Youth Through Privileging Narratives

Lauren Christian Gibson

ABSTRACT

Empowering children in the research process requires giving youth a voice to actively engage in the production of knowledge. One way to do this is through narrative inquiry. This qualitative study privileges the voices of the Haitian immigrant community in New York City by examining how Haitian adolescents comprehend their own educational adaptations. The narratives that emanate from this study demonstrate the complexities of the educational adaptations of adolescent immigrants. Participants' cumulative stories illuminate the dissonance that exists between the Haitian community and U.S. schools in terms of teachers' roles, methods of learning and assessment, and perceptions of education. The author addresses the agency of Haitian adolescents to improve the schooling process for immigrants by constructing an understanding of their home culture and lives in U.S. classrooms. Moll, Amanti, Neff, and Gonzalez's (1992) notion of "funds of knowledge" focuses on building on the knowledge and cultural capital that children of marginalized groups bring to school. Funds of knowledge examines the strengths and resources

Participatory Methodologies to Elevate Children's Voice and Agency, pages 405–422
Copyright © 2019 by Information Age Publishing
405

of adolescents with the premise that people have expertise that comes from their life experiences, and students' home cultures are a resource for education. Narrative inquiry gives children a voice to articulate the funds of knowledge they use to understand and shape their lives in the United States while navigating U.S. schools.

Researchers have begun to explore the role of children and youth as contributors in the research process, resulting in increased studies involving young people as agents in the production of knowledge (Alderson, 2015; Christensen, 2004; Gallacher & Gallagher, 2008; Groundwater-Smith, Dockett, & Bottrell, 2015; Kellett, Forrest, Dent, & Ward, 2004; Tisdall, 2017). Despite an increase in studies involving youth, very few studies have involved Haitian adolescent immigrants attending U.S. schools (Paez, 2009).

Haitian immigrants are a group that has steadily increased in numbers, especially in urban centers such as New York City, Boston, and Miami. Estimates suggest that over 30,000 Haitian students attend the New York City (NYC) public schools (Joseph, 2010). Although a significant number of Haitians attend NYC schools and U.S. schools, there is a dearth of research involving Haitian immigrant youth in the United States (Doucet, Schwartz, & Debraggio, 2011; Doucet & Suárez-Orozco, 2006; Nicolas, DeSilva, & Rabenstein, 2009). Including and empowering children, particularly Haitian adolescents, in the research process requires giving youth a voice to actively engage in the production of knowledge. One way to do this is through narrative inquiry.

Narrative inquiry is a case-centered approach best suited for capturing the life experiences and stories of a small group of people (Creswell & Poth, 2017; Riessman, 2008). "Simply put, narrative inquiry is the study of experience understood narratively" (Clandinin, Caine, Lessard, & Huber, 2016, p. 15). Narrative inquiry allows the researcher to gain an understanding of adolescents from their own perspectives. As Seidman (2006) argues, narrative inquiry "is a powerful way to gain insight into educational and other important social issues through understanding the experience of the individuals whose lives reflect those issues" (p. 14).

METHODOLOGY: EMPOWERING ADOLESCENT HAITIAN IMMIGRANTS IN RESEARCH

This study utilized narrative inquiry in order to examine how Haitian transnational adolescents understood their own educational adaptations. Transnationalism is the term used to explain the "process by which transmigrants, through their daily activities, forge and sustain multi-stranded social, economic, and political relations that link together their societies of origin and settlement, and through which they create transnational social fields that cross national borders" (Basch, Glick-Schiller, & Szanton-Blanc, 1994, p. 6). Based on the literature, it is clear that family, community, and adolescent Haitian students' transnational lives, including their previous educational experience in Haiti, play a strong role in how they adapt to the new culture and invest U.S. schools (Doucet, 2005; Doucet & Suárez-Orozco, 2006; Paez, 2009; Zephir, 2001, 2004).

Narrative inquiry as a methodology privileges the voice of the immigrant student, which contrasts with previous studies that focused on acculturation from a stance ascribed by the dominant group rather than from understanding immigrant adaptation from *their* perspective (Kelley, 1982; Stauble, 1981). Thus, this study provides insight into how adolescent Haitian immigrant students in NYC, who lead transnational lives, invest in their schooling.

RESEARCHER'S POSITIONING

Narrative inquiry is situated in relationships, including the relationship between the participants and the researcher. Clandinin et al. (2016) note that "it is not the experience of the other that we are studying; rather, we are studying our experience as inquirers in relation with the experience of participants" (p. 25). Clandinin et al. (2016) stress the importance of the researcher positioning herself into the research by "beginning with autobiographical narrative inquiries, or what we call narrative beginnings" (p. 25). Hence, it is important that I write myself into the story as I filtered participants' experiences through my own life history.

I am a White woman from Kentucky who visited Haiti often as a teenager with my family in order to conduct aide or missionary work. I remember confronting linguicism[1] for the first time in a bank in Port-au-Prince, Haiti. I had gone to the bank with my mother, sister, and an interpreter. In the line beside us was a Haitian gentleman who spoke Creole but did not speak French. The teller refused to conduct business with him in Creole, insisting that he speak French. Our interpreter ended up interpreting in French and Creole for this man in order to help him make his transaction. When he turned away to leave, however, I heard the teller speaking Creole with the teller beside her. Yet, the teller refused to speak Creole with the gentleman who was a monolingual Creole speaker, denigrating him for his inability to conduct the transaction in French. This experience led me to see how linguistic discrimination can disempower people, and spurred my interest in giving voice to marginalized groups including marginalized immigrants, specifically Haitian youth, in the United States.

It is not surprising, then, that I would choose narrative inquiry as a methodology for this study, as it is consistent with my own belief in positioning research from an emic perspective. I believe that hearing and understanding the adolescents' stories from the perspective of the community and in the community is the best way to provide insight into how Haitian immigrant students in New York City, who lead transnational lives, invest in their schooling. Seidman (2006) asserts that researchers interview because they value others' stories. "Most simply put, stories are a way of knowing" (Seidman, 2006, p. 7). Hence, I have a favorable predisposition towards hearing the Haitian students' stories through their voices.

My position as an outsider, a White American adult woman in academia researching the Haitian community, influenced the research process and analysis of the data, as I did not speak Creole but relied on interpreters and the limited English of newcomers in order to hear participants' stories. In addition, I filtered participants' stories through the lens of my experiences as an American woman who attended school in the United States system and grew up speaking English, a language of power in the United States. Furthermore, it is likely that because participants viewed me as an outsider, the stories they shared and the information they gave me may have differed from what they would have told an insider.

CONTEXT

This study took place at a community-based organization (CBO), Haitian Adolescent Immigrant Group (HAIG). HAIG, a CBO for Haitian English Language Learners ages 14 to 21, is the only CBO in New York City to focus exclusively on servicing and meeting the educational adaptation needs of adolescent Haitian immigrants. It is located in the heart of the Caribbean community in Brooklyn, NY in Flatbush. Flatbush is a neighborhood in community District 14 (Brooklyn Neighborhood Reports, 2012). According to the Brooklyn Neighborhood Reports (2012), the top five places of birth of residents of community District 14 were New York State (48.4%), Haiti (7.2%), Trinidad and Tobago (3.9%), Mexico (3.6%), and Jamaica (2.6%), underscoring the presence of Caribbean immigrants and the high Haitian population in this neighborhood. The transnational lifestyle of many of the residents in this neighborhood is indicated by colorful Caribbean storefronts; Caribbean music blasting from cars; stores that sell barrels, which are used to send all kinds of necessities back to the Caribbean; restaurants that serve "Caribbean American" food; travel agencies advertising special rates to the Caribbean; and shops that sell "phone cards" to call to the Caribbean.

HAIG was founded in 2005 by a Haitian woman who has undergone the immigration process herself, so she serves as a cultural broker between Haitian immigrants and the dominant U.S. society. Active members of HAIG consist of around 60 to 70 youth, most of whom are ages 17 to 21. This CBO offers programs and services to help students adapt to U.S. culture and to U.S. schools. For example, HAIG assists Haitian English Language Learners in accessing appropriate high schools within the NYC public school system that can meet their needs; provides a space for students to discuss experiences and educational issues, allowing youth to reach out to their peers; and organizes cultural activities to provide students with learning experiences that facilitate the acquisition of critical thinking skills and leadership skills at the same time as building self-esteem as well as strengthening community ties and cultural awareness (Daniella, personal communication, December 15, 2010).

Because HAIG is informally organized with divergent activities and events that students can engage in at different levels, adolescents' participation at HAIG varies from regularly using the computers to participating in a weekly literacy circle for middle-school aged girls, to attending an annual special event such as the Haitian Flag Day celebration. Furthermore, HAIG is a dominant force in disseminating news and information to the Haitian community in New York City by using radio, a common means of communication for Haitians. For instance, on radio, the director notes the importance of students enrolling in school as soon as they arrive in the United States rather than waiting until they have learned English (Daniella, personal communication, December 15, 2010).

PARTICIPANTS

For this study, there are six participants, five students and the center director. From the five students, three were selected as focal participants. Much like Doucet, Grayman-Simpson, and Wertheim's (2013) study, three focal participants were selected from the five adolescents as an adaptation of Glaser and Strauss' (1967) concept of theoretical sampling. This notion calls for researchers to intentionally identify participants who can represent or illustrate specific theoretical constructs to examine as many facets of a phenomenon as possible. Though I did not choose my participants for the study in this manner, after my data collection was completed I selected focal participants from my five student participants whose stories best illuminated the educational adaptations of adolescent Haitian immigrants.

The selection process consisted of two levels based on certain criteria. The five adolescent students from HAIG who served as participants met the following criteria: they were born in Haiti, involved in HAIG, and attended an NYC public school at the time of the interviews. The adolescent participants attended a range of schools with differing language programs provided. Once participants were identified, I selected adolescent focal participants who represented an array of grade levels from 9th grade to 12th grade and a range of length of time of involvement in HAIG from 2 months to 3 years.

The focal participants were representative of the larger group in many ways, yet I chose to focus on them because they all seemed to demonstrate qualities of leadership, determination, and ability to overcome struggle, important attributes necessary for educational adaptation. The focal participants' narratives were the focus of member checking supported by relevant data from the secondary participants. Table 18.1 illustrates characteristics of the participants from HAIG with an asterisk beside the focal participants and brief descriptions of the focal participants and the director of HAIG.

Claudette is a petite girl who dresses femininely and conservatively. When she lived in Haiti, her school was shut down for nearly seven months due to the 2010 earthquake until it could be moved and reopened on the top of a mountain. At the time of the interviews, she had been in the United States for only 2½ years, yet she had the best English of any of the adolescent participants I interviewed, and she chose to conduct her interviews entirely in English. She is a very confident and articulate young lady. Due to her advanced English proficiency and her ability to critically reflect on her educational adaptations, her narrative tended to dominate her fellow adolescents' stories.

Casseus is a young man who initially appeared shy but was eager to tell the story of his life in Haiti and the United States. He lives in the United

TABLE 18.1 Profile of Participants at HAIG

Pseudonym	Gender	Age	Grade	Length of Residence in the United States	Length of Time in HAIG	Language Programs Offered at Participants' School(s)
Claudette*	Female	14 years	9th	2.5 years	2 months	ESL (Middle) ESL (High)
Casseus*	Male	18 years	11th	3 years	3 years	ESL
Gina*	Female	18 years	12th	2 years	2 years	ESL (1st School) ESL (2nd School)
Reginald	Male	16 years	9th	4 months	4 months	ESL
Marylin	Female	13 years	8th	2 years	2 months	ESL

Note: ESL programs employ strategies for English language development as well as some native language support (Department of English Language Learners and Student Support, 2015). At the time of this study, ESL was the term used for these programs. Currently, the Division of English Language Learners and Student Support (2017) has replaced the term ESL with a new term, English as a New Language Programs (ENL).

States with his grandmother, aunt, and uncle; his father passed away, and his mother lives in Haiti. Casseus is dedicated to improving his English and is involved in several after-school clubs and programs both in Creole and in English. Despite Casseus' limited English proficiency, he desired to conduct his interviews in English, rarely utilizing the interpreter, and choosing to tell stories that illustrated his point when he did not have the desired English vocabulary rather than asking the interpreter to interpret when he needed to negotiate meaning.

Gina is a very slim young lady who speaks barely above a whisper. Despite her quiet nature, she is a strong leader who arranged for a group of students to change schools in order to attend safer schools. Gina lives with her adoptive parents, who are her aunt and uncle, and her two older sisters who are her best friends. Having the most limited English proficiency of all of the focal participants, Gina often struggled to convey her message but appeared to feel shame and embarrassment at having to use the interpreter. Often I had to probe her to use the interpreter and remind her that this was not an English test.

The director of HAIG, Daniella, is a tall lady with a huge smile and a strong voice. She started HAIG in 2005 in response to her experiences teaching ESL in the community and working with adolescents who had not been successful in completing high school in NYC. She spent some of her elementary years in a boarding school in Haiti, learning to read and write in Creole from the director's nephew, a priest, who went against the wishes of his aunt by introducing the students to Creole literacy and the mindset of speaking Creole in social situations where French was expected. She migrated to the United States at the age of 13 and began to learn English in NYC public schools.

DATA COLLECTION

In order to collect data for this narrative inquiry, I used "in-depth, phenomenologically based interviewing" (Seidman, 2006, p. 15). A "phenomenological study describes the meaning for several individuals of their lived experiences of a concept or a phenomenon" (Creswell, 2007, p. 57). I chose phenomenological interviews because I was examining several individuals' experiences, as opposed to a single individual's experience, with respect to a particular phenomenon—in this case, Haitian immigrants educational adaptations. My goal in using this method was to have the participants reconstruct their experiences regarding their educational adaptations by investigating and building upon participants' responses to interview questions. According to Seidman (2006), "people's behavior becomes meaningful and understandable when placed in the context of their lives and the lives of those around them. Without context there is little possibility of exploring the meaning of an experience" (pp. 16–17).

Dolbeare and Schuman (Schuman, 1982) designed the series of three interviews that distinguish this model. The first interview creates the context of the participants' experience. The second asks participants to recount the details of their experiences within the context that the experiences occurred. The third allows participants to make meaning from their experiences (Seidman, 2006).

Given the logistical constraints of conducting three interviews with each participant, I conducted only two interviews with each participant, incorporating meaning making into both interviews one and two in order to collect data for my study. I used interviews solely because of the logistical difficulty of getting other data (e.g., observations, assessment instruments, etc.) from a CBO, which is informally organized in terms of assessments, and student attendance is inconsistent. During the first interview, I asked participants about their lived experiences as students up to the time they came to the United States and the meaning of their lives then. The second interview focused on the participants' lived experiences as students in the United States and the meaning of their lives now. In addition, I asked them about their educational adaptations. The length of time of each interview was a minimum of 30 minutes but total length was flexible to account for open-ended questions.

Participants were given the choice as to the language, English or Creole, in which they would prefer to conduct interviews. For interviews that were conducted in Creole, an interpreter was present. I had access to two Haitian Creole/English interpreters through the director of HAIG. She put me in contact with two college students who attended HAIG as adolescents but currently work as interpreters while pursuing their college degrees. Although the interpreters were provided with the intention of giving participants a language choice in conducting interviews, participants often viewed the interpreters as part of the conversation, including them in the interviews as a community resource on the Haitian adaptation process rather than simply resources to facilitate interviews in two different languages.

The adolescent participants, with the exception of one, were very reluctant to use the interpreter to conduct interviews in Creole, evidencing a forceful desire to use English and assimilate to the dominant culture. The students' tendency to use English in the interviews impacted the findings. As a result of limited English proficiency, some of the adolescents' responses were vague or pat, restricting the context of conversation. Nevertheless, the adolescents' choice to primarily use English provided an important example of agency to assert themselves inside this identity of English speaker in their decision of the language in which to express themselves.

DATA ANALYSIS

The data collected in this study were analyzed using thematic narrative analysis. Riessman (2008) posits that in thematic narrative analysis, concern is placed on the content of what is told rather than the interaction, language, or form of the telling of the story. By gleaning themes from in-depth interviews, this study captured "momentous, historical experiences" as well as found and reconstructed "the compelling in the experiences of everyday life" (Seidman, 2006, p. 123) of adolescent Haitian immigrants as they adapted educationally to life in the United States.

I analyzed the interviews that I had conducted using Seidman's (2006) method of thematic narrative analysis. This method consisted of reading through the transcripts, marking data themes. Throughout this process, I wrote notes about the passages I found significant in order to articulate my thinking process in choosing certain ones as important and selecting some over others. In instances where an interpreter was used to collect data, I met with them to invite their perspective on the interviews as a cultural broker. Hence, I partnered with participants and interpreters to "negotiate the meaning of the stories, adding a validation check to the analysis" (Creswell, 2007, p. 57).

VOICES OF ADOLESCENT HAITIAN IMMIGRANTS: TRANSNATIONAL PERSPECTIVE ON VIEW OF U.S. SCHOOLS

In giving Haitian adolescents a voice to describe their educational adaptations, the focal adolescent participants in my study and the supporting cast of participants, along with the director of HAIG, discussed their engagement in transnational practices by viewing U.S. schools through a Haitian lens. Adolescent participants viewed U.S. schools through the lens of their experiences of Haitian schools. For example, Claudette viewed the U.S. school system as a means to finish her secondary education and possibly receive a scholarship for college. However, she felt that the basis of her education, as well as the motivation to study and succeed, came from her experiences in Haiti. With the exception of the difficulty of learning the English language, Claudette asserted that U.S. schools are "easy" for Haitian students. In discussing U.S. schools, Claudette noted, "I found it easier because most of the things, we did it in Haiti and it is like actually doing it again" (Claudette, May 22, 2013). Even though Claudette claimed to like the US education system better due to an ease in content, she gravitated towards Haitian teachers and school employees, describing the difficulty she experienced with some of the U.S. teaching methods, such as collaborative work, with which she had little to no experience from her Haitian educational background.

Like Claudette, Marylin, a secondary participant, noted that free public schools were a positive aspect of the U.S. education system. This philosophical judgment, based on the idea that free education is something good, demonstrated a deeper appreciation of free schooling based on the more impoverished backgrounds in Haiti from which most of the participants came. Marylin also asserted that schools were easier in the United States because she did not have to memorize large quantities of material, referencing an ease in approach to learning.

> I think an advantage that we have is that we don't need to study like we used to study in Haiti. So we could have good grades but we don't really have to study like we used to study. It used to be like a big chapter and you gotta think everything and you not gonna go slow. You gonna go fast 'cause you not gonna, like, say the thing like one after another. Like it's gonna be four of us standing in front of the teacher and she's watching four of us like that and we got to say it fast. (Marylin, May 20, 2013)

Despite celebrating that U.S. schools were "easier," Marylin also emphasized that she was bored with the U.S. education system.

> The reason that I don't really like it the way that I used to like the Haiti school is because in my school they don't really have things that could make us want to learn. If every day we learn English, Science, Social Studies, Math, and Gym, we have to do, they gotta put dance in the school so the kids, some of us, we think it boring. (Marylin, May 20, 2013)

Mariyln desired added enrichment such as dance classes to make school more rewarding and fun. Ironically, however, when asked to explain what made school in Haiti more enjoyable, she described relationships rather than enrichment. "The teachers be making fun of the kids. It's fun. We making fun of each other . . . the teachers have like a relationship with us" (Marylin, May 20, 2013). She juxtaposed the relationship she had with the Haitian teachers with her interactions with U.S. teachers who would openly say, "the reason that I come here is to just to teach, not to be your friend" (Marylin, May 20, 2013). Interestingly, Mariyln also noted that the teachers in Haiti were treated with more respect than the U.S. teachers, even though the students had more "fun" with the Haitian teachers, reinforcing the high value that participants, coming from the collectivist culture of Haiti, placed on relationships, community, and respect (Ballenger, 1992).

Casseus also described his experiences in U.S. schools through the lens of the circumstances of his Haitian schools. He spoke of getting "beat up" by his Haitian teachers for not knowing his lessons (Casseus, January 28,

2013), resulting in a high affective filter that caused an inability to learn as quickly in Haitian schools when compared to U.S. schools. He expressed an enjoyment for schools in the U.S., which was not present in Haiti. "Like in Haiti, I didn't like the school. Now I like the school. That's a big change that happened in my life" (Casseus, January 28, 2013). Unlike the Haitian system, in U.S. schools he was able to thrive due to an ease in discipline that differed sharply from the rigidity of Haitian schools, reflecting participants' appreciation for no corporal punishment in schools, as they came from a Haitian educational environment where such punishment was often used (Ballenger, 1992; Dejean, 2010).

Casseus expressed disdain for the Haitian school system, contrasting starkly with his heavy engagement in Haitian organizations in the U.S. education system such as HAIG and his school's Haitian Club. Casseus gave an example of one of the discussions they had in Haitian Club where they had parties and brainstormed about ways to make Haiti better, describing how they "talk about Haiti, how did the earthquake happen, how we supposed to resolve that problems, to make Haiti became more pretty" (Casseus, January 28, 2013).

Gina's discussion of schools in Haiti and the U.S. highlighted a difference between the two systems in perception of assessment. "My school in Haiti is different from here. In Haiti, you have to study, study, like, keep it in your head, and when you study you have to recite the lessons you have received, that they teach you" (Gina, January 31, 2013). Gina detailed the difficulty of the Haitian system of rote memorization of the textbook and teachers' notes (Zainuddin, Yahya, Morales-Jones, & Ariza, 2002). Yet, she asserted that she had never been punished for forgetting her lesson in Haiti because she had learned how to succeed in that system. She appreciated that she always knew what would be assessed in Haitian schools, differing from U.S. schools, where material that she studied was often not assessed.

Though Gina commented on the ease in approach to learning in U.S. schools, she noted that she was retaking her Living Environments class as she had failed this Regents exam twice. Gina's experience underscored the complexity of students' struggles in the U.S. system that does not require as much rote memorization but demands abstract reasoning, critical thinking, an ability to identify main ideas, and connect content to other disciplines as well as real life while deciphering what is most important to understand (De-Capua & Marshall, 2010). Participants from a Haitian system that values rote memorization often find this critical aspect of the U.S. system challenging.

Perhaps the most potent example of differences in the U.S. and Haitian school systems came from Reginald, a secondary participant, who had been in the United States for 4 months at the time of his interviews. In his NYC school, he had been placed in the ninth grade even though he had just completed sixth grade in Haiti. He was the only adolescent participant who chose to use an interpreter throughout all of the interviews, as he was the newest arrived adolescent immigrant. During our sessions, he kept his eyes averted downward, gave short responses in Creole, and appeared nervous. When asked about why he came to the United States, he replied in a barely audible voice, "because it's better in here" (Reginald, May 23, 2013). I probed his answer to find out what he meant, to which his only response was that "everybody goes to school here" (Reginald, May 23, 2013). In a similar manner, when I inquired about his teachers in Haiti, he said that he liked them "because they help me to learn very well" (Reginald, May 23, 2013).

After the interviews were concluded and Reginald had exited the building, the interpreter asserted that Reginald was a product of the Haitian school system that encourages students to regurgitate memorized responses, or commonly held beliefs, without questioning their own beliefs or being able to think for themselves. The interpreter also stated that this was probably Reginald's first time sharing his experiences with someone in an interview setting, a type of interaction that is not common in Haitian culture. Reginald's interviews were seemingly short and simple, yet the message of his former style of schooling and his context as a recently arrived Haitian immigrant came out strongly in the manner in which he spoke and in what he didn't say.

Reginald provided a glimpse of a student who had been schooled almost exclusively in the Haitian system, which was reflected in his perspective of U.S. schools through the lens of experiences in Haitian schools. His response that the United States was better than Haiti because everyone attended school in the United States was another philosophical judgment based on the idea that universal education is something good. In addition, his statement underscored participants' deeper appreciation of educational access, coming from the Haitian reality of limited access to schools. Reginald's response reinforced findings from M. Suárez-Orozco's (1987) study on recent arrivals from El Salvador, Guatemala, and Nicaragua who noted the importance of access to U.S. schools, which they compared to the limited opportunities for schooling in their home countries. In addition, Daniella pointed out:

> Especially in Haiti, education is not so accessible to everyone so there is that for families. When young people coming here they have many challenges because if you're an individual or your parents could pay your school for you then it was good. For many students that wasn't the case. There is a public school in Haiti. It's the opposite, 80% private, 20% public. Not too many kids get into the public school. The rest the parents have to pay. Paying for school and everything that comes with it is very difficult. (Daniella, January 28, 2013)

Haitian immigrant students, like Reginald, took a transnational perspective on their views of U.S. schools, influenced by their experiences in Haiti.

Moreover, in discussing perspectives of easiness that were filtered through the lens of another culture, participants demonstrated an approach to learning that was socialized in Haiti while simultaneously struggling with differing expectations of U.S. schools. Hence, adolescents illustrated a mismatch in Haitian cultural expectations and the reality of U.S. schools.

DISCUSSION: MISMATCH IN HAITIAN CULTURAL EXPECTATIONS AND REALITY OF U.S. SCHOOLS

There are numerous disconnects between the U.S. school system and the Haitian schooling community from which the youth came. In spite of the fact that the majority of newly arrived immigrants, including the Haitian participants in this study, live transnational lives, most schools do not acknowledge this reality (Sánchez, 2004, 2007, 2008; Sánchez & Machado-Casas, 2009). The adolescent participants discussed the difficulty in enrolling in the U.S. system, echoing Zephir's (2001) assertion that entering the New York City public schools is a very difficult, overwhelming, and unfamiliar process for Haitian immigrant students and their parents. Daniella explained, "the Department of Education itself doesn't do a great job of letting parents know what's involved and what exists and doesn't exist. We have to do that" (Daniella, January 28, 2013).

In addition, adolescent participants frequently reinforced Locher's (2010) assertion that grade placement for newly-arrived Haitian immigrants in the United States could be problematic as students discussed being forced to repeat a grade that they had completed in Haiti or placed in a grade that was significantly higher than what they had participated in in Haiti. For example, Gina completed 10th grade in Haiti and was placed back in 10th grade when she arrived in New York at the age of 16 years old. At the time of our interviews, she was 18 years old and in 11th grade.

Although visible differences such as enrollment and grade placement were problematic, subtle cultural differences and misunderstandings that came as a result of transnational practices and understandings appeared to cause the greatest difficulty as the differences were often interpreted as deficits rather than differences. Claudette asserted that in Haiti the teachers care enough about the students to punish them so that they won't repeat incorrect behavior, but in the United States, teachers might not spend the necessary time and energy to correct students' poor behavior. Subtlety in difference is a matter of interpretation as Claudette interpreted the U.S. teachers' behavior as lack of caring based on her cultural frame of reference in terms of how teachers are expected to behave. She noted that in the United States, "not all teachers are going to spend their time talking to you when you did something bad. They are going to be like, 'get out of the classroom,' and they are done with you" (Claudette, May 22, 2013). She juxtaposed the response of teachers in the United States with teachers in Haiti.

> They are going to say, "you are going to stay on one feet," or "you are going to stand up in the classroom." Everybody is sitting there and then after 1 hour or 30 minutes, they will be like, "you can sit down now." And you will be like, "oh, what I did was wrong," and you not going to do it again to not stand up by yourself in the classroom. (Claudette, May 22, 2013)

The adolescent participants' interviews also revealed that the underlying attitudes, beliefs, values, and worldviews that differ from the wider U.S. attitudes, created tension and misunderstanding in the classroom. Marylin noted that she was "smarter" than her fellow classmates from the United States because she treated her teachers with more respect, demonstrating that her judgment of one's intellect was based on Haitian cultural beliefs that place a high emphasis on respecting teachers and elders. "I think I'm smarter than them. Not only the knowledge, but the way that I act. I don't act the way, the foolish way that they act" (Marylin, May 20, 2013).

The adolescents illuminated the differences, difficulties, and tensions for Haitian youth in U.S. schools, illustrating the dissonance between the Haitian community and schools. Thus, the participants' stories provide opportunities for change in the education of Haitian youth in the United States.

CONCLUSION: AGENCY OF HAITIAN YOUTH IN VOICING FUNDS OF KNOWLEDGE

By empowering students to share their stories through narrative inquiry, Haitian adolescents demonstrate agency to improve the schooling process for immigrants by constructing an understanding of their home culture and lives in U.S. classrooms. Moll, Amanti, Neff, and Gonzalez's (1992) notion of "funds of knowledge" focuses on building on the knowledge and cultural capital that children of marginalized groups bring to school. Funds of knowledge examines the strengths and resources of adolescents with the premise that people have expertise that comes from their life experiences, and students' home cultures are a resource for education.

Narrative inquiry gives Haitian youth a voice to articulate the funds of knowledge they use to understand and shape their lives in the United States while navigating U.S. schools. Teachers, administrators, and stakeholders must build on the Haitian community's funds of knowledge in order to expand on participants' strengths and make schooling relevant. Delpit (2006) stresses the importance of learning about children's lives in order to learn their strengths. "Not knowing students' strengths leads to our 'teaching down' to children from communities that are culturally different from that of the teachers in the school" (p. 173). Similarly, Darling-Hammond (1997) asserts that schools must build family and community connections in order to gain knowledge about students, which allows schools to teach effectively and to strengthen relationships that promote child development.

Questions for Reflection

1. The implementation of narrative inquiry as a research methodology can be complex as the researcher is directly involving participants who often lead busy, intricate, and, at times, difficult lives. In the case of this particular study, what were some of the unique factors that impacted the data collection and analysis process?
2. The researcher's positioning as an English-speaking, White, American, adult, female in academia impacted the process of using narrative inquiry to give a voice to Haitian immigrant adolescents to share their stories. How can the researcher address position when using narrative inquiry as a methodology?
3. Revisit a study that you have recently read involving children. Was narrative inquiry used as a methodology to engage the children in the active production of knowledge? In not, how could narrative inquiry have been an alternative or additional methodology to enrich the findings and empower the participants?

Suggestions for Further Reading

Clandinin, D. J., Caine, V., Lessard, S., & Huber, J. (2016). *Engaging in narrative inquiries with children*. New York, NY: Routledge.

Creswell, J. W., & Poth, C. N. (2017). *Qualitative inquiry and research design: Choosing among five approaches* (4th ed.). Thousand Oaks, CA: SAGE.

Riessman, C. K. (2008). *Narrative methods for the human sciences*. Thousand Oaks, CA: SAGE.

Seidman, I. (2013). *Interviewing as qualitative research: A guide for researchers in education and the social sciences*. New York, NY: Teachers College Press.

NOTE

1. Phillipson (1992) defines linguicism as the "ideologies, structures, and practices which are used to legitimate, effectuate, and reproduce an unequal division of power and resources (both material and immaterial) between groups which are defined on the basis of language" (p. 47).

REFERENCES

Alderson, P. (2015). Ethics of research with children. In O. Saracho (Ed.), *Handbook of Research Methods in Early Childhood Education* (pp. 633–654). Charlotte, NC: Information Age.

Ballenger, C. (1992). Because you like us: The language of control. *Harvard Educational Review*, 62(2), 199–208.

Basch, L. G., Glick-Schiller, N., & Szanton-Blanc, C. (1994). *Nations unbound: Transnational projects, postcolonial predicaments, and deterritorialized nation-states*. New York, NY: Gordon and Breach Science.

Brooklyn Neighborhood Reports. (2012). Retrieved from http://www.brooklyncommunityfoundation.org/your-community/information-for-action/brooklyn-neighborhood-reports

Clandinin, D. J., Caine, V., Lessard, S., & Huber, J. (2016). *Engaging in narrative inquiries with children*. New York, NY: Routledge.

Christensen, P. H. (2004). Children's participation in ethnographic research: Issues of power and representation. *Children & Society*, 18(2), 165–176.

Creswell, J. W. (2007). *Qualitative inquiry and research design: Choosing among five approaches* (2nd ed.). Thousand Oaks, CA: SAGE.

Creswell, J. W., & Poth, C. N. (2017). *Qualitative inquiry and research design: Choosing among five approaches* (4th ed.). Thousand Oaks, CA: SAGE.

Darling-Hammond, L. (1997). *The right to learn: A blueprint for creating schools that work*. San Francisco, CA: Wiley.

DeCapua, A., & Marshall, H. W. (2010). Students with limited or interrupted formal education in US classrooms. *Urban Review*, 42, 159–173.

Dejean, Y. (2010). Creole and education in Haiti. In A. K. Spears & C. M. B. Joseph (Eds.), *The Haitian Creole language: History, structure, use, and education* (pp. 199–216). Lanham, MD: Lexington Books.

Delpit, L. D. (2006). *Other people's children: Cultural conflict in the classroom*. New York, NY: The New Press.

Department of English Language Learners and Student Support. (2015). Retrieved from http://schools.nyc.gov/Academics/ELL/default.htm

Division of English Language Learners and Student Support. (2017). Retrieved from http://schools.nyc.gov/Academics/ELL/default.htm

Doucet, F. (2005). Divergent realities: The home and school lives of Haitian immigrant youth. *Journal of Youth Ministry*, 3(2), 37–65.

Doucet, F., Grayman-Simpson, N., & Wertheim, S. S. (2013). Steps along the journey: Documenting undergraduate White women's transformative processes in a diversity course. *Journal of Diversity in Higher Education*, 6(4), 276–291.

Doucet, F., Schwartz, A. E., & Debraggio, E. (2011). *Beyond Black: Diversity among Black immigrant students in New York City public schools*. Washington, DC: Migration Policy Institute's National Center on Immigrant Integration Policy.

Doucet, F., & Suárez-Orozco, C. (2006). Ethnic identity and schooling: The experiences of Haitian immigrant youth. In L. Romanucci-Ross, G. De Vos, & T. Tsuda (Eds.), *Ethnic identity: Creation, conflict, and accommodation* (4th ed., pp. 163–188). Walnut Creek, CA: Altamira Press.

Gallacher, L.-A., & Gallagher, M. (2008). Methodological immaturity in childhood research? Thinking through 'participatory methods'. *Childhood, 15*(4), 499–516.

Glaser, B. G., & Strauss, A. L. (1967). *The discovery of grounded theory: Strategies for qualitative research.* Chicago, IL: Aldine.

Groundwater-Smith, S., Dockett, S., & Bottrell, D. (2015). *Participatory research with children and young people.* Los Angeles, CA: SAGE.

Joseph, C. M. B. (2010). Haitians in the U.S.: Language, politics, and education. In A. K. Spears & C. M. B. Joseph (Eds.), *The Haitian Creole language: History, structure, use, and education* (pp. 229–248). Lanham, MD: Lexington Books.

Kellett, M., Forrest, R., Dent, N., & Ward, S. (2004). 'Just teach us the skills please, we'll do the rest': Empowering ten-year-olds as active researchers. *Children & Society, 18*(5), 329–343.

Kelley, J. P. (1982). *Interlanguage variation and social/psychological influences within a developmental stage* (Unpublished master's thesis). University of California Los Angeles, Los Angeles, CA.

Locher, U. (2010). Education in Haiti. In A. K. Spears & C. M. B. Joseph (Eds.), *The Haitian Creole language: History, structure, use, and education* (pp. 177–198). Lanham, MD: Lexington Books.

Moll, L. C., Amanti, C., Neff, D., & Gonzalez, N. (1992). Funds of knowledge for teaching: Using a qualitative approach to connect homes and classrooms. *Theory into Practice, 31*(1), 132–141.

Nicolas, G., DeSilva, A., & Rabenstein, K. (2009). Educational attainment of Haitian immigrants. *Urban Education, 44*(6), 664–686.

Paez, M. (2009). Predictors of English-language proficiency among immigrant youth. *Bilingual Research Journal, 32*, 168–187.

Phillipson, R. (1992). *Linguistic imperialism.* Oxford, England: Oxford University Press.

Riessman, C. K. (2008). *Narrative methods for the human sciences.* Thousand Oaks, CA: SAGE.

Sánchez, P. (2004). *At home in two places: Second-generation Mexicanas and their lives as engaged transnationals* (Doctoral dissertation). Retrieved from ProQuest Dissertations & Theses Database. (3165549)

Sánchez, P. (2007). Urban immigrant students: How transnationalism shapes their world learning. *The Urban Review, 39*(5), 489–517.

Sánchez, P. (2008). Coming of age across borders: Family, gender, and place in the lives of second-generation transnational Mexicanas. In R. Marquez & H. Romo (Eds.), *Transformations of la familia on the U.S.–Mexico border* (pp. 185–208). Notre Dame, IN: Notre Dame Press.

Sánchez, P., & Machado-Casas, M. (2009). At the intersection of transnationalism, Latina/o immigrants, and education. *The High School Journal, 92*(4), 3–15.

Schuman, D. (1982). *Policy analysis, education, and everyday life.* Lexington, MA: Heath.

Seidman, I. (2006). *Interviewing as qualitative research: A guide for researchers in education and the social sciences.* New York, NY: Teachers College Press.

Stauble, A. M. (1981). *A comparative study of a Spanish-English and Japanese- English second language continuum: Verb phrase morphology* (Unpublished doctoral dissertation). University of California Los Angeles, Los Angeles, CA.

Suárez-Orozco, M. M. (1987). "Becoming somebody": Central American immigrants in U.S. inner-city schools. *Anthropology & Education Quarterly, 18*(4), 287–299.

Tisdall, E. K. M. (2017). Conceptualising children and young people's participation: Examining vulnerability, social accountability and co-production. *The International Journal of Human Rights, 21*(1), 59–75.

Zainuddin, H., Yahya, N., Morales-Jones, C. A., & Ariza, E. N. (2002). *Fundamentals of teaching English to speakers of other languages in K–12 mainstream classrooms.* Dubuque, IA: Kendall Hunt.

Zephir, F. (2001). *Trends in ethnic identification among second-generation Haitian immigrants in New York City.* Westport, CT: Bergin & Barvey.

Zephir, F. (2004). *The Haitian Americans.* Westport, CT: Greenwood Press.

CHAPTER 19

CO-CREATING SPACE FOR VOICE

Reflections on a Participatory Research Process With War-Affected Youth Living in Canada

Myriam Denov, Natasha Blanchet-Cohen, Alusine Bah, Leontine Uwababyeyi, Jean Kagame, and Andie (Saša) Buccitelli

ABSTRACT

This chapter explores the conditions that enable war-affected young people to assert and articulate their voices within the context of participatory research. While Quebec and Canada have seen an increase in war-induced migration of children and families, limited attention has been paid to war-affected young people's active participation in research. Yet the contributions of young people in the research process are considered essential to providing more responsive services and programs. In this chapter, we take a critical look at how to engage war-affected young people in ways that can be empowering, transformational, and knowledge generating. Based on a collaborative inquiry with war-affected youth who participated in a 2-year youth

Participatory Methodologies to Elevate Children's Voice and Agency, pages 423–442
Copyright © 2019 by Information Age Publishing

423

forum alongside a multidisciplinary research team, we critically reflect back on the process to understand the challenges and opportunities in relation to participatory methodologies. Dominant themes that we pay attention to center around the roles and ways of creating space for: (a) the (un)structuring of the youth forum; (b) the need to navigate ethical issues, including power and privilege and the complex roles of researchers as both insiders and outsiders; and (c) the value of trust, relationship building, and art as a form of expression and change. The chapter, co-authored by both youth and adult researchers, will contribute to understandings of the considerations in ensuring that war-affected youths' participation on research teams be empowering (and not disempowering).

As a consequence of armed conflict, there are currently 125 million people in need of humanitarian assistance, and 60 million people who have been forced to flee their homes as internally displaced persons or refugees (Ki-Moon, 2016). Children comprise 52% of the 59.5 million forcibly displaced by war worldwide (UNHCR, 2015). Each year, thousands of children fleeing war zones enter Canada (Stewart, 2011). In the province of Quebec, between 2003 and 2012, 7 of the top 10 source countries for accepted refugees were war-affected nations, representing nearly 27,000 people (Ministère de l'Immigration et des Communautés Culturelles, 2015). This influx of war-affected child refugees and asylum-seekers from diverse countries calls for a better understanding of their realities and perspectives.

Conventionally research has focused on research *on* war-affected children, but there is growing recognition that research *with* those who have experienced war is crucial. Particularly, participatory research with its dual function of generating knowledge, as well as social change, is welcomed as a method potentially sensitive and empowering to participants. Intended to be generative and transformative, carrying out research in this way poses, however, several challenges, including paying attention to the processes that enable reaching these diverse research purposes.

In this chapter, we critically reflect back on the involvement of war-affected youth in a "youth forum" that operated alongside an adult research team. Drawing on fieldnotes undertaken during the 2 years of the forum, as well as 6 reflection meetings carried out in the context of co-writing this chapter, we discuss elements of co-creating space for youth voice: (a) the (un)structuring of the youth forum; (b) the need to navigate ethical issues, including power and privilege and the complex roles of researchers as both insiders and outsiders; and (c) the value of trust, relationship building, and art as a form of expression and change. To frame our research, we begin by a review of critical issues to consider in doing participatory research with youth and specifically with war-affected youth.

CRITICAL ISSUES IN DOING PARTICIPATORY RESEARCH
WITH YOUTH

Given the profound and complex power relations inherent to the research process, researchers are increasingly turning to participatory approaches as a means to undo the monopoly over knowledge production by universities and into the hands of local actors and communities (Bennett, 2004). Participatory research promotes the generation of knowledge through a merging of academic and local knowledge to provide marginalized groups with tools for analyzing their life condition. A strength of participatory approach is the "integration of researchers' theoretical and methodological expertise within nonacademic participants' real-world knowledge and experiences into a mutually reinforcing partnership" (Cargo & Mercer, 2008, p. 327). It can be used as a powerful tool that reflects local ways of knowing, being, and doing that are culturally endemic to diverse communities (Evans & Foster, 2009). The approach can lay the foundations for non-hierarchical relationships, participant empowerment, and reciprocal learning by participants and researchers.

When conducting research with children and youth, the approach may not only help to neutralize power differentials, ethical concerns, and engage children and youth as active citizens, but also increase data quality, reliability, and validity (Veale, McKay, Worthen, & Wessells, 2013). It may also help to facilitate reflection, debate, argument, dissent, and consensus to stimulate the articulation of multiple voices and positions. While Veale (2005) argues that the participatory research process should be experienced by participants as transformative, and based on principles of social justice, it is in no way a panacea. Ayala (2009) suggests that inviting individuals to participate in change can bring both feelings of empowerment and vulnerability, especially when partners must go against complex social and political dynamics. Bennett (2004) also notes that there is a danger that participants may become alienated from their community by virtue of their association with a research project. In addition, a heightened awareness by a marginal group of its oppression can increase unhappiness. At the other extreme, participatory work can result in the creation of a participating elite among local people—ultimately fostering factionalism within a community.

While ethical issues are unquestionably present in all forms of participatory research—issues of power in the researcher-participant relationship may present themselves more sharply when study participants are young people (Denov, 2010). As such, within the participatory paradigm, researchers conducting research with children and youth have increasingly aimed to develop youth–adult partnerships in various forms. Rationale for youth engagement on research teams has included recognizing youth rights (Brown & Galeas, 2011), engaging young people's abilities (Kincheloe, 2007), fostering youth learning and development (Brown, 2010); and expanding youth voice, agency, and empowerment (Lind, 2008). Moreover, there have been documented benefits of including youth on research teams including expanded voice, agency, critical thinking, activism, and justice (Brown, 2010).

Also, the idea of youth voice is a common, yet understudied feature of this work, associated simultaneously with agency and citizenship. As highlighted by Caron, Raby, Mitchell, Théwissen-Leblanc, and Prioletta (2015), critiquing and studying youth voice, especially public voice, is key to deepening the understanding of participatory research. When young people have experienced trauma, often forced into silence to survive, how do participatory methods provide for finding "voice" safely, in ways that are empowering, transformational as well as knowledge generating? How do issues of power, relationship building, and ethics come into play within the co-creation of research space?

This chapter explores the opportunities and challenges associated with co-creating a space for youth voice within the context of an emerging research team focusing on war-affected youth living in Canada. Drawing upon the perspectives of both adult and youth research team members, we reflect on the creation of a youth forum and highlight some of the strengths and pitfalls of co-creating a space for youth affected by war on an adult-led research team.

WAR-AFFECTED YOUTH IN CANADA: CONTEXT AND PROJECT RATIONALE

The broader context for the research was a recognition that with war-induced migration[1] currently on the rise, its impact on children and youth deserves far greater attention. Research has shown that for war-affected children and youth who make their way to new countries, war-related mental health distress may occur alongside poverty, discrimination, isolation, language barriers, and difficulties in school (Denov & Bryan, 2014). As refugees, war-affected children and youth may require additional support given the multiple challenges encountered in their countries of origin (Denov & Blanchet-Cohen, 2016). In the Canadian context, the Standing Senate Committee on Human Rights noted: "Migrant children [across Canada] face a number of obstacles to settlement and integration . . . too often slipping through the cracks in service provision" (Crowe, 2006, p. 12). Understanding, through research, the complexity of war-affected young people's needs and experiences both during flight and following resettlement, alongside the development of appropriate services, can act as a preventive measure, and build on existing individual and community strengths.

In response to the need for research and practice with this unique population of young people, we initiated the Research Group on Children and

Global Adversity housed at McGill University and funded by the Fonds de Recherche du Québec sur la Société et la Culture. Since 2012, our research group has been working collectively to tackle the theoretical, methodological and service provision considerations pertinent for war-affected youth in Quebec and Canada, and in particular, the implications for policy and practice. Our multidisciplinary team of researchers and practitioners has been designed with three core objectives. First, we aimed to mobilize isolated research projects on children affected by armed conflict. There is an ongoing global initiative, promoted by the United Nations, emphasizing the importance of bridging disciplines and sectors in relation to children facing global adversity. UNICEF (2008) has articulated that the merging of law, education, social services and clinical intervention are key to ensuring the healthy development and protection of children. Despite such assertions, researchers working in the area of children in adversity in Québec have tended to work in isolation. We therefore sought to bring together a group of 15 researchers from four Québec universities from five disciplines.

Second, a great deal of research has centered on children's maladaptive, antisocial behavior in the aftermath of war, as well as negative, physical and mental health outcomes (Barber & Schluterman, 2008; O'Callaghan, McMullen, Shannon, & Rafferty, 2015; Stark & Wessells, 2013). While providing important insights into the well-being of children facing adversity, scholarship may inadvertently reinforce popular discourses of war-affected children as inherently victimized, pathological, and "at risk" (Denov & Bryan, 2014), often overlooking children and youth's capacities, adaptability, and resilience (Lenz, 2017). We therefore sought to employ research approaches and intervention practices that not only address the challenges faced by war-affected populations, but also recognize and build upon their capacities, moving beyond paradigms of trauma and distress. At the same time, we have been cautious not to overemphasize resilience by assuming that all will or have the capacity to "bounce back." Indeed, there is a danger of creating conceptual binaries whereby war-affected populations are presented as either profoundly affected by traumatic events on the one hand, or "resilient" on the other (Denov & Akesson, 2017). Research has increasingly shown that the lives of war-affected populations are characterized by *both* traumatic experiences, alongside powerful stories of survival (Denov & Blanchet-Cohen, 2016; Wessells, 2006). In our work, we have therefore sought to recognize the importance of addressing the complexity of experiences—acknowledging both adversity and capacity, trauma and resilience. This included conducting an exploratory qualitative research study addressing the wartime, flight and resettlement experiences of a sample of war-affected youth living in Quebec (Denov & Blanchet-Cohen, 2014; Blanchet-Cohen & Denov, 2015; Denov & Blanchet-Cohen, 2016).

Finally, and most importantly for this chapter, was the emphasis on considering and giving space for youth participation. Reflecting conventional notions of power, and what is regarded as "expert knowledge," youth who have been caught up in circumstances of war and genocide rarely have opportunities to articulate their perspectives, concerns and needs, or actively contribute to scholarly discussions. In spite of provisions in the UN Convention on the Rights of the Child that children hold fundamental participation rights, scholarly inquiry and the design of services rarely incorporate child participation (Hilker & Fraser, 2009). Until recently, social science research has been critiqued for contributing to children's marginalization by using methods and approaches that regard them as "objects" of research, rather than active participants (Denov, 2010). With the new sociology of childhood, tangible and significant shifts in the conceptualization of children and childhood have occurred whereby children and adolescents are now viewed as social agents able to influence their immediate contexts (Morrow, 2008). Indeed, children and youth possess knowledge and perceptions of their social environment that is valid, and their voices need to be part of the research (Morrow & Richards, 1996).

Drawing upon this approach, our research group engaged four war-affected youth (two male and two female) originally from Colombia, Sierra Leone, and Rwanda to form a "youth forum" that was to work alongside the larger research group. The youth forum was facilitated by two individuals—one a war-affected youth originally from Sierra Leone, and the other an experienced social worker who had vast experience working with marginalized youth—particularly from the LGBTQ community. With the creation of the forum, our research group sought to enhance the knowledge, quality, and direction of the research group, as well as encourage and promote youth participation and empowerment. Our hope was that by engaging youth on the research team, we would inform our overall learning on youth participation more generally. Over a 2-year period, members of the youth forum met once per month. Below, we discuss issues raised related to co-creating space for youth voice that emerged from the field notes and discussion groups with three of the four youth and two adult researchers, one who spearheaded the project, and another member of the team.

RESEARCH CO-CREATION AND YOUTH VOICE

"Structuring" the Youth Forum

In developing the youth forum, it was critical for our team to ensure that the forum was a space that meaningfully represented war-affected young people's voices and experiences, and that the youth played a leading role in the development of the forum's objectives, structures, activities, and culture. The four youth were recruited by the youth facilitator from Sierra Leone, through a snowball sampling technique. As such, once the four youth consented to being part of the group, the group collectively established the goals and objectives of the forum and its activities. In developing the forum, it was critical that it be organic: We hoped that it would be something that struck a chord with the youth in such a way that they felt that their involvement was meaningful to their lives and was empowering. In the field notes prior to the first meeting, the facilitators noted:

> The goal should not be to lure the youth in so that they can fulfill the research group's objective of "integrating" youth voices. Alternatively, the goal should be to offer the necessary resources and support to facilitate the youth's development of the forum, as they see fit. The larger group is only providing the avenue through which youth can mobilize and define their own objectives, activities and structure. This also includes their definition of the presenting problem. Thus far, the research members have been defining the problem, agenda and approach, but these may not align themselves with those identified by the youth. In order for the group to be successful, they must have a vested interest in the forum and its relationship to the larger research group. The concept of the forum has to resonate with the youth: in order for it to be successful, it has to be something that they feel is relevant and has the potential to change current social and political dynamics with the overarching objective of improving their and their peers' lives. If this is absent, what incentive is there for them to engage in the process?

This unstructured approach to the forum, in some ways, brought a degree of uncertainty to the group, as the entire team entered into the process not knowing what activities and content would make up the forum. However, in reflecting back on the process, this female youth participant explained how the unstructured approach was preferable to a more structured approach:

> When it is well-structured, it makes it too professional and then it puts pressure on people. Then [the group becomes] like an expectation. So it might discourage some people because they may say "this is what they want from me, so if I don't do this this might happen"... [Because] [the youth forum] was free [unstructured], then I didn't feel any pressure...The other one [participatory project I was involved in] I felt pressured, but this one never. They were like "we have to do this, and that." [In this forum] we were able to find a balance between structured and unstructured. [In the other project, I felt that] I have to be there because I feel pressured. If I am late, I don't go because I know it is not going to be good. But this forum, you guys allowed us to feel free. If someone called in, and said he is late, you guys are ok with it.

Another key aim of the forum was to build a place and space of trust and safety, developing a sense of cohesion, belonging, and community amongst the youth. This meant that the principles of social justice, anti-racist, and anti-oppressive practice were to be embedded in forum's content and approach. We sought to avoid reinforcing oppressive structures and power dynamics, which the youth were likely to have experienced to varying degrees.

Throughout the course of the meetings, the youth came up with a set of ground rules and structure. Each meeting began with a group ice-breaker exercise (a fun and interactive game) to make people feel at ease and comfortable. This was followed by individual "check-in" to see how each member was doing and if there was anything in particular they were hoping to share or address. The meeting then included a debrief and feedback session of the previous meeting. Each meeting then discussed a main theme that the group brought forward as an area of interest or concern. Examples of key themes discussed during the course of the forum included: the meaning of war and armed conflict, the challenges associated with migration and resettlement, and policy and service provision needs. Meetings ended with a wrap up game, as well as a discussion of suggestions for the theme and format of the next meeting.

Before the youth forum began, the research team was unsure as to how the youth would be connected to the larger adult research team. The youth decided how and what that would look like. Below we reflect on the ethical issues that arose and needed to be navigated as we worked through such questions.

Navigating Ethical Minefields

Power relations and ethical considerations are vital when considering the realities of young people affected by armed conflict. Those who are still suffering from the trauma of war and genocide and their related effects could experience heightened anxiety by "reliving it" through participatory research. Individuals who have begun to come to terms with their experiences of violence and armed conflict are beginning to move forward in their lives may feel that they are being asked to reopen old wounds. Additional difficulties can arise as a result of participants' discomfort and anxiety in openly discussing their experiences, or their fear of reprisal as a result of sharing their stories through participatory approaches. Respondents could also worry of social stigmatization and judgment as a result of speaking about their direct involvement in violence. These diverse issues undoubtedly represented a few of the "ethical minefields" (Boyden & De Berry, 2004) that required constant care, attention, and mitigation.

On Power and Privilege

Other ethical issues presented themselves throughout the process of the youth forum. Giving greater control to participants is paramount and ensures that the research process works to empower them, and assures that the research process serves their interests. However, this can potentially bring forth ethical dilemmas. Key questions included: "Who holds the "last word" in relation to forum decision-making?"; "What do adult researchers do when they perceive the project moving in an 'inappropriate' direction, or in situations where children may be putting themselves or others at risk?" "In such situations, to whom are the researchers accountable?"; and "Who ultimately holds the reins and the power and authority to control and decide?" The dangers and risks of tokenistic power are significant. Reflections on power and privilege became paramount throughout the process. This facilitator of the youth forum reflected in their field notes:

> I have begun to reflect a great deal on my position within the forum and the larger research program, more generally. I have a strong investment in the forum and feel that it is providing a unique and beautiful space for all its members. However, I also question whether my position of privilege and power in the forum (i.e., as a researcher attached to an elitist institution) is doing more harm than good. Is this program simply a post-colonial/imperialist process? Are we seriously devolving power to the youth in all aspects of the research project? Whose interests are we serving? Is it really the youth's? Or is it more so the interests of the university in terms of producing research for the sake of bolstering the institution's prestige and power? I reflect on how the vast majority of the researchers of the program are white, likely privileged, individuals who may have never experienced anything similar to the youth forum members. As I have stressed in previous reflections, this is something that I constantly think of. I have practiced self-scrutiny and self-reflexivity throughout this process…I feel like this is a necessity in order to identify one's privilege, power and potential complicity to processes of re-marginalization, exploitation and imperialism. These thoughts leave me feeling disillusioned and conflicted. As I continue to navigate this complex issue, my dedication to and investment in the youth forum and its members will not change. The forum I feel has provided much to the members as well as to me.

Another facilitator of the youth forum reflected on the challenge of power relations with members of the adult research team. He reflected that while he trusted the adult members of the research team, he was unable to fend off the reality that they were ultimately in an authority position:

> The power struggle is [there]…I trust [adult researcher] I have known [adult researcher] for a while. But I always have at the back of my mind— she is my boss. That's the truth…It is also a cultural thing for me…that it doesn't matter how close my relationship [with her] is…it's not equal. And

that's how we are brought in the society [I was raised in]. No matter what, people who are at a certain level [of education and status have to be treated in a certain way] ... you just have to maintain that fact.

However, power is not always top–down. When conducting research with children and youth, Barker and Smith (2001) maintain that the conceptualization of the research relationship as "adult as all powerful" is overly simplistic. They argue that because children are the "experts of the day-to-day spaces of childhood, adults' lack of experience of such places means that they are often the 'novice' or incompetent adult" (p. 146). In this sense, power in the research relationship, whether with child, youth, or adult participants, is never statically and evenly distributed. Instead, it can be characterized as fluid, negotiable, unpredictable, and fluctuates depending on the different constellations of identity and power at play (Mutua & Blue Swadener, 2004). Thapar-Bjorkert and Henry (2004) encourage researchers to question the rigid demarcation between oppressor (researcher) and oppressed (participant) and to critically appropriate a framework which imagines power as shifting, multiple, and intersecting. In this sense,

> power is understood as not only top–down, but dispersed through both research relationships and the research process ... this reconceptualization allows researchers to reimagine [their] participants as agents ... the researched as powerless and the researcher as all powerful, while still acknowledging that there are differences and inequalities between researchers and research participants. (Thapar-Bjorkert & Henry 2004, p. 364)

This conceptualization of power is fitting with the current research space, as shifts in power were noted throughout the process. This was particularly apparent in terms of the relationship between the adult research team and the youth forum, and in particular, how and in what ways, the youth wanted to be connected to the adult research team. At the outset, the youth chose to have a separate forum from the adult research team. As such, a major obstacle was finding an effective means of communicating between the youth forum and the adult research team members. This issue was discussed during a youth forum meeting:

> If the program's goal is to have the forum act as an advisory body, information disseminated one way or another must be done in such a way that is accessible and culturally competent. We cannot presume that the nature of the feedback that the youth provide is going to be done in a language or style that conforms to academic cultural expectations. More importantly, information concerning the research group's activities must be vulgarized in such a way that it is accessible to and usable by the youth.

In the end, it was left up to the youth forum participants to decide if they wanted to join the larger team of adult researchers. After much discussion, and reflecting shifting power relations and structures, the youth collectively decided that they preferred to remain a unique and separate group from the adult research team. The trust was not there that they would feel safe, comfortable among a team of academics, with whom they felt a limited connection to. Thus, the linkage with the adult-team was done by the facilitators of the youth forum, who reported to the research team during the team meetings.

Multiple and Complex Roles

Another challenge related to the facilitators and the ways in which they struggled to navigate multiple and competing roles. There is often an assumption that as researchers, we are either "insiders" or "outsiders"—we are either members of the communities that we study—or we are outside of these communities. However, it appears to be far more complex than that, as we can be both "insiders" and "outsiders" at the same time. For example, one of the facilitators was himself a war-affected individual from Sierra Leone. In the following quote, this facilitator reflected on his dual role as both "insider" and "outsider":

> I have to say it was difficult. Because...you know, here I am as a referee. Yet at the same time you are watching a game, but you are also part of the game...You know it was very emotional. At the same time, you want to help these [youth] by listening to them, but at the same time, what they are telling you is close to you. It was a difficult process. I was playing a dual role, at the same time dealing with emotions.

The other facilitator who had not directly experienced war or armed conflict, reflected on the experience of being an "outsider" and its implications:

> I experienced today's forum as both difficult and powerful. We reflected upon the theme of war and violence and the meaning these phenomena have in our lives. I at first found it challenging to participate in the discussion given my privilege in never having experienced war. As such, I took the position of a deep listener. Everyone shared their experience of war and how it has impacted them. It was difficult and moving to hear these stories. We spoke about the difficulties related to forgiveness and healing. Forgiveness is possible, but often takes time. One participant noted that forgiveness is important, but that forgetting was not so easily achieved, particularly when one has lost their entire family as a result of war. Other participants spoke about their implication in conflicts and the challenges in making sense of this. I felt that, for many, this was the first time they had a chance to really engage in dialogue with others who shared similar experiences. There seemed to be a degree of trust and comfort in the room. The energy was very unique.

This same facilitator also reflected on their struggle to address issues of power and privilege both personally, as well as within the group:

> I could not stop experiencing bodily shivers when hearing about people's stories as well as how they have come to terms with their experiences over the years. I experienced a great deal of anger, frustration, and sadness. I reflected on how Canada, along with other countries of the Global North, are complicit in processes of violence in the Global South. How the legacy of both past and contemporary processes of oppression (including colonialism and neoliberalism) have contributed to the pain that the participants have experienced. I reflected on my complicity in these processes, my membership to the Global North, my immense privilege as a white person who has never had to negotiate an insecure status…

At the same time, this same facilitator eventually made connections with their own experiences of violence and oppression based upon their gender identity and expression, which made them an "insider" to having experienced profound instances of violence, discrimination, and marginalization:

> In hearing the stories, I began to understand how the participants' experiences of oppression and violence share some parallels with my own experiences of oppression and violence. I reflected on the various forms of violence I used to experience throughout much of my childhood for being effeminate and for being an English speaker in a francophone Québec town (e.g., verbal assaults, physical attacks, bullying, and micro-aggressions). I reflected on the current forms of violence, both cover and overt, I experience in light of my gender identity and expression (i.e., I identify as genderqueer, specifically I experience my gender as woman/agender). I thought of the ways I constantly look down when I am in public out of fear of being judged or aggressed. I thought of how having been through experiences of violence in addition to my membership to a minority group greatly influences my psyche, how I perceive myself, how I experience and move through the world…I am not suggesting that my experience of violence in any way mirrors those of the participants. I will never fully feel what they feel, but I sense that my understanding and capacity to feel what the participants feel is enhanced when I can identify similar sites of repression. I feel that this is important in order to build community and solidarity with others and in fostering radically inclusive and critically conscious spaces where mutual support and healing can occur.

These reflections suggest that co-creating space for voice with experiential youth and facilitators involves accepting that the boundaries between researcher/researched roles will be fluid, and that knowledge-sharing within the group can be enhanced by giving time to nurture safety. It may, at times, remain internal to the group processes and at other times be publically shared. Questions of power and inequalities between youth and adults and amongst youth cannot however be denied. Embracing the complexity and the tensions is part of navigating and deepening the relationships that lead to creating spaces for meaningful sharing.

Trust, Relationship Building, and Art as a Form of Expression and Change

While the challenges raised in the youth forum were numerous, it is important to underscore the trust and relationship building that occurred within the context of the forum. This was particularly significant as youth participants reported that war and armed conflict were topics that were largely taboo and difficult to address with their Canadian-born peers. This participant reflected on discussing their lives in the context of the youth forum:

> Here you can say anything you want and nobody will judge. We were very comfortable with everyone...At [the other group I participated in] I didn't feel like trusting anyone in the group. I only have few people that I trust.

Building trust among group members did not occur immediately, but was instead a lengthy and sometimes difficult process. One of the facilitators discussed the initial reticence among participants to share personal stories of war and genocide, as well as their direct involvement in armed violence, for fear of judgment or reprisal. The facilitator explained the process of trust and relationship building within the group:

> Ahhhhh.... for me I was a bit worried because these people didn't know me at all. One of the...participants was also from [Sierra Leone] and he never discussed details about [his past]...I was just a bit cautious...He told me that [he] was in Liberia. I was like "Ohhh Liberia! To do what?" He was like: "You know what I mean." I said, "No, I don't." Then he started telling me...what he did [his involvement in an armed group] and which [armed] group he was part of...[Another participant] also talked about what they went through in Colombia, what their family went through...I felt like I could no longer keep [my experience to myself]. But [my past] is something that I reserve, reserve all the time...I don't want to go into the details. But when they...talked about their experiences, I just felt overwhelmed...I could trust them...So, for me, trust was very important. I already felt that that was a space I could share with them. I don't have to fear because I already know what they have been through and this is something that I have also lived through.

This same facilitator later described how, following an extended period of relationship building among members of the group, he eventually felt comfortable enough to disclose that he had been a former child soldier to other members of the youth forum. Here, he described how he came to a point where he felt comfortable enough to disclose this most personal and difficult experience:

> For me, I was still dealing with it in my head. Okay, how do you go about [sharing] this?...But at some point in time, you know, you feel that something should get out of your mind...After two, three months, it's a lot of meeting before [I shared] and then one day it came out. There are so many reasons, but one reason was I felt that its good for them to hear. That they are not only sharing, but also, I am listening all the time. But I also have something to say...I felt so much relief because most of the time I have this guilt [for what I did]...that I didn't want to disclose to them...Since then I felt like I don't have any guilt. This is what happened to me, and I had no choice. I started feeling good about myself. It was a moment for me to say, you know I realized this is something I wanted to talk about. I was not like [I was] compelled to say it—like you have to say this. But the environment made it easier for me to say, well you know what, I can say it. They provided the opportunity, and I had the space to say it.

Given the tragedy of war and genocide, words and narrative alone often cannot adequately capture the realities and complexity of conflict-related experiences. As such, researchers are increasingly turning to the arts to enable multiple forms of participant expression, as well as for the therapeutic, restorative, and empowering qualities of arts-based techniques (Leavy, 2009). Scholarship has begun to highlight the psychological benefits of using arts-based approaches within research, such as drawing or photography, as they provide a way to safely access traumatic memory, ultimately helping with traumatic recovery (Gantt & Tinnin, 2009). Theater, art-making and storytelling became a natural and organic part of the youth forum. Youth individually and collectively suggested the use of theater, drama, drawing, and storying as a means of expression, cohesion and relationship-building. One facilitator described how the process of using theater came about within the group:

> And [one of the participants] just said, I have an idea. We said: "What?" She said, "Next week." A normal week came and she said, "Everybody stand up." Everybody stood up. She said, "We're gonna do something different"...She said it's called the 'theater of the oppressed'...but if you don't want to participate its ok." And then she gave us the directions, you can express your feelings and don't need to say a word just express it. And boy oh boy, it was like talking to a therapist or something or a psychologist. It was amazing...from there on, I realized people started really opening up...I am expressing myself in different way. At one point, the theater of the oppressed was very significant to me....I was acting [out through pantomime] like somebody who is traumatized and he is violent and can do anything without saying a word. Something psychologically, I was feeling like bringing something back to

me.... It's only kind of social drama thing, right? But it gets to you. Because if you lived through it, you wanna reenact the same thing and you feel like you are doing it in real life. So, for me...oh it felt real.

Art was also used during several sessions using the process of body-mapping. In this method, participants lay on a large sheet of paper while other participants used markers to trace an outline of his or her body. Having colored in the drawn figure, the youth identified specific parts of their body that were significant to them and added concepts that related to their past, present, and future. For example, one participant had lost her entire family during the Rwandan genocide, and had come to Canada alone and unaccompanied. She explained the meaning and significance of her completed body map which featured the words "hope," "strength," "love," "friendship," "peace," and "resilience" on different parts of her drawn figure:

Hope represents my future. *Strength* is for strong. *Love* and *Friendship* is about my friends are my family and my families are my friends. *Peace* is what I want. *Resilience* is what people tell me I am...I think the body-mapping was more about what we felt about ourselves and what other people see in us. I think we do share the same ideas. I remember some participants drew something similar to me...I came from a country of genocide so I think resilience is something I see in myself. Yeah, I came to Canada a few years ago so people helped me to adjust to this society and now I am willing to give back to society. As for hope, when I look at my future, I think my future will be better than my past. And that is why hope is important to me. I believe that I will always be a strong person. It is important for me to have friends because they are like my family.

Ultimately, the process of art-making and sharing stories was not only expressed as helpful to each individual participant, or to the group as a collective, but that sharing their stories, through art or through narrative, was seen as an important catalyst for change. As this group member explained:

Because sometimes, like often times you know all those histories of oppression you only focus on the negative side of it. But if you help [people] understand how powerful their stories are...I mean the history is like a treasure that can be passed on to other generations. I think it can be something that even though it might take time for [others] to understand, your history can actually change other people. It can maybe contribute into something. I think it can be something powerful which also comes with informing people what's the purpose of the group...I think making people believe that their history is a treasure, [that it is] something valuable, not just like something that's just gonna haunt them in a negative way. So, like a powerful piece.

It is indeed through the maps that the youth chose to publicly present their process and stories. At conferences, they presented alongside the adult research team members by sharing these and their stories. For adult-researchers on the team, it was an opportunity to listen, with humility as the stories were being shared from a place where young people felt empowered.

CONCLUDING REFLECTIONS

Ultimately, our experience highlights the ways in which participatory research processes can be empowering and transformative when youth are provided the opportunity to define their own space. However, the process is also demanding, messy, and complex involving ongoing navigation and negotiation between and amongst adult and youth researchers, offering both positive and challenging experiences for both.

For war-affected youth, the participatory process involved taking the time to find their voice by building relationships amongst youth who were commonly war-affected, to create a collective space where they felt comfortable sharing their stories. This co-created space included providing for multiple mediums of experience. Through the process of finding and articulating their voices, youth healed and grew. This is reflected by the fact that today all of the youth are undertaking undergraduate studies. For the adult-team, it was about respecting the decisions and processes of the youth, and that finding and articulating voice meant for youth holding, to an extent defending, their own process, and that knowledge-sharing would often remain at the group level. Embracing participatory processes meant accepting that youth need time to find and articulate their voices, to be able to decide the terms on which they wanted to share, when and how, and whether they wanted or not to engage with adults in the sensemaking of their stories.

In this case, the fact that despite 2 years of activities there was never a merging of youth and the adult-led team points to the importance of paying attention to readiness of youth and adult researchers. For the youth who had experienced traumatic experiences, sharing, and sensemaking was empowering at the group level, amongst youth and facilitators that they could relate to, and had built a relationship of trust. While the adult researchers may have been well intended, it seems that much remains to be learned about creating spaces that are truly welcoming, inclusive, and empowering for youth amongst adult researchers. Moving forward involves continuing to learn how youth voice can be enabled and nurtured in ways that are both empowering and generative of individual and broader knowledge in both adult and youth-led spaces in order to bridge the divide.

Questions for Reflection

1. What participatory processes provide for youth who have experienced trauma safe and empowering spaces to find voice in research?
2. How can adult-led research teams create contexts that welcome experiential youth to participate directly as researchers? How does one determine readiness of adult and youth?
3. How can the ethical minefields to doing participatory research with war-affected youth be navigated? How does awareness of power and privilege enhance research?
4. How do youth navigate among the complex and multiple roles they play in sharing and facilitating knowledge-creation at the group and broader collective levels?
5. How does one find balance between the discovery, sensemaking, social change and generating knowledge roles of participatory research?

Suggestions for Further Reading

Boyden, J., & De Berry, J. (2004). *Children and youth on the front line.* Oxford, England: Berghahn Books.

Cargo, M., & Mercer, S. (2008). The value and challenges of participatory research: Strengthening its practice. *Annual Review of Public Health, 29*, 325–350.

Denov, M., & Akesson, B. (Eds.). (2017). *Children affected by armed conflict: Theory, method, and practice.* New York, NY: Columbia University Press.

Gardner, M., Brown, L., Young, E., Young, A., McCann, A., & Myles, C. (2016). Feeling like research partners as a young-adult team. *Canadian Journal of Action Research, 17*(3), 20–38.

Jacquez, F., Vaughn, L. M., & Wagner, E. (2013). Youth as partners, participants or passive recipients: A review of children and adolescents in community-based participatory research. *American Journal of Community Psychology, 51*(1–2), 176–189.

Leavy, P. (2009). *Method meets art: Arts-based research practice.* London, England: The Guilford Press.

Morrow, V. (2008). Ethical dilemmas in research with children and young people about their social environments. *Children's Geographies, 6*(1), 49–61.

NOTE

1. "War-induced migration" refers to migration that occurs as a result of fleeing war and/or armed conflict.

REFERENCES

Ayala, J. (2009). Split scenes, converging visions: The ethical terrains where PAR and borderlands scholarship meet. *The Urban Review, 41*(1), 66–84.

Barber, B. K., & Schluterman, J. M. (2008). An overview of the empirical literature on adolescents and political violence. In B. K. Barber (Ed.), *Adolescents and war: How youth deal with political violence* (pp. 35–61). Oxford, England: Oxford University Press.

Barker, J., & F., Smith. (2001). Power, positionality and practicality: Carrying out fieldwork with children. *Ethics, Place and Environment, 4*(2), 142–147.

Bennett, M. (2004), A review of the literature on the benefits and drawbacks of participatory action research. *First Peoples Child and Family Review, 1*(1),19–32.

Blanchet-Cohen, N., & Denov, M. (2015). War-affected children's approach to resettlement: Implications for child and family services. *Annals of Anthropological Practice, 39*(2), 120–133.

Boyden, J., & De Berry, J. (2004). *Children and youth on the front line.* Oxford, England: Berghahn Books.

Brown, T. (2010). Arise to the challenge: Partnering with urban youth to improve educational research and learning. *Perspectives on Urban Education, 7*(1), 4–14.

Brown, T., & Galeas, K. (2011). Confronting "limit situations" in a youth/adult educational research collaborative. In B. D. Schultz (Ed.), *Listening to and learning from students: Possibilities for teaching, learning, and curriculum* (pp. 13–26). Charlotte, NC: Information Age.

Cargo, M., & Mercer, S. (2008). The value and challenges of participatory research: Strengthening its practice. *Annual Review of Public Health, 29*, 325–350.

Caron, C., Raby, R., Mitchell, C., Théwissen-Leblanc, C., & Prioletta, J. (2015, June). *Youth voices on YouTube: A multimodal approach.* Paper presented at the Canadian Communications Association, Ottawa, Canada.

Crowe, S. (2006). *Immigrant and refugee Children in middle childhood: An overview.* Ottawa, Canada: National Children's Alliance.

Denov, M. (2010). *Child soldiers: Sierra Leone's revolutionary united front.* Cambridge, England: Cambridge Press.

Denov, M., & Akesson, B. (2017). (Eds.), *Children affected by armed conflict: Theory, method, and practice.* New York, NY: Columbia University Press.

Denov, M., & Blanchet-Cohen, N. (2014) The rights and realities of war-affected refugee children and youth in Quebec: Making children's rights meaningful. *Canadian Journal of Children's Rights, 1*(1), 18–43.

Denov, M., & Blanchet-Cohen, N. (2016). Trajectories of violence and survival: Turnings and adaptations in the lives of two war-affected youth living in Canada. *Peace and Conflict: Journal of Peace Psychology, 22*(3), 236–245.

Denov, M., & Bryan, C. (2014). Social navigation and resettlement: Separated children in the context of Canada. *Refuge: Canada's Periodical on Refugees, 30*(1), 25–34.

Evans, M., & Foster, S. (2009). Representation in participatory video: Some considerations from research with Métis in British Columbia. *Journal of Canadian Studies, 43*(1), 87–108.

Gantt, L., & Tinnin, L. W. (2009). Support for a neurobiological view of trauma with implications for art therapy. *The Arts in Psychotherapy, 36*(3), 148–153.

Hilker, L. M., & Fraser, E. (2009). *Youth exclusion, violence, conflict and fragile states* (Report prepared for the DFID's Equity and Rights Team). Retrieved from http://www.gsdrc.org/docs/open/con66.pdf

Ki-Moon B. (2016). *One humanity: Shared responsibility.* Report of the Secretary-General for the world humanitarian summit. New York, NY: United Nations.

Kincheloe, J. (2007). Clarifying the purpose of engaging students as researchers. In D. Thiessen & A. Cook-Sather (Eds.), *International Handbook of Student Experience in Elementary and Secondary School* (pp. 745–774). Netherlands: Springer.

Leavy, P. (2009). *Method meets art: Arts-based research practice.* London, England: Guilford Press.

Lenz, J. (2017). Armed with resilience: Tapping into the experiences and survival skills of formerly abducted girl child soldiers in Northern Uganda. In M. Denov & B. Akesson (Eds.), Children affected by armed conflict. *Theory, method, and practice* (pp. 112–136). New York, NY: Columbia University Press.

Lind, C. (2008). Knowledge development with adolescents in a PAR process. *Educational Action Research, 16*(2), 221–233.

Ministère de l'Immigration et des Communautés culturelles. (2015). *Présence en 2014 des immigrants admis au Québec de 2003 à 2012* [Presence in 2014 of immigrants admitted to Quebec from 2003–2012]. Gouvernement du Québec. Retrieved from http://www.midi.gouv.qc.ca/publications/fr/recherches-statistiques/PUB_Presence2014_admisQc.pdf

Morrow, V. (2008). Ethical dilemmas in research with children and young people about their social environments. *Children's Geographies, 6*(1), 49–61.

Morrow, V., & Richards, M. (1996). The ethics of social research with children: An overview. *Children and Society, 10*(2), 90–105.

Mutua, K., & Blue Swadener, B. (2004). Introduction. In K. Mutua & B. Blue Swadener (Eds.), *Decolonizing research in cross-cultural contexts* (pp. 1–27). Albany: State University of New York Press.

O'Callaghan, P., McMullen, J., Shannon, C., & Rafferty, H. (2015). Comparing a trauma focused and non trauma focused intervention with war affected Congolese youth: A preliminary randomised trial. *Intervention, 13*(1), 28–44.

Stark, L., & Wessells, M. (2013). The fallacy of the ticking time bomb: Resilience of children formerly recruited into armed forces and groups. In C. Fernando & M. Ferrari (Eds.), *Handbook of resilience in children of war* (pp. 95–106). New York, NY: Springer.

Stewart, J. (2011). *Supporting refugee children: Strategies for educators.* Toronto, Canada: University of Toronto Press.

Thapar-Bjorkert, S., & Henry, M. (2004). Reassessing the research relationship: Location, position and power in fieldwork accounts. *International Journal of Social Research Methodology, 7*(5), 363–381.

UNHCR. (2015). *World at War: Forced Displacement in 2014.* Geneva, Switzerland: UNHCR.

UNICEF. (2008). *UNICEF child protection strategy.* New York, NY: Economic and Social Council. Retrieved from https://www.unicef.org/protection/CP_Strategy_English(1).pdf

Veale, A. (2005). Creative methodologies in participatory research with children. In S. Greene & D. Hogan (Eds.), *Researching children's experience* (pp. 253–272). Thousand Oaks, CA: SAGE.

Veale, A., McKay, S., Worthen, M., & Wessells, M. (2013). Participation as principle and tool in social reintegration: Young mothers formerly associated with armed groups in Sierra Leone, Liberia, and northern Uganda. *Journal of Aggression, Maltreatment & Trauma, 22*(8), 829–848.

Wessells, M. (2006). *Child soldiers: From violence to protection.* Cambridge, MA: Harvard University Press.

ABOUT THE CONTRIBUTORS

Amanda Ajodhia received her PhD from the Ontario Institute for Studies in Education/ University of Toronto. She also holds an Honors BSc (psychology specialist) from the University of Toronto, and a MA (early childhood studies) from Ryerson University. Her research interests focus on school inclusion and equity for ethnically diverse young people with disabilities. Additionally, she explores young people's participation in research, notions of difference and normalcy, qualitative methods of inquiry, and international perspectives of inclusive education. In 2016 she published a book, *Voices and Visions From Ethnoculturally Diverse Young People With Disabilities* with Sense Publishers, and more recently in 2017 she published a chapter entitled "Arts/Image-Based Creative Co-Research with Disabled Children: Practical Dilemmas of the Research Process" in M. Emme and A. Kirova (Eds.), *Good Question! Creative Research Collaborations with Kids* (pp. 92–120) with The Canadian Society for Education through Art. She previously served as a lecturer and faculty advisor in the School of Early Childhood at Ryerson University, Toronto, and more recently as an assistant professor in the Graduate School of Education at Nazarbayev University, Astana, Kazakhstan.

Johanne April, PhD, is a full professor in the Department of Educational Sciences at the Université du Québec in Outaouais (Saint-Jérôme campus). Her recent research interests include the practices of preschool teachers and school transitions in a low SES environment. She is also the author of the book *L'activité Psychomotrice au Préscolaire* published by Chenelière Education in 2015.

Participatory Methodologies to Elevate Children's Voice and Agency, pages 443–455
Copyright © 2019 by Information Age Publishing
All rights of reproduction in any form reserved.

443

Alusine Bah was 14 years old when his town was attacked by the R.U.F (Revolutionary United Front) rebels in Sierra Leone. He fled into the forest and it wasn't long before he was found by the Sierra Leone Army and forced to become one of their many child soldiers. Alusine was a child soldier in the army for 2 years. He was sent to a rehabilitation center to begin the long and difficult recovery and normalization of his life. In November 1996, Alusine was chosen to come to New York to speak at the United Nations about how children's rights are being violated in war-affected countries and the impact of war on children. In 2003, Alusine started a new life in Montreal. Since then he has returned to school after an 8-year interruption. Alusine also helps youth by motivating them about nonviolence through conferences in schools all over Montreal and in Canada. He wants to raise awareness of Canadian youth to the history and reality of his country, and to the plight of children and youth affected by war everywhere. In 2007, Alusine was awarded the YMCA peace medal award for helping youth in advocating for peace. And in 2008, he was recognized for helping youth in community program and received the Martin Luther King Jr. Legacy Award in Montreal. Alusine graduated from Concordia University in 2011 and is currently a research assistant at McGill University.

Michael Baizerman is professor of Youth Studies, School of Social Work, University of Minnesota. He is a leading scholar in the fields of youth studies and youth work with over 60 articles and books on topics ranging from the social construction of adolescence to the everyday lives of young people. He consults internationally with governments, universities, and community organizations and international nongovernmental organizations to build effective and sustainable youth work practice and programs.

Jane E. Baker is an associate professor of early childhood education in the Department of Curriculum and Instruction at Tennessee Tech University, where she teaches undergraduate and graduate courses in early literacy, content methods, family collaboration, and at-risk populations. Her research interests include early literacy methods, classroom discourse, family collaboration, and family STEM education.

Tiffany Barnikis is currently a PhD candidate in the Department of Education at York University, Toronto, Canada. She holds a Master of Arts degree in early childhood studies from Ryerson University, Toronto, Canada. This chapter draws upon her major research project, which she conducted as part of her MA, and a subsequent follow-up study. Tiffany's areas of research include children's perceptions of the world around them, particularly of their experiences in different learning environments, approaches to participatory research with children, and varied conceptualizations of children and childhood.

Rachel Berman earned an MA in human development and family relations at the University of Connecticut, and a PhD in family studies at the University of Guelph in Guelph, Ontario. She is currently an associate professor and the graduate program director in the School of Early Childhood Studies at Ryerson University. She is the editor of *Corridor Talk: Canadian Feminist Scholars Share Stories of Research Partnerships* published by Inanna Publications in 2014 and a lead researcher on the Can We Talk About Race? Confronting Color-Blindness in Early Childhood Settings, a project funded by the Social Sciences and Humanities Research Council of Canada.

Ilene R. Berson, PhD, is a professor of early childhood at the University of South Florida and coordinates the early childhood doctoral program in the Department of Teaching and Learning. Dr. Berson teaches courses on early childhood integrated social studies, humanities, and arts; ICT in the early years; visual research methods; and early childhood advocacy and leadership. She has been recognized for her outstanding contributions and excellence in teaching, research, and service by the USF Institute on Black Life, USF Office of Undergraduate Research, USF College of Education, American Educational Research Association Special Interest Group Research in Global Child Advocacy, U.S. Department of Health and Human Services Substance Abuse Mental Health Services Administration, and the National Child Labor Committee. She leads international studies on integrating social justice and child advocacy into early childhood teacher preparation, and conducts participatory research to explore young children's civic engagement through multiple literacies. Moreover, Dr. Berson studies the intersection of technology and the pedagogy of inquiry in the early years with a focus on children's affordances of digital innovations. She has extensively disseminated her research through publications and presentations worldwide. Dr. Berson has been the principal investigator on numerous grants from organizations such as the Spencer Foundation, the Library of Congress, the Florida Department of Health, and the U.S. Department of Health and Human Services Substance Abuse Mental Health Services Administration to develop innovative solutions that promote young children's well-being and educational outcomes.

Michael J. Berson, PhD is a professor of social science education at the University of South Florida and a senior fellow in The Florida Joint Center for Citizenship. He coordinates the USF College of Education PhD program in curriculum and instruction with a concentration in social science education. Dr. Berson instructs courses in social studies methods, technology innovation in the social studies, elementary school social studies, and visual research methods in education. He has received the USF Outstanding Undergraduate Teaching Award, was twice chosen as the USF nominee for the United States Professor of the Year Program sponsored by CASE and The

Carnegie Foundation for the Advancement of Teaching, and has received international recognition for integrating emerging technologies into instruction and modeling innovative pedagogy. He also was honored with the National Council for the Social Studies President's Award for outstanding contribution to the field and was selected for the Florida Council for the Social Studies International Relations Award for his research in global child advocacy. Dr. Berson has served as an advisor on cybersecurity and the integration of technology into education to companies and organizations throughout the world. Among his leadership positions, he was elected chair of the College and University Faculty Assembly of the National Council for the Social Studies, vice president of the Society for Information Technology and Teacher Education, a member of the board of directors for the Social Science Education Consortium, and a member of the advisory board for the International Society for the Social Studies. Dr. Berson has extensively published books, chapters, and journal articles and presented his research worldwide. He was named the Association of Educational Publishers Distinguished Achievement Award Winner in the learned article category. He has been the principal investigator, co-principal investigator, or primary partner on grants from the United States Department of Education, Florida Department of Education, the Spencer Foundation, and the Library of Congress. Dr. Berson conducts research in the areas of global child advocacy and technology in social studies education.

Natasha Blanchet-Cohen is an associate professor in the Department of Applied Human Sciences at Concordia University and graduate director of the Youth Work diploma. Dr. Blanchet-Cohen's work focuses on child rights and participation, resiliency, social inclusion, and systems change and innovation. As an interdisciplinary scholar, she has led national research initiatives on building resilient communities through youth engagement, and holds a particular interest in immigrant and indigenous youth. Her work explores the opportunities and limitations for immigrant and indigenous young people in being change agents in their schools, homes, and communities, as well as the perspectives of youth in providing for rights-based and culturally-safe services and programs. She has been a member of the research team on children and global adversity for the past 4 years.

Joyce E. Bronteng is a bilingual and literacy lecturer at University of Cape Coast, Ghana but currently a doctoral candidate at the University of South Florida. Her research focuses on bilingual and literacy studies involving young learners, parents, and teachers. She has co-published textbooks for public Basic Schools in Ghana as well as articles on enhancing early literacy acquisition in linguistically diverse classrooms.

Andie (Saša) Buccitelli is a community worker, educator, and advocate who works as a teacher in the Social Service Program at Dawson College and as a support worker at a youth empowerment organisation in Montreal. Intersectionality, trans and queer positionality, healing, collective care, art, and emotional consciousness are central considerations and practices in their life and work. Their community endeavours have included anything from organizing a photovoice art exhibit with young parents, to facilitating workshops on sexual health, consent and gendered cyberviolence in various settings. In their teaching practice, they strive to attend to the overt and insidious ways trauma, oppression, guilt, shame and fear are reproduced in the classroom in an attempt to nurture learning spaces grounded in critical consciousness, healing, self/collective compassion, accountability, creativity and trust.

Heilyn Camacho is an assistant professor at Aalborg University, associated with the e-Learning Lab—the Center for User Driven Innovation, Learning, and Design. She completed her PhD in the field of developing ICT competences in small- and medium-sized companies using action learning, the triple helix method, and problem-based learning to propose a multilayer integration methodology for organizational development. Her current research interest is design for change, combining different bodies of knowledge from organizational and learning theories to facilitate organizational change. Her current research projects are: (a) action research projects pursuing change in low socioeconomic status schools, (b) transforming traditional teaching to problem-based learning approaches, and (c) moving schools to become learning organizations through the use of ICT. She uses participatory research and action research approaches, and is currently involved in several international projects where she collaborates with European and Latin American universities.

Elisabeth De Schauwer works as a Visiting Professor in Disability Studies at Ghent University. She works closely together with children, parents, and schools in inclusive education. Her PhD was around the lived experiences of stakeholders in inclusive education of children with severe communicative difficulties. As activism, research, and working with students go hand in hand, following people, their stories, and the connection with disability are a never-ending source of inspiration in her work and daily life. Her research focuses on disability and the influence on pedagogical relationships. She is interested in strengthening interdisciplinary links between pedagogy and other disciplines like philosophy, feminism, anthropology, etc.

Myriam Denov holds the Canada Research Chair in Youth, Gender, and Armed Conflict, and is a full professor of social work at McGill University. A former Commonwealth Scholar (PhD University of Cambridge), she has conducted extensive research on children and families affected by war and migration, child soldiers, refugee youth, and children's rights. A specialist in participatory research, she has worked with war-affected children and families in Asia, Africa, and the Americas. She has presented expert evidence in court on child soldiers and has advised government and nongovernmental organizations on children in armed conflict and girls in armed groups. She has written several books including *Child Soldiers: Sierra Leone's Revolutionary United Front* (Cambridge University Press). In 2014, she was awarded a Trudeau Fellowship to study the realities of children born in LRA captivity in northern Uganda. In 2015, she was inducted into the College of the Royal Society of Canada. Her current work is exploring the intergenerational effects of wartime sexual violence in northern Uganda, Cambodia, and Rwanda. She also leads a multi-institutional research team on children and global adversity.

Jill Dunn is a senior lecturer in Stranmillis University College, Belfast where she teaches early years literacy across BEd, PGCE (Early Years), PGCE (International) and Master's programs. Her main research interests lie in children's culture, including digital technology, and participatory research with children. She has also been involved in a number of funded research projects on literacy and the use of iPads in early years education and has published in these areas.

Carlo Fabian, professor, is a senior researcher, project leader, and lecturer at the University of Applied Sciences and Arts Northwestern Switzerland (FHNW), Institute for Social Planning, Organisational Change, and Urban Development. He has a master's degree in health and social psychology, is a specialist psychologist in health psychology (FSP) and has a Master of Advanced Studies (MAS) in coaching studies. After several years as a researcher and lecturer at the University of Zurich (1997–2001), the Swiss Institute for Health and Addiction Research (1999–2000), and the FHNW (2001–2008), he worked at RADIX (2008–2012), a Swiss not-for-profit organization, where he developed and implemented many projects in municipalities and schools with a focus on participation. Since 2011 he has led projects at the FHNW addressing the subject of urban development, participatory planning, and well-being.

Michelle Finnerty is a lecturer in music at the School of Music and Theatre, University College Cork, Cork, Ireland. Her research interests include; Irish traditional music, music in education, early years' arts education, music in community contexts, and teaching and learning in higher education. Michelle has recently completed her PhD dissertation where she was awarded a prestigious 3-year doctoral scholarship from the Department of Children and Youth Affairs, Ireland. As part of this work, Michelle carried out research with children in a range of in-school and out-of-school context examining children's perspectives on their musical worlds and cultural lives in Ireland. Her research findings are presented to policy makers in the context of the National Children's Strategy in Ireland. In addition to performing music in many contexts, Michelle has overseen a diverse range of music education research projects funded by The Arts Council of Ireland, Cork Arts and Health Board, St Patrick's College Drumcondra, Cork City Council, and Music Generation Cork City. In 2012, she was research advisor and partner to the published Tiny Voice—Early Years Report (2013). In 2013 and 2014, Michelle facilitated the development of a traditional music program for young children in Cork city in partnership with Club Ceoil, Ballyphenane, Creative Tradition, and Music Generation Cork City. She is currently the primary investigator of an Early Years Pilot Project in collaboration with Cork City Childcare and Music Generation Cork City. She is a founding member of the Society for Music Education in Ireland (2010) and was assistant secretary from 2010–2014 and secretary from 2014–2016. She was treasurer of the Irish Council for Traditional Music (2014–2015).

Lauren Christian Gibson is an adjunct professor in the Florida State University Panama City College of Education Elementary Education program where she teaches courses and supervises student teachers. She has a bachelor's degree in elementary education from Asbury University, a master's degree in teaching English to speakers of other languages (TESOL) from Inter American University of Puerto Rico, and a doctorate in TESOL from New York University. Dr. Gibson began her teaching career as an elementary English as a Second Language (ESL) teacher in Lexington, Kentucky. Later, she taught courses at the graduate and undergraduate levels in TESOL, education, and English at New York University, LaGuardia Community College/City University of New York, The College of New Rochelle, Medgar Evers College/City University of New York, University of Kentucky, Inter American University of Puerto Rico, and Florida State University Panama City. Her research focuses on the educational and linguistic adaptations of Haitian immigrant families and youth from a community perspective as well as the roles of Haitian Creole and French in schools in Haiti. She presents widely at conferences such as American Educational Research Association (AERA), TESOL, and National Association of Bilingual Education (NABE), and she has served as a proposal reviewer for TESOL and NABE. She resides in Panama City Beach with her husband and their young son and daughter.

Colette Gray is a principal lecturer at Stranmillis University College where she teaches research methods in education and early childhood studies across BA (Hons), BEd, and Master's programs. A chartered developmental psychologist, her primary expertise is in children's cognitive development. Her research interests lie in participatory research involving young children, traditional and emerging theoretical paradigms, and in the development of research methods that offer an authentic window into the young child's world experiences. Until very recently she was the editor of the *International Journal of Early Years Education* and remains a member of the editorial board and, for 5 years, was also head of the International Participatory Research Special Interest Group organized under the auspices of EECERA. She has a significant publication record and is currently involved in the production of several books on aspects of participatory research involving young children and a third edition of her book *Learning Theories in Childhood*.

Susan Groundwater-Smith is an honorary professor in the Sydney School of Education and Social Work at the University of Sydney. She co-founded the Coalition of Knowledge Building Schools that had among its stated desiderata the need to engage children and young people in research both in schools and other cultural institutions concerned with the investigation of practice. Her attention has been particularly directed to concepts of action research in its various forms and manifestations.

Timo Huber works for DOK Impuls, the specialist unit for child-friendly urban development of the umbrella organization for open work with children in the city of Bern, Switzerland (DOK). He was a research assistant at the University of Applied Sciences and Arts Northwestern Switzerland (FHNW), School of Social Work (HSA), Institute for Social Planning, Organisational Change, and Urban Development. He is currently attending a master's study in social work, focusing on community development at the University of Applied Sciences Fulda and the University of Applied Sciences RheinMain, Wiesbaden, Germany.

Edith Jolicoeur is an invited professor in remedial education of oral and written language at Université du Québec à Rimouski. She has a doctorate in education from the Université du Québec network on social representations of autism spectrum disorder. Dr. Jolicoeur did her postdoctoral training at Université Laval where she is a member of the Centre de Recherche et d'Interventions sur la Réussite Scolaire (CRIRES). Her postdoctoral research focused on language learning (both oral and written) among individuals with intellectual disabilities. She teaches courses in language instruction for students with disabilities and on interventions that promote their inclusion in mainstream classrooms.

Jean Kagame is an undergraduate MasterCard Foundation Scholar from Kigali, Rwanda. He is pursuing a bachelor's of social work and a minor in international development studies at McGill University in Montreal, Canada. Since 2015, Kagame has been a member in a research project exploring the lives and realities of children born of war rape across multiple contexts, notably in Northern Uganda, Rwanda, and Cambodia. In 2016, he served as the president of McGill African Students' Society. Now he is working as a resident assistant (floor fellow) at McGill University. Kagame's previous professional experience includes over two years of work for Agahozo-Shalom, a youth village and a residential community that provides education, psycho-social support, and care to restore the rhythm of life for the most talented and needy orphans in Rwanda. He also interned with Survivors Fund Rwanda, a UK NGO based in Rwanda which provides financial support to the Survivors of the 1994 genocide committed against Tutsi in Rwanda. Having grown up in post-Genocide Rwanda, he has the lived experience of confronting and navigating the issues faced by children and young adults in the aftermath of war. It is primarily for this reason that he is deeply inspired to work as a professional with war-affected populations, particularly in developing countries. Kagame's additional interests include learning how indigenous knowledge and practices can be applied by international NGOs for the betterment of lives after tragedies, such as war.

Joanne Lehrer is associate professor of preschool education at Université du Québec en Outaouais and president of the Canadian Association for Research in Early Childhood. Her research interests include educational transitions in early childhood, children's perspectives, and relationships with families. She holds a master's in child study from Concordia University and a PhD in education from Université du Québec à Montréal.

Joseph Levitan is an assistant professor in the Department of Integrated Studies of Education at McGill University. His research interests include reflexive and affective leadership skills, community-driven education reform, social justice in education, and identity and learning. He is also the director of education at the Sacred Valley Project, a nonprofit dedicated to facilitating culturally grounded and socially just education with indigenous communities.

Maggie MacNevin is a registered early childhood educator who holds a Master of Arts degree in early childhood studies from Ryerson University. She has worked as an early childhood educator in childcare and family resource settings, and as a part-time instructor at Ryerson University's School of Early Childhood Studies. Since 2014, Maggie has been involved in the ongoing research project entitled Can We Talk About Race? Confronting Colour Blindness in Early Childhood Settings. She is currently enjoying a year of parental leave with her young son.

Colleen McMillan is a practicing clinical social worker and associate professor at the School of Social Work at the University of Waterloo in Canada. As a qualitative health researcher her work focuses on issues of power within the medical paradigm and employs participatory and collaborative methods towards empowering those with whom she works. Her standpoint as a feminist informed practitioner within a medical clinic has allowed her to identify spaces of tension regarding questions around expertism, power, and knowledge holders. As such her role regularly expands to that of a change agent in partnership with those with whom she works toward creating change in traditional healthcare systems. Working with vulnerable groups such as women, children, individuals with severe physical disabilities, and older adults has allowed her to identify methods that make central the voice of the individual as the owner of their lived experience and as such, a form of knowledge. Understanding that voice is only one method to understand the narratives of children; her work often takes the shape of dance, performance, artwork, and games to fully support and make visible knowledge in a way that is relevant, equitable, and child directed.

Denise Mitchell has taught early years pedagogy across a wide range of modules and programs over her time as senior lecturer in Stranmillis University College. She was involved in setting up the early childhood studies degree in Stranmillis University College and her research interests were in literacy in the early years. She is now enjoying retirement after an extensive and very committed career in education.

Nicole Mockler is an associate professor in the Sydney School of Education and Social Work at the University of Sydney. She is co-author/editor of 14 books, including *Questioning the Language of Improvement and Reform in Education: Reclaiming Meaning, Engaging With Student Voice in Research, Education and Community: Beyond Legitimation and Guardianship*, and *Teacher Professional Learning in an Age of Compliance: Mind the Gap.* Her research interests are in inquiry-based teacher professional learning, education policy and politics, particularly as they impact upon teachers' work. She is currently editor-in-chief of *The Australian Educational Researcher*, and a member of the international advisory board of the *British Educational Research Journal* and *Educational Action Research.*

Pamela Moffett is a senior lecturer at Stranmillis University College where she delivers courses in mathematics pedagogy on the BEd (primary), PGCE (early years), PGCE (international), and CPD programmes. She has participated in a number of mobility visits within Europe and has delivered professional development courses in Malaysia and India. Her research interests include the development of early number sense and the use of meaningful contexts for children's learning in mathematics. She has been involved in a number of funded research projects and has recently co-authored *Number Talk*, a teaching resource book to promote understanding and use of number language in the early years.

Aaron Osafo-Acquah is a senior lecturer in educational psychology at the University of Cape Coast in Ghana. His research interest is early childhood education and pupil performance at the basic education level in Ghana. He has published articles including "Early Childhood Education in the Central Region of Ghana—Challenges, Opportunities, and the Way Forward" and "Impact of Quality Improvement in the Primary Schools Program (QUIPS) in the Academic Performance of Pupils in the New Edubiase District of Ghana."

Mathieu Point holds a doctorate in education and is a professor in the department of educational sciences at the Université du Québec à Trois-Rivières. He is a regular researcher member of the Normand-Maurice research chair and the International Laboratory on educational inclusion. His work focuses on play, inclusive pedagogy, psychomotor development, and social interactions in early childhood.

Rosemary Richards, PhD, is a senior lecturer at Toi Ohomai Institute of Technology (Rotorua, New Zealand) in early childhood and adult education undergraduate and postgraduate programs. She previously taught at Australian Catholic University (Sydney) and Massey University, New Zealand. As a teacher, artist, and researcher she is especially passionate about supporting young children's arts and educational experience and helping teachers to do likewise. Research projects include New Zealand children's drawing self-efficacy and the messages children gave and received about their drawing; Australian children's perspectives on their art experiences as they transitioned between homes, early childhood centers, and schools; and international students' experiences within a New Zealand tertiary setting. It is Rosemary's belief that relationships are at the heart of effective pedagogy and curriculum development should be informed by understandings about the ways learners experience education and develop relationships. Her research interests include narrative inquiry, art education pedagogical theory and knowledge, child-sensitive methodologies, children's perspectives, self-efficacy beliefs, ethnography, visual methodologies, and international students' experiences. Rosemary co-convened of the 2nd International Art in Early Childhood Conference held in NSW in 2007, and co-edited the inaugural *International Art in Early Childhood Research Journal*. She continues to publish her work in books, journals, and conferences and reviews for several international early childhood and education journals. By invitation, she presented at the "15th Neuroscience, Early Childhood Development and Pedagogical Arts" conference in Mexico (2015) and the "4th Annual Global Congress of Knowledge Economy—2017" in China.

Julie Ruel, PhD, is an adjunct professor at the Université du Québec en Outaouais and an associate researcher at the Centre Intégré de Santé et de

Services Sociaux de l'Outaouais. Since 2011 she has been co-holder of the interdisciplinary chair in research on literacy and inclusion. A psychologist by training, she has worked for more than 35 years in the health and social services sector. She has carried out a number of research projects on educational transitions, especially transitions to kindergarten.

Myriam D. Savage, PhD, RDT-BCT, is a board member of the North American Drama Therapy Association (NADTA) and held office as inaugural SoCal NADTA chapter president. Dr. Savage, a registered drama therapist and board-certified trainer is founder-director at SoCal Drama Therapy Center in Los Angeles. A lecturer for the Visual Arts and Performance Arts Education program at UCLA, her drama therapy work history has entailed facilitating various populations in both educational and clinical settings. A founding faculty member of UCLArts and Healing, Social Emotional Arts (SEA) program, she teaches professional development to educators, artists, and clinical practitioners on the uses of expressive therapies in practice. She is a recipient of the Drama Therapy Fund professional research grant (2014) and a pilot grant from Lesley University (2015) for her work with homeless women on skid row. Dr. Savage has a doctorate in expressive therapies, leads drama therapy groups for adolescents in dual diagnosis, and publishes and lectures on drama therapy.

Harry Shier was born in Belfast, Ireland, in 1954, and worked in England for many years, first in children's play, then in children's rights and participation. In 1981 he founded Playtrain, an independent training agency specializing in children's rights, play, and creativity. In the 1990s he worked and wrote extensively on children's participation rights, developing the "Article 31 Children's Consultancy Scheme," which enables children to act as consultants to the management of cultural institutions, helping them make facilities and programs child-friendly. This experience was crystallized in his 2001 paper "Pathways to Participation," which introduced a tool for analyzing children's participation in decision-making that is now widely used throughout the world. In 2001 he moved to Nicaragua, Central America, where he worked with a local organization, CESESMA, supporting child workers on the region's coffee plantations in defending their rights. He continued to write and research with children, and published works on child rights and participation in both English and Spanish. He also wrote the report on the violation of children's right to play around the world that convinced the UN Committee on the Rights of the Child to issue guidance to the world's governments on the right to play. In 2016 he was awarded a PhD at Queen's University Belfast for his study on Nicaraguan children's perceptions of human rights in school. He is currently based in Ireland as Learning and Development Officer with Misean Cara, and is a member of UNICEF's International Expert Group on Adolescent Participation. His published writing, in English and Spanish, and a full CV are available at: www.harryshier.net.

Cara Sisk PhD, CCLS is an assistant professor and the child life program director for the School of Human Ecology at Tennessee Technological University. Cara's clinical practice experience as a certified child life specialist serving children and adolescents in health care was critical in her professional development and foundational to her academic interests. Cara is dedicated to doing research to positively impact the health care of children with special health care needs and disabilities. Her dissertation research integrated her interest of children in health care with a therapeutic tool she often used in her practice as a child life specialist: medical play.

Leontine Umubyeyi was born and raised in Rwanda. She came to Canada 8 years ago. During Tutsi Genocide, Leontine lost her entire family; she is the only survivor of her family. Leontine Left Rwanda for Canada in 2008 due to lack of safety. In recent years, the Rwandan government has adopted a law of truth and reconciliation, where killers come out of prisons and ask forgiveness from their victims. During this process, Leontine met the men who murdered her family and that was when she decided to leave Rwanda. She has been involved in different research and advocacy projects, and she has worked with different organizations as a public speaker. Today Leontine is a social work student at McGill University and she feels she is in the right place where she can make a difference in our society.

Hanne Vandenbussche is connected to the field of disability studies at Ghent University. She has specific interest in the relationship between disability studies and philosophy. In her research she focuses on belonging and inclusive citizenship. Hereto she cooperates with parents, children, and young adults following inclusive trajectories.

Geert Van Hove, Prof. Dr. works as a full professor at Ghent University (Belgium) in the Department of Special Needs Education and is Director of Studies for the Faculty of Psychology and Educational Sciences. His research concerns the lived experiences of children and adults with disabilities.

Ross VeLure Roholt is associate professor of youth studies, and director, youth development leadership program, School of Social Work, University of Minnesota. He is an active public engaged scholar with current projects on civic youth work and youth-led social innovation, with emphasis on the social determinants of violence. He consults internationally with governments and community organizations on youth involvement in social and community development.

Printed in Great Britain
by Amazon